THE TEBTUNIS PAPYRI

VOLUME IV

THE
TEBTUNIS PAPYRI

VOLUME IV

EDITED WITH TRANSLATIONS AND NOTES BY

JAMES G. KEENAN

AND

JOHN C. SHELTON

Graeco-Roman Memoirs, No. 64

PUBLISHED FOR

THE BRITISH ACADEMY

BY THE

EGYPT EXPLORATION SOCIETY

3 DOUGHTY MEWS, LONDON WCIN 2PG

1976

PRINTED IN GREAT BRITAIN
AT THE UNIVERSITY PRINTING HOUSE, CAMBRIDGE
(HARRY MYERS, UNIVERSITY PRINTER)
AND PUBLISHED FOR
THE BRITISH ACADEMY
BY THE EGYPT EXPLORATION SOCIETY
3 DOUGHTY MEWS, LONDON WC1N 2PG

PREFACE

Professors Keenan and Shelton write as follows:—

"WITH this volume the wish expressed by Crönert, *WKlPh* 20, col. 489, that the numerous and extensive papyri briefly treated in the *Descriptions* at the back of P. Teb. I should soon be made fully available to scholars, is after 70 years fulfilled only in part; for we have included only letters, petitions, and such accounts as bear on land and taxation at Kerkeosiris. The work was begun in the summer of 1968 and essentially completed in that of 1973. We have observed a division of labour: the letters and petitions were prepared by James Keenan, the lists by John Shelton; and despite a good deal of mutual assistance and advice, each editor remains responsible for that part of the book which appears under his name.

So large an undertaking is not easily brought to completion without support from others. The greater portion of the land and tax lists were prepared by Dr Shelton while he was on a leave of absence from the University of Georgia under a Junior Fellowship from the National Endowment for the Humanities; the University also supplied him with several hundred dollars' worth of photographs, and permitted him twice in five years so to arrange his teaching schedule as to leave six consecutive months free for research. Dr Keenan would like to thank the University of California for the research support which he received during his five years as a faculty member of the Classics Department at Berkeley, and for a sabbatical leave during the Fall Quarter 1971 to continue work on this project. We are indebted to Professor Herbert C. Youtie for reading an earlier draft of this book and making a number of valuable corrections; to Professor Eric G. Turner for his helpful comments on the manuscript and for proposing its publication by the Egypt Exploration Society; to the Bancroft Library and its Director, Professor James D. Hart, for permission to publish these texts. Finally, we wish to express special thanks to Mrs Leslie Clarke and the Rare Books staff for their courteous assistance over the past years."

The General editors wish to thank these two scholars for their dedicated concentration on their task; the Alexander von Humboldt Foundation for a subsidy towards the necessarily high cost of printing a book such as this; and the Cambridge University Press for the care and attention bestowed on a complicated piece of composition. They would like also to thank Dr W. E. H. Cockle for some help with parts of the proof-reading.

P. J. PARSONS
J. R. REA
E. G. TURNER
General Editors of the Graeco-Roman Memoirs

November 1975

CONTENTS

TEXTS

TABLES AND CHARTS

INDICES

TABLE OF PAPYRI

CLASSIFICATION OF PAPYRI ACCORDING TO CROCODILES

In considering whether two texts which cannot be physically joined may not nevertheless belong to the same document, and for other purposes, it is often useful to know which papyri were found in the same mummy; and also which mummies were buried together as a group, since long documents were sometimes divided between two or more crocodiles that were mummified together. Two such groups contain Menches papyri, those which in vol. I xvi–xvii are called groups (b) and (c), consisting respectively of mummies 7, 9, and 28, and mummies 8, 12, 13, 14, 15, 16, 17, and 27. In addition to these two groups, crocodiles 20 and 23 have produced texts belonging to this archive.

Crocodile 9. **1113**, **1131**.
12. **1095**, **1096**.
13. **1105**, **1138**.
14. **1099**, **1104**, **1147**.
15. **1106**.
16. **1118**, **1120**.
20. **1094**, **1108**, **1117**, **1121**, **1135**, **1142**.
23. **1112**, **1116**, **1122**, **1123**, **1146**.
27. **1097**, **1101–3**, **1110**, **1114–15**, **1124**, **1126–9**, **1132**, **1134**, **1139–41**, **1143–5**, **1148–50**.
28. **1100**, **1109**, **1111**, **1119**, **1130**, **1133**, **1136–7**.

1107 was divided among crocodiles 12, 14, 15, and 27 (group c). The source of **1098** is not known.

CONCORDANCE BETWEEN P. TEB. I AND P. TEB. IV

P. Teb. IV	P. Teb. I
1094	125
1095	126
1096	127
1097	UC 2399
1098	UC 2485
1099	142
1100	239
1101	237
1102	161
1103	141v + 63v
1104	246
1105	162
1106	163v
1107	94 + 163r + 247–9
1108	143
1109	147(b)
1110	141r
1111	147(a)
1112	146
1113	72(a)
1114	144
1115	145r
1116	152
1117	151
1118	173r
1119	215
1120	173v
1121	255
1122	187
1123	86v
1124	233v
1125	149
1126	71v
1127	233r
1128	170
1129	235 + 236
1130	174r
1131	238
1132	169
1133	205
1134	13v(b)
1135	159r
1136	174v

P. Teb. I	P. Teb. IV
13r	1140
13v(a)	1150
13v(b)	1134
16r	1143
63v	1103
71v	1126
72(a)	1113
86v	1123
94	1107
116r	1146
125	1094
126	1095
127	1096
141r	1110
141v	1103
142	1099
143	1108
144	1114
145r	1115
145v	1145
146	1112
147(a)	1111
147(b)	1109
149	1125
151	1117
152	1116
159r	1135
159v	1142
161	1102
162	1105
163r	1107
163v	1106
169	1132
170	1128
171	1144
173r	1118
173v	1120
174r	1130
174v	1136
187	1122
197	1138
199	1139
205	1133

1137	214	214	1137
1138	197	215	1119
1139	199	218	1148
1140	13r	219	1141
1141	219	232	1149
1142	159v	233r	1127
1143	16r	233v	1124
1144	171	235	1129
1145	145v	236	1129
1146	116r	237	1101
1147	245	238	1131
1148	218	239	1100
1149	232	245	1147
1150	13v(a)	246	1104
		247	1107
		248	1107
		249	1107
		255	1121
		UC 2399	1097
		UC 2485	1098

NOTE ON EDITORIAL PRACTICE AND LIST OF ABBREVIATIONS

THIS volume consists entirely of non-literary texts, which we have printed in modern style, resolving abbreviations and symbols, and adding punctuation and accents. Faults of spelling and grammar have been pointed out in a critical apparatus or discussed in textual notes when they could not be conveniently indicated in the text itself. Iota adscript has been printed where it appears on the papyrus, and used in restorations and in resolutions of abbreviations; in the very few instances where the adscript was omitted by a scribe, we have printed iota subscript. Square brackets [ ] indicate a lacuna, parentheses ( ) resolution of an abbreviation or symbol, angular brackets ⟨ ⟩ a mistaken omission in the original, double square brackets ⟦ ⟧ a deletion by the scribe, braces { } superfluous letters, and high strokes \` ´ superlinear additions, but not letters raised to mark an abbreviation. We have carefully observed a distinction between open and closed brackets at line ends: thus, for example, *Πε]τεςούχου* [δ would indicate that in our belief the supplements provided were required, but might not be sufficient to complete the line at either end; whereas [*Ὧροc Πε*]*τεcούχου* [δγ́] would indicate that no further supplement was expected.

Dots within brackets, or numerals within brackets, indicate the approximate extent of a lacuna; dots outside brackets indicate illegible letters, and dots under letters indicate uncertain readings. Strokes over numerals are reproduced as they occur, check marks by a scribe are reproduced in the text or described in the introduction. All writing runs parallel to the fibres unless otherwise noted.

Heavy numerals refer to Tebtunis papyri in this and earlier volumes, ordinary numerals to lines. The number of the crocodile mummy from which a given papyrus was extracted may be found by referring to the *editio princeps* of each text in vol. I; of the pieces which have not previously been mentioned, **1097** came from crocodile 27, and the source of **1098** is not known. A table of the mummies and the texts they produced is given on p. xi.

All documents in Part One are translated as fully as the condition of the texts permits. A full translation of the voluminous, repetitious, but for the most part straightforward land and tax lists seems inappropriate. As a guide to the reader who may find the terse accounting-office Greek of these texts unfamiliar, however, we have provided an English version of, usually, the first well-preserved column of each document, or series of closely related documents, in so far as such a guide seemed of value; and particularly difficult passages are translated or explained in the notes.

Abbreviations of papyrus editions and scholarly journals are those in common use. In addition, the following shortened references are employed:

COP. M.-Th. Lenger, *Corpus des Ordonnances des Ptolémées*, Acad. royale de Belgique, Mémoires LVI, 5. Brussels, 1964.

Crawford, *Kerkeosiris*. Dorothy J. Crawford, *Kerkeosiris: an Egyptian Village in the Ptolemaic Period*. Cambridge, 1971.

Crown Tenants. J. C. Shelton, 'Land Register: Crown Tenants at Kerkeosiris' in *Collectanea Papyrologica: Texts published in Honor* of H. C. Youtie (A. E. Hanson, editor). Bonn, 1976.

Henne, *Liste des stratèges*. H. Henne, *Liste des stratèges des nomes égyptiens à l'époque gréco-romaine*. Cairo, 1935 (*Mémoires de l'Institut Français d'Archéologie Orientale du Caire* 56).

Herrmann, *Bodenpacht*. J. Herrmann, *Studien zur Bodenpacht im Recht der graeco-ägyptischen Papyri*. Munich, 1958 (*Münch. Beitr.* 41).

Lesquier, *Institutions militaires*. J. Lesquier, *Les institutions militaires de l'Égypte sous les Lagides*. Paris, 1911.

Mayser, *Grammatik*. E. Mayser, *Grammatik der griechischen Papyri aus der Ptolemäerzeit mit Einschluss der gleichzeitigen Ostraka und der in Ägypten verfassten Inschriften*. Leipzig and Berlin, 1906–.

NB. F. Preisigke, *Namenbuch enthaltend alle griechischen, lateinischen, ägyptischen, hebräischen, arabischen und sonstigen semitischen und nichtsemitischen Menschennamen, soweit sie in griechischen Urkunden (Papyri, Ostraka, Inschriften, Mumienschildern usw.) Ägyptens sich vorfinden*. Heidelberg, 1922.

Onomasticon. D. Foraboschi, *Onomasticon alterum papyrologicum: Supplemento al Namenbuch di F. Preisigke*. Milan, 1967–. (*Testi e documenti per lo studio dell'antichità* 16, Serie papyrologica 2).

Otto, *Priester und Tempel*. W. Otto, *Priester und Tempel im hellenistischen Ägypten*. Leipzig–Berlin, 1905–8.

Packman, *Taxes*. Zola M. Packman, *The Taxes in Grain in Ptolemaic Egypt: Receipts from the Granary of Diospolis Magna, 164–88 B.C.* New Haven–Toronto, 1968 (*American Studies in Papyrology* 4).

PPt. W. Peremans and E. van 't Dack, *Prosopographia Ptolemaica*, in *Studia Hellenistica* 6 (1950), 8 (1952), 11 (1956), 12 (1959), 13 (1963), 17 (1968).

Préaux, *L'économie royale*. Cl. Préaux, *L'économie royale des Lagides*. Brussels, 1939.

Preisigke, *Girowesen*. F. Preisigke, *Girowesen im griechischen Ägypten*. Strassburg, 1910.

Rostovtzeff, *Kolonat*. M. Rostovtzeff (Rostowzew), *Studien zur Geschichte des römischen Kolonates*. Leipzig–Berlin, 1910 (*Archiv* Beiheft 1).

Rostovtzeff, *SEHHW*. M. Rostovtzeff, *The Social and Economic History of the Hellenistic World*. 3 vols., Oxford, 1941.

Schnebel, *Landwirtschaft*. M. Schnebel, *Die Landwirtschaft im hellenistischen Ägypten*. Munich, 1925 (*Münch. Beitr.* 7).

Schwarz, *Die öffentliche und private Urkunde*. A. B. Schwarz, *Die öffentliche und private Urkunde im römischen Ägypten*. Leipzig, 1920 (*Abh. sächs. Akad.* 31, 3).

Taubenschlag, *Law*[2]. R. Taubenschlag, *The Law of Greco-Roman Egypt in the Light of the Papyri*. 2nd edition, Warsaw, 1955.

WB. F. Preisigke, *Wörterbuch der griechischen Papyrusurkunden mit Einschluss der griechischen Inschriften, Aufschriften, Ostraka, Mumienschilder usw. aus Ägypten*. Berlin, 1925–.

INTRODUCTION

A. The Papyri

The papyrus collection held by the University of California at Berkeley was acquired as a result of excavations conducted by Grenfell and Hunt in the winter of 1899/1900 at the ancient village Tebtunis on the southern fringe of the Fayum. The excavations were financed by Mrs Phoebe Apperson Hearst, and the papyri which were uncovered were found in three main groups. They came from: (1) the cartonnage of mummified crocodiles; (2) the ruins of the Roman town, including houses within the area of the Temple of Soknebtunis; and (3) the cartonnage of mummified human corpses (*Archiv* 1 [1901], 376–8, P. Teb. I Preface; cf. E. J. Goodspeed, *The Independent* 57 [1904], 1066–70). With the exception of a number of Demotic rolls sent to Cairo (cf. **42** and **59** introdd.), the papyri were removed to Oxford, England for editing. Those of Group 1, mainly texts of the late second–early first centuries B.C. and including the archive of Menches, village scribe of Kerkeosiris (for at least a second time) from 119 to 111/110, were published in volume I of *The Tebtunis Papyri* (1902). The papyri from the Roman town were published several years later in P. Teb. II (1907), while those from the cartonnage of mummified human remains, texts of the third and second centuries B.C., were published in P. Teb. III, which appeared in two parts (1933, 1938), with extended delays in publication owing first to Grenfell's lengthy illness and death, then to the death of Hunt (see Prefaces to P. Teb. III, 1 and 2; for necrologies of the two great men: *Proc. Brit. Ac.* 12 [1926], 357–64, 20 [1934], 323–33). In 1935 the papyri were transferred from Oxford to the British Museum (P. Teb. III, 2 Preface); and in 1938, upon completion by C. C. Edgar of P. Teb. III, Part 2, the collection was shipped to Berkeley where, in the summer of 1940, over 1700 pieces were catalogued and mounted by Edmund H. Kase, Jr. (*TAPA* 71 [1940], xliv–xlv; for additional details on the collection: *ibid.* and *Collectanea Papyrologica in Honor of H. C. Youtie*, p. 91). These now form part of the Rare Books Collections in the Bancroft Library.

The papyri edited in the present volume, with but two exceptions (**1097**, **1098**), are exclusively from the *descripta* at the back of P. Teb. I. All, with the exception of two (**1116**, **1129**) whose inclusion is justified by their material relevance to the other documents, are from the Menches archive. Of the Menches documents not included here, some are fragmentary land surveys and tax lists which may be included in a future volume, others (e.g. **128**, **129**) are petitions which have so far resisted satisfactory decipherment. Nonetheless, for all practical intents and purposes the archive's evidence is exhausted in the present volume.

The importance of the archive as a primary source of information concerning

Ptolemaic Egypt, particularly its economic and administrative structure, will hardly be disputed by those who have interested themselves in such studies. That portion of the archive which was published in volume I has recently been the subject of penetrating analysis by Dorothy J. Crawford (*Kerkeosiris: an Egyptian Village in the Ptolemaic Period*, Cambridge Classical Studies, Cambridge, 1971); the reader is referred to this book for an orientation to past studies of our village and the long bibliography on specialized points of Ptolemaic social and economic history.

In view of the amplitude and quality of past scholarship – in addition to Mrs Crawford, the contributions of Rostovtzeff, Wilcken, Otto, Préaux, Peremans, Van 't Dack, and Uebel may be singled out for mention here – a full discussion of Kerkeosiris and its economy need not be undertaken afresh in this edition. However, the reader may well find a brief general sketch of the land and taxes of the village useful, particularly for the study of the great mass of detailed, often confusing, and excessively tedious lists which constitute the second part of this volume. It need hardly be stressed that the following sections of the Introduction refer to Kerkeosiris during the time when Menches was the village scribe, and that conclusions here drawn may not be valid for other times or other parts of Egypt.

B. Land and Taxes at Kerkeosiris

The total area of Kerkeosiris in the 52nd year of Ptolemy Euergetes II, 119/118 B.C., is given by **60**. 3 as 4700 arouras, about 3150 acres. This figure must have remained stable: not only does 4700 look artificially even, but the area of *βαcιλικὴ γῆ* for the following year is calculated simply by deducting all other land categories from 4700 and accepting the remainder as *βαcιλική*. This method presupposes a static figure for the village total.

One may conveniently divide Ptolemaic land into two broad categories – that from which the Crown could hope to collect rent in grain, and that from which it could not. The latter consisted of land which by its nature was incapable of yielding crops, of land rented for cash instead of grain, and of land for which the Crown forbore to ask rent. In the first division fall such items as roads, waterways, threshing-floors and dovecotes, which made up the *ὑπόλογος ἄφορος ἐκτὸς μιcθώcεως*. In the second division Kerkeosiris possessed 175$\frac{3}{8}$ arouras of sandy grazing land, *νομαὶ ἐκτὸς μιcθώcεως πρὸς χαλκὸν διοικούμεναι* (**61**(a). 154–5; **1121**. 11). The third division consisted of *ἱερὰ γῆ* held by the temples, as well as cleruchic grants to various military and civil officials. In other parts of Egypt *ἰδιόκτητος* was found as well, though we do not know of such private land at Kerkeosiris. The village itself, *κώμη cὺν περιcτάcει*, may have fallen into a fourth division, though in the presence of buildings and roads it closely resembles *ὑπόλογος ἄφορος*. For fiscal purposes garden land in the *περίcταcιc* was treated differently from the *κώμη* proper (**60**. 5–6).

When these types of land are subtracted from the village total, the remainder is *βαcιλικὴ γῆ*, Crown land, subject to *ἐκφόριον* or *cιτικὴ μίcθωcιc*, a term which does not require that rents be collected in grain, but only that they be so calculated. The *cιτική* μίcθωcιc of Kerkeosiris included even cash payments (**1105** introd.; **1104**. 2 note), which are distinguished from rent collected on νομαὶ αἱ πρὸc χαλκόν in that the former were an adaeratio, though a required one, and the latter were not. Included in the cιτικὴ μίcθωcιc also were portions of the βαcιλική which in fact produced no revenue whatever owing to the poor condition of the land. So e.g. **1116** distinguishes regularly between such entries as a dike ἐκτὸc μιcθώcεωc (line 60) and waterlogged land ἐν μιcθώcει (line 42); for the latter had an assigned rent calculated in grain, though not collectable, whereas the former had no rent assigned at all.

It is not altogether clear whether the Ptolemaic administration itself used a single term to encompass all land which was not subject to the cιτικὴ μίcθωcιc, that is, all land exclusive of the βαcιλική. If it did so, that term was most probably the much-discussed ἐν ἀφέcει γῆ (cf. most recently *CE* 46, 1971, 113–19). Such passages as **63**. 2–3 κατὰ φύλλον ἱερᾶc καὶ κληρουχικῆc καὶ τῆc ἄλληc τῆc ἐν ἀφέcει show clearly that land ἐν ἀφέcει did include temple and cleruchic land; and **27**. 54–5, τὴν βαcιλικὴν καὶ τὴν ἐν ἀφέcει γῆν, together with the absence of Crown land from **62**, **63**, and **1108–15**, shows that it did not include βαcιλική. **85** styles itself a εὐθυμετρία κατὰ περίχωμα τοῦ cπόρου (= τῆc βαcιλικῆc) καὶ τῆc ἱερᾶc καὶ τῆc κληρουχικῆc καὶ τῆc ἄλληc τῆc ἐν ἀφέcει. Since **85** and similar texts (**84**, **1116–21**) cover not only βαcιλική subject to rents, ἱερά, and κληρουχική, but also ὑπόλογοc ἐκτὸc μιcθώcεωc and νομαὶ αἱ πρὸc χαλκόν, the latter two species of land must be included among that described as ἡ ἄλλη ἡ ἐν ἀφέcει or the title of **85** must be inaccurate: for it is not possible, in the face of such passages as **61**(a). 157–9, to suppose that they were classed as βαcιλική.

If land ἐν ἀφέcει included not only farm land but also such topographical features as drainage ditches which in the nature of things cannot be cultivated, we shall certainly be right in agreeing with Herrmann (*CE* 30, 1955, 97–8) that it is senseless to speak of land ἐν ἀφέcει as that the *cultivation of which* the Crown has left to others: what the Crown has renounced will be not the working of the land, but its claim to a grain rental. It must be pointed out, however, that no land other than cleruchic, sacred, and private is ever explicitly said to be ἐν ἀφέcει; and the κατὰ φύλλον lists of ἡ ἐν ἀφέcει do not include either νομαὶ or ὑπόλογοc ἐκτὸc μιcθώcεωc. (A possible exception is **62**. 335, but one fears that that notation may not be strictly connected with the document as headed). On the other hand, inclusion of uncultivable land and perennial pastures in planting reports would have been pointless.

With the possible exception of κώμη proper, all land ἐν ἀφέcει, if this is the correct term to use, might under certain circumstances return to the Crown and be reclassified as βαcιλική, or be placed into a different group ἐν ἀφέcει. The confiscation of cleroi for various causes is a familiar feature of Ptolemaic life, and the cancellation of temple holdings too is known (**74**. 59–60; **75**. 77–8). In an uncertain village, probably Magdola, cleroi were assigned freely from νομαὶ ἐκτὸc μιcθώcεωc (**79**). Even ὑπόλογοc ἐκτὸc μιcθώcεωc was not exempt from reclassification: channels go dry or fill up, roads may be abandoned, dovecotes and threshing-floors may be relocated. So in **1103**. 157–8 two arouras of erstwhile ὑδραγωγός are cultivated at a rent, and in **61**(b). 103 ff. we hear of fairly large-scale farming of land that was once part of τοῦ ἐκτὸς μισθώσεως ὑπολόγου.

Conversely, cleruchic and temple land was regularly taken from βασιλική.

Crown land formed the most extensive in acreage and much the most productive part of the territory of Kerkeosiris. It seems likely that all land was ultimately the property of the king, but Crown land was that most immediately under his control, being let out by his agents to tenant farmers who paid not only a series of land taxes but above all a substantial rent. In so leasing this land the king vis-à-vis the peasant maintained a landlord–tenant relation no different in principle from that maintained by most of the larger land-holders of Egypt, though the king's representatives were of course officials rather than private men and the immensity of his property made collection procedures immeasurably more complex.

Crown domains included both land good enough to find willing tenants, and other land too poor to cultivate at a profit. Such useless property was called ὑπόλογος, 'deduction', or ἐν ὑπολόγωι, because it represented a deduction which officials responsible for rent collection could make from the sum which they would otherwise have had to deliver.[1] Hence we occasionally find ὑπόλογος used also of land which in itself was good, but for some other reason would not yield a rent: so σπόριμος wrongly assigned to cleruchs in **72**. 177 ff. was counted ἐν ὑπολόγωι.

During the main period of our documentation, ὑπόλογος at Kerkeosiris is regularly specified as falling into one of two classes, that which went out of cultivation before the revolt of 131 B.C., and that which went out of cultivation afterwards (ἕως τοῦ λθ ἔτους *versus* ἀπὸ τοῦ μ ἔτους): and the precise year in which each plot was placed ἐν ὑπολόγωι was generally available from such detailed lists as **61** and **72**. In **1116**, which may antedate Euergetes' return to power, the term ὑπόλογος is not used; but other early texts employ the 12th year of Philometor as an analogous turning point (e.g. **827**. 2–3; vol. I, p. 578): presumably major surveys were conducted in those years. The government's interest in the dating of ὑπόλογος is no doubt due not only to desire to avoid fraudulent return of σπόριμος in this category, but to help estimate what land would best repay attempts at reclamation, or could with least probable loss to the Crown be sold, or given up to cleruchs. Annual reports on ὑπόλογος were required of each village (cf. **74**, **75**), and data from these were later assembled for the meris or nome as a whole.

Governmental efforts to reclaim derelict land took many forms. Long-term leases were granted at nominal rent or none at all to persons who were willing to bring the land back into cultivation: cf. **61**(b). 1–87, 121–9, 346–414; **72**. 24–34; Rostovtzeff, *Kolonat* 30 ff. Many military cleruchs received χέρσος in the expectation that they would work the land not only for their own profit but to pay certain dues to the state; and in instances where cleruchs were allowed to retain allotments wrongly made from arable land, local

[1] Cf. now the definition in a document of the Roman age, P. Oxy. XXXVIII 2847. 13–15: καλεῖτα[ι δὲ] ὑπόλογος ἐπειδὴ ὑπολογεῖται ἐκ τοῦ μέτρου τ[ῆς γ]ῆς τοῦ κατὰ πεδίον ὡς ὑπολειφθῆναι τὸ λοιπὸν ἔμφορον (3rd cent. A.D.).

officials at fault were required to lease out an equal amount of χέρcοc (**61**(b). 228–9). It was a condition of Menches' reappointment as komogrammateus that he reclaim 10 arouras of ὑπόλογοc (**10**. 2–4), and later he was granted a cleros of 20 arouras more (**75**. 50–1; **1115**. 185–6). We may guess that similar proceedings were commonplace. Further, if reclamation of derelict land was not a positive condition of holding office, many officials nonetheless found engaging in such projects advisable (**61**(b). 9–18 with notes; **75**. 19–20, 33–4).

In following the various attempts at reclamation mentioned in vol. I, it will be observed that those aimed at recovering land most recently gone out of cultivation are in general the most frequent and the most successful. One notes that in the case of cleruchs distinction is made between ὑπόλογοc which was and was not suitable for their grants. In one case we are told that the καθήκων ὑπόλογοc for a cleros of Philometor's 31st year was that which had gone out of use the year before; i.e., that reclamation should be as easy for the recipient as possible (**61**(b). 241–5 = **72**. 179–83). On the other hand, the allotment which Menches received in 113/112 B.C. was taken from the least hopeful land, that which had been unproductive for 20 years or more (**75**. 51).

Despite the Crown's obvious anxiety to reclaim as much waste land as possible, it was not permitted merely to seize such property for oneself without due administrative and fiscal process. So in **1125** we find that men who have reclaimed (κατειρ[γάcθαι]) small portions of land in addition to their legitimate farms are charged with the clearly punitive rent of 5 artabs per aroura. This is the same rent that Menches was required to pay in **10**, where the high rate is to be regarded as at once a price of office and a negative incentive to bring the land to full use as quickly as possible.

If all other efforts to gain tenants failed, derelict property might be sold outright (**1101**). The Kerkeosiris archive gives us no example of an ordinary farmer who was forced to reclaim land against his will.

Productive Land and Rents at Kerkeosiris (see p. 6)

Date	Arouras sown	Artabs charged	Reference
124/23	1227$\frac{3}{4}$	4858$\frac{2}{3}$	**1129**. 10
123/22	?	?	—
122/21	1308$\frac{3}{4}$	5274$\frac{7}{12}$	**66**. 18
121/20	1185$\frac{1}{4}$	4847$\frac{1}{2}$	**66**. 93
120/19	?	?	—
119/18	1139$\frac{1}{4}$	4642$\frac{1}{12}$	**67**. 4
118/17	1139$\frac{1}{4}$	4642$\frac{1}{12}$	**60**. 55
117/16	1182$\frac{1}{4}$	4609$\frac{1}{12}$	**68**. 86
116/15	1179$\frac{1}{4}$	4594$\frac{1}{12}$	**1103**. 292
115/14	1193$\frac{3}{4}$	4665$\frac{5}{12}$	**69**. 5
114/13	1193$\frac{3}{4}$	4665$\frac{5}{12}$	**69**. 38 n.
113/12	1261$\frac{9}{16}$	4645$\frac{2}{3}$	**75** introd.
112/11	1263$\frac{1}{16}$	4653$\frac{1}{12}$	**70**. 4
111/10	1263$\frac{1}{16}$	4653$\frac{1}{12}$	**70**. 62

The counterpart to ὑπόλογος with its various subspecies (flooded, sanded, salty, etc.) was cπόριμος, or land ἐν ἀρετῆι, land which should *prima facie* yield a worthwhile crop if cultivated. This productive area varied from year to year, as did the rents collectable. The totals known to us are listed at the foot of of p. 5: cf. vol. I, pp. 562–3; Crawford, *Kerkeosiris* 117.

In addition to these figures **160** gives us 1261$\frac{5}{12}$ arouras rented for 4745$\frac{2}{3}$ artabs in an uncertain year, most probably 120/119 B.C.

As evidence of economic trends these figures must be used with caution. About 35 more arouras were sown in the last year of the series than in the first, but these brought in about 5 per cent less rent. On the other hand, 39 arouras of good land had been taken from the βαcιλική and distributed to cleruchs in 121/120; and 20 arouras which had been removed from ὑπόλογος in 113/112 do not appear here because they were allotted as a cleros for Menches. And while rents from βαcιλικοὶ γεωργοί declined, charges on cleruchs were increased over the same period (below, 11–12).

Crown land at Kerkeosiris was farmed by persons in many walks of life, individually and in associations; they included not only men known to us exclusively in their role of βαcιλικοὶ γεωργοί, but also cleruchs, priests, and men of other professions, as well as temples; for details see *Crown Tenants*, pp. 114–17. But no woman is found in possession of land at Kerkeosiris.

By whom rents on Crown land were fixed – the komogrammateus, the komomisthotes of **183**, or some other official – is not clear. But the range of permissible rents was clearly limited: during most of the period covered by our archive the only rents in use for non-cleruchic tenants were probably 4$\frac{11}{12}$, 4$\frac{1}{2}$, 4, 3$\frac{1}{2}$, 3$\frac{1}{4}$, 3, 2$\frac{1}{2}$, 2, and 1 artab per aroura; and of these rent at 3$\frac{1}{4}$ artabs appears to have been limited to certain land leased to the shrine of Petesouchos (**1103**. 176 note). In years 4 and 5 of Soter II, special reduced rates of $\frac{1}{2}$ and $\frac{1}{4}$ artabs were introduced in favour of tenants of recent ὑπόλογος (**74**. 11–18; **94**. 32–5). For rent at 5 artabs, see pp. 5 and 8, **1126**. 7 note.

Unless special arrangements to the contrary had been made, the rental class to which a given lot was assigned might change from year to year, most probably in accordance with the value of the land under changing flood conditions. Peasants were also able to exchange holdings with one another in whole or in part whether or not the rent had been changed; cf. especially **85**, **1103**, **1105–7**, **1117–20**. Nevertheless, most men farmed much the same land from year to year under much the same terms. They called the land their own (**42**. 10–11; **50**. 4–5), and their sons might farm it after them (cf. e.g. **84**. 104–5 with **1118**. 97–8). Under these circumstances, fear of being dispossessed from the land by an offer of higher rent cannot have been very lively, and may not have existed at all except for those who undertook long-term leases at special rates. Even then it may have been necessary at times for the new bidder to demonstrate negligence on the part of the first lessee (cf. **72**. 421–2).

The fluctuations in rental which we may observe taking place in this archive are not compatible with the theory of land tenure developed by Rostovtzeff and Wilcken (*Kolonat* 47 ff., *Gdz*. 272–8), according to which Crown land was rented for indefinite periods by means of large-scale διαμιcθώcειc which fixed with great rigidity the conditions to be met up to such time as popular outrage or government avarice brought about another διαμίcθωcιc. It has elsewhere been suggested that this theory be abandoned (my *Crown Tenants*, p. 120 with note 28).

Texts in vol. I distinguish between two primary modes of acquiring a tenancy – land is either μεμιcθωμένη or it is let ἄνευ cυναλλάξεωc: **61**(b). 21–2, 20–88 vs. 89–106; cf. **72**. 68. The same verbal opposition is met also in respect to ἱερὰ γῆ in **6**. 30–2. The distinguishing feature of the land which these texts call μεμιcθωμένη, then, is that it alone is the object of lease agreements called cυναλλάξειc. By the descriptions of those portions of μεμιcθωμένη which are preserved for us in **61**(b) and **72**, we know that the conditions of such cυναλλάξειc varied greatly; and indeed a dioecetes investigating such land had to inquire not only who the lessees were (and the lessors), but ἐπὶ τίcι, 'on what conditions' the land had been let (**61**(b). 41). The variety of conditions found (cf. **61**(b). 1–87, 121–9, 346–414; **72**. 24–34; further **710**, **737**, **807**) forbids us to suppose that this procedure was followed in leasing land to most Crown tenants, as a greater degree of standardization must have been necessary on practical grounds. On the contrary, these are long-term arrangements, often emphyteutic, aimed at the reclamation of derelict land rather than the ordinary cultivation of cπόριμοc.

The consequence of these observations is that ordinary Crown land was either leased ἄνευ cυναλλάξεωc or by some third method, but a mid-course between leases with and without special terms is hard to find. References to land farmed ἄνευ cυναλλάξεωc in **61**(b) and **72** we therefore take to mean nothing more than land let as normal βαcιλική in contrast to its previous special status. A more sinister view is expressed in *Kolonat* 53–7.

Concerning the normal terms on which Crown land was let, however, we are not at all well informed. Leases of such from the period have not been found and can hardly be expected if cυναλλάξειc were reserved for special arrangements. But the impression given by our tax rolls and land surveys is that this land was leased from year to year for what it was worth; that rates fluctuated annually according to the condition of the land; that renewal of the lease was automatic not only to the farmer but his heirs so long as the land was desired and the dues were met, but that giving up the land or acquiring new parcels was easy and commonplace. Registration in such tax rolls as **1105** and **1107**, with cadastral information recorded in registers like **1116–21**, is perhaps all that was officially needed to assure a tenant rights and responsibilities over a given piece of land. In so small a hamlet as Kerkeosiris, verbal understanding with the komogrammateus was probably sufficient to bring this about; a more formal request was required in the larger Euhemeria (P. Jand. 134; cf. also **808**).

The rental of land according to its worth (ἐκ τῆc ἀξίαc) has generally been regarded as an emergency measure allowed by the Ptolemaic administration only when the peasantry could no longer be forced or cajoled into paying higher rents (cf. *Kolonat* 33); but the remarkable thing in fact is not that land should be rented at its worth, but rather that it was ever rented otherwise. The chief exception to rental ἐκ τῆc ἀξίαc has already been discussed – the letting of *ὑπόλογος* on special terms over long periods, during which a set rent was to be paid apparently in disregard of actual flood conditions. In such cases rent was set low enough that the lessee nevertheless stood to make sufficient profit from the good years if he succeeded in working the land. Rents in excess of the land's true value also seem to have been assigned as punishments, and as the price of office (above, p. 5).

In some cases rents were to all appearances established with regard to the status of the lessee: cleruchs often leased Crown land at either 5 or 5⅓ artabs per aroura. (5 artabs: **84**. 75, 77, 79, 83, 86 (p. 161 below), 88, 96; **1103**. 66; **1117**. 12; **1120**. 44, 71, 72, 74, 75, 78, 81, 84, 95, 111; **1122**. 25; **1124**. 5⅓ artabs: **98**. 1–26; **1103**. 264–86; **1120**. 25; **1133**. 76–7; **1148**. 4–5.) Where such parcels can be located in surveys, they are invariably adjacent to the tenant's own cleruchic plot. It is surprising to find this ordinarily favoured class paying higher rent than the peasantry, but it seems likely that this disadvantage was more than counterbalanced by a remission of taxes (**1105**. 40, **1107**. 279 notes).

By whatever means land was rented, Crown tenants had their names registered in great tax rolls stating the amount of property held by each and the dues owed thereon, with space left under each entry to record payments as these were made (**94**+**1107**, **1105**+**93**). The dues recorded in these rolls included not only rental itself, but also a series of taxes discussed in the introductions to **1105** and **1128**. It is clear that not all taxes were applicable to all land, but we cannot at present determine the principles which lay behind individual assessments.

Rent and taxes were apparently due on all land that with normal care should have yielded a crop. We find instances of rent collected on land that went unsown (**1103**. 69, 108, 116–17, 290; **1119**. 55; cf. **1148**. 2 n.), but in such cases summary crop reports state that individual or collective negligence by the tenants was at fault (**61**(a). 176–7; **66**. 56–74; **67**. 70–88; **68**. 83–5).

All known dues for Crown land at Kerkeosiris were stated in terms of wheat, but within clearly defined limits other modes of payment were accepted. Taking the village as a whole, cash payments were made on land sown with aracus, up to the value of $39\frac{5}{12}$ artabs of wheat; the price was probably 400 copper drachmas per artab (**1104**. 2 note). Five hundred artabs of lentils were taken for the same amount of wheat; and a predetermined quantity of barley, which varied from year to year, was accepted at the ratio 5 art. barley = 3 art. wheat. As late as 123 B.C. dues could also be paid in beans and aracus, 7 artabs of either being reckoned as 3 of wheat (**1129**. 57 n.); but this was not done in later texts.

The manner in which it was determined what crop each man should pay – how far this was a matter of personal choice and how far prescribed by the Crown – is quite unclear. The theoretical arrangement of rents in **1104** appears to have nothing to do with this question, but it is worth noting that the amount of barley required for 113 B.C. (**89**. 10) exceeds the total rent due on land planted with barley that year according to **69**. 13. Lists were kept of those who paid in crops other than wheat (lentils: **1134**; **1137**. 44–67; **1138**. 43–62; barley: **1137**. 32–43, 68–77; **1138**. 64–79; cf. **1135**).

Grain collection began in Pharmouthi (18 April–17 May at this period), was at its heaviest in this and the following month, and was all but over by the end of Payni (**89**, **1129–31**). In the one complete collection record which we have all rent due was in by the end of the calendar year (**89**, from 113 B.C.). The rolls **1105**+**93** and **94**+**1107** show clearly that most men paid in a series of instalments which might take several months to complete, and in this respect Kerkeosiran practice differs in no way from that found in Upper Egypt (cf. Packman, *Taxes* 62–3). Grain apparently could be delivered at Kerkeosiris either to the royal granary or to that owned by the shrine of Petesouchos (**61**(b). 386; **1140**. 93). It could also be delivered at a neighbouring village and credited to a farmer in Kerkeosiris by giro transfer (**89**. 71; **1129**. 34–6). Finally, dues could be paid from grain held in private accounts by means of a simple banking transaction (e.g. **1105**. 7). Such liberal procedure conflicts with the usual interpretation of **27**, a rather obscure document which is in need of further study.[1]

The artab referred to in our tax documents contained 36 choinikes; in **61**(b). 390 it is called δοχικόν (*sc.* μέτρον) to distinguish it from an artab of 42 choinikes used in the Souchieion. The suggestion has been made that in reports to the government neither of these artabs was used, but instead one of 40 choinikes, a most confusing procedure which would lend itself handily to official fraud (**61**(b). 317–19 note). In fact there is no 40-choinix artab in these papers: the calculation by which the editors of vol. I arrive at that measure (p. 227) is dependent on the assumption that a tax called τριχοίνικον was collected on all land under cultivation, an assumption which we now know to be false (**1105** introd.). It is to be noted further that in the one case known to us where grain paid for dues had been reckoned in terms of an artab other than δοχικόν, this fact was stated and the figures were

[1] This text, a circular emanating from the office of the dioecetes, cites an oath to be administered to the γενηματοφύλακες. Among other things, they must swear (60 ff.) παρακομ[ίζειν δὲ] ἐπὶ τοὺς ἀποδεδειγμένους [τόπου]ς καὶ μηθὲν τούτων καταπ̣ρ̣ο̣ήςε[cθαι ἀλλὰ (?)] | ἐπὰν καὶ {περὶ} τὸ περὶ τῆς [ἀφέςε]ω̣ς πρόγραμμα ἐκτεθῆι ἐὰ̣ν μὴ̣ πάντ[ων] | ὧν δέον ἐςτὶ παραδοθέντω[ν καὶ] τῶν ἐφελκομένων πρὸς τοὺς ἔμ[π]ροςθεν χρόνους | ἐκπληρωθέντων ἐπις[. The Greek is extraordinarily difficult and possibly corrupt, but the general thought is fairly clear: 'to convey [the crops] to the appointed places, and release no portion of them in advance, but when the announcement concerning crop release has been posted, [and not even then] unless all necessary charges, including arrears from previous years, have been paid in full'. The restoration of [ἀφέςε]ω̣ς can hardly be doubted: all other instances of ἄφεςις in the sense of 'crop release' concern cleruchic holdings (P. Petrie II 2(1). 10; P. Amh. II 43. 9; **815** frag. 2 verso 20, 3 recto 12, 5. 32, 6. 28), but land ἐν ἀφέςει as well as Crown land is also involved here (l. 55).

What, however, is the understood object of παρακομ[ίζειν and καταπ̣ρ̣ο̣ήςε[cθαι, and what crops are covered by the περὶ τῆς [ἀφέςε]ω̣ς πρόγραμμα? If the regular rental of Crown grain-land is meant (see as representative W*Gdz* 331 introd.; Préaux, *L'économie royale* 126–9), then the Roman-age practice envisaged in e.g. P. Petaus 53, and the Sicilian procedure which Cicero considered outrageous (*In Verrem* 3. 36) would be parallel. But as this is plainly not the way such charges were collected in Kerkeosiris, or in the Upper Egyptian texts studied by Packman (*Taxes* 62 f.), we should then have to consider this oath a dead letter, perhaps an innovation which failed to put itself through.

The context of the oath, however, and the tenor of the letter in which it is contained, suggest rather that the text deals not with the regular grain harvest, but with fodder and second crops (χλωρῶν καὶ τῶν ἄλλων ἐπιςπόρων, 55–6), which are otherwise known to have been subject to special regulations that would not be reflected in the tax lists of the present volume. See Rostovtzeff, *JEA* 6 (1920), 174–5.

then converted (**61**(b). 385–90). Accounts usually state whether grain was received by a measure called *εἰcδέξιμον* (or *δέξιμον*) or by that which was *ἐξαχοίνικον*, but these seem simply to be accounting terms indicating that grain received was or was not subject to a cleaning charge (**1105** introd.).

The Ptolemaic (and pre-Ptolemaic) practice of granting parcels of land to various army, police, and civil officials in the form of cleroi is well known. At Kerkeosiris this cleruchic land occupied an area surpassed only by the *βαcιλική*, the arable portion of which it exceeded by some hundreds of arouras. In the 52nd year of Euergetes II some $1581\frac{11}{32}$ arouras of this land existed about the village, taken in part from the *cπόριμοc βαcιλική* and in part from *ὑπόλογοc*, according to the terms of the various grants. This figure was soon reduced to $1574\frac{27}{32}$ by the removal of an *ἑπτάρουροc μάχιμοc* (**62**. 307 n.), and despite numerous re-allocations of individual cleroi in consequence of inheritance, promotions, or cessions, the total remained stable until an additional 20 arouras were assigned to Menches in 113/112. Cleruchs were for the most part not absentee landlords, but present and active in Kerkeosiris, as may be seen not only in that many of them tilled their allotments personally (cf. Index IX, s.v. *γεωργὸc αὐτόc*), but also from complaints against individuals recorded in numerous petitions. By the time of our archive allotments were hereditary (**124**. 32–3), and many instances of son succeeding to father or brother to brother are found in the present volume. Women are not found in possession of cleroi, any more than in possession of Crown land at Kerkeosiris in this period.

Such land lists as **1108–15** regularly distinguish between catoecic and non-catoecic cleruchs, detailing catoecic grants from a given year or reign before proceeding to non-catoecic. The latter consisted not only of various police officers, but also native troops enrolled within a laarchy, cavalry as well as foot. Greek names are preponderant among all cleruchs except these native troops; and while this preponderance is due in part to the adoption of Greek names by higher echelons of Egyptian society (cf. vol. I, 546–7), there seems little doubt that a division in nomenclature so thorough-going as that found in our texts should reflect a true racial difference. Cf. also **1107**. 279 note.

Military cleruchs, both catoecic and non-catoecic, often bear a title which reflects the size of their allotments: so we find at Kerkeosiris *ἑπτάρουροι μάχιμοι*, *εἰκοcιάρουροι* and *τριακοντάρουροι ἱππεῖc*, an *ἑβδομηκοντάρουροc*, *ὀγδοηκοντάρουροι*, and *ἑκατοντάρουροι*. In addition there was a *τριακοντάρουροc χερcέφιπποc* among the police, if indeed his was a civil and not a military post. Among catoecs a chronological pattern appears: Philopator gave land to an *ἑβδομηκοντάρουροc*, Epiphanes to *ὀγδοηκοντάρουροι*, and so far as can be determined later grants, with the exception of five 80-aroura cleroi in the 31st year of Philometor, went to *ἑκατοντάρουροι*. These titles rarely correspond to the actual amount of land held at Kerkeosiris: real sizes were generally much smaller, though occasionally somewhat larger, than the nomenclature would suggest. In a minority of cases we are told that more of the allotment was to be found at a different village.

A particular complication in determining cleros sizes arises from the native troops introduced under Euergetes II, for we find that the amount of land attributed to these is reckoned differently according as the reference is taken from land lists or tax accounts. Thus:

	Land lists	Tax accounts
machimoi	6½ arouras	7 arouras
5 hippeis	19	20½
1 hippeus	15	16½
1 hippeus	5	5¼
1 hippeus	5	5⅜

In **61**(b). 333–40 the higher figures are obtained by adding to the lower ones a *διάφορον cχοινιcμοῦ*, supposedly the difference between the amount of land to which each man was entitled and the amount which a survey had determined to be in his possession. The results, however, are too uniform to be genuine; and the cleroi of two machimoi in **1122**. 16 and 26 are in fact measured at 6 7/16 and 6 9/16 arouras, both closer to 6½ than to 7. Even these figures are likely to be high (**87** introd.).

With the exception of the very smallest holdings, cleroi seldom occupied solid blocks of land, but were divided into scattered parcels; none the less, the survey lists **84**, **85**, **1117–20** show that parcels belonging to cleroi of a given class tend to be found in clusters.

The earliest text of this archive which provides unambiguous evidence concerning dues on cleruchic land is **61**(b). 327–45 from 118/117 B.C. In that year *ἔφοδοι*, *φυλακῖται*, *ἐρημοφύλακες*, and the native troops enrolled in laarchies were required to pay a *ἡμιαρτάβιον* tax – ½ artab per aroura – on such holdings as were at least partially cultivated (*ἧc μέροc ἐcπάρθαι* as contrasted with *ὅλο(ιc) ὑπολόγου*, which was exempt). In addition, ephodoi, phylakitai, and eremophylakes owed 1 artab per man for scribal fees, *γραμματικόν*. In calculating *ἡμιαρτάβιον* due, the cleros size used was that found after the addition of *διάφορον cχοινιcμοῦ*.

In the course of the next few years most of these dues increased in a manner reminiscent of the chronologically graduated stages of rent in long-term leases of Crown land. By 113 B.C. (**89**. 48–76), ephodoi, phylakitai, and native troops were assessed on unsown as well as sown holdings, and the rates charged to ephodoi doubled to 1 artab/aroura, the tax now being called *ἀρταβιεία*. In the same year, eremophylakes were subject to an additional *εἰcφορά* of 15 artabs, though it is not clear whether this was an assessment at 1½ artabs per aroura or was a *κατ' ἄνδρα* charge. Scribal fees remained unchanged, unless 2 artabs charged to a *χερcέφιπποc* was an innovation.

The following year (**98**+**1147**) the *ἡμιαρτάβιον* on *ἱππεῖc* was increased to an *ἀρταβιεία* of 1 artab/aroura; and one 20-aroura cavalryman who in fact held only 16½ arouras in Kerkeosiris paid for a full 20½-aroura cleros (**98**. 70). Conceivably he received exemption from the tax in the village where the remainder of his cleros was located. At the same time, the tax on machimoi was raised to ¾ artab per aroura: in **98**. 77 the new assessment is called τὸ (ἥμιcυ) (τέταρτον) but other texts retain the old name ἡμιαρτάβιον. Eremophylakes that year apparently paid no γραμματικόν, and the εἰcφορά was lowered to 10 artabs (**98**. 53–7); but the exemption for unsown land may have been removed. Over the period of our documentation, then, only phylakitai were left with an undisturbed tax rate.

Two apparent anomalies in this system should be noted: a 30-aroura cavalryman with $5\frac{3}{8}$ arouras at Kerkeosiris paid $2\frac{2}{3}$ artabs in 118/117 but $2\frac{3}{4}$ in 113 (**61**(b). 333 vs. **89**. 51 and 59); and in 112 he was assessed at $5\frac{1}{4}$ but actually paid $5\frac{1}{3}$ (**98**. 59–60; ες in the last line is a mistake for εγ́). Further, a 20-aroura cavalryman with $5\frac{1}{4}$ arouras pays $5\frac{1}{3}$ artabs (**98**. 72). The second case we cannot explain; but the first is due simply to governmental insistence that the Crown receive at worst no less than its due, the original charges of $2\frac{2}{3}$ and $5\frac{1}{4}$ artabs both being slightly under the accurate but unpayable sums of $2\frac{11}{16}$ and $5\frac{3}{8}$.

In addition to these regular and predictable charges, we find payments of 1, $1\frac{1}{2}$ or 2 artabs from cleruchs of various grades in **1140**. 86–7, **1144**. 34–40 and **1145**. But the purpose of these payments is not stated and they may not have been due on cleroi as such. **75**. 6 ff. mentions an ἀρταβιεία which fell upon three catoecs, but as no document in the archive records assessment or collection of this tax from persons other than these three individuals there may have been special circumstances involved; the same applies to a ἡμιαρτάβιον apparently connected with a catoec in **64**. 80, if τὸ ∠ in that text is indeed this tax. Cleruchs were further subject to a προcλήψεως cτέφανος on receipt of their allotments; but as this was paid only once (though sometimes in instalments) it is not surprising that we have no examples in the present volume. For other cleruchic dues see Lesquier, *Institutions militaires* 212–23.

A chart giving the history of cleruchic allotments found in Kerkeosiris after the grant to Menches in 113/112 B.C. may be found on p. 15 below. Abundant evidence on the agricultural use of this land published in vol. I has been minutely examined by Crawford, *Kerkeosiris* 53–85, with Tables III, IV, VI, VII, IX, and XV–XVIII.

Shrines and temples in or near Kerkeosiris held a total of $291\frac{7}{8}$ arouras, about $\frac{1}{6}$ of the village area, in the form of ἱερὰ γῆ. Scholars have sometimes emphasized that according to Egyptian thought sacred land was the property not of temple, shrine, or priesthood but of the god himself;[1] but this is not altogether true. It is the shrine that is named as proprietor in such references as ἰβιῶνος, ἰβίων τροφῆς, or simply ἐλαccόνων (**1109**. 2–3, **1110**. 29, **1120**. 38); and certain Crown land is spoken of indifferently as leased to pastophoroi of the god Mestasytmis, or to Mestasytmis himself (**72**. 24–34 vs. **94**. 34–5).

Chief holder of sacred land in Kerkeosiris was Souchos, with $141\frac{1}{2}$ arouras unequally divided between 20 arouras of garden or vineyard and $121\frac{1}{2}$ of grainland. Most of our texts refer to this property as water-logged and unproductive, but such was not its

[1] 'Der Eigentümer des Landes ist *der Gott*' – Rostovtzeff, *GGA* 1909, p. 623, italics R.'s. Similarly Bouché-Leclercq, *Histoire des Lagides* III 191. Cf. W*Gdz* 278.

permanent condition: we find wheat growing in **1119**. 52–3, 115/114 B.C.; and it is hard to explain the vegetable garden of **1121**. 2 otherwise than as the property of Souchos.

It has been proposed that in view of the generally bad condition of this land tenants may have worked only under compulsion (Crawford, p. 96). But the references just cited show that the land was not so bad as previous evidence would lead one to believe, and it is to the highest degree doubtful whether any temple was able to commandeer cultivators in the Ptolemaic period (see pp. 17 ff., *Crown Tenants* pp. 121 ff.). The possibility that the men whom such texts as **1110**. 5–15 list as being in charge of the land were in fact priests, as is the case in all similar instances at Kerkeosiris, should not be dismissed; for although the priesthood of Soknebtynis worked their land *κοινῆι*, that of Souchos may have preferred a division *nominatim*. The location of the temple itself is undetermined. Arsinoe remains the best suggestion: others are Medinet Madi and Kerkeosiris itself (vol. I, p. 544; Crawford, p. 89 n. 9).

The temple of Souchos is not known to have had other regular revenue from Kerkeosiris. There is no indication that taxes were ever levied against its property in the village.

In the 41st and 42nd years of Euergetes II a temple of Soknebtynis, presumably the *λόγιμον ἱερόν* of Tebtunis, received at Kerkeosiris a total of 131 arouras of arable land dedicated by native troops enrolled in Chomenis' laarchy, who received cleruchic grants in those years. It is possible that it was the dedication of this land which reduced the size of cleroi given to machimoi from a nominal 7 arouras to 6½, and those given to cavalrymen from 20 to 19; if this is so, however, dedications from a much wider area than the village itself must have been centred at Kerkeosiris, since the *Χομηνιακοί* in residence could account for only a little over 20 arouras. This land was invariably booked to the priests of the temple, who farmed it themselves from at least the 51st to the 54th years of Euergetes. The following year they let the land to others (**63**. 18–23 = **1110**. 16–22), and our evidence fails after that date. In addition to its holdings of *ἱερὰ γῆ* the temple leased a small quantity of Crown land which it sublet to one Petermouthis son of Amenneus; neither this man nor the tenants of the sacred land proper are known to have had other temple connections. One-third the revenues from certain dovecotes were also a perquisite of Soknebtynis.

This temple is listed in **61**(b). 324 as owing a tax of ½ artab per aroura on land under cultivation, a total of 65 artabs per year; and this is the amount paid in **98**. 28.

Kerkeosiris encompassed some 13 village shrines listed in **88** (cf. my *Crown Peasants*, p. 116 n. 14), but of these only five owned sacred land for farming. The largest of the *ἐλάccονα ἱερά* was a shrine to Petesouchos, of sufficient stature to possess a ceremonial entrance way, *δρόμοc*, and a granary of its own; the 6-choinix measure here used was accepted as a standard in both public and private transactions (**61**(b). 386; **105**. 40–1), and grain for public dues could be paid at this granary (**61**(b) loc. cit.; **1140**. 94; cf. **852**. 96 for Ptolemais Arabon). Petesouchos being a local form of Souchos, his shrine was called a *Coυχιεῖον*; this rather confusing nomenclature has misled one recent scholar into supposing that the first-class temple of Souchos was also located in the village (Crawford, 89–90).

We have no record of crop production on the $5\frac{3}{8}$ arouras of *ἱερὰ γῆ* belonging to Petesouchos. On the other hand, this shrine was one of the most important lessees of *βασιλική* (cf. *Crown Tenants*, 121–4; **1104**. 1–9 with note). No fewer than seven sub-lessees are known from our texts, none of them with any apparent priestly status. In addition to revenue derived herefrom, the shrine received 5 artabs a year in required donations (**88**. 4–15).

Three shrines to Thoth/Hermes with associated ibis feeding stations and burial grounds were found in Kerkeosiris: that under the care of Hergeus and his brothers owned 4 arouras, those under Pnepheros son of Peteimouthes (later succeeded by another (?) Hergeus) and Cheyris and brothers owned 5 each. A payment for *μίcθωcιc* credited to the first of these in **1146**. 29 indicates that it too rented Crown land.

Finally, a shrine to Onnophris held one aroura of sacred land.

All five of these shrines were subject to a tax of $\frac{1}{2}$ artab per aroura, which one infers from **61**(b). 326 should have been collected only if the land was at least partly sown. Such is also the most natural interpretation of **98**. 27 ff.; but at least four of the shrines which pay dues in that text had only barren land that year (**1114**. 1–5). In 115/114 all the shrines were *ἐν ὑπολόγωι*: but the following year $21\frac{1}{6}$ artabs were collected from *ἐλάccονα ἱερά* at Kerkeosiris (**89**. 67), a figure so high that it is tempting to suppose the *ἡμιαρτάβιον* had been increased for sacred as well as cleruchic land. It is conceivable, however, that the payments in **89** tacitly include an *εἰcφορά*, which we know from **1149**. 53–8 to have been levied against the land of Petesouchos, Orsenouphis, and at least one of the ibis shrines on occasion.

How and whether the undeniable fact that these shrines and the temple of Soknebtynis (but apparently not that of Souchos) were taxed can be reconciled with the decree **5**. 57–61, which orders that neither *κ̣[οι]ν̣ω̣ν̣ι̣(κὰ) μηδὲ cτεφά(νουc) μηδὲ τὰ ἀρτ̣ά̣(βια)* be exacted from *τῶν ἀνιερωμένων τοῖc θε[οῖc* is a matter of highest importance which these texts in no way help to solve. The long-standing proposal to distinguish between *ἀνιερωμένη* and *ἱερὰ γῆ* can hardly be maintained (cf. *Crown Tenants*, pp. 122 f.). But it is not lightly to be assumed that a decree granting privileges to priesthood in a land so noted for piety as Egypt was ignored, particularly when one considers that the regulation against collecting *cτέφανοι* on sacred property was apparently extended to cover even Crown land leased by Petesouchos (**93**. 55 ff.).

Cleruchic Land in Kerkeosiris, 112/111 B.C.

The chart below is based on **1115**. For similar data 8 years earlier, see Crawford, p. 147, Tables I and II.

Date	Cleruchs	Size of Cleros titular/actual
207/206 Philopator, year 16	1 katoikos	70/70
	1 chersephippos	30/34 $\frac{3}{32}$
205/180 Epiphanes	3 katoikoi	
	one at	80/80
	one at	80/16
	one at	80? or 30?/18 $\frac{3}{8}$
180/45 Philometor	3 syngeneis katoikon	
	one at	100/40*
	two at	100/5 $\frac{3}{8}$*
	1 eremophylax	—/10
151/50 year 31	5 katoikoi	80/40
150/49 year 32	2 eremophylakes	—/10
149/48 33	2 phylakitai	—/10
148/47 34	5 katoikoi	
	one at	100/60
	two at	100/24
	two at	100?/10
137/36 Euergetes, year 34	1 katoikos	100?/12
	2 ephodoi	—/12
135/34 36	3 katoikoi	
	one at	100?/12
	one at	100/34
	one at	100?/10
134/33 37	10 katoikoi	
	two at	100/50
	two at	100/40
	one at	100/30
	one at	100/25
	two at	100/20
	two at	100/10
130/29 41	1 hippeus	30/5 or 5 $\frac{3}{8}$*
	7 hippeis	
	five at	20/19 or 20 $\frac{1}{2}$
	one at	20/15 or 16 $\frac{1}{2}$*
	one at	20/5 or 5 $\frac{1}{4}$*
	30 machimoi	7/6 $\frac{1}{2}$ or 7
129/28 42	4 machimoi	7/6 $\frac{1}{2}$ or 7
125/24 46	15 machimoi	
	14 at	7/6 $\frac{1}{2}$ or **7**
	1 at	7/3*
121/20 50	5 machimoi	7/6 $\frac{1}{2}$ or **7**
118/17 53	1 katoikos	100/25
113/12 Soter II, year 5	Menches	—/20

* More of the cleros is located outside Kerkeosiris.

C. Quality of Life in Kerkeosiris

'By the end of the long reign of Ptolemy Euergetes II agriculture was running down... The standard of living, consistently low, dropped even further.

'It is on this note of poverty and despair...that one may suitably leave Kerkeosiris, the land, the village and its inhabitants.' So concludes the most comprehensive survey of our village ever written (Crawford, p. 139).

That Kerkeosiris was poor in modern terms is patently true. But what of despair?

The nature of available evidence strictly limits the statements which may be made concerning Kerkeosiris. Regarding such land and taxes as fell within the scope of our archive, we are extraordinarily well informed. So vast is the quantity of material at our disposal that even arguments from silence in some cases take on considerable force. So for example the absence of grain payments by catoecic cleruchs most probably indicates that the *ἀρταβιεία* required of three such in **75**. 4–11 was due to special circumstances and was not a recurring charge on catoecs as a class.

But our knowledge of day-to-day life apart from taxes and farming is virtually nil. Even in agriculture we are limited for the most part to grain and a handful of other crops grown on the *πεδίον* surrounding Kerkeosiris as opposed to such fruits, vines, and vegetables as may have been raised in home gardens, and in taxation for the most part to grain dues on the *πεδίον* as opposed to money taxes for any purpose. Assuredly, the village included men whose livelihoods never led them to take up hoe or scythe, but we hear almost exclusively of the farmer. Women and children are altogether absent from our tax accounts, and even from the letters and petitions we learn little about them.

We are well informed concerning the amount of grain which a peasant paid for his land, but not about the amount with which he was left. It is often said that the Crown tenant lost half his crop or a little more to the state, and the cleruch about one quarter; but these are mere guesses, and that for the cleruch probably much too high. A fifty-per-cent rental should at all events have placed no excessive burden upon the peasant: it would be in line with the rates for share-leasing that were commonplace between private individuals in the Roman period (cf. Herrmann, *Bodenpacht* 204 ff.), and with the very slight evidence for private Ptolemaic share-leasing listed by Seidl, *Ptolemäische Rechtsgeschichte* 130 n. 11.[1]

The fact is that we cannot determine whether the average inhabitant of Kerkeosiris considered himself well or badly clothed, housed, or fed; nor do we know whether his supply of food and other necessities would be considered sufficient for reasonable well-being today. The impression which Egypt gave outside visitors in the ancient world was one of abundance and comparative ease (e.g. DS 1 80. 5–6).

Class favouritism was of course a plain fact of life. Taxation on cleruchic land of any

[1] The rent charged for Crown land at Kerkeosiris compares rather favourably with the rates found in leases between private persons cited by Hennig, *Bodenpacht* 185–8, so far as the scant evidence and the difference in land quality permits a judgement. Cf. further **1099** introd.

status was low, and catoecic land may have been tax-free. Terms of land rental, too, regarded not only the character of the land but the status of the tenant, cleruchs and temples both apparently receiving tax advantages. But the *βαcιλικοὶ γεωργοί* too had privileges, which other classes seem sometimes to have been willing to pay to receive (**1103** introd.).

Perhaps the most galling feature of life in Ptolemaic Egypt as it is often understood, however, is the regimentation and uncertainty of peasant life.[1] The peasant's dues were fixed, we are told, with so little regard to real land value that rental *ἐκ τῆc ἀξίαc* was the exception rather than the rule, an alleviatory measure reserved for cultivators who could no longer meet dues established according to the theoretical 'Bonitätsklassen'.[2] Having received his issue of seed-grain, the peasant was then bound to the land until harvest;[3] and when this came he was compelled to pay the last grain of charges due before the crop could be touched for his own purposes (cf. p. 9 n. 1). And in paying his dues he was most probably victimized by a clever cheat; for the officials did not account for the grain collected by the same measure with which it was taken in (**61**(b). 317–19 n.). As if this were not bad enough, peasants were regularly compelled to till temple property, which was handled identically to Crown land by Crown officials.[4] Finally, if a man did find some Crown land at reasonable rates, he could be dispossessed at any time by whoever made a better offer.[5]

The baselessness of these views has for the most part been handled in the preceding sketch of land tenure and in *Crown Tenants*, pp. 118 ff. There is no evidence of Crown management of temple lands, but on the contrary even in rental of *βαcιλική* temples enjoyed a privileged status; land dues were regularly paid over a long interval, to all appearances at any granary convenient to the taxpayer; transfer of land between Crown tenants was commonplace, rents were adjusted yearly, there is no indication that the movements of the Crown tenant were unduly restricted by law.

The question remains to what extent these men were free to rent or refuse land as they chose. In reference to *ἱερὰ γῆ*, **6**. 30–2 has often been taken as proof that compulsory farming was a standard feature of Egyptian life: *ἐνίουc μιcθουμέν̣[ου]c̣ γᾶc τε καὶ ἕτερα ἐπὶ πλείονα χρόνον, τινὰc δὲ καὶ βιαζομέν[ου]c ἄνευ cυναλλάξεων*, 'some long-term lessees of land and other properties, and even some compelled without agreements'. But *βιαζο-*

[1] 'Everything was for the State and through the state, nothing for the individual, except the mere possibility of a gray existence which saved the worker from starvation' – Rostovtzeff, *JEA* 6 (1920), 164. 'Kein freier Schritt wird ihnen...gestattet, stets steht hinter ihnen ein beobachtender Beamter' (*Kolonat* 82). Cf. the grim machinery outlined in Tarn–Griffith, *Hellenistic Civilization* 177–209; Bevan, *History of Egypt* 145; *CAH* VII 137.

[2] *Kolonat* 33; W*Gdz* 276; Crawford 104.

[3] W*Gdz* 275 with earlier literature; *L'économie royale* 497; *CAH* VII 137.

[4] Otto, *Priester und Tempel* II, 86 f.; *L'économie royale* 481; W*Gdz* 278; *PWK* vA, I, col. 269; *CAH* VII 137 f.; cf. Partsch, *Bürgschaftsrecht* 629–36.

[5] 'The State was not bound by any contract with the "cultivator"; if at any moment it desired to dismiss one "cultivator" and replace him with another, it could do so' – Bevan 146. Similarly Tarn–Griffith 188; Rostovtzeff, *JEA* 6 (1920), 166.

μέν[ου]ϲ was interpreted as middle, not passive, by the first editors ('some who even take forcible possession without any contracts', vol. I, p. 62; so also COP p. 117); and the continuation of the sentence, *μὴ τελεῖν τοὺϲ καθή[κοντ]αϲ φόρουϲ*, shows that this is right: the temple could hardly have had strength to force men to till its land, yet lack strength to collect its rent. And *βιαζομένουϲ* used absolutely in the sentence would be very harsh, while governing *γᾶϲ* it is quite smooth. The priests' complaint is very similar to that of a cleruch in P. Lille 1.

One other verbal echo of wide-spread force has been detected in these papers: **61**(b) and other documents repeatedly refer to land farmed *διὰ τῶν κατὰ μέροϲ γεωργῶν*; the word *μέροϲ* Rostovtzeff suggests is equivalent to *μεριϲμόϲ* (*Kolonat* 57). But this is an impossible use of the word: 'by various tenants' is the right translation; cf. **61**(b). 50 note.

We have in fact no instance at Kerkeosiris during the years covered by the present volume in which compulsory cultivation of any type of land is clearly demonstrable or even reasonably probable, with one possible exception. In **1103**. 115–19 and 288–90 the tenants of Kerkeosiris are collectively held responsible not only for the pastures which they normally rent, but also for 9½ arouras charged with 28½ artabs rent: and of this only two arouras were sown. It is quite possible that we have here, if not compulsion directed at individuals, at least communal responsibility for land dues. Even this is not certain. On the whole, Grenfell and Hunt's long note on *βία* in **61**(b). 33 seems the most accurate judgement that has yet been passed on the subject.

PART ONE

PETITIONS, CORRESPONDENCE, AND REGULATIONS

BY

JAMES G. KEENAN

1094. Petition to the Komogrammateus

P. Teb. 125 — (*a*) 2·2 × 5·2 cm. (*b*) 5·5 × 5·7 cm. (*c*) 2·2 × 3·7 cm. — 114/113 B.C.

Three fragments from the beginning of a petition to Menches (line 1 restored) from Apollodoros, ὁ ἐξειληφὼς τὴν διάθεςιν καὶ τὸ τέλος τοῦ ἐλαίου. Since Apollodoros' activities as known from other texts (**38** = *WChr* 303, **39** = Sel. Pap. II 276, **157** [17 Epeiph, line 15 ined.], **212**) are limited to the year 4 (114/113 B.C.), it is likely that the present text should be assigned to the same year.

Very little survives – enough, however, to show that the complaint being brought is the same as that introduced in **38**. 10 ff., viz. the tax-farmer's business was suffering because of persons who were engaging in the sale of 'kolpitic', i.e. 'smuggled' or 'contraband', oil; cf. line 3 note. On the other hand, verbal differences between line 2 of the present text (note *ad loc.*) and **38**. 11 indicate that **38**. 10 ff. is not an exact copy of which the present text is the original; and because line 4 of our text cannot be restored from **38**, we must conclude that the incidents described in the two texts, though similar, are not identical. Cf. **38** introd.

The hand is very small, letters ranging in size from less than 0·2 cm. in height to (in exceptional cases: e.g. phi, line 1, psi, line 2) more than 0·5 cm. The norm is roughly 0·3 cm. This is not the hand which wrote **39**, also addressed to Menches from Apollodoros. With the exception of the second half of line 2, restorations below are supplied from **38**. 10–12.

For earlier bibliography on Ptolemaic tax-farming, see Rostovtzeff, *SEHHW* III 1396 f. (n. 125); for discussion on the oil monopoly in particular, see Préaux, *L'économie royale* 65–93. See now also Bingen, *CE* 21 (1946), 127–48, Préaux, *CE* 29 (1954), 312–27, and Wickersham, *BASP* 7 (1970), 45–51. The komogrammateus was concerned with all local matters involving the royal revenues. This explains why the present petition, concerning the illicit sale of oil, and **1095**, in which the plaintiff alleges that he was hindered in collecting land rents (lines 8–10, 24–6), were addressed to Menches. In **1096** there is nothing to suggest that the royal revenues were in any way directly affected, but the plaintiff is a βαςιλικὸς γεωργός, and Crown tenants regularly resorted to the komogrammateus as a first source of appeal (Rostovtzeff, *Kolonat* 68 ff., E. Berneker, *Münch. Beitr.* 22, 1935, 122–7). There is a recent listing and discussion of Ptolemaic petitions to the komogrammateus in P. Yale I, pp. 157 ff., where particular attention is paid to the competence of the komogrammateus vis-à-vis that of the komarch. **1094** should, like **38–9**, be classified as a προςαγγελία or προςάγγελμα; for lists and discussion thereon, see E. Berneker, *Zur Geschichte der Prozesseinleitung im ptolemäischen Recht* (Ansbach, 1930), 36–40, M. Hombert–Cl. Préaux, *CE* 17 (1942), 259–86, and A. di Bitonto, *Aegyptus* 48 (1968), 53 ff.

[Μεγχεῖ κ]ωμογραμ[ματεῖ Κερκεοϲίρεωϲ παρ' Ἀπο]λ̣λοδώρου
τοῦ ἐξειληφότ[οϲ] τὴν διάθεϲ̣[ιν καὶ]
[τὸ τέλοϲ το]ῦ ἐλα[ίου τῆϲ αὐτῆϲ εἰϲ τὸ δ (ἔτοϲ). τῆ]ϲ
ἐγλήμψεωϲ ἐν οὐ τ[ῆι τ]υχούϲ̣[ηι ἐνδείαι
[χάριν τῶν παρ]ε̣ι̣ϲ̣φ[ερόντων εἰϲ τὴν κώμην καὶ παραπωλ]ο̣ύ̣ν̣των
κολπιτεικὸν [ἔλαιον καὶ κίκι
[± 12]ω.[± 18 π]ερὶ τοῦ Πτολεμ[
[± 30].ου ἔλαιον τ̣[
. . . .

2 l. ἐκλήψεωϲ   3 l. κολπιτικόν

'To Menches, komogrammateus of Kerkeosiris, from Apollodoros, the contractor for the retailing and the tax upon oil at the same village for the year 4. My tax-farming contract...into extraordinary poverty because of those who are smuggling into the village and illicitly selling contraband oil and kiki...'

2 Cf. **38**. 11: τῆϲ ἐγλήμψεωϲ εἰϲ τέλοϲ καταλελ[ειμμέν]ηϲ, κτλ.

ἐγλήμψεωϲ (= ἐκλήψεωϲ): in context of the 'Staatspacht', synonymous with ὠνή: WO I p. 539 n. 1.

ἐν οὐ τ[ῆι τ]υχούϲ̣[ηι ἐνδείαι: for the use of τυγχάνω see *WB* II s.v. The appropriateness of the restoration ἐνδείαι is suggested by P. Rev. Laws (new ed. Bingen, SB Beiheft I) Cols. 45. 16 and 47. 9. At the end of the present line, and perhaps running over into the beginning of the next, a participle in agreement with ἐγλήμψεωϲ is needed. Perhaps γενομένηϲ, πεϲούϲηϲ, or simply οὔϲηϲ, the resulting phrase being a substitute for καταλελειμμένηϲ in **38**. 11.

3 κολπιτεικόν: originally taken to mean 'Kolpitic', i.e. imported from Syria (**38**. 12 note, H. Maspero, *Les finances de l'Égypte sous les Lagides* 74). On its subsequent identification as meaning 'smuggled' or 'contraband' (lit. bought or sold 'under the cloak'), see **709**. 9 note, Rostovtzeff, *Gnomon* 12 (1936), 51, *BL* III 240–1, Préaux, *L'économie royale* 90 with n. 5. Cf. P. Phil. 35. 22: κολπιτευόμενον. Part of the present line is transcribed in the note to **38**. 12. Variations from the transcription offered here are presumably due to slight deterioration in the condition of the papyrus.

4 Πτολεμ[: probably the personal name Ptolemaios.

1095. Petition to the Komogrammateus

P. Teb. 126 — 8·2 × 29·8 cm. — 113 B.C.

This petition and the following belong to a series which also includes **45** (*MChr* 40), **46** (*MChr* 41), and **47**, all addressed to Menches by βαϲιλικοὶ γεωργοί whose houses had been broken into and robbed by Pyrrhichos son of Dionysios, a catoecic cavalryman, and a villager, Herakleios son of Poseidippos, at the head of a large armed band (ϲὺν ἄλλοιϲ πλείϲτοιϲ ἐν μαχαίραιϲ). The plaintiffs were victims of a concerted raid which took place on 8 Mesore of the year 4 (23 August 113 B.C.), evidently during the daytime, for the petitions from this group which give details on the whereabouts of the victims at the time of the raid indicate that Pyrrhichos and Herakleios struck while the men of the households they plundered were away from home, at work in the fields (**47**. 3 ff.), or assisting in the collection of land rents (**45**. 9 ff., **1095**. 8–10 and note).

For the hand of these petitions, which is the same throughout, cf. the reproduction of **47** in pl. VII at the back of vol. I.

Μεγχεῖ κ̣[ωμογραμματεῖ]
Κερκεοσίρεω̣[ϲ]
παρὰ Τεῶτος [τοῦ ± 7]
βασιλικοῦ γεωρ[γοῦ τῶν]
ἐκ τῆς αὐτῆς. τῆι̣ ῆ̄ τοῦ
Μεσορὴ τοῦ δ (ἔτους) ὄντος μου
σὺν τοῖς ἄλλοις π̣ρεσβυτέροις
[τῶ]ν γεωργῶν πρὸς τῆι
πρακτορε̣ί̣α̣ι̣ τῶν ἐ̣ν̣οφειλο-
μ̣[έ]νων [πρὸ]ς τὴν μίσθωσιν
τοῦ αὐτοῦ ἔτ̣ο̣υς, ἐπελθόντες
ἐπὶ τὴν ὑπ[ά]ρ̣χουσάν μοι
οἰκίαν Πύρ̣ρ̣ι̣χος Διονυσίου
τῶν κα(τοίκων) ἱπ(πέων) καὶ Ἡράκλε[ι]ος Ποσει-
δίππο̣υ̣ τ̣ῶ̣ν ἐκ [τῆς] αὐτῆς
κώμης σὺν ἄ[λλο]ις πλείστοις
ἐν μαχαίραις κ̣[αὶ ο]ὐδενὶ
κόσμωι̣ χ̣ρ̣η̣[σ]ά̣μενοι συν-
[τ]ρ̣ί̣ψαν[τε]ς̣ τὰς θύρας
[γενό]μενοι ἔνδον ἀπη-
[νέγκαν]το θύραν καὶ
[± 6] οὐθενὸς ἁπλῶς
[ὄντος μοι] πρὸς αὐτούς,
[δι' ἣν] αἰτίαν ἐμπε-
ποδίσθαι ἐν τοῖς κατὰ τὴν
πρακτορείαν. διὸ ἐπιδίδω-
μί σ[οι] ὅπως περὶ ἑκάστων
ὑπ[ογρ]αφὴν ποιήσηι προσ-
υπο̣[τ]άξαντα καὶ τοῦ
ὑπομνή(ματος) ἀντίγρ(αφον) οἷ[ς] καθήκει
ἵν' ἐγὼ μὲν κομίσωμαι

τὰ ἐμαυτοῦ, αὐτοὶ δὲ τύχωcι
τῆc ἁρμοζούcηc ἐπιπλήξεωc.
εὐτύχει.

28–9 l. προcυποτάξαc

'To Menches, komogrammateus of Kerkeosiris, from Teos son of..., Crown tenant and inhabitant of the same village. On 8 Mesore of year 4 while I was engaged with the other elders of the tenants in the collection of sums owing for the land rent of the same year, Pyrrhichos son of Dionysios, a catoecic cavalryman, and Herakleios son of Poseidippos, an inhabitant of the same village, with very many other persons armed with swords, suddenly came upon my house and, having thrown off all restraint, they shattered the doors. Having made an entry, they carried off a door and..., although there was no dispute whatever between me and them. For this reason we were impeded in our duties of collection.

'I therefore present to you this complaint in order that you may subscribe to my statements, having added below a copy of the petition for the competent authorities, so that I may recover my own property and the accused may receive the punishment they deserve.

'Farewell.'

2 *Κερκεοcίρεω[c]*: nothing more is needed to fill out the line; cf. **45**. 2, **46**. 2, **1096**. 2.

3 *Τεῶτοc* [*τοῦ* ±7]: a *Τεῶc Πετεχῶντοc* is included in a list of persons *ἀπὸ τῶν πρεcβυτέρων* (**1137**. 8 ff., 23), but there is insufficient space in the lacuna of the present line to accommodate *Πετεχῶντοc* (**45**. 3, **46**. 3, and **1096**. 3 prove that *τοῦ* is required in the lacuna). On the other hand, one cannot discount the possibility that the patronymic was abbreviated, e.g. as *Πετεχῶ(ντοc)*. This *Πετεχῶν* had two sons named *Τεῶc*; see Index VI s.v.

5–6 *ῃ̣*: badly damaged, but guaranteed by **45**. 6, **46**. 6, **47**. 2, **1096**. 5.

7–8 *π̣ρεcβυτέροιc* [*τῶ*]*ν γεωργῶν*: in contemporary texts from Kerkeosiris the presbyteroi appear engaging in a number of tasks: inspecting with the komogrammateus and the komarch the dike works in the vicinity of the village (*περὶ τὴν κώμην χωματικὰ ἔργα*: **13**. 5 f.; see further on their concern for the dikes **50**. 20 ff.); working with the komarch to collect wheat, some of which was a special levy (*ἐπιγραφή*) for the visit of the king (*πρὸc τὴν τοῦ βαcιλέωc παρουcίαν*: **48**. 13 f. with editors' note on line 12); collecting land rents (the present text, lines 8 ff.; cf. **128** desc.). In addition, the presbyteroi were purportedly influential enough to help insure a friendly reception among the villagers for a worried tax-farmer (**40**. 17 ff.). For a full discussion on the presbyteroi, see A. Tomsin, 'Étude sur les *πρεcβύτεροι* des villages de la *χώρα* égyptienne', *BAB* 38 (1952), 95–130 with earlier bibliography given p. 95 n. 1, and specifically for the late second century B.C., pp. 111 ff. Tomsin's article is continued in the same volume on pp. 467–532. More recently, on the activities of the presbyteroi in conjunction with the komarch: P. Yale I p. 160.

8–10 *πρὸc τῆι πρακτορ̣ε̣ί̣α̣ι̣, κτλ.*: cf. **45**. 9 ff. where Demas son of Seuthes claims to have been involved in the same collection duties at the time of the raid. For *μίcθωcιc* as the rent due on Crown land, see above, pp. 2 ff. According to **89**. 26, where *μιc( )* should be resolved as *μιc(θώcεωc)*, 199¾ artabs of lentils were collected for rent on Crown land between Mesore 1 and 10 in year 4. These were the last in a series of instalment payments which had begun on Pharmouthi 1 (**89**. 14). It may therefore be suggested that *ἐνοφειλομένων* in our text does not refer to 'arrears', but rather to amounts owing on account for the current regnal/fiscal year. Cf. above, p. 9 and **1105**. 7 note.

13 *Πύρρ̣ιχοc Διονυcίου*: in all likelihood, son of Dionysios son of Pyrrhichos, *τῶν μεταβεβηκότων εἰc τὴν κατοικίαν ἐκ τῶν τριακονταρούρων Φυλέωc* (**45**. 14 note, *PPt* 2632, 2690, cf. below, Index VI for additional references). It is striking that he does not hold a cleros at Kerkeosiris even though he is already a *κάτοικοc ἱππεύc*. His friend Herakleios is not known apart from this raid.

17 *ἐν μαχαίραιc*: **16**. 14 note.

21 *θύραν*: cf. **45**. 37 and **47**. 35 when *θύραι μυρίκιναι* are declared stolen.

28–9 *προcυπο̣[τ]άξαντα* (= *προcυποτάξαc*): for the anacoluthon cf. **38**. 26, **45**. 29, **46**. 25, **47**. 28, **50**. 36, **1096**. 19, **1097**. 6–7. See further Mayser, *Grammatik* II, 1, 342–3 (n. 1).

30 *ὑπομνή(ματοc) ἀντίγρ(αφον)*: written in full in **50**. 37 and **1097**. 8–9.

1096. PETITION TO THE KOMOGRAMMATEUS

P. Teb. 127 — 7·8 × 27 cm. — 113 B.C.

Μεγχεῖ κωμογραμματεῖ Κερκε[οϲ]ίρεωϲ π̣[αρ]ὰ Πόρτιοϲ τοῦ Πόρτιοϲ βαϲ̣ιλικοῦ γεωργοῦ τῶν ἐκ τῆϲ αὐτῆϲ. τῆι η τοῦ Μεϲορὴ τοῦ δ (ἔτουϲ) ἐπ[ελ-] θόντεϲ ἐπὶ τὴν ἀνεκτιϲ- μ̣[ένην μοι οἰκίαν] Πύρριχοϲ [Διονυϲίου τῶν κα(τοίκων) ἱπ(πέων) καὶ Ἡράκλει]οϲ [Ποϲειδίππου τῶν ἐκ τῆϲ αὐτῆϲ ϲ]ὺν [ἄλλοιϲ π]λ̣είϲτοιϲ [ἐν μαχαίραιϲ γενόμ]ενοι ἔνδον [ἀπηνέγκ]α̣ντο [τὰ ὑπογ]ε̣γραμμένα, [οὐθενὸϲ ἁπ]λ̣ῶϲ ὄντοϲ μοι [πρὸϲ αὐτούϲ.] διὸ ἐπι- [δίδωμί] ϲ̣οι ὅπωϲ περὶ [ἑκάϲτων ὑ]π̣ο̣γρ(αφὴν) ποιήϲ̣[ηι] [προϲ]υποτάξαντα καὶ τοῦ [ὑπο]μ̣νή(ματοϲ) ἀντίγρ(αφον) οἷϲ καθήκει [ἵνα τῶν ἐγκαλουμ]ε̣ν̣ων [καταϲταθέντων ἐγ]ὼ̣ μὲν [κομίϲωμ]α̣ι τὰ ἐμαυτοῦ, αὐτοὶ δ̣[ὲ τύχ]ω̣ϲι τῆϲ ἁρμο- ζούϲη[ϲ ἐπι]πλήξεωϲ.

εὐτύχει.

ἔϲτι̣ν̣ δ̣[ὲ] τ̣ὸ̣ [κ]αθ' ἕν·
ἱμάτιον γυ(ναικεῖον) ἄξι(ον) χα(λκοῦ) ʼΓω
χειτῶνα παιδι(κ) φ
ποτή(ριον) κ̣[
προϲκ[εφάλαιον

19 l. προϲυποτάξαϲ   29 i.e. χιτὼν παιδι(κόϲ)

'To Menches, komogrammateus of Kerkeosiris, from Portis son of Portis, Crown tenant and inhabitant of the same village. On 8 Mesore of year 4 Pyrrhichos son of Dionysios, a catoecic cavalryman, and Herakleios son of Poseidippos, an inhabitant of the same village, with very many other persons armed with swords, suddenly came upon the house that I have rebuilt. Having made an entry, they carried off the articles listed below, although there was no dispute whatever between me and them.

'I therefore present to you this complaint so that you may subscribe to my statements, having added below a copy of the petition for the competent authorities, so that, when the accused have been presented for trial, I may recover my own property and the accused may receive the punishment they deserve.

'Farewell.

'The itemized list is: a woman's robe worth 3800 copper (drachmas); a child's chiton, 500 (drachmas); a cup . . . ; a pillow . . . '

3 *Πόρτιος τοῦ Πόρτιος*: since the name *Πόρτις* has a number of variant terminations (cf. *NB* s.v.), this man is probably identical with the *Πόρτιος τοῦ Πόρτου* of **164**. 22. For other references in the present volume, see Index VI.

5 *η*: the superlinear stroke is not evident on the papyrus, but must have been there originally. It is very clear in **45**. 6, **46**. 6, and **47**. 2, though these strokes were not printed in vol. I.

7–8 *ἀνεκτισμ[ένην*: not the expected *ὑπάρχουσαν*.

11 For the exceptional shortness of this line, cf. lines 13–14.

12–14 *γενόμ]ενοι, κτλ.*: restored from **45**. 23 ff. For the shortness of lines 13 and 14, cf. line 11.

21–3 Restored from **45**. 31 ff.; cf. **50** (= *WChr* 329) lines 38 f.

28 Cf. **46**. 33 where the plaintiff lists among the articles stolen from him by Pyrrhichos and Herakleios *ἱμάτιον γυ(ναικεῖον) ἄξι(ον) (ταλάντου) α ʼΔ*.

1097. FRAGMENT OF A PETITION

UC 2399 | 10 × 11 cm. | Late second century

Ten lines from the end of a petition. Lines 1–3 contain damaged remnants from the conclusion of the complaint; lines 4–9, a formulaic request that the official concerned subscribe to the plaintiffs' statements, having added below a copy of the petition (cf. **1095**. 26 ff., **1096**. 16 ff., **45**. 27 ff., **46**. 22 ff., **47**. 25 ff., **50**. 35 ff.) so as to have it placed on record (*ἐν χρηματισμῶι*: cf. **44**. 25 f., **49**. 19 f.). Salutation in line 10. A left-hand margin of 1·7 cm.; bottom margin: 3·5 cm.

Not included among the vol. I *descripta*, but catalogued now as UC 2399, this papyrus came from the cartonnage of crocodile 27; for other papyri yielded by this mummy, see vol. I, p. xvii and above, p. xi. The hand is typical of the late second century, much like, if not in fact identical with, that which wrote the Pyrrhichos–Herakleios group of petitions. The formulaic closing of the present text, which parallels the formula of other Kerkeosiris petitions even as to the anacoluthon (lines 6–7, cf. **1095**. 28–9 note), makes it likely that this petition was directed to Menches. The substance of the complaint cannot be recovered.

. . . . . .

1 ạ.[

τοῦ βασιλ[. . . . .].λισεως

διὰ πλειόνων .[......].cομεν.
διὸ ἐπιδίδομέν c[οι ὅπω]c περὶ
ἑκάcτων ὑπογραφὴν
ποιήcηι προcυποτά-
ξαντα καὶ τοῦ ὑπομνή-
ματοc ἀντίγραφον ἵν' ὑπ̣ά̣ρ̣χ̣ηι̣
ἡμῖν ἐν χρηματιcμῶι.
εὐτύχει.

6–7 l. προcυποτάξαc

(Lines 4 ff.) 'We therefore present to you this complaint so that you may subscribe to our statements, having added below a copy of this petition so that we may have it on record.

'Farewell.'

1098. Fragments of a Petition

UC 2485	(*a*) 1 × 2·3 cm.	*c.* 114 B.C.
	(*b*) 2·5 × 2 cm.	
	(*c*) 1·6 × 3 cm.	
	(*d*) 7·2 × 7·8 cm.	

Four fragments of a petition, not previously mentioned, but catalogued as UC 2485. The number of the crocodile mummy which yielded this piece is unknown.

Of the three smaller fragments, (a) preserves a slight left-hand margin and must therefore have come from the left side of the original text; (b) and (c) each preserve middle sections of several lines of text, but their position with respect to each other and with respect to (a) is uncertain. All three must, however, precede (d), the largest fragment, which contains the end of the petition together with a bottom margin of 3·2 cm. An approximate date for the document and its connection with the Menches archive are indicated by the reference to the strategos Ptolemaios son of Philinos in lines 13–14 (see note *ad loc.*).

(fragment a)	(fragment b)	(fragment c)
ἐ̣κ̣[	ὁρμήc]αc εἰc φυ[γήν	].[
μ[	] ο̣ὐδὲ̣ ἐ̣νθε[	]. cυνεcτ̣[
	]ων παραχρῆ[μα	\`τῶ]ν αὐ(τῶν)'
		ἀ]πὸ δὲ τῶν [
		]....ν[

(fragment d)

διὸ ἐπιδίδω-]

[μι] ὑμῖν ὅπω̣ς̣ . . . [. . . . .]
ὁ δηλούμενος κατ̣α̣ς̣τ̣α̣[θῆι]
ἐπὶ Πτολεμαῖον Φ[ι]λίνου
τὸν στρατηγὸν ἵνα ἐγὼ μὲν
τὰ ἐμαυτοῦ \`κομ[ίς]ωμαι´, αὐτὸ̣ς δὲ
μὴ ἀθῶιος διαφύγη[ι].
εὐτυχ{ι}εῖτε.

(Lines 10 ff.) 'I therefore present to you this complaint so that...the above-named may be brought to trial before Ptolemaios son of Philinos, the strategus, so that I may recover my own property and the accused may not escape unpunished.

'Farewell.'

3 ὁρμήc]αc εἰc φυ[γήν: cf. **38**. 23: ε]ἰc φυγὴν ὡρμηκέναι; **48**. 24: εἰc φυγὴν ὁρμῆcαι; **230** desc.: εἰc φυγὴν ὥρημcαν. A description of the beating inflicted on the plaintiff by the accused and/or mention of articles stolen from the plaintiff must have preceded.

8 \`τῶ]ν αὐ(τῶν)´: written very small, between the lines.

10–11 διὸ ἐπιδίδω|μι]: restored *exempli gratia*. The rest of line 11 was perhaps filled with a passive participial form of ἀναζητέω or ἀcφαλίζω, in agreement with ὁ δηλούμενοc in line 12.

13–14 A Ptolemaios son of Philinos is known for his activity in reclaiming land ἀπὸ τοῦ ὑπολόγου in the year 49 (122/21 B.C.) (vol. I, p. 570, cf. Index VIII in that volume for full references), and a Ptolemaios, without patronymic, is known to have been strategus in 114 B.C. (**13**. 2, **15**. 15, cf. **28**. 1, **42**. 1, *PPt* 318). Appearance of the strategus with patronymic in the present text now makes it likely that the two persons are identical. His father Philinos is possibly (though unprovably) identical with the strategus of 125/4 B.C. (**700**. 18–19, 97, *PPt* 341, Henne, *Liste des stratèges* p. 6, Mussies, P.L. Bat. XIV, p. 16, no. 43).

15 τὰ ἐμαυτοῦ: refers to articles stolen from the plaintiff by the accused. Lists were sometimes appended at the bottom of petitions (e.g. **45–7**, **1096**); in other instances, as evidently in the present case, the items stolen are mentioned in the body of the text (e.g. **1095**). Cf. above, line 3 note.

16 Cf. **44**. 28.

17 εὐτυχ{ι}εῖτε: the scribe first wrote εὐτύχι (= εὐτύχει), then changed to the plural in order to conform to the number of officials addressed in the petition (cf. ὑμῖν, line 11), without cancelling the iota.

1099. LETTER FROM MENCHES TO HOROS

P. Teb. 142 30·2 × 11·5 cm. 114 B.C.

A letter from Menches informing Horos the basilikogrammateus that the *βαcιλικοὶ γεωργοί* of Kerkeosiris had retired (*ἀνακεχωρηκέναι*: line 4) to the temple at Narmouthis. The text is a fair copy of **26**. 11–24 (= *WChr* 330), with some omissions (cf. **142** desc.), written across the fibres on a dark brown, extremely brittle papyrus. A horizontal crack running through line 2 renders some of the readings in that line doubtful as to detail.

The anachoresis had occurred on 19 Phaophi of year 4 (**26**. 20 f.) while Menches was in Ptolemais Euergetis, the nome metropolis some 18 miles (160 stades: **92**. 4–5, **1102**. 3–4 [restored], cf. vol. II, pp. 397–400) from Kerkeosiris, for an auditing of his accounts. The wording *τῶν ἐπαιτουμένων λόγων* (lines 2–3) leaves doubt as to the nature of these accounts (Crawford, *Kerkeosiris* 25). It may be that this was a special, rather than a regular audit. Cf. **20**. 7 f.: *καὶ ἐὰν τὰ λογάρια ἀπαιτῶνται, κτλ.* On the auditing of Menches' accounts, see Harper, *Aegyptus* 14 (1934), 22 f.

The flight of the Crown tenants to the temple at Narmouthis indicates that the temples at Kerkeosiris did not possess asylia (Otto, *Priester und Tempel* II, 298 n. 6; generally on asylia: Fr. von Woess, *Münch. Beitr.* 5, 1923, cf. Rostovtzeff, *SEHHW* III, 1549 n. 180). This accords with what is otherwise known about the Kerkeosiris temples. They were of second or lesser rank (*δεύτερα* or *ἐλάccονα ἱερά*); some may have been of third rank. Two first-rank temples owned land near the village, but are not likely to have been situated there (see vol. I, p. 543 and above, p. 13). The expression *τὸ ἐν Ναρμοῦθι ἱερόν* in our text need not imply that there was only one temple at Narmouthis. Rather it suggests that there was only one temple at Narmouthis with asylia, and for this reason Menches considered additional specification unnecessary.

The reason for the anachoresis is unknown. Préaux (*L'économie royale* 501), followed by Braunert (*JJP* 9–10, 1955–6, 253 n. 66), believes that the Crown tenants here fled because the rent was too high. Such an explanation is possible, though not necessarily compelling. It may be noted that a brief statement composed by Menches on the same day as the anachoresis-report (**71**, Col. 2 of the papyrus which contains **26**) reveals that almost all the arouras sown in the year 3 had been irrigated by Phaophi 20 of the year 4, and that the sowing of these had just begun (104 arouras completed). The anachoresis may then have had something to do with the work of sowing. Even if so, its effects were temporary: later in the year 4, **1105+93** shows Crown tenants paying rents at the usual rates – and on time. In the only other instance of anachoresis attested for Kerkeosiran Crown tenants (**41**; **61**(b). 351 ff. and **72**. 341 ff. apparently concern long-term leases under special conditions), the reasons given are harassment of their wives and extortion attempts by Marres the topogrammateus and others.

For discussions concerning anachoresis, see Braunert, *JJP* 9–10 (1955–6), 240–93 with the works cited in the footnotes on those pages and, more recently, Walter Schmidt, *Der Einfluss der Anachoresis im Rechtsleben Ägyptens zur Ptolemäerzeit* (Diss. Köln, 1966).

Μ[εγχῆ]ς κωμ{μ}ογραμματεὺς Κερκεοσίρεως τῆς Π̣ολέμωνος μ[ε]ρίδος Ὥρωι
χ[α]ί̣ρ̣[ειν.] ὄ̣ν̣τι μ[οι] ἐν Π̣τ̣ο̣λ̣ε̣μ̣α̣ί̣δ̣ε̣ι̣ [Εὐ]εργέτ[ι]δι πρὸς τῆι ἐ̣[πιδόcει] τῶν ἐ̣[παιτου-]
μένων λόγων προcέπεcεν ἡμῖν τοὺc ἐκ τῆc κώμ̣η̣[c βαcι]λ̣ι̣κοὺc γεωργοὺc
ἀνακεχωρηκέναι ἐπὶ τὸ ἐν Ναρμοῦθι ἱερόν. καλῶc̣ [ἔ]χειν [ὑπέ]λ̣α̣βον π̣ρ̣ο̣cαν̣[ε-]
νέγκαι ὅπωc εἰδῆ̣c.

ἔρρωcο. (Ἔτουc) δ Φαῶφι κ̄.

Verso: *Ὥρωι.*

2 l. *Πτολεμαίδι*

'Menches, komogrammateus of Kerkeosiris of the division of Polemon, to Horos, greetings. When I was at Ptolemais Euergetis for the delivery of the accounts which were demanded, I happened to hear that the Crown tenants of the village had retired to the temple at Narmouthis. I considered it right to report the fact for your information.

'Good-bye. Year 4, Phaophi 20.'

(Verso): 'To Horos.'

1 Ὥρωι: it is clear from **26** that the basilikogrammateus is meant.

2 For Ptolemais Euergetis (or Euergetou), the nome metropolis, see **1102**. 3 and note. ἐ̣[πιδόcει]: restored from **26**. 13.

4 Ναρμοῦθι: the modern Medinet Madi; cf. *ZNW* 37 (1938), 274 ff., *CE* 14 (1939), 88, A. Grohmann, *From the World of Arabic Papyri* (Cairo, 1952), 10 and 214 n. 11. On its proximity to Kerkeosiris: vol. II, p. 391, Layton, *ZPE* 6 (1970), 184 with n. 8.

4–5 π̣ρ̣οcαν̣[ε]νέγκαι: **26**. 22 should accordingly be restored with first, not second aorist.

6 The date is 9 November 114 B.C.; cf. **71**. 8 note.

1100. Correspondence Concerning the Cession of Catoecic Land

P. Teb. 239 — (*a*) 13·4 × 12·8 cm. (*b*) 14·1 × 13·8 cm. — 114 B.C.

Correspondence concerning the cession (παραχώρηcιc) of catoecic land, here specifically a cleros of 5 arouras, to Philonautes son of Apollonios. Parallel texts are **30** (= W*Chr* 233) and **31**.

The situation in the present text is the same as that in the other two texts: the land had been ceded to Philonautes, but not yet recorded under his name in the official registers. He therefore addressed a petition (ὑπόμνημα) to Aristippos, ὁ πρὸc τῆι cυντάξει τῶν κατοίκων ἱππέων. It was this petition, mentioned in line 8, but lost at the end of our papyrus, which initiated this series of letters. What the papyrus does contain is, in chronological order (which the papyrus reverses), as follows:

1. Copy of a letter (8 ff.) from Aristippos to Apollonios, the basilikogrammateus. He states that the parachoresis has been substantiated by the scribes in his own office and presumably asks (this is also missing from our text, but cf. line 10 note) that the basilikogrammateus have the transfer registered in his list as well.

2. Copy of a letter (6–7) from Horos, who had succeeded Apollonios as basilikogrammateus by 19 Mecheir of year 3 (line 7), to Marres, the topogrammateus. He encloses a copy of Aristippos' letter.

3. Letter (2–5) from Marres to Menches. Enclosed is the copy of Horos' letter together with the rest of the correspondence in the series. This was received in Menches' office on 24 Mecheir of year 3 (line 1; cf. **30**. 1 and **31**. 1).

Relevant to the present text are the introductory discussions to **30** and W*Chr* 233; also W*Gdz* 176 f. and Kunkel, *ZSS*, Röm. Abt. 48 (1928), 285 ff., esp. 292 f. and 301. For the procedures ordinarily involved in parachoresis, see Kunkel, art. cit., Préaux, *L'économie royale* 474 f., Taubenschlag, *Law*² 228 f. and notes. Cf. below, line 3 note.

ἐλ(ήφθη) (ἔτουϲ) γ Μεχεὶρ κ̅δ̅.
(m. 2) Μαρρῆϲ Μεγχεῖ χαίρειν. τῆϲ πα̣[ρὰ Ὥρου βαϲ]ι̣λικοῦ γραμμα̣τ̣έ̣ω̣ϲ̣ ἐπιϲτολῆϲ περὶ ὧν δηλοῖ
π̣αρακεχωρῆϲθαι Φιλοναύτει Ἀπ[ολλων]ί̣ο̣υ̣ κ̣λ̣ή̣ρ̣ου [πε]ρὶ Κερκεοϲῖριν (ἀρουρῶν) ε τὸ ἀντίγραφ[ον]
ὑποτετάχαμεν ὅπω[ϲ εἰδὼϲ κατακολουθῇϲ τοῖϲ ἐπεϲταλμένοιϲ].
ἔρρωϲο̣. (ἔτουϲ) γ Μεχεὶρ κ̅α̅.
Ὧροϲ Μαρρεῖ χαίρειν. τ[ῆϲ παρὰ Ἀριϲτίππου τοῦ πρὸϲ τ]ῆι ϲυντάξει τῶν κατοίκων ἱππέων
ἐπιϲτολῆϲ ἀντίγραφον ὑ̣π̣ό̣κ̣ε̣ι̣τ̣[αι. ἔρρωϲο. (ἔτουϲ) γ Μεχ]εὶρ ι̅θ̅.
Ἀ̣ρ̣ί̣ϲ̣τιπποϲ Ἀπολλωνίωι χαίρε[ιν. τοῦ δεδομένου ἡμ]ῖ̣ν̣ ὑπομνήματοϲ παρὰ Φιλοναύτου
[τὸ ἀντίγρ]αφον ὑπόκ[ειται. ἐπεὶ οὖν καὶ οἱ παρ' ἡμῶν γραμματ]ε̣ῖϲ ἀ[νενη]ν̣όχαϲι γεγονέναι αὐτῶι
[τὴν παραχώρηϲιν τῶν ε (ἀρουρῶν), κτλ.

. . . .

Verso: Μεγχεῖ.

'Received, year 3, Mecheir 24.

(2nd hand) 'Marres to Menches, greetings. I have appended a copy of the letter from Horos, the basilikogrammateus, about the cession which he states has been made to Philonautes son of Apollonios of a holding of 5 arouras in the vicinity of Kerkeosiris in order that you, being informed, may execute its instructions. Good-bye. Year 3, Mecheir 21.

'Horos to Marres, greetings. I have appended a copy of the letter from Aristippos, superintendent for the assignment of the catoecic cavalry. Good-bye. Year 3, Mecheir 19.

'Aristippos to Apollonios, greetings. I have appended a copy of the petition given to me by Philonautes. Therefore, since my scribes have also reported that the cession has in fact been made to him...'

(Verso): 'To Menches.'

1 ἐλ(ήφθη): $\stackrel{\lambda}{\epsilon}$ pap. For the resolution, cf. PSI III 169. 1 note, *BASP* 7 (1970), 97. Not ἐλ(άβομεν) or ἔλ(αβον), the resolutions suggested in vol. I (**19** introd.). The date here is 13 March 114 B.C.

2 [Ὥρου]: supplied from line 6.

3 π̣αρακεχωρῆϲθαι: used technically of the transfer of catoecic land; cf. *MGdz* 112, 181, *WChr* 233. 3 note, Taubenschlag, *Law*^{2} 228 n. 19, P. Wisc. I p. 36. Such transfer was normally initiated by means of a ὁμολογία παραχωρήϲεωϲ between the alienator (in the present case, unknown) and alienee (here, Philonautes). No examples survive from Kerkeosiris. See, however, the texts cited by Schwarz, *Die öffentliche und private Urkunde*, 211 n. 1, BGU VIII 1731–4 with Kunkel's discussion in *ZSS*, Röm. Abt. 48 (1928), 285 ff.

Philonautes son of Apollonios appears nowhere else in the Kerkeosiris papyri. It is possible that he was not confirmed in the cession, or that he died before he could take over the land.

4 The lacuna is supplied from **30**. 4.

5 Mecheir 21: March 10.

6 [Ἀριϲτίππου]: supplied from line 8.

7 Mecheir 19: March 8.

9 The lacuna is supplied from **30**. 11.

10 Continue καλῶϲ ποιήϲειϲ ϲυντάξαϲ καὶ παρὰ ϲοὶ ἀναγράφειν εἰϲ αὐτὸν ἀκολούθωϲ (**30**. 12–13, cf. **31**. 13–14).

P. Teb. 237 14 × 14·5 cm. c. 113 B.C.

The text, though extremely fragmentary, can be seen to contain a series of letters concerning the State sale of *ὑπόλογος*, land which had suffered a loss of productivity, thereby causing a reduction in the total revenue (see above, pp. 4 f). Procedures involved in the sale of land by the State in the Roman period are well-known (recent summaries in P. Petaus, pp. 108 ff., with bibliography cited on p. 109, and Paul R. Swarney, *The Ptolemaic and Roman Idios Logos*, *A.S.P.* VIII, Toronto, 1970, 53 ff.). For the Ptolemaic period, the crucial text is P. Eleph. 14, the best discussion, Rostovtzeff, *Kolonat* 18 ff.

What is particularly striking about the present text is its affinities with papyri of the Roman period which contain similar series of correspondence – notably, P. Amh. II 68 (= *WChr* 374), of the late first century from the Hermopolite Nome, and P. Lond. Inv. 1876 (= SB V 7599), edited by Roberts and Skeat as 'A Sale of *ὙΠΟΛΟΓΟΣ* at Tebtunis in the Reign of Domitian', *Aegyptus* 13 (1933), 455–71. (See further P. Petaus 17–23.) It is, in fact, the closeness to these Roman documents which permits our identifying the nature of the present series of letters (for details, see commentary below, *passim*); but the incompleteness of our text (an indeterminate number of lines has been lost at the top) and the fragmentary condition of the extant lines (particularly lines 1–2 and 13–15) make conclusive interpretation difficult. For specific points the reader is once again referred to the commentary.

Preserved on the papyrus are the following items, in chronological order (which the papyrus reverses):

1. A short letter (lines 13–15) to Asklepiades, *ὁ ἐπὶ τῶν προσόδων* (cf. **27**. 94 and 98–9, *PPt* 975), in all probability from Eirenaios the dioecetes (cf. on this and generally on the sequence of parties concerned in the present series of letters, **27** Cols. I and IV).

2. A letter (lines 9–12) from Eirenaios to Horos, the basilikogrammateus, enclosing part 1 and ordering the dispatch of the *σχηματογραφίαι* (below, line 6 note).

3. End of what appears to be a circular letter (lines 1–7, with salutation restored in line 8) from Horos to either the topogrammateis or the komogrammateis of the nome (cf. **27**. 85: *τοπογραμματεῦσι* emended to *κωμογραμματεῦσι*), or both (cf. **27**. 2). The second and third possibilities appear more likely: if, however, the circular was addressed only to the topogrammateis, then it must be assumed, since this set of letters ultimately came to Menches' office, that a fourth item, a letter to Menches from the topogrammateus (at this time, Marres: **41** introd., cf. **1100**), has been completely lost.

At no point in our text has a date been preserved (dates were probably given in the lacunae of lines 8 and 12); nonetheless, an approximate date is suggested by the three officials whose names occur in the papyrus, all of whom are concerned in **27** (113 B.C.). Presumably, procedures such as those attested in the present text led to the creation of ἰδιόκτητοc γῆ at Kerkeosiris; but this is not corroborated in the surveys, which, however, extensive as they are, are incomplete.

. . . .

τὴν π̣αρά̣δειξ[ι]ν ὧν ἐμν[ήcα]τ̣[ο (ἀρουρῶν) ± 18]
ἀπὸ τῶν ἐπικεχωρ̣ημένων εἰδ[ῶν ± 16]
ὑπολόγου περὶ τὰ̣c ὑπ[ο]cημα̣[ιν]ο̣μέναc [κώμαc(?) cτοχαcάμενοι]
τοῦ μηθὲν ἐν τούτοιc ἀγνοηθῆ[ναι μηδὲ πρὸc χάριν οἰκο-]
νομηθῆναι, τῶν δὲ παραδειχθη[cομένων (ἀρουρῶν) πέμψαθ' ἡμῖν]
τὰc cχηματογραφίαc διccὰc εὐcήμω̣[c, ἐπιθέντεc τὰ μέτρα]
καὶ γειτνίαc ὅπωc τἄλλα οἰκονομη[θῆι καθάπερ ἐπέcταλται.]
[ἔρρωcθε. Date]
Εἰρηναῖοc Ὥρωι χαάρειν. τῆc πρὸc Ἀ[cκληπιάδην]
ἐπιcτολῆc ἀντίγραφον ὑπόκειται. [± 12]
ἀκολούθωc καὶ ὑποπαραδειχθηc̣[ομένων (ἀρουρῶν) αἱ cχηματο-]
γραφίαι πεμφθήτωcαν ἡμῖν εὐc[ήμωc. ἔρρωcο. Date]
Ἀcκληπιάδει. τοῦ μετενη[νεγμένου ἡμῖν ± 11]
ὑπὲρ τῆc ἐπικεχωρημέ[νηc
τοῖc ἡμετέροιc . . οιc καὶ ο̣υ̣[

'. . . the report of the arouras which he mentioned . . . from the permissible kinds (sc. of land) . . . derelict land in the vicinity of the villages(?) noted below, making it your aim to omit no particulars in these matters and to show no favours in taking care of them. Send me the plans of the arouras to be reported, in duplicate, clearly written, having added the measurements and the boundaries, so that the rest may be taken care of in accordance with the instructions.

'(Good-bye. Date.)'

'Eirenaios to Horos, greetings. I have appended a copy of the letter to Asklepiades . . . accordingly, and let the plans of the arouras to be reported below be sent to me clearly written. (Good-bye. Date.)'

'To Asklepiades. The (bid?) brought to me concerning the . . . permitted . . . to my . . .'

1 π̣αρά̣δειξ[ι]ν: evidently here, as in P. Amh. II 68. 33, a report based upon personal inspection (ἐπίcκεψιc) of the land for sale. In the lacuna supply, probably, something like προcφωνήcατε εἴ εἰcιν. We take the flow of thought in lines 1–5 to be: going on the spot and carrying out an inspection of the land mentioned, report to us if it is of the proper sort, and send us a plan of it.

2 ἐπικεχωρημένων εἰδ[ῶν: ἀπ[ὸ τοῦ εἰ]c πρᾶcιν ἐπικεχωρημένου ὑπολόγου (Roberts–Skeat text = SB 7599. 3); ἀπὸ [τοῦ] καθήκοντοc ὑπολόγου καὶ cυνκεχωρημένου εἰ[c] π[ρᾶ]cιν (P. Amh. 68. 3, cf. lines 7, 25, and 34), but εἰc cannot be read here. For εἴδη of land at Kerkeosiris, cf. **61**(a) 156. After εἰδ[ῶν, possibly something like καὶ μὴ ἀπὸ ἐμβρόχου; cf. SB 7599. 3. The exclusion from sale of ἔμβροχοc in the SB text is presumably owing to its being the easiest variety of ὑπόλογοc to reclaim.

3 [κώμαc(?): perhaps less doubtful than the query might suggest, particularly if this is in fact part of a circular letter addressed to the komogrammateis and/or topogrammateis. See introd.

cτοχαcάμενοι]: cf. P. Amh. 68. 4, SB 7599. 5. Plural if the letter is a circular; otherwise, singular.

4 Restored from SB 7599. 6. Cf. P. Amh. 68. 10.

5 παραδειχθη[cομένων: 'to be reported'; but the sense here is not absolutely clear. In this case the word may mean 'to be sold by (the procedures of) paradeixis'. See P. Petaus 17. 3 note.

πέμψαθ' ἡμῖν: cf. πεμφθήτωcαν, line 12, and for the plurals, **27**. 7, 88.

6 ϲχηματογραφίαϲ: reading suggested by Professor Youtie, and certainly correct; cf. P. Meyer (Gr. Texte) I. 20 and PSI X, 1118. 10. It replaces the χωματογραφίαι of the vol. I description of this text, and that word can now be excised from our lexica. Presumably, the ϲχηματογραφίαι here are plans of the parcels of land for sale, perhaps similar to, though probably more detailed and clearly drawn (cf. the insistence that they be drawn εὐϲήμωϲ: this line and line 12) than the type of sketches in **1122–3**. Cf. Crawford, *Kerkeosiris* 14.

ἐπιθέντεϲ τὰ μέτρα]: P. Amh. 68. 9. Perhaps παραθέντεϲ; cf. **14**. 10.

7 ὅπωϲ τἆλλα, κτλ: what follows is supplied from **27**. 9 as corrected by Crönert, *WKlPh* 20 (1903), 457; cf. Wilcken's re-edition of **27** Cols. I–III as *Chr* 331.

11 ὑποπαραδειχθηϲ[ομένων: *addendum lexicis*.

12 πεμφθήτωϲαν: for the imperative ending in -ϲαν, see Blass–Debrunner–Funk, *A Greek Grammar of the New Testament*, p. 44, Mayser, *Grammatik* I (2nd ed.), 2, 89.

13 Roman parallels suggest a restoration of ἀναφορίου or χρηματιϲμοῦ (cf. P. Petaus 17. 2, 8 notes, Roberts–Skeat, art. cit., p. 461), of which the latter more closely suits the available space.

14 Restore γῆϲ or some appropriate category of derelict land, e.g. χέρϲου or ἁλμυρίδοϲ.

15 ..οιϲ: υ̣ἱ̣οῖϲ looks almost unavoidable, but presents difficulties of interpretation. τόποιϲ cannot be read.

1102. Regulations for the Transport of Grain

P. Teb. 161 — (*a*) 10·8 × 14·7 cm. (*b*) 3·5 × 14·3 cm. — 116/115 B.C.

Two fragments which do not (apparently) join. (a) is a fair copy of **92**, with additional lines, dated at the top to the year 2 (116/115 B.C.). Lines 2–5 give the location of Kerkeosiris (cf. **92**. 1–7); 5–8, instructions for collecting grain in the village, with the charges to be assessed (cf. **92**. 7 ff.); 9 ff. concern the transport of grain by pack animal to some harbour in the Herakleopolite Nome, and from there – to judge from the damaged remains of line 11 – by boat downriver to Alexandria, with additional charges specified (cf. **92**. 12–13 and **92** introd. where lines 9–13 of the present text are transcribed).

Fragment (b) may belong to the lower part of (a) (cf. **92** introd.). Mentioned therein are the villages Berenikis Thesmophorou (lines 20 and 24) and Tali (line 22), both of which were situated near Kerkeosiris in the southern part of the Fayum (**17**. 5 note, vol. II pp. 373, 402 f., Crawford, *Kerkeosiris* 46 ff.; cf. **1117**. 125 note and on Tali, see now most fully E. Nestola, *Aegyptus* 50, 1970, 155–212). The fragment probably contained instructions similar, or supplementary to those of (a), but the remains are too scanty for definitive interpretation.

As suggested by Grenfell and Hunt, the condition and contents of these two fragments indicate that **92** was left unfinished by its scribe. He broke off at the word ὑποζυγίων (line 13), apparently in mid-sentence. Fragment (a) lacks the village name Κερκεοϲίρεωϲ found at the top of **92**. It preserves a top margin (measured from the top of line 2) of 3·3 cm. In this margin the year has been added, perhaps, though not necessarily, by a second hand. Also in this margin, at the middle of the upper edge of the papyrus, is a smudge of ink, but no clearly defined traces of writing. The fragment is in good condition; nevertheless, several tiny pieces have flaked off from the main fragment. Two of these contain together three damaged, uncertain letters which have not been joined to the main text.

All restorations in (a) are based on **92**. At the bottom of (b), a margin of 3·9 cm. On State transport of grain in Ptolemaic and Roman Egypt, see Rostovtzeff, *Archiv* 3 (1906), 201 ff.; Kunkel, *Archiv* 8 (1927), 169 ff.; Zilliacus, *Aegyptus* 19 (1939), 59 ff.; E. Börner, *Der staatliche Korntransport im griechisch-römischen Ägypten* (Diss. Hamburg, 1939); Schwartz, *BIFAO* 47 (1948), 179 ff.; Guéraud, *JJP* 4 (1950), 107 ff.; Świderek, *Eos* 58 (1969–70), 63–6; P. Petaus, pp. 222–3.

(fragment a)

(Ἔτουϲ) β
[τῆϲ] μὴ φρουρουμένηϲ [μη]δ̣ʼ οὔϲηϲ ἐπὶ [τοῦ μεγάλου ποταμοῦ]
μη[δʼ] ἐπʼ ἄλλου πλωτοῦ, ἀπ̣εχούϲηϲ δʼ εἰϲ [Πτολεμαίδα Εὐεργέτου]
τὴν μητρόπολιν τ̣[οῦ νομοῦ] ϲτάδια [ρξ, εἰϲ δὲ Μοῖριν τὴν]
ϲύνεγγυϲ φρουρουμένην ϲτάδια [ρνθ, ὁ δʼ ἐξ αὐτῆϲ ϲυνα-]
γόμενοϲ ϲῖτοϲ παράγετα[ι ε]ἰ̣ϲ̣ τὸν ἐ[ν τῇ κώμῃ βαϲιλικὸν θη-]
ϲ̣α̣υ̣ρ̣ό̣ν, μετρουμένων [ε]ἰϲ τὰϲ καθά[ρϲειϲ καὶ]
[τὸ] κ̣οϲκινευτικὸν τ̣[ῶν] ρ (ἀρταβῶν) (ἀρταβῶν) γ [ἐπίμετρον β καὶ]
[ἐν]τεῦθεν κατάγεται δ̣[ιʼ ὑπ]ο̣ζυγί[ων εἰϲ ± 5]
[Ἡρα]κλεοπολίτου τὴν οὖϲ̣α̣[ν ± 25]
[. .]ν εἰϲ Ἀλεξάνδρε⟨ι⟩αν εξα[± 27]
[τ]ῶ̣ν ρ (ἀρταβῶν) (ἀρταβ. .) η, ἐπ̣[± 30]
[τ]ῆ̣ϲ δὲ κώμη[ϲ
[ ]. .[

. . . .

3 ἄλλου: λο corrected from ου. 4 ϲτάδια: stroke over final α. 5 ϲύνεγγυϲ: ϲύνενγυϲ, **92**. 6; ϲτάδια: stroke over ϲ, stroke over final α. 6 παράγετα[ι: παρέγεται, **92**. 8. 7 μετρουμένων: προϲμετρουμένων, **92**. 9–10. 9 [ἐν]τεῦθεν κατάγεται [διʼ ὑποζυγίων (space for 16 letters): **92** introd. 12 ἐπ̣[: ἐπ̣ι̣[, **92** introd.

(fragment b)

. . . . .

]φορολογ[
α]γωγὴν .[
]ων γε[
]ϲ φακληρου .[
τὴν] αὐτὴν κ[ώμην
Βερενι]κίδα Θεϲμοφ[όρου

]. ο̣π̣ε̣ ἀπὸ του[
]κατὰ Ταλὶ κ̣[
]ων εἰϲ τὴ[ν
24 Βερ]ενικίδα Θε[ϲμοφόρου

(Fragment a) 'Year 2. (Sc. at Kerkeosiris) which is unguarded and is not situated on the great river or on any other navigable stream, and is 160 stades distant from Ptolemais Euergetou the nome metropolis and 159 stades from Moiris where there is a guarded point nearby, the grain is collected and conveyed to the royal granary in the village, 3 artabs measured (i.e. as extra payment) on every 100 artabs for cleansing and sifting, 2 artabs for extra measure. It is transported from there by pack animals to...in the Herakleopolite (Nome)...to Alexandria..., 8 artabs on every 100 for...the village...

1 The year 2 is 116/115 B.C.

2 [τοῦ μεγάλου ποταμοῦ]: cf. **92**. 3, **25**. 22–3. The Nile rather than the Baḥr Yusuf according to **92**. 2 note. Cf. Calderini, *Aegyptus* 1 (1920), 42 and *contra* Rostovtzeff, *Archiv* 3 (1906), 210 n. 2.

3 [Πτολεμαίδα Εὐεργέτου]: vol. II pp. 398–400, *WB* III 16a s.v. Πτολεμαίϲ. In the Roman period, most commonly referred to as Ἀρϲινοιτῶν πόλιϲ: P. Petaus, p. 23.

7–8 For the charges cf. **92**. 9–11 note, F. Preisigke, *Girowesen im griechischen Ägypten* (Strassburg, 1910), 113, P. Berl. Leihg. pp. 275 ff., and **851**. 1 note.

9 κατάγεται: κατάγειν was one of 'the regular terms for transport of goods to points of embarkation' – **703**. 74 note. It also indicated movement downriver toward Alexandria, but it is the former sense which is required in this line of our text. See further P. Giss. Univ.-Bibl. VI p. 33, P. Petaus 53. 15 note.

ὑπ]ο̣ζυγί[ων: usually meaning donkeys (ὄνοι): Schnebel, *Landwirtschaft* 334; (les ânes): Préaux, *L'économie royale* 229.

11 εξα[: a form of ἐξάγω or ἐξαγωγή? Cf. line 16 where some compound of ἀγωγή (perhaps καταγωγήν) seems to be required.

12 ἐπ̣[: ἐπ[ίμετρον? Cf. line 8 as restored from **92**. 11.

15 A case of φορολογία or φορολόγοϲ, or perhaps a form of φορολογέω.

PART TWO

LAND LISTS AND TAX LISTS

BY

JOHN C. SHELTON

1103. LIST OF LAND AND RENTS

P. Teb. 141v+63v *c.* 286 × 32 cm. 116/115 B.C.

The text below, found on the combined versos of **141** = **1110** and **63**, has been fully published in *Collectanea Papyrologica* 1976 pp. 111–51, 'Land Register: Crown Tenants at Kerkeosiris', from which article most of the following discussion is taken verbatim. The contents are: (1) a listing of every tenant of Crown land in Kerkeosiris in 116/115 B.C., together with the size of his holding, the rent charged thereon, and the crops planted, plus a description of any changes in the size or rent of the holding as compared with the preceding year (lines 1–286); (2) a brief but sometimes obscure summary of the foregoing list (287–95); (3) a résumé of the final figures of size and rent for each holding, taken from part 1, with totals calculated at irregular intervals (296–402); (4) a list of holdings rented chiefly at $5\frac{1}{3}$ artabs per aroura, which cannot be matched with the list of land at that rate which concludes part 1 (403–12); (5) a mutilated column which adds together the subtotals scattered throughout part 3 (413–23).

That the list in part 1 is complete is shown by a comparison with part 3: column 18 breaks off at line 325 with an entry which corresponds to lines 120–1, near the bottom of the last column of **1110**v; line 326 corresponds to line 131, the first entry preserved on the verso of **63**. After lines 120–1, **1110**v contains four entries; and between lines 325 and 326 papyrus sufficient to hold just four lines has fallen away. One must conclude that the loss between the two versos is zero. That the list treats of all the cultivated Crown land in Kerkeosiris can hardly be doubted. The total in line 292, $1179\frac{1}{4}$ arouras at $4594\frac{1}{12}$ artabs, is to be compared with $1182\frac{1}{4}$ arouras at $4609\frac{1}{12}$ artabs for the year before this text (**66**. 86) and $1193\frac{3}{4}$ at $4665\frac{5}{12}$ the year after (**69**. 5).

Few documents offer more difficulties to decipherment. The scribe writes a cramped cursive in comparatively pale ink, and his cancellations and corrections are numerous and often confusing. The papyrus itself has suffered seriously from holes and tears, and the surviving surface is often hopelessly abraded or discoloured. In addition, the plastic mounting (cf. p. 1) has in several places been sealed over the written text and cannot be removed without destroying the papyrus. But fortunately the scribe is repetitious: often after stating the quantity of land concerned he breaks it down into various components according to rent, then restates the total and breaks it down again according to crops sown, and finally states the total once more. This allows considerable scope for cross-checking, so that we are rarely unable to determine at least the area and rent for a given holding. Moreover, parts 1 and 3 complement each other in such a way that figures lost from one are generally recoverable from the other. As a result, we remain ignorant of the size of only six holdings for the year (57–9, 84–6, 111–14, 250, 283, 286); but the last two fall in a special category (cf. p. 8), the size of the holding in 111–14 was either 14 or 15 arouras, and in only the first of the remaining three passages is the rent lost as well as the area.

This is the only papyrus which provides us with data for Crown land as detailed and complete as that which **62**, **63**, and **1108–15** supply for the holdings of cleruchs and temples. Since **63** = **1110** covers land ἐν ἀφέσει for 116/115, and **1103** covers βασιλικὴ γῆ for the same period, we can now determine the distribution and use of almost every aroura of land at Kerkeosiris in that year. We find as lessees 148 individuals or partnerships. As concerns the average Crown tenant, however, this figure is misleading:

1. It includes $69\frac{1}{2}$ arouras at $88\frac{1}{2}$ artabs which were a communal responsibility of all the farmers (γεωργοὶ κοινῆι, lines 115–19, 289–90).

2. It includes four parcels of land leased to the god Petesouchos, totalling 20 arouras for $80\frac{11}{12}$ artabs (172–9).

3. It includes 22 cleruchs who leased for the most part a single aroura at $5\frac{1}{3}$ artabs (264–86).

For a discussion of these special categories, see *Crown Tenants*, pp. 120–5 and p. 8 above. When these are excluded, we are left with 121 tenancies, among which were distributed slightly less than 1062 arouras paying slightly less than $4322\frac{3}{4}$ artabs. If the leases of Crown land at Kerkeosiris in 116/115 were averaged out, the average farm would comprise $8\frac{3}{4}$ arouras rated at $35\frac{3}{4}$ artabs. There were, however, no average βασιλικοὶ γεωργοί in Kerkeosiris that year. Five approached average to a quarter of an aroura ($8\frac{1}{2}$ arouras, line 247; 9 arouras, lines 79, 88, 229, 246), but the most common holding of Crown land was 5 arouras; for details, see chart p. 39. No fewer than 71 tenancies, 60 per cent, were $8\frac{1}{2}$ arouras or smaller; and 32, more than a quarter of the total, fell between 4 and 6 arouras. Cf. **56**, where a peasant seeking land sufficient to support self and family asks for 5 arouras.

Of the 121 tenancies, at least ten per cent were held by two or more men in partnership: 12 such are preserved, and others may have been listed in portions of the papyrus that are now lost.

Farming land in association with others, besides its more obvious advantages, brought a tax advantage. The charges θέμα and γεωμετρία, at $\frac{1}{2}$ artab apiece, and λοχι( ), at $\frac{1}{6}$, were due from every tenancy regardless of its size (**1105** introd.). If, then, A, B, and C farm land independently of one another, they must pay $3\frac{1}{2}$ artabs for these 3 taxes; if they farm the same land in partnership, the charge is only $1\frac{1}{6}$ artabs. In compensation for the $2\frac{1}{3}$ lost artabs, the Crown will have tripled the number of persons who can be held directly responsible for the remaining dues.

A further, though slighter, advantage might accrue to tenants if by combining holdings they eliminated fractions of an aroura. Two holdings of $4\frac{1}{2}$ arouras at $4\frac{11}{12}$ artabs, for example, must pay $22\frac{1}{6}$ artabs rent apiece, total $44\frac{1}{3}$; one holding of 9 arouras pays only $44\frac{1}{4}$, a saving of $\frac{1}{12}$ artab.

Partnerships were often based on family ties; we find father and son together in lines 20, 31, and 136; two brothers in 87, 120, and 151; four brothers plus father in 95. In five further cases no relationship is apparent (39, 43, 48, 103, 160). There was of course nothing to prevent a man from holding property both as an individual and as a member of a partnership; cf. 43, 87, 151 notes.

Two holdings farmed in common by at least three associates draw attention because

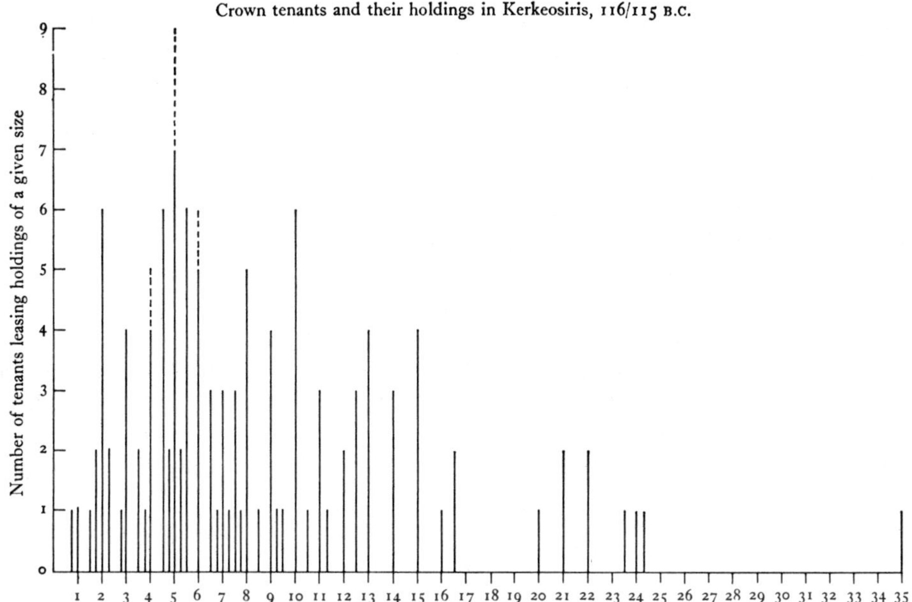

Size in arouras of Crown holdings, lines 1–263, omitting 57–9, 83–6, 111–14, 250. Standard Crown holdings – solid lines; 4 holdings of god Petesouchos added in broken lines. Irregular fractions are rounded down to the nearest ¼ aroura.

of their small size, only 3½ and 1¾ arouras (43, 103). The primary business of associations with such modest holdings can hardly have been the farming of Crown land. One might suspect that the property was rented not so much to raise crops as to acquire for the individuals concerned the status of *βαϲιλικὸϲ γεωργόϲ* with its attendant privileges (5. 138–43 = 155–61, 168–77, 207–47; Rostovtzeff, *Kolonat* 63 ff.). Onnophris son of Horos (43) was a *βαϲιλικὸϲ γεωργόϲ* in his own right (223), but we know nothing of his *μέτοχοι*, to whom such advantages as freedom from personal execution for debt and limited exemption from military quartering and other requisitions may well have seemed cheaply acquired at the cost of renting a little land.

1103 allows one to observe in greater detail than any other text the changes that might be made in Crown holdings between two consecutive years: out of 121 tenancies, 34 at least were altered in some way from the year before. This amounts to 28 per cent of the holdings; and the actual figure was no doubt higher, since many entries give no information concerning the previous year and in 16 cases the data are lost. For the most part these differences came from re-allocations of property between one tenant and another; in at least one instance a reduction of rent accompanied the change (34–5 note). A further probable reduction of rent in 227, and an increase in 93, apparently did not involve property exchange. Other changes in rental have probably been obscured by simultaneous re-apportionment of the land involved; cf. **85**, where this complicating factor does not arise.

There is no reason to believe that re-allocation of property among these tenants was anything other than voluntary. It is impossible to understand, for instance, why the Crown would have had an interest in seeing to it that 4 arouras of land farmed by Demetrius son of Sentheus at $4\frac{1}{12}$ artabs per aroura (128) should instead be farmed by Harmiysis son of NN at the same rent (2). These changes are official, and not to be confused with any private arrangements the tenants may have made by way of sub-lease; cf. 65–6 note, where the accidental listing of a sub-tenant necessitated a correction in the text. For the significance of these changes as regards the modality of leasing Crown land, see *Crown Tenants*, 118 ff.

Lines 296–402 are cross-referenced to parts 1 and 5 of the text (1–286 and 413–23). A simple reference to line numbers indicates that the figures agree in both passages; square brackets mean that textual mutilation has prevented confirmation; round brackets mean that the figures disagree; and a dash opposite line 401 means that no counterpart can be located. A complicated array of check strokes and dots has been omitted for convenience in printing.

1110 verso.

Traces of writing that have been washed out. Then:

Col. I

ἔτους β κατ' ἄν[δ]ρ̣α καὶ φ̣ύ̣λ̣λον

Ἁρμιῦσις [δ] (ἀρτάβαι ?) ιδ καὶ με(μερισμέναι) ἀπ[ὸ τῆς (πρότερον) Μαρρε]ί̣ους

τ̣ο̣ῦ̣ Μαρρείους ς (ἀρτ.) κθ∠ καὶ ἀπὸ τῆς [(πρότερον)] Δημητ[ρίου] τοῦ
Σενθέως δ (ἀρτ.) ιθ̣β̣́, (γίν.) ι (ἀρτ.) μθς́, (γίν.) ιδ (ἀρτ.) [ξ]γς́.
σπό(ρος) (πυρῶι) η (ἀρτ. ?) [λ]θγ́, κ(ριθῆι) α (ἀρτ.), γ, φα(κῶι) γ (ἀρτ.) ιδ∠d, τή(λει) β (ἀρτ.) ς, (γίν.) ιδ (ἀρτ.) ξ[γίβ́]

Ἁρυ̣ώ̣[της] Φαήσιος ι (ἀρτ.) μ. σπό(ρος) (πυρῶι) ς (ἀρτ.) κδ, φασή(λωι) β (ἀρτ.) η̣[
]. . . . . . (γίν. ?) ι (ἀρτ. ?) μ

] ις∠ (ἀρτ.) πα∠. σπό(ρος) (πυρῶι) ια∠ (ἀρτ.) ν[ς∠γ́ίβ́],
ἀ̣ρ̣ά̣(κωι) β̣ (ἀρτ.) θ∠γ́, φασή(λωι) γ (ἀρτ.) ιδ∠̣[d, (γίν.) ις∠ (ἀρτ.) πα∠]

[Ἀθεμ]μ̣εὺς Πετεσούχου .[±15]. . .

] (γίν. ?) κ̣β (ἀρτ. ?) ϛδ̣∠ḍ. ϲπό(ροϲ) (πυρῶι) ια (ἀρτ.) ν∠,
φ[α(κῶι)
ἀρά(κωι) δ (ἀρτ.) ι̣β̣, (γίν.) κβ (ἀρτ.) ϛδ∠d

Ἁρφα̣ῆϲιϲ Ὀννώφριοϲ α∠ (ἀρτ.) ζγ́ιβ́ κ[αὶ] ἀπὸ τ[ῆ]ϲ (πρότερον) Πετ[οϲίριοϲ
τοῦ]
Ἁρκοίφιοϲ ∠ (ἀρτ.) β∠, (γίν.) β (ἀρτ.) θ∠̣γ́

Ἁρβῆχ[ιϲ Ἑρ]γέωϲ ιγ (ἀρτ.) κε. ϲπό(ροϲ) (πυρῶι) ι κρι(θῆι) γ [
. . . . .ϲπό(ροϲ) (ἀρτ.) δ (ἀρτ.) ια∠, φα(κῶι) δ (ἀρτ.) η∠, χο(ρτο)νο(μῶν)
ε (ἀρτ.) ε, (γίν.) [ιγ (ἀρτ.) κε]

Ἁρμαχόροϲ Ἁρμαχόρου δ (ἀρτ.) ιε. ϲπό(ροϲ) (πυρῶι) β (ἀρτ.) η̣, κ(ριθῆι)
β (ἀρτ. ?) ζ, (γίν.) δ (ἀρτ.) ιε

⟦Ἁρφαῆϲιϲ Ὀ̣ν̣[ν]ώφριο̣ϲ̣ α (ἔτουϲ) α∠ (ἀρτ.) ζγ́ιβ́, καὶ με(μεριϲμένον)
ἀπὸ τῆϲ (πρότερον) Πετοϲίρ[ι]οϲ του⟧
⟦ Ἁρκοίφιοϲ [∠] (ἀρτ. ?) β∠, (γίν.) β (ἀρτ.) θ∠γ́. ϲπό(ροϲ) (πυρῶι)⟧

Θῶνιϲ Ὀρϲεν[ού]φιοϲ καὶ Ὀρϲενοῦφιϲ α [(ἔτουϲ)] ζ∠d (ἀρτ.) λα, β (ἔτουϲ)
ἴϲο(ν). δ ἀ̣[ν(ὰ) δ]∠γ́ιβ́ (ἀρτ.) ιθβ́,
γ∠d ἀν(ὰ) γ [(ἀρτ.) ια]d, (γίν.) ζ∠d (ἀρτ.) λα. ϲπό(ροϲ) (πυρῶι)
⟦δ∠ (ἀρτ.) ιθβ́⟧ \ϛ (ἀρτ.) κεβ́, κ(ριθῆι) α⟨∠⟩d (ἀρτ.) ε̣γ́,
(γίν.) ζ∠d (ἀρτ.) λα

Πετερμοῦθιϲ Ὥ̣[ρο]υ̣ ἀπὸ τῆϲ (πρότερον) Πετεϲού(χου) τοῦ Ϲοκμή(νιοϲ) η∠d
(ἀρτ.) μβιβ́, καὶ τῆϲ (πρότερον)
Ἁρχύψιοϲ τοῦ Πετεήϲιοϲ εd (ἀρτ.) κε∠γ́, (γίν.) ιδ (ἀρτ.) ξ⟦ϛβ́⟧ \η∠γ́/.
ϲπό(ροϲ) (πυρῶι) η (ἀρτ.) λβ̣ϛ́ [
]. .[
[(γίν.) . (ἀρτ.)] υ̣⟦α∠⟧ \γ́/

Col. II

Κατῦτιϲ Κατύτιοϲ α (ἔτουϲ) κγ∠ (ἀρτ.) ρδιβ́, β̣ (ἔτουϲ?) ἴ̣ϲο̣(ν). ι̣η∠̣
ἀ̣ν̣(ὰ) δ∠γ́ι̣β̣́ (ἀρτ.) ⟦ϛα⟧ \πθ̣ι̣β̣́,/
ε ἀν(ὰ) γ ιε, (γίν.) κγ∠̣ (ἀρτ.) ρδιβ́. ϲπό(ροϲ) (πυρῶι) ιε∠ (ἀρτ.)
ξ⟦δϛ̣́⟧ \εḍ,/ φα(κῶι) ε (ἀρτ.) κδιβ́,
ἀρά(κωι) γ (ἀρτ.) ιδ∠d, (γίν.) κγ∠ (ἀρτ.) ρδιβ́

⟦῾Αρμαχόρος ῾Αρμαχόρου καὶ οἱ μέ(τοχοι)⟧ \`Κατῦτις Cιcούχου {καὶ} ⟦τὴν (πρότερον) Κατύτιος τοῦ Cιcούχου ̣ . .]′ η (ἀρτ.) κδ (ὧν) (πυρῶι) ϵ (ἀρτ.) ιϵ, κρι(θῆι) γ (ἀρτ.) θ, (γίν.) η (ἀρτ.) κδ

Κέντις Κατύτιος α (ἔτους) ϵd (ἀρτ.) κϵ∠γ́. cπό(ρος) (πυρῶι) γ (ἀρτ.) ιδ∠d, φα(κῶι) βd (ἀρτ.) ιαίβ́, (γίν.) ϵd (ἀρτ.) κϵ∠γ́

Παπνϵβτῦνις Cοκέωc καὶ Κολλούθηc α (ἔτουc) ι∠ (ἀρτ.) μζ∠, β (ἔτουc ?) ἴcο(ν).
ϵ∠ [ἀν(ὰ) δ∠]γ́ίβ́ [(ἀρτ.) κζ]ίβ́, ϵ ἀν(ὰ) δ (ἀρτ.) κ. cπό(ρος) (πυρῶι) ϛ (ἀρτ.) κϛ∠d, κρι(θῆι) β (ἀρτ.) ηγ́
[. β∠ (ἀρτ.) ι]βγ́ίβ́, (γίν.) [ι]∠ (ἀρτ.) μζ∠

[῾Αρχῦψιc] Πϵτϵήcιοc α (ἔτουc) ἀπὸ ϛ∠ή (ἀρτ.) λα adή (ἀρτ.) δ∠, καὶ μϵ(μϵριcμένον) ἀπὸ τῆc (πρότϵρον)
Τοθοήουc τοῦ Φαγάτου ∠d (ἀρτ.) γ, (γίν.) βή (ἀρτ.) ζ∠ (ὧν) αή ἀν(ὰ) δ (ἀρτ.) δ∠
α ἀν(ὰ) γ. cπό(ρος) (πυρῶι) αἱ πᾶ(cαι)

Μαρρῆc Πϵτοcίριοc α (ἔτουc) ιϛ∠ (ἀρτ.) νϛd, β (ἔτουc) ἴcο(ν). (ὧν) ι ἀν(ὰ) δ (ἀρτ.) μ
ϛ∠ ἀν(ὰ) β∠ (ἀρτ.) ιϛd. cπό(ρος) (πυρῶι) ι∠ (ἀρτ.) μd, κρι(θῆι) δ (ἀρτ.) η, φα(κῶι) β (ἀρτ.) η, (γίν.) ιϛ∠ (ἀρτ.) νϛd

Μϵcταcῦτμιc Πϵτϵcούχου καὶ οἱ μέ(τοχοι) α (ἔτουc) ⟦κϛ⟧ \`λϵ′ (ἀρτ.) ⟦ξ∠⟧ \`ο′, β (ἔτουc) ἴcο(ν). cπό(ρος) (πυρῶι)

Μαρρῆc Πϵτϵcούχου \`α (ἔτουc)′ δ (ἀρτ.) ιθβ́, β (ἔτουc) ἴcο(ν). cπό(ρος) (πυρῶι) αἱ πᾶ(cαι)

᾿Οννῶφριc Φατρήουc α (ἔτουc) ϛ∠ (ἀρτ.) λβ, β (ἔτουc) ἴcο(ν). cπό(ρος) (πυρῶι) γ (ἀρτ.) ιδ∠, φα(κῶι) ∠d γ∠d,
κρι(θῆι) γ (ἀρτ.) ιδ∠d, (γίν.) ϛ∠d (ἀρτ.) λβd, καὶ ἀπὸ {τοῦ} τῆc (πρότϵρον) Πϵτοcί(ριοc) τοῦ ῞Ωρου d (ἀρτ.) α∠d, (γίν.) ϛ∠d (ἀρτ.) λγd

᾿Οννῶφριc ῞Ωρου καὶ οἱ μέ(τοχοι) α (ἔτουc) γ∠ (ἀρτ.) ι∠, β (ἔτουc) ἴcο(ν). cπό(ρος) (πυρῶι) β (ἀρτ.) ϛ,
κρι(θῆι) α∠ (ἀρτ.) δ∠, (γίν.) γ∠ (ἀρτ.) ι∠

Πετερμοῦθις Μαρρήους α (ἔτους) ιβ ἀν(ὰ) β∠ (ἀρτ.) λ, β (ἔτους) ἴσο(ν). σπό(ρος) (πυρῶι) ϛ (ἀρτ.) ιε, ἀρά(κωι) ϛ (ἀρτ.) ιε, (γίν.) ιβ (ἀρτ.) λ

Πετεσοῦχος Νεκτενίβιος α (ἔτους) κ (ἀρτ.) μ, β (ἔτους) ἴσο(ν). σπό(ρος) φα(κῶι) αἱ πᾶ(σαι)

Τεῶς Θοτορταίου καὶ Ἀνεμπεὺς ἀπὸ τῆς (πρότερον) Σενθέως τοῦ Ἁρκοίφιος ε∠ (ἀρτ.) κζί́β. σπό(ρος) (πυρῶι) αἱ πᾶ(σαι)

*(γίνονται) ρμβ∠*d *(ἀρτ.) υπεϛ́*

Col. III

*Πετοσῖρις Ἁρκοίφιος α (ἔτους) ι∠*d *(ἀρτ.) μϛ*d, *β (ἔτους) [ζ ἀν(ὰ) δ∠γ́ί́β (ἀρτ.) λδγ́ί́β γ ἀν(ὰ) γ (ἀρτ.) θ̣, (γίν.) ι (ἀρτ.) μγγ́ί́β. σπό(ρος) (πυρῶι) ζ (ἀρτ.) λδγ́ί́β, χό(ρτωι) γ (ἀρτ.) θ̣*

Πόρτεις μέ(γας) Τεῶτος α (ἔτους) ϛ̣ (ἀρτ.) ιϛ∠, β (ἔτους) ἴσο(ν). [γ] ἀν(ὰ) γ θ, γ ἀν(ὰ) β∠ ζ∠. σπό(ρος) (πυρῶι) γ (ἀρτ.) ζ∠, τή(λει) α (ἀρτ.) γ, φασή(λωι) β (ἀρτ.) ϛ, (γίν.) ϛ [(ἀρτ.)] ιϛ∠

Πετοσῖρις Ὥρου α (ἔτους)⟦. .⟧ *\`ϛ∠´ (ἀρτ.)* ⟦*κε*⟧ *κδ∠*d, *β (ἔτους) ἴσο(ν). β̣∠*d *ἀν(ὰ) δ∠γ́ί́β (ἀρτ.) ιγγ́ί́β, γ∠*d *ἀν(ὰ) γ (ἀρτ.) ια*d, *(γίν.) ϛ∠ (ἀρτ.) κδ∠*d. *σπό(ρος) (πυρῶι) γ (ἀρτ. ?) ιγ*d, *κρι(θῆι) α∠ (ἀρτ.) .∠, φα(κοῦ) β (ἀρτ.) ε∠γ́, (γίν.) ϛ̣∠ (ἀρτ.) κδ∠*d

Παπνεβτῦνις Π̣[ε]τοσίριος α (ἔτους) . (ἀρτ.) δ[±5]ϛ́, β (ἔτους) . . . κ̣α̣ὶ̣ ἀπὸ τῆς (πρότερον) Πετῶτος τοῦ Μαρρήους [τή(λει) α (ἀρτ.) δ [

Πετοσῖρις Φαήσιος α̣ (ἔτους ?) ζ (ἀρτ.) κα, [β] (ἔτους) [ἴσο(ν).] (πυρῶι) γ∠ (ἀρτ.) ι∠, κρι(θῆι) γ∠ [(ἀρτ.)] ι∠, (γίν.) ζ (ἀρτ.) κα

Πετεσοῦχος Πετοσίριος α (ἔτους) ιγ (ἀρτ.) . . . . [β (ἔτους). . . .] ⟦*σπό(ρος) (πυρῶι) ζ∠ (ἀρτ.) λεί̣β*⟧ *\` . . . . . . . . . ἀ̣ν̣(ὰ) δ∠̣γ́ί́β´ φα(κῶι) α ἀν(ὰ) δ∠γ́ί́β, τή(λει) β∠ [(ἀρτ.)* ⟦*β∠γ́*⟧ *\`βγ́´, χό(ρτωι) β (ἀρτ.) η, (γίν.) ιβ∠ (ἀρτ.) . . . . .*

Πετερμοῦθις Ἀμεννέως α (ἔτους) γ (ἀρτ.) ιδ∠d, β (ἔτους) [ἴcο(ν).] ϲ̣π̣ό̣(ρος) (πυρῶι) αἱ πᾶ(σαι)

Διονύϲιοϲ δι' αὐ(τοῦ)

Πνεφερῶϲ Πετειμούθου α (ἔτους) ζ (ἀρτ.) λ̣δγ′[ιβ′, β] (ἔτους) β (ἀρτ.) ι

Τοθοῆϲ Ἀγοννούφιοϲ α (ἔτους) δ∠ (ἀρτ.) κβϛ′, καὶ ἀπὸ τῆϲ (πρότερον) Παλλαμούνιοϲ α (ἀρτ.) δ∠γ′ιβ′, (γίν.) ε∠ (ἀρτ.) κζ[ι′]β′. ϲπό(ροϲ) (πυρῶι) γ (ἀρτ.) ι̣δ∠̣d, ἀρά(κωι) α∠ ζγ′ιβ′,
ἀϲπό(ρου) α (ἀρτ.) δ∠γ′ιβ′

(γίν.) ϛ∠d (ἀρτ.) λγ′ιβ′

Φαῆϲιϲ Πετεήϲιοϲ α (ἔτους) ϛ∠ (ἀρτ.) λβ, β (ἔτους) ἴϲο(ν). ϲπό(ροϲ) (πυρῶι) γ∠ (ἀρτ.) ιζ′ιβ′,
κρι(θῆι) γ (ἀρτ.) ιδ∠d, (γίν.) λβ

Τοθοῆϲ Φαγάτου α (ἔτους) α∠d (ἀρτ.) ϛ∠, β (ἔτους) [α] (ἀρτ.) γ. ϲπό(ροϲ) (πυρῶι)

Φμοῦιϲ Παθήβιοϲ τὴν (πρότερον) Ὥρου τοῦ Παθήβιοϲ [α] (ἔτους ?) ε ἀν(ὰ) δ (ἀρτ.) κ, β (ἔτους) ἴϲο(ν)
ϲπό(ροϲ) (πυρῶι) β (ἀρτ.) η, κρι(θῆι) α δ, φα(κῶι) β (ἀρτ.) η, (γίν.) ε [(ἀρτ.)] κ̣

(γίνονται) ο . ∠̣d (ἀρτ.) [. . .]δ∠γ′

Col. IV

Φαγάτηϲ Μικίωνοϲ α (ἔτους) η (ἀρτ.) λθγ′, β (ἔτους) ἴϲο(ν). (πυρῶι ?) ϛ′ (ἀρτ. ?) [κθ∠]
φα(κῶι) β (ἀρτ.) θ∠γ′, (γίν.) η (ἀρτ.) λθγ′

Φαῆϲιϲ Ἁρυώτου α (ἔτους) θ (ἀρτ.) μβγ′, β (ἔτους) ἴϲο(ν). η ἀν(ὰ) [δ∠γ′ιβ′],
α ἀν(ὰ) γ. ϲπό(ροϲ) (πυρῶι) ζ (ἀρτ.) λβ∠, φαϲή(λωι) β (ἀρτ.) θ∠γ′, (γίν.) θ (ἀρτ.) μβγ′

Ὧροϲ Πετεϲούχου `α (ἔτους)′ ιζ (ἀρτ.) ν̣, β (ἔτους) ι ἀνὰ β∠ (ἀρτ. ?) [κε].
ϲπό(ροϲ) (πυρῶι) ε (ἀρτ.) ιβ∠, φαϲή(λωι) ε (ἀρτ.) ιβ∠, (γίν.) ι (ἀρτ.) κε

Ὧροϲ Ὀρϲενούφιοϲ α (ἔτους) δ∠ (ἀρτ.) κβϛ′, β (ἔτους) ἴϲο(ν). ϲ̣π̣ό̣(ροϲ) (πυρῶι ?) α̣[ἱ πᾶ(ϲαι)]

῟Ωρος Πετεχῶ̣ν̣τος α (ἔτους) [
ε ἀν(ὰ) δ∠γʹιβʹ (ἀρτ.) κδ∠ιβʹ, ι ἀν(ὰ) [
cπό(ρος) (πυρῶι) ιγ (ἀρτ.) ξδ∠ιβʹ, φα(κῶι) δ (ἀρτ.) ι, χ[ο(ρτο)]νο(μῶν) . . .[

`῟Ωρος καὶʹ Θῶνις Κεντ̣ί̣ς̣ι̣ος καὶ ⟦῟Ωρος Πετ[ε]χῶντος⟧ ἀπὸ τῆς (πρότερον) [
θ ἀν(ὰ) δ∠γʹιβʹ (ἀρτ.) μ̣δd. cπό(ρος) (πυρῶι) αἱ πᾶ(cαι)

῟Ωρος Πετενεφιήους `α (ἔτους)ʹ ι ἀν(ὰ) δ∠γʹιβʹ (ἀρτ.) μθϛʹ, [β (ἔτους) ἴcο(ν).]
ς̣π̣ό̣(ρος) (πυρῶι) δ̣∠̣ḍ (ἀρτ.) κδ∠ιβʹ, ἀρά(κωι) β (ἀρτ.) θ∠γʹ, φα(κῶι) γḍ
(ἀρτ.) ιδι̣β̣ʹ

῟Ωρος Μικίωνος α (ἔτους) ι (ἀρτ.) λδ∠d, β (ἔτους) ἴcο(ν). [cπό(ρος) . ϛ]
(ἀρτ.) κ̣β∠d,
φα(κῶι) β ϛ, φαcή(λωι) β ϛ, (γίν.) ι (ἀρτ.) λδ∠d

Πετεcοκονοῦρις Κεφάλωνος α (ἔτους) η (ἀρτ.) ιδ̣, [β (ἔτους)] η (ἀρτ.) [ιϛ].
cπό(ρος) (πυρῶι) ϛ (ἀρτ.) ιβ, ἀρά(κωι) β (ἀρτ.) δ, (γίν.) η (ἀρτ.) ιϛ

Πετεcοῦχος Χεύριος καὶ Χεῦρις καὶ οἱ ἀ̣δ̣ε̣λ(φοὶ) α (ἔτους)
κβ (ἀρτ.) πδ∠, β (ἔτους) ἴcο(ν). (ὧν) ϛ ἀν(ὰ) δ∠γʹιβʹ (ἀρτ.) κθ∠,
ζ ἀν(ὰ) δ (ἀρτ.) κη,
θ ἀν(ὰ) γ (ἀρτ.) κζ ⟦. .γ∠ . .ι .⟧. cπό(ρος) (πυρῶι) ιβ (ἀρτ. ?) μ̣⟦θ∠d⟧
`ε∠dʹ, ἀρά(κωι) ζ (ἀρτ.) κθ[∠d],
χό(ρτωι) α γ, φαcή(λωι) α γ, φα(κῶι) α (ἀρτ.) γ, (γίν.) κβ (ἀρτ.) π̣δ̣∠̣

Τοθοήους γ ἀν(ὰ) δ∠γʹιβʹ ιδ∠d

Πετεcούχου γ ἀν(ὰ) δ∠γʹιβʹ ιδ∠d, γ ἀν(ὰ) δ ιβ, (γίν.) κϛ∠d. Χεῦρις μι(κρὸς)
δ [(ἀρτ.) ιϛ]
Χεῦρις ε (ἀρτ.) ι[ε]
Τεεφῖβις δ ἀν(ὰ) γ (ἀρτ.) ιβ, (γίν.) κβ̣ (ἀρτ.) πδ∠

Col. V

Π̣ᾶ̣cις Πανετβεῦις καὶ οἱ μέ(τοχοι) α∠d (ἀρτ.) εβʹ. [c]πό(ρος) (πυρῶι)
[Παᾶ]π̣ις Πετοςίριος β∠d (ἀρτ.) θ `(ὧν) ∠d ἀν(ὰ) δ (ἀρτ.) γ, β ἀν(ὰ) γ (ἀρτ.) ϛʹ
(ὧν) (πυρῶι) ∠d (ἀρτ.) γ
]α̣(κωι) β (ἀρτ.) ϛ, (γίν.) β∠d (ἀρτ.) θ

]ις Πετοςίριος α (ἔτους) δ (ἀρτ.) ιθḍ . . . . κ̣α̣ὶ̣ ἀ̣π̣ὸ̣ τῆς (πρότερον)
] Π̣ε̣τεcού(χου) ε ἀν(ὰ) δ (ἀρτ.) κ, (γίν.) θ (ἀρτ.) λθβʹ. (πυρῶι)

ϛ (ἀρτ.) ....
]εν . . .β (ἀρτ.) ⟦. .⟧ κ∠ ἀςπ̣ό̣ρ̣ο̣υ̣ [
(γίν.) ϛ∠ (ἀρτ.) λβ
]∠ḍ (ἀρτ.) γ. ςπό(ροс) (πυρῶι)
] . . (ἀρτ.) μζ∠, β (ἔτουс) ιε (ἀρτ. ?) μζβ̣́
] ε ἀν(ὰ) δ (ἀρτ.) κ, α ἀν(ὰ) γ
ς]π̣[ό(ροс)] (πυρῶι) θ (ἀρτ.) λζ∠d, μελα(νθίωι) α δ∠̣γ́ι̣β̣́,
. . . α (ἀρτ.) ε, (γίν.) ιδ (ἀρτ.) μ̣ζβ́
οἱ γεωργοὶ κοινῆι νομῶν ξ (ἀρτ.) ξ
ἀ̣ςπόρ̣ο̣υ̣ α∠ (ἀρτ.) ζ∠
καὶ τῆς (πρότερον) Ἁρυώτ̣ο̣υ̣ Ἁρυώτου ϛ (ἀρτ.) ιε ἀςπόρου
καὶ τὴν (πρότερον) Ϲενθέως β (ἀρτ.) ϛ. ςπό(ροс) χό(ρτωι)
(γίν.) θ∠ (ἀρτ.) κη∠
⟦Κεφαλᾶς⟧ \`Ἀπῦγχις καὶ Κεφαλᾶς οἱ̣ β′ Πετεςούχου α (ἔτουс) ε (ἀρτ.) κδ∠ι̣β́,
β (ἔτουс) ζ∠ (ἀρτ.) λβίβ́.
ςπό(ροс) (πυρῶι) δ∠ (ἀρτ.) ιζγ́, φα(κῶι) β (ἀρτ.) θ∠γ́, φαςή(λωι) α
(ἀρτ.) δ∠γ́ίβ́, (γίν.) ζ∠ (ἀρτ.) λβίβ́
Ἁρμιῦςις Πετεύριος ζd ἀν(ὰ) δ∠γ́ίβ́ (ἀρτ.) λεβ́. ςπό(ροс) ⟨(πυρῶι)⟩ εd (ἀρτ.)
κε∠̣γ́
φα(κῶι) β (ἀρτ.) θ∠γ́, (γίν.) ζd (ἀρτ.) λε̣β́
Ἁρμιῦςις Πετεςούχου \`Λάγου′ δ∠ ἀν(ὰ) δ∠γ́ίβ́ (ἀρτ.) κβϛ́. ςπό(ροс) (πυρῶι) γ
(ἀρτ.) ιδ∠d,
φα(κῶι) α∠ (ἀρτ.) ζγ́ίβ́, (γίν.) δ∠ (ἀρτ.) κβϛ́ ⟦. . . .⟧
Ἁρυώτης Ἀμεννέως δ ἀν(ὰ) δ∠γ́ίβ́ (ἀρτ.) ιθβ́ (ὧν) (πυρῶι) β (ἀρτ.) θ∠γ́,
φα(κῶι) α δ∠γ́ίβ́, φαςή(λωι) α δ∠γ́ίβ́, (γίν.) δ (ἀρτ.) ιθβ́
Δημήτριος Ϲενθέως α (ἔτουс) η (ἀρτ.) λεβ́, β (ἔτουс)
δ (ἀρτ.) ιϛ, καὶ με(μεριςμένη) ἀπὸ τῆς (πρότερον) Χολῶτος α (ἀρτ.) δ∠γ́ίβ́,
(γίν.) ε (ἀρτ.) κα. ςπό(ροс) (πυρῶι) αἱ πᾶ(ςαι)

63 verso

Col. VI

Ἀμεννεὺς Ἀθε[μ]μέως α (ἔτουс) γ∠ (ἀρτ.) ιζγ́ίβ́, β (ἔτουс) ἴςο(ν). ςπό(ροс)
(πυρῶι) αἱ πᾶ(ςαι)

Πετεcοῦχοc Ὀρcε[νο]ύφιοc ε ἀν(ὰ) δ (ἀρτ.) κ, β (ἔτουc) ἴcο(ν). cπό(ροc)
(πυρῶι) γ (ἀρτ.) ιβ,
ἀρά(κωι) β (ἀρτ.) η, (γίν.) ε (ἀρτ.) κ

Θοτ̣ο̣ρταῖc Πετ[οc]ίριοc α (ἔτουc) ε∠ (ἀρτ.) κζγ´ιβ´, β (ἔτουc) ἴcο(ν). cπό(ροc)
(πυρῶι) γ∠
(ἀρτ.) ιζγ´ιβ´, φα(κῶι) α̣ (ἀρτ. ?) δ∠γ´ιβ´, φαcή(λωι) α (ἀρτ.) δ∠γ´ιβ´,
(γίν.) ε∠ (ἀρτ.) κζγ´ιβ´

Μαρρῆc Ἰμούθου καὶ Ἀμεννεὺc α (ἔτουc) ια (ἀρτ.) λβγ´, β (ἔτουc) ἴcο(ν),
(ὧν ?) β̣ ἀ̣ν̣(ὰ) δ∠γ´ιβ´ (ἀρτ.) [θ]∠γ´, θ ἀν(ὰ) β∠ (ἀρτ.) κβ∠, (γίν.) ια
(ἀρτ.) λβγ´.
cπό(ροc) (πυρῶι) δ (ἀρτ.) ι, κρι(θῆι) ε (ἀρτ.) ιβ∠, ἀρά(κωι) β
(ἀρτ.) θ∠γ´, (γίν.) ια [(ἀρτ.) λβγ´]

Μεcταcῦτμιc Σοκέωc α (ἔτουc) η (ἀρτ.) λθγ´, β (ἔτουc) [ἴ]cο(ν).
cπό(ροc) (πυρῶι) ε (ἀρτ.) κδ∠ιβ´, φα(κῶι) α δ∠γ´ιβ´, ἀρά(κωι) β θ∠γ´,
(γίν.) η (ἀρτ.) λθγ´

*Μ̣ε̣γχ̣ῆ̣c̣ Δημ̣ητ̣ρ̣ί̣ο̣υ̣ γ∠*d *(ἀρτ.) [ι]ηγ´ιβ´. cπό(ροc) (πυρῶι) αἱ πᾶ(cαι)*
Ἁ̣ρ̣φ̣α̣ῆ̣c̣ι̣c̣ Πε[τ]εcούχου ια ἀν(ὰ) δ∠̣γ´ι̣β̣´ (ἀρτ.) ν̣διβ´. cπό(ροc) (πυρῶι) ς
(ἀρτ.) κθ∠,
*φα(κῶι) β (ἀρτ.) θ∠γ´, ἀρά(κωι) γ ιδ∠*d, *(γίν.) ι̣α̣ (ἀρτ.) νδιβ´*
[ ]θ̣[. .] . . . . .[
[ ]

Μ̣α̣ρ̣ρ̣ῆ̣c̣ Π[ετε]χ̣ῶντοc α (ἔτουc) η (ἀρτ.) λθγ´, καὶ με(μεριcμένην) τὴν
(πρότερον) διὰ . . . . .
τοῦ . . .δ̣( ) δ∠ (ἀρτ.) κβς´, (γίν.) ι̣β̣∠̣ (ἀρτ. ?) ξα∠. cπό(ροc) (πυρῶι)
η (ἀρτ.) λθ∠,
*φα(κῶι) α∠ (ἀρτ.) ζγ´ι̣β̣´, ἀρά(κωι) γ (ἀρτ.) ιδ∠*d

*[Πετεcο]ῦχοc Ἰμούθου δ∠*d *(ἀρτ.) κγ∠*d. *cπό(ροc) (πυρῶι) β∠ (ἀρτ.) ιβγ´ιβ´,*
φα(κῶι) α (ἀρτ. ?) δ̣∠̣γ´ι̣β̣´,
*ἀ̣ρ̣ά̣(κωι) α*d *(ἀρτ.) δ∠γ´ιβ´, (γίν.) δ∠*d *(ἀρτ.) κγ∠*d

[Πε]τ̣ῶ̣c̣ Μαρρείουc καὶ Πετερμοῦθιc α (ἔτουc) κε∠ (ἀρτ.) ρκ̣ε̣ι̣β̣´,
[β (ἔτουc) κ̣α̣ (ἀρτ.) ϙ̣β∠γ´. cπό(ροc) (πυρῶι) ιε̣ (ἀρτ.) ξ̣α̣γ´, κ̣ρ̣ι̣(θῆι)
*γ (ἀρτ.) ιδ∠*d, *ἀρά(κωι) γ ιδ∠*d

Col. VII

Πετεcοῦχοc Cοκμήνιοc α (ἔτουc) `ἀπὸ´ ι∠ήίϛ (ἀρτ.) νββ,
β (ἔτουc) β ἀ̣ṿ(ὰ) δ∠γ'ίβ (ἀρτ.) θ∠γ', καὶ ἀπὸ τῆc (πρότερον) Πνεφερῶτοc τοῦ
Πετειμούθου ε (ἀρτ.) κδ∠ίβ, (γίν.) ζ (ἀρτ.) λδγ'ίβ. {cπό(ροc) (πυρῶι)}
cπό(ροc) (πυρῶι) ε (ἀρτ.) κδ∠ίβ, φα(κῶι) `α´ δ∠γ'ίβ, ἀρά(κωι) α (ἀρτ.)
δ∠γ'ίβ

Φαγάτηc Πετεcούχου α (ἔτουc) ϛ καὶ ὑ[δ]ρα(γωγοῦ) ∠, (γίν.) ϛ∠ (ἀρτ.) λβ,
β (ἔτουc) ἀπὸ τῆc διὰ Κεντείcιοc καὶ Ἀρυ(ώτου) [τοῦ Ἀμ]εννẹ́(ωc) . .
τοῦ ὑδρα(γωγοῦ) α∠ (ἀρτ.) ζ∠, {(γίν.)}
(γίν.) η (ἀρτ.) λθγ'. cπό(ροc) (πυρῶι) ϛ (ἀρτ.) κθ∠ φ[α(κῶι) β] (ἀρτ.)
θ∠γ', (γίν.) η (ἀρτ.) λθγ'

Φατρῆc Πάcιτοc καὶ Ὧροc Θοτορταί[ου] . .
β (ἔτουc) μẹ(μεριcμέν-) ἀ̣π̣ὸ̣ τ̣ῆ̣ϲ̣ (πρότερον ?) [
cπό(ροc) (πυρῶι) ζ (ἀρτ.)[(γίν.) ιαd] (ἀρτ.) ṿ[.]∠

Φαῆcιc Φίβιοc [
φα(κῶι) β (ἀρτ.) θ∠γ', .[

Slight traces of perhaps 3 lines, then probably at least 1 line lost.

ε∠ (ἀρτ.) κ]ζίβ

] . . . . .ου τὴν (πρότερον) . . . . . .ω( ) βd (ἀρτ.) ϛ∠̣ḍ
(traces) *(γίν. ?) β̣d (ἀρτ.) ϛ∠d*
[ ]θε . . .[
[ ] . . .[
[ι]ẹ (ἀρτ.) να.
c̣π̣ό̣(ροc) (πυρῶι ?) [ ] (ἀρτ.) . ., ἀρά(κωι) [. (γίν.)] ιε
(ἀρτ.) να

Col. VIII

[Π]ẹτεcοῦχοc θε(ὸc) δι' Ἁρφαήcιοc καὶ οἱ μέ(τοχοι) ε ἀν(ὰ) γ (ἀρτ. ?) ιε.
cπό(ροc) ἀρά(κωι) αἱ πᾶ(cαι)

Πετεcοῦχοc θε(ὸc) διὰ Πετοcίριοc τοῦ Ἀμεννέ(ωc) ϛ (ἀρτ.) κθ∠.
cπό(ροc) (πυρῶι) δ (ἀρτ.) ιθβ, κ̣ρ̣ι̣(θῆι) β θ∠γ', (γίν.) ϛ (ἀρτ.) κθ∠

Πετεcοῦχοc θε(ὸc) διὰ Πετεcούχου τοῦ Πακύ(ρριοc) ẹ ἀν(ὰ) γd ⟦ιδ̣d⟧ `ιϛ∠d´.
cπό(ροc) (πυρῶι) β∠ (ἀρτ.) η∠, χό(ρτωι) β∠ (ἀρτ.) ηd, (γίν.) ε (ἀρτ.) ιϛ∠d

Πετεcοῦχοc θε(ὸc) διὰ Μ[α]ρρείουc τοῦ Πακύ(ρριοc) δ (ἀρτ.) ιθβ́.
    cπό(ροc) (πυρῶι) β̣ (ἀρτ.) θ∠γ́, ἀρά(κωι) β (ἀρτ.) θ∠γ́, (γίν.) δ (ἀρτ.) ιθβ́

Πτόλλιc Ὀ[ρcείουc τὴν (πρότερον)] διὰ Μεcταcύ(τμιοc) ε (ἀρτ.) κδ∠ίβ́.
    [cπό(ροc)   (γίν.) ε (ἀρτ.)] κδ∠ίβ́
[   ] .[
[   ] ⟦ϛη∠ίβ́⟧ \`ργϛ́´
    [   ]
[   ] . .[   ] . . . . κδd
    [(ἀρτ.) ρδ
[   ] . .[
[   ] (ἀρτ.) κ .[

[Ἁρ]μιῦcιc Ἁρ[μιύcιοc ϛ (ἀρτ.)] κθ∠. cπό(ροc) (πυρῶι) δ (ἀρτ.) ⟦ιδ∠d⟧ \`ιθβ́´,
        . . β̣ (ἀρτ.) θ̣[∠]γ́, (γίν.) ϛ (ἀρτ.) κθ∠
[. . . . .] . .ιϛ . .[±8] (γίν.) δ (ἀρτ.) ιθβ́. cπό(ροc) (πυρῶι) β (ἀρτ.) θ∠γ́,
        κ(ριθῆι) β (ἀρτ.) θ∠γ́
[. . . . .] . . .ετ̣ . . .[±8 Κε]ντείcιοc α∠ (ἀρτ.) ζ∠.

[   ] β (ἀρτ.) θ∠γ́, κρι(θῆι) β (ἀρτ.) θ∠γ́, (γίν.)
        δ (ἀρτ.) ιθβ́

[δ ἀν(ὰ) δ] (ἀρτ.) ιϛ. cπό(ροc) (πυρῶι) β (ἀρτ.) η,
        φαcή(λωι) β (ἀρτ.) η

Col. IX

⟦one line washed out⟧

Ἁρμαχόροc Θοτορταίου βḍ ἀν(ὰ) γ (ἀρτ.) ϛ∠d.
    cπό(ροc) (πυρῶι) αἱ πᾶ(cαι)

Ἁρμιῦcιc Πετοcίριοc δ∠ ἀν(ὰ) δ (ἀρτ.) ιη.
    κρι(θῆι) β∠ (ἀρτ.) ι, τή(λει) α (ἀρτ.) δ, φαcή(λωι) α (ἀρτ.) δ, (γίν.)
        δ (ἀρτ.) ιη

Ἁρμιῦcιc Πετώυτοc ιβ∠ (ἀρτ.) νϛ∠.
    cπό(ροc) (πυρῶι) ζ∠ (ἀρτ.) λϛ∠γ́ίβ́, χό(ρτωι) γ θ∠d, φα(κῶι) ⟨β⟩ θ∠γ́,
        (γίν.) ιβ∠ (ἀρτ.) νϛ∠

Ἀπολλώνιοc Διοκλείουc ε (ἀρτ.) ιε.
    cπό(ροc) (πυρῶι) δ (ἀρτ.) ιβ, φαcή(λωι) α (ἀρτ.) γ, (γίν.) ε (ἀρτ.) ιε

Ὧρος Νεοπτολέμου ε (ἀρτ.) ιε. σπό(ρος) (πυρῶι) δ (ἀρτ.) ιβ, φασή(λωι) α (ἀρτ. ?) γ, (γίν.) ε (ἀρτ.) ιε

Δημήτριος Ἡρακλείδου ι (ἀρτ.) ι. σπό(ρος) (πυρῶι) αἱ πᾶ(σαι)

Θῶνις μέ(γας) Κεντίσιος ιγ (ἀρτ.) ξγ∠γ́ιβ́, β (ἔτους) με(μερισμέναι) ἀπὸ τῆς (πρότερον) Πετεή̣σ̣ι̣ος τοῦ Πάσιτος β (ἀρτ.) θ∠γ́, (γίν.) ιε (ἀρτ.) ογ∠d. σπό(ρος) (πυρῶι) .[ ] κ̣ρ̣ι̣(θῆι) δ (ἀρτ.) ιθ̣[β́], φα(κῶι) β (ἀρτ.) θ∠γ́, ἀρά(κωι) δ (ἀρτ.) ιθβ́, (γίν.) ιε (ἀρτ.) ογ∠d

Θῶνις μι(κρὸς) Κ̣ε̣ν̣τ̣ί̣[σιος] ε̣ (ἀρτ.) κδ∠ιβ́, β (ἔτους) δ∠ (ἀρτ.) κβς́, με(μερισμένη) ἀπὸ τῆς (πρότερον) Φ̣ρ̣α̣μ̣ή̣ν̣ι̣ο̣ς̣ τ̣ο̣ῦ̣ Π̣ε̣τ̣ο̣σίριος α∠ (ἀρτ.) ζγ́ιβ́, (γίν.) ς (ἀρτ.) [κθ∠]. σπό(ρος) (πυρῶι) ε̣ (ἀρτ. ?) κδ∠ιβ́, φα(κῶι) α (ἀρτ.) δ∠γ́ιβ́, (γίν.) ς (ἀρτ.) κ[θ∠]

Θοτεὺς Διο[δώρου] .[ ] . .δ (ἀρτ.) [

Ἰλῶ[ς Ὥρου] (ἀρτ.) ι, (γίν.) [ἀρά(κωι) γ∠ (ἀρτ.) . . . . . β (ἀρτ.) . .[

Μαρρῆς Μαρρείους . . . ±12 . . . ., β (ἔτους) [γ (ἀρτ.) ιδ]∠d. σπό(ρος) (πυρῶι) α̣ἱ̣ π̣ᾶ̣(σαι)

Ὀννῶφρις Πετεχῶ̣ν̣τ̣ο̣ς̣ ιγ (ἀρτ.) ξγ∠γ́ιβ́. σπό(ρος) (πυρῶι) θ (ἀρτ.) μ̣δ̣ḍ, κ̣ρ̣ι̣(θῆι) β̣ (ἀρτ. ?) θ̣∠̣γ́, φα(κῶι) β (ἀρτ.) θ∠γ́, (γίν.) ιγ (ἀρτ.) ξγ∠γ́ιβ́

Ὀρσῆς Ὀρσείους ε∠ ἀ̣ν̣(ὰ) δ̣∠̣γ́ι̣β̣́ (ἀρτ. ?) κζς́. σπό(ρος) (πυρῶι) αἱ πᾶ(σαι)

Ὀννῶφρις Ὥρου θd ἀν(ὰ) δ∠γ́ιβ́ με∠. σπό(ρος) (πυρῶι) δd (ἀρτ.) κ∠γ́ιβ́, φα(κῶι) γ (ἀρτ.) ιδ∠d, τή(λει) β (ἀρτ.) θ∠γ́, (γίν.) θ̣ḍ (ἀρτ. ?) με∠

Col. X

Πετενοῦπις [Πετοσίριο]ς ε̣ḍ ἀν(ὰ) δ∠γ́ιβ́ [(ἀρτ.)] κε∠γ́. σπό(ρος) (πυρῶι) γ (ἀρτ.) [ιδβ́, . βd (ἀρτ.)] ιαιβ́, (γίν.) εd (ἀρτ.) κε∠γ́

Πᾶσις Πετεσούχ[ου ιε] ἀν(ὰ) δ∠γ́ιβ́ ⟦ογ∠d⟧ \`ναd´. σπό(ρος) (πυρῶι) ι (ἀρτ.) λαd, φα(κῶι) ε (ἀρτ.) κ, [(γίν.) ιε] (ἀρτ.) ναd

Πορεγέβθις Ἀπύ[γχιος θ] (ὦν) γ ἀν(ὰ) δ∠γ́ιβ́ ιδ∠d, ς ἀν(ὰ) γ (ἀρτ.) ιη,

(γίν.) θ (ἀρτ.) λβ∠d.
σπό(ρος) (πυρῶι) γ (ἀρτ.) ι[δ]∠̣[d, . γ (ἀρτ.) θ], ἀρά(κωι) γ (ἀρτ.) θ,
(γίν.) θ (ἀρτ.) λβ∠d.

Πετεσοῦχος Σωτ[ηρίδου θ]∠ (ὤν) γ∠ ἀν(ὰ) δ∠γ´ιβ´ ιζd, ς ἀν(ὰ) δ (ἀρτ.) [κδ],
(γίν.) θ∠
(ἀρτ.) μαd. σπ[ό(ρος) . ς (ἀρτ.) κ]δ, φα(κῶι) γ∠ (ἀρτ.) ιζ∠, (γίν.)
θ∠ (ἀρτ.) μα[d]
Νίκων Ἀμενν̣[έως ι] ἀν(ὰ) δ∠γ´ιβ´ (ἀρτ.) μθς´.
σπό(ρος) τήλει [αἱ πᾶ(σαι)]

Μαρρῆς Σεν[θέως β] ἀν(ὰ) γ (ἀρτ.) ς. σπό(ρος) (πυρῶι) αἱ πᾶ(σαι)

Πετεσοῦχος Σ[αραπίωνος] δ̣∠̣ ἀν(ὰ) δ (ἀρτ.) ιη.
σπό(ρος) (πυρῶι) β∠ [(ἀρτ.) ι, . α (ἀρτ.)] δ̣, τή(λει) α (ἀρτ.) δ,
(γίν.) δ∠ (ἀρτ.) ιη

Πνεφερῶς [ι]γ (ἀρτ.) μα∠d (ὤν) ε∠ ἀν(ὰ) δ∠γ´ιβ´ (ἀρτ.) κζ∠ιβ´,
∠ . . [(ἀρτ.)] ιδ, (γίν.) ιγ (ἀρτ.) μα̣∠d.
σπό(ρος) [

[ ] ἀν(ὰ) γ, (γίν.) ιδ (ἀρτ.) μδ∠d.
[σπό(ρος)] γ (ἀρτ.) ιδ∠d, ἀρά(κωι) β (ἀρτ.) ς,
(γίν.) ιδ (ἀρτ.) μδ∠d

[*Πετερμοῦθις Σι*]*εφμοῦτος* ια (ἀρτ.) νδ∠ιβ´,
[(ὤν) α ἀν(ὰ) δ∠, ι ἀν(ὰ)] δ∠γ´ιβ´. σπό(ρος) (πυρῶι) η (ἀρτ.) λθ̣γ´,
φα(κῶι) β (ἀρτ.) θ∠γ´, ἀρά(κωι) α (ἀρτ.) δ∠,
[(γίν.) ια] (ἀρτ.) νδ∠ιβ´

[θ] (ἀρτ.) μ̣α∠d. σπό(ρος) (πυρῶι) ς̣ (ἀρτ.) κζ,
φα(κῶι) γ (ἀρτ.) ιδ∠d

[ς]∠̣ ἀ̣ν̣(ὰ) δ∠γ´ιβ´ (ἀρτ.) λβ, β ἀν(ὰ) γ (ἀρτ.) ς,
(γίν.) η∠ (ἀρτ.) λη.
[σπό(ρος) . α∠] (ἀρτ.) ζγ´ιβ´, . . ζ (ἀρτ. ?) λ̣δ̣∠ι̣β´, (γίν.) η∠ (ἀρτ.) λη

[ ] ε∠η´ (ἀρτ.) κζ⟦ιβ´⟧ \`∠γ´ιβ´'
[ ] . (ἀρτ.) λβ∠

[β] (ἀρτ.) θ∠γ´

Col. XI

Ψενῆcιc Θώνιοc δ∠d ἀν(ὰ) δ∠γ́ίβ́ (ἀρτ.) κγγ́.
σπό(ροc) (πυρῶι) β∠ḍ (ἀρτ.) ι̣γ∠̣, φα(κῶι) β (ἀρτ.) θ∠γ́, ⟨(γίν.) δ∠d⟩ (ἀρτ.) κγγ́
Χῦψιc Πετεcούχου ζ∠ ἀν(ὰ) δ∠γ́ίβ́ (ἀρτ.) λϛ∠γ́ίβ́.
σπό(ροc) (πυρῶι) γ∠ (ἀρτ.) ιζd, φα(κῶι) δ (ἀρτ.) ιθβ́, (γίν.) ζ∠ (ἀρτ.) λϛ∠γ́ίβ́

Ὧροc Κεντείc̣ι̣οc εή (ἀρτ.) κεd.
σπό(ροc) (πυρῶι) γή (ἀρτ.) ιεγ́ίβ́, φα(κῶι) β (ἀρτ.) θ∠γ́, (γίν.) εή̣ (ἀρτ.) κεd

Ὧροc μέ(γαc) Κεντείcιοc ιε∠ (ἀρτ.) οαγ́ίβ́, ιγ∠ ἀν(ὰ) δ∠γ́ίβ́ (ἀρτ.) ξγ∠γ́ίβ́, β∠ ἀν(ὰ) γ (ἀρτ.) ζ∠, (γίν.) ιε∠ (ἀρτ.) οα̣γ́ίβ́. β̣ (ἔτουc) με(μεριcμένον) ἀπὸ τῆc (πρότερον)
Πετε . . . . ∠ (ἀρτ.) β, (γίν.) ιϛ (ἀρτ.) ογγ́ίβ́.
σπό(ροc) (πυρῶι) ι∠ (ἀρτ.) μ . ∠γ́, φα(κῶι) γ (ἀρτ.) ιδ∠d, ἀρά(κωι) [β]∠̣ [(ἀρτ.)] οη∠γ́

Ὧροc Ὀρcείουc ιγ∠ ἀν(ὰ) δ∠γ́ίβ́ (ἀρτ.) ξϛ, β̣ (ἔτουc ?) [ιγ (ἀρτ.) ξγ∠γ́ίβ́].
σπό(ροc) (πυρῶι) ϛ (ἀρτ.) κθ∠, φα(κῶι) γ (ἀρτ.) ιδβ̣́, ἀρά(κωι) β (ἀρτ.) θ̣∠γ́, τή(λει) β̣ [(ἀρτ.) θ∠γ́], (γίν.) ιγ (ἀρτ.) ξγ∠̣γ́ί̣β̣́

Θοτεὺc Φολήμιοc α (ἀρτ.) εγ́. σπό(ροc) [
Ἁροννῶφριc Ὥρου α (ἀρτ.) εγ́. σπό(ροc) [
Ἀμοῦνιc Πικάμιοc α∠ (ἀρτ.) ζ∠. σπό(ροc) (πυρῶι ?)
Ἁρμιῦcιc Φατρήουc α [(ἀρτ.)] εγ́. σπό(ροc) (πυρῶι)
Ἁρυώτηc Ἁρυώτου α (ἀρτ.) εγ́. σπό(ροc) (πυρῶι)
Ἁρυώτηc Φαεῦτοc β (ἀρτ.) ιβ́. σπό(ροc) (πυρῶι)
Ὀρcῆc Ἁρονήcιοc α (ἀρτ.) εγ́. σπό(ροc) (πυρῶι)
Μεcταcῦτμιc Ὥρου β (ἀρτ.) ιβ́. σπό(ροc) (πυρῶι)
Ὧροc Ὥρου α∠ (ἀρτ.) η. σπό(ροc) (πυρῶι)
Πετεcοῦχοc Π̣ετεc[ούχ]ου β∠ (ἀρτ.) ιγ. σπό(ροc) (πυρῶι)

Col. XII

Παcῶc Ὀρc̣ε̣[ίουc α] (ἀρτ.) εγ́. σπό(ροc) (πυρῶι)
Παcῶc μέ(γαc) Φ[ανήcιοc] α (ἀρτ.) εγ́. σπό(ροc) (πυρῶι)
Πᾶcιc μέ(γαc) [Καλατύτ]ιοc α (ἀρτ.) εγ́. σπό(ροc) μελα(νθίωι)

Πᾶϲιϲ μι(κρὸϲ) [Καλατύτιο]ϲ ∠ (ἀρτ.) ββ̣́. ϲπό(ροϲ) (πυρῶι)
Φαεὺϲ [Σοκέωϲ] α (ἀρτ.) εγ́. ϲπό(ροϲ) (πυρῶι)
Πετ[ ] τὴν (πρότερον) Κεφαλᾶ̣τ̣ο̣ϲ̣ τ̣ο̣ῦ̣ Πετεϲού(χου)
γ (ἀρτ.) ι̣ϛ̣. ϲ̣π̣ό̣(ροϲ) (πυρῶι)
Ψενῆϲιϲ [Στεφάνου] α (ἀρτ.) εγ́. ϲπό(ροϲ) χό(ρτωι)
Ἁρψάλ[ιϲ Στεφάνου] β∠ (ἀρτ.) ιγ. ϲ̣π̣ό̣(ροϲ) (πυρῶι ?)
] ϲπό(ροϲ) (πυρῶι)
] α̣∠̣ḍ (ἀρτ.) η∠d. ϲπό(ροϲ) (πυρῶι)
] α (ἀρτ.) ε̣γ́. ϲπό(ροϲ) (πυρῶι)
] ϲπό(ροϲ) (πυρῶι)

Col. XIII

π .τιμη( ) δ∠ (ἀρτ.) κβϛ́
νομῶν ξ (ἀρτ.) ξ
γεω(ργοὶ) κοινεῖ β (ἀρτ.) ϛ
ἀϲπό(ρου) ζ∠ (ἀρτ.) κβ∠
(γίν.) οδ (ἀρτ.) ριβ́

ἀπὸ (ἀρουρῶν) ͵Αροθ̣d (ἀρτ.) ͵Δφϙδίβ
ε̄ ϙε (ἀρτ.) ρμαβ́ Σ̣
. . . . (ἄρουραι ?) ο̣δ (ἀρτ.) ριβ́
ἐλ( ) κα (ἀρτ.) λα

Col. XIV (foot of papyrus, between cols. XI and XII)

ιδ ξγϛ́ 2–5
ι μ 6–7
ιϛ∠ πα∠ 8–9
κβ ϙδ∠d 10–12
β̣ θ∠γ́ 13–14 = 18–19
ιγ κε̣ 15–16
δ ιε 17
ζ∠d λα 20–1
ιδ ξη[∠γ́] 22–3
κγ∠̣ [ρδίβ́] 26–8
η [κδ] 29
(γίν.) ρλγ∠̣ḍ 413

Col. XV (under XII)

[εd] κε∠[γ́] 30
[ι∠] μζ∠ 31–3
breaks off

Col. XVI (foot, between XII and XIII)

[ϛ∠] λβ̣ 71–2

α γ 73
ε κ 74–5
(γίν.)
η λθή 77–8
breaks off

Col. XVII (under XIII)

] πβ [84–6]
[θ] μδς́ (87–8)
[ι] μθς́ 89–90
[ι] λδ∠d 91–2
[η] ι̣[ς] 93–4
breaks off

Col. XVIII (under XIII)

α∠d εβ́ 103
β∠d θ 104–5
β ι (106–9)
∠d γ 110
ι̣[.] μζ∠ (111–14)
[ζ∠] λ̣β̣ίβ́ 120–1
breaks off

Col. XIX (right of and lower than XIII)

γ∠ ιζγ́ίβ́ 131
(γίν.) ξε Σ̣. γ́ίβ́ 417
ε κ 132–3
ε∠ κζγ́ίβ́ 134–5
ια λβγ́ 136–8
η λθγ́ 139–40
γ∠d ιη (141)
ια νδίβ́ 142–3
γ θ [144]
δ∠ κβς́ [145]
ιβ∠ ξα∠ 146–8
[δ]∠d κγ∠[d] 149–50
[γ ιδ∠d] 151–2

Col. XX

ζ λδ[γ́ί]β́ 153–6
η λθγ́ 157–9
ιαd ν[.]∠ 160–2
ιβ [ ] [163–4]
δ∠ [κβ]ς́ [ ]
α∠d [η]β́ [ ]
ε∠ κγίβ́ 165
βd ς∠d 166–7
ζ∠ ζ∠ [168]
ς κθ∠ [169]
ιε να 170–1
ε̣ ιε 172–3
ς κθ∠ 174–5
(γίν.) ϙδ∠d τ̣ν̣γ∠̣γ́ 419
ε ις∠d 176–7
[δ] ι̣θβ́ 178–9
[ε] κ̣δ̣∠̣ί̣β́ 180–1
κ̣α πα 182
κ̣δ ργς̣́ 183
κδd ρδ 185–6
γ ι̣δ 187
β γ∠ (188)
ς κ[θ]∠ 189–90
δ [ιθβ́] 191
[α∠ ζ∠] 192
[δ ιθβ́] 193
[δ ις] 194

Col. XXI

βḍ ς∠d 196–7
δ∠ ιη 198–9
ιβ∠ νς∠ 200–1
ε ιε 202–3
ε ιε 204–5
δ ιθβ́ (206–7)

ιε ⟦θ̣γ∠d⟧ `ογ∠d´ 208–10
ε∠d κηβ́ (211–13)
ϛ ιη 214
ιε ξ 215–16
γ ιδ∠d 217–18
ιγ ξγ∠γ́ίβ́ 219–20
ε∠ κζϛ́ 221–2
(γίν.) ⟦ϙε∠⟧ `ϙϛ∠´ ⟦τνϛϛ́⟧ `υμ̣ηϛ́´ 420
θd με∠ 223–4
εd κ̣ε̣∠̣γ́ 225–6
ιε ξαd (227–8)
θ λβ∠d 229–30
θ∠ μαd 231–2
ι μθϛ́ 233–4
β ϛ 235
δ∠ ιη 236–7
ιγ μα∠d 238–40
α γ (241–2)
ια νδ∠ίβ́ 243–5
θ μα∠ḍ 246
[λβ]∠ 250
[β] θ̣∠̣γ́ 251

Col. XXII
η∠ λη 247–8
ε∠ή κζίβ́ (249)
δ∠d κγγ́ 252–3
ζ∠ λϛ∠γ́ίβ́ 254–5
εή κεd 256–7
ιζ οη∠γ́ (258–61)
ιγ∠ ξγ∠γ́ίβ́ 262–3
ϛ∠ λδd —
(γίν.) ξη∠ 421

α εγ́
β ιβ́
α∠ η
β∠ ιγ
γ ιϛ
α∠ η
γ ιε
γ∠ ιηγ́
α∠d η∠d
(γίν.) ιθ∠d (ἀρτ.) ργίβ́

Col. XXIII
ᾱ (ἄρουραι) ρλγ∠d 307
β̄ ρ⟦μβd⟧ `λβd´ (ἀρτ.) [
γ̄ ρνθd [
ριε∠ [(ἀρτ.)] . .[
ξε (ἀρτ.) Σ .[γ́ίβ́ 327
ϙ (ἀρτ.) .[
ϙ̣δ∠d (ἀρτ.) τ̣[νγ∠γ́ (?) 352

.ζd (ἀρτ.) .[
ϛϛ̣́∠ (ἀρτ.) υμη[ϛ́ 372
] (ἀρτ.) υ̣η̣ .[
ξ̣η∠ (ἀρτ.) τ . . .[402

56 1st κδ corrected from κε 116 ἀcπόρου corrected from καί 172 οἱ μέ(τοχοι): read τῶν με(τόχων)

Col. II. 'Katytis son of Katytis. Year 1, $23\frac{1}{2}$ arouras paying $104\frac{1}{2}$ artabs. Year 2, the same: $18\frac{1}{2}$ arouras at $4\frac{11}{12}$ art. per aroura, $89\frac{1}{12}$ art.; 5 at 3, 15. Total, $23\frac{1}{2}$ arouras, $104\frac{1}{12}$ art. Crops $15\frac{1}{2}$ arouras in wheat, paying $65\frac{1}{4}$ art.; 5 in lentils, $24\frac{1}{12}$ art.; 3 in aracus, $14\frac{3}{4}$ art. Total, $23\frac{1}{2}$ arouras: $104\frac{1}{12}$ art.

'Katytis son of Sisouchos. 8 arouras paying 24 art. Of these 5 are in wheat, 15 art. due; 3 in barley, 9 art. Total, 8 arouras, 24 art.

'Kentis son of Katytis. Year 1, $5\frac{1}{4}$ arouras paying $25\frac{5}{6}$ art. Crops: 3 arouras in wheat, $14\frac{3}{4}$ art.; $2\frac{1}{4}$ in lentils, $11\frac{1}{12}$ art. Total, $5\frac{1}{4}$ arouras, $25\frac{5}{6}$ art.

'Papnebtynis son of Sokeus, and Kollouthes. Year 1, $10\frac{1}{2}$ arouras, $47\frac{1}{2}$ art. Year 2, the same: $5\frac{1}{2}$ at $4\frac{11}{12}$, $27\frac{1}{12}$ art.; 5 at 4, 20 art. Crops: 6 in wheat, $26\frac{3}{4}$ art.; 2 in barley, $8\frac{1}{3}$ art.; $2\frac{1}{2}$ in . . ., $12\frac{5}{12}$ art. Total, $10\frac{1}{2}$ arouras, $47\frac{1}{2}$ art.

'Harchypsis son of Peteesis. Year 1, out of $6\frac{5}{8}$ arouras paying 31 art., $1\frac{3}{8}$ arouras paying $4\frac{1}{2}$ art.; and apportioned from the land formerly held by Tothoes son of Phagates, $\frac{3}{4}$ aroura paying 3 art. Total, $2\frac{1}{8}$ arouras paying $7\frac{1}{2}$ art. Of these, $1\frac{1}{8}$ rent for 4 art. per aroura, $4\frac{1}{2}$ art. due; and 1 is rented at 3 art., all in wheat.

'Marres son of Petosiris. Year 1, $16\frac{1}{2}$ arouras paying $56\frac{1}{4}$ art. Year 2, the same. Of these 10 rent for 4 art. apiece, 40 art. due; $6\frac{1}{2}$ at $2\frac{1}{2}$, $16\frac{1}{4}$ art. due. Crops: $10\frac{1}{2}$ in wheat, $40\frac{1}{4}$ art.; 4 in barley, 8 art.; 2 in lentils, 8 art. Total, $16\frac{1}{2}$ arouras, $56\frac{1}{4}$ art.

'Mestasytmis son of Petesouchos, and associates. Year 1, 35 arouras paying 70 art. Year 2, the same. Crop: wheat.

'Marres son of Petesouchos. Year 1, 4 arouras paying $19\frac{2}{3}$ art. Year 2, the same. Crop: all in wheat.

'Onnophris son of Phatres. Year 1, $6\frac{1}{2}$ arouras paying 32 art. Year 2, the same. Crops: 3 arouras in wheat, $14\frac{1}{2}$ art.; $\frac{3}{4}$ in lentils, $3\frac{3}{4}$; 3 in barley, $14\frac{3}{4}$. Total, $6\frac{3}{4}$ arouras, $32\frac{1}{4}$ art. And out of the land formerly held by Petosiris son of Horos, $\frac{1}{4}$ aroura paying $1\frac{3}{4}$ art. Total, $6\frac{3}{4}$ arouras, $33\frac{1}{4}$ art.

'Onnophris son of Horos, and associates. Year 1, $3\frac{1}{2}$ arouras, $10\frac{1}{2}$ art. Year 2, the same. Crops: 2 arouras in wheat, 6 art. due; $1\frac{1}{2}$ in barley, $4\frac{1}{2}$ art. Total, $3\frac{1}{2}$ arouras, $10\frac{1}{2}$ art.

'Petermouthis son of Marres. Year 1, 12 arouras at $2\frac{1}{2}$ art., 30 art. Year 2, the same. Crops: 6 arouras in wheat, 15 art.; 6 in aracus, 15 art. Total, 12 arouras, 30 art.

'Petesouchos son of Nektenibis. Year 1, 20 arouras paying 40 art. Year 2, the same. Crop: all in lentils.

'Teos son of Thotortaios, and Anempeus. Out of land formerly held by Sentheus son of Harkoiphis, $5\frac{1}{2}$ arouras paying $27\frac{1}{12}$ art. Crops: all in wheat.

'Total for the column: $142\frac{3}{4}$ arouras paying $485\frac{1}{6}$ artabs.'

2 με(μεριcμέναι): or perhaps με(μιcθωμέναι), though in **61**(b) and **72** that word seems limited to special long-term arrangements. *Μερίζω* does not of itself carry an implication of force (cf. e.g. **739**. 5); as applied to compulsory land assignments in UPZ 110. 48 and 66 it may be euphemistic. Cf. also **1137**. 8.

τῆc (πρότερον) Μαρρε]ί̣ουc: cf. 217.

τῆc [(πρότερον)] Δημητ[ρίου: cf. 128.

5 (ἀρτ.) ξ[γίβ]: I have restored the correct total of the items in line 5, although it falls $\frac{1}{12}$ short of $63\frac{1}{6}$ (line 4). Cf. 32 note.

13 τ[ῆ]c (πρότερον) Πετ[οcίριοc: cf. 51.

14 (ἀρτ.) θ∠̣γ́: this sum was not reached by adding $7\frac{5}{12}$ to $2\frac{1}{2}$ (= $9\frac{11}{12}$), but by multiplying the

total 2 arouras by $4\frac{11}{12}$ art./ar. The rental on the $\frac{1}{2}$ aroura lot was $4\frac{11}{12}$, not 5 art./ar.

16 *cπό(ρος) (ἀρτ.) δ*: the artab sign is a mistake. Probably (*πυρῶι*) was intended.

χο(ρτο)νο(μῶν): cf. **60**. 82 note.

18–19 The entry was cancelled because it repeats 13–14.

20 *'Ορcενοῦφιc*: Thonis' father.

21 (*γίν.*) *ζ∠d* (*ἀρτ.*) *λα*: really $30\frac{11}{12}$ art., but this is consistent with an error farther along in the line, where the rent on $1\frac{3}{4}$ aroura (at 3 art./ar.) is reckoned as $5\frac{1}{3}$ rather than $5\frac{1}{4}$ art.

22 *τῆc (πρότερον) Πετεcούχου*: cf. 153–4.

μβίβ: since the calculation in the next line shows that the $8\frac{3}{4}$ arouras here were rated at $4\frac{11}{12}$ art., $42\frac{1}{12}$ is an error for $43\frac{1}{12}$.

23 (*ἀρτ.*) *ξ⟦ϛβ⟧ ʽη∠γ′*: $68\frac{5}{6}$ is the product of 14 ar. × $4\frac{11}{12}$ art./ar., not the sum of the foregoing rents ($42\frac{1}{12} + 25\frac{5}{6} = 67\frac{11}{12}$). Cf. 14 note.

26–8 Written over an earlier text poorly washed out.

31 *Κολλούθηc*: Papnebtynis' son.

32 The rent here calculated according to the value of the land totals $47\frac{1}{12}$ art.; the rent actually charged in lines 31 and 33 is $47\frac{1}{2}$ art. The discrepancy may have been caused by the tenant's using parcels with fractions of an aroura at $4\frac{11}{12}$ for the various crops. Cf. lines 4–5.

34 [*'Αρχῦψιc Π*]*ετεήcιοc, κτλ.*: cf. 23.

34–5 *τῆc (πρότερον) Τοθοήουc*: cf. 73. This $\frac{3}{4}$ aroura is now rated at 4 art./ar. It was higher the year before, when $3\frac{1}{2}$ art. were charged.

41–2 For a clarified version of this bungled account see **1107**. 44, *'Οννῶφριc* [*Φατρεί*]*ουc β ϛ∠* (*ἀρτ.*) *λβ*, *Κε(ρκεούρεωc) λι(βὸc) d* (*ἀρτ.*) *αd*, (*γίν.*) *ϛ∠d* (*ἀρτ.*) *λγd* 'Onnophris son of Phatres. $6\frac{1}{2}$ arouras at 32 art. in the Second Perichoma, $\frac{1}{4}$ ar. at $1\frac{1}{4}$ art. in the Western Kerkeouris Perichoma, total $6\frac{3}{4}$ at $33\frac{1}{4}$ art.' The scribe here wrote incorrectly that Onnophris' holding was the same in year 2 as in year 1; then in detailing the crops he realized that the total was larger than it should be, so he added out of place the land transferred from Petosiris (cf. 55 note). But he added the rents incorrectly ($32\frac{1}{4}$ instead of 33 or $33\frac{1}{4}$), and gave the rental of the new parcel as $1\frac{3}{4}$ instead of $1\frac{1}{4}$ art.

43 Onnophris son of Horos appears independently of his associates in 223.

45 *Πετερμοῦθιc Μαρρείουc*: cf. 151 note.

τῆc (πρότερον) Cενθέωc: cf. 118.

50 The correct totals were $152\frac{5}{8}$ arouras, $495\frac{1}{6}$ artabs.

51 Of the $\frac{3}{4}$ aroura which this man gave up between years 1 and 2, $\frac{1}{2}$ is accounted for in 13–14, the remainder perhaps in 42; cf. 55 n.

55 *β* (*ἔτουc*) *ἴcο(ν)*: if this is right, then the statement in 42 that Onnophris son of Phatres is farming $\frac{1}{4}$ aroura which once belonged to this individual is wrong, or refers to an earlier year. But between years 1 and 2 Petosiris son of Harkoiphis gave up $\frac{3}{4}$ aroura, of which only $\frac{1}{2}$ is accountable elsewhere (13–14), so *"Ωρου* in 42 may be an error for *'Αρκοίφιος*.

κδ∠d: the items detailed in the rest of the line total $24\frac{2}{3}$ art. (really $24\frac{5}{6}$, because the rent on the $2\frac{3}{4}$ aroura lot should have been $13\frac{7}{12}$ rather than than $13\frac{5}{12}$).

56 (*ἀρτ.*) . ∠: no number before the (*ἥμιcυ*) sign will make the arithmetic come out right.

57 *τῆc (πρότερον) Πετῶτοc*: cf. 151.

65–6 In year 1, Pnepheros was booked for 7 arouras at $4\frac{11}{12}$ art. each. In year 2 this was changed to 2 ar. at 5 art.; but in fact these were not booked to Pnepheros, but to the cleruch Dionysios son of Pyrrhichos, from whom Pnepheros merely sublet the land. The insertion of line 65 was intended to make this clear. Cf. **1117**. 11–12; and for the land given up by Pnepheros see 154–5.

71 (*ἀρτ.*) *ιζίβ*: really $17\frac{1}{4}$, which would make the addition correct.

73 Cf. 34–5 n.

84–6 The lost figures included 82 art. rent; cf. 315.

87 Kentisis had 2 sons named Thonis and also 2 named Horos; we cannot tell which are meant here. All four held Crown land in their own names apart from this partnership (208, 211, 256, 258).

88 *μδd*: line 316 erroneously has $44\frac{1}{6}$.

95 *καὶ οἱ ἀ̣δ̣ε̣λ̣(φοί)*: sc. the brothers of Petesouchos, not of his father Cheyris.

99–102 These lines give the individual holdings of each member of the family group in lines 95–8.

100 *Χεῦρις μι(κρός)*: usually *μικρός* in this context means the younger of 2 brothers with the same name, but here it is apparently used to distinguish Cheyris son of Cheyris from his father.

105 *φ]α̣(κῶι)* or *ἀρ]ά̣(κωι)*.

111 *β (ἔτους) ιε*: only 14 in 114; line 324 does not help.

115 *νομῶν ξ*: up to year 53 of Euergetes II (118/117) there had been only 30 arouras of pasture bringing in a grain rental at Kerkeosiris. After the sowing of that year, a further 29 arouras were added; and since 60 arouras are found here and in later texts, 1 more must have been reclaimed in year 54 of Euergetes = 1 of Soter. Cf. **68**. 72 note. In addition Kerkeosiris possessed $175\frac{3}{8}$ arouras for which the rental was collected in cash (**61**(a). 154–5).

117 Cf. **68**. 83–5.

124 *Λάγου*: apparently the grandfather's name, not a correction of *Πετεσούχου*. If the addition was intended to distinguish between two persons with the same name, we cannot tell whether it means that this was or was not the *machimos*.

128 Cf. 3–4.

130 *(ἀρτ.) κα*: should have been $20\frac{11}{12}$.

136 *'Αμεννεύς*: Marres' son.

141 *[ι]ηγ́ιβ́*: 18 in 332. At $4\frac{11}{12}$ art./ar., one expects $18\frac{1}{2}$.

144–5 According to lines 334–5 the figures lost are respectively 3 arouras paying 9 artabs and $4\frac{1}{2}$ paying $22\frac{1}{6}$.

150 *κγ∠d*: the individual items total only $22\frac{1}{4}$. No doubt the rent on the land planted in aracus is too low.

151 *Πετερμοῦθις*: presumably the brother of Petos who appears independently in line 45. For some of (?) the land given up after year 1 cf. 57–8.

153–4 The $8\frac{11}{16}$ arouras given up by Petesouchos after year 1 appear as $8\frac{3}{4}$ in line 22.

154 *τῆς (πρότερον) Πνεφερῶτος*: cf. 66.

157 *ὑ[δ]ρα(γωγοῦ)*: so again in the next line. Irrigation canals are normally *ὑπόλογος ἐκτὸς μισθώσεως*: this one is subject to rental because it is used for growing crops, and has therefore either gone dry or been filled up (cf. the actions of one Lykos in **50**). For a similar situation cf. *TAPA* 101 (1970), 490, lines 3–4.

163–71 For the figures restored, or lost in lines where restoration cannot be reasonably attempted, see 342–9.

176 *ιϛ∠d*: right was $16\frac{1}{4}$. The mistake was carried over from the year before (**68**. 24), but had been caught by year 4 (**69**. 10). Those texts include no more land at this rate.

182–7 Cf. 356–9.

188 *(ἀρτ.) κ.[*: according to 360 this man farmed 2 arouras paying $3\frac{1}{2}$ art., but it does not seem possible to reconcile that with the traces here.

192 The lessee was NN *καὶ* NN *Κεντίσιος* or NN *τὴν (πρότερον) Κεντίσιος* (or some equivalent expression).

206 *ι (ἀρτ.) ι*: line 371 gives this as 4 ar. at $4\frac{11}{12}$ art. That is probably a mistaken reference to an earlier year; cf. **1117**. 159–61.

208, 211 Cf. 87 note.

217 Cf. 2–3 and 376.

221 *κζϛ́*: right was $27\frac{1}{12}$.

223 Cf. 43.

227 ⟦*ογ∠d*⟧ \`*ναd*': the first figure was correct at $4\frac{11}{12}$ art.; apparently the rate on some of the land was lowered. Line 382 copies the second figure incorrectly as $61\frac{1}{4}$.

244 *[(ὧν) α ἀν(ὰ) δ∠, ι ἀν(ὰ)] δ∠γ́ιβ́*: the following crop details show that the restoration is right but there is a mistake in the total due (lines 243, 245), since $4\frac{1}{2}+49\frac{1}{6}$ is only $53\frac{2}{3}$. The scribe may have absent-mindedly calculated the dues on all 11 arouras at $4\frac{11}{12}$, but even then there is an error, for the correct total would be $54\frac{1}{12}$, as is found in **1107**. 141.

249–51 Probably a line with crop details has been lost after each entry.

252 *κγγ́*: should have been $23\frac{5}{12}$.

256 *῟Ωρος Κεντείς̣ι̣ος*: the younger of this name, since his older brother follows in 258. Cf. 87 n.

258 *(ἀρτ.) ξγ∠γ́ιβ́*: a mistake for $66\frac{5}{12}$; the scribe calculated rent on 13 instead of $13\frac{1}{2}$ arouras.

261 Without knowing how the crops were distributed over parcels of different value the lost and mutilated figures cannot be calculated. It is also doubtful whether the total to be aimed for is $73\frac{5}{12}$ (line 260) or $78\frac{5}{6}$, which cannot be arrived at from the plots as listed but is repeated in 399.

262 ξϛ: should be $66\frac{5}{12}$.

287 π.τιμη( ): or perhaps [.]π.τιμη( ). I cannot explain the term.

289 γεω(ργοὶ) κοινει̑ (read κοινῆι) β (ἀρτ.) ϛ: refers to 118. In fact the tenants in common were responsible for all the property in lines 288–90, if not 287–90, but the 2 arouras are singled out because they alone produced a crop.

290 Cf. 116, 117.

291 Totals correct.

293 Obscure to me.

295 ἐλ( ): ἐλ(είφθηcαν), 'remainder'? The following figures result from subtracting line 294 (= 291) from 293.

307 ρλγ∠ḍ: right was $134\frac{3}{4}$.

313 (γίν.): the figures were never filled in.

352 (γίν.) ϙδ∠d τṛγ∠γ́: there are $92\frac{1}{4}$ arouras listed in this column. The artabs cannot be checked.

379 ϙϛ∠, ʽυμ̣ηϛ́ʼ: $96\frac{1}{2}$ is right; the artabs should have been $427\frac{1}{3}$.

392–3 These two lines should have followed 395.

402, 412 Totals correct.

403–12 No convincing correspondence with 264–86 is apparent. Line 409 gives a calculation at 5 instead of $5\frac{1}{3}$ art./ar.

413–15 ᾱ, β̄, γ̄: apparently not column numbers (our cols. 14–16), but '1st total, 2nd total, 3rd total'.

1104. Register of Land and Rents

P. Teb. 246 19·5 × 30·5 cm. Late second century B.C.

Like **1103**, the following fragment lists Crown tenants together with the amount of land booked to each, the rental paid thereon, and the crops planted; like **94+1107**, it states also the περίχωμα in which each parcel was located; cf. notes to lines 4 and 7 and Crawford, *Kerkeosiris* 110–11.

The chief interest of the text lies in the scribe's practice of breaking down rental first assessed as wheat into component portions of wheat, barley, olyra, and cash. A comparison with **1011** leaves no doubt that this represents a γενιcμὸc ἐκ τῆc ὑποθήκηc, of which several summary specimens are found in this archive (**67**. 5 note), but for which no κατ' ἄνδρα at Kerkeosiris has previously been known (cf. **832** for Oxyrhyncha). These theoretical classifications of rents by the γένη in which they were to be paid bears little relation to the crops sown or to the form in which dues were actually collected: thus olyra is prominent in γενιcμοὶ ἐκ τῆc ὑποθήκηc (cf. lines 12 and 17 below and the passages cited in **67**. 5 note) although we have no instance of charges at Kerkeosiris being paid in that crop, and only one instance of land so planted (10 arouras in 121/20, **66**. 36); whereas lentils, of which 500 artabs were taken in as land rent each year (**1105**, introd.), play no role in the ὑποθήκη. Only in the requirement that the equivalent of $39\frac{5}{12}$ artabs wheat be paid in cash does the γενιcμὸc ἐκ τῆc ὑποθήκηc correspond to real practice at Kerkeosiris during this period. In reckoning equivalences, 5 artabs of barley were treated as worth 3 of wheat, and 5 of olyra as worth 2; the price in cash was probably 400 copper drachmas per artab of wheat (2 note). Cf. P. Lond. VII pp. 98 f.

In lines 4, 10, and 15 dots surmount the figures for arouras; the meaning of a similar dot over *Μεϲταϲύτμιοϲ* in line 7 is not clear.

[Πετεϲούχου θε(οῦ)] κ̣ρ̣ο̣κ̣ο̣(δείλου) διὰ Πετεϲούχου τοῦ Πακύρριοϲ [
  [ε] (ἀρτ.) ιϛ (ὧν) (πυροῦ) η, κ(ριθῆϲ) ηγ´ αἷ (πυροῦ) ε,
    χα(λκοῦ) ξ (ἀρτ.) γ.
  ϲ̣π̣ό̣(ροϲ) (πυρῶι) γ (ἀρτ.) θ∠, χό(ρτωι) β (ἀρτ.) ϛ∠.
Πετεϲούχου θε(οῦ) κροκο(δείλου) διὰ Μαρρείουϲ τοῦ Πα̣κ̣ύ̣ρρ[ιοϲ] Κε(ρκεούρεωϲ)
    λι(βὸϲ) δ̇ ἀν(ὰ) δ∠γ´ιβ´ (ἀρτ.) ιθβ´ (ὧν)
  (πυροῦ) ιδβ´, κ(ριθῆϲ) ηγ´ αἷ (πυροῦ) ε.
  ϲπό(ροϲ) (πυρῶι) β∠ (ἀρτ.) ιβγ´, ἀρά(κωι) α∠ (ἀρτ.) ζγ´.
Πετεϲούχου θε(οῦ) διὰ Μεϲταϲύ̣τμιοϲ τοῦ Πακύρριοϲ γ̄ νό(του) ε ἀν(ὰ) [δ∠γ´ιβ´]
    (ἀρτ.) κδ∠[ιβ´ (ὧν)]
  [(πυροῦ) ι]δγ´ιβ´, κ(ριθῆϲ) ιϛβ´ αἷ (πυροῦ) ι.
  ϲπό(ροϲ) (πυρῶι) γ (ἀρτ.) ιδ∠d, φα(κῶι) α (ἀρτ.) δ∠γ´ιβ´, ἀρά(κωι) α
    (ἀρτ.) δ[∠γ´ιβ´,] (γίν.) ε (ἀρτ.) κδ∠̣ι̣β̣´.
Πετεῆϲι[ϲ] Τ̣εῶτοϲ Κοι(ρι) η ἀν(ὰ) γ (ἀρτ.) κδ, ε̇ ἀν(ὰ) α (ἀρτ.) ε,
    [θ ἀν(ὰ)] δ̣ (ἀρτ.) λϛ, (γίν.) κβ (ἀρτ.) ξε,
  Κε(ρκεούρεωϲ) ἀπη(λιώτου) ε̣ [ἀν(ὰ) γ (ἀρτ.)] ιε, ι ἀν(ὰ) δ (ἀρτ.) μ,
κ(ριθῆϛ) δ   (γίν.) (ἄρουραι) ιε (ἀρτ.) νε, (γίν.) λζ (ἀρτ.) ρκ̄ πᾱ (ὧν)
  (πυροῦ) να, [κ(ριθῆϲ) λγ]γ´ αἷ (πυροῦ) κ, ὀλ(υρῶν) κε αἷ (πυροῦ) ι.
κ(ρ.) α, ἀρά(κου) δ   ϲπό(ροϲ) (πυρῶι) . .[± 5] ., κρι(θῆι) δ (ἀρτ.) ιϛ,
    φα(κῶι) δ (ἀρτ.) ιϛ [?
13 Ὧροϲ Πε[. . . . . .]οϲ καὶ Μαρρῆϲ ιγ (ἀρτ.) κ[± 6] . . .[
14 ϲπό(ροϲ) (πυρῶι) [± 5] κρι(θῆι) δ (ἀρτ.) ιβ.
Μαρρῆϲ Πετ .[. . . . .]ϲ̣ Κοι(ρι) ιγ´, . ιά, (γίν.) κδ ἀν(ὰ) δ (ἀρτ.) ϙϛ[
  (γίν.) λβ (ἀρτ.) [. . . . .] . τε .( ) δ, λο(ιπαὶ) κη (ἀρτ.) ρ[ι]β (ὧν)
    (πυροῦ) ξβ, κ(ριθῆϲ) ν [αἷ (πυροῦ) λ,]
  ὀλ(υρῶν) ν αἷ (πυροῦ) [κ.] ϲπό(ροϲ) (πυρῶι) ιε (ἀρτ.) ξ, κ(ριθῆι) ε
    (ἀρτ.) κ, φα(κῶι) δ (ἀρτ.) ιϛ [
[ ]ω̣̂ντοϲ Κοι(ρι) ε ἀν(ὰ) δ (ἀρτ.) κ̣, [Κ]ε(ρκεούρεωϲ) . . ε
    ἀν(ὰ) . . . . [
  ] .ηϲ δ (ἀρτ.) ιϛ´, (γίν.) ιδ (ἀρτ.) νδ (ὧν) (πυροῦ) λδ, κ(ριθῆϲ)
    λγγ´ [αἷ (πυροῦ) κ.]

[ϲπό(ροϲ) . ιβ (ἀρτ.)] λ̣, φα(κοῦ) δ (ἀρτ.) ιϛ, ἀρά(κωι) β (ἀρτ.) η.
ϛγ (ἀρτ.) τμηd

Col. II

Ἁρμιῦϲιϲ Ἁ̣[ρμιύϲιοϲ
(πυροῦ)
. . .[

breaks off

Lines 1–9. 'Petesouchos the crocodile god, represented by Petesouchos son of Pakyrris... 5 arouras renting for 16 artabs. Toward these he is to pay 8 art. wheat; $8\frac{1}{3}$ art. barley, which equals 5 of wheat; and 60 copper pieces, equivalent to 3 art. wheat. Crop: 3 arouras in wheat, rental $9\frac{1}{2}$ art.; 2 arouras in grass, rental $6\frac{1}{2}$ art.

'Petesouchos the crocodile god, represented by Marres son of Pakyrris, 4 arouras at $4\frac{11}{12}$ art. apiece in the West Kerkeouris Basin, $19\frac{2}{3}$ artabs. Toward these he is to pay $14\frac{2}{3}$ art. wheat and $8\frac{1}{3}$ art. barley, which equals 5 of wheat. Crops: $2\frac{1}{2}$ arouras in wheat, $12\frac{1}{3}$ art.; $1\frac{1}{2}$ arouras in aracus, $7\frac{1}{3}$ art.

'Petesouchos the crocodile god, represented by Mestasytmis son of Pakyrris, 5 arouras at $4\frac{11}{12}$ in the South Third Basin, $24\frac{7}{12}$ artabs. Toward these he is to pay $14\frac{5}{12}$ [*sic* for $14\frac{7}{12}$] art. wheat and $16\frac{2}{3}$ art. barley, which equals 10 of wheat. Crops: 3 arouras in wheat, $14\frac{3}{4}$ art.; 1 in lentils, $4\frac{11}{12}$ art.; 1 in aracus, $4\frac{11}{12}$ art.; total, 5 arouras, $24\frac{7}{12}$ art.'

1–9 For other lists of Crown holdings by this god see **93**. 55–71; **1103**. 172–9; cf. also **84**. 73, 111; **1117**. 9; **1118**. 6, 74; **1120**. 31, 40, 92, 121; my *Crown Tenants*, pp. 121 ff.

1 At the end of the line has been lost at least the name of the perichoma in which the property was located; cf. next note.

[ε] (ἀρτ.) ιϛ: the number of arouras is assured by line 3. The average rental is $5\frac{1}{5}$ artabs per aroura, a rate which is not found in **66–70** and is improbable of itself, since $\frac{1}{5}$ does not belong to the series of fractions normally used in reference to artabs. The god Petesouchos, represented by Petesouchos son of Pakyrris, rented 5 arouras at $3\frac{1}{4}$ artabs in the Fourth Perichoma from 118 to at least 112 B.C. (**84**. 111–12; **1103**. 176; **1120**. 121); if the same property is meant here (as $6\frac{1}{2}$ art. charged for 2 arouras in line 3 rather suggests), then 16 is a mistake for $16\frac{1}{4}$ and $9\frac{1}{2}$ in line 3 for $9\frac{3}{4}$. Otherwise, the end of line 1 must have broken down the 5 arouras into two or more parcels rented at some combination of standard rates, though there does not seem to be much room for this.

2 χα(λκοῦ) ξ (ἀρτ.) γ: the equivalence of 20 copper pieces with 1 art. wheat is well known in these texts; cf. **68**. 60 note; **832**. 3 note; T. Reekmans, 'The Ptolemaic Copper Inflation', *Studia Hellenistica* 7 (1951), 82 and 106. If the unit of currency understood is the drachma, the price is astonishingly low for a period in which wheat sold for from 500 to 2200 copper drachmas per artab (*ibid.*, pp. 111–12). Reekmans explains the anomaly on the grounds that 'this is, of course, a merely arbitrary price, which has no connection with the market price' (p. 82). That the government's rate for adaeratio of wheat dues was in principle completely arbitrary is hard to believe; that it was set at $\frac{1}{25}$ to $\frac{1}{100}$ the value of the goods it was to replace seems altogether incredible. In **68**. 60; **70**. 6, 63; **93**. 59, 69; **94**. 22; and an unpublished fragment from Box 19, folder 71, the unit of money in question is described as χα(λκοῦ) κ (δραχμ). In **373**. 12 (A.D. 110/11) the phrase χαλκοῦ εἰκοϲι-δράχμου is found as the name of a tax; and on analogy with that passage the editors suggest the same reading for the Ptolemaic passages, with the conclusion '**94**. 22 χα(λκοῦ) (εἰκοϲιδράχμου) Σ (ἀρτάβαι) ι would now be most naturally explained by supposing that 200 20-drachmae pieces were the value of 10 artabas, i.e. 400 copper dr. for an artaba, though this does not accord very well with the other evidence concerning the value of wheat in the papyri contemporary with **94**'. This explanation seems inevitable, though we should prefer to read (εἰκοϲιδράχμων) rather than (εἰκοϲιδράχμου). The editors of vol. II apparently understood the latter as an adjective in agreement with χα(λκοῦ), but one expects the name of a unit of money. The expansion (εἰκοϲιδράχμων) would complete our lexico-

graphy for the Egyptian series of coins, *δίδραχμον* for the kite, *τετράδραχμον* for stater, and now *εἰκοσίδραχμον* for deben. The expression in **373**. 12 (and now P. Strasb. 218. 10) uses the noun in the singular, but the Ptolemaic passages require a plural.

If this is right, the price of 400 dr. per artab is still low but not incomprehensible. It was probably correct near the end of the reign of Epiphanes (data on wheat prices are missing, but cf. Reekmans' charts p. 111), and may have been maintained thereafter from the natural sluggishness of Ptolemaic bureaucracy. In **94**. 23, however, the same currency is called *χα(λκοῦ) (δραχμὰς) (εἰκοσιδράχμους)*, unless the first drachma sign is to be cancelled; and in **160** and perhaps **1009**. 16 *(δραχμαί)* is the term used. BGU VI 1217 certainly employs drachmas and not debens, but the text is confusing and a 20:1 proportion is not altogether clear. The balance of the evidence favours debens rather than drachmas in the Kerkeosiris texts.

4 *Μαρρείους τοῦ Πα̣κ̣ύρρ[ιος]*: cf. **1103**. 178.

Κε(ρκεούρεως) λι(βός): the name is written in full in **1117**. 124, where the eastern portion is meant. Other *περιχώματα* at Kerkeosiris which occur in this volume are the *Θεμίστου* (cf. **13**. 12), the *Κοι(ρι)* (**84**. 202–3), the *Παω( )*, and the *Ψιναρα( )* or *Ψιναρά* (**60**. 43), as well as the numbers 2–4, of which the 3rd is usually specified further as north or south (7 note). In addition, a *Πτολεμαίου νό(του) περίχωμα* is surveyed in **85**. 4, and probably the northern portion of the same basin is meant in **85**. 112. A further perichoma, referred to under two names in **61**(b). 170 and **72**. 82–3, does not seem to have been used in Kerkeosiris at this period; and it is uncertain whether *α* in **91**. 18 (cf. note) is evidence for a Perichoma Nr. One. At Magdola dike-surrounded basins of presumably the same sort were called *γύαι*, but that term does not seem to play a role in the topography of Kerkeosiris; cf. next note and **1117** introd.

7 *γ̄ νό(του)*: the south portion of the Third Perichoma; *γύ(ου) νό(του)* is not possible. The editors of **62** chose that expansion, which is palaeographically plausible in their text, because they misinterpreted the *β* which sometimes follows *γ̄* as a numeral instead of *β(ορρᾶ)*.

8 *ι]δγ´ιβ´*: a mistake for $14\frac{7}{12}$.

11–12 The point of the marginalia is obscure to me.

11 *ρκ̄ πᾱ*: the second figure is apparently intended to replace the first one, though the reason for this is unclear. 120 is the correct total of the assigned wheat rental, 65+55 artabs; but the following *γενισμός* totals only 81.

12 Perhaps *κ̣[θ (ἀρτ.) μ]θ*, which would complete the reckoning for 37 arouras and 81 artabs. But the initial traces favour *ι̣δ̣* rather than *κ̣*, and a further entry may have been lost at the end of the line. After the lacuna, *ϛ* or *∠̣* could be read as well as *θ̣*.

13 *Ὧρος Πε[. . . . . .]ος*: *Πε[τεχῶντ]ος* or *Πε[τοσίρι]ος* would fit the space; both men had brothers named Marres. **93**. 31 has an account for Horos son of Petosiris very different from that given here, but this does not necessarily favour *Πε[τεχῶντ]ος*, since Crown holdings were subject to rapid changes.

15 After *Μαρρῆς*, *Πετε̣[χῶντο]ς̣* is perhaps preferable to *Πετο̣[σίριο]ς̣*; apart from the palaeography, cf. notes to 16 and 18.

.ιά: the name of the perichoma has been so clumsily written that it seems a mere inkblot, but probably *Κε(ρκεούρεως)* was intended. At the end of the line entries for 8 more arouras are expected; cf. the total 32 in line 16.

16 *(ἀρτ.) [. . . . .]. τε.( ) δ, λο(ιπαὶ) κη*: the lacuna must contain, in addition to rent on the 32 arouras, some indication that the following 4 arouras are to be deducted, so as to leave only 28 for Marres. If *τε.( )* is the name of the person to whom the 4 arouras were transferred, one might suggest *ὧν εἰ]ς* or *πρὸ]ς Τεῶ̣(ν)*. Marres son of Petechon had a brother named Teos, and it is not improbable that line 19 of the next entry, for a man with the patronymic Petechon, concerns these same 4 arouras. If so, they were rated at 4 art. apiece like the rest of Marres' property, and the rental lost in the lacuna will have been *ρκη*.

17 At the end of the line has been lost the crop on 4 arouras paying 16 artabs.

18 The tenant is *[Τεῶς Πετεχ]ῶ̣ντος* if the 4 arouras in line 19 are those referred to in line 16 above; cf. note.

[Κ]ε(ρκεούρεως) λ̣ι̣(βός) or *ἀ̣π̣η(λιώτου)* are equally possible.

ε ἀν(ὰ) . . . . [: the papyrus is damaged and the figure for rent appears to have undergone correction. The total booked to this man was 14 arouras paying 54 artabs, of which 9 arouras and 36 artabs are accounted for elsewhere (18 and 19). The total charge on these 5 arouras was therefore 18 artabs; this corresponds to an average rate of 3⅗ artabs, a figure which could hardly have been charged and was certainly not written. As the last trace of ink visible in the line is probably (ὧν), the scribe no doubt intended to specify that the 5 arouras consisted of 4 at 4 art. plus 1 at 2, or some other combination of standard rents that will yield 18 art. due.

19].ηϲ: neither βαϲιλ]ικῆϲ nor simply γῆϲ is attractive. In **1119**. 80 a piece of land is characterized as αλαγηϲ, which could well be read here. If the word intended is ἀλλαγῆϲ, the land may have been acquired by some kind of exchange; then it is tempting to identify the land here with the 4 arouras of line 16, one brother gaining what the other lost.

20 For reasons of space, only one crop can have been lost after [ϲπό(ροϲ).

21 ϛγ (ἀρτ.) τμd: the column really lists at least 106 arouras; the figure for artabs cannot be checked.

1105. Register of Rents and Taxes

P. Teb. 162 | 54 × 30·5 cm. | 114/113 B.C.

1105–7 contain further portions of the tax rolls **93** and **94**: **1105** consists of the three columns which immediately precede **93**, **1107** is the continuation of **94**, and **1106** is a set of work notes for **1107**. 134–9. When complete, these registers listed every Crown tenant at Kerkeosiris in their respective years, the size of each man's holding, and the rents and taxes charged. Generous space was left between entries, and in this space payments were recorded as they were made. These texts leave no doubt that at Kerkeosiris, as in Upper Egypt, grain dues were ordinarily paid in a series of instalments that might stretch over several months; cf. Packman, *Taxes*, esp. 62–3; Shelton, *CE* 46. 91 (1971), 115 n. 1.

The charges fall into three groups: ἐκφόριον, the land rental proper, with which **1103** and **1104** are concerned exclusively; a set of six comparatively small imposts discussed below; and the γεωμετρία and ϲτέφανοϲ taxes, the first invariably ½ artab and the second assessed at ½ artab per aroura (**1128** introd.). In addition, ½ artab for praktor's fees is sometimes found (**1105**. 43, 55; **93**. 10, 24, 59, cf. 15; **1107**. 77, 86, 92, 174; cf. **91**. 4, 7, 17, 19, 26; **95**. 8. 1½ artabs charged in **1106**. 9 and **1107**. 138 is the total due from 3 sets of tenants). A small handling charge occurs in **1105**. 44 and **1107**. 96 (cf. **847**. 17–18 n.), and a 2-artab γραμματικόν in addition to the usual scribal fees is found in **1105**. 4 and **93**. 23 and 46. The circumstances under which these three taxes would be exacted are unclear.

Of the six taxes which typically follow the sum due for land rental, three, τετρακαιεικοϲτή (cf. vol. I, p. 413), θηϲαυροφυλακικόν, and κράϲτιϲ (cf. **61**(b). 317–19 n.) show no clear relation to the amount of land held or the rental paid. For θέμα, presumably a charge to defer costs of maintaining personal grain accounts at the granary, ½ artab was collected, and scribal fees were assessed at ¼ artab per aroura (exceptions: 1 art. on 2⅞ arouras, line 9 below and **1107**. 105; 1 art. on 5⅛ ar., **93**. 14; 1 art. on 6⅛ ar., line 43 below). The τριχοίνικον (cf. **61**(b). 317–19 n.) was assessed at $\frac{1}{12}$ art. per aroura, and a tax abbreviated λοχι( ), for which $\frac{1}{6}$ art. was charged, remains obscure; cf. vol. 1, p. 413; Crönert, *WKlPh* 1903, 485.

These six taxes, plus *γεωμετρία* and *cτέφανος*, fell upon most but not all the Crown tenants of Kerkeosiris. The exceptions are as follows:

1. No charge except rent: **1105**. 40; **93**. 31, 48; **94**. 18, 22, 28, 32; **1107**. 82. It is likely that two of these lessees received special terms based on their cleruchic status (**1105**. 40; **94**. 18); and an association headed by a machimos (**94**. 28) held a special contract briefly described in **74**. 21–6. There is no obvious explanation for the remaining cases.

2. No charge except rent and loans of seed: **93**. 26; **1107**. 159. The plots have in common their very small size, $\frac{3}{4}$ and 1 aroura respectively. The charge on the second holding was reduced from the previous year, when it paid *γεωμετρία* in addition to *δάνειον*, which was at the same time somewhat higher (**1105**. 52). All these passages are exceptions to the usual quota of 1 artab seed per aroura.

3. No charge except rent, *δάνειον*, *γεωμετρία*: **1105**. 52.

4. Rent, *δάνειον*, *γεωμετρία*, *cτέφανος*: **1105**. 21. This holding is slightly larger than the foregoing, $1\frac{1}{2}$ arouras; cf. notes to **1105**. 21 and **1107**. 124–5.

Δάνειον as a stated charge occurs only in the instances just cited, although many more loans than these must have been granted; cf. e.g. **1136**.

5. Rent, *τετρακαιεικοcτή*, and *τριχοίνικον*: **93**. 32; **94**. 20, 34; **1107**. 88, 199, 201, 220, 283, 345. The last of these passages refers to pastures tended by the *γεωργοὶ κοινῆι*, and the reference in **94**. 32 is to land rented under special terms by the god Mestasytmis. The other instances have no striking feature.

6. Rent, *τετρ.*, *θέμα*, *τριχ.*, *γραμματικόν*: **1107**. 275.

7. Same, plus *γεωμετρία*: **1105**. 36.

8. Rent, *τετρ.*, *θέμα*, *τριχ.*, *λοχι( )*, *γραμ.*: **1107**. 146, 341.

9. Standard charges less *γραμματικόν*: **1107**. 79.

Exceptions so numerous as these cannot well be all ascribed to scribal vagary, particularly inasmuch as reasonable explanations for several of the cases can be put forward. It would appear that the terms on which Crown land was leased included not only the amount of *ἐκφόριον* which was to be paid, but an understanding as to which taxes were applicable. The guidelines which governed such decisions are not discoverable on present evidence.

All charges are calculated in terms of wheat, but payment was accepted also in cash, barley, and lentils. Money payments were taken only to the value of $39\frac{5}{12}$ art. of wheat in rental of land sown with aracus (**67**. 44–50; **68**. 56–60; **70**. 44–8), and instances of such payment are accordingly scarce (**93**. 59, 69; **94**. 22; cf. **1104**). Five artabs of barley were accepted as equivalent to three of wheat; whether the decision to pay in wheat or barley rested with the tenant is unclear. Lentils were taken at par with wheat, but only to the total of 500 artabs for the village (**67**. 15 n.). The total rent due on land planted in lentils was always substantially more than that (cf. vol. 1, p. 562), and the method by which the 500 artabs were distributed among the villagers is unknown. Such statements of payments still to be collected as **1107.** 43, which distinguish between wheat still due and lentils still due (but never barley still due); and such lists as **1137.** 44 ff., show that lentil payments were not simply taken on a first-come-first-served basis. Payments are recorded only for late Payni and early Epeiph.

Grain was accepted by two measures, *ἑξαχοίνικον* and *δέξιμον* or *εἰcδέξιμον* (the explanation of P. Berl. Leihg. p. 288, according to which these terms would be not adjectives but abstract nouns, seems too subtle). Wheat and barley received by the *δέξιμον* measure was subject to cleaning, which reduced the quantity of wheat by about 5 per cent and that of barley by about $7\frac{1}{2}$ to 8 per cent. The deduction here called *κάθαρcιc* probably included not only lost bulk from the removal of impurities, but a fee for sifting and the surcharge *ἐπίμετρον*; cf. P. Berl. Leihg. p. 283. Grain received by *ἑξαχοίνικον* measure had apparently already been cleaned, since deductions are not made for that purpose: in the awkwardly worded passage **93.** 10–11, *πυροῦ (ἑξα)χ(οινίκωι) ἀπὸ ιθ∠ κα(θάρcεωc) α λο(ιπαὶ) ιη∠ θ*d, one must refer *(ἑξα)χ(οινίκωι)* to the $9\frac{1}{4}$ clean artabs credited to the account, not to the $19\frac{1}{2}$ which underwent cleaning. The measure used with lentil payments is not specified, nor are cleaning fees mentioned in these texts, though such occur in unpublished portions of **172.**

A comparison of **1105.** 1–2 and **93.** 6–7 with **1103.** 62 and 71 shows that our text is later than the 2nd year of Soter II. A comparison of lines 15–23 with **1107.** 123–5 shows that **1105** precedes that text, which dates to year 5. Year 3 appears to be excluded: cf. **93.** 49 with **1134.** 14; **1105.** 1–2 with **1119.** 33; and see **1128** introd. Moreover, two errors in **1107** (lines 134, 150, notes) seem to have been copied from **1105**, a circumstance which most naturally suggests year 4 for this text. The holding of Petesouchos son of Cheyris and his brothers in lines 27–31 below is different from that in **1106**, which is explicitly dated to year 4; but the differences can be explained (**1106** introd.). Only two payments in **1139** (46 and 47; cf. introd.), which also refers to year 4, have a discoverable relationship to **1105+93**, but the interpretation of **1139** is too uncertain for this to be taken as a serious objection to the date.

This register treats of 28 individuals or partnerships that farmed Crown land; one of these, the crocodile god Petesouchos, is given four entries according to his various human representatives (**93.** 55 ff.). To judge from the data of **1103**, the preserved papyrus probably amounts to between $\frac{1}{5}$ and $\frac{1}{4}$ of its original size. Its entries parallel those of **1107.** 94–183, which should be studied in conjunction with this text.

As it is not practical to convert separately each of the hundreds of dates in **1105+93** and **94+1107**, we have supplied for the reader's convenience a chart giving Julian equivalents of Egyptian days in the 5th regnal year of Soter II, to which most of the precise dates in vols. I and IV refer. Dates taken from the chart later than Choiak 14 (i.e., all dates in the present text) are also correct for year 4, and conversions will be accurate to within a few days for any document in this volume. Note that at this period the Julian calendar is one day in advance of the Gregorian calendar now in use, so that, e.g., Pachon 1, which the chart identifies as 18 May, was May 17th in modern-day terms.

Date Conversions, Year 5 of Soter II

	Thoth	Phaophi	Hathyr	Choiak	Tybi	Mecheir	Phame-noth	Phar-mouthi	Pachon	Payni	Epeiph	Mesore	Epago-menai
1	9/20	10/20	11/19	12/19	1/18	2/17	3/19	4/18	5/18	6/17	7/17	8/16	9/15
2	9/21	10/21	11/20	12/20	1/19	2/18	3/20	4/19	5/19	6/18	7/18	8/17	9/16
3	9/22	10/22	11/21	12/21	1/20	2/19	3/21	4/20	5/20	6/19	7/19	8/18	9/17
4	9/23	10/23	11/22	12/22	1/21	2/20	3/22	4/21	5/21	6/20	7/20	8/19	9/18
5	9/24	10/24	11/23	12/23	1/22	2/21	3/23	4/22	5/22	6/21	7/21	8/20	9/19
6	9/25	10/25	11/24	12/24	1/23	2/22	3/24	4/23	5/23	6/22	7/22	8/21	
7	9/26	10/26	11/25	12/25	1/24	2/23	3/25	4/24	5/24	6/23	7/23	8/22	
8	9/27	10/27	11/26	12/26	1/25	2/24	3/26	4/25	5/25	6/24	7/24	8/23	
9	9/28	10/28	11/27	12/27	1/26	2/25	3/27	4/26	5/26	6/25	7/25	8/24	
10	9/29	10/29	11/28	12/28	1/27	2/26	3/28	4/27	5/27	6/26	7/26	8/25	
11	9/30	10/30	11/29	12/29	1/28	2/27	3/29	4/28	5/28	6/27	7/27	8/26	
12	10/1	10/31	11/30	12/30	1/29	2/28	3/30	4/29	5/29	6/28	7/28	8/27	
13	10/2	11/1	12/1	12/31	1/30	3/1	3/31	4/30	5/30	6/29	7/29	8/28	
14	10/3	11/2	12/2	1/1	1/31	3/2	4/1	5/1	5/31	6/30	7/30	8/29	
15	10/4	11/3	12/3	1/2	2/1	3/3	4/2	5/2	6/1	7/1	7/31	8/30	
16	10/5	11/4	12/4	1/3	2/2	3/4	4/3	5/3	6/2	7/2	8/1	8/31	
17	10/6	11/5	12/5	1/4	2/3	3/5	4/4	5/4	6/3	7/3	8/2	9/1	
18	10/7	11/6	12/6	1/5	2/4	3/6	4/5	5/5	6/4	7/4	8/3	9/2	
19	10/8	11/7	12/7	1/6	2/5	3/7	4/6	5/6	6/5	7/5	8/4	9/3	
20	10/9	11/8	12/8	1/7	2/6	3/8	4/7	5/7	6/6	7/6	8/5	9/4	
21	10/10	11/9	12/9	1/8	2/7	3/9	4/8	5/8	6/7	7/7	8/6	9/5	
22	10/11	11/10	12/10	1/9	2/8	3/10	4/9	5/9	6/8	7/8	8/7	9/6	
23	10/12	11/11	12/11	1/10	2/9	3/11	4/10	5/10	6/9	7/9	8/8	9/7	
24	10/13	11/12	12/12	1/11	2/10	3/12	4/11	5/11	6/10	7/10	8/9	9/8	
25	10/14	11/13	12/13	1/12	2/11	3/13	4/12	5/12	6/11	7/11	8/10	9/9	
26	10/15	11/14	12/14	1/13	2/12	3/14	4/13	5/13	6/12	7/12	8/11	9/10	
27	10/16	11/15	12/15	1/14	2/13	3/15	4/14	5/14	6/13	7/13	8/12	9/11	
28	10/17	11/16	12/16	1/15	2/14	3/16	4/15	5/15	6/14	7/14	8/13	9/12	
29	10/18	11/17	12/17	1/16	2/15	3/17	4/16	5/16	6/15	7/15	8/14	9/13	
30	10/19	11/18	12/18	1/17	2/16	3/18	4/17	5/17	6/16	7/16	8/15	9/14	

Traces of a column to the left.

Πετεσοῦχος Πετοσίριος. θ∠d (ἀρτάβαι) μ⟦ϛ∠d⟧ \`ζ∠ḍ', καὶ ἀπὸ τῆς (πρότερον)
Ὀρσείους β (ἀρτάβαι) ιι´β´, (γίνονται) ια∠d (ἀρτάβαι) ν⟦ϛ∠γ´⟧ \`ζ∠γ´'.
(τετρακαιεικοστῆς) ∠ι´β´, θέ(ματος) ∠,
(τρι)χ(οινίκου) α, θη(σαυροφυλακικοῦ) γ´ι´β´, κρά(στεως) γ´ι´β´, λοχι(   ) ϛ´,
γρ(αμματικοῦ) γ, (γίνονται) ϛι´β´, (γίνονται) ξ⟦β∠γ´ι´β´⟧ \`γ∠γ´ι´β´'.
γρ(αμματικοῦ) β καὶ γεω(μετρίας) ∠, στεφά(νου) ε∠d, (γίνονται) ϛd, (γίνονται)
⟦ξθϛ´⟧\`οϛ´ .(ὧν) με(τρηθεῖσαι) Φαρμοῦ(θι) ῑ
(πυροῦ) (ἑξα)χ(οινίκωι) λϛγ´. \`⟦Παῦνι⟧' κθ̄ (πυροῦ)(ἑξα)χ(οινίκωι) κα,
(γίνονται) νζγ´. λ̄ (πυροῦ) ε∠γ´. Παῦνι ῑ
ἀπ[ὸ] θέ(ματος) αὐ(τοῦ) (πυροῦ) αγ´. ιθ̄ φα(κοῦ) δ, (γίνονται) εἰς (πυροῦ)
ξη∠. καὶ γρ(αμματικοῦ) β, (γίνονται) ο∠.
⟦λο(ιπαὶ) ϛ (ὧν) (πυροῦ) β̣ φạ(κοῦ) δ̣⟧

Π̣αᾶπις Πετοσίριος. β∠dη´ (ἀρτάβαι) θγ´. (τετρακαιεικοστῆς) ϛ´, θέ(ματος) ∠,
(τρι)χ(οινίκου) d, θη(σαυροφυλακικοῦ) ϛ´, κρά(στεως) [ϛ´],
λ̣ο̣χι(   ) [ϛ´, γρ(αμματικοῦ) α,] (γίνονται) [β]γ´ι̣´β̣´, (γίνονται) ια∠d.
καὶ γεω(μετρίας) ∠, στεφά(νου) α̣[d, (γίνεται) α∠d,
(γίνονται) ιγ∠.]
[(ὧν) με(τρηθεῖσαι) ± 6] κ̣ζ̄ κ(ριθῆς) κβ (ὧν) κạ(θάρσεως) α̣β̣´,
λο(ιπαὶ) κγ´ αἳ (πυροῦ) ιβϛ´. Π̣α̣[
[(γίνεται) εἰ]ς (πυροῦ) αγ´.

Πνεφερῶς Πετεσούχου. βιϛ´ [(ἀρτ.) ϛ]γ´. (τετρ.) ι̣´β´, θέ(μ.) ∠, [(τρι)χ. ϛ´,]
θη(ς.) ι´β´, κρά(ς.) ι´β´, λοχι(   ) ϛ´, γρ(α.) ∠, (γίν.) α∠ι´β´. καὶ γεω(μ.) ∠,
ς̣[τεφά(νου) α,]
[(γίν.)] α̣∠, (γίν.) θ∠.

Πετεσοῦχος Σαραπίωνος. δ∠η´ (ἀρτ.) ιη∠. (τετρ.) d, θέ(μ.) ∠, (τρι)χ. [γ´ι´β´,]
θη(ς.) d, κρά(ς.) d, λοχι(   ) ϛ´, γρ(α.) αd, (γίν.) γι´β´, (γίν.) κα∠ι´β´.
καὶ γεω(μ.) [∠,]
στεφά(νου) βd, (γίν.) β∠d, (γίν.) κδγ´. (ὧν) με(τ.) Φαρμοῦθι ̣
[κ(ριθῆς) ιθ (ὧν)]
κα(θ.) α∠, λο(ιπαὶ) ιζ∠ αἳ (πυροῦ) ι∠. Π̣α̣χὼν ιθ̄ (πυροῦ) δε(ξίμωι)
ιδ (ὧν) κα(θ.) ∠ḍ, [λο(ιπαὶ) ιγd,]
(γίν.) κγ∠d. λ̄ (πυροῦ ?) ∠̣ι´β̣´, (γίν.) κδ[γ´.]
λο(ιπὸν) ∠ι´β´.

Col. II

[Π]ᾶϲιϲ Ὥρου. αd (ἀρτ.) ϛγ́ίβ́, δα(νείου) αγ́, (γίν.) ζ∠d. καὶ γεω(μ.) ∠,
ϛ̣[τ]εφά(νου) ∠, (γίν.) α, (γίν.) η∠d. Παχὼν λ̄ (πυροῦ) (ἑξα)χ(οινίκωι)
ζ∠γ́ίβ́.
λο(ιπὸν) ∠̣γ́.

Π̣ορεγέβθιϲ Ὥρου. δ∠dή (ἀρτ.) κδd. (τετρ.) d, θέ(μ.) ∠, (τρι)χ. γ́ίβ́, θη(ϲ.) d,
κρά(ϲ.) d, λοχι(   ) ϛ́, γρ(α.) αd, (γίν.) γίβ́, (γίν.) κζγ́. καὶ γεω(μ.) ∠,
ϲτεφά(νου) βd.
(γίν.) β∠d, (γίν.) λίβ́. (ὧν) με(τ.) Παχ(ὼν) η̄ (πυροῦ) δε(ξίμωι) λα
(ὧν) κα(θ.) α∠ίβ́, λο(ιπαὶ) κθγ́ίβ́.

Πετε[ϲοῦ]χοϲ Χεύριοϲ καὶ οἱ ἀδελ(φοί). κα (ἀρτ.) ⟦ϙγ. (τετρ.)⟧ \`πε∠´.
Π[ε]τεϲοῦχοϲ ζή (ἀρτ.) λα∠, Τεεφῖβιϲ δd (ἀρτ.) κ,
Χεῦριϲ δd (ἀρτ.) ιη∠, Μαρεμῆνιϲ καὶ Πρε(   ) ⟦εd⟧ \`ϛ´ (ἀρτ.) ι⟦ε∠⟧ \`η´,
(γίν.) κα [(ἀρτ.)] πε∠. (τετρ.) α, θέ(μ.) ∠, (τρι)χ. αβ́, θη(ϲ.) α,
κρά(ϲ.) α, λοχι(   ) ϛ́, γρ(α.) ε, (γίν.) ιγ́,
(γίν.) ϙεγ́. καὶ γεω̣(μ.) ⟦β⟧ \`∠´, ϲτεφά(νου) ι̣, (γίν.) ι⟦β⟧ \`∠´,
(γίν.) ρ⟦ζγ́⟧ \`ε∠γ́´. (ὧν) με(τ.) Φαρμοῦθι κδ
(πυροῦ) δε(ξίμωι) λ̣α (ὧν) κα(θ.) α∠ίβ́, λο(ιπαὶ) κθγ́ίβ́. Παχ(ὼν) η̄
(πυροῦ) δε(ξίμωι) νδ (ὧν) κα(θ.) β∠d, λο(ιπαὶ) ναd,
(γίν.) πβ́.
[λο(ιπαὶ)] κβίβ́.
] . (πυροῦ)

Πᾶϲιϲ Πετεϲούχου. κ∠ (ἀρτ.) ρ∠γ́. (τετρ.) α, θέ(μ.) ∠, (τρι)χ. αβ́, γρ(α.) ε,
(γίν.) ζϛ́,
(γίν.) ρη. καὶ γεω(μ.) ∠.

Col. III

ιβ∠ ϛ (ὧν)
με(τ.)
Ταυρίϲκοϲ Ἀπολλωνίου. β (ἀρτ.) ι. {(ὧν) με(τ.)}
// με(τ.) Παχ(ὼν) κθ̄ (πυροῦ) ι.

Τεῶϲ Θοτορταίου. ϛή (ἀρτ.) λ. (τετρ.) γ́, θέ(μ.) ∠, (τρι)χ. ∠, κρά(ϲ.) ḍ
[θη(ϲ.) ∠ίβ́,]
πρα(κτορικοῦ) ∠ λοχι(   ) ϛ́, γρ(α.) α, (γίν.) γγ́, (γίν.) λγγ́. καὶ γεω(μ.) ∠,

cτεφά(νου) γ, (γίν.) [γ∠,]
(γίν.) λ⟦ζ⟧ \`ς∠', χ̣ε(ιρicτικοῦ ?) α∠, (γίν.) λή. με(τ.) Φαρμοῦθι ῑ
(πυροῦ) δε(ξίμωι) ιη (ὧν) κα(θ.) ∠γ́ίβ́, λ̣ο̣(ιπαὶ) ι̣ζ̣ίβ̣.
Παχ(ὼν) κζ̄ (πυροῦ) (ἑξα)χ(οινίκωι) ιϛ∠, (γίν.) λγ∠ίβ́. Παῦ(νι) ῑ̣
(πυροῦ) α∠γ́ίβ́. ιϛ φα(κοῦ) β,
(γίν.) γ∠γ́ίβ́, (γίν.) λζ∠.

Τοθοῆc Ἀγοννούφιοc. ϛ∠dή (ἀρτ.) λδίβ́. (τετρ.) γ́, θέ(μ.) ∠, (τρι)χ. ∠̣ίβ́,
(γίν.) λδγ́ίβ́ *κρά(c.) d, θη(c.) d, λοχι(   ) ς́, γρ(α.) α∠d, (γίν.) γ∠γ́, (γίν.) λζ∠γ́ίβ́.*
καὶ γεω(μ.) ∠,
cτεφά(νου) γ∠, (γίν.) δ, (γίν.) μα∠γ́ίβ́. (ὧν) με(τ.) Φαρμοῦθι κε̄
⟦λο(ιπ.) . . ∠d⟧ *(πυροῦ) δε(ξίμωι) ἀπὸ ϙϛ̄ λϛ (ὧν) κα(θ.) α∠γ́, λο(ιπαὶ) λδς́. Παῦνι*
ῑ \`ἀπὸ' (πυροῦ) ιδ∠d
⟦(πυροῦ) ιδd⟧ *(πυροῦ) ζ∠ίβ́. ιθ̄ φα(κοῦ) ββ́, (γίν.) (πυροῦ) μγ̣∠ίβ́, φα(κοῦ) ββ́,*
(γίν.) μϛd.

Τοθοῆc Φαγάτου. α (ἀρτ.) γς́, δα(νείου) αγ́, (γίν.) δ∠. καὶ γεω(μ.) ∠.

Τοθοῆc Cενθέωc. δή (ἀρτ.) ιη∠γ́. (τετρ.) d, θέ(μ.) ∠, (τρι)χ. γ́,
θη(c.) ς́, κρά(c.) ς́, λοχι(   ) ς́, γρ(α.) α, (γίν.) β∠ίβ́, (γίν.) καγ́ίβ́.
καὶ γεω(μ.) ∠,
πρα(κ.) ∠ *{(γίν.)} cτεφά(νου) ∠d, (γίν.) αd, (γίν.) κββ́. (ὧν) με(τ.) Φαρμοῦθι κθ̄*
(πυροῦ) δε(ξίμωι) ιδ (ὧν) κα(θ.) ∠d, λο(ιπαὶ) ιγd. Παῦνι ιδ̄ ἀπὸ
(πυροῦ) (ἑξα)χ(οινίκωι) θ̄ ζγ́ίβ́, (γίν.) (πυροῦ) κβ́.
λο(ιπαὶ) φα(κοῦ) β.

The text continues directly with **93**.

28 ζή : ή corrected from d.

Lines 1–10. 'Petesouchos son of Petosiris, $9\frac{3}{4}$ arouras renting for $47\frac{3}{4}$ artabs;[1] and out of the property formerly held by Orses, 2 ar. for $10\frac{1}{12}$ art.;[2] total, $11\frac{3}{4}$ arouras, $57\frac{5}{6}$ artabs. $\frac{7}{12}$ art. for 24th tax, $\frac{1}{2}$ for deposit charges, 1 for trichoinikon, $\frac{5}{12}$ for granary-guard tax, $\frac{5}{12}$ for fodder tax, $\frac{1}{6}$ for lochi( ), 3 for scribal fees. Total for taxes, $6\frac{1}{12}$; total rent and taxes, $63\frac{11}{12}$. Plus $\frac{1}{2}$ art. survey fee and $5\frac{3}{4}$ for crown tax, total $6\frac{1}{4}$. Grand total, $70\frac{1}{6}$. (*marginal note*) 2 art. for scribal fees. Of these were paid: Pharmouthi 10th, $36\frac{1}{3}$ art. wheat by 6-choinix measure. 29th, 21 art. wheat by 6-choinix measure, total $57\frac{1}{3}$. 30th, $5\frac{5}{6}$ art. wheat. (*from line* 7) Remainder 6, of which 2 are wheat and 4 lentils. (*line* 5) Payni 10th, from his private deposit, $1\frac{1}{3}$ art. wheat. 19th, 4 art. lentils. Total reckoned in terms of wheat, $68\frac{1}{2}$. Plus 2 art. scribal fees, total $70\frac{1}{2}$.

'Paapis son of Petosiris, $2\frac{7}{8}$ ar. renting for $9\frac{1}{3}$ art. $\frac{1}{6}$ art. 24th tax, $\frac{1}{2}$ for deposit charges, $\frac{1}{4}$ trichoinikon, $\frac{1}{6}$ granary-guard tax, $\frac{1}{6}$ fodder tax, $\frac{1}{6}$ lochi( ), 1 for scribal fees. Total for taxes, $2\frac{5}{12}$, total rent and taxes, $11\frac{3}{4}$. Plus $\frac{1}{2}$ art. survey fee and $1\frac{1}{4}$ crown tax, total $1\frac{3}{4}$. Grand total, $13\frac{1}{2}$. Of these were paid: . . .27th, 22 art. barley, from which $1\frac{2}{3}$ was lost in cleaning or deducted for cleaning fees; remainder, $20\frac{1}{3}$ art. barley, which equals $12\frac{1}{6}$ art. wheat.'

[1,2] *Sic* for 48 and $9\frac{5}{6}$ art. respectively; see 1–7 n.

1–7 Cf. **1103**. 62–3; **1107**. 94–8. The rents ascribed to the land here, in particular to the 2 arouras once held by Orses, look bizarre, especially as the total of $11\frac{3}{4}$ arouras at $57\frac{5}{8}$ artabs is that expected for a holding uniformly rated at $4\frac{11}{12}$ artabs per aroura. There has apparently been an error in arithmetic: $47\frac{3}{4}$ art. for $9\frac{3}{4}$ ar. at $4\frac{11}{12}$ is $\frac{1}{4}$ too low; the scribe compensated for this by making the rent on the remaining plot $\frac{1}{4}$ too high.

4 γρ(αμματικοῦ) β: paid in l. 6. Two art. γρ. in addition to the tax of the same name which was reckoned at $\frac{1}{4}$ art./ar. is found also in **93**. 23 and 46. It is the amount charged for *γραμματικὸν ἱερέων* in **97**. 21, but there is no evidence that any of the 3 taxpayers in **1105+93** were priests.

6 ἀπ[ὸ] θέ(ματος) αὐ(τοῦ): i.e., paid by giro transfer.

7 λο(ιπαὶ) ϛ: the difference between $63\frac{1}{8}$ art. paid up to and including Pachon 30 and $69\frac{1}{8}$, the uncorrected figure of l. 4.

One cannot determine from the statements introduced by λο(ιπαί) in this text and **94+1107** any official date after which accounts fell into arrears: the remainder in l. 20 was calculated after Pachon 19 but before Pachon 30; here, after Pachon 30 but before Payni 10; in line 57, after Payni 14. In **1095** dues are described as ἐνοφειλόμενα on Mesore 8, but this may mean simply 'still due' rather than 'in arrears' in the modern sense.

10 The lacuna would be best filled by Φαρμοῦ(θι).

Π̣α̣[: Π̣α̣[χ(ών) or Π̣α̣[ῦ(νι).

12–14 No payments for this account were recorded.

14 θ∠: right was $9\frac{5}{12}$.

20 λο(ιπὸν) ∠ιβ́: paid on Pachon 30, l. 19.

21–3 The land was later taken over by Petesouchos son of Sarapion; cf. **1107**. 124–5.

21 αd: a mistake for $1\frac{1}{2}$; cf. **1107**. 124–5.

27 κα and πε∠: see 30 n.

29 Πρε( ): only here. Presumably not simply πρε(σβύτερος) to refer to the elder Cheyris, father of the brothers; for even if this were acceptable Greek idiom, we should expect to find him in the heading if he were one of the tenants, as in **1103**. 95. Cf. **1106** introd.

30 κα [(ἀρτ.)] πε∠: 21 is the sum of the uncorrected subtotals $7\frac{1}{4}$ (cf. *app. crit.*), $4\frac{1}{4}$, $4\frac{1}{4}$, and $5\frac{1}{4}$; $85\frac{1}{2}$ is the sum of the uncorrected subtotals $31\frac{1}{2}$, 20, $18\frac{1}{2}$, and $15\frac{1}{2}$. The right figures after correction would have been $21\frac{5}{8}$ arouras, 88 artabs.

31 ϙεγ́: right was $95\frac{5}{8}$.

34 λο(ιπαὶ) κβιβ́: right was $25\frac{1}{6}$.

36 ζϛ́: right was $8\frac{1}{6}$.

38–9 Obscure notations in the upper margin.

40 Tauriskos is a catoecic cleruch: he pays a higher rent for his land than any other Crown tenant in the list, but apparently no taxes. Cf. **94**. 18, where Maron son of Petosiris (there were a catoec and a machimos by that name) likewise pays no taxes. Cf. also **1107**. 279 n. and p. 8.

44 λ⟦ζ⟧ `ϛ∠΄: right was $36\frac{5}{8}$.

48 (γίν.) λδγ́ιβ́: obscure marginal note.

51 μγ∠ιβ́: right was $41\frac{3}{4}$. Apparently the scribe used 36 instead of $34\frac{1}{8}$ as the payment on Pharmouthi 25.

μϛd: an overpayment of $4\frac{1}{3}$ art.

53–7 In **1107**. 161–4 the same amount of land rents for 20 art., but it does not seem to be the same property; cf. note ad loc.

54 θη(ς.) ϛ́, κρά(ς.) ϛ́: $\frac{1}{4}$ apiece in **1107**. 162.

55 (γίν.)...κββ́: written over an erasure.

1106. Register of Rents and Taxes

P. Teb. 163v — 16 × 11 cm. used — 114/113 B.C.

While the reckoning for Petesouchos son of Cheyris and his brothers in years 1 and 2 of Soter II offers no difficulties (**1103**. 95–101), considerable confusion is shown in later accounts, particularly in the numerous and not always accurate 'corrections' in **1105**. 27–31. The following text, written on the back of **1107**, was apparently intended as a set of work notes for ll. 134–9 of that document. Dated explicitly to year 4, it diverges seriously from **1105**, which refers to the same year: in **1105**. 29 Cheyris rents $4\frac{1}{4}$ arouras, and Maremenis and Pre( ) together rent $5\frac{1}{4}$ (using the original figure); in **1106** and **1107** the mysterious Pre( ) has disappeared, and Cheyris and Maremenis have consolidated their $9\frac{1}{2}$ arouras. It seems, then, that **1106** represents a re-arrangement of holdings later in year 4 than **1105**, occasioned probably by the removal of Pre( ).

Contrary to the other accounts, **1106** itemizes man by man not only the holdings and rents, but also the taxes due. This procedure was probably not legitimate, as it leads to results rather different from those obtained by treating the partnership as a whole: *θέμα* and *λοχι( )* are charged three times each instead of once, and the total due for *τετρακαιεικοστή*, *θηcαυροφυλακικόν* and *κράcτιc* is in every case $\frac{1}{6}$ artab higher than that of the recto text **1107**. Significantly, these calculations are ignored in reckoning the final sum due: the recto total for taxes due is used instead (9 note).

δ (ἔτουc)
Πετεcοῦχοc. ζ, λ∠d. προ(   ) ή, ∠d. (γίν.) λά∠. γγ́, (γίν.) λδίβ́.
(τετρ.) γ́ίβ́, θέ(μ.) ∠, (τρι)χ. ∠ίβ́, θη(c.) d, κρά(c.) d, λοχι(   ) ς́,
γρ(α.) α∠d, (γίν.) δ, (γίν.) λε̣∠̣.
Τεεφῖ(βιc). δ (ἀρτ.) ιθβ́, προ(   ) ή (ἀρτ.) γ́, (γίν.) δή (ἀρτ.) κ̇. (τετρ.) d,
θέ(μ.) ∠, (τρι)χ. γ́, θη(c.) d, κρά(c.) ḍ, λ̣ο̣χι(   ) ς́, γρ(α.) α,
(γίν.) β∠d, (γίν.) κβ∠d.
Χεῦριc καὶ Μαρεμῆνιc. θ∠ (ἀρτ.) λεd, προ(   ) α, (γίν.) λς́d.
(τετρ.) ∠, θέ(μ.) ∠, (τρι)χ. ∠γ́, θη(c.) γ́, κρά(c.) γ́, λοχι(   ) ς́,
γρ(α.) β∠, (γίν.) ε̣ς́,
(γίν.) μαγ́ίβ́.
(γίν.) τὸ (πᾶν) ϙθ∠γ́ίβ́. cτεφά(νου) ι, πρα(κ.) α∠, (γίν.) ια∠, (γίν.) ριας́.

Col. II

(*c.* 8·5 cm. blank)

δ (ἀρτ.) ιη. (τετρ.) d, θέ(μ.) ∠, (τρι)χ. γ́, θη(c.) ḍ, κρά(c.) ς́,
λοχι(   ) ς́, γρ(α.) β́, (γίν.) β∠̣[
Τε{τ}εφῖ(βιc) δ (ἀρτ.) ιθβ́[

Χεῦ(ρις) κ∠. Μ̣αρεμῆ(νις) ι̣ε̣∠̣ḍ [

(τρι)χ. ∠γ́, θη(c.) d, κρά(c.) d, λοχ[ι(   ) ς́

(γίν.) . . .[

(ὧν) με(τ.) οηβ́.

λο(ιπαὶ) ϛ̣d.

2–6 Dots over λα∠, κ, and λϛd mark these figures as the total rent due.

2 γγ́, (γίν.) λδίβ́: if $34\frac{1}{12}$ is meant as the sum of $31\frac{1}{2}$ and $3\frac{1}{3}$, it is a surprising mistake for $34\frac{5}{6}$. Palaeographically, these figures might be taken as a correction of δ, (γίν.) λε̣∠̣ in the line below, but if so it is not easy to see how they could have been arrived at. For *προ*(   ) see **1107** introd.

3 (γίν.) δ: right was $3\frac{11}{12}$; cf. next note.

8 μαγ́ίβ́: the true total of $36\frac{1}{4}+5\frac{1}{6}$ is $41\frac{1}{2}$; the sum here, by falling $\frac{1}{12}$ short of that figure, compensates for the overcharge of $\frac{1}{12}$ in line 3.

9 ϛθ∠γ́ίβ́: this is $83\frac{3}{4}$ artabs rent plus the *recto* total for taxes, $12\frac{1}{6}$ artabs (**1107**. 139).

cτεφά(νου) ι: the expected charge on 21 arouras is $10\frac{1}{2}$ artabs, as in **1107**. 139; but 10 is also found in **1105**. 31.

πρα(κ.) α∠: i.e., $\frac{1}{2}$ artab apiece from Petesouchos, Teephibis, and the partnership of Cheyris and Maremenis.

ριας́: right was $111\frac{5}{12}$.

10 δ (ἀρτ.) ιη: apparently refers to Cheyris alone; cf. **1105**. 29, where the figures given probably include $\frac{1}{4}$ aroura *προ*( ) at $\frac{1}{2}$ artab. In line 13 also the dues of Cheyris and Maremenis are stated separately.

1107. Register of Rents and Taxes

P. Teb. 94+163r+247+248+249   *c.* 273 × 30·5 cm.   113/112 B.C.

Various fragments of this papyrus were used in the mummies of no fewer than four crocodiles (12, 14, 15, 27, all from tomb c), and were published or described under five numbers in vol. I. Owing to different circumstances of preservation, adjoining passages sometimes have strikingly different colorations; but the identity of hands, date, and format leaves no doubt that the pieces belong together even when they can no longer be physically joined. United, they constitute a large part of a roll similar to but more detailed than **1105+93**. The order in which Crown tenants are listed is virtually the same as that in the latter text and in **1128**, and this order has served as a guide in placing otherwise uncertain fragments. The first column printed below is the unpublished col. IV of **94**; line numeration has been continued from that text. Despite the imposing length of **94+1107** as preserved, its 81 entries can hardly represent more than about two-thirds of the original document, since one expects approximately 120 ordinary tenancies of Crown land in a given year (**1103**, introd.); and indeed some earlier columns of the papyrus mentioned in **94** introd. can no longer be located.

94+1107 at first follows the practice of **1104** of locating various holdings according to *περίχωμα*; but after line 90 this is given up. A particularly noteworthy feature of the text is the thorough-going distinction made between standard holdings of Crown land and other parcels which are introduced by the abbreviation *προ*( ). This cannot be simply the name of a perichoma, for a tenant's holdings and rents in various perichomata are always summed up before the *προ*( ) is added as something extra. The editors of **82**. 44 note (cf. **94**. 2 note) hesitantly suggest *πρό*(*c*), 'additionally', referring to **81**, wherein land holders at Magdola who farmed more land than had been booked to them are listed after the pattern, so-and-so, *πρόc* the land he is entitled to farm, so much in excess (e.g. line 16, *πρὸc ι* (*πυρῶι*) ∠dή, 'in addition to 10 arouras, ⅞ aroura planted in wheat'. But while the preposition *πρόc* in **81** is intelligible enough, an adverbial *πρόc* in our text seems impossibly harsh.

There can be little doubt, though, that the word intended is the same as that in **82**. 44 and **83**. 2 and 29. In these passages the abbreviation is followed not as in **81** by the official holding of each man, but by the amount which each was found by *ἐπίcκεψιc* to possess in excess of that area. If the same is meant here, the expansion is presumably *προ*(*cηγμένηc*) or a similar participle, and the land so designated will be those small parcels noted as *πλ*(*είω*) which frequently occur in such detailed land surveys as **87**, **1122**, and **1123**. The amounts of land so listed here are always very small: the largest area is 1 aroura (**94**. 2), the most common only ⅛. The rents charged correspond to rates from as low as 1⅜ artabs per aroura (line 99) to as high as 8⅓ (245). As neither these nor several other unusual figures are found in **66–70**, it seems likely that rents were improvised parcel-by-parcel without attempting to follow a standard canon.

These parcels are different from the land *πρόc τιcιν γεωργίοιc* rented at 5 artabs per aroura in **1125**; no doubt *κατειρ*[*γάcθαι*] in line 3 of that text implies deliberate reclamation of derelict land, which was presumably not the case here. Some of the land noted as excess in the surveys resulted merely from the inaccuracy of procedures used (**87**, introd.), but it is not likely that the men in this text were required to make payments for fictitious holdings assessed at a series of complex rates. The problem of farmers deliberately or accidentally seizing land to which they were not entitled was a common one in Egypt; cf. e.g. **5**. 36–43; **6**. 31–2.

The quantity of extra land understandably bears no detectable relation to the size of the original holding, and a few tenants have no such extra land at all. This is the case for three long-term leases drawn up to begin in the 4th and 5th years of Soter II (**94**. 28–35) and for several other tenants who have no further feature in common. In **1105** no distinction is made between *προ*( ) and primary holdings, any more than between land in different perichomata, but all is summed up together.

The editors of **94** placed the text in 'about the 5th year' of Soter II (34 note, where our l. 57 is meant). The 5th year is guaranteed by a comparison of the barley payments in ll. 40, 151, 163, 174, 203, and 256 with **1135**. 16, 18, 10, 12, 14, and 15.

94, Col. IV

Νικάνωρ Πτολεμ̣[αίο]υ. Κοι(ρι) γ ἀν(ὰ) δ∠γ́ιβ́, ιδ∠d. β̄ τὴν
χ (πρότερον) Θώνιος τοῦ
Ὀρcενούφιος καὶ Φαῆcις ι ἀν(ὰ) δ∠γ́ιβ́, μθϛ́. (γίνονται) ιγ
(ἀρτάβαι) ξγ∠γ́ιβ́.
προ( ) ḍ (ἀρτάβη) αγ́, (γίνονται) ιγd (ἀρτάβαι) ξεd. (τετρακαιεικοcτῆc) β́, θέ(ματος) ∠, (τρι)χ(οινίκου) αίβ́,
θη(cαυροφυλακικοῦ) ∠, κρά(cτεως) ∠, λοχι( ) ϛ́,
γρ(αμματικοῦ) γd,
(γίνονται) ϛβ́, (γίνονται) οα∠γ́ιβ́ (cτεφά(νου) ϛ∠, (γίνεται) τὸ
(πᾶν) οηγ́ιβ́) γεω(μετρίας) ∠, (γίνονται) οβγ́ιβ́.
με(τρηθεῖcαι) Φαρμοῦθι ιη̄ κ(ριθῆc) λδ∠ (ὧν) κα(θάρcεως) β∠ίβ́, λο(ιπαὶ)
λα∠γ́ιβ́ αἳ (πυροῦ) ιθ. Παχ(ὼν) ῑ (πυροῦ) εἰcδε(ξίμωι)
λγ (ὧν) κα(θάρcεως) αβ́,
κα(θαροῦ) λαγ́, (γίνονται) εἰc (πυροῦ) νγ́. (m. 2) Ἐπεὶφ ᾱ
φα(κοῦ) ϛ. β̄ (πυροῦ) α.
ῑ cτεφ(άνου) (πυροῦ) ϛ̣∠.
(m. 1) λο(ιπαὶ) κη∠ίβ́ (ὧν) (πυροῦ) κβίβ́ φα(κοῦ) ϛ∠.

Ὀννῶφρις [Φατρεί]ο̣υ̣c. β̄ ϛ∠ (ἀρτάβαι) λβ. Κε(ρκεούρεως) λι(βὸc) d
χ (ἀρτάβη) αd. (γίνονται) ϛ∠d (ἀρτάβαι) λγd.
προ( ) ή (ἀρτάβηc) ∠d, (γίνονται) ϛ∠dή (ἀρτάβαι) λδ.
⟦λο(ιπαὶ) δ̣γ́ιβ́⟧ (τετρακαιεικοcτῆc) γ́, [θ]έ̣(ματος) [∠, (τρι)χ(οινίκου) ∠,
θη(cαυροφυλακικοῦ) ϛ́,] κ̣ρ̣ά(cτεως) ϛ́, λοχι( ) ϛ́,
γρ(αμματικοῦ) α∠d, γγ́ιβ́, (γίνονται) λζγ́ιβ́. cτεφ(άνου)
γd, γεω(μετρίας) ∠, (γίνονται) μαϛ.
(ὧν) με(τρηθεῖcαι) .[κ(ριθῆc) (ὧν) κα(θάρcεως) , λο(ιπαὶ) ιϛ]∠γ́
αἳ (πυροῦ) ιίβ́. λ̄ (πυροῦ) εἰcδε(ξίμωι) κδ∠ (ὧν) κα(θάρcεως) αd, λο(ιπαὶ) κ⟦γd⟧ \`β∠d´, (γίνονται) λγγ́.
[ ] . . (ὧν ?) [
[λο(ιπαὶ) ζ∠]γ́ (ὧν) (πυροῦ ?) δ∠ίβ́ φα(κοῦ) γd.

Ὀννῶφρ̣ι[c] Ὥρου καὶ Ἑραθρῆc. β̄ δ, Κε(ρκεούρεως) εd, (γίνονται) θd
χ ἀν(ὰ) δ∠γ́ιβ́, (ἀρτάβαι) με∠. προ̣( ) ή (ἀρτάβηc) ∠γ́ιβ́,
(γίνονται) θdή (ἀρτάβαι) μϛγ́ιβ́. (τετρακαιεικοcτῆc) ∠, θέ(ματος) ∠,
(τρι)χ(οινίκου) ∠d, θη(cαυροφυλακικοῦ) γ́, κρά(cτεως) γ́,

λοχι(   ) ϛ́, γρ̣(αμματικοῦ) βd, (γίνονται) δ∠γ́, (γίνονται) ναd.

στεφά(νου) δ∠, γεω(μετρίας) ∠, (γίνονται) ε, (γίνεται) τὸ (πᾶν) νϛd.

με(τρηθεῖcαι) Φαρμοῦ(θι) ιζ̄ (πυροῦ) εἰcδε(ξίμωι) ἃc Πετεcοῦχοc
Ἰμούθου ἀπὸ μ̄ ιγγ́ (ὧν) κα(θάρcεωc) β́, λο(ιπαὶ) ιββ́.

λ̄ (πυροῦ) εἰcδε(ξίμωι) κϛ (ὧν) κα(θάρcεωc) αγ́, λο(ιπαὶ) κδβ́, (γίνονται)
(πυροῦ) λζγ́. Παῦ(νι) ιθ̄ (πυροῦ) (ἑξα)χ(οινίκωι) ι,
(γίνονται) μζγ́.

Ἐπεὶφ ᾱ (πυροῦ) δ φα(κοῦ) δ∠.

(τετρακαιεικοcτῆc) ∠ιβ́, θέ(ματοc) ∠, (τρι)χ(οινίκου) ∠γ́ιβ́, θη(cαυροφυλακικοῦ) ∠, κρά(cτεωc) ∠, λοχι(   ) ϛ́, γρ(αμματικοῦ) β∠d,
γεω(μετρίαc) α.

λο(ιπαὶ) η∠γ́ιβ́ (ὧν) (πυροῦ) δ φα(κοῦ) δ∠.

ϛ (ἔτουc) Ὀννῶ(φριc) κεβ́, γ́ιβ́, ∠, (γίνονται) κθd, β∠,
(γίνονται) λα∠d, ιd, (γίνονται) μβ.

με(τρηθεῖcαι) κϛ (ὧν) κα(θάρcεωc) αγ́, λο(ιπαὶ) κδ̣β́, (ἑξα)χ(οινίκωι) ιγβ́, (γίνονται) ληγ́, λο(ιπαὶ) γβ́.

Col. V (**163**, Col. I)

λα. (τετρακαιεικοcτῆc) ∠, θέ(ματοc) ∠, (τρι)χ(οινίκου ?) . . . .
κρά(cτεωc) ., λοχι(   ) ϛ́, ... γεω(μετρίαc) ∠,
(γίνονται) λϛ̣d. μ̣ε̣(τρηθεῖcαι ?)

Π̣ετοcῖρ̣ι̣ϛ̣ Ὥ̣ρου καὶ Ἁρμαχόρ(οc). Κοι(ρι   ) ζ∠ ἀ̣ν̣(ὰ) γ, (ἀρτάβαι ?) κ̣β̣∠̣.
Κε(ρκεούρεωc) γ ἀν(ὰ) δ∠γ́ιβ́, ιδ∠d.

(γίνονται) ι∠ (ἀρτάβαι) λζd. προ(   ) d (ἀρτάβη) α. (γίνονται)
ι∠d (ἀρτάβαι) ληd. (τετρακαιεικοcτῆc) ∠, θέ(ματοc) ∠,
(τρι)χ(οινίκου) ∠γ́, θη(cαυροφυλακικοῦ) ∠, κρά(cτεωc) ∠,
λοχι(   ) ϛ́, γρ(αμματικοῦ) β̣∠̣,

(γίνονται) ε∠, (γίνονται) μγ∠d. (στεφά(νου) εd, (γίνεται) τὸ (πᾶν) μθ.)
γεω(μετρίαc) ∠̣, (γίνονται) μ̣δ̣ḍ.

μ̣ε̣(τρηθεῖcαι) Παχ(ὼν) β̄ (πυροῦ) εἰcδε(ξίμωι) λη∠ (ὧν) κ̣α̣(θάρcεωc)
α̣∠γ́ιβ́, λο(ιπαὶ) λϛ∠ιβ́. (m. 2) Ἐπεὶφ ζ̄

(m. 3 ?)]κβ∠

ζ̣∠ (m. 2) ϛ (ἔτουc) Φαρμοῦ(θι) (πυροῦ) ιεϛ́, κδ̄ (πυροῦ) κα-
(θαροῦ) θ∠, [.] (πυροῦ) [κ]α(θαροῦ) . . . ., (γίνονται)

μβ́.
(γίνονται) λ̣δ̣γ́.

(m. 1) Π̣ε̣τ̣ε̣ρ̣μοῦθις Ὥρου. γ̄ ς, Κε(ρκεούρεως) η, (γίνονται) ιδ ἀν(ὰ) δ∠γ́ιβ́,
(ἀρτ.) ξη∠γ́. προ( ) ḍί̣ς́ (ἀρτ.) α∠, (γίν.) ιδdίς́
(ἀρτ.) ο̣γ́.
(τετρ.) ∠d, θέ(μ.) ∠, (τρι)χ. αγ́, θη(c.) ∠, κρά(c.) ∠, λοχι( ) ς́,
γρ(α.) γ∠, (γίν.) ζίβ́, (γίν.) ο̣ζγ́ίβ́. στεφά(νου) ζ,
(γίν.) τὸ (πᾶν) πδγ́ίβ́.
γεω(μ.) ∠, (γίν.) οζ∠γ́ίβ́.

με(τ.) Φαρμοῦθι λ̄ (πυροῦ) εἰcδε(ξίμωι) νζ (ὧν) κα(θ.) β∠γ́, λο(ιπαὶ)
νδς́ (m. 2 ?) [Ἐπεὶ]φ ᾱ φα(κοῦ) κ, β̣̄ (πυροῦ) γ∠d.
θ̄ στεφά(νου) (πυροῦ) ζ.
(m. 3 ?) β̣∠ ιβγ́ίβ
ζ∠ κβ∠

(m. 1) λο(ιπαὶ) λ∠d (ὧν) (πυροῦ) ι∠d φα(κοῦ) κ.

Παπνε̣β̣τ̣ῦ̣νις Cο̣κέως καὶ Κολλούθης. β̄ ε ἀν(ὰ) δ, κ. Κ̣ε̣(ρκεούρεως) ε̣∠
ἀν(ὰ) δ̣∠̣γ́ίβ́, κζ{∠γ́}ίβ́.
(γίν.) ι∠ (ἀρτ.) μζίβ́. προ( ) d (ἀρτ.) αd, (γίν.) ι[∠d] (ἀρτ.) μηγ́.
(τετρ.) ∠, θέ(μ.) ∠̣, (τρι)χ. ∠γ́, θη(c.) ∠, κρά(c.) ∠,
λοχι( ) ς́, γρ(α.) β∠, (γίν.) ε∠,
(γίν.) νδ. γεω(μ.) ∠, (γίν.) ν̣δ̣∠̣. (στεφά(νου) ε̣d, γεω(μ.) ∠,
πρα(κτορικοῦ) ∠, (γίν.) ςd, (γίν.) τὸ (πᾶν) ξ̣∠̣d.)

. . . .

Col. VI

Πετερμοῦθις Μαρρείους. Κοι(ρι) ιβ ἀν(ὰ) β∠, λ. προ( ) ∠ (ἀρτ.) αd.
χ // (γίν.) ιβ∠ (ἀρτ.) λαd. (τετρ.) ∠, [θέ(μ.) ∠,]
(τρι)χ. α, θη(c.) ∠, κρά(c.) ∠, λοχι( ) ς́, (γίν.) γς́, (γίν.) λδγ́ίβ́.
στεφά(νου) ς, γεω(μ.) ∠, πρα(κ.) ∠, (γίν.) ζ, (γίν.)
τὸ (πᾶν) μαγ́[ίβ́].

μ̣ε̣(τ.) [Πα]χ(ὼν) ζ̄ (πυροῦ) (ἑξα)χ(οινίκωι) ἀ[πὸ] πς̄ λγ∠. (m. 2 ?)
Ἐπεὶφ ῑ στεφά(νου) (πυροῦ) ς.

(m. 1) λο(ιπαὶ) (πυροῦ) ς.

Π̣ετεςοῦχος Νεκτενίβιος. Κο(ιρι) κ ἀν(ὰ) β, (ἀρτ.) μ. {(ὧν) με(τ.)}
χ // με(τ.) Φαρμοῦθι γ̄ κ(ριθῆς) (ἑξα)χ(οινίκωι) ξϛβ́ αἶ (πυροῦ) μ.

Πετοςῖρις Ἁρκοίφιος Κο(ιρι) ζ ἀν(ὰ) δ∠γ́ιβ́, λδγ́ιβ́. γ ἀν(ὰ) γ, θ. (γίν.)
ι (ἀρτ.) μγγ́[ιβ́. προ( ) d (ἀρτ.) αd.]
(γίν.) ιd (ἀρτ.) μδβ́. (τετρ.) ∠, θέ(μ.) ∠, (τρι)χ. ∠γ́, θη(ς.) γ́,
κρά(ς.) γ́, λοχι( ) ϛ́, γρ(α.) β∠, (γίν.) εϛ́, (γίν.)
μθ∠̣γ́. [(ςτεφά(νου) ε,]
(γεω(μ.) ∠, πρα(κ.) ∠, (γίν.) ϛ, (γίν.) τὸ (πᾶν) νε∠γ́. (ὧν) με(τ.))
γεω(μ.) ∠, (γίν.) νγ́.

με(τ.) Φαρμοῦθι ιζ̄ (πυροῦ) εἰςδε(ξίμωι) \`ἀπὸ´ νθ̣ \`νγ́´ (ὧν) κα(θ.) ββ́,
λο(ιπαὶ) νγ́.

Πετεςοῦχος Τεεφίβιο̣ς. ϛ∠ (ἀρτ.) ιϛ∠. (τετρ.) d, (τρι)χ. ∠, (γίν.) ∠d,
χ (γίν.) ιζd.
(m. 2) με(τ.) Ἐπεὶφ ζ̄ φα(κοῦ) ι.

(m. 1) Παπνεβτῦνις Πετοςίριος. Κ( ) δ∠ (ἀρτ.) κβϛ́, προ( ) ή (ἀρτ.)
χ ∠, (γίν.) δ∠ή (ἀρτ.) κββ́.
(τετρ.) d, θέ(μ.) ∠, (τρι)χ. γ́ιβ́, [θη(ς.) d, κρά(ς.) d, λο]χι( ) ϛ́,
γρ(α.) α, (γίν.) β[∠γ́], (γίν. ?) κ̣ε̣∠. (ςτεφά(νου) βḍ,
γεω(μ.) ∠, (γίν.) β∠̣ḍ,
π̣ρ̣α(κ.) ∠, (γίν.) γḍ, [(γίν.) τὸ (πᾶν) κη]∠d.)
[με(τ.) ± 15] .[. .] [. . . . .] . (ἑξα)χ(οινίκωι) βϛ́. (m. 2 ?)
Ἐπ[εὶφ] ζ̄ φα(κοῦ) .

. . . .

Col. VII

χ Πετεςοῦχος Πετοςίριος. ι (ἀρτ.) μθϛ́. (τετρ.) ∠, θέ(μ.) ∠, (τρι)χ. ∠γ́,
θη(ς.) γ́, κρά(ς.) γ́,
λοχι( ) ϛ́, γρ(α.) β∠, (γίν.) εϛ́, (γίν.) νδγ́. γεω(μ.) ∠, (γίν.) νδ∠γ́.

με(τ.) Παχ(ὼν) ιγ̄ (πυροῦ) εἰςδε(ξίμωι) μϛ (ὧν) χει(ριςτικοῦ) ϛ́
κα(θάρςεως) βγ́, (γίν.) β∠, λο(ιπαὶ) μγ∠. Παῦνι ιε̄
(πυροῦ) (ἑξα)χ(οινίκωι) γ,
(γίν.) μϛ∠. (m. 2 ?) Παῦνι ιθ̄ (πυροῦ) β∠d. Ἐπεὶφ ζ̄ φα(κοῦ) ε,
θ̄ ςτεφά(νου) (πυροῦ) ε, κ̄ (πυροῦ) ∠γ́.

(m. 1) ? λο(ιπαὶ) ιβ∠d (ὧν) (πυροῦ) ζ∠d φα(κοῦ) ε.

Πετεϲοκονοῦριϲ Κεφάλωνοϲ. η (ἀρτ.) ιϛ, προ(   ) ∠ (ἀρτ.) ∠γ́, (γίν.)
χ // η∠ (ἀρτ.) ιϛ∠γ́.
(τετρ.) ∠̣, θέ(μ.) ∠, (τρι)χ̣. β́, θη(ϲ.) γ́, κρά(ϲ.) ϛ́, λοχι(   ) ϛ́,
γρ(α.) β, (γίν.) δ⟦∠⟧ \`γ́', (γίν.) κ⟦α⟧ \`∠γ́'. γεω(μ.) ∠,
(γίν.) καγ́.

(ὧν) με(τ.) Παῦ(νι) ϛ̄ (πυροῦ) εἰϲδε(ξίμωι) ἀπὸ κζ∠ κγ (ὧν) κα(θ.) αϛ́,
λο(ιπαὶ) κα∠γ́.
(m. 2) Ἐπεὶφ ᾱ ϲτεφά(νου) (πυροῦ) δ.

(m. 1) λο(ιπαὶ) (πυροῦ) δ.

Παᾶπιϲ Πετοϲίριοϲ. β∠d (ἀρτ.) θ, προ(   ) ή (ἀρτ.) γ́, (γίν.) β∠dή (ἀρτ.) θγ́.
χ (τετρ.) ϛ́, θέ(μ.) ∠,
(τρι)χ. d, θη(ϲ.) ϛ́, κρά(ϲ.) ϛ́, λοχι(   ) ϛ́, γρ(α.) α, (γίν.) βγ́ιβ́,
(γίν.) ια∠d.
με(τ.) Φαρμοῦθι ῑ κ(ριθῆϲ) ιϛ∠ (ὧν) κα(θ.) αd, λο(ιπαὶ) ιεd αἶ
(πυροῦ) θίβ́. [   ]ζ̄ (ἑξα)χ(οινίκωι) δ αἶ (πυροῦ) βγ́.
(γίν.) ιαγ́ίβ́. (m. 2) Ἐπεὶφ θ̄ ϲτεφ(άνου) (πυροῦ) αd.
(m. 1) λο(ιπαὶ) β∠ίβ́ (ὧν) (πυροῦ) αd φα(κοῦ) αγ́.

Ποτάμων Ἀμεννέωϲ. ι̣[α] (ἀρτ. ?) [νδί]β̣́, προ(   ) d (ἀρτ.) αd, (γίν.)
χ // ιαd (ἀρτ.) νεγ́.
(τετρ.) ∠, θέ(μ.) ∠, (τρι)χ. α, θη(ϲ.) γ́, κρά(ϲ.) γ́, λοχι(   ) ϛ́,
γρ(α.) γ, (γίν.) ε∠γ́, (γίν.) ξαϛ́. γεω(μ.) ∠, (γίν.) ξ̣α̣β̣́.

με(τ.) Παχ(ὼν) θ̄ (πυροῦ) (ἑξα)χ(οινίκωι) λδ. Παῦ(νι) ιζ̄ [(πυροῦ)]
(ἑξα)χ(οινίκωι) ι. [.] (πυροῦ) (ἑξα)χ(οινίκωι) ιη.
(γίν.) ξβ.
(m. 2 ?) [Ἐπ]εὶφ θ̄ ϲτεφά(νου) (πυροῦ) δ.
(m. 1) λο(ιπαὶ) ε∠ (ὧν) ϲτεφά(νου) δ⟦∠⟧ φακ(οῦ) α∠, (γίν.) ϛ.

Col. VIII

Πα{α}υϲῖριϲ καὶ Ὧροϲ. δ (ὧν) α ἀνὰ δ, γ ἀνὰ γ, θ, (γίν.) δ (ἀρτ.) ιγ.
προ(   ) ή (ἀρτ.) ∠, (γίν.) δ̣ή̣ [(ἀρτ.)] ιγ∠.
(τετρ.) d, θέ(μ.) ∠, (τρι)χ. γ́, θη(ϲ.) d, κρά(ϲ.) d, λοχι(   ) ϛ́,
γρ(α.) α, (γίν.) β∠d, (γίν.) ιϛd.

με(τ.) Φαρμοῦθι ῑ κ(ριθῆς) ιε (ὧν) ⟨κα(θ.)⟩ αϛ́, λο(ιπαὶ) ιγ∠γ́ αἳ
(πυροῦ) ηd. Παῦ(νι) ιζ̄ (πυροῦ) (ἑξα)χ(οινίκωι) [ζβ́],
(γίν.) ιε∠γ́ιβ́. λο(ιπὸν) ∠γ́.
(m. 2 ?) Ἐπεὶφ ζ̄ φα(κοῦ) ∠γ́, ιδ̄ στεφά(νου) (πυροῦ) α, κ̄ (πυροῦ) α, (γίν.) β.
(m. 1) β∠γ́ (ὧν) (πυροῦ)

Πνεφερῶς Πετεσούχου. β (ἀρτ.) ϛ, προ( ) ιϛ́ (ἀρτ.) γ́, (γίν.) βιϛ́ (ἀρτ.) ϛγ́.
χ // (τετρ.) ιβ́, θέ(μ.) ∠, (τρι)χ. ϛ́, θη(ς.) ιβ́, κρά(ς.) ιβ́,
λοχι( ) ϛ́, γρ(α.) ∠, (γίν.) αγ́ιβ́, (γίν.) ζ∠γ́ιβ́. γεω(μ.) ∠,
(γίν.) ηγ́ιβ́. (ὧν) με(τ.) Παχ(ὼν) λ̄ (πυροῦ) εἰςδε(ξίμωι)
\`ἀπὸ´ $\overline{\text{ιδ∠}}$ (ὧν) κα(θ.) ∠d,
λο(ιπαὶ) ιγ∠d, ηγ́ιβ́. (m. 2) Ἐπεὶφ ᾱ (πυροῦ) α.
(m. 1) λο(ιπὴ) α.

Πετεσοῦχος Σαραπίωνος. δ∠ (ἀρτ.) ιη, προ( ) ή (ἀρτ.) ∠, (γίν.) δ∠ή
χ (ἀρτ.) ιη∠. (τετρ.) d, θέ(μ.) ∠, (τρι)χ. γ́ιβ́, [θη(ς.) d,]
κρά(ς.) d, λοχι( ) ϛ́, γρ(α.) αd, (γίν.) γιβ́, (γίν.) ḳ[α]∠̣ιβ́. καὶ
τῆς εἰς Πᾶσιν Ὥρου αd (ἀρτ.) ϛd, [προ( ) d (ἀρτ.)] ϛ́,
(γίν.) α̣∠̣ (ἀρτ. ?) ϛ̣γ́ιβ́. (τετρ.) ιβ́, θέ(μ.) ∠, (τρι)χ. ιβ́, [θη(ς.) ι]β́,
κρά(ς.) ϛ́, λοχι( ) ϛ́, [γρ(α.) d,] (γίν.) αγ́, (γίν.) ζ∠d,
(γίν.) τῶν β ἀνδ̣(ρῶν) [ϛ (ἀρτ.) κ]θγ́.
στεφά(νου) γ, γεω(μ.) ∠, (γίν.) γ∠, (γίν.) λβ∠γ́. (m. 2 ?)
(ὧν) με(τ.) Ἐπεὶφ β̄ (πυροῦ) δ∠, ϛ̄ φα(κοῦ) κδ∠, (γίν.) κθ.
Ἐπεὶφ θ̄ στεφά(νου) (πυροῦ) βd, ῑ ∠d.
λο(ιπαὶ) (πυροῦ) γ∠γ́.

(m. 1) Πορεγέβθις Ὥρου. [δ]∠d (ἀρτ.) κ[δ, προ( ) ή (ἀρτ.)] ḍ, (γίν.) δ∠dή
// (ἀρτ. ?) κδd. (τετρ.) d, θέ(μ.) ∠, (τρι)χ. γ́ιβ́,
θη(ς.) d, κρά(ς.) d, λοχι( ) ϛ́, γρ(α.) αd, (γίν.) γιβ́, (γίν.) [κζγ́,
καὶ γεω(μ.) ∠, στε]φά(νου) βd.
με(τ.) Φαρμοῦθι λ̄ (πυροῦ) εἰςδε(ξίμωι) ι̣θ [± 12] Ὥρωι γ[
(m. 2) Ἐπεὶφ ῑ στεφά(νου) (πυροῦ) ββ́.
(m. 1 ?) λο(ιπαὶ) βd.

Col. IX

Πετεσοῦχος Χεύριος καὶ οἱ ἀδελ(φοί). κα (ἀρτ.) ϙγ (ὧν)

Πετεσοῦχος ζ (ὧν) γ ἀν(ὰ) δ∠γ´ιβ´, (ἀρτ.) ιδ∠d, δ ἀνὰ δ, ις, (γίν.)
χ ζ (ἀρτ.) λ̣[∠d, προ( ) ή (ἀρτ.) ∠d,]
(γίν.) ζή (ἀρτ.) λα∠. Τεεφῖβις δ (ἀρτ.) ιθβ̣´, π̣ρο( ) ή (ἀρτ.) γ´, (γίν.) δ̣[ή (ἀρτ.) κ.]
Χεῦρις Χεύριος καὶ Μαρεμῆνις θ∠ (ὧν) δ∠ ἀνὰ δ∠, (ἀρτ.) κd, ϵ̣ [ἀνὰ γ, (ἀρτ.) ιϵ,]
(γίν.) θ∠ (ἀρτ.) λ̣ϵd, προ( ) d (ἀρτ.) α, (γίν.) θ∠d (ἀρτ.) λϛd, (γίν.) τὸ (πᾶν) (ἄρουραι) κα̣ (ἀρτ.) πζ[∠d. (τετρ.) α, πρα(κ.) α∠,]
θέ(μ.) ∠, (τρι)χ. α∠d, θη(ς.) α, κρά(ς.) α, λοχι( ) ϛ´, γρ(α.) ϵ̣d, (γίν.) ιβϛ´, (γίν.) τὸ (πᾶν) ϙθ∠γ´ιβ´. ‵γεω(μ.) ∠,′ στεφά(νου) ι∠, [(γίν.) ια, (γίν.) ρι∠γ´ιβ´.]

μϵ(τ.) Φαρμοῦθι ιη̄ ἃς Τεεφῖβι κ(ριθῆς) ιϵ∠, (ὧν) κα(θ.) αϛ´, λο(ιπαὶ) ιδγ´ αἳ (πυροῦ) η∠. Πα̣χ(ὼν) [. ἃς]
λο(ιπ.) κβ∠d (ὧν) χλω̣(ρῶν) ζ (πυροῦ?) ιϵ∠d Πετεσοῦχος (πυροῦ) εἰςδε(ξίμωι) νβ (ὧν) κα(θ.) ββ´, λο(ιπαὶ) μθγ´.
ζ̄ ἃς Χεῦρις (πυροῦ) εἰςδε(ξίμωι) κβ (ὧν) [κα(θ.) αϛ´,]
λο(ιπαὶ) κ∠γ´, (γίν.) εἰς (πυροῦ) οηβ´. (m. 2 ?) Ἐπεὶφ ϛ̄ φα(κοῦ) ι. θ̄ στεφά(νου) (πυροῦ) [

(m. 1 ?) λο(ιπαὶ) κα (ὧν) (πυροῦ) ι∠ φα(κοῦ) ι∠.

Πᾶσις Πετεσούχου. κ∠ (ἀρτ.) ρ∠γ´. (τετρ.) α, θέ(μ.) ∠, (τρι)χ. αβ´, λοχι( ) ϛ´, γρ(α.) ϵ, (γίν.) ηγ´, (γίν.) τὸ (πᾶν) ρθ[ϛ´.]

μϵ(τ.) Παχ(ὼν) θ̄ (πυροῦ) (ἑξα)χ(οινίκωι) οϵ∠. ιγ̄ (πυροῦ) (ἑξα)χ(οινίκωι) ιϛ∠, (γίν.) ϙβ. (m. 2 ?) Ἐπεὶφ ζ̄ φα(κοῦ) ζϛ´, (γίν.) ϙθϛ´, λο(ιπαὶ) ι.

(m. 1 ?) λο(ιπαὶ) ζϛ´

. . . .

Col. X (**249**, Col. I)

Τεῶς Θοτορταίου. ϛ (ἀρτ.) κθ∠, προ( ) ή [(ἀρτ.) ∠, (γίν.) ϛή (ἀρτ.) λ.
χ (τετρ.) γ´, θέ(μ.) ∠, (τρι)χ. ∠, κρά(ς.) d, θη(ς.) ∠ιβ´, λοχι( ) ϛ´,]
γρ(α.) α∠, (γίν.) γγ´, (γίν.) λγγ´. γεω(μ.) ∠, (γίν.) λ[γ∠γ´, καὶ στ]εφά(νου) γ, (γίν.) λϛ∠γ´.

[με(τ.) Φ]αρμοῦθι ιη̄ κ(ριθῆς) κδ (ὧν) κα(θ.) α∠γ́, λο(ιπαὶ) κβς́ αἳ
(πυροῦ) ιγd. Παῦ(νι) κ̄ (πυροῦ) δε(ξίμωι) ιη,
κα(θ.) ∠γ́ιβ́, λο(ιπαὶ) ιζιβ́, (γίν.) λγ́. (m. 2) Ἐπεὶφ β̄ (πυροῦ) α.
ζ̄ φα(κοῦ) γ. θ̄ στεφά(νου) (πυροῦ) γ.

(m. 1) λο(ιπαὶ) ζ (ὧν) (πυροῦ) δ φα(κοῦ) γ.

Τοθοῆς Ἀγοννούφιος. ς∠d (ἀρτ.) λγd, προ( ) ή, ∠γ́, (γίν.) ς∠dή (ἀρτ.)
// λδιβ́. (τετρ.) γ́, θέ(μ.) ∠,
[(τρι)]χ. [∠]ι̣β̣́, θη(ς.) d, κρά(ς.) d, λοχι( ) ς, γρ(α.) α∠d, (γίν.) γ∠γ́,
(γίν.) λζ∠γ́ιβ́. γεω(μ.) ∠, (γίν.) ληγ́ιβ́, στεφά(νου) γ∠̣,
(γίν.) μα∠γ́ι̣β̣́.
με(τ.) [±5] ε̣ἰ̣ςδε(ξίμωι) (πυροῦ) κη∠ (ὧν) κα(θ.) αγ́ιβ́, λο(ιπαὶ)
κζιβ́. Παῦ(νι) ι̣ (πυροῦ ?) (ἑξα)χ̣(οινίκωι) η, (γίν.) λειβ́.
(m. 2 ?) Ἐπεὶφ ᾱ φ̣α̣(κοῦ) [
ζ̄ [±6] ζ, (γίν.) μβ∠γ́ιβ́.

(m. 1) λο(ιπαὶ) ς∠γ́ (ὧν) (πυροῦ) ε̣∠ φα(κοῦ) α̣γ́.

[Τοθ]ο̣ῆς Φαγάτου. α (ἀρτ.) γς́, δα(νείου) ας́, (γίν.) δ̣γ́.
με(τ.) Παῦ(νι) ις̄ ἃς Μαρρῆς Πετεσούχου (πυροῦ) (ἑξα)χ(οινίκωι) γγ́.
(m. 2) Ἐ̣π̣ε̣ὶφ θ̄ α.

(m. 1) Τοθοῆς Σενθέως. β∠ (ἀρτ.) ιβ∠, καὶ ἀπὸ τῆς (πρότερον) Πετεήσιος α∠
(ἀρτ.) ζγ́ιβ́,
[(γίν.)] δ̣ (ἀρτ.) ιθβ́. προ( ) ή (ἀρτ.) γ́, (γίν.) δή (ἀρτ.) κ.
(τετρ.) d, θέ(μ.) ∠, (τρι)χ. γ́, θη(ς.) d, κρά(ς.) d,
λοχι( ) ς́, γρ(α.) α, (γίν.) β∠d.

με(τ.) Φ[α]ρμοῦθι ιη̄ [κ](ριθῆς) ιη∠̣ (ὧν) κα(θ.) α∠̣, λο(ιπαὶ) ιζ αἳ
(πυροῦ) ις. Παχ(ὼν) θ̄ (πυροῦ)
ε∠γ́, (γίν.) ις.

Col. XI

. . . .

[λο(ιπαὶ) . (ὧν)] (πυροῦ) γ φ̣α̣(κοῦ) .

Φμούεις Παθήβιος. ε (ἀρτ.) [κ, προ( ) ή (ἀρτ.) ∠, (γίν.) εή (ἀρτ.) κ∠.
// (τετρ.) d, θέ(μ.) ∠, (τρι)χ. γ́ιβ́, θη(ς.) ∠, κρά(ς.) d,

λοχι(   ) ϛ',]
γρ(α.) αd, (γίν.) γίβ', (γίν.) κ̣γ∠ίβ. γεω(μ.) ∠, (γίν.) κ̣δίβ'.

με(τ.) Παχ(ὼν) ῑ (πυροῦ) εἰςδε(ξίμωι) ἀπὸ ν̅ϛ̅ κγ (ὧν ?) κα(θ.) αϛ',
λο(ιπαὶ) κα∠γ'. (m. 2 ?) Ἐπεὶφ ᾱ [φα(κοῦ β∠̣.
θ̄ ςτεφά(νου) (πυροῦ) β∠̣.

(m. 1) λο(ιπαὶ) ϵ (ὧν) (πυροῦ) β∠ φα(κοῦ) β̣∠.

Φαῆςις Ἀρυώτου. θ (ὧν) η ἀν(ὰ) δ∠γ'ίβ', (ἀρτ.) λθγ', α ἀν(ὰ) γ, (γίν.) θ
χ /   (ἀρτ.) μβγ'. προ(   ) d (ἀρτ.) α,
(γίν.) θd (ἀρτ.) μγγ'. (τετρ.) ∠, θέ(μ.) ∠, (τρι)χ. ∠d, θη(ς.) γ',
κρά(ς.) γ', λοχι(   ) ϛ', γρ(α.) βd, (γίν.) δ∠γ', (γίν.)
μηγ'.
γεω(μ.) ∠, (γίν.) μη∠γ'.

με(τ.) Φαρμοῦθι ιη̅ κ(ριθῆς) ιϛ (ὧν) κα(θ.) αγ', λο(ιπαὶ) ιδβ' αἱ (πυροῦ)
η∠. κδ̄ (πυροῦ) λθ∠ (ὧν) πρα(κ.) ∠.
(m. 2 ?) Ἐπεὶφ ζ̄ φα(κοῦ) βγ'ίβ'   θ̄ ςτεφά(νου) (πυροῦ) δ∠.
λο(ιπαὶ) βγ'ίβ'.

(m. 1) λο(ιπαὶ) ϵγ'.

. . . .

Col. XII . . . .

Ὧρο[ς Τιμοθέου
ἐξη( )
γρ(α.) α, (γίν.) [
λο(ιπαὶ) δγ'
με(τ.) Φαρ[μοῦθι

Ὧρος Πετοςίρ[ιος
με(τ.) Φα[ρμοῦθι
ἐξη( )

(fragment b)

Col. XIII = **247** Col. I

αλ
Ὧρος Ὀρςενούφ[ιος
με(τρηθεῖςαι) Ἐπεὶφ γ̄ φα(κοῦ) ββ'. λο(ιπαὶ) β[
Ὧρος Πετῶτ[ος

με(τ.) Ἐπεὶφ ῑ φα(κοῦ) ιβ [
Ὧρος Κατύτ[ιος
χ γρ(αμματικοῦ) α, (γίν.) α∠, με(τ.) Ἐπεὶφ κ̅ϛ̅ (πυροῦ ?) [
Ὧρος Μικίωνος ἀπὸ κδ [

(*c*. 3·5 cm. blank)

Κέντις Θ̣[ώνιος] . [
με(τ.) Ἐπεὶφ γ̅ (πυροῦ) α, . . γ´ιβ´, . . .[
Θῶνις μι(κρὸ)ς Κεντίς[ιος] ἀπὸ κ∠γ´ [
Πετεσοῦχος Χεύ[ριος
] . [
. . . .

(fragment c)

Col. XIV

[Ὀνν]ῶφρις Τεῶτος. η∠γ´ (ὧν) ζ ἀν(ὰ) γ, κα, α∠γ´ ἀν(ὰ) β∠, δ, (γίν.) η∠γ´
(ἀρτ. ?) [κ]ε̣. (τετρακαιεικοστῆς) ∠, (τρι)χ(οινίκου) β´,
(γίν.) αϛ´, (γίν.) κϛϛ´. (ὧν) με(τ.) Ἐπεὶφ ϛ̅ φα(κοῦ) κϛ.

[Πετεῆσις] Τεῶτος. κδ∠ (ἀρτ.) πγ∠, προ( ) ∠ (ἀρτ.) β∠, (γίν.) κε (ἀρτ.)
πϛ. [(τετρ.)] α̣d, (τρι)χ. βιβ´, (γίν.) γγ´,
(γίν.) πθ∠. (ὧν) με(τ.)
[Φα]ρ̣[μο]ῦθι ⟨ι⟩η̅ κ(ριθῆς) νϛ∠ (ὧν) κα(θάρσεως) δd, λο(ιπαὶ) νγd αἳ
(πυροῦ) λαγ´. Παχ(ὼν) γ̅ (πυροῦ) ἀπὸ ϙγ∠ ξ (ὧν)
κα(θ.) γ, λο(ιπαὶ) νζ. (γίν.) πηγ´.

Τεῶς Πετεχῶντος καὶ Ὧρος. κδ∠ (ἀρτ.) ρε. (τετρ.) αd, θέ(ματος) ∠,
(τρι)χ. β, θη(σαυροφυλακικοῦ) γ´ιβ´, κρά(στεως) γ´ιβ´,
λοχι( ) ϛ´, γρ(α.) ϛ´, (γίν.) ι∠d, (γίν.) τὸ (πᾶν) ρις∠d.
με(τ.) Παχ(ὼν) γ̅ (πυροῦ) (ἑξα)χ(οινίκωι) ἀπὸ ϙ̅β̅ οα. (m. 2 ?)
Ἐπεὶφ β̅ (πυροῦ) ζ∠. ε̅ \`ἃς Θέω(ν)´ φα(κοῦ) ι∠,
καὶ ἃς αὐ(τοὶ) ι̣δ∠ḍ.

(m. 1) [Μ]αρρῆς Πετεχῶντος καὶ Πετεσοῦχος Ὀρσενούφιος. καd (ἀρτ.) πε,
προ( ) ∠ (ἀρτ.) β, (γίν.) κα∠ḍ (ἀρτ.) πζ. (τετρ.) αιβ´, θέ(μ.) ∠,
(τρι)χ. β, θη(σ.) ∠, κρά(σ.) ∠, λοχι( ) ϛ´, γρ(α.) ε∠,
(γίν.) ιd,
(γίν.) τὸ (πᾶν) ϙζd.

μ̣ε̣(τ.) *Φαρμοῦθι* κδ̄ . .[. . . .] .ζ. *Παχ(ὼν)* γ̄ ἃς *Θέω(ν)* (πυροῦ) (ἑξα)χ(οινίκωι) .[. .] . ο .[
Παῦ(νι) κ̄ (πυροῦ) (ἑξα)χ(οινίκωι) βd. (m. 2 ?) *Ἐπεὶφ* β̄ ἃς
Θέω(ν) (πυροῦ) (ἑξα)χ(οινίκωι) δ. ϛ̄ ἃς *Θέω(ν)*
φα(κοῦ) η, ἃς *Πετεcοῦ(χος)* *Ὀρcε(νούφιος)* φα(κοῦ) ε.
(ὧν) *Πετεcούχου* *Ὀρcενού(φιος)* . . ἀπὸ (ἀρτ.) ϛδ∠ μζd, (ὧν)
με(τ.) λ̣δ, (γίν.) μαβ̣́[
μγd . . .

Col. XV

(m. 1) Ὧροc [Ὀρcείουc.] ιγ∠ (ἀρτ.) ξϛ∠, προ( ) d (ἀρτ.) αγ́, (γίν.) ιγ∠d
χ (ἀρτ.) ξζ∠γ́. (τετρ.) β́, [
216 κ]ρά(c.) d, λοχι( ) ϛ́, γρ(α.) γd, (γίν.) ϛd, (γίν.) οδ̣ίβ. γεω(μετρίας) ∠,
(γίν.) οδ∠ιβ́.
με(τ.) *Φαρμοῦθι* κδ̄ (πυροῦ) νη∠ (ὧν) κα(θ.) β∠ιβ́, \`λο(ιπαὶ) νε∠ιβ́'.
Παῦ(νι) ϛ̄ (πυροῦ) εἰcδε(ξίμωι) κ (ὧν) κα(θ.) α,
λο(ιπαὶ) ιθ, (ὧν) αὐ(τὸc) [
[λο(ιπ.) (πυρ.) .] φα(κ.) ζ *Παῦ(νι)* κ̄ (πυροῦ) (ἑξα)χ. ε∠, (γίν.) ξηιβ́. *Ἐπεὶφ* ϛ̄
φα(κοῦ) ϛ. ζ̄ φα(κοῦ) α̣.
θ̄ (πυροῦ) ϛ∠.

220 Ἡράκλειοc *Π̣ε̣τάλου*. θ∠ (ἀρτ.) μϛ̣∠̣ḍ (τετρ.) ∠, (τρι)χ. ∠γ́, (γίν.) αγ́,
(γίν.) μη̣ί̣β̣́.
[με(τ.)] *Φαρμοῦθι* κϛ̄ (πυροῦ) (ἑξα)χ. ιζ∠. (m. 2) *Ἐπεὶφ* ϛ̄
(πυροῦ) ιϛ. ζ̄ β. η̄ ε. θ̄ .[
(Blank space of *c*. 12 cm.)
νθ (ὧν) κα(θάρcεωc) γ, λο(ιπαὶ) νϛ ιθ ε∠ιβ́ φα(κοῦ) ζ, (γίν.) πζ∠ (ὧν) ιβ∠,
λο(ιπαὶ) οε.

(fragment d)

Col. XVI = **248** Col. II

[*Μαρρῆc Πετε*]*cούχου*. δ (ἀρτ. ?) ι̣θ̣β́[
] *Π̣ετοcίριοc* . . . .αυ . . . . .[± 11] (γίν.) . . [
225] κ̣είβ. (τετρ.) d, [θέ(μ.)] ∠, (τρι)χ. γ́ιβ, θη(c.) d, κρ̣ά̣(c.) ḍ,
λοχι( ) ϛ́, [γρ(α.) αϛ́, (γίν.)] γίβ. [γεω(μ.) ∠,
(γίν.) κηβ́.]

με(τ.) Παῦ(νι) ιγ̄ (πυροῦ) (ἑξα)χ. γ∠. Ἐπεὶφ ᾱ φα(κοῦ) .. στεφά(νου)
(πυροῦ) β.
—β́.

Νῖνις Φαήσιος. γ, ιδ∠d, πρ[ο( )] ή́ (ἀρτ.) γ́, (γίν.) γή́ (ἀρτ. ?) ιε̣ίβ́.
χ (τετρ.) d̤, θέ(μ.) ∠, (τρι)χ. d̤, θη(ς.) ς́, κρά(ς.) ς́,
λοχι( ) ς́, γρ(α.) α, (γίν.) β∠, (γίν.) ιζ∠ίβ́. γεω(μ.) ∠, (γίν.)
ιηί̣β́.
μ̣ε̣(τ.) Παχ(ὼν) ς̄ ἃς Πετεσοῦχο[ς Π]α̣αλαμ̣ο(ύνιος) (πυροῦ) δε(ξίμωι)
[ἀπὸ] ... ι (ὧν) ∠, λο(ιπαὶ) θ∠.
Παῦ(νι) ιθ̄ (πυροῦ) ς, (γίν.) (πυροῦ) ιε∠. (m. 2 ?) [Ἐ]πεὶφ ς̄
(πυροῦ) α φα(κοῦ) α.
(m. 1) λο(ιπαὶ) β∠ίβ́.

Νί̣[κων] Ἀ̣μεννέως. ι (ἀρτ.) μθς́, προ( ) ήίς́ (ἀρτ.) α̣, (γίν.) ιήίς́ (ἀρτ.) νς́.
χ (τετρ. ?) ., θ̣έ̣(μ.) ∠̣, (τρι)χ. ∠γ́,
[θη(ς.) .,] κρά(ς.) d, λοχι( ) ς́, γρ(α.) β̇∠, (γίν.) ε, (γίν.) νες́.
γεω(μ.) ∠, (γίν.) νεβ́. (ὧν) με(τ.) Παῦ(νι) ιη̄
[(πυροῦ) δε(ξίμωι) κδ∠γίβ́] (ὧν ?) κα(θ.) α∠, [λο(ιπαὶ)]
κγίβ́. λο(ιπαὶ) λβ∠ίβ́. (m. 1) Ἐπεὶφ β̄ (πυροῦ) ιη. ζ̄ φα(κοῦ) ε.
(m. 1) (πυροῦ) ιηίβ́, φα(κοῦ) ε.

Πετεσοῦχος Πετεσούχου. ια (ἀρτ.) νδ∠ίβ́, προ( ) ∠ (ἀρτ.) α, (γίν.) [ια∠
χ (ἀρτ.) νε∠ίβ́. (τετρ.) ∠ίβ́,]
θέ(μ.) ∠, (τρι)χ. ∠γίβ́, θη(ς.) γ́, κρά(ς.) γ́, λοχι( ) ς́, γρ(α.) β∠d,
(γίν.) ε∠ίβ́, (γίν.) τὸ (πᾶν) ξ[ας́. γεω(μ.) ∠, (γίν.) ξαβ́.]
με(τ.) Φαρμοῦθι κβ̄ (πυροῦ) (ἑξα)χ. ξ ἃ̣ς̣ Μαρώνιο( ) θυ( )
λογι( ) α, (γίν.) ξ[α
(Slight traces of one line, remainder stripped away)

. . . .

Col. XVII = **247** Col. IV (UC Catalogue 1783+1786a)

Πετεσοῦχος ⟦.......⟧ Μικίωνος κ̣α̣ὶ̣ Ἡ̣ρ̣[ακλείων
[±15].[...].[±7]....[
Παῦ(νι) ιζ̄ ἃς Ἡρακλεί(ων) (πυροῦ) κα(θαροῦ) ιβ. Ἐπεὶφ ζ̄ φα(κοῦ) [
] στεφά(νου) (πυροῦ) β∠.

(Papyrus stripped for 5 cm.)

Πετῶς Μαρρείους. κα (ἀρτ.) ϙβ∠γ́, προ( ) d [(ἀρτ.)] β̣ι̣β́, (γίν.) κ̣α̣[d (ἀρτ.)] ϙδ∠γ̣́ι̣β́. (τετρ. ?) α̣ιβ́,
χ
θέ(μ.) ∠, (τρι)χ. α∠γ́ιβ́, θη(c.) ∠, κρά(c.) ∠, λοχι( ) ς́, γρ(α.) εd, (γίν.) θ̣∠γ́ιβ́, (γίν.) ρδ∠γ́. γεω(μετρίας) ∠, (γίν.) ρεγ́.
[με(τ.)] Φαρμοῦθι κδ̄ (πυροῦ) (ἑξα)χ. λε. Παχ(ὼν) θ̄ (πυροῦ) εἰ[c]δε(ξίμωι) ξ (ὧν) κα(θ.) γ, λο(ιπαὶ) νζ, (γίν.) ϙβ.
(m. 2) Ἐπεὶφ ᾱ (πυροῦ) ες́ φα(κοῦ) ς. ῑ (πυροῦ) δ∠.
(m. 1) λο(ιπαὶ) ιεβ́.
[Πε]τεcοῦχος Cοκμήνιος. ζ∠ (ἀρτ.) λς∠γ́ιβ́, προ( ) ή (ἀρτ.) ∠d, (γίν.) ζ∠ή (ἀρτ.) λζβ́.
(τετρ.) γ́ιβ́, θέ(μ.) ∠, (τρί)χ. ∠ιβ́, θη(c.) d, κρά(c.) d, λοχι( ) ς́, γρ(α.) α̣∠d, (γίν.) γ∠γ́ιβ́, (γίν.) τὸ (πᾶν) μ⟦α∠ιβ́⟧ \`βιβ́΄.
μ̣ε̣(τ.) Παχ̣(ὼν) ς̄ (πυροῦ) εἰcδε(ξίμωι) ἀπὸ μς̄ λ̣ς (ὧν) κα(θ.) α̣∠γ́, λο(ιπαὶ) λδς́.
(m. 2) Ἐπεὶφ ᾱ (πυροῦ) β∠ φα(κοῦ) γ∠. β̄ (πυροῦ) γ∠γ́.
(m. 1) Πετεcοῦχος Ὀννώφριος. δ (ἀρτ.) ις, προ( ) ή (ἀρτ.) ∠, (γίν.) δή (ἀρτ.) ις̣∠̣.
(τετρ.) d, θέ(μ.) ∠, (τρι)χ. γ́, θη(c.) d, κρά(c.) d, λοχι( ) ς́, γρ(α.) α, (γίν.) β∠d, (γίν.) ιθd. γεω(μ.) ∠, (γίν.) ιθ∠d.
με(τ.) Φαρμοῦθι ιη̄ κ(ριθῆc) ς∠ (ὧν) ∠ λο(ιπαὶ) ς αἱ (πυροῦ) ε∠. (πυροῦ) ι (ὧν) κα(θ.) ∠ λο(ιπαὶ) [θ∠,]
(γίν.) ιε. (m. 2 ?) Ἐπεὶφ ῑ τὰ ἐν θέ(ματι) αὐ(τοῦ) διὰ Πετεcού(χου) (πυροῦ) δ.
(m. 1) τοπάρχῃ χρή(αc) (ἑξα)χ(οινίκωι) δ, γρ(α.) β, (γίν.) ς.

Col. XVIII

[±25].∠ή (ἀρτ.) κζ∠ιβ́.
χ (τετρ.) d, θέ(μ.) ∠, [(τρι)]χ̣[, θη(c.) κρά(c.) , λοχι( ) ς́, γρ(α.) , (γίν.)] λ̣β́, cτεφά(νου) β∠, (γίν.) λγς́.
[με(τ.) Ἐπεὶ]φ ζ̄ φα(κοῦ) β, (γίν.) . ., (γίν.) εἰc (πυροῦ)
. . . .[ ].
Φαῆcιc Φ[ίβιος.] ς (ἀρτ.) κθ∠, [π]ρο( ) ή (ἀρτ.) ∠ιβ́, (γίν.) ςή (ἀρτ.) λιβ́.
χ (τετρ.) d, θέ(μ.) ∠, (τρι)χ. ∠,
θη(c.) d, κρά(c.) d, λοχι( ) [ς́, γρ(α.)] α̣∠, (γίν.) γ∠, (γίν.) λ̣διβ́.

με(τ.) Παχ(ὼν) θ̄ (πυροῦ) εἰς[δε(ξίμωι) λα∠] (ὧν) κα(θ.) α∠ιβ́,
λο(ιπαὶ) κθ∠γ́ιβ́. (m. 2 ?) Ἐπεὶφ ς̄ φα(κοῦ) β∠.
(m. 1) λο(ιπαὶ) β∠.

Χαιρήμων [Πε]τοςίριος. δ∠ (ἀρτ.) κ̣βς́, προ( ) ή (ἀρτ.) ∠, (γίν.) δ∠ή
χ // (ἀρτ.) κββ́.
(τετρ.) d, θέ(μ.) ∠, [(τρι)χ. γ́ιβ́,] θη(ϲ.) d, κρά(ϲ.) d, λοχι( ) ς́,
γρ(α.) [α]d, (γίν.) γ́ιβ́, (γίν.) κε̣∠d
με(τ.) Παχ(ὼν) θ̄ (πυροῦ) [εἰϲδε(ξίμωι)] κ̣δ (ὧν) κα(θ.) αd,
λο(ιπαὶ) κβ∠d. (m. 2 ?) Ἐπεὶφ ς̄ (πυροῦ)
α φα(κοῦ) β, (γίν.) γ, (γίν.) κε∠d.
(m. 1) λο(ιπαὶ) γ.

Ὧρος Πετες[ούχο]υ̣. βd (ἀρτ.) ς∠d, προ( ) ις́ (ἀρτ.) d, (γίν.) βdις́
χ // (ἀρτ.) ζ. (τετρ.) ιβ́,
θέ(μ.) ∠, (τρι)χ. ς́, [θη(ϲ.) ιβ́, κρά(ϲ.)] ιβ́, λοχι( ) ς́, γρ(α.) ∠̣, (γίν.) α∠ιβ́,
(γίν.) η∠d. γεω(μ.) ∠, (γίν.) θd.
(ὧν) με(τ.) Παῦ(νι) β̄ (πυροῦ) εἰϲδ[ε(ξίμωι) η] (ὧν) κα(θ.) γ́ιβ́, λο(ιπαὶ)
ζ∠ιβ́. κ̄ (πυροῦ) (ἑξα)χ(οινίκωι) α∠, (γίν.) θιβ́.
(m. 2 ?) Ἐπεὶφ η̄ ϲτεφά(νου) (πυροῦ) α.

(m. 1) Ἰλῶϲ Ὥρου καὶ Ἁρφαῆϲιϲ Πετεχῶντοϲ. ιη (ἀρτ.) ξθ∠d. (τετρ.) ∠γ́,
χ θέ(μ.) ∠, (τρι)χ. α∠,
γρ(α.) δd, (γίν.) ζ̣ι̣β́, (γίν.) τὸ (πᾶν) οςβ́.
με(τ.) Παχ(ὼν) ῑ (πυροῦ) (ἑξα)χ. νη. (m. 2 ?) Ἐπεὶφ ζ̄ φα(κοῦ) η.
(*c.* 4 cm. blank)
(m. 1) . . κγ

Col. XIX

Ἑλλήνων γεωργ[ῶν
Ἁρμι̣ῦ̣[ϲιϲ Ἁ]ρμιύϲιοϲ. ς (ἀρτ.) κθ∠, προ( ) ή (ἀρτ.) β́, (γίν.) ςή
⧣ (ἀρτ.) λς́. (τετρ.) d,
θέ(μ.) ∠, (τρι)χ. γ́, θη(ϲ.) d, κρά(ϲ.) d, λοχι( ) ς́, γρ(α.) α∠,
(γίν.) γ∠γ́, (γίν.) λ⟦γ∠⟧ \`δ´. γεω(μ.) ∠, (γίν.) λδ̣∠.
με(τ.) Φαρμοῦθι κδ (πυροῦ) (ἑξα)χ(οινίκωι) ἀπὸ μς̄ λδ∠.

Ἁρφαῆϲιϲ Πετ[ο]ϲίριοϲ. δ (ἀρτ.) ιβ. (τετρ.) d, [(τρι)]χ. γ́, (γίν.) ∠ιβ́,
⧣ (γίν.) ι̣β̣[∠ιβ́].

με(τ.) Φ̣αρμοῦθι κδ̄ κ(ριθῆς) (ἑξα)χ(οινίκωι) κ αἳ (πυροῦ) ιβ.

ʽΑρμαχόρος Θοτορταίου. ε∠d (ὧν) γ∠ ἀν(ὰ) δ∠γ́ιβ́ (ἀρτ.) ιζγ́ιβ́, βd ἀν(ὰ)
χ γ ς∠d.
(γίν.) ε∠d (ἀρτ.) κδς́. προ( ) ή (ἀρτ.) ∠, (γίν.) ε∠dή (ἀρτ.) κδβ́.
(τετρ.) d, θέ(μ.) ∠, (τρι)χ. γ́ιβ́, θη(c.) d, κρά(c.) d,
λοχι( ) ς́, γρ(α.) ας́, (γίν.) γ́ιβ́, (γίν.) κζ∠d. γεω(μ.) ∠, (γίν.) κηd.
με(τ.) Παχ(ὼν) κς̄ (πυροῦ) εἰcδε(ξίμωι) ιζ (ὧν) κα(θ.) ∠γ́, λο(ιπαὶ) ιςς́.
Ἐπεὶφ ζ̄ .....ς́.
λο(ιπὴ) αίβ́.

ʽΑρμιῦcιc Πετοcίριοc. δ̣∠̣ (ἀρτ.) ιη, π̣ρο( ) ή (ἀρτ.) ∠, (γίν.) δ∠ή
χ (ἀρτ.) ιη∠. (τετρ.) d, θέ(μ.) ∠,
(τρι)χ. γ́ιβ́, θη(c.) d, κρά(c.) d, λοχι( ) ς́, γρ(α.) α, (γίν.) β∠γ́,
(γίν.) καγ́. γεω(μ.) ∠, (γίν.) κα∠γ́.
με(τ.) Παχ(ὼν) β̣̄ (πυροῦ) εἰcδε(ξίμωι) κα (ὧν) κα(θ.) αίβ́, λο(ιπαὶ)
ιθ∠γ́ιβ́. Ἐπεὶφ θ̄ cτεφ(άνου) (π̣υροῦ) βd.

Θοτεὺc Διοδώρου. ς ιη, προ( ) d (ἀρτ.) β́, (γίν.) ςd (ἀρτ.) ιηβ́. (τετρ.) d,
θέ(μ.) ∠,
(τρι)χ. ∠, θ[η(c.)] d, κρά(c.) d, λ̣ο̣χι( ) ς́, γρ(α.) α∠̣, (γίν.) γγ́ιβ́
(γίν.) κβίβ́. γεω(μ.) ∠, (γίν.) κβ∠ίβ́.
λο(ιπὴ) α∠ίβ́ ἄλ(λαι) βd, (γίν.) γ∠γ́. με(τ.) Φαρμοῦθι ιη̄ κ(ριθῆς) ιθ (ὧν) κα(θ.) α∠, λο(ιπαὶ) ιζ∠ αἳ
(πυροῦ) ι∠. Παχ(ὼν) κζ̄ (πυροῦ) (ἑξα)χ(οινίκωι) η∠,
(γίν.) ιθ. (m. 2 ?) Παῦ(νι) κ̄ (πυροῦ) (ἑξα)χ(οινίκωι) β. Ἐπεὶφ [.]
(πυροῦ) α∠.
θ̄ cτεφά(νου) (πυροῦ) γ.

Col. XX

Μαρρῆc Cενθέωc. β (ἀρτ.) ς, προ( ) ή (ἀρτ.) d, (γίν.) βή (ἀρτ.) ςd.
(τετρ.) ς́, θέ(μ.) ∠, (τρι)χ. ς́,
θη(c.) ς́, [κρά(c.) γ́, λοχ]ι( ) ς́, γρ(α.) α, (γίν.) β⟨∠⟩, (γίν.) η∠d.
γεω(μ.) ∠, (γίν.) θd.
με(τ.) Παχ(ὼν) ιγ̄ ἃc Cοκμῆ(νιc) ἀπὸ (πυροῦ) (ἀρτ.) λ[
Ἐπεὶφ ῑ cτεφά(νου) α.

Ὀρcῆc Ὀρcείουc καὶ Πτόλλιc. θ (ἀρτ.) μ[δγ́ιβ́,] προ( ) d (ἀρτ.) ∠γ́ιβ́,
(γίν.) θd (ἀρτ.) μεγ́.

(τετρ.) [γ́, θ]έ(μ.) ∠, (τρι)χ. ∠d, θη(c.) d, κρά(c.) d, λοχι( ) ϛ́,
λο(ιπαὶ) ζϛ́ γρ(α.) βd, (γίν.) δβ́, (γίν.) ν. γεω(μ.) ∠, (γίν.) ν∠.
με(τ.) Φαρμοῦθι ῑ ἃc Χολῶc ἀπὸ (πυροῦ) λη∠ λ (ὧν) κα(θ.) α∠,
λο(ιπαὶ) κη∠.
Παῦ(νι) ιζ̄ (πυροῦ) (ἑξα)χ(οινίκωι) ιδ∠γ́ίβ́, (γίν.) μ̣γγ́. Ἐπεὶφ ᾱ
φα(κοῦ) ε. β̄ (πυροῦ) βϛ́.
θ̄ cτεφά(νου) (πυροῦ) δ∠.

Πετενοῦπις Πετοcίριος. ζ∠d (ἀρτ.) ληϛ́, προ( ) ήίϛ́ ∠d, (γίν.) ζ∠dήίϛ́
λο(ιπαὶ) εγ́ (ἀρτ.) λη∠γ́ίβ́. (τετρ.) γ́ίβ́, θέ(μ.) ∠, (τρι)χ. β́, θη(c.) γ́,
ἃc [Ἀπ]ο̣λλω( ) α∠,
λο(ιπαὶ) γ∠γ́ κρά(c.) γ́, λοχι( ) ϛ́, γρ(α.) α∠d, (γίν.) δϛ́.
(γίν.) μγίβ. γεω(μ.) ∠, (γίν.) μγ∠ίβ.
με(τ.) Φαρμοῦθι δ̄ (πυροῦ) εἰcδε(ξίμωι) ιη∠ (ὧν) \`κα(θ.)ʹ ∠γ́ίβ́,
λο(ιπαὶ) ιζ∠ίβ. Παχ(ὼν) κϛ̄ (πυροῦ) εἰcδε(ξίμωι)
\`ἀπὸʹ κϛ̄ {(ὧν)}
κα∠ίβ́ (ὧν) κα(θ.) αίβ, λο(ιπαὶ) κβ́, (γίν.) ληd. (m. 2 ?)
Ἐπεὶφ ϛ̄ φα(κοῦ) γγ́ίβ́. θ̄ cτεφά(νου) (πυροῦ) γ∠d.

(m. 1) Πορεγέβθις Ἀπύγχιος. θ (ἀρτ.) λα∠d, προ( ) d (ἀρτ.) α, (γίν.) d
χ (ἀρτ.) λβ∠d. (τετρ.) ∠
θέ(μ.) ∠, (τρι)χ. ∠γ́, θη(c.) d, κρά(c.) d, λοχι( ) ϛ́, γρ(α.) βd,
(γίν.) δ∠d. (γίν.) λζ∠. γεω(μ.) ∠, (γίν.) λη. (ὧν)
λο(ιπαὶ) δ∠ με(τ.) Φαρμοῦθι ̣̄ (πυροῦ) εἰcδε(ξίμωι) ἀπὸ νϛ̄ (ὧν) κα(θ.) κθ∠.
Παῦ(νι) ιζ̄ (πυροῦ) δ.
(m. 2) Ἐπεὶφ ᾱ φα(κοῦ) δ∠, (γίν.) (blank). θ̄ cτεφά(νου) (πυροῦ) δ∠.

(m. 1) Πετεϲ̣ο̣ῦχος Cω̣τ̣ηρίδου. θ (ἀρτ.) λη∠d (ὧν) γ ἀν(ὰ) δ∠γ́ίβ́ [(ἀρτ.) ιδ∠d,
ϛ ἀν(ὰ) δ (ἀρτ.)]
κδ, (γίν.) θ (ἀρτ.) λη∠ḍ. προ( ) ή (ἀρτ.) ∠γ́ίβ́, (γίν.) θή (ἀρτ.) λθβ́.
(τετρ.) ∠, θ[έ(μ.) ∠, (τρι)χ. ∠d, θη(c.) , κρά(c.) ,]
λοχι( ) ϛ́, γρ(α.) βd, (γίν.) δ∠γ́ίβ́, (γίν.) μδ∠ίβ. cτεφά(νου) δ∠,
{(γίν.)} γεω(μ.) [∠, (γίν.) μθ∠ίβ́.]
με(τ.) Παχ(ὼν) θ̄ ἃc Ἁρμιῦcιc (πυροῦ) (ἑξα)χ(οινίκωι) κβ∠. ιγ̄
(πυροῦ) εἰcδε(ξίμωι) κϛ∠ (ὧν) κα(θ.) αγ́, [λο(ιπαὶ) κεϛ́.]
Ἐπεὶφ ῑ cτεφά(νου) (πυροῦ) ἀπὸ δ∠̄ α∠d.
λο(ιπὴ) (πυροῦ) α∠d.

Col. XXI

[Πετερμοῦθι]ς Σιεφμοῦτος. ια (ἀρτ.) νδίβ́, προ(   ) d (ἀρτ.) αϛ́,
(γίν.) ιαd (ἀρτ.) ν⟦αd⟧ \`εd´.
(τετρ. ?) ∠̣ίβ́, θ̣έ̣(μ.) ∠̣, (τρι)χ. ∠γ́ίβ́, θη(ς.) γ́, κρά(ς.) γ́, λοχι(   ) ϛ́,
γρ(α.) β∠d, (γίν.) ε∠ίβ́, γεω(μ.) ∠, (γίν.) ϛίβ́, (γίν.) ξαγ́.
[με(τ.)] Φαρμοῦθι ῑ (πυροῦ) κγ (ὧν) κα(θ.) αϛ́, λο(ιπαὶ) κα∠γ́.
Παχ(ὼν) ιϛ̄ (πυροῦ) εἰσδε(ξίμωι) λη∠ [(ὧν)]
κα(θ.) α∠γ́ίβ́, λο(ιπαὶ) λϛ∠ίβ́, (m. 2 ?) (γίν.) εἰς (πυροῦ) νηγ́ίβ́.
Ἐπεὶφ ϛ̄ φα(κοῦ) γ.
] στεφά(νου) (πυροῦ) ε∠.

(m. 1) [Πετεσο]ῦχος Ὀρσενούφιος Βε(   ). ε ἀν(ὰ) δ (ἀρτ.) κ, προ(   ) ∠
(ἀρτ.) β, (γίν.) ε∠ (ἀρτ.) κβ.
(τετρ.) d, θέ(μ.) ∠, (τρι)χ. γ́ίβ́, θη(ς.) d, κρά(ς.) d, λοχι(   ) ϛ́,
γρ(α.) αd, (γίν.) γίβ́, (γίν.) κείβ́. γεω(μ.) ∠, (γίν.) κε∠ίβ́.
με(τ.) Φαρμοῦ(θι) ῑ (πυροῦ) κϛ (ὧν) κα(θ.) αγ́, λο(ιπαὶ) κδβ́. (m. 2 ?)
Ἐπεὶφ ῑ τὰς ἐν θέ(ματι) αὐ(τοῦ) (πυροῦ) . .

(m. 1) Σοκμῆνις Ὀρσείους. ε ἀν(ὰ) γ ιε, προ(   ) ή (ἀρτ.) ∠, (γίν.) εή
(ἀρτ.) ιε∠. (τετρ.) d, θέ(μ.) ∠, (τρι)χ. γ́ίβ́,
θη(ς.) d, κρά(ς.) d, λοχι(   ) ϛ́, γρ(α.) αd, (γίν.) γίβ́, (γίν.) ιη∠ίβ́.
γεω(μ.) ∠, (γίν.) ιθίβ́.
με(τ.) Παχ(ὼν) ιϛ̄ (πυροῦ) εἰσδε(ξίμωι) ἀπὸ λ̄ κ (ὧν) κα(θ.) α, λο(ιπαὶ)
ιθ. (m. 2 ?) Ἐπεὶφ γ̣̄ (πυροῦ) β∠.
(m. 1) ?] (τετρ. ?) d, θέ(μ.) ∠, (τρι)χ. ∠ίβ́, θη(ς.) γ́ίβ́, κρά(ς.) γ́ίβ́, λοχι(   ) ϛ́,
γρ(α.) β, γεω(μ.) α.

Τεῶς Ὥρου. θ (ἀρτ.) μα∠, προ(   ) d (ἀρτ.) ∠γ́ίβ́, (γίν.) θd (ἀρτ.) μβγ́ίβ́.
(τετρ.) γ́ί̣β́, θ̣έ̣(μ.) ∠̣,
(τρι)χ. ∠γ́, θη(ς.) γ́, κρά(ς.) γ́, λοχι(   ) ϛ́, γρ(α.) βd, (γίν.) δ∠γ́,
(γίν.) μζd. γεω(μ.) ∠, (γίν.) μζ∠d.
με(τ.) Παχ(ὼν) β̄ (πυροῦ) (ἑξα)χ(οινίκωι) \`ἀπὸ´ ν̄ μθ∠γ́, πλ(είω) βίβ́.
Ἐπεὶφ θ̄ στεφά(νου) (πυροῦ) δ∠.

Φραμῆνις Πετοσίριος. η∠ (ἀρτ.) λδ. (τετρ.) γ́, θέ(μ.) ∠, (τρι)χ. ∠d,
λοχι(   ) ϛ́,
γρ(α.) β, (γίν.) γ∠ίβ́, (γίν.) λζ∠d.

μϵ(τ.) Παχ(ὼν) β̄ (πυροῦ) ϵἰϲδϵ(ξίμωι) κγ∠ (ὧν) κα(θ.) αϛ´, λο(ιπαὶ)
κβγ´. Παῦ(νι) ιθ̄ (πυροῦ) δ, (γίν.) κϛγ´.
Ἐπεὶφ ⟨ ̣⟩ φα(κοῦ) ϛ, (γίν.) λβγ´.

(fragment e)

Col. XXII

γϵωργοὶ κοινῆι. νο(μῶν) ξ (ἀρτ.) ξ. (τϵτρ.) γ, (τρι)χ. ϵ, (γίν.) η,
(γίν.) ξη. μϵ(τ.)
Παχ(ὼν) ιᾱ Μαρρῆϲ Πακύ(ρριοϲ) (πυροῦ) αγ´.
(Blank space of *c.* 19 cm.)
Πϵτοϲίριοϲ Κατύτιοϲ καὶ Πᾶϲιϲ. ηd (ἀρτ.) κϵ̣. (τϵτρ. ?) ∠, θϵ́(μ.) ∠,
(τρι)χ. β´,
θη(ϲ.) d, κρά(ϲ.) d, λοχι(   ) ϛ´, γρ(α.) β, (γίν.) δγ´. καὶ
⟦ϲτϵφά(νου)⟧ γϵω(μϵτρίαϲ) ∠, (γίν.) [δ]∠̣γ´, (γίν.) κθ∠γ´.
(ὧν) μϵ(τ.) Φαρμοῦθι ζ̄ κρι(θῆϲ) μβ (ὧν) κα(θ.) γ̣γ´, λο(ιπαὶ) λ̣[η]β̣´
αἶ (πυροῦ) κγd.
λο(ιπαὶ) ϛ∠ιβ´.

Traces of a further column and several disconnected fragments do not merit publication.

37 Φαήϲιοϲ 50 1st ∠ corrected from d 99 1st ∠ corr. from α 100 καγ´: γ´ corr. from ∠ 134 κα: α corrected from δ 173 μη∠γ´: γ´ corrected from ιβ´ 249 ιϵβ´ corrected from ιϵϛ´ 339 (τρι)χ. ∠γ´ corrected from (τρι)χ. ∠d

Lines 36–43. 'Nikanor son of Ptolemaios, 3 arouras in the Koiri( ) Perichoma at $4\frac{11}{12}$ artabs apiece, $14\frac{3}{4}$ art., and in the Second Perichoma 10 arouras at $4\frac{11}{12}$ formerly held by Thonis son of Orsenouphis and Phaesis, $49\frac{1}{6}$ art. Total, 13 arouras, $63\frac{11}{12}$ art. In addition, $\frac{1}{4}$ renting for $1\frac{1}{3}$ art., total $13\frac{1}{4}$ for $65\frac{1}{4}$ art. $\frac{2}{3}$ art. for 24th tax, $\frac{1}{2}$ for deposit charges, $1\frac{1}{12}$ for trichoinikon, $\frac{1}{2}$ for granary-guard tax, $\frac{1}{2}$ for fodder tax, $\frac{1}{6}$ for lochi( ), $3\frac{1}{4}$ for scribal fees, total $6\frac{2}{3}$. Grand total, $71\frac{11}{12}$. For crown tax, $6\frac{1}{2}$ art., all together $78\frac{5}{12}$ (*in brackets*). Survey fee, $\frac{1}{2}$ art., total $72\frac{5}{12}$.

'Paid Pharmouthi 18, $34\frac{1}{2}$ art. barley less $2\frac{7}{12}$ lost in cleaning or deducted for cleaning charges; remainder $31\frac{11}{12}$, which equals 19 art. wheat. Pachon 10, 33 art. wheat by receiving measure, less $1\frac{2}{3}$ art. for cleaning; i.e., $31\frac{1}{3}$ art. clean wheat. Total reckoned in terms of wheat, $50\frac{1}{3}$ art. (*line* 43) Remainder, $28\frac{7}{12}$ art., of which $22\frac{1}{12}$ are wheat and $6\frac{1}{2}$ are lentils. (*2nd hand*) Epeiph 1, 6 art. lentils. 2nd, 1 art. wheat. 10th, $6\frac{1}{2}$ art. wheat for crown tax.'

37 Θώνιοϲ τοῦ Ὀρϲϵνούφιοϲ καὶ Φαῆϲιϲ: for the partnership, cf. **1144**. 25, 101.

39 The scribe's curved brackets are used to set off the stephanos charge for some reason, not to cancel it; cf. 68 note.

40 κ(ριθῆϲ) λδ∠: cf. **1135**. 16.

43 λο(ιπαὶ) κη∠ιβ´: $78\frac{11}{12}$ artabs (the sum of the bracketed $78\frac{5}{12}$ of line 39 plus $\frac{1}{2}$ art. survey fee) less $50\frac{1}{3}$ art. paid through Pachon.

49 Ὀννῶφρι[ϲ] Ὥρου καὶ Ἑραθρῆϲ: brothers. The first lot of land is probably located in **1119**. 63, though Herathres is not mentioned there; and the second in **1117**. 42, where he is replaced by one Menches.

52 ἆς Πετεσοῦχος Ἰμούθου ἀπὸ $\overline{\mu}$ ιγγ´: that is, Petesouchos brought to the granary 40 artabs, of which 13⅓ were credited to Onnophris and Herathres.

54 These payments make up the deficit noted in line 56.

55 and 57–9. The connection of these lines with each other and with the rest of the account is not very clear. Onnophris in line 59 is presumably the son of Horos, and 25⅔ is nearly the rent on 5¼ arouras at $4\frac{11}{12}$ artabs (line 49; exact would be 25⅚); but $\frac{11}{12}$ art. trichoinikon in line 55 must refer to a plot of 11 arouras. Year 6 is 112/111 B.C.; cf. 65.

56 η∠γ´ιβ´: the correct difference between 56¼ due (52) and 47⅓ paid (53). The breakdown into wheat and lentils ignores $\frac{5}{12}$ art.

57 κθd: the correct total of 25⅔, $\frac{5}{12}$, and ½ is $26\frac{7}{12}$.

60–6 This account does not balance, and some details are obscure.

60 Κε(ρκεούρεως) γ: probably located in **1117**. 109 though Harmachoros is not mentioned there.

65 Cf. line 57. A part of the payment here may have been arrears for year 5.

66 (γίνονται) λ̣δ̣γ´: obscure.

67 $\overline{\gamma}$ ϛ: located in **1120**. 49.

68 ζιβ´: right was 7¼.

στεφά(νου): although the charge for stephanos is not bracketed, it is ignored in the total in line 69.

70 The payments in Epeiph make up the deficit noted in 74.

74 λο(ιπαὶ) λ∠d: the total due, never expressed above, was $77\frac{11}{12}$ from line 69 plus 7 art. stephanos, = $84\frac{11}{12}$. 30¾ is the difference between this amount and 54⅙ paid in line 70.

(πυροῦ) ι∠d: 7 art. stephanos plus 3¾ for other charges (paid 70–1).

75 καὶ Κολλούθης: son of Papnebtynis.

76 μζιβ´: tacitly corrects the error in the last figure of 75.

77 νδ: correct was 53⅚.

γεω(μ.): occurs twice in this line, no doubt by error.

78 The land is located in **84**. 33 = 214.

81 λο(ιπαὶ) (πυροῦ) ϛ: paid for stephanos in line 80. But 6 art. remainder plus 33½ paid line 80 amount to only 39½ of the $41\frac{5}{12}$ due. Possibly a further payment of 1½ artabs has been lost because of a tear in the papyrus.

82–3 Twelve arouras of this land are located in **84**. 17.

87 The first νγ´ (50⅓) is a mistake for 53.

89 φα(κοῦ) ι: there is a slight tear in the papyrus which might have contained a further figure, but the space would not have sufficed for anything larger than a narrowly written d.

90 Κ( ): a mark above κ seems to be simply an abbreviation sign, and gives no particular support to either Κο̣(ιρι) or Κε̣(ρκεούρεως).

97 $\overline{\kappa}$ (πυροῦ) ∠γ´: brings the total paid to ⅚ above the deficit noted in line 98 and ¼ above the true total due (cf. next note).

98 λο(ιπαὶ) ιβ∠d: 12¾ was paid Payni 19 and Epeiph 7 and 9. But the true difference between 46½ paid through Payni 15 and 59⅚ due (54⅚ from line 95, plus 5 art. stephanos) was 13⅓ art.

100 κ⟦α⟧ `∠γ´': correct was 21⅙.

101 κα∠γ´: ½ art. more than was due according to the faulty calculation of line 100, and ⅙ more than was actually due.

103 λο(ιπαὶ) (πυροῦ) δ: refers to the stephanos, though this was not mentioned in the account of charges due.

106 [ ]ζ̄: the lacuna is sufficient to accommodate Παχ(ὼν) or Παῦ(νι), or simply [ι]ζ or [κ]ζ.

108 λο(ιπαὶ) β∠ιβ´: the difference between 11⅚ artabs due (105) and $11\frac{5}{12}$ paid (107) is only 1⅓ art., 2¼ less than the figure given here. 1¼ of this is accounted for by the stephanos charge, but the explanation for the remaining artab is obscure; cf. 113 note.

111 ξβ: an overpayment of ⅙ art.

113 λο(ιπαὶ) ϵ∠: 4 of this is for stephanos, but the remaining 1½ artabs are puzzling, especially in view of the fact that the payments in Payni actually exceeded the amount due.

στεφά(νου) δ⟦∠⟧: 4 is the final figure given in **1128**. 58 also, but one expects 5½ here.

(γίν.) ϛ: an error for 5½, left uncorrected after the cancellation of ∠ from the figure for stephanos.

114 *Ὧρος*: brother of Paysiris.

116 λο(ιπὸν) ∠γ′: this agrees with the figure paid for lentils in line 117, and is implied by 118, since 2 of the 2⅝ there are for stephanos. But the true difference between 16¼ due and 15 11/12 paid is only ⅓.

117 Both wheat payments are for stephanos.

118 (ὧν) (πυροῦ): the figures, which the scribe did not fill in, would have been (πυροῦ) ⟨β, φα(κοῦ) ∠γ′⟩.

120 (γίν.) αγ′ιβ′: right was 1 7/12.

121 The payment in Epeiph was no doubt for stephanos; it meets the deficit noted in line 122.

123 Petesouchos's 4½ arouras are located in **84**. 49 = 224.

124 καὶ τῆς εἰς Πᾶσιν: cf. **1105**. 21–3; and for the formula, **82**. 18–21.

125 (τετρ.) κτλ.: Pasis himself was charged only δάνειον, γεωμετρία, and στέφανος in **1105**.

131 The mutilated portion of the line includes payments which make up all of Poregebthis' dues, since the figure for the remainder in line 133 is entirely stephanos and his name is marked with the double strokes which indicate payment in full. But it has not proved possible to integrate Ὥρωι (reading certain) into the line satisfactorily. One might think of [καὶ ἃς *NN*] Ὥρου but Ὥρου cannot be read.

132 ββ′: should have been 2¼; cf. lines 130, 133.

134 (ἀρτ.) ϙγ: individual rents detailed in lines 135–8 total only 87¾, correctly given in 138; but the uncorrected figure in **1105** at this point (line 27) was also 93, and that may have been unthinkingly copied here.

135 γ ἀν(ὰ) δ∠γ′ιβ′: located in **1119**. 15.

δ ἀν(ὰ) δ: located in **1119**. 19.

136 Τεεφῖβις δ: located in **84**. 41.

137 Χεῦρις Χεύριος: one of the brothers rather than the father Cheyris, whose patronymic is unknown.

Μαρεμῆνις: son of Petesouchos and grandson of Cheyris, if he is to be identified with the *Μαραμῆνις Πετεσούχου* of **172** VI 14 ined. The partnership of Cheyris and Maremenis apparently began in 114/113 B.C.; cf. **1106**.

138 πζ[∠d: cf. 134 note.

(τετρ.) α, πρα(κ.) α∠: the second charge is taken from **1106**. 9. The amount of the first is required arithmetically, and agrees with **1105**. 30.

141–3 The arithmetic in the marginal account is correct, but I cannot relate it to any other item in the text.

145 λο(ιπαὶ) κα: the true difference between 78⅝ art. paid and 110 11/12 due (139) is 32¼.

146–8 Parcels of this land, all at 4 11/12 art., are located in **84**. 100 and 108 = **1118**. 101 = **1120**. 117; **1118**. 92 and 95 = **1120**. 109 and 113.

146 λοχι( ) ς′: this charge is omitted in **1105**. 36.

148 Following this line an entry for Tauriskos son of Apollonios (**1105**. 40–1) may have been lost.

150 γρ(α.) α∠: only one art. for this charge in **1105**. 43, but 1½ is expected at the usual rate.

γγ′: a mistake for 3⅝, apparently copied from **1105**. 43, where 3⅓ was correct.

153 λο(ιπαὶ) ζ: this figure tacitly corrects the error in line 150 (cf. note). It is the difference between 37⅓ art. actually due (36⅝ line 150, wrongly) and 30⅓ paid.

156 The month was probably Παχ(ών). There is not room for Φαρμοῦθι unless it was abbreviated, which is generally not done in this account; and Παῦ(νι) would probably not have been repeated farther on in the line if it had already occurred earlier.

157 μβ∠γ′ιβ′: an overpayment of 1 art.

161 (ἀρτ.) ιβ∠: it is more probable that this is an error for 12⅓ than that the 2½ arouras were really rented at 5 art. apiece, especially since the total 19⅝ is that expected on 4 arouras uniformly rated at 4 11/12.

162 (γίν.) δη′ (ἀρτ.) κ: in **1105**. 53, 18⅝ art. were charged for the same amount of land, but the property was probably not the same; for it is more likely that Tothoes gave up 1½ arouras of land after year 4 and then acquired the same amount, at a higher valuation, from Peteesis, than it is that

τῆϲ (πρότερον) Πετεήϲιοϲ here is tacitly included in the $4\frac{1}{8}$ arouras of **1105**. Phrases of this sort normally refer to land acquired since the immediately preceding crop, whereas that interpretation would refer it back at least 2 years.

θη(ϲ.) d, κρά(ϲ.) d: only $\frac{1}{8}$ apiece in **1105**. 54. This suggests that the assessment of these taxes was related to the valuation as well as the quantity of land involved; cf. **1105** introd.

(γίν.) β∠d: completes the line; no total for taxes and rents together was given.

163 [κ](ριθῆϲ) ιη∠: cf. **1135**. 10.

164 ιϛ: does not complete the payments due, but no statement of deficit is preserved.

165 Presumably this line is the end of the account for Phaesis son of Peteesis, since Φαῆϲιϲ Πετοϲίριοϲ and Φαῆϲιϲ Πετεήϲιοϲ, in that order, intervene between Tothoes and Phmouis in **1105**+**93** and **1128**.

166 $4\frac{1}{2}$ arouras are located in **1117**. 143; cf. **1123**. 6–11.

167 γρ(α.) ad: only 1 art. in **93**. 14.

(γίν.) γίβ: this is the total given in **93**. 14, where it was correct; here it should have been $3\frac{1}{3}$. For similar confusion cf. 134 and 150 notes.

170 λο(ιπαὶ) ε: $2\frac{1}{2}$ of this is for stephanos. The remaining $2\frac{1}{2}$ is the difference between $21\frac{5}{6}$ art. paid and $24\frac{1}{3}$ really due, as opposed to the erroneous $24\frac{1}{12}$ of line 167. For a similar tacit correction, cf. 153 note.

174 κ(ριθῆϲ) ιϛ: cf. **1135**. 12.

175 φα(κοῦ) βγ́ίβ: meets the arrears in line 176, but it is not easy to see how the latter were determined. The payment on Pharmouthi 24 left only $\frac{5}{6}$ art. plus stephanos owing.

177 λο(ιπαὶ) εγ́: $4\frac{1}{2}$ art. stephanos plus $\frac{5}{6}$, the difference between $48\frac{5}{6}$ due and 48 paid.

179 εξη( ): so again in l. 195. I do not know whether it can be connected with εξηχ( ) in P. Mich. IV 224. 353 and 354.

186 αλ: clear. Does it mean col. 30 of roll 1? No other column is so headed.

194 Κέντιϲ Θ̣[ώνιοϲ: not Ὧ̣[ρου, who is accounted for in **94**. 1.

196 μι(κρὸ)ϲ: for the manner of abbreviation cf. φυλ(ακίτη)ϲ **81**. 20; γρ(αμματικ)ο(ῦ) **89**. 53 n.

196–7 Restore probably [καὶ ἃϲ] / Πετεϲοῦχοϲ Χεύ[ριοϲ, since the man is already entered in 134 ff.

201 [Πετεῆϲιϲ]: suggested by **1104**. 10–11, which reveals this man as the most substantial farmer with the patronymic Teos; and confirmed by **1135**. 14.

202 πθ∠: right was $89\frac{1}{3}$.

203 [Φα]ρ̣[μο]ῦθι ⟨ι⟩η̄: not [Φα]ρ̣[μο]ῦθ(ι) ιη̄ ; cf. **1135**. 14.

λο(ιπαὶ) νγd: right was $52\frac{1}{4}$.

205 Τεῶϲ Πετεχῶντοϲ: one cannot tell whether the older or younger man of this name is meant; in any case, Horos is his brother.

207 Θέω(ν): presumably the brother of the lessees is meant; cf. ll. 211 and 212.

214 Obscure.

215 ιγ∠: $6\frac{1}{2}$ arouras are located in **1117**. 32, the remaining 7 in **1119**. 67.

217 ʽλο(ιπαὶ) νε∠ίβʹ: $\frac{1}{12}$ too much.

218 [λο(ιπ.) (πυρ.) .]: perhaps 12 art., the sum of $6\frac{1}{2}$ art. stephanos paid in line 219 and the mysterious $5\frac{1}{2}$ paid Payni 20.

(γίν.) ξηίβ: it is not clear how this figure was reached. The total of $55\frac{7}{12}+19$ (line 217) in itself equals the $74\frac{7}{12}$ due line 216.

222 The notations are obscure.

224] Π̣ετοϲίριοϲ: no doubt preceded by καὶ ἀπὸ τῆϲ (πρότερον), but Petosiris may be either the former tenant or the former tenant's patronymic. $\frac{5}{12}$ trichoinikon suggests a total of 5 arouras.

226 ϲτεφά(νου) (πυροῦ) β: appropriate for only 4 arouras; cf. preceding note.

227 Obscure.

236 (πυροῦ) ιηίβ, φα(κοῦ) ε: the payments on Epeiph 2 were no doubt intended to meet these dues, though the figure for wheat is $\frac{1}{12}$ smaller than here. The total implied as due in this line is $23\frac{1}{12}$, as against the correct $32\frac{7}{12}$ of line 235. The scribe appears to have mistaken the first figure in that line as a total due rather than an amount paid, then subtracted from that the sum due in lentils to find the sum due in wheat.

241 κ̣α̣ὶ̣ Ἡρ̣[ακλείων: cf. **1130**. 96 and line 243 below.

244 *ϲτεφά(νου) (πυροῦ) β∠*: cf. **1128**. 96, where the same amount is due from Petesouchos alone.

249 *λο(ιπαὶ) ιεβ́*: this is the amount paid in Epeiph (248), but the true difference between $105\frac{1}{3}$ due and 92 paid was $13\frac{1}{3}$.

251 *μ⟦α∠ιβ́⟧ ʻβιβ́ʼ*: the final figure includes *γεωμετρία*.

256 *κ(ριθῆϲ) ϛ∠*: cf. **1135**. 15.

258 *τοπάρχῃ χρή(αϲ)*: 'to the toparch for his office.' Whether this curious note is to be connected with the foregoing account is not clear.

264 *(γίν.) γ∠*: right was $3\frac{5}{12}$.

(γίν.) λ̣διβ́: right was $33\frac{7}{12}$, unless the figure given is meant to include *γεωμετρία*; cf. 251 n.

272 *(γίν.) η∠*ḍ: right was $8\frac{7}{12}$.

276 *τὸ (πᾶν) οϛβ́*: right was $76\frac{5}{6}$.

278 Obscure.

279 *Ἑλλήνων γεωργ̣[ῶν*: the phrase occurs only here, and has been taken as a heading for the column (cf. **247**). The men who follow, however, appear to be ordinary Egyptian peasants. Harmiysis son of Harmiysis (280) was a teacher (**1139**. 92), but that would hardly qualify him as *Ἕλλην*. More probably this line is an entry in itself. If so, it may refer to those cleruchs who rented bits of land at special rates (p. 8; **1105**. 40 n.), and who are treated individually for this year in **98**. There is room here for a total statement of land and rent, but not for taxes; in **98** only stephanos payments appear sporadically in addition to rent. The cleruchic lessees of Crown land listed in **98** are in fact all native troops, but the term *Ἕλλην* may have survived from an earlier period when only or primarily Greek cleruchs were involved.

287 *(γίν.) γιβ́*: right was 3.

290 Located **1119**. 30.

295–7 The initial figure of the marginal account is the difference between $22\frac{7}{12}$ art. due and 19 paid by Pachon 27. Why $2\frac{1}{4}$ art. were added is unclear.

304 Orses and Ptollis are brothers.

315 *λο(ιπαὶ) κβ́*: right was $20\frac{1}{2}$.

326 $3\frac{1}{2}$ arouras are located in **84**. 71 = **1118**. 71, the remainder in **1117**. 105.

331 *Βε( )*: not *Κε(ρκεούρεωϲ)*. Perhaps *Βε(ρενικίτηϲ)*, but there is no other evidence that this man came from Berenikis Thesmophorou.

337 The readings are clear enough, but the point of the line is obscure.

340 *πλ(είω) βιβ́*: i.e., the payment $49\frac{5}{6}$ art. was $2\frac{1}{12}$ larger than needed to meet $47\frac{3}{4}$ due.

341 Located **84**. 23 and 26.

342 *(γίν.) γ∠ιβ́*: right was $3\frac{3}{4}$.

345 Cf. **1103**. 115 note.

1108. List of Holders of Temple and Cleruchic Land

P. Teb. 143 | 130 × 29 cm. | 124/121 B.C.

With **1108** we begin a series of texts parallel to **62** and **63**. **63** and **1110** are titled *κατὰ φύλλον ἱερᾶϲ καὶ κληρουχικῆϲ καὶ τῆϲ ἄλληϲ τῆϲ ἐν ἀφέϲει*, 'detailed report on the crops of sacred, cleruchic, and other released land'; but whatever may be meant by the latter term (cf. p. 3), only sacred and cleruchic land is in fact listed in the texts here published, together with the name of the owner, the cultivator, and the crops, if any, that were sown. Unlike corresponding lists for Crown land (**1103–7**), no statement of dues is given; for *μίϲθωϲιϲ* in itself was not charged, and separate *ἀπαιτήϲιμα* for taxes on land *ἐν ἀφέϲει* were kept (**98**+**1147**).

The natural presumption is that all 'released' land about Kerkeosiris was to be listed. **1100** mentions a catoecic cession in 114 B.C. which finds no reflection in any of our lists or surveys, but such affairs were not handled very promptly (**30, 31**) and it is possible that our documentation breaks off before the transfer was properly recorded; or the cession may have failed for some reason. A bid to purchase derelict land in about the same year, which should have resulted in the creation of *ἰδιόκτητοϲ γῆ* in the village, likewise fails to appear in any of these documents (**1101**).

Temple and cleruchic land has enjoyed an abundance of accurate scholarship: see Crawford, 53–102, with copious bibliography; cf. pp. 10–15 above. Crop information in this and the following texts is to be compared with that analysed by Crawford, 148–59 and 174–5.

1108 was written after a transfer of cleruchs from the Herakleidou Meris which took place in year 46 of Euergetes II, 125/124 B.C. (lines 118 ff.), but before the transfer from Ibion Eikosipentarouron which took place in year 50 (**62**. 294 note). A comparison of the preserved portions of this text with corresponding sections of **62** (year 52, 119/118 B.C.) reveals no deaths among the many persons named. The interval between the two documents cannot therefore have been very great.

Col. I

. . . .

[γ]ίνονται . . .[. .] . .[
καὶ τῆϲ ἐπὶ τοῦ πατρὸϲ [τοῦ βαϲιλέωϲ, τῶν δι' Ἑρμαφίλου]
[(ὀγδοηκοντ]αρούρων) Καλλικράτ[η]ϲ Φιλοξέν[ου] π. (πυρῶι) λγ κρι(θῆι) [
[ἐν] κα- . . . γεω(ργὸϲ) Φα[ῆϲ]ιϲ [Φα]ῆϲ̣ι̣ο̣ϲ̣
[το]χῆ
κ̣αὶ τῶν ἀναζευ(ξάντων) εἰϲ τὴν Θηβ(αίδα) ἀπὸ τῶν 'Δ̣ ἀ̣ν̣δ̣[ρῶν]
Κ̣αλλικράτηϲ Πτολεμαίου ἀβρόχου ιϛ
κ̣αὶ τῶν μεταβεβη(κότων) εἰϲ τ[ὴν] κα(τοικίαν) ἐκ τῶν Φυλέωϲ
Διονυϲίου τοῦ Πυρρί̣χου ιηdή (ὧν) (πυρῶι) ε̣
φα(κῶι) ηdή ἀρά(κωι) ε, γεω(ργὸϲ) Πετῶϲ Μ̣α̣ρρείουϲ
γίνονται κατοίκων ριδdή (ὧν ?) ϲπο(ρίμου) . . . . ἀβ[ρό(χου)]
ἐρημοφυλάκων Σειλ[η]νὸϲ Δημητ̣ρ̣ί̣ο̣υ̣
ὃν με(τειληφέναι) Ἡρακλείδην [τ]ὸν υἱὸν ι̣ . . . .[
γίνονται τῆϲ ἐπὶ τοῦ π[α]τ̣ρὸϲ ρκ̣δ̣dή
ϲπο(ρίμου) ρηdή ἀβρ[ό(χου)] ι̣ϛ
καὶ τῆϲ ἐπὶ τοῦ ἀδελ[φοῦ τοῦ βαϲιλέωϲ, ϲυγγενῶν κατοίκων ἱππέων]
Διοδότου Μικίων[οϲ καὶ Ἀπολ(λώνιοϲ) ἀδελ(φὸϲ) οὗ τὸ λο(ιπὸν) τοῦ
κλ(ήρου) περὶ τὸν Ἰβιῶ(να) τῶν (εἰκοϲιπενταρούρων)]
ι∠dή (ὧν) (πυρῶι) ι̣ κρι(θῆι) [γεω(ργὸϲ)

Λυσίμ[αχος Πύ]ρ̣ρου̣ [οὗ τὸ λο(ιπὸν) τοῦ κλ(ήρου)] περὶ τ[ὸν Ἰβιῶ(να)
τῶν (εἰκοσιπενταρούρων)]
μ [(ὧν)] ιε [

Col. II

γίνονται ἀνδ(ρῶν) β (ἄρουραι) ν∠dή σπο(ρίμου)
καὶ τῶν ἐν τῶι λα (ἔτει) διὰ Διονυσίου εἰς τοὺς κα(τοίκους) ἱπ(πεῖς)
Διόδοτος Ἀπολλωνίου μ (ὧν) (πυρῶι) ιβ κρι(θῆι) η ἀρά(κωι) ε
φα(κῶι) ε χο(ρτο)νο(μῶν) ι
ἐν κατοχῆ γεωργὸς Πετοσῖρις
Λέοντος τοῦ Λεοντίσκου μ (ὧν) (πυρῶι) ι ἀρά(κωι) ιε χό(ρτωι) ιε,
γεω(ργὸς) Θοτορταῖς
Ἀπολλωνίωι Ἀπολλωνίου μ (ὧν) (πυρῶι) κ ἀρά(κωι) ε κρι(θῆι) β
χό(ρτωι) θ, (γίνονται) λϛ
ἐμβρόχου δ, γεωργὸς αὐτός
Δώρωι Πετάλου μ (ὧν) (πυρῶι) ιε ἀρά(κωι) ιε φα(κῶι) γ, (γίνονται) λγ,
ἐμβρόχου ζ
γεωργὸς Φαῆσις
Βρομερὸς Ζηνοδώρου μ̣ (ὧν ?) (πυρῶι) ι φα(κῶι) ιε ἀρά(κωι) ι κρι(θῆι) ε,
(γίνονται) μ
ἐν κατοχῆ γεωργὸς Πετεσοῦχος Ἁρυωτος
γίνονται ἀνδ(ρῶν) ε (ἄρουραι) Σ (ὧν) σπο(ρίμου) ρπθ̣ ἀσπό(ρου) ια
καὶ τῆς ἐν τῶι λδ (ἔτει) Ἀπολλοδώρωι Πτολεμαίου ξ (ὧν)
ἐν κατοχῆ (πυρῶι) κ φακῶι κ̣ε ἀρά(κωι) ιε, (γίνονται) ξ, γεω(ργὸς)
Ἀθεμμεὺς Πετεσούχου
καὶ τῶν μετα̣[βε]βη(κότων) εἰς τ̣ὴ̣ν κ̣α(τοικίαν) ἐξ ἐφό̣δ̣ων
Ἀπολλωνίωι Πτολεμαίου κδ (ὧν) (πυρῶι) η φασή̣(λωι) [ ] χο(ρτο-)
νο(μῶν) \`ζ', γεω(ργὸς) αὐ(τός)
⟦ γεω(ργὸς) αὐ(τὸς) ⟧
⟦γ̣ί̣ν̣ο̣ν̣τ̣α̣ι̣ ἀ̣ν̣δ(ρῶν) β (ἄρουραι) μη σπο(ρίμου)⟧
καὶ ἐκ τῶν ἐρη(μο)φυ(λάκων) Ἀρτάβαι Πανταύχου ι (ὧν) (πυρῶι) ε ἀρά(κωι) ε,
γεω(ργὸς) αὐ(τός)
Νεκτενῖβις Ὥρου ι (ὧν) κρι(θῆι) ε̣ ἀρά(κωι) ε, γεω(ργὸς) αὐ(τός)
(γίνονται) κατοίκων τοη∠dή (ὧν) σπο(ρίμου)
ἐρη(μο)φυ(λάκων) τῶν ἐν τῶι λβ (ἔτει)
Πτολεμαῖος Ϲ̣αραπίωνος ι (ὧν) (πυρῶι) ε ἐμβρό(χου) ε, γεω(ργὸς)

α[ὐ(τός)]
Λαγῶς Διοδώρου ι ἀράκωι, γεω(ργὸς) Πελῶις
φυλακιτῶν τῶν ἐν τῶ[ι] λγ (ἔτει)
Ἀπολλων[ίο]υ τοῦ Ἀχιλλέως ὃν με(τειληφέναι) Ἀκουσίλαον τὸν υἱὸν
ι σπό(ρος) (πυρῶι) ε χό(ρτωι) ε, [γ]ε̣ω(ργὸς) Πορεγέβθις
Μάρων τὸν καὶ Νεκ̣τ̣ς̣άφθιν Πετοσίριον χο(ρτο)νο(μῶν) ι, γεω(ργὸς)
αὐ(τός)
Ἐτφεμοῦνις Ἀμορταίου ὃν με(τειληφέναι) Ἡρακλ̣είδην τὸν
υἱὸν ι̣ σπό(ρος) (πυρῶι) ε ἀρά(κωι) γ φα(κῶι) β, γεωργὸ[ς] αὐ(τός)
γίνονται τ̣ῆ̣ς̣ ἐπὶ τοῦ ἀδελφοῦ υκη∠d́ή (ὧν) σπο(ρίμου)

Col. III

. . . .

]. .ε. .δ[. .]δια[. .]. . . .[
] ἀ̣ρά(κωι) ε φα(κῶι) ε, (γίνονται) . . , ἀσπόρ[ο]υ κε
]εω̣[. . . .] μ̣ετεπιγεγρ(αμμένας) Πρωτάρχωι
ἀπὸ] τ̣[ῶ]ν (πρότερον) . . ν (ὧν ?) (πυρῶι) κε κ̣ρ̣ι̣(θῆι) ιε ἀρά(κωι) ι,
γεω(ργὸς) Σενθεὺς
[Ἡλιοδώρου τ]οῦ Διονυσίου χέ(ρσου) ν
[Ἡλιοδώρου] τοῦ Μηνοδώρου χέ(ρσου) ν
[Χαιρήμονος] τοῦ Κρατείνου ἀσπό(ρου) κ
(γίνονται) (ἄρουραι ?)] τκ (ὧν) σπο(ρίμου) ρμε ἀσπό(ρου) νε χέ(ρσου) ρ
ἀβρό(χου) κ
[καὶ τῶν μεταβ]ε̣βη(κότων) ἐξ ἐφό(δων) τῶν ἐν τῶι λδ (ἔτει) καταμεμετρη-
(μένων)
[ ] κδ (ὧν) (πυρῶι) ιβ ἀρά(κωι) ιβ γεω(ργὸς) αὐ(τός)
[[καὶ ἐν τῶι λς (ἔτει)]. . . . . . .κδ. . .[ ]]
φα]σή(λωι) β χο(ρτο)νο(μῶν) ε, (γίνονται) ιβ, ἀσπό(ρου) ιβ,
γεω(ργὸς) αὐτός
[[[ ]]]
] ἀσπόρου ιβ, (γίνονται) κα(τοίκων) υβ
[ἐφόδων τῶν ἐν τῶι λδ (ἔτει)]
[Μενίσκο]υ̣ τ̣ο̣ῦ̣ Πτολεμαίου ὃν με(τειληφέναι)
[Πτολεμαῖον τὸν υἱὸν κδ (ὧν)] ἐμβρό(χου) ιβ, γεω(ργὸς) α̣ὐ̣τ̣ό̣ς̣
[καὶ τῆς διαμεμετρη(μένης) τοῖς δ]ι̣ὰ̣ Χο(μήνιος) ἐν τῶ̣ι̣ μ̣α̣ (ἔτει ?)
[(τριακονταρούρων) Ἁρυώτης Φαεῦτος οὗ τὸ λο(ιπὸν) τοῦ κλή(ρου) περὶ

Τ]εβτῦ(νιν) ε cπό(ροc) (πυρῶι) [γεω(ργὸc)
[(εἰκοσιαρούρων) γε]ω̣[ρ]γὸc Ὧροc Ἁρ .[
[ ] ε̣, γεω(ργὸc) Χελῶc Ϲ̣[ιcούχου
[ ] . . γεω(ργὸc) Κατῦτι[c
[ ] ἀρ̣ά̣(κωι) δ, γεω(ργὸc) . .[

. . . .

Col. IV

Φμέρcιc Ὥ[ρου οὗ τὸ λο(ιπὸν) τοῦ κ]λή(ρου) περὶ Τεβτῦ(νιν) ε (πυρῶι) γεωρ̣[γὸc
γίνονται (εἰκοσιαρούρων) ἀνδ(ρῶν) [ζ (ἄρουραι) ρι]ε̣, (γίνονται) ἱππεῦcι cπο(ρίμου) ρκ
[μ]αχίμοιc (ἑπταρούροιc)
Πορεγέβθιc Ἀπύγχιοc ϛ∠ (ὧν) (πυρῶι) γ∠ ἀρά(κωι) γ, γεω(ργὸc) αὐτόc
Ὥρωι Θοτορταίου ϛ̣∠ (ὧν) (πυρῶι) γ∠ ἀρά(κωι) γ, γεω(ργὸc) Πᾶcιc Παcίω(νοc)
Ὥρωι Ὥρου ϛ∠ (ὧν) (πυρῶι) δ ἀρά(κωι) β∠, γεω(ργὸc) Δημήτριοc
Ἁρχύψει Πετοcίρειοc ϛ∠ (ὧν) (πυρῶι) δ φα(κῶι) β∠, γεω(ργὸc) αὐ(τόc)
Ἁρθώνει Ἁρφαήcειοc ϛ∠ (ὧν) (πυρῶι) γ∠ φα(κῶι) γ, γεω(ργὸc) αὐ(τόc)
[ἐ]ν [κ]α(τοχῆ) Ἁρψή[θ]ει Κολλούθου ϛ∠ (ὧν) (πυρῶι) δ∠ [. . ( )] β, γεω(ργὸc) ⟦Ν̣ο̣υ̣μῆνιc⟧ \`Μαρρῆ(c) Πύρρου´
[ἐ]ν κ̣α(τοχῆ) Κανῶc Πετοcίριοc̣ ϛ∠ (ὧν) (πυρῶι) δ φα(κῶι) β∠, γεω(ργὸc) Μαρρῆc Πύρρου
Ἁρcύτμει Πετοcίρ[ι]οc ϛ∠ (ὧν) (πυρῶι) γ∠ ἀρά(κωι) γ, γεω(ργὸc) αὐτόc
Ὥρωι μι(κρῶι) Κολλούθο̣υ̣ ϛ∠ (ὧν) (πυρῶι) γ∠ ἀρά(κωι) γ, γεω(ργὸc) αὐτόc
Πετεcούχωι Τοθοή[ο]υc ϛ∠ (ὧν) (πυρῶι) γ∠ ἀρά(κωι) γ, γεω(ργὸc) Μαρρῆc
Ὥρωι Φαγώμιοc ϛ∠ (ὧν) (πυρῶι) γ∠ φα(κῶι) γ, γεω(ργὸc) Ἀπῦγχιc Πυρρίχου
Φατρεῖ Ὥρου ϛ∠ (ὧν) (πυρῶι) γ∠ ἀρά(κωι) γ, γεω(ργὸc) αὐ(τόc)
Μεcταcύτμει Ὥρου ϛ∠, (πυρῶι) δ ἀρά(κωι) β̣∠, γεω(ργὸc) αὐ(τόc)
Φαεὺc Cοκέωc ϛ∠, (πυρῶι) γ∠ ἀρά(κωι) γ, γεω(ργὸc) {αὐ(τὸc)} Ἀρτεμίδω(ροc) Τ̣α( )
Θοτεὺc Φολήμιοc ϛ∠ (πυρῶι) γ∠ ἀρά(κωι) γ, γεω(ργὸc) αὐ(τόc)
Ὥρωι Ἁρφαήcει[οc] ϛ∠, (πυρῶι) γ∠ φα(κῶι) γ, γεω(ργὸc) Ἀπῦγχιc Πυρρίχου
Ἁρμιῦcιc Cοκονώπιοc ϛ∠ (πυρῶι) δ ἀρά(κωι) β∠, γεω(ργὸc) Πνεφερῶc
Τεῶc Τεῶτοc ϛ∠, (πυρῶι) δ ἀρά(κωι) β∠, γεω(ργὸc) Παπνεβτῦ(νιc) Cοκέ(ωc)

Νεκ̣τενῖβις Ὥρου ϛ∠, (πυρῶι) γ∠ φα(κῶι) γ, γεω(ργὸς) αὐ(τός)
Κάςτωρ Πνεφερῶτ[ο]ς ϛ∠ (πυρῶι) γ∠ ἀρά(κωι) γ, γεω(ργὸς) Πινοῦπις
Ἀπῦγχις Ποώριος ϛ∠, (πυρῶι) γ∠ φα(κῶι) γ, γεω(ργὸς) Νεκτενῖβις Τα( )
Κολλούθης Ὥρου ϛ∠, (πυρῶι) γ∠ ἀρά(κωι) γ, γεω(ργὸς) αὐ(τός)

Col. V

Ὕλλος Πάιτο̣ς̣ ϛ∠, (πυρῶι) [
Πᾶςις μέ(γας) Καλατ̣ῦ̣τιος ϛ∠ [
Πᾶς̣ι̣ς̣ μ̣ι̣(κρὸς) Κ̣αλατύτιος ϛ̣∠ [(πυρῶι)] δ φα(κῶι) β∠, γεω(ργὸς) αὐ(τός)
Ἁρφαῆςις Ὥ̣ρ̣ου ϛ∠ [(πυρῶι)] γ φα(κῶι) γ∠, γεω(ργὸς) αὐ(τός)
Κολλούθει Πετοςίριος [ϛ∠, (πυρῶι)] γ∠ ἀρά(κωι) γ, γεω(ργὸς) αὐ(τός)
Ὀννώφρει Πετερμ[ούθιος ϛ∠,] (πυρῶι) δ ἀρά(κωι) β∠, γεω(ργὸς) Μεγχῆς
Ἀμοῦνι Πικάμιος [ϛ∠, (πυρῶι) γ]∠ ἀρά(κωι) γ, γεω(ργὸς) Ἕρμων
[Ἀ]μοῦνι Τεφνάχθ[ιος ϛ∠, (πυρῶι)] δ̣ ἀρά(κωι) β∠, γεω(ργὸς) Ἕρμων
γίνονται ἀνδ(ρῶν) λ (ἄρουραι) ρϞε
γίνονται τῆς ἐν τῶι μα (ἔτει) ἄρ[ουραι τιε]
καὶ τῆς ἐν τῶι μβ̣ (ἔτει) ὁμοίως (ἑπταρούροις) μαχίμ̣[ο]ις
Ἁρυώτει Ἁρ̣υώτου ϛ∠ ἀρά(κωι) κα(τανενεμημένωι), γεω(ργὸς) αὐτός
Χεῦρις Σοχ̣ώτου ϛ∠, [(πυρῶι) δ]∠ ἀρά(κωι) β, γεω(ργὸς) αὐ(τός)
ἐπις(κεφθεῖςαι) Ὥρωι Ὀρςενούφιος ϛ∠, (πυρῶι) γ∠ ἀρά(κωι) γ, γεω(ργὸς) αὐ(τός)
Πᾶςις Σοκονώπιος ϛ∠, (πυρῶι) γ ἀρ[ά(κωι) γ∠, γεω(ργὸς)] αὐ(τός)
γίνονται ἀνδ(ρῶν) δ ςπο(ρίμου) κϛ
γίνονται τοῖς διὰ Χομήνιος τμ[α]
καὶ ἐν τῶι μϛ (ἔτει) τοῖς ἐκ̣ τῆς Ἡρακλ[εί]δ̣ο̣υ μερίδος μετα-
κεκληρουχημένοις̣ ἀπὸ τῶ̣ν̣ πρ[οςλ]ημφθέντων
δι' Ὥρου καὶ Πεςούριος εἰς̣ τὴ̣ν̣ τ̣ῶ̣[ν μα]χί̣μ̣ων ςύνταξιν
οὓς καὶ γέγραφεν Πτολεμαῖος καὶ Ξένω̣ν̣ οἱ γραμματεῖς
τῶν [μ]α̣χίμων φέ[ρ]ειν ὑπὸ τὴν Χομή̣[νι]ος [λ]α̣α̣[ρ]χί̣α̣ν̣
Ὀννῶφρις [Μεςταςύτμιος ϛ∠
Ὥρου τοῦ Πα̣[ώπιος ϛ∠ γεω(ργὸς)] Ἀςκ̣λ̣ηπ̣ι̣(άδης ?)
Πτολεμαῖος [Σενθέως οὗ τὸ λο(ιπὸν) τοῦ κλή(ρου) περὶ]
Ἄρεως [κώμην γ γεω(ργὸς) Ὀ]ρ̣ςείους
Πεςύθει [Παχώτου ϛ∠] (ὧν) (πυρῶι) γ∠ φα(κῶι) γ, γ̣ε̣ω̣(ργὸς) Πετεςο̣ῦ(χος)
Μαρρεί(ους)
Π[αςῶς μέ(γας) Φανήςιος ϛ∠ (ὧν) δ].( ) β∠, γεω(ργὸς) αὐτός

Col. VI

[*Φθαῦς Πετεήςιος* ς∠

[*ʽΑρμιῦςις Πετεςούχ*]*ου* ς∠ (*ὧν* ?) (*πυρῶι*) [

[*Παςῶς μι*(*κρὸς*) *Φανήςιος*] ς∠ (*ὧν*) (*πυρῶι*) δ *ἀρά*(*κωι*) β̣∠, *γ*ε̣ω̣(*ργὸς*) [

[*Σοκονῶπις Πάςιτος* ς]∠ (*ὧν*) (*πυρῶι*) γ∠ *ἀρά*(*κωι*) γ, *γεω*(*ργὸς*) *αὐτός*

Παςῶς ᾿Ορςείους ς∠ (*πυρῶι* ?), *γεω*(*ργὸς*) *αὐτός*

Πετεςούχου τοῦ Πετεςούχου ς∠, (*πυρῶι*) δ *ἀρά*(*κωι*) β∠, *γεω*(*ργὸς*) *αὐ*[*τός*]

᾿Ορςῆς ʽΑροννήςιος ς∠ (*πυρῶι*), *γεω*(*ργὸς*) *αὐτός*

γίνονται ἀνδ(*ρῶν*) ιβ (*ἄρουραι*) οδ∠

καὶ τοῖς διὰ Πτολεμαίου τοῦ Πετενούπιος

Μαρρεῖ Παάπιος ς∠ (*πυρῶι* ?), *γ*ε̣ω̣(*ργὸς*) α̣ὐ̣*τός*

ʽΑροννῶφρις ῝Ωρου ς̣∠̣ (*πυρῶι* ?), *γ*ε̣[*ω*(*ργὸς*)] *αὐτός*

[.]α̣*λῆτος τοῦ Πάςιτος* ς∠, (*πυρῶι*) γ∠ *ἀρά*(*κωι*) γ, *γεω*(*ργὸς*) *Ψοςναῦς*

[± 12]*ύφιος* ς∠, (*πυρῶι*) δ *ἀρά*(*κωι*) β̣∠, *γεω*(*ργὸς*) *αὐ*(*τός*)

[*ʽΑρμάις Πατ*]*ορςείους* ς∠ (*πυρῶι*), *γεω*(*ργὸς*) *Πετεςοῦ*(*χος*) *Πακύρ*[*ιος*]

γ[*ίνο*]*νται* α̣ν̣[*δ*(*ρῶν*)] ε̣ (*ἄρουραι* ?) λβ∠ *μαχίμων ἀνδ*(*ρῶν*)

[*γίνο*]*νται τῆς ἐπὶ τοῦ βαςιλέως* ωϙη

[*ὥς*]*τ᾿ εἶναι κλη*(*ρουχικῆς*) (*ἄρουραι*) *᾿Αφνε*dίς́λβ́ *ςπο*(*ρίμου*)

(Seven cm. left blank)

31 *ʽΑρυώτου* 48 *Πετοςίριος* 81 (*πυρῶι*) δ: δ corrected 84 (*πυρῶι*) δ∠: δ corr. from γ 85 *Μαρρῆ*(*ς*) corr. from *αὐτός*

1 One expects *γίνονται τῆς ἐπὶ τοῦ πάππου* (*ἄρουραι*) ρδίς́λ́β́ (cf. **62**. 36), but it does not appear to have been written.

4–5 [*ἐν*] *κα*[*το*]*χῆ*: or perhaps [*ἐν*] *κα*[*το*]*χῆ*(*ι*), since the final η is raised. For the reading cf. ll. 24, 31, 34, 84, 85. See Lesquier, *Institutions militaires* 225 ff.

17–18 Like **62**. 59–61, this text treats Mikion's two sons as a single entity (cf. l. 21). Later documents give a separate entry for each.

17 [*οὗ*: so **62**. 61, for *ὧν*.

21 *ἀνδ*(*ρῶν*) β: counting Diodotos and Apollonios (17–18) as one person.

32 *ἀςπό*(*ρου*) ια: the total of entries for *ἐμβρόχου* in ll. 27 and 28; cf. 59 n.

36 After *φαςή*(*λωι*) a number alone may have been lost, or both a number and another crop.

37–8 In later texts *᾿Αςκληπιάδης Πτολεμαίου* is found in this position, but the erasure here is too thorough to permit verification of any reading. The reason for sponging out the lines is obscure; similar cancellations occur in 62 and 64 below. Cf. perhaps **1113**, in which three cleruchs unaccountably disappear from the lists for one year.

41 (*γίνονται*) *κατοίκων τοη*∠dή: the correct total of ll. 17–40, if one includes 24 arouras belonging to the promoted ephodos whose name was cancelled in l. 37. No figure was filled in after *ςπο*(*ρίμου*); cf. 51, 145.

48 *Μάρων τὸν καὶ Νεκ*τ̣ς̣*άφθιν*: for *Μάρων ὁ καὶ Νεκτςάφθις*. The same confusion of cases as in **62**. 110 and **84**. 115, 124–5.

51 Cf. 41 n.

54 *μετεπιγεγρ*(*αμμένας*): cf. Lesquier p. 189 with n. 2.

Πρωτάρχωι: the patronymic *Διονυσίου* is probably to be restored in the next line.

55 *ἀπὸ*] *τ*[*ῶ*]*ν* (*πρότερον*) seems inevitable, but the following traces cannot belong to more than two letters, of which the second has a descender suitable for rho, iota, or phi. Protarchos' land had previously been held by Chairemon son of Theon (**64**(a). 57), but the traces do not seem to fit an abbreviation of *Χαιρήμονος*. Still earlier the property had been farmed as Crown land by tenants who are listed in **73**. 8–14.

56 [*Ἡλιοδώρου τ*]*οῦ Διονυσίου*: 3 catoecic cavalrymen with the patronymic *Διονυσίου* received land in year 37 of Euergetes II: Apollonios, Protarchos, and Heliodoros. Of these Protarchos occurred in the previous entry, and Apollonios should have been listed still earlier, in the lost portion of the document.

59 *ἀσπό(ρου)*: it is striking that 'unsown' land is treated here as distinct from *χέρσου* and *ἀβρόχου*, which were likewise unsown. But it does not necessarily imply negligently uncultivated land as opposed to that which was left barren because of natural conditions; cf. 32 n., where water-logged property is listed as *ἀσπόρου*.

62 and 64 Cf. 37–8 n.

65 *υβ*: total of ll. 59–65. All 82 arouras held by promoted ephodoi are counted here despite the cancellation of ll. 62 and 64.

78 [*μ*]*αχίμοις* (*ἐπταρούροις*): usually *ἐπταρούροις μαχίμοις*.

92 *Ṭα*( ): not *Πα*( ); cf. 99, where the same abbreviation occurs.

112 *ἀρά(κωι) κα(τανενεμημένωι)*: cf. **1119**. 15 n.

114 *ἐπισ(κεφθεῖσαι)*: i.e., the information here given had been checked by survey.

137 *Πτολεμαίου τοῦ Πετενούπιος*: identical with the scribe mentioned above, l. 121 (*PPt* 2479), as is shown by e.g. **1110**. 215. The patronymic is not given elsewhere.

145 *'Αφνεdίςλβ*: cf. vol. I, p. 553.

For the omission of the figure after *σπο(ρίμου)*, cf. 41 n. The text it as stands most naturally means that all $1555\frac{11}{32}$ arouras were sown, but as this is not the case one should perhaps insert ⟨(*ὧν*)⟩ before *σπο(ρίμου)*.

1109. List of Holders of Temple and Cleruchic Land

P. Teb. 147(b) 28·5 × 12 cm. Before 119/118 B.C.

Two mutilated columns described as **147** were dated by the editors to 113/111 B.C. In fact the papyrus fragments come from separate rolls and refer to quite different years: fragment a (**1111**) cannot be earlier than the 3rd year of Soter II, 115/114, while the present document belongs to the preceding reign. Cf. lines 7, 12, and 13, where Philopator and Epiphanes are described respectively as grandfather and father of the king. The text moreover antedates **62** (119/118 B.C.), since line 1 books to one Peteimouthes a plot which in later texts is ascribed to his son Pnepheros.

The preserved text corresponds to **1110**. 30–52.

ἄλλου ἰβιῶνος διὰ Π̣ετειμούθου καὶ τῶ[ν ε

ἄλλου ἰβιῶνος διὰ Χ̣εύριος καὶ τῶν ἀδ[ελ(φῶν) ε

[γίνον]ται αἱ προκεί(μεναι) (ἄρουραι) κdή

[ὥστ' εἶναι] ἱερᾶς (ἄρουραι) Σϛα∠dή, (ὧν) ἀμ(πελώνων) κ, κα(ταλείπονται)

[Σοα∠dή]

[κληρο]υ̣χικῆϲ τῆϲ ὑπαρχούϲηϲ ἕω̣ϲ̣ [τοῦ . . (ἔτουϲ)
ὧν ἐϲτίν·
[τῆϲ] ἕωϲ τοῦ ιϛ (ἔτουϲ) ἐπὶ τοῦ πά[ππου τοῦ βαϲιλέωϲ]
[(ἑβδομηκονταρούρων) Ἀφθ]ονήτου τοῦ Ἑβδομίωνοϲ [ο (ὧν) ϲπό(ροϲ)
ἁλμυ(ρίδοϲ) κδ, γεω(ργο) Θῶνι[ϲ
[(τριακονταρούρων) χερϲεφ]ίππων
[Πα]νταύχου τοῦ Πανταύχο̣υ̣ [λδίϛʹλβʹ
[γίνοντ]α̣ι τῆϲ ἐπ̣ὶ τοῦ πάπ̣που [ρδίϛʹλβʹ]
[καὶ τῆ]ϲ ἐπὶ τοῦ πατρὸϲ (ὀγδοηκονταρούρων ?)
[Φιλο]ξένου τοῦ Καλλικράτο[υ ὃν με(τειληφέναι) Καλλικράτην]
τ̣ὸ̣ν υἱὸ̣ν̣ [π] (ὧν) ϲπ̣[ό(ροϲ)] (πυρῶι ?) [
[καὶ τ]ῶ̣ν εἰϲ τὴν [Θηβαΐδα ἀπὸ τῶν 'Δ ἀνδρῶν]
[Καλλ]ικράτου τοῦ Πτολεμαίου [ιϛ
[καὶ τ]ῶ̣ν μεταβεβη(κότων) εἰϲ τὴν κατοικ̣[ίαν ἐκ τῶν (τριακονταρούρων)
Φυλέωϲ]
[Δ]ιονυϲίου τοῦ Πυρρίχου ιηdή [(ὧν) ϲπό(ροϲ)
ἐμβρόχου δdή, γεω(ργὸϲ) αὐτόϲ
[γίνονται] κ̣[α]τοίκων

1 *Π̣ετειμούθου*: by the time of **62**. 24, this land was farmed by Pnepheros son of Peteimouthes and his brothers, who are no doubt this man's sons.

1 and 2 The restorations of the figures are correct unless there was an otherwise unattested change in the holdings of these ibis shrines between this text and later documents.

5 The number of arouras to be restored at the end of this line cannot be calculated because it is uncertain (a) whether this text postdates or antedates the transfer of cleruchs from Ibion Eikosipentarouron in Euergetes II's 50th year; and (b), how many machimoi this text included among those enrolled by Ptolemaios and Xenon.

7 ἕωϲ τοῦ ιϛ (ἔτουϲ): cf. **1114**. 9, τῆϲ ἐν τῶι ιϛ (ἔτει). The year of this land assignment was not previously known. Year 16 of Philopator is 207/206 B.C.

9 γεω(ργο) Θῶνι[ϲ: perhaps simply γεω(ργὸϲ) Θῶνι[ϲ, possibly followed by a patronymic. But **62**. 33 suggests γεω(ργοὶ) Θῶνι[ϲ καὶ Ἀνεμπεύϲ].

13 (ὀγδοηκονταρούρων?): the symbols for 80 and for aroura appear here in the reverse of their usual order (ὦπ instead of πῶ).

21 [γίνονται] κ̣[α]τοίκων: if the figure (114⅜ arouras) was filled in, it was separated from κ̣[α]τοίκων by more than 3 cm., since that much space is left blank before the papyrus breaks off on the right.

1110. List of Holders of Temple and Cleruchic Land

P. Teb. 141 recto 140 × 32 cm. 116/115 B.C

This long papyrus duplicates most of the information in **63**, and is written in the same hand as that text. The variant readings from **63** which it presents are sufficiently numerous and interesting to justify a full transcript here. These variants are sometimes of such a nature as to preclude the possibility that either text was copied from the other, for both **1110** and **63** contain information that could not be derived directly from the other document: lines 22, 31, 115, and 116 state details omitted from the corresponding sections of **63**; while **63**. 34, 81–2 and 99 add data not found in **1110**. The texts further contain notable differences in matters of fact or of wording: cf. notes to lines 10, 14 and 15, 28, 32, 50, 52, 58, 89, 96, 99, 112, 128, 130–1, 151, 175, and 230. To these passages some scores of purely verbal differences could be added. Apparently **63** and **1110** represent not so much copies as independent recensions of basically the same material. Cf. further line 36 note.

The text notes below offer only a partial collation of the two papyri: variations in the method of abbreviating certain words (e.g., *φα(κῶι)* vs. *φακ(ῶι)*, *ἐμ(βρόχου)* vs. *ἐμβρό(χου)*) are normally passed by without comment, as are some details of spelling.

The verso was used for **1103**. The difficulties in the way of decipherment described in the introduction to that text apply to a lesser degree here, as the recto side of the papyrus is better preserved: and most of the lacunae can be filled from **63** or from **64**(a).

Lines 1–8 have been published with photograph in *CE* 46. 91 (1971), 113 ff.

Col. I

Ἔτους β, παρὰ Μεγχείου[ς κωμογραμματέ]ῳς
Κερκεοσίρεως. κατὰ φ[ύλλον ἱερᾶς καὶ κλη]ρ̣[ουχ]ικῆς
καὶ τῆς ἄλλης τῆς ἐ[ν ἀφέσει τοῦ αὐτοῦ] (ἔτους).
ἱερᾶς γῆς (πρώτων) ἱε[ρῶν]
Σούχου θεοῦ μεγ[άλου μεγάλου ἐμβρόχο]υ ρμα∠
[ὧν ἐστίν·]
Πετ[ενεφιγῆς Πετενεφιείους] κε
Ὧ[ρος Ἁρσιγήσιος καὶ οἱ μέ(τοχοι) ι]ε
[Ἀπολλώνιος Ποσειδωνίου] ν
[Χαιρήμων Ἀσκληπιάδου τὴν (πρότερον) Σ]αραπίωνος [λ]
Π̣[ετειμούθης Πετεσούχου ι]
Π̣[ετεσοῦχος Πετεσούχου] ϛ̣
Πετερμοῦθις [Πε]τ̣εήσιος [γ]
Μαρρῆς Ψοσναῦτος ἀπὸ τῆς (πρότερον) [Πετεσούχου β καὶ]

ἀπὸ τῆϲ (πρότερον) Πετειμούθου ∠, (γίνονται) β∠. (γίνονται) ἐμβρό(χου)
ρμα∠
Ϲοκνεβτύνει⟨οϲ⟩ θεοῦ μεγάλου μẹ[γάλ]ου διὰ τῶν
ἱερείων κοινεῖ ἀπὸ τῆϲ ἀν[ι]ερωμένηϲ ὑπὸ
τῶν προϲλημφθέντων δ[ι]ạ̀ Χομήνị[ο]ϲ̣
ἱππεῦϲι καὶ (ἑπταρούρων) μαχί(μων) ἐν τῶ[ι] μα (ἔτει) ρ̣, καὶ
ἐν τῶι μβ (ἔτει) λ, (γίνονται) ρλ̣ (ὧν) (πυρῶι) πε φα(κῶι) θ
φαςή(λωι) κε ἀρά(κωι) ϛ, (γίνονται) ρλ, γ[εω(ργοὶ) Πετοςῖριϲ Ἁρ]κοίφιοϲ
καὶ Πετενοῦπιϲ κạ̣ὶ Χαλ̣[. . .]τηϲ καὶ οἱ μέ(τοχοι)
γίνονται (πρώτων) ἱερῶν (ἄρουραι) [Ϲ]οα∠
ἐλαϲϲόνων ἱερῶν τῶν ἐ[ν] τῆι κώ(μηι) θεῶν
Πετεϲούχου θεοῦ κροκο(δείλου) τ[ῆ]ϲ κώμηϲ
διὰ Μαρρείουϲ καὶ τῶν με(τόχων) ἀϲπόρου εd́ή
Ὀρϲενοῦφιϲ θεοῦ με(γάλου) δι' Ὀρϲενούφιοϲ καὶ τῶν
μετόχων ἐμβρόχου α
ἰβίων τρο(φῆϲ) δι' Ἑργέωϲ καὶ τῶν με(τόχων) ἐμβρόχου δ
ἄλλου διὰ Χεύριοϲ καὶ τῶν ἀδελ(φῶν) ⟦ἀϲπόρου⟧ ε
ἄλλου διὰ Πνεφερῶτοϲ τοῦ Πετειμούθου
καὶ τῶν ἀδελ(φῶν) ἐμβρόχου ε
(γίνονται) ἐλαϲϲόνων κdή

Col. II

ὥϲτ' εἶναι τῆϲ ἱερᾶϲ (ἄρουραι) Ϲϙα∠dή
κληρουχικῆϲ τῆϲ ὑπαρχούϲηϲ ἕωϲ τοῦ α (ἔτουϲ)
τῆϲ ἐπὶ τοῦ `πρ[ο]΄πάππου τοῦ βαϲιλέωϲ
(ἑβδομηκονταρούρων) Ἀφθονήτου τοῦ Ἑβδομίωνοϲ ο (ὧν) (πυρῶι) κ
ἀρά(κωι) λ, (γίνονται) ν, ὑπολό(γου) ἁλμυ(ρίδοϲ) κ, γεω(ργὸϲ) Πετερμοῦθιϲ
(τριακονταρούρων) χερϲεφίππων
Πανταύχου τοῦ Πανταύχου χέ(ρϲου) λδίςλβ
(γίνονται) τῆϲ ἐπὶ τοῦ `πρ[ο]΄πάππου ρδίςλβ
[καὶ τῆϲ ἐπὶ τοῦ πάππου] τ̣ο̣ῦ̣ β̣[αϲιλέω]ϲ, τῶν
[δι' Ἑρμαφίλ]ου
[(ὀγδοηκονταρούρων) Καλλ]ικράτηϲ Φιλοξένου π [(ὧν) (πυρῶι) κ]
ἀρά(κωι) ε φαςή(λωι) ιε κρι(θῆι) ε, (γίνονται) με, ὑπολό(γου)
ἐμ(βρόχου) λ⟨ε⟩, γεω(ργοὶ) Ὧρ[οϲ] καὶ

Πετερμοῦθιϲ
καὶ τῶν ἀναζευξάντων εἰϲ τὴν Θηβαί(δα) ἀπὸ τῶν 'Δ ἀνδ(ρῶν)
Καλλικράτηϲ Πτολεμαίου ἐμβρόχου ιϛ
καὶ τῶν μεταβεβη(κότων) εἰϲ τὴν κα(τοικίαν) ἐκ τῶν (τριακονταρούρων)
Φυλέωϲ
Διονυϲίου τοῦ Πυρρίχου ιηdή (ὧν) (πυρῶι) ϛ φα(κῶι) γ φαϲή(λωι) δ
(γίνονται) ιγ, ἐμβρό(χου) εdή, γεω(ργὸϲ) 'Ανεμπεύϲ
γίνονται κατοίκων ριδdή
ἐρη(μο)φυ(λάκων) Ἡρακλείδου τοῦ Ϲιλανίωνοϲ ι ϲπό(ροϲ) φακῶι, γεω(ργὸϲ)
'Οννῶφριϲ
γίνονται τῆϲ ἐπὶ τοῦ πάππου (ἄρουραι) ρκδdή
καὶ τῆϲ ἐπὶ τοῦ {ἐπὶ τοῦ} ἀδελ(φοῦ) τοῦ πατρὸϲ̣ τοῦ βα(ϲιλέωϲ), ϲυγγε(νῶν)
κα(τοίκων) ἱπ(πέων)
Διοδότου τοῦ Μικ[ί]ωνοϲ οὗ τὸ λ̣ο̣(ιπὸν) τοῦ κλ(ήρου)
περὶ ἄλλαϲ κώ(μαϲ) ἀβρόχου εdήιϛ
'Απολλωνίου τοῦ Μικίωνοϲ οὗ τὸ λο(ιπὸν) τοῦ κλ(ήρου)
περὶ τὸν 'Ιβιῶ(να) τῶν (εἰκοϲιπενταρούρων) ἀβρόχου εdήιϛ
Λυϲιμάχωι Πύρρου οὗ τὸ λο(ιπὸν) τοῦ κλ(ήρου) περὶ τὸν
'Ιβιῶ(να) τῶν (εἰκοϲιπενταρούρων) μ (ὧν) (πυρῶι) ιε ἀρά(κωι) ιε,
(γίνονται) λ,
ἐμβρό(χου) ι, γεω(ργὸϲ) Μαρρῆϲ

Col. III

γ[ίνονται ἀνδ(ρῶν)] γ̄ (ἄρουραι) ν∠dή
κ[α]ὶ τῶ̣ν̣ [ἐν τῶι λ]α̣ (ἔτει) διὰ Διονυϲίου εἰϲ τοὺϲ κα(τοίκουϲ) ἱπ(πεῖϲ)
Διοδότου τοῦ 'Α[πο]λλωνίου μ (ὧν) (πυρῶι) ιε φα(κῶι) ε, (γίνονται) κ,
ἐμβρό(χου) κ, [γεω(ργὸϲ)] Ὧροϲ Ὥρου
Λέοντοϲ τοῦ Λεοντίϲκου μ (ὧν) (πυρῶι) ιε ἀρά(κωι) ι, (γίνονται) κε,
ἐμβρό(χου) ι[ε], γ̣ε̣ω̣(ργὸϲ) αὐ(τόϲ)
'Αμμωνίου τ[οῦ] 'Απολλωνίου ὃν με(τειληφέναι)
'Αμμώνιο[ν] τὸν υἱὸν μ (ὧν) (πυρῶι) ιε φα(κῶι) ε ἀρά(κωι) ε,
(γίνονται) κε
ἐμβρόχου [ι]ε̣, γ̣ε̣ω̣(ργὸϲ) αὐ(τόϲ)
Δώρου τοῦ [Πετάλου μ]
[Βρομεροῦ τοῦ Ζηνοδώρου μ (ὧν) (πυρῶι) ιε ἀρά(κωι)] ε φαϲή(λωι) ε

[τή(λει) ε, (γίνονται) λ, ἐμβρό(χου) ι, γεω(ργὸϲ) Φαῆϲιϲ
Πετ]ο̣ϲί[ριοϲ]
(γίνονται) [ἀνδ(ρῶν) ε̄ (ἄρουραι) Σ]
καὶ τῆϲ ἐν̣ [τ]ῶι λδ (ἔτει)
Ἀπολλοδώ̣[ρο]υ̣ τοῦ Πτολεμαίου ξ (ὧν) (πυρῶι) κε ἀρά(κωι) ε
φαϲή(λωι) ι, (γίνονται) μ, [ἐμ]β̣ρ̣ό̣(χου) κ, γεω(ργὸϲ) Ἀθεμμε̣ύ̣ϲ
καὶ τῶν με[τα]βεβη(κότων) εἰϲ τὴν κα(τοικίαν) ἐξ ἐφόδων
Ἀπολλων[ίου τοῦ] Πτολεμαίου ὃν με(τειληφέναι)
Πτολ[εμ]αῖον τὸν υἱὸν ἀϲπόρου κδ
Ἀϲκληπ[ιάδ]ου τοῦ̣ Πτολεμαίου ἀϲπόρου κδ
(γίνονται) ἀνδ(ρῶν) β̄ (ἄρουραι) μη
καὶ ἐκ τῶ[ν] ἐρημοφυλάκων
Ἀρταβά[ζα] τ̣ο̣ῦ̣ Πανταύχου ἀϲπόρου ι
Πτολε[μαίου τοῦ] Ἀπολλωνίου ἀϲπόρου ι
(γίνονται) ἀνδ(ρῶν) β̄ (ἄρουραι) κ
γίνονται [κα]τ̣οίκων (ἄρουραι) τ⟦κη⟧ \`οη∠dή´
ἐρη(μο)φυλάκ̣ων τῶν ἐν τῶι λβ (ἔτει)
Πτολεμ̣[αίο]υ τοῦ Σαραπίωνοϲ ἐμ(βρόχου) ι
Λάγου τ[οῦ] Διοδώρου ἀϲπόρου ι

Col. IV

φυλακιτῶν τῶν ἐν τῶι λγ (ἔτει)
Ἀκουϲιλάου τοῦ Ἀπολλωνίου ι (ὧν) (πυρῶι) γ φαϲή(λωι) δ,
(γίνονται) ζ, ἐ̣μ(βρόχου) γ
γεω(ργὸϲ) αὐ(τόϲ)
Ἡρακλείδου τοῦ Ἐφθεμούνιοϲ ι (ὧν) (πυροῦ) δ ἀρά(κωι) γ, (γίνονται) ζ,
ἐμβρό(χου) γ, γεω(ργὸϲ) Πετεϲοῦχοϲ
(γίνονται) ἀνδ(ρῶν) β̄ (ἄρουραι) κ
γίνονται τῆϲ ἐπὶ τοῦ πάππου υκη∠dή
καὶ τῆϲ ἐπὶ τοῦ πατρὸϲ τοῦ βαϲιλέωϲ, τοῖϲ
προϲειλημμένοιϲ εἰϲ τοὺϲ διὰ Κρίτωνοϲ
κατοίκουϲ ἱππεῖϲ ἐν τῶι λζ (ἔτει)
Ἀκουϲιλάου τοῦ Ἀϲκληπιάδ̣ου ἐμβρόχου λ
Βακχίωι Μουϲαίου κ (ὧν) (πυρῶι) ιβ φαϲή(λωι) γ, (γίνονται) ιε
ἐμβρό(χου) ε, γεω(ργὸϲ) Ἰλῶϲ

Ἀπολλωνίου τοῦ Διονυςίου ἀςπόρου ν
Πρώταρχος Διονυςίου ν (ὧν) (πυρῶι) κ ἀρά(κωι) ε φαςή(λωι) ε,
(γίνονται) λ, ἐμβρό(χου) κ, γεω(ργοὶ) Μαρεμῆνις καὶ οἱ μέ(τοχοι)
Πολέμων Ἀμμωνίου̣ ἀςπόρου κ
Ἀθηνίων Ἀρχίου μ (ὧν) (πυρῶι) ιε φαςή(λωι) ι, (γίνονται) κε
ἐμβρόχου ιε, γεω(ργὸς) Πετεῦρις
Ἡρώδης Ἡλιοδώρου ἀπὸ τοῦ (πρότερον) Ἡλιοδώρου
τοῦ Διονυςίου χέρςου μ
Ἡφαιςτίων Στρατονίκου χέ(ρςου) ι
Λεπτίνης Στρατονίκου χέρςου κε
Μελάνιππος Ἀςκληπιάδου ἀπὸ τοῦ (πρότερον)
Πολέμωνος τοῦ Ἀμμωνίου ι ςπό(ρος) (πυρῶι), γεω(ργὸς) ι
(γίνονται) ἀνδ(ρῶν) ι (ἄρουραι) Σϛε
καὶ τῶν μεταβεβη(κότων) εἰς τὴν κα(τοικίαν) ἐξ ἐφόδων, τῶν
ἐν τῶι λδ (ἔτει) καταμεμετρημένων
Δημητρίου τοῦ Ἡρακλείδου ἀςπόρου ιβ
Ταυρίςκου τοῦ Ἀπολλωνίου ἀπὸ τοῦ (πρότερον)
Δημητρίου τοῦ Ἡρακλείδου ἀςπόρου ιβ

Col. V

Ἀςκληπιάδου τοῦ Ἀςκληπιάδου κ[δ, καὶ]
ἀπὸ τοῦ (πρότερον) Πολέμωνος τοῦ Ἀμμω̣ν̣ί̣ο̣υ̣ ι̣, (γίνονται ?) [λδ (ὧν)]
ςπό(ρος) (πυρῶι) ιδ φαςή(λωι) ι, (γίνονται) κδ, ἐμβρό(χου) ι,
γεω(ργὸς) αὐ(τός)
Ἀκουςίλα⟨ο⟩ς Ἀςκληπιάδου ἀςπόρου ι
(γίνονται) ἀνδ(ρῶν) ι (ἄρουραι) [ ]
καὶ τῶν παρακεχωρημένων εἰς τὸ β (ἔτος) ὑπὸ τῶν ἐ̣[κ τοῦ]
ἱππικοῦ λογι(στηρίου) κατὰ τὸν παρ' Ὀννώφριος τοῦ τοπογρα(μματέως)
χρη(ματισμὸν) οὗ χρό(νος) (ἔτους) β Τῦβι κη Διδυμάρχωι Ἀπολλων̣[ίου]
τὸν (πρότερον) Πέτρων⟨ος⟩ τοῦ Θέωνος ἐφό(δου) μεταβεβη(κότος)
ἀςπόρου [κδ]
καὶ ἐκ τ[ῶν φυλακι]τῶν [τῶν ἐ]ν̣ τ̣ῶι [λγ (ἔτει)]
Μάρω̣ν̣ος τ[οῦ Διονυςίου] ἀςπόρου [κε]
γίνονται κατοίκω[ν (ἄρουραι) υιβ]
ἐφόδων τῶν ἐν τῷ̣ι λδ̣ (ἔτει ?)

Πτολεμαίου τοῦ Μενίϲκου [ἐ]μ̣β̣ρ̣[ό(χου) κδ]
Ἀπολλωνίου τοῦ Πτολεμαίου κδ (ὧν) [(πυρῶι) ιβ φαϲή(λωι) γ, (γίνονται) ιε]
ἐμβρό(χου) θ, γεω(ργὸϲ) αὐ(τόϲ)
(γίνονται) ἀνδ(ρῶν) β̄ (ἄρουραι) κ
καὶ τῆϲ καταμεμετρημένηϲ τοῖϲ [δι]ὰ̣ Χομήνιοϲ
ἐν τῶι μα (ἔτει) ἱππεῦϲι καὶ (ἑπταρούροιϲ) μ[α]χ̣ί̣μ̣ο̣ι̣ϲ̣
(τριακονταρούρων) Ἁρυώτηϲ Φαεῦτοϲ οὗ τὸ λο(ιπὸν) τ[οῦ κλ(ήρου)] π̣ερὶ
Τεβτῦ(νιν) ε ϲπό(ροϲ) (πυρῶι), γεω(ργὸϲ) α[ὐτόϲ]
(εἰκοϲιαρούρων) Πετεῆϲιϲ Πάϲιτοϲ ιθ (ὧν) (πυρῶι) ι φ[αϲή(λωι) ϛ
φα(κῶι) γ, γεω(ργὸϲ) αὐ(τόϲ)
Ἁρμιῦϲιϲ Πτολεμαίου ἀϲπόρου ιθ
Ἀκριϲίωι Ἀκριϲίου ὃν με(τειληφέναι) Χομῆνιν τ[ὸ]ν̣ υἱὸν ιθ,
(πυρῶι) ι φα(κῶι) γ φαϲή(λωι) ϛ, γεω(ργὸϲ) αὐ(τόϲ)
Κεφαλᾶϲ Πετεϲούχου ἀϲπόρου [ιθ]
Τεῶϲ Τεῶτοϲ οὗ τὸ λο(ιπὸν) τοῦ κλ(ήρου) περὶ Τ[εβτῦ(νιν)] ιε,
(πυρῶι) ζ∠ φαϲή(λωι) ζ∠, γεω(ργὸϲ) αὐ(τόϲ)
Φμέρϲιϲ Ὥρου οὗ τὸ λο(ιπὸν) τοῦ κλ(ήρου) περὶ Τε[βτῦ(νιν)] ε
ϲπό(ροϲ) (πυρῶι), γεω(ργὸϲ) α̣ὐ(τόϲ)
Ἁρμιῦϲιϲ Φατρήουϲ ἀϲπόρου ιθ
(γίνονται) ἀνδ(ρῶν) η (ἄρουραι) ρκ

Col. VI

(ἑπταρούρων) μαχίμων
Π̣ορεγέβθιϲ Ἀπύγχιο̣ϲ̣ ϛ̣∠ (ὧν) (πυρῶι) δ∠ φα(κῶι) β, γεω(ργὸϲ) αὐ(τόϲ)
Ὧ̣ροϲ Ὥρου [ϛ∠] (ὧν) (πυρῶι) γ∠ φα(κῶι) α∠ φαϲή(λωι) α∠, γεω(ργὸϲ)
αὐ(τόϲ)
[Ὧ]ροϲ Θοτορταίου ϛ̣∠ (ὧν) (πυρῶι) δ∠ φα(κῶι) β, γεω(ργὸϲ) αὐ(τόϲ)
Ἁ̣ρχῦψιϲ Πετοϲίριοϲ ϛ∠ (ὧν) (πυρῶι) δ∠ ἀρά(κωι) β, γεω(ργὸϲ) αὐ(τόϲ)
Ἁ̣ρθῶνιϲ Ἁρφαήϲιοϲ ϛ∠ (ὧν) (πυρῶι) δ∠ φαϲή(λωι) β, γεω(ργὸϲ) αὐ(τόϲ)
Κανῶϲ Πετοϲίριοϲ ϛ∠ ἀϲπόρου
Ἁρϲῦτμιϲ Πετοϲίριοϲ ϛ∠ ἀϲπόρου
Ὧροϲ μι(κρὸϲ) Κολλούθου ϛ∠ ἀ̣ϲ̣π̣ό̣ρ̣ο̣υ̣
Ἁρψῆθιϲ Κολλούθου ϛ∠ (ὧν) (πυρῶι) γ∠ [ἀρά(κωι) β φα(κῶι) α, γεω(ργὸϲ)
αὐ(τόϲ)]
[Πετεϲοῦχοϲ Τοθο]ήουϲ ϛ̣∠̣ ϲπό(ροϲ) (πυρῶι), γεω(ργὸϲ) α[ὐ(τόϲ)]

[Ὧρος Φαγώμιος] ς∠ (ὧν) (πυρῶι) γ∠ φασή(λωι) γ, γεω(ργὸς) [αὐ(τός)]
Φ̣ατρῆ[ς] Ὥ̣ρου ς∠ (ὧν) (πυρῶι) γ∠ ἀρά(κωι) γ, γ[ε]ω(ργὸς) [αὐ(τός)]
Μεςταςῦτμις Ὥρ[ο]υ ς∠ ςπό(ρος) (πυρῶι), γεω(ργὸς) [αὐ(τός)]
Φαεὺς Σοκέως ς∠ (ὧν) (πυρῶι) γ∠ φα(κῶι) γ, γεω(ργὸς) αὐ(τός)
Θοτεὺς Φολήμιος ς∠ (ὧν) ⟨(πυρῶι)⟩ γ∠ φασή(λωι) γ, γεω(ργὸς) αὐ(τός)
Ὧρος Ἁρφαήςιος ς∠ ἀςπόρου
Ἁρμιῦςις Σοκονώπιος ς̣∠̣ (ὧν) (πυρῶι) [γ]∠ τή(λει) γ, γεω(ργὸς) αὐ(τός)
Τεῶς Τεῶτος ς∠ ςπό(ρος) φαςήλωι, γεω(ργὸς) αὐ(τός)
Πᾶςις μι(κρὸς) Καλατύτιος ς∠ (ὧν) φα(κῶι) β φαςή(λωι) δ∠, γεω(ργὸς) αὐ(τός)
Νεκτενῖβι⟨ς⟩ Ὥρου ς∠ (ὧν) (πυρῶι) δ ἀρά(κωι) β∠, γεω(ργὸς) αὐ(τός)
Φολῆμις Νεκτενίβιος ς∠ (ὧν) φα(κῶι) β∠ ἀρά(κωι) β φαςή(λωι) β, γεω(ργὸς) αὐ(τός)
Ἀπῦγχις Ποώριος ς∠ ἀςπ[ό]ρου
Κολλούθης Ὥρου ς∠ ἀ̣[ςπόρο]υ
Ὕλλος Πάιτος ς∠ (ὧν) (πυρῶι) γ[∠ ἀ]ρά(κωι) γ, γεω(ργὸς) αὐ(τός)
Πᾶςις μέ(γας) Καλατύτιος ς∠ ςπό(ρος) μελανθε(ίωι), γεω(ργὸς) αὐ(τός)
Ἁρφαῆςις Ὥρου ς∠ ἀςπόρου
Κολλούθης Πετοςίριος ς∠ ςπό(ρος) [(πυρῶι) δ]∠̣ ἀρά(κωι) β, γεω(ργὸς) αὐ(τός)
Ὀννῶφρις Πετερμούθιος ς∠ [ςπό(ρος)] φακῶι, γεω(ργὸς) αὐ(τός)
Ἀμοῦνις Πικάμιος ς∠ (ὧν ?) [(πυρῶι) γ]∠ φαςή(λωι) γ, γεω(ργὸς) αὐ(τός)
Ἀμοῦνις Τεφνάχθιος ς∠ (ὧν ?) [(πυρῶι) γ]∠ φα(κῶι) γ, γεω(ργὸς) αὐ(τός)
(γίνονται) ἀνδ(ρῶν) λ (ἄρουραι) ρϙε

Col. VII

γίν[ον]τ̣α̣ι̣ τῆς ἐν [τῶι μα (ἔτει) (ἄρουραι) τιε]
καὶ τῆς ἐν τῶ[ι] μ̣β̣ (ἔτει)
Ἁρυώτης [Ἁ]ρ̣[υώτ]ο̣υ [ς∠ ςπό(ρος) (πυρῶι), γεω(ργὸς) α]ὐ̣(τός)
Χεῦρις Σοχώτου [ς∠ (ὧν) . . ( ) δ∠ φα(κῶι) β, γεω(ργὸς) αὐτό]ς
Ὧρος Ὀρςενούφιος [ς∠ (ὧν) . . ( ) . ἀρά(κωι) . ∠,] γεω(ργὸς) αὐ(τός)
Πᾶςις Σοκονώπιος [ς∠ (ὧν) . . ( ) γ∠ . . α̣( ) γ, γεω(ργὸς) αὐ(τός)]
(γίνονται) ἀνδ(ρῶν) δ (ἄρουραι ?) κ̣ς̣
γ̣ί̣νονται τοῖς διὰ Χομήνι[ος (ἄρουραι) τμα]

[καὶ τ]ῆc ἐν τῶι μϛ (ἔτει) τ[οῖc ἐκ τῆc]
[Ἡρα(κλείδου) με(ρίδοc) μετακεκληρ]ο̣υ̣χημέν[οιc ἀπὸ τῶν (πρότερον) δι' Ὥρου καὶ]
[Πεcούριοc προcλημφθέντων εἰc τὴν]
[τῶν μαχίμων cύνταξιν, οὓc καὶ γέγραφεν Πτολεμαῖοc καὶ]
Ξένων οἱ γραμματεῖc [τῶν μαχίμων φέρειν ὑπὸ τὴν]
Χομήνιοc λααρχίαν (ἑπταρούρων) [μαχίμων]
Ὀννῶφριc Μεcταcύτ[μιοc] ϛ∠ (ὧν) ἀρ[ά(κωι)] γ∠ φα(κῶι) γ, γεω(ργὸc) αὐ(τόc)
Πτολεμαῖ[οc Cενθέωc οὗ τὸ λο(ιπὸν) τοῦ κλ(ήρου) περὶ] Ἄρε(ωc) κώ(μην) γ c̣π̣ό̣(ροc) (πυρῶι), γεω(ργὸc) αὐ(τόc)
Ὧροc [Παώπιοc ϛ]∠ cπό(ροc) (πυρῶι), γεω(ργὸc) αὐ(τόc)
Πεcύθηc Πα̣χ̣ῶτοc ϛ̣∠̣ (ὧν ?) (πυρῶι ?) γ∠ φαcή(λωι) γ, γεω(ργὸc) αὐ(τόc)
Cοκονῶπιc [Πάcιτοc ϛ∠] (ὧν) (πυρῶι) β∠ φα(κῶι) β ἀρά(κωι) β, γεω(ργὸc) αὐ(τόc)
Παcῶc μι(κρὸc) Φα̣ν̣[ήc]ι̣οc [ϛ∠ (ὧν) φα(κῶι) α φαcή(λωι) ε∠, γεω(ργὸc) αὐ(τόc)
Παcῶc Ὀρcείουc ϛ∠̣ (ὧν) (πυρῶι) β∠ φα(κῶι) α∠ φαcή(λωι) α∠, γεω(ργὸc) αὐ(τόc)
Ὀρcῆc Ἁροννήcιοc ϛ∠̣ ἀcπόρου
Φθαῦc Πετεήcιοc [ϛ]∠ (ὧν) φα(κῶι) β ἀρά(κωι) β∠ φαcή(λωι) [β], γεω(ργὸc) αὐ(τόc)
Ἁρμι̣ῦcιc Πετεcούχου [ϛ]∠̣ cπό(ροc) (πυρῶι), γεω(ργὸc) αὐ(τόc)
Παcῶc μέ(γαc) Φανήcιοc [ϛ]∠ cπό(ροc) (πυρῶι), γεω(ργὸc) αὐ(τόc)
Πετεcοῦχοc Πετεcού[χου] ϛ∠ (ὧν) (πυρῶι) β φα(κῶι) β φαcή(λωι) β, γεω(ργὸc) αὐ(τόc)
(γίνονται) ἀνδ(ρῶν) ιβ (ἄρουραι) οδ∠
ὥcτ' εἶναι τῆc διὰ Χομήνιοc (ἄρουραι) υιε∠
καὶ τοῖc διὰ Πτολεμαίου καὶ Ξένωνοc
Μαρρῆc Παάπιοc ϛ∠ (ὧν) (πυρῶι) γ∠ φαcή(λωι) γ, γεω(ργὸc) αὐ(τόc)

Col. VIII

[Ἁ]ροννῶφριc Ὥρου ϛ∠
cπό(ροc) (πυρῶι) γ∠ ἀρά(κωι) β φαcή(λωι) α̣, γεω(ργὸc) αὐ(τόc)

ʽΑρμάις Πανορϲείουϲ ϛ∠
ϲπό(ροϲ) (πυρῶι) γ∠ φαϲή(λωι) γ, γεω(ργὸϲ) αὐ(τόϲ)
(γίνονται) ἀνδ(ρῶν) γ̄ (ἄρουραι) ιθ∠
καὶ τῆϲ ἐν τῶι να (ἔτει)
καταμεμετρη(μένηϲ) τοῖϲ δ[ιὰ] Χομή(νιοϲ)
ἀντὶ τῆϲ ἀνειλη(μμένηϲ) αὐτῶν
περὶ τὸν ʼΙβιῶ(να) τῶν (εἰκοϲιπενταρούρων)
Κόμων Πεχύϲιοϲ ϛ∠
ϲπό(ροϲ) (πυρῶι) γ∠ ἀρά(κωι) γ, γεω(ργὸϲ) αὐ(τόϲ)
Λαβόιϲ Φατρήουϲ ὃν με(τειληφέναι)
Κολλούθην τὸν ἀδελ(φὸν) ἀϲπόρου ϛ∠
Παῶπιϲ Πετεϲούχου [ϛ∠ ϲπό(ροϲ) (πυρῶι) β]
φα(κῶι) β φαϲή(λωι) β∠, γεω(ργὸϲ) αὐ(τόϲ)
ʽΑρψάλιϲ Cτεφάνου ϛ∠
(πυρῶι) γ∠ [χό(ρτωι)] γ, γεω(ργὸϲ) αὐ(τόϲ)
Ψενῆϲιϲ Cτεφάνου ϛ∠ ἀϲπόρου
(γίνονται) ἀνδ(ρῶν) ε (ἄρουραι) λβ∠
ὥϲτʼ εἶναι κλη(ρουχικῆϲ)

17 ἱερέων κοινῆι 19 ἱππέων 27 ʼΟρϲενούφιοϲ 50 γ corrected from β 164 γ∠: γ corrected from δ

3 τῆϲ ἄλληϲ τῆϲ: the editors of **63**. 3 wrongly restored [γῆ]ϲ at this point; see *CE* 46. 91 (1971), 113 ff.

7 Πετ[ενεφιγῆϲ for Πετενεφιῆϲ: so spelled in **63**. 7; cf. note ad loc. Similarly ʽΑρϲιγήϲιοϲ in the next line.

10 [Χαιρήμων ʼΑϲκληπιάδου τὴν (πρότερον) C]αραπίωνοϲ [λ]: cf. **63**. 10–11, Cαραπίων Cαραπίωνοϲ ἣν [read ὃν] με(τείληφε) Χαιρήμων ʼΑϲκληπιάδου λ.

14 and 15 (πρότερον): διά in **63**. 15 and 16.

16 Cοκνεβτύνει⟨οϲ⟩: spelled correctly in **63**. 18.

17 ἱερείων: other instances of short e represented by ει before ω are listed in Mayser I, pp. 72 f. Spelled correctly in **63**. 18.

κοινει: cf. **1118**. 176 note. Omitted from **63**.

19 ἱππεῦϲι for ἱππέων: so also **63**. 20.

(ἑπταρούρων) μαχί(μων): **63**. 20 shows that the expansions should be in the correct genitive rather than dative to correspond with ἱππεῦϲι.

20 Between (ὧν) and (πυρῶι) **63**. 21 inserts ϲπό(ροϲ): and so regularly throughout the rest of the text.

21 The order of the entries for φαϲή(λωι) and ἀρά(κωι) is reversed in **63**. 21. The entries total only 125 arouras in both texts. Possibly 5 arouras went unsown and were omitted.

22 κα̣ὶ̣ Χαλ̣[...]τηϲ: omitted from **63**. The man is not known elsewhere.

27 ʼΟρϲενοῦφιϲ for ʼΟρϲενούφιοϲ: spelled correctly in **63**. 27.

με(γάλου): omitted from **63**

28 ἐμβρόχου: ἀϲπόρου in **63**.. 27.

30 *ἄλλου*: masculine *ad sensum*, since *ἰβίων τροφή* = *ἰβιῶν*.

⟦*ἀςπόρου*⟧: not cancelled in **63**. 29. The scribe may have intended to replace this word with *ἐμβρόχου*, as was done in **1115**. 67.

31 *Πνεφερῶτος τοῦ Πετειμούθου*: the patronymic is not given in **63**.

32 *ἐμβρόχου*: *ἀςπόρου* in **63**. 30.

34 *ὥςτ' εἶναι*: corresponds in **63**. 31 to the stroke which is usually resolved (*γίνονται*); cf. note 52 below.

τῆς: not in **63**. *γῆς* cannot be read, even if it produced an acceptable word order.

36 *`πρ[ο]'πάππου*: the same superlinear correction was made in line 41 below. This strongly suggests that our text was modelled after a document dated in the preceding reign before news of the death of Euergetes II (28 June, 116 B.C.) had reached Menches' office.

38 *ἀρά(κωι)*: *ἀρά(κωι) κ̣α(τανενεμημένωι)*, **63**. 34.

44 *Καλλ]ικράτης*: **63**. 40 uses the genitive.

45 *ἐμ(βρόχου) λ⟨ε⟩*: *ἐμβρό(χου) λε*, **63**. 41.

50 *φαςή(λωι) δ*: **63**. 45 incorrectly reads 5 arouras here. Cf. note ad loc.

52 *γίνονται*: represented by a stroke in **63**. 47.

ριδdή: correct. **63**. 47 reads *ρ⟨ι⟩δdή*.

55 *γίνονται*: not in **63** as presently read, but probably to be restored as a stroke in line 50 of that text.

56 *καί*: regularly used to introduce new classes of land in this papyrus, but not in **63**.

ἱπ(πέων): not in **63**.

58 *περὶ ἄλλας κώ(μας)*: *περὶ τὸν Ἰβιῶ(να) τῶν (εἰκοςιπενταρούρων)* in **63**. 54.

61 *Λυςιμάχωι*: **63**. 57 uses the genitive.

63 *ἐμβρό(χου)*: **63**. 58 has *ὑπολό(γου) ἐμβρό(χου)*; so also in many passages.

85 *καὶ ἐκ τῶ[ν] ἐρημοφυλάκων*: [*ἐξ ἐρημοφυλάκ*]*ων*, **63**. 79.

86 *Ἀρταβά[ζα]*: this is the most common genitive of the name (cf. **1114**. 61; **1115**. 183), though *Ἀρταβάζου* is found in **64**(a). 33. The form *Ἀρτάβα* restored in **63**. 80 and **62**. 95 should be discarded.

87 *Πτολε[μαίου τοῦ] Ἀπολλωνίου*: **63**. 81–2 adds *ἀπ[ὸ τοῦ (πρότερον) Νεκτενίβιος τοῦ] Ὥρου*.

89 *τ*⟦*κη*⟧ *`οη∠dή'*: **63**. 83 has the correct figure only.

96 *Ἐφθεμούνιος*: *Ἐτφεμούν*[*ιος* in **63**. 91.

99 *πάππου*: a mistake for *ἀδελφοῦ τοῦ πατρός*, which **63**. 94 correctly reads.

104 *Βακχίωι*: genitive in **63**. 98.

105 *Ἰλῶς*: **63**. 99 (cf. *BASP* 7, 1970, p. 9) adds *Ὥρου*.

107 *Πρώταρχος*: genitive in **63**. 101.

109 *Πολέμων*: genitive in **63**. 103.

112 *Διονυςίου*: the correct reading. **63**. 107 wrongly has *Μηνοδώρου*; see note ad loc.

115 *χέρςου κε*: the figure was omitted in **63**. 109.

116 *Μελάνιππος*: genitive in **63**. 110.

116–17 *ἀπὸ κτλ.*: not in **63**.

117 *γεω(ργὸς) ι*: *sic*. *γεω(ργὸς) αὐ(τός)* **63**. 110.

128 *ι*: a mistake for δ, which **63**. 121 reads correctly. The number of arouras should be 68, but the error in the number of cleruchs suggests that the scribe may have wrongly copied the figures of line 118 instead.

130 *ἱππικοῦ*: confirms the expansion *ἱπ(πικοῦ?)* in **63**. 122.

λογι(ςτηρίου): expanded as *λογι(ςμοῦ)* in **63**. 122, but cf. Préaux, *L'éc. roy.* 474 n. 3.

130–1 *κατὰ τὸν παρ' Ὀννώφριος τοῦ τοπογρα(μματέως) χρη(ματιςμόν)*: cf. **63**. 123, [*κατὰ*] *χρη(ματις- μὸν) Ὀννώφριος τοῦ τοπογραμματέως*. See **30**.

132 *τόν*: *τοῦ* in **63**. 124. *τόν* is more precise, since the cession encompassed the whole of the kleros and not just a part of it.

Πέτρων⟨ος⟩: spelled correctly in **63**. 124.

μεταβεβη(κότος): **63**. 125 adds *εἰς τὴν κα(τοικίαν)*.

142 *μ[α]χ̣ί̣μ̣ο̣ι̣ς̣*: **63**. 135 wrongly reads *μαχίμων*.

151 *αὐ(τός)*: *Μαρρῆς* **63**. 144.

165 *Τοθο]ήους*: *Τοθοείους* **63**. 158.

175 *Νεκτενῖβι⟨c⟩*: more probably an accidental slip than an intentional dative in this long list of otherwise nominative names.

ἀρά(κωι): *φαcή(λωι)* **63**. 168.

179–86 In **63** the corresponding lines, 172–80, are lost or mutilated. They should be restored to follow the text here.

185 *Τεφνάχθιοc*: wrongly restored *Νεφνάχθει* in **63**. 178.

194 *τοῖc*: *τῆc* **63**. 187.

216 *Μαρρῆc*: dative in **63**. 211.

222 *να (ἔτει)*: so also **63**. 215 for the correct year 50; cf. **62**. 294 note.

228–9 *Λαβόιc Φατρήουc κτλ.*: this entry was at first omitted from **63**, then inserted in ll. 218–19.

229 *τὸν ἀδελ(φόν)*: since Kolluthes's patronymic was *Ὥρου* (cf. **1147**. 179–80; **84**. 20 = 205), *ἀδελφόc* here means 'half-brother'.

230 *Πετεcούχου*: so usually, but *Πετείουc* in **63**. 222 and **1124**. 1.

236 *ὥcτ' εἶναι κλη(ρουχικῆc)*: omitted from **63**. The figure was not filled in.

1111. List of Holders of Temple and Cleruchic Land

P. Teb. 147(a) 11 × 16 cm. 115/114 B.C.(?)

The mention of year 2 of Soter II (116/115 B.C.) in lines 4 and 8 of this text would be compatible with a date in that or a later year. Comparison with **63** = **1110** excludes year 2, leaving 115/114 as the earliest possible date. In all probability 115/114 (year 3) is precise: years 4 and 5 of the reign are represented by **1113** and **1114**, and it is on general grounds unlikely that the trivial changes in land-holding referred to in this papyrus would continue to be specified in a document of year 6 or later. Alternatively, one may suppose that **1111** comes from a duplicate of one of the following documents: the example of **63** and **1110** shows that the possibility of duplicates is a real one. But this is hardly necessary, as no feature of the text is inconsistent with a date in year 3.

1111 offers the only detailed treatment of Souchos's temple land apart from **63** = **1110** and **64**(a), all three from 116/115 B.C. Since that year, $8\frac{1}{2}$ arouras formerly under the charge of Petesouchos son of Petesouchos and his brother or son Peteimouthes had been recalled by the temple and redistributed. In the present text the new allocation of 8 arouras can be traced; the remaining $\frac{1}{2}$ will have been accounted for in a portion of the papyrus now lost. For details see notes. Restorations of names and figures not otherwise discussed are taken from **63**.

The editors of **147** wrongly described this text as belonging to the same roll as **1109**; see introd. there.

[Coύχου θεοῦ μεγάλου με]γ̣άλου (ἄρουραι) [ρμα∠]
[ὧν ἐcτί]ν̣
[Ὧροc Ἁρcιήcιοc καὶ οἱ μέ(τοχοι)] ι̣[ε χέ]ρ̣[cου, καὶ ἀπὸ] τ̣ῆc διὰ
Πετειμού[θο]υ
[τῆc ἀναλη(φθείcηc) ἐν τῶι] β (ἔτει) ἀπὸ (ἀρουρῶν) η∠ ε, (γίνονται) κ̣

[*Πετενεφιῆϲ*] *Πετενεφιείουϲ χέρϲου κε*
[*'Απολλωνίου*] *τοῦ Ποϲειδω̣νίου χέρϲου ν*
[*Πετεϲούχου*] *τοῦ Πετεϲούχο̣υ̣ ε, καὶ αἱ ἀν⟨α⟩λη(φθεῖϲαι)*
[*ἐν τῶ*]*ι β* (*ἔτει*) *παρὰ Πετειμούθου καὶ Πετε̣ϲούχ*[*ου*]
[*ἀπὸ* (*ἀρουρῶν*)] *η∠* *γ*, (*γίνονται*) *η χέρϲ*[*ου*]
[*Πετειμούθη*]*ϲ Πετε*[*ϲού*]*χου καὶ Πετεϲοῦχοϲ χέρ*[*ϲου β∠*]
[± 10 *C*]*αραπίωυ̣*[*οϲ*] *χέρϲου λ̣*
. . . .

4 *ἀναλη(φθείϲηϲ)*: for the restoration cf. lines 7–8, *αἱ ἀν⟨α⟩λη(φθεῖϲαι)* [*ἐν τῶ*]*ι β* (*ἔτει*). *'Αναλαμβάνω* is often used of confiscation by the Crown, but here it is used of an action taken by the temple administration itself; for it is clear that the lands *ἀναληφθεῖϲαι* here not only remained in control of the temple but were in part redistributed to the same individuals as had farmed the property before (cf. line 9, note). Apparently the temple administration had decided to change the terms on which 8½ arouras had been leased: it therefore took these away from the former tenants Peteimouthes and Petesouchos (*ἀναλαμβάνειν*) and let them out again. Petesouchos (lines 7–8) agreed to continue working three of these arouras under the new conditions, and Horos took five of the remainder.

ἀπὸ (*ἀρουρῶν*) *η∠ ε*: in line 3 this property is described as *τ̣ῆϲ διὰ Πετειμού*[*θο*]*υ*, but in lines 8–9 clearly the same 8½ arouras are said to have been taken away from both Peteimouthes and Petesouchos. The two statements are reconciled if one assumes that the 5 arouras acquired here by Horos included land from Peteimouthes' holding only. Cf. lines 7 and 9, notes.

7 [*Πετεϲούχου*]: so restored because the only alternative, *Πετειμούθηϲ*, occurs in line 10 below.

ε: in **63**. 13 = **1110**. 12, Petesouchos was farmer of 6 arouras. The 5 arouras here were left after the recall of land in year 2; the amount of land taken away from Petesouchos at that time was therefore 1 aroura.

9 [*ἀπὸ* (*ἀρουρῶν*)] *η∠ γ*: these 8½ arouras are the total recalled from both Petesouchos and Peteimouthes. Since the amount taken from Petesouchos alone was 1 aroura (cf. preceding note), Peteimouthes lost 7½. Of these 5 are accounted for in line 4, leaving a maximum of 2½ from Peteimouthes here. One must conclude that the 3 arouras added to Petesouchos's original 5 in this passage included at least ½ aroura that he himself had farmed before its recall by the temple.

10 [*Πετειμούθη*]*ϲ Πετε*[*ϲού*]*χου καὶ Πετεϲοῦχοϲ*: Peteimouthes was an independent farmer in **63**, but here he has gone into partnership with Petesouchos.

β∠]: the 10 arouras of **63**. 12 less 7½ arouras recalled by the temple (cf. line 9 note).

11 It is not clear what preceded *C*]*αραπίωυ̣*[*οϲ*] in this line. One expects [*Χαιρήμων 'Αϲκληπιάδου τὴν* (*πρότερον*) *C*]*αραπίωυ̣*[*οϲ*] (cf. **1110**. 10), but there is scarcely room for all that. Possibly one or more of the names were abbreviated. Or, perhaps more simply, *Cαραπίων Cαραπίωνοϲ* himself may have taken over the land again.

1112. Land and Tax Lists

P. Teb. 146 — 27·5 × 29 cm. — 115/114 B.C.

We have ordered this text among the lists of holders of temple and cleruchic land because the information contained in cols. I and II is of the same type as that given by **1108–11** and **1113–15**, although the format is rather different. Cleruchs are not named in their usual order, and the frequent use of abbreviations led the first editors to suggest that the document may be only a rough draft. A third column records grain payments received on Epeiph 30 from various *βαcιλικοὶ γεωργοί*, among whom appear several cleruchs and the god Petesouchos.

The text was written before the succession of Ptolemaios son of Apollonios to his father's cleros, so before year 4 of Soter II (cf. line 15 with **1113.** 35); but Pankrates son of Lagos is already in possession of the land his father held in year 2 (17–18; cf. **1110.** 92). This necessitates a date in year 3, 115/114 B.C.

At the bottom of col. II are found the ends of some lines from a draft of an official report, written in an extremely cursive hand: [1]]ϲ̣ι̣ν διὰ τοῦ προτέρου [2]προcαγγ]έλματος εξων. [3]]c εὑρῆcθαι \`ἐπακάcθαι´* ἐκ τῆc [4][ὑπὸ NN το]ῦ̣ βα(cιλικοῦ) γρ(αμματέωc) γεγενημένηc [5]ἐπ̣ι̣c̣κ]έψεωc εὑρηθ̣έντοc (*sic*)[6]]. κβ̄ τοῦ Ἐπεὶφ μ̣η̣(νὸc) [7]ἐ]π̣ι̣cκέψεωc διὰ τοῦ αὐτοῦ [8]ἐν] ὑπολό(γωι) ἀναφερόμενον. Lines 1–2 and 3–5 appear to read smoothly with the minimal supplements provided; there are no palaeographical indications as to whether the loss may in fact have been greater.

1112 is not part of **1111** from probably the same year.

. . (ὧν) μετρεῖν

κληρ̣ο̣ύ(χων). (εἰκοcιαρούρων) Χο(μήνιοc)
Κεφ̣α̣λᾶc Πετεcούχου ιθ
[(πυρῶι)] θ̣ κ(ριθῆι) ε φαcή(λωι) ε
[γεω(ργὸc)] Ὧρ̣ο̣ς̣ Νεοπτολ(έμου)

(2 cm. blank; then mutilated ends of perhaps 10 lines)

Col. II

Ἀκουcιλάου τοῦ Ἀcκ̣λ̣η(πιάδου)
ἀπὸ ῑ {ε} (ὧν) (πυρῶι) ε ἀρά(κωι) ε
γεω(ργὸc) αὐ(τόc)
Βρο(μεροῦ) τοῦ Ζη(νοδώρου) ἀπὸ μ̄ ιε [(ὧν) (πυρῶι) ι]ε
κ(ριθῆι) ι τή(λει) ε, (γίν.) λ, ἀcπ[όρου ι]
γεω(ργὸc) Πτο( )
Ἀθη(νίωνοc) τοῦ Ἀρχί(ου) ἀπὸ μ̄ (ὧν)
(πυρῶι) ιε ἀρά(κωι) ιε φαcή(λωι) ι
γεω(ργὸc) Ἁρυ(ώτηc)
Ἀ̣π̣ολλω(νίου) τοῦ Πτο(λεμαίου) ἀπὸ κδ̄ (ὧν)
(πυρῶι) ιε ἀρά(κωι) θ, γεω(ργὸc) αὐ(τόc)
[ἐ]ρη(μο)[φ]ύ(λακοc) Λάγου τοῦ Διοδώρου
ὃ̣ν̣ με(τειληφέναι) Πα̣γκρά(την) τὸν υἱὸν ι (ὧν)
(πυρῶι ?) ε χ̣ό̣(ρτωι) ε, γεω(ργὸc) αὐ(τόc)

* Read ἐπηναγκάcθαι or ἐπενέγκαcθαι?

Col. III

Ἐπεὶφ λ̄
Νίκων Ἀμεννέως .[
Πετῶς Μαρρείους .[
Ἁροννῶφρις Ὥρου [
    Χολῶς ἀπὸ τοῦ λο(ιποῦ) β, ἃς Μεςταςῦ(τμις) C[οκέως
Ἁρμαχόρος Θοτορταίου [
Θῶνις Ὀρςενούφιος φα(κοῦ) [
Πετεςοῦχος Cωτηρίδ[ου
Χῦψις Πετεςούχου [
Πνεφερῶς Ὥρου [
(Ὧρος Κεντίςιος τọ̀ λο(ιπὸν) [
Τεῶς Πετεχῶνṭọς̣ [
    Πετεςου(χο) [
    Ὀννῶ̣φρις .[
Φ̣ρ̣α̣μ̣ῆνις Πετοςίριọ[ς
    αὐ(τὸς) ε∠, ἐπις(τατικοῦ) [
Ἁρμιῦςις Π̣[
Ἀθεμμεὺς Π[ετεςούχου
(m. 2) ἐπις(τατικόν)
(m. 1) Πετερ̣μοῦθις [
Πετεςοῦχος Ἰμ[ούθου
Ἀμεννεὺς Ἀ[θεμμέως
Πετεςοῦχος θε(ὸς) διὰ [
[Δ]ημᾶς Cενθ̣[έως
    (γίνονται) ρμ[
    .μθ∠
    ρμδ[

6 Ἀκουςιλάου: the promoted ephodos, not the homonymous hekatontarouros, as is shown by the amount of land.

11 Πτο( ): Πτό(λλις) (cf. **1114**. 50?) or Πτο(λεμαῖος).

24, 32, 33, 35 Inset lines record persons who delivered grain on behalf of those named in the main entry; supply ἃς before each.

32 Πετεςοῦ(χος) or Πετεςού(χου).

35 ἐπις(τατικοῦ): much more likely than ἐπις(κεφθεῖςαι) or ἐπις(κέψεως) in a text of this nature. Cf. **97** introd.

1113. List of Holders of Temple and Cleruchic Land

P. Teb. 72(a) 30 × 30 cm. 114/113 B.C.

Two fragmentary columns from a long papyrus the remainder of which has been printed as **72**. For the date, see introd. to that text.

1113 is noteworthy for two enigmatic omissions: Bromeros son of Zenodoros has disappeared from the list of catoecic cavalrymen enrolled by Dionysios, and the entire category of eremophylakes who had been promoted to the *katoikia* under Philometor is missing. The absence of Bromeros may be in some way connected with the irregularities reported in **61**(a). 20–9, where see note; but no plausible reason for the absence of the promoted eremophylakes (at this date Sosikles son of Menneias and Ptolemaios son of Apollonios) suggests itself. All three persons are found in possession of their land again the following year (**1114**. 49, 60–3).

The lines printed below correspond to **1110**. 49–94.

Col. I

[καὶ τῶν] μετ[α]βεβηκότων εἰς τὴν κατοικίαν ẹ̓κ τῶν
[(τριακονταρούρων) Φυλέως]
[Διονυσίου τοῦ] Πυρρίχου ιηδή (ὧν) σπό(ρος) (πυρῶι) ε φακ(ῶι) ε φασή(λωι) ε̣,
(γίνονται) ιε
[ἀσπό]ρ[ου] γδή, γεω(ργὸς) Ἀνεμπεύς
[γίνοντα]ι κατοίκων ριδδή
[ἐρημοφυλάκω]ν Δημητρίου τοῦ Cε̣ιληνοῦ ὅν με(τειληφέναι)
[Cειληνὸν] τ̣ọ̀ν υἱόν, καὶ παρὰ τούτου Ἡρακλείδην
[τὸν υἱὸν] ι (ὧν) σπόρος (πυρῶι) η, ἐμβρόχου β, γεω(ργὸς) Πτο(λεμαῖος)
[γίνονται τῆς] ἐπὶ τοῦ Ἐπιφανοῦς ρκδδή
[καὶ τῆς] ἐπὶ τοῦ Φιλομήτορος βασιλέως
[συγγε]ν̣ῶν κατοίκων ἱππέων
[Διοδότ]ου τοῦ Μικίωνος οὗ τὸ λο[ι]π̣ὸν τοῦ κλήρου
[πε]ρὶ ἄλλας κώμας ἀς[π]ọ́ρου εδή
[Ἀπολλω]νίου τοῦ Μικίωνος οὗ [τὸ] λοιπὸν τοῦ κλήρου
[περὶ ἄλ]λας κώμας ἀς[π]όρου εδή
[Πύρρου τοῦ] Πτολεμαίου οὗ τὸ λοιπὸ̣ν τοῦ κλήρου
[περὶ τὸν Ἰβι]ῶνα (εἰκοσιπενταρούρων) ὅν με(τειληφέναι) Λυσίμαχον
τὸν υἱὸν μ (ὧν)
] κ ἀρά(κωι) ι, (γίνονται) λ, ἐμβρό(χου) ι, γεω(ργὸς) Πελῶις
[καὶ τῶν ἐν τῶι λ]α (ἔτει) διὰ Διονυσίου

[Ἀπολλωνίου] τοῦ Ἀπολλωνίου ὃν ὁ κωμογραμματεὺϲ
[γράφει με(τειληφέναι) Διόδο]τον τὸν υἱὸν μ (ὧν) (πυρῶι) ιε
ἀρά(κωι) ε, (γίνονται) [κ], ἀϲπόρου
[τῆϲ ἐν] τῶι γ (ἔτει) ϲπαρείϲηϲ ι, τῆϲ ἕωϲ τοῦ γ (ἔτουϲ) ι, (γίνονται) κ
γεω(ργὸϲ) Τεῶϲ Ὥρου

Col. II

Λεοντίϲκου τοῦ Λεοντίϲκο[υ] ὃν μετει[ληφέναι]
Λέοντα τὸν υἱὸν μ (ὧν) (πυρῶι) [.] ἀρά(κωι) ι, ἀϲπόρου [
γεω(ργὸϲ) Πετεϲοῦ(χοϲ)
Ἀμμωνίου τοῦ Ἀπολλωνί[ου μ] (ὧν) (πυρῶι) ι ἀ̣ρ̣άκωι ι
χόρτωι ε, (γίνονται) κε, ἀϲπό[ρου ι]ε̣, [γεω(ργὸϲ)
Πετάλου τοῦ Φιλοξένου ὃν με(τειληφέναι) Δῶρον τὸν υἱὸν μ (ὧν) [
χόρ(τωι) ε, (γίνονται) ιε, ἀϲπόρου κε, γεω(ργὸϲ) αὐ(τόϲ)
γίνονται ἀνδρῶν δ [(ἄρουραι) ρξ]
[κα]ὶ τῶν ἐν τῶι λδ (ἔτει)
Ἀπολλοδώρωι Πτολεμαίου [ξ
καὶ τῶν μεταβεβηκότων εἰ[ϲ] τὴν κ[ατοικίαν ἐξ ἐφόδων]
Ἀπολλ[ων]ίωι Πτολεμαίου ὃν ὁ κωμογρ(αμματεὺϲ) γ[ράφει με(τειληφέναι)
Πτολεμαῖον]
τὸν υἱὸν ἀϲπ[ό]ρου κδ
Ἀϲκληπιάδου τοῦ Πτολεμαίου ἀϲπόρου [κδ]
γίνονται κατοίκων ἱππέων [Σξη]
ἐρημοφυλάκων τῶν ἐν τῶι λβ (ἔτει)
Σαραπίωνοϲ τοῦ Διονυϲίο[υ] ὃν ὁ κω[μογρ(αμματεὺϲ) γράφει με(τειληφέναι)]
Πτολεμαῖον τὸν υἱὸν ἐμβρ[όχου ι]
Διοδώρου τοῦ Εὐκτήμονοϲ ὃν με(τειληφέναι) [Λαγῶν τὸν υἱόν,]
παρὰ δὲ τούτου Παγκράτην [τὸν υἱὸν ι
(m. 2) γεω(ργὸϲ) αὐτόϲ
γίνονται κ
φυλακιτῶν τῶν ἐν τῶι λ[γ] (ἔτει)
Ἀπολλωνίου τοῦ Ἀχιλλέωϲ ὃν με(τειληφέναι) [Ἀκουϲίλαον τὸν υἱὸν ι (ὧν)]
ϲπό(ροϲ) (πυρῶι) ε χό(ρτωι) β, (γίνονται) ζ, ἐμβρό(χου) γ, [γεω(ργὸϲ)

8 Πτο(λεμαῖοϲ): the expansion assumes that this is the same lessee as in **1114**. 29 and **1115**. 10. Leases of cleruchic land in Ptolemaic Egypt were often for only a single year (Crawford, p. 80 n. 4), but these lists point to a number of longer-term or repeated leases: cf. **1108**. 24, 34, 47, 81 with

62. 70, 86, 109, 183; **1109.** 9 note with **62.** 33; **1112.** 11 note with **1114.** 50; **1114.** 26, 38, 42 with **1115.** 7, 18, 23.

13 and 15 The figures are only approximate. Correct was $5\frac{7}{16}$ apiece.

17 Ἰβι]ῶνα (εἰκοcιπενταρούρων): elsewhere the papyri in vols. I and IV use τῶν before (εἰκοcιπενταρούρων). Omission of τῶν in the name became standard in Roman times and occurs sporadically in Ptolemaic texts; cf. **731.** 1; **793,** viii, 29.

20 Apollonios' patronymic was not known before.

21–2 ἀcπόρου [τῆc ἐν] τῶι γ (ἔτει) cπαρείcηc ι, τῆc ἕωc τοῦ γ (ἔτουc) ι: 'unsown land: 10 arouras that were sown in year 3, and 10 (left unsown) up to and including year 3'. With the second phrase understand not cπαρείcηc but ἀcπόρου. This 40-aroura cleros had earlier been fully cultivated (**1108.** 23 and **62.** 68), but by year 2 of Soter II 20 arouras had become water-logged (**63.** 61 = **1110.** 66–7). The passage here indicates that 10 of these had been reclaimed in the 3rd year, but had immediately fallen out of cultivation again; these plus the 10 arouras for which no attempt at reclamation had been made make up the 20 arouras unsown in year 4. Such detail concerning the history of cleruchic plots does not occur in other texts.

23 Τεῶc Ὥρου: no doubt the brother or son of Ὧροc Ὥρου, who farmed the land in year 2 (**63.** 62 = **1110.** 66). Teos continued to lease this cleros for at least three more years (**1114.** 42 and **1115.** 23).

24 Leontiskos's patronymic was not known before.

27 Ἀμμωνίου τοῦ Ἀπολλωνί[ου: this can hardly be correct. Ammonios son of Apollonios had already been replaced by his son Ammonios by 116/115 B.C. (**63.** 65 = **1110.** 70), and this second Ammonios had been replaced by an Apollonios who was doubtless his own son or brother by 113/112 (**1114.** 45). One must either supply ⟨ὃν με(τειληφέναι) Ἀμμώνιον τὸν υἱόν⟩ or assume that the scribe here reversed the names of father and son.

29 Petalos's patronymic was not known before.

31 γίνονται ἀνδρῶν δ̅ [(ἄρουραι) ρξ]: other texts list 5 men with 200 arouras; cf. introd.

1114. List of Holders of Temple and Cleruchic Land

P. Teb. 144 86 × 31 cm. 113/112 B.C.

A terminus post quem for this text is provided by the succession of Philonautes son of Leon to the cleros which in year 4 of Soter II had still belonged to his father (cf. ll. 43–4 with **1113.** 24–5). On the other hand, Menandros son of Pantauchos is still listed as possessor of a cleros which he ceded to Dionysios son of Dionysios in year 2. As Menches' office became cognizant of that cession by late Phamenoth of year 5 (**31.** 1), one may confidently date the present document to the first half of that year, 113/112 B.C., before the cession to Menches reported in **1115.** 185.

On the back of Col. I are written against the fibres the two words Ἱερῶc / Ἱερῶν: the second name may be accusative of the first, or a variant form of the nominative. Ἱερῶc is not found in the *Namenbuch* or *Onomasticon*, but is an easy variant of Ἱερεύc.

Col. IV verso contains a short account, likewise written against the fibres:

1 (πυροῦ) ϛ μη η ιε, (γίνονται) οζ
2 ἀρά(κου) ιζ ϛ ε, (γίνονται) κη
3 φα(κοῦ) ιε
4 φαcή(λου) ι

'Wheat: 6+48+8+15 = 77. Aracus: 17+6+5 = 28. Lentils: 15. Beans: 10.'

The addition in the first two lines is correct. No connection with the recto is apparent.

Col. I

Ὀρcενούφιος θεοῦ μεγά(λου) δι' Ὀρcενούφιος καὶ
τῶν με(τόχων) ἀcπόρου α
Ἰ[βί]ων τροφῆc διὰ Χεύριος καὶ τῶν με(τόχων) ἀcπόρου δ
ἄλ[λ]ου δι' Ἐργέως καὶ τῶν με(τόχων) ἀcπόρου ε
ἄλλου διὰ Πνεφερῶτος καὶ τῶν ἀδελ(φῶν) ἀcπόρου ε
(γίνονται) ἐλ(αccόνων) κdή
[ὥc]ṭ' εἶναι ἱερᾶc (ἄρουραι) ΣϚα∠dή
(Blank space of *c.* 4·5 cm.)
κληρουχικῆc τῆc ὑπαρχούcηc ἕως [τοῦ δ (ἔτους)]
τῆc ẹ̓ν τῶι ιϚ (ἔτει) ἐπὶ τοῦ Φιλοπάτορ[οc βαcιλέωc]
(ἑβδομηκονταρούρων) Ạ̓φθονήτου τοῦ Ẹ̔β[δο]μ̣ίωṇ[οc ο (ὧν) cπό(ροc)
φακῷ̣[ι
(τριακονταρούρων) [χερcεφίπ]π̣ων
[Πανταύ]χου τοῦ Πανταύχο̣υ ὃν με(τειληφέναι) Μένανδρον
[τὸν] υἱὸν χέρcου λδίςλ́β
[γίνονται] ṭῆc ἐπὶ τοῦ Φιλοπάτοροc βαcιλέωc
[καὶ τῆ]ς̣ [ἐπ]ὶ̣ τοῦ πάππου τοῦ βαcιλέωc, τῶν
[δι' Ἑρ]μ̣αφίλ{ιλ}ου (ὀγδοηκονταρούρων)
[Κα]λλικράτηc Φιλοξ̣ένο̣υ π (ὧν) cπό(ροc) (πυρῶι) ιβ κρι(θῆι) γ
ἀρά(κωι) ε φα(κῶι) ε, (γίνονται) κε
ἀcπόρου νε, γεω(ργὸc) Μαρρῆc

Col. II

καὶ τῶν ἀναζευξάντων εἰc τὴν Θηβα(ίδα)
ἀπὸ τῶν 'Δ ἀνδρῶν
ϡ Καλλικράτηc Πτολεμαίου ιϚ (ὧν) (πυρῶι) δ κρι(θῆι) δ, (γίνονται) η,
ἀcπόρου η, γεω(ργὸc) Λιμναῖοc
καὶ τῶν μεταβεβη(κότων) εἰc τὴν κατοικίαν ἐκ τῶν (τριακονταρούρων)
Φυλέωc Διονυcίου τοῦ Πυρρίχου ιηdή (ὧν) (πυρῶι) ζ
φακῶι ε ἀρά(κωι) γ ἐμβρό(χου) γdή, γεω(ργὸc) Ἀνεμπεύc
γίνονται κατοίκων (ἄρουραι) ριδdή
ἐρημοφυλάκων

Ἡρακλείδου τοῦ Cειλα̣νίωνος ι ϛ̣[πό(ρος) ἀ]ρ̣ά̣(κωι), γεω(ργὸς) Πτ[ολε-
μαῖος]
γίνοντ̣α̣ι̣ τῆς ἐπὶ τοῦ π̣[ά]π̣[που (ἄρουραι)] ρκδdή
καὶ τῆς ἐπὶ τοῦ Φιλομήτορος βασιλέως
συγγενῶν κατοίκων ἱππέων
Διοδότου τοῦ Μικίωνος οὗ τὸ λο(ιπὸν) τοῦ κλή(ρου) περὶ τὸν Ἰβιῶνα
τῶν (εἰκοσιπενταρούρων) εdήίς̸ σπό(ρος) ἀρά(κωι), γεω(ργὸς) Τοθοῆς
Ἀπολλωνίου τοῦ Μικίωνος οὗ τὸ λο(ιπὸν) τοῦ κλή(ρου) περὶ τὸν Ἰβιῶνα
τῶν (εἰκοσιπενταρούρων) εdήίς̸ σπό(ρος) ἀρά(κωι), γεω(ργὸς) Τοθοῆς
Λυσιμάχωι Πύρρου οὗ τὸ λο(ιπὸν) τοῦ κλή(ρου) περὶ τὸν Ἰβιῶνα̣
τῶν (εἰκοσιπενταρούρων) μ (ὧν) σπό(ρος) (πυρῶι) κ ἀρά(κωι) ιε,
(γίνονται) λε, ἐμβρό(χου) ε, γεω(ργὸς) Πελῶις
(γίνονται) ἀνδ(ρῶν) γ (ἄρουραι) ν∠dή

Col. III

καὶ τῶν ἐν τῶι λα (ἔτει) διὰ Διονυσίου εἰς τοὺς κα(τοίκους) ἱπ(πεῖς)
ٲ *Διοδότου τοῦ Ἀπολλωνίου μ (ὧν) σπό(ρος) (πυρῶι) κ ἀρά(κωι) ι*
ἀσπόρου ι, γεω(ργὸς) Τεῶς Ὥρου
Λέοντος τοῦ Λεοντίσκου ὃν με(τειληφέναι) Φιλοναύτην
τὸν υἱὸν μ (ὧν) σπό(ρος) (πυρῶι) κ ἀρά(κωι) ιε, ἀσπόρου ε, γεω(ργὸς)
ٲ *Ἀπολλωνίου τοῦ Ἀμμωνίου ⟦ ⟧*
⟦ ⟧ μ (ὧν) σπό(ρος) (πυρῶι) ιε ἀρά(κωι) ε φα(κῶι) ε,
(γίνονται) κε, ἀσπόρου ιε, γεω(ργὸς) Πευκέστης
Δώρου τοῦ Πετάλου μ (ὧν) σπό(ρος) (πυρῶι) ιε ἀρά(κωι) η, (γίνονται) κγ,
ἀσπόρου ιζ
γεω(ργὸς) Ἀθεμμεύς
Βρομεροῦ τοῦ Ζηνο̣δώρου μ (ὧν) σπό(ρος) (πυρῶι) ιε κρι(θῆι) ε \`ἀρά(κωι) ε,ʹ
(γίνονται) κ, ἀσπόρου ιε,
γεω(ργὸς) Πτόλ[λι]ς̣
[γίνο]ν̣ται ἀνδρῶν ε (ἄρουραι) Σ
[καὶ τῶν ἐν τῶ]ι λ̣[δ (ἔτει)]
ٲ *Ἀ̣π̣ο̣λ̣[λοδ]ώρ̣ο̣υ̣ τ̣[οῦ Πτολεμα]ί[ου] ξ (ὧν) [σ]πό(ρος) (πυρῶι) κε̣*
ἀρά(κωι) ιε φασ[ή(λωι)] ι, (γίνονται) ν
ἀσπόρου ι, γεω(ργοὶ) [Πετο]σῖρις Ἁρκοίφιος καὶ οἱ μέ(τοχοι)
καὶ τ̣ῶν μεταβε[β]η(κότων) [εἰ]ς̣ τ̣ὴ̣ν̣ κατοικίαν ἐξ ἐφόδων

Πτολεμαίου τ̣[ο]ῦ̣ Ἀπολλωνίου κδ (ὧν) σπό(ρος) (πυρῶι) γ χό(ρτωι) γ̣, (γίνονται) ϛ,
ἀσπόρου ιη, [γ]ε̣ω(ργὸς) αὐτός
Ἀσκληπιάδ̣ο̣υ̣ τοῦ Πτολεμαίου ἀσπόρου κδ
(γίνονται) ἀνδ(ρῶν) β̣ (ἄρουραι ?) μ̣η̣
καὶ \`ἐ̣κ̣´ τῶν ⟦ἐξ⟧ ἐρημοφυλάκων
Σωσικλείους τοῦ Μεννείο̣υ̣ τ̣ὸ̣ (πρότερον) Ἀρταβάζα̣
Πανταύχου ι (ὧν) σπό(ρος) κ̣ρ̣ι̣(θῆι ?) . . . . .
Πτολεμαίου το̣ῦ̣ Ἀ̣π[ολλωνίου ι
(γίνονται) ἀνδ(ρῶν) β (ἄρουραι) κ´
γίνονται κατοίκ[ων] (ἄρουραι ?) τ̣ο̣η∠ḍή

Col. IV

ἐρημοφυλάκων τῶν ἐν τ̣ῶι λβ (ἔτει)
Πτ̣ο̣λ̣εμαίου τοῦ Σαρ̣απίωνος ι (ὧν) χο(ρτο)ν̣ο̣(μῶν) ε, ἀ[σπό]ρου ε
γεω(ργὸς) αὐτός
Λ̣ά̣γ̣ο̣υ̣ τοῦ Διοδώρου ὃν με(τειληφέναι) Παγκράτην
τὸν υἱὸν ι (ὧν) σπό(ρος) (πυρῶι) ε χό(ρτωι) ε, γεω(ργὸς) αὐτός
φυλα̣[κι]τῶν τῶν ἐν τῶι λγ (ἔτει)
Ἀ̣κ̣ο̣υ̣σιλάου τοῦ Ἀπ[ο]λλωνίου ι (ὧν) σπό(ρος) (πυρῶι) ζ χό(ρτωι) γ,
γεω(ργὸς) αὐ(τός)
Ἡρακλείδου τοῦ Ἐτ̣[φ]ε̣μ̣ούνιος ι (ὧν) σπό(ρος) (πυρῶι) ϛ φα(κῶι) δ,
γεω(ργὸς) Πετεσοῦ(χος)
(γίνονται) ἀνδ(ρῶν) β (ἄρουραι) κ
γίνονται τῆς ἐπὶ [τοῦ Φιλομή]τορος (ἄρουραι) υκη∠ḍή
καὶ τ̣[ῆς ἐ]πὶ τοῦ πα̣τ̣[ρὸς τοῦ βασιλέως] τοῖς [προ]ς̣-
ειλ̣η̣μ̣μ̣ένοις εἰς τοὺς [διὰ Κ]ρ̣[ί]τ̣[ωνο]ς κατοίκου[ς] ἱπ(πεῖς)
Ἀ̣κ̣ουσιλάου τοῦ Ἀσκ[λ]ηπ{π}ιάδου τὸ (πρότερον) Θέωνος τοῦ
Θέωνος λ (ὧν) σπό(ρος) χόρτωι ι, ἀσπόρου κ, γεω(ργὸς) αὐ(τός)
Β̣α̣κ̣χ̣ί̣ο̣υ̣ τοῦ Μουσαίου κ (ὧν) σπό(ρος) (πυρῶι) ιε χό(ρτωι) ε, γεω(ργὸς)
Ὧρος
Ἀπ̣ο̣λλωνίου τοῦ Διονυσίου ν (ὧν) σπό(ρος) (πυρῶι) κε φασή(λωι) ι
. . κωι ι, (γίνονται) με, ἀσπόρου ε, γεω(ργὸς) Ἀγαθοκλῆς
Π̣ρ̣ω̣τ̣άρχου τοῦ Διονυσίου ν (ὧν) σπό(ρος) (πυρῶι) λ̣[ε] φακῶι ε
ἀ̣ρ̣ά̣(κωι) ε, ἀσπόρου ε, γεω(ργοὶ) Τεῶς Ὥρου καὶ Μεστασῦ(τμις)

Π̣[ολέμωνος το]ῦ Ἀμμωνίου ἀcπόρου κ
[Ἀθηνίωνος τοῦ] Ἀρχίου μ (ὧν) cπό(ροc) (πυρῶι) κβ ἀρά(κωι) ιγ,
(γίνονται) λε
ἀcπόρο̣υ̣ ϵ̣, γεω(ργὸc) Ὧροc Κεντίcιοc
[Ἡρώδου τοῦ] Ἡλιοδώρου ἀcπόρου μ
Ἡ[φ]α̣[ι]cτίων Cτρατονίκου ἐμβρόχου ι

Col. V

Λ[επτίνηc Cτρατονίκου κε
˥ Μ[ελάνιπποc Ἀcκληπιάδου ι
[(γίνονται) ἀνδ(ρῶν) ι (ἄρουραι) Σϛε]
καὶ τ[ῶν μεταβεβη(κότων) εἰc τὴν κατοικίαν ἐξ ἐφόδων]
˥ Δ[ημητρίου το]ῦ Ἡ̣ρακ̣λ̣ε̣ί̣[δου ιβ (ὧν) cπό(ροc)
]ο̣υ̣ . γεω(ργὸc) αὐτόc
ˎ Τ[αυρί]c̣κου τοῦ Ἀπολλωνί̣[ου ιβ (ὧν) cπό(ροc)
ἀcπόρου δ, γεω(ργὸc) Ἁφθ̣ο̣ῆ̣ριc
Ἀcκληπιάδου τοῦ Ἀcκληπ[ιάδου κδ, καὶ ἀπὸ τοῦ (πρότερον)]
Πολέμωνοc τοῦ Ἀμμωνίο[υ ι, λδ, (ὧν) cπό(ροc)
ἀcπόρου ιθ, γεω(ργὸc) Πετεc̣[οῦ(χοc) ?]
Ἀκουcιλάου τοῦ Ἀcκληπ[ιάδου ι
(γίνονται) ἀνδ(ρῶν) δ (ἄρουραι) ξη̣
καὶ ἐν τῶι β (ἔτει) Διδυμά[ρχωι Ἀπολλωνίου τὸν (πρότερον)]
Πέτρωνοc τοῦ Θέωνο[c κδ (ὧν) cπό(ροc)
ἀcπόρου ιη γεω(ργὸc) αὐτ[όc]
καὶ ἐκ τῶν φ[υλ]α̣κιτῶν
Μάρω̣ν̣ο̣c̣ τοῦ Διονυcίου [κε
(γίνονται) κατοίκων (ἄρουραι) [υιβ]
ἐφόδων τῶν ἐν τῶι λ[δ (ἔτει)]
Πτολεμαίου τοῦ Μενί[cκου κδ
Ἀπολλωνίου τοῦ Πτολε[μαίου κδ (ὧν) cπό(ροc)
ἀcπόρου . , γεω(ργὸc) α̣[
(γίνονται) ἀνδ(ρῶν) β (ἄρουραι) μ̣η

13 ο in 2nd *Πανταύχου* corrected from ϵ 56 1st γ corrected from ϛ 97 Ἁφθ̣ο̣ῆριc corrected from αὐτόc

3 and 4 Either the names or the figures in these lines should be reversed, since all other texts state that it was Hergeus and associates who farmed 4 arouras, Cheyris and associates who farmed 5; cf. e.g. **1110**. 29–30.

9 ἐ̣ν τῶι ις (ἔτει): cf. **1109**. 7 n.

13 This is the earliest reference to Menandros, who promptly ceded the cleros to Dionysios son of Dionysios. Cf. introd. and **1115**. 176–7 n.

15 The number of arouras ($104\frac{3}{32}$) was never filled in.

21 I do not know the meaning of the mark before *Καλλικράτης*. It recurs in lines 41, 45, 53, 91, 94 and, perhaps, made more hurriedly, 96.

43 Philonautes succeeded to his father's cleros at Kerkeosiris between year 4 and 5 of Soter II; cf. introd. An individual with the same name, likewise a catoecic cavalryman, is found at Berenikis Thesmophorou as early as year 3 (**13**). The system of cleruchic allotment is not sufficiently well known to permit positive denial or assertion that the two men may be identical.

44 γεω(ργός): nothing further was written.

45–6 The space of the cancellation is sufficient to accommodate the name of a successor to Apollonios, written by mistake. The ink was so thoroughly sponged out that no reading can be verified beyond the probability that the last letter of l. 45 was ny.

49 (γίνονται) κ: does not include the entry for aracus that was added above the line.

82 . . κωι: the traces are compatible with either φ̣α̣κῶι or ἀ̣ρ̣ά̣κωι.

103 For the cession to Didymarchos see **30**.

1115. List of Holders of Temple and Cleruchic Land

P. Teb. 145 recto | 146 × 30·5 cm. | 111/110 B.C. or later

This list can be placed no earlier than year 7 of Soter II, 111/110 B.C.: line 185 mentions year 5, and a comparison with **1114** rules out a date in that year itself; year 6 is eliminated by a comparison of l. 84 with **107**. No terminus ante can be certainly fixed, but the text so closely resembles **1114** in respect of the lessees named for various cleroi and the amounts of sown and unsown land that it is unlikely the two documents refer to years very far apart.

Cols. IV–VIII are so mutilated and discoloured that decipherment would have been impossible without the aid of the parallel texts in vols. I and IV, and above all of the list of 30-, 20-, and 7-aroura cleruchs for year 5 given by **98+1147**. Extensive restoration of names in ll. 93 ff. is based on that text.

On the back is **1145**.

Col. I

[καὶ τῶν ἀναζευ]ξάντων εἰς τὴν Θηβαείδα
[ἀπὸ τῶν ʼΔ ἀνδρ]ῶν
[Καλλικράτης Π]τολεμαίου ις (ὧν) (πυρῶι) ς κρι(θῆι) β, (γίνονται) η
]η γεω(ργὸς) Λ[ι]μναῖος
[καὶ τῶν μεταβεβηκότω]ν̣ εἰς τὴν κα(τοικίαν) ἐκ τῶν (τριακονταρούρων) Φυλέως
[Διονυςίου τοῦ] Πυρρίχου ιηδ́ή (ὧν) (πυρῶι) η φακῶι δ
γ] ἐμβρόχου γδ́ή γεω(ργὸς) ʼΑνεμπεύς
[(γίνονται) κατοίκ]ων (ἄρουραι) ριδδ́ή

[ἐρημοφυλάκων]
[Ἡρακλείδου τοῦ] Cειλανίωνος ι cπό(ροc) (πυρῶι) γεω(ργὸc) Πτολεμαῖοc
[(γίνονται) τῆc ἐπὶ τ]οῦ πάππου ρκδdή
[τῆc ἐπὶ τοῦ Φι]λομήτοροc βαcιλέωc
[cυγγενῶν κατοί]ḳων ἱππέων
[Διοδότου τοῦ Μι]κίωνοc οὗ τὸ λο(ιπὸν) τοῦ κλή(ρου) περὶ τὸν Ἰβιῶ(να)
[τῶν (εἰκοcιπενταρούρων)] εdήίς cπό(ροc) κρι(θῆι) γεω(ργὸc) Τοθοῆc
[Ἀπολλωνίου το]ῦ Μικίωνοc οὗ τὸ λο(ιπὸν) τοῦ κλή(ρου) περὶ τὸν Ἰβιῶ(να)
[τῶν (εἰκοcιπενταρούρων)] εdήίς cπό(ροc) (πυρῶι) γεω(ργὸc) Τοθοῆc
[Λυcιμάχου τοῦ Πύ]ρρου οὗ τὸ λο(ιπὸν) τοῦ κλή(ρου) περὶ τὸν Ἰβιῶ(να)
τῶν (εἰκοcιπενταρούρων)
[μ (ὧν) cπό(ροc)] ἀρά(κωι) ι χόρτωι ι, (γίνονται) λε
ἐμβρόχου ε γεω(ργὸc) Πελῶι̣[c]
[γίνονται ἀνδρ]ῶν γ (ἄρουραι) ν∠dή

Col. II

καὶ τῶν ἐν τῶι λα (ἔτει) διὰ Διονυcίου εἰc τοὺc κα(τοίκουc) ἱπ(πεῖc)
Διοδότου τοῦ Ἀπολλων̣ί̣ου μ (ὧν) (πυρῶι) ιε ἀρά(κωι) ε
φαcή(λωι) ι, (γίνονται) λ, ἀcπόρου ι γεω(ργὸc) Τεῶc Ὧρου
Λέοντοc τοῦ Λεοντίcκου ὃν με(τειληφέναι) Φιλοναύτην
τὸν υἱὸν μ̣ (ὧν) ιε̣ ἀρά(κωι) ι χόρτωι ι, (γίνονται) λε
ἀcπόρου ε
γεω(ργὸc) Πελῶιc
Ἀπολλωνίου τοῦ Ἀμμωνίου μ (ὧν) (πυρῶι) ιζ ἀρά(κωι) η, (γίνονται) κε
ἀcπόρου ιε γεω(ργὸc) αὐτόc
Δ̣ώρ̣[ο]υ τοῦ Πετάλου μ (ὧν) (πυρῶι) ιζ ἀρά(κωι) δ, (γίνονται) κα
ἀcπόρου ιθ γεω(ργὸc) Ἀθεμμεύc
[Βρο]μεροῦ τοῦ Ζηνο̣δ̣ώρου μ (ὧν) (πυρῶι) ιε κρι(θῆι) ε ἀρά(κωι) ε,
(γίνονται) κε
ἀcπόρου ιε γεω(ργὸc) Πετεcοῦχοc
γ[ί]ν[ο]νται ἀνδρῶν ε (ἄρουραι) Σ
καὶ τῆc ἐν τῶι λδ (ἔτει)
Ἀπολλοδώρωι Πτολεμαίου ξ (ὧν) (πυρῶι ?) λ, ἀρά(κωι) ι φαcή(λωι) ι
(γίνονται) ν
ἀcπόρου ι γεω(ργοὶ) Cενθεὺc καὶ οἱ μέ(τοχοι)

καὶ τῶν μεταβεβη(κότων) εἰς τ[ὴν] κα(τοικίαν) ἐ̣ξ̣ ἐφόδων
Πτολεμαίου τοῦ Ἀπο̣λ̣λ̣ω̣ν̣ί̣ο̣υ̣ κ̣δ̣ (ὧν) (πυρῶι) δ ἀρά(κωι) β, (γίνονται) ϛ
ἀςπόρου ιη γ̣ε̣ω̣(ργὸς) Τ̣εῶς
[Ἀ]ςκλ̣ηπιάδου το[ῦ] Πτολεμαίου ἀςπόρου κδ
(γίνονται) ἀνδ(ρῶν) β (ἄρουραι) μ̣η̣
καὶ [ἐκ τῶ]ν̣ ἐρημοφυλάκ̣ω̣ν̣
Πτολεμαίου τοῦ Ἀπολλωνίου ι (ὧν) (πυρῶι) ε ἀρά(κωι) ε
γεω(ργὸς) αὐ̣τ̣ό̣ς̣

Col. III

ἐρημοφυλάκων τῶν ἐν τῷ̣ι λβ (ἔτει)
Πτολεμαίου τοῦ Cαραπίω[νο]ς̣ ἀςπόρου ι
Λάγου τοῦ Διοδώρου ὃν με(τειληφέναι) Παγκ̣ράτην τὸν
υἱὸν ι (ὧν) (πυρῶι) ε̣ ἀρά(κωι) ε γεω(ργὸς) α̣[ὐ]τός
φυλακιτῶν τῶν ἐν τῶι λγ (ἔτει)
Ἀκουςιλάου τοῦ Ἀπολλων̣[ίου] ι (ὧν) (πυρῶι) ε τήλ̣ε̣ι̣ ε
γεω(ργὸς) αὐτός
Ἡρακλείδου τοῦ Ἐτφεμ[ούνιο]ς̣ ι (ὧν) (πυρῶι) ε ἀρά(κωι) ε
γεω(ργὸς) Πετεςοῦχος
(γίνονται) ἀνδ(ρῶν) β (ἄρουραι) [κ]
γίνον{ον}ται τῆς ἐπὶ [τοῦ Φιλομ]ή̣τορος υιη∠dή
καὶ τῆς ἐπὶ τοῦ πατρὸς τ̣[οῦ βαςιλ]έως τοῖς προς-
ειλημμένοις εἰς τοὺς δ̣ι̣ὰ̣ Κ̣ρ̣ί̣[τω]νο[ς] κα(τοίκους) ἱπ(πεῖς)
Ἀκουςιλάου τοῦ Ἀςκληπιάδου [τὸν] (πρότερον) Θέωνος τ̣[οῦ]
Θέωνος λ (ὧν) ςπό(ρος) (πυρῶι) ι [ἀ]ς[πόρου] κ γεω(ργὸς)
α[ὐτός]
Βακχίου τοῦ Μουςαίου [κ
Ἀπολλωνίου τοῦ Διονυςίου [ν (ὧν)
φακῶι ιε, (γίνονται) με ἀςπόρου ε γ̣ε̣ω̣(ργὸς) [
Πρώταρχος Διονυςίου ν̣ [(ὧν)
(γίνονται) με [ἀ]ςπόρου ε γ[εω(ργὸς)
Πολέμων Ἀμ̣μωνίου [κ
Ἀθηνίων Ἀρχίου μ (ὧν) (πυρῶι) [
⟦ἀςπόρου⟧ ἐμβρόχου ε

Col. IV

Μελάνιππος Ἀσκληπιάδου ι (ὧν) (πυρῶι) ϵ κρι(θῆι) ϵ γ̣ϵ̣ω̣(ργὸς) α̣ὐ̣(τός)
Ἡρώδης Ἡλιοδώρου ἀσ̣π̣ό̣ρου μ
Ἡ̣φαιστίων Στρατονίκου ἐμβρόχ[ο]υ̣ ι
Λεπτίνης Στρατο̣ν̣[ί]κ̣ου ἐμβρόχ̣ο̣υ̣ κ̣ϵ̣
[(γίνονται)] ἀνδ(ρῶν) ι̣ [(ἄρουραι)] Σϙϵ
κ̣α̣ὶ̣ τ̣ῶ̣ν̣ μ̣ϵ̣τ̣[αβεβη(κότων) ἐξ ἐφόδων]
Δ̣ημ[ητρίου τοῦ Ἡρακλείδου ιβ (ὧν)
(γίνονται) .[
Τα[υρίσκου τοῦ Ἀπολλωνίου ιβ
[Ἀσκληπιάδου τοῦ Ἀσκλη]π[ιάδου λδ
[Ἀκουσιλάου τοῦ Ἀ]σκληπιάδου ι (ὧν) (πυρῶι) [
[(γίνονται)] ἀ̣ν̣δ(ρῶν) δ̣ (ἄρουραι ?) ξη
[καὶ ἐκ τῶν φυλα]κ̣ιτῶν
[Μάρων]ο̣ς τοῦ̣ Διονυσίου ἀσπόρου κϵ
[(γίνονται)] κ̣α̣τ̣ο̣ί̣κων (ἄρουραι) τπη
ἐφόδων τῶν ἐν τῶι λδ (ἔτει)
Πτολεμαίου τοῦ Μενίσκου ἀσπόρου κ̣δ̣
Ἀπολλωνίου τοῦ Πτολεμαίου κ̣δ̣ [(ὧν)
ἀσπόρου γ γεω(ργὸς) αὐτός
(γίνονται) ἀ̣ν̣δ̣(ρῶν) β (ἄρουραι) μη
καὶ τῆς καταμεμετρημένης τοῖς διὰ Χομή̣ν̣[ιος]
ἱππεῦσι καὶ (ἑπταρούροις) μαχίμοις

Col. V

(τριακονταρούρων ?) Ἁρυώτης Φ̣α̣εῦτος οὗ τὸ λο(ιπὸν) τοῦ κλή(ρου) περὶ
Τεβτῦνιν [ϵ σπό(ρος)] (πυρῶι ?) γ̣ϵ̣ω̣(ργὸς) αὐτός
(εἰκοσιαρούρων) [Μ]ϵ̣στασῦτμις [Φαγάτου ιθ
[Λυσίμαχος Χομήνιος ιθ
[Χομῆνις Ἀκρισίου ? ιθ
[Ζώπυρος Διονυσίου ιθ
[Θοτεὺς Ὀρσείους οὗ τὸ λο(ιπὸν) τοῦ κλή(ρου) περὶ Τεβτῦ(νιν) ιϵ (ὧν)
σπό(ρος)
φασή(λωι) δ [
Φμέρ̣σ̣ι̣ς̣ Ὧρ[ου οὗ τὸ λο(ιπὸν) τοῦ κλή(ρου) περὶ Τεβτῦ(νιν)] ϵ̣

φạcή(λωι) . [
Ἁρμιῦcιc Φ̣[α]τρείọυ̣c̣ [ιθ] (ὧν) (πυρῶι?) δ̣ κρι(θῆι) ε φαcή(λωι) ι̣
γεω(ργὸc) αὐ̣τόc
(γίνονται) ἀνδ(ρῶν) η (ἄρουραι) ρκ
[(ἑπταρούρων) μαχίμων]
Πορεγέβθιc Ἀπύγχιοc ϛ∠ (ὧν) (πυρῶι) γ∠ κρι(θῆι) γ γεω(ργὸc) αὐτόc
Ὧροc Ὥρου ϛ∠ (ὧν) (πυρῶι) γ∠̣ ἀρά(κωι) γ γε̣ω̣(ργὸc) Ἁρυώτηc
Ὧροc Θοτορταίου ϛ∠ (ὧν) (πυρῶι) γ ἀρά(κωι) γ∠ γεω(ργὸc) αὐτόc
Ἁρχῦψιc Πετοcίριοc ϛ∠ (ὧν) [. .] . . . . . γ̣ε̣ω̣(ργὸc) ạὐ̣τ̣ọ́c̣
Πετεcοῦχοc Τεῶτọc ϛ∠ (ὧν) [. . .] . . . .
Κανῶc Πετοcίριοc ϛ∠ (ὧν) (πυρῶι ?) [. .] . . . . .

Col. VI

Ἁρcῦ[τμιc Πετοcίριοc ϛ∠
Ἁ̣ρ̣[cεν]θεὺ̣c [Cιεφμοῦτοc ϛ∠
Ἁρ̣[ψῆθιc] Κολλ̣ọύ̣[θου ϛ∠
Π̣ε̣τ̣ε̣cοῦχ̣οc Τ̣οθοε[ίουc ϛ∠
Ὧροc Φαγώμιοc ọ̔̃ν [με(τειληφέναι)
ϛ∠ (ὧν) (πυρῶι) γ ἀρά(κωι) γ∠ [γεω(ργὸc)
Φατρῆ̣c̣ Ὥρου [ϛ]∠ [
[Μεc]ταcῦ[τμιc Ὥρου ϛ∠
Φαεὺc [Cοκέωc ϛ∠
Θοτεὺc [Φολήμιοc ϛ∠
Μ̣αρρῆ̣c̣ [Πακούρριοc τὸν (πρότερον) Ὥρου τοῦ]
Ἁρφαή[cιοc ϛ∠
Ἁρμιῦcιc [Cοκονώπιοc ϛ∠ γ]εω(ργὸc) αὐτόc
Τ̣ε̣ῶc [Τεῶτοc ϛ∠ γ]εω(ργὸc) αὐτόc
Πᾶcιc μι(κρὸc) Κ[αλατύτιοc ϛ∠] γεω(ργὸc) αὐτόc
Πᾶcιc μέ(γαc) [Καλατύτιοc ϛ∠ γεω(ργὸc) αὐτό]c̣
Νεκτενῖβ[ιc Ὥρου ϛ∠] γεω(ργὸc) αὐτόc
Φολ̣ῆμιc [Νεκτενίβιοc ϛ∠ γεω(ργὸc) α]ὐ̣τ̣όc
Ἀπῦγχιc [Ποώριοc ϛ∠ γεω(ργὸc) αὐτ]όc
Κολλούθ̣η̣c̣ [Ὥρου ϛ∠
Ὕλλοc Πάιτ[οc ϛ∠

Col. VII

[Ἁρφαῆσις] Ὥ̣ρου ς∠ (ὧν) (πυρῶι) γ∠ [ἀρ]ά(κωι) γ γεω(ργὸς) α̣ὐ̣(τός)
[Κολλούθης] Π̣ετοσίριος ς∠ (ὧν) (πυρῶι) γ∠ φα(κῶι) γ γεω(ργὸς) α̣ὐ̣τ̣ό̣ς̣
[Ὀννῶφρις] Πετερ[μούθιος ς∠
[Τεῶς μι(κρὸς) Πε]τεχ̣ῶν̣[τος ς∠
[Ἀμοῦνις Τεφνάχθιος ς∠
[(γίνονται) ἀνδ(ρῶν) λ (ἄρουραι) ρϛε]
[γίνονται τῆς ἐν τῶι μα (ἔτει) (ἄρουραι) τιε]
[καὶ τῆς ἐν τῶι μβ (ἔτει)]
[Ἁρυώτης Ἁρυώτου ς∠
[Χεῦρις Σοχώτου ς∠
[Ἀρχίβιος Ὥρου ς∠
[Πᾶσις] Σοκ̣[ονώπιος ς∠
(γίνονται) ἀ̣ν̣[δ(ρῶν)] δ [(ἄρουραι) κς]
γίνονται τοῖς διὰ Χομήνιος [(ἄρουραι)] τμα
καὶ τῆς ἐν τῶι μς (ἔτει) τοῖς ἐκ τῆς Ἡρακλείδου μερίδος
μετακεκληρουχημένοις ἀπὸ τῶν (πρότερον) δι' Ὥρου καὶ
Πεσούριος προσλημφθέντων εἰς τὴν τῶν
μαχίμων σύνταξιν οὓς καὶ γέγραφεν
Πτο̣λ̣[εμαῖος] καὶ Ξένων οἱ γραμματεῖς τῶν
μαχίμων φέρειν ὑπὸ τὴ̣ν̣ τ̣ο̣ῦ Χομήνιος
λααρχίαν (ἑπταρούρων) μαχίμων
Ὀννῶφρις Μεστασύτμιος ς̣∠ (ὧν ?) (πυρῶι) γ∠ ἀρά(κωι) γ γ̣εω(ργὸς) αὐ(τός)

Col. VIII

Πτολεμαῖος Σε̣[νθέως οὗ τὸ λο(ιπὸν) τοῦ κλή(ρου) περὶ]
Ἄρεως κώ(μην) γ [
[Ὧ]ρ̣ος Π[α]ώπιο[ς ς∠
[Πεσύθης Παχῶτος ς∠
[Μαρρῆς Ἁράπιος ς∠
[Φθαῦς Πετεήσιος ς∠] γεω̣(ργὸς) αὐ[τός]
[Πασῶς μι(κρὸς) Φανή]σ̣ι̣ο̣ς̣ [ς∠ (ὧν) γ∠] φασή(λωι) γ γεω(ργὸς)
αὐτός
[Πασῶς Ὀρσε]ίους ς∠ (ὧν) (πυρῶι) γ∠ ἀρά(κωι) γ γεω(ργὸς) αὐτός
[Πετεσοῦχο]ς Πετεσούχου ς∠ (ὧν) (πυρῶι) γ∠ φασή(λωι) γ γεω(ργὸς) αὐτ[ός]

['Ορςῆς 'Αρο]ννήςιος [± 7] Πετοςίριος [
τὸν ἀδελ(φὸν) ϛ∠ (ὧν) (πυρῶι ?) γ∠ ἀρ[ά(κωι)] γ γεω(ργὸς) αὐτός
'Αρμιῦςις Πετε̣ς̣ο̣ύχ̣ο̣υ̣ [
. Cαραπίωνος τὸν ἀδελ(φὸν) ϛ∠ (ὧν) (πυρῶι) γ∠ φας̣ή(λωι) γ γεω(ργὸς) αὐ(τός)
Παςῶς [μέ]γ(ας) Φανήςιος ϛ̣∠ (ὧν) (πυρῶι) γ∠ ἀρά(κωι) γ γεω(ργὸς) αὐτ[ός]
(γίνονται) [ἀνδ(ρῶν)] ιβ (ἄρουραι) οδ∠
ὥςτ' ε̣ἶ̣ν̣α̣ι̣ [τοῖς] διὰ Χομήνιος (ἄρουραι) υιε∠
καὶ τοῖς διὰ Πτ̣[ο]λεμ̣α̣ίου καὶ Ξένωνος
Μαρρῆς Π̣α̣άπ̣ι̣ο̣ς̣ ϛ∠ (ὧν) (πυρῶι) γ∠̣ φαςή(λωι) γ γεω(ργὸς) αὐτός
'Αροννῶφρι̣ς̣ "Ω̣ρ̣ο̣υ̣ ϛ[∠ (ὧν)] (πυρῶι ?) [γ∠] .( ) γ γεω(ργὸς) αὐτός
'Α̣ρμ̣ά̣ις Πανορς̣ε̣ί̣ο̣υ̣ς̣ ϛ∠ (ὧν) (πυρῶι) γ∠ . .( ) γ γεω(ργὸς) αὐτός
(γίνονται) ἀνδ(ρῶν) γ (ἄρουραι) ιθ∠

Col. IX

(*c*. 8 lines lost)

[(γίνονται) ἀνδ(ρῶν) ε . (ἄρουραι) λ]β̣∠
[γίνον]τ̣α̣ι̣ τ̣[ῆς ἐπ]ὶ τοῦ πατρὸς ϡ̣γ∠
[καὶ] τ̣ῆς ἐπὶ τοῦ βαςιλέως τῶν ἐν τῶι β (ἔτει)
[πα]ρ̣α̣κεχωρημένων
Διονυςίωι Διονυςίου τὸν (πρότερον) Μενάνδρου τοῦ
Πανταύχου λδίϛ΄λβ΄ (ὧν) (πυρῶι) ε ἀςπόρου κθίϛ΄λβ΄
Διδυμάρχου τοῦ 'Απολλωνίου τὸν (πρότερον) Πέτρωνος
τοῦ Θέωνος κδ (ὧν) (πυρῶι) γ ἀρά(κωι) γ, (γίνονται) ϛ ἀςπόρου ιη
γεω(ργὸς) αὐτός
Cωςικλῆς Μεννείου τὸν (πρότερον) 'Αρταβάζα τοῦ
Παν[τ]αύχου ι (ὧν) (πυρῶι) β ἀρά(κωι) γ, (γίνονται) ε ἀςπόρου ε
γεω(ργὸς) αὐτός
καὶ τῆς ἐν τῶι ε (ἔτει) καταμεμετρη(μένης) Μεγχεῖ Πετεςούχ̣[ου]
κωμογραμματεῖ ἀπὸ τοῦ περὶ τὴν κώ(μην) ὑπολό(γου) (ἄρουραι) κ
ὥςτ' εἶναι κλη(ρουχικῆς)

177 Second ω in παρακεχωρημένων corrected from η

36 Cενθεὺς καὶ οἱ μέ(τοχοι): in **1114**. 54 this association was headed by Sentheus' brother Petosiris.

55 υιη∠δή: $418\frac{7}{8}$ rather than the $428\frac{7}{8}$ of previous years because 10 arouras belonging to Sosikles

son of Menneias have been removed from the category of cleroi belonging to promoted eremophylakes and placed in a special section, 183 f.

67 *ἐμβρόχου*: written below, rather than above, the cancelled *ἀςπόρου* to replace the latter. This practice is exceedingly rare; I cannot cite another certain example.

82 *τπη*: correct. Not 412 arouras as previously because 24 ar. belonging to a promoted ephodos have been treated separately, 180–2. Cf. 55 n.

93–6 For the restorations see the list of *εἰκοςιάρουροι* for year 5 in **98**. 61 ff.

94 *Χομῆνις Ἀκριςίου*: or perhaps his successor Homeros (**1120**. 65).

162–5 It is rather tempting to read [*Ὀρςῆς Ἁρο*]*ννήςιος* [*ὃν με(τειληφέναι) Ὧρον*] *Πετοςίριος* / *τὸν ἀδελ(φόν)* and *Ἁρμιῦςις Πετεςο̣ύχο̣υ̣* [*ὃν με(τειληφέναι) Ἁρμιῦςιν*] / . *Caραπίωνος τὸν ἀδελ(φόν)*, with *ἀδελφόν* bearing in both cases the meaning 'half-brother', as in **1110**. 229. A Horos son of Petosiris appears in a list of cleruchs in **1124**. 16, a Harmiysis son of Sarapion in **98**. 17. But this would raise serious chronological problems, since Harmiysis son of Petesouchos and his supposed successor would then appear in the same document (**98**. 17 and **1147**. 166); and **1124**. 16 may antedate **1147**. 62, in which Horos's supposed predecessor is still active.

175 *ϡγ∠*: not 927½ as earlier; cf. 82 n.

176–7 *τῶν ἐν τῶι β (ἔτει)* [*πα*]*ρ̣ακεχωρημένων*: in a note to the parallel passage **65**. 24 the editors of vol. I assert that the cession to Dionysios (178–9) took place in year 5 rather than year 2, but on insufficient grounds: it is the correspondence to correct continued false registration of the land, not the cession itself, that **31** dates to year 5. Year 2 is certainly correct in the case of Didymarchos (180–2; cf. **30**); and the other two cessions listed here may very well have taken place late that year also, after **63** and **1110** were drafted. Cf. Uebel, *Kleruchen*, p. 173.

1116. LAND SURVEY

P. Teb. 152 — (*a*) 15·5 × 30·5 cm. (*b*) 19 × 30·5 cm. (*c*) 30 × 30·5 cm. — 134/121 B.C. (134/132?)

1116–23 are records of the land survey at Kerkeosiris. The topic has most recently been treated by Crawford, pp. 5–38, to which the reader is referred for bibliography and analysis of parallel texts. **1116–21**, like **84** and **85**, list farms, roads, waterways, and other topographical features in the order in which they were inspected. The orientation of each piece of land is given in relation to the parcel last mentioned, the name of the responsible land-holder is given, and in the case of Crown land we are almost invariably told the rent charged. This is sufficient cadastral information for tax purposes, and such lists might also be used at the end of the flood season to restore boundaries that had been washed away or silted over (cf. Strabo 17. 1. 3, where this specific use of surveying is cited as the source of Greek geometry). Lists like these do not, however, provide an adequate basis for a true cadastre, because only two boundaries are generally determined; and of these the dimensions are given very rarely, and the angles involved not at all. For this reason such sketches of limited areas of Kerkeosiris as have been offered by Calderini (*Aegyptus* I, 1920, 48–9), Crawford (pp. 160–1), and myself (**1117**. 1–13 n.) are of very limited value. Surveys were also made in much greater detail than shown by these documents, but our specimens are neither extensive nor well preserved (**1122–3**).

The terminus a quo for **1116** is year 37 of Euergetes II, when the class of land held by

Heliodoros son of Menodoros (76) came into being. The text is assuredly no later than year 48, since it mentions rent at $5\frac{41}{48}$ and $5\frac{11}{12}$ artabs per aroura, rates which had fallen out of use at Kerkeosiris by year 49 (**66**); and it is quite likely much earlier than that, probably antedating the revolt of 131 B.C. Only such an early date seems to yield a plausible hypothesis concerning the most remarkable feature of the document – the discrepancies in cleruchic allotments as detailed here and in later texts. These are as follows.

1. Pantauchos son of Pantauchos had $34\frac{3}{32}$ arouras. A lot of $4\frac{7}{8}$ is located in l. 91, but later his land falls into two parcels, one of 20 arouras and one of $14\frac{3}{32}$ (**84**. 17, 182).

2. Philoxenos son of Kallikrates had 80 arouras. Lots of 58 and 5 ar., ll. 30 and 36 below, are irreconcilable with lots of 51 and 32 later (**1117**. 83 = **1118**. 183; **85**. 92. These total 83, which is too high; the note, later cancelled, in **85**. 92 (*ὧν*) *ἀποβιαζομένης ἐν cυ(γκρίcει)* (*ἄρουραι*) δ, is probably connected with this excess).

3. Heliodoros son of Menodoros holds one block of 50 arouras in l. 76. By year 52 he had ceded 10 of these to Athenion son of Archias (**61**(a). 1 n.). These 10 and the remaining 40 are located in **84**. 150 and 187, where they appear to be widely separated lots.

4. If *Θέων*]*οc* is the right supplement to l. 75 (see note), then what is here a divided holding was later consolidated into one block of 30 arouras (**84**. 167, **1118**. 143).

Textual mutilation prevents identification of the cleroi in ll. 24, 28, 29, and 33, but 60 arouras held by an *ὀγδοηκοντάρουροc* in 97 have left no trace in later texts. Only those cleroi of lines 65 and 94–5 seem to have remained stable over the years.

Reorganization of individual holdings has nothing to do with cessions such as are recorded in **30**, **31**, and **1100**, and we have no information as to how or why they were brought about or whether they were voluntary. One might cautiously suggest, however, that the large-scale cleruchic settlements made after the conclusion of the revolt of 131 involved also a redistribution of land for some earlier cleruchs. Should this be the case, **1116** is no doubt to be dated before the arrival of numerous native troops at Kerkeosiris in Euergetes' 41st year; and this would explain the otherwise remarkable absence of their ubiquitous cleroi from a text which covers approximately $\frac{1}{5}$ of the village. A date in years 37 or 38 would further explain the failure of this text to divide derelict land into that which fell out of use before and after year 39. It would raise the question also whether the failure of numerous tenants with impressively Greek names either to recur themselves in later lists or to leave progeny named after themselves could have been occasioned by their removal in the course of the revolt.

The usual formulas of Kerkeosiris land surveys are discussed in **84**. 16 n., **86** introd., and **1117**. 3, 5 notes. Striking variations in the present document are as follows:

1. Changes of direction in the survey often occur without a warning *ἀρχό*(*μεναι*); cf. 46–7, 47–8, 52–3, 60–1, 88–9, 91–3, 17 n., 55 n.

2. Changes of direction are not limited to right angles; cf. 44, *βο*(*ρρᾶ*) *ἐχό*(*μεναι*) *ἀρχό*(*μεναι*) *βο*(*ρρᾶ*); 41, *βο*(*ρρᾶ*) *ἐχό*(*μεναι*) *ἀρχό*(*μεναι*) *νό*(*του*); the opposite change without

ἀρχό(μεναι) 60–1; λι(βὸς) ἐχό(μεναι) l. 47 vs. ἀπη(λιώτου) ἐχό(μεναι) in 48. See **1117**. 5 note.

3. The order of elements in describing land held by cleruchs is: orientation of land, name of cleruch, status of cleruch, κλ(ήρου) (ἄρουραι), extent of holding. In one case the cleros is described with an adjective (75, ἱππαρ[χ]ικοῦ κλ(ήρου)); but 91, χερϲεφίππου κλ(ήρου), shows that one should not assume an extension of this practice to all ambiguous passages. We therefore prefer the expansion (ὀγδοηκονταρούρου) as in other texts to (ὀγδοηκονταρουρικοῦ), ἐφό(δου) to ἐφο(δικοῦ), and other instances similarly (**1117**. 5 n.).

Much of the text is mutilated and obscure. References to cleruchic land which are preserved or certainly restorable include 5 parcels totalling 169 arouras held by ὀγδοηκοντάρουροι (24, 30, 33, 36, 97); 1 of 20 by an ephodos (95); 1 of ten by an hipparches (75), and 1 of 50 by (another) ἑκατοντάρουροϲ (76). A chersephippos had a plot of $4\frac{7}{8}$ arouras (91), a cleruch of uncertain status one of 10 (28). Sacred land is mentioned twice, $2\frac{1}{2}$ arouras belonging to Souchos (96) and an uncertain amount for an ibis feeding station (52).

The majority of the land belonged to a class which is never identified but which must be βαϲιλική. Preserved or restorable are 25 parcels totalling $214\frac{1}{4}$ arouras rented at $4\frac{11}{12}$ artabs per aroura (3–7, 10–14, 19, 21, 22, 66, 67, 71, 72, 74, 80–3, 85, 86, 90); 14 parcels amounting to more than 117 arouras at $5\frac{19}{48}$ art. (19, 20, 66, 67, 71, 72, 80–6, 89); 1 parcel of 5 arouras at $5\frac{41}{48}$ art. (8); and 1 of 5 at $5\frac{11}{12}$ (9). There are in addition eight lots totalling $75\frac{1}{2}$ arouras for which the rent is not stated (1, 2, 15–17, 31, 35, 68). The higher rates here were gradually abandoned at Kerkeosiris; by 120 the two highest figures had been given up altogether, and rent at $5\frac{19}{48}$ was applied to only 142 arouras for the village, as opposed to more than 117 in this fragment alone (cf. **66**. 30, 44, 45); by 118 this rate too had vanished (**67**).

Col. IV of **1116** has been published with a plate by Crawford, pp. 141–3.

Col. I

νό(του) ἐχό(μεναι) Ὥρου τοῦ Ἁρχύψιοϲ (ἄρουραι) ιϛ
νό(του) ἐχό(μεναι) Θέων Πολυκράτου η
νό(του) ἐχό(μεναι) Διδύμου τοῦ Ἀντικράτου ιγ ἀν(ὰ) δ∠γ´[ιβ´]
νό(του) ἐχό(μεναι) Ἀλεξάνδρου τοῦ Ἡρακλείδου ϛ ἀν(ὰ) δ∠γ´ιβ´
νό(του) ἐχό(μεναι) Διονυϲίου τοῦ Cωτηρίδου ϛ ἀν(ὰ) δ∠γ´ιβ´
νό(του) ἐχό(μεναι) ἀρχό(μεναι) ἀπη(λιώτου) Χαριδήμου τοῦ Ἀπολλωνίου
ιβ ἀν(ὰ) δ∠γ´ιβ´
λι(βὸϲ) ἐχό(μεναι) διὰ τοῦ αὐτοῦ ι ἀν(ὰ) δ∠γ´ιβ´
λι(βὸϲ) ἐχό(μεναι) Φιλοξένου τοῦ Νικάνοροϲ ε ἀν(ὰ) ε∠γ´μη´
λι(βὸϲ) ἐχό(μεναι) ἀρχό(μεναι) βο(ρρᾶ) Πτολεμαίου τοῦ Νικάνοροϲ ε ἀν(ὰ) ε∠γ´ιβ´
βο(ρρᾶ) ἐχό(μεναι) Θέωνοϲ τοῦ Πολυκράτου β ἀν(ὰ) δ∠γ´ιβ´
βο(ρρᾶ) ἐχό(μεναι) διὰ τοῦ αὐτοῦ η ἀν(ὰ) δ∠γ´ιβ´

παρα(κείμεναι) νό(του) ἐχό(μεναι) Πάτρωνος τοῦ Πτολεμαίου ιη ἀν(ὰ) δ̣∠γ΄ιβ΄
νό(του) ἐχό(μεναι) ἀρχό(μεναι) ἀπη(λιώτου) Ζωπύρου [το]ῦ Ζωπύρου ιγ ἀν(ὰ)
δ∠γ΄ιβ΄
[λι(βὸς) ἐ]χό(μεναι) Θέωνος τοῦ Πολυκρά[το]υ̣ κβ ἀν(ὰ) δ∠γ΄ιβ΄
[λι(βὸς) ἐχό(μεναι)] ἀ̣ρχό(μεναι) νό(του) Πετερμοῦθις Σαμ[ῶτο]ς θ
[βο(ρρᾶ) ἐχό(μεναι)] Πακῦρρις Μαρρείους δ
ἐχό(μεναι)] Ἀθεμμεὺς Ἀθεμμέως ις
ἐχό(μεναι) Ἀ]πολλωνίδου τοῦ Φαίδρου καὶ Πετεχῶντος κθ (ὧν)
. . ιε ἀν(ὰ) ϵdήμή ιδ [ἀν(ὰ)] δ∠γ΄ιβ΄
παρα(κείμεναι) λι(βὸς) ἐχό(μεναι) Διονύσιος Ἑρμί̣[ου] ιζ ἀν(ὰ) ϵdήμή
[λι(βὸς) ἐχό(μεναι) Ἀ]πολλώνιος Διονυσοδ̣ώρου ιβ ἀν(ὰ) δ∠γ΄ιβ΄
[λι(βὸς) ἐχό(μεναι) Π̣ετεχῶν Ὥρου ιδ ἀν(ὰ) δ∠γ΄ιβ΄

(fragment b)

Col. II

] . . . . ιβ
Πτο]λεμαίου (ὀγδοηκοντ[αρούρου])
κ̣λ(ήρου) (ἄρουραι) κς
]ώ̣σεως β∠d
] μ̣ισθώ(σ) ϵ∠d
] β
] Διο̣ν̣υ̣σ̣[ίου] κλ(ήρου) (ἄρουραι) ι
] . . . . . . (ὀγδοηκονταρούρου) κλ(ήρου) (ἄρουραι) ι
Φιλο]ξένου τοῦ Καλλικ[ράτ]ου (ὀγδοηκονταρούρου)
κλ(ήρου) (ἄρουραι) νη
Ἀλεξ]ά̣ν̣δρου τοῦ Ἀπολλωνί[ο]υ (ἄρουραι) ϵ
] . . . . . .ϵ( ) δια ζ
] . . . .οδώρου (ὀγδοηκονταρούρου) κλ(ήρου)
(ἄρουραι) κ
] . . . .ς̣ ἐν μισθώσει ι̣ς∠
] . τοῦ προσημ[. . . .] (ἄρουραι) δ
Φιλο]ξένου τοῦ Καλλικράτου (ὀγδοηκονταρούρου)
κλ(ήρου) (ἄρουραι) ϵ
] μ̣ι̣σθώ(σ) ἣν καὶ ἐπ̣εξύσθαι π[
χ]άριν τῶν ἐπικ̣ε̣ι(μένων) ὑδάτων

] μεγά(λου) περιχώματος
[γίνονται τοῦ] περιχώματος

Col. III

βο(ρρᾶ) ἐχό(μεναι) ἀρχό(μεναι) νό(του) ἐν τῶι λεγομένωι .[περιχώματι]
ἐμβρόχου ἐν μιςθώςει .[
βο(ρρᾶ) ἐχό(μεναι) ἁλμυρίδος ἐν μιςθώςει [
παρα(κείμεναι) βο(ρρᾶ) ἐχό(μεναι) ἀρχό(μεναι) βο(ρρᾶ) Τεεφίβιος Ἁρκοίφιο[ς
νό(του) ἐχό(μεναι) Σαραπίων Πτολεμαίου [
νό(του) ἐχό(μεναι) Πετεσọῦχος Τεῶτος θ[
παρα(κείμεναι) λι(βὸς) ἐχό(μεναι) ἀβρόχου ἐν μιςθώ(ςει) ἣν ἐπικε .[
παρα(κείμεναι) ἀπη(λιώτου) ἐχό(μεναι) ἀρχό(μεναι) βο(ρρᾶ) Ἴ̣ς̣τρου τοῦ
Πτολεμαίọυ̣ [
νό(του) ἐχό(μεναι) Ἑριεὺς Τοθοείους [
νό(του) ἐχό(μεναι) Ὀνν[ῶ]φρις Ἁρχύ̣ψιος [
νό(του) ἐχό(μεναι) ἀρχό(μεναι) ἀπη(λιώτου) Ἑριεὺς Τοθοείους [
λι(βὸς) ἐχό(μεναι) ἰβίων τρο(φῆς) δ[ιὰ
παρα(κείμεναι) νό(του) ἐχό(μεναι) Νίκωνος [
νό(του) ἐχό(μεναι) Πολεμάρχου τ[οῦ
νό(του) ἐχό(μεναι) [
παρα(κείμεναι) ἀπη(λιώτου) [ἐχό(μεναι)] ἁ̣λμυ(ρίδος) ἐν̣ [μιςθώςει
ἀπη(λιώτου) ἐχό(μεναι) ἀρχό(μεναι) βο(ρρᾶ) ἁλμυ(ρίδος) [
χάριν τῶν ἐπικει[μένων ὑδάτων
μεγάλου περιχ[ώματος
νό(του) ἐχό(μενον) χῶμα ἐκτὸς̣ [μιςθώςεως
παρα(κείμεναι) βο(ρρᾶ) ἐχ[ό(μεναι)] ἀρχό(μεναι) λι(βὸς) ε[
ἐξαγω(γοῦ) χάριν̣ [
π̣[

(fragment c)

Col. IV

ἐν τῶι λεγομέν]ωι Θεμίςτου περιχώματι
Ἀςκληπιάδου τοῦ] Πτολεμαίου ἐφό(δου) κλ(ήρου) μεταβεβη(κότος)
εἰς κα(τοικίαν) (ἄρουραι) κδ
] Θ̣ο̣τ̣ο̣ρταίου (ἄρουραι) ε (ὧν) β∠ ἀν(ὰ) εdήμή β∠
ἀν(ὰ) δ∠γίβ

]ι̣μο̣ύθου καὶ τοῦ ἀδελ(φοῦ) θ (ὧν) δ̣∠ ἀν(ὰ) ϵ dήμή
δ∠ ἀν(ὰ) δ∠γ́ίβ́
] Διονυϲοδώρου ιγ∠
ἐν] μ̣ι̣ϲ̣θώϲει ἣν γεγονέναι γύην β̣d
] . . . . τοῦ Πετοϲίριοϲ (ἄρουραι) .∠d (ὧν)
ἀν(ὰ) ϵdήμ]ή γd ἀν(ὰ) δ∠γ́ίβ́
] ιβ (ὧν) ϛ [ἀ]ν̣(ὰ) ϵdήμή ϛ ἀν(ὰ) δ∠γ́ίβ́
] γεγονέναι γύην (ἄρουρα) α∠
το]ῦ Μ̣ε̣νίϲκου ϵ ἀν(ὰ) δ∠γ́ίβ́
]οϲ τοῦ Θέωνοϲ ἱππαρ[χ]ικοῦ κλ(ήρου) (ἄρουραι) ι
Ἡλιοδώρ]ου τοῦ Μηνοδώρου (ἑκατονταρούρου) κλ(ήρου) (ἄρουραι) ν
] ἐ̣κτὸϲ μιϲθώϲεωϲ (ἄρουραι) ζ∠d
ἕωϲ τῶν π]ε̣ρὶ Βερενικίδα Θεϲμοφόρου πεδίων λι(βὸϲ)
]βρόχου τοῦ ἐν μιϲθώϲει ιϵ∠dλ́β́
] Πᾶϲιϲ Πεϲούριοϲ ϛ (ὧν) γ ἀν(ὰ) ϵdήμή γ ἀν(ὰ) δ∠γ́ίβ́
] .ωνίδου τοῦ Πτολεμαίου ιβ (ὧν) ϛ ἀν(ὰ) ϵdήμή
ϛ ἀ̣[ν(ὰ) δ]∠γ́ί[β́]
]ώ̣ρου τοῦ Διονυϲοδώρου ϛ (ὧν) γ ἀν(ὰ) ϵdήμή
γ [ἀν(ὰ)] δ̣∠γ́[ίβ́]
]ενῆϲιϲ η (ὧν) δ [ἀ]ν̣(ὰ) ϵdήμ̣ή δ ἀν(ὰ) δ∠γ́ίβ́
Κο]μοάπιοϲ ιϵ ἀν(ὰ) ϵdήμή
]νωρο̣υ ι (ὧν) ϵ ἀν(ὰ) ϵdή[μ]ή ϵ ἀν(ὰ) δ∠γ́ίβ́

Col. V

ἐχό(μεναι) ἀρχό(μεναι)] λ̣ι̣(βὸϲ) Πετεχῶν Τ̣εῶτοϲ ι (ὧν) ϵ ἀν(ὰ) ϵdήμή
δ ἀν(ὰ) δ∠γ́ίβ́
ἀπ[η(λιώτου)] ἐχ[ό(μεναι)] ἐμβρό(χου) ἐμ μιϲθώϲει ιϵ
βο(ρρᾶ) ἐχό(μεναι) Πᾶϲιϲ Πεϲούριοϲ (ἄρουραι) μθ (ὧν) λα ἀν(ὰ) ϵdήμή
ιη ἀν(ὰ) δ∠γ́ίβ́
[βο(ρρᾶ) ἐχό(μεναι) Π]α̣ν̣ταύχ[ο]υ τοῦ Π[αν]ταύχου χερϲεφίππου
κλ(ήρου) (ἄρουραι) δ∠dή
παρα(κειμένη) [ἀ]πη(λιώτου) ἐχο(μένη) ἐμβρόχου ἐν μιϲθώϲει αd
παρα(κείμεναι) [ἀπη(λιώτου)] ἐ̣χό(μεναι) ἀρχό(μεναι) νό(του) Μενίϲκου τοῦ
Πτολεμαίου
ἐφό(δου) κλ(ήρου) (ἄρουραι) κ

[β]ο(ρρᾶ) ἐχ[ό(μεναι)] ἱερᾶc γῆc Cούχου θεοῦ μεγάλου με(γάλου) β∠

[βο(ρρᾶ) ἐ]χ̣[ό(μεναι)] Cυμμάχου τοῦ Θεοδώρου (ὀγδοηκονταρούρου) κλ(ήρου) (ἄρουραι) ξ

[βο(ρρᾶ) ἐ]χό(μεναι) ἐμβρόχου ἐν μιcθώcει ιγ∠

π̣αρα(κειμένηc) βο(ρρᾶ) ἐχο(μένηc) ἀρχο(μένηc) λ[ι(βὸc)] καλάμου κεντρ[ί]του ∠δή

ἀπη(λιώτου) ἐχό(μεναι) ἀρχό(μεναι) νό(του) ἐμβρό(χου) ὃν καὶ γεγονέν[αι γύην] γ∠

γίνονται τοῦ περιχώματοc

Remainder of column blank. Traces of a further column do not merit publication.

47 ἀβρόχου corr. from ἐμβρόχου   50 ψ in Ἀρχύψιοc corr. from μ

Col. I. 'Adjacent on the south, Horos son of Harchypsis, 16 arouras. Adjacent on the south, Theon son of Polykrates, 8. Adjacent on the south, Didymos son of Antikrates, 13 at $4\frac{11}{12}$. Adjacent on the south, Alexandros son of Herakleides, 6 at $4\frac{11}{12}$. Adjacent on the south, Dionysios son of Soterides, 6 at $4\frac{11}{12}$. Adjacent on the south (and the survey now proceeds from east to west), Charidemos son of Apollonios, 12 at $4\frac{11}{12}$. Adjacent on the west, farmed by the same man, 10 at $4\frac{11}{12}$. Adjacent on the west, Philoxenos son of Nikanor, 5 at $5\frac{41}{48}$. Adjacent on the west (and the survey now proceeds from north to south) Ptolemaios son of Nikanor, 5 at $5\frac{11}{12}$. Adjacent on the north [*sic*], Theon son of Polykrates, 2 at $4\frac{11}{12}$. Adjacent on the north [*sic*], farmed by the same man, 8 at $4\frac{11}{12}$. Lying alongside, adjacent on the south, Patron son of Ptolemaios, 18 at $4\frac{11}{12}$. Adjacent on the south (and the survey now proceeds from east to west), Zopyros son of Zopyrus, 13 at $4\frac{11}{12}$. Adjacent on the west, Theon son of Polykrates, 22 at $4\frac{11}{12}$. Adjacent on the west (and the survey now proceeds from south to north), Petermouthis son of Samos, 9. Adjacent on the north, Pakyrris son of Marres, 4. Adjacent on the...Athemmeus son of Athemmeus, 16. Adjacent on the..., Apollonides son of Phaidros and Petechon, 29, of which 15 are rented at $5\frac{19}{48}$ and 14 at $4\frac{11}{12}$. Lying alongside, adjacent on the west, Dionysios son of Hermias, 17 at $5\frac{19}{48}$. Adjacent on the west, Apollonios son of Dionysodoros, 12 at $4\frac{11}{12}$. Adjacent on the west, Petechon son of Horos, 14 at $4\frac{11}{12}$.'

2 Θέων Πολυκράτου: recurs ll. 10, 14. For the 3rd decl. gen. in -ου, common in this text but rare in the rest of vols. I and IV, see Mayser, I, p. 247.

10 and 11 βο(ρρᾶ) is a mistake for νό(του), which the scribe wrote rightly in 12 and 13 without going back to correct himself here.

15 Πετερμοῦθιc Cαμ[ῶτο]c: the only Crown tenant in this text who can be identified elsewhere; cf. **1129**. 54 and 66 (123 B.C.).

17 The natural restoration is βο(ρρᾶ), but by l. 20 the survey is proceeding toward the west, and the change of direction may have occurred earlier, in 17 or 18, without a warning ἀρχό(μεναι).

25 Probably ἐκτὸc μιcθ]ώ̣cεωc (cf. 60, 78), but possibly a name.

26 ἐν] μιcθώ(cει) or ἐκτὸc] μιcθώ(cεωc). See p. 3.

28 Διο̣ν̣υ̣c̣[ίου: space limitations forbid Διο̣ν̣υ̣c̣[οδώρου.

30 For Philoxenos see introd.

32 δια: obscure.

35 προcημ[. . . .]: προcημ[αινο(μένου)]?

36 ἐπεξύcθαι: probably 'heaped up' with sand, the opposite of κατεξύcθαι (**84**. 16 n.). The word does not seem to have occurred previously in a comparable context.

37 π[: perhaps π[ᾶcαν or π[αρά; probably not = 80.

38 χ]άριν τῶν ἐπικε̣ι̣(μένων) ὑδάτων: cf. 58 and the instances of water damage reported in **61**(b). 132–69, **74**, and **75**.

39 At the beginning of the line supply perhaps [τῶν ἀπὸ τοῦ].

40 [γίνονται τοῦ] περιχώματος: cf. 101; **1118**. 1 note.

41 The name of the perichoma probably began with pi. If so, this will be the name elsewhere abbreviated Παω( ).

55 Line 56 shows that the direction of the survey changes here, so perhaps [ἀρχό(μεναι) λι(βόϲ) is to be restored. But that is not certain in this text; cf. introd.

56 A stroke may have been lost before this line; cf. 61 n.

58–9 Cf. 38–9.

61 ε[: the stroke before the first word of the line probably indicates that the land is out of cultivation; cf. 42, 43, 47, 57, 58, 60, and 56 note. If so, E as the first letter of a name would be out of place.

64 Θεμίϲτου περιχώματι: cf. **84**. 140.

65 'Αϲκληπιάδου τοῦ] Πτολεμαίου: cf. **84**. 152; **1118**. 131; **32**.

ἐφό(δου) κλ(ήρου) μεταβεβη(κότοϲ): clumsy word order; see the passages just cited for a smoother version. Crawford's expansion ἐφό(δου) κλ(ηρούχων) μεταβεβη(κότων) is unconvincing not only because it lacks a parallel, but because it implies that catoecs occupied a higher grade than cleruchs, whereas they were cleruchs themselves.

66 C. supplies Τεῶτοϲ τοῦ before Θοτορταίου.

67 'Ι̣μ̣ο̣ύθου or Πετε]ι̣μ̣ο̣ύθου.

τοῦ ἀδελ(φοῦ): τοῦ λο(ιποῦ) κλ(ήρου) C.

70 . ∠d: the sign before looks more like an aroura symbol repeated by mistake than like any numeral. C. reads ϵ∠d.

75 The editors of **152**, followed by C., print Θέων]οϲ τοῦ Θέωνοϲ ἱππαρ[χι]κοῦ κλ(ήρου). The ι of ἱππαρχικοῦ should not be bracketed; and Θέων]οϲ is very bold. The discrepancy between the form of the holding here and later perhaps weighs little in this text (cf. introd.), but though the later Theon was hippeus there is no indication that he was hipparches. Still, it may be so.

76 For Heliodoros cf. introd.

78 ἕωϲ τῶν π]ε̣ρὶ κτλ.: cf. **84**. 189.

79 ἀ]βρόχου or ἐμ]βρόχου. For the following masculine article instead of the usual feminine, cf. l. 100, ὅν.

85]ν Ὥρου or]νώρου.

86 The figures given total 9, not 10 arouras.

88 ἐμ = ἐν.

91 For Pantauchos see introd.

94 Μενίϲκου τοῦ Πτολεμαίου: cf. his son's land, **84**. 176.

99 καλάμου κεντρ[ί]του: not land 'cultivated' with prickly reeds (**61**(b). 426 n.), but out of cultivation because overgrown with them.

100 ὅν: cf. 79 n.

1117. Land Survey

P. Teb. 151 (a) 17 × 18·5 cm. 120/119 B.C.
(b) 16 × 26 cm.
(c) 68 × 29·5 cm.

Three non-contiguous fragments of a survey similar to **84**, **85**, **1116**, and **1118–21**. A terminus a quo for the text is supplied by the reference to year 51 of Euergetes II in line 166, a terminus ante by Petron son of Theon, the transfer of whose cleros to Didymarchos son of Apollonios was known to Menches' office by Tybi 29, year 2 of Soter II (**30**. 1). A comparison of the crop information in line 6 with that in **62**. 187, **61**(a). 70, and **1110**. 159 shows that **1117** does not refer to years 52 or 53 of Euergetes or 2 of Soter, and year 54 = 1 is accounted for in **1118**. Only year 51, 120/119 B.C., remains possible.

The reader who attempts a close study of **84** and **1117–21** will often find the similarities and dissimilarities between passages which clearly cover approximately the same territory rather bewildering. Apart from annual changes wrought by the flood, and exchanges of property among various tenants, the order in which lots are named varies according to the whim of the surveyors, who sometimes followed the same path from year to year but sometimes did not. But however the team meandered from lot to lot, in this group of texts the topographical subdivisions of the fields of Kerkeosiris, called *περιχώματα*, seem always to have been surveyed following a basic order: Koiri( ), Second, Third South, Third North, Fourth, Themistou, Pao( ), Kerkeouris West, Kerkeouris East, and Psinara( ).

It is often difficult, however, to determine at which point in a given list a dividing line has been crossed, because such headings as are found in **84**. 66, 140, 193 (where *Παω*( ) should be restored), and 203; **1117**. 97, 124; and **1121**. 3 are comparatively unusual. Most often the perichoma with which a given fragment deals can be determined only by comparison with parallel texts, or by cross-checks with **94**+**1107** and **62**. The first of these rolls is of very limited value for this purpose, since the Crown holdings it describes were not very permanent and often cannot be located in texts from different years; and **62**, dealing with land *ἐν ἀφέcει*, is so difficult to follow that the first editors believed the locations it named were not perichomata at all but *γύαι*. Crawford, p. 110, agrees, but the word *gyes* is based on false readings; see **1104**. 7 note. The term *γύηc* is indeed found at Kerkeosiris, but it apparently meant simply 'field'; cf. **105**. 13 n., where our text **1116** (ll. 69, 73, 100) is cited under the number **152**.

The difficulty arises from two basic sources:

1. The scribe of **62** is often guilty of irritating and misleading negligence: with few exceptions, he names only one perichoma per cleruch, however widespread the property may in fact have been. For this reason parcels of the larger cleroi are not a safe guide in determining the perichoma to which a survey fragment refers.

2. The boundary between the Fourth Perichoma and the Third North was apparently so indistinct that survey teams crossed over it easily, and we therefore find under the

heading δ̄ farms which according to **62** were really in the γ̄ *βο(ρρᾶ)*: so **84**. 97, 106, 113, 117, 119 and parallel texts.

Despite these difficulties, the following chart is probably a fairly accurate index to the content of these papyri.

	1117 (120/119)	**84** (118/117)	**1118** (117/116)	**1119** (115/114)	**1120** (late)	**1121** (?)
Koiri( )	—	5–57; 201–end	—	—	—	—
Second	—	—	—	all	—	—
Third South	—	—	—	—	1–37	—
Third North	1–53	—	2–68	—	38–91	—
Fourth	—	66–138	69–124	—	92–end	—
Themistou	—	139–192	125–158	—	—	—
Pao( )	54–96	193–198	159–end	—	—	—
Kerkeouris West	97–123	—	—	—	—	—
Kerkeouris East	124–end	—	—	—	—	—
Psinara( )	—	—	—	—	—	all

The order in which perichomata were surveyed is probably different in **1116** because of its much earlier date. **85** presents a different and presently insoluble problem, inasmuch as it lists under the heading *Πτολεμαίου λεγομένου νό(του) περιχώ(ματος)* (**85**. 4) cleroi which according to **62** were in the Koiri( ). The *βορρᾶ περίχωμα* of **85**. 112 may be an extension of the Ptolemaiou Notou. Neither of these perichomata recurs elsewhere in our archive; perhaps they are simply the Koiri( ) under a less common name.

Col. I

(*c*. 8 lines lost)

ἱερᾶς γῆς ἐλ(αςςόνων) διὰ Πνεφερῶ(τος) τοῦ Π]ẹτειμ̣ούθ̣ο̣υ
[καὶ τῶν] ἀδελ̣(φῶν) ϵ cπό(ρος) (πυρῶι)
[λι(βὸς) ἐχό(μεναι) Χῦψις Π]ẹτεςούχου γ καὶ ἀπὸ τῆς (πρότερον) Ἁρχύψιος
[τοῦ Πετεής]ιος α, (γίνονται) δ ἀν(ὰ) δ∠γ́ιβ́ cπό(ρος) ἀρά(κωι) ἐν
μ̣ε(λανθείωι)
[λι(βὸς) ἐχό(μ.) ἀρχό(μ.) βο(ρρᾶ) κλ(ήρου) (ἑπταρούρου) Χο(μήνιος)
Ἁρχ]ῦψις Πετοςίριος ς∠ τοῦ αὐ(τοῦ) βα(ςιλικῆς) ∠ ἀν(ὰ) ϵ,
(γίνονται) ζ (ὧν)
[cπό(ρος) φ]α(κῶι) ϵ ἀρά(κωι) β γεω(ργὸς) Πτόλλις
[νό(του) ἐχό(μ.) ἀρχό(μ.) λι(βὸς) κλ(ήρου) (ὀγδοηκονταρούρου) Ἀμ]μωνίου
τοῦ Ἀπολλωνίου ιη (ὧν) cπό(ρος) (πυρῶι) ι
[κρι](θῆι) δ φα(κῶι) δ γεω(ργὸς) Φαῆςις Φίβιος

[ἀπη(λιώτου) ἐχό(μ.) ἀρχό(μ.) βο(ρρᾶ) Πε]τεσọύχου θε(οῦ) διὰ Πετεσούχου
ε ἀν(ὰ) γ σπό(ρος) (πυρῶι)
[νό(του) ἐχό(μ.) κλ(ήρου) ἐφό(δου) Ἀπολ]λωνίου τοῦ Πτολεμαίου ϛ
σπό(ρος) (πυρῶι) γεω(ργὸς) αὐ(τός)
[νό(του) ἐχό(μ.) Διο]νυσίου τοῦ Πυρρίχου διὰ Πνεφερῶτος
[τοῦ Πετει]μούθου β ἀν(ὰ) ε σπό(ρος) (πυρῶι)
[νό(του) ἐχό(μενον) Διο]νυσίου τοῦ Πυρρίχου παρα(δείσου) ẹρή(μου) d

Col. II

(c. 9 lines lost)

/[
/λ[ι(βὸς) ἐχο(μ.)
/λι(βὸς) ἐχο(μ.) ἀρχο(μ.) νό(του) Ὧρ[ος
/βο(ρρᾶ) ἐχο(μ.) \`ἀρχο(μ.) ἀπη(λιώτου)´ Ψ[ε]ṇῆσις Σ[
/λι(βὸς) ἐχο(μ.) ἀρχο(μ.) βο(ρρᾶ) Φατρ[ῆς
/νό(του) ἐχό(μ.) ἀρ[χό(μ.)] ἀπη(λιώτου) κλ(ήρου) (ἑπτ[αρούρου)
/[τοῦ αὐτοῦ] β̣α(σιλικῆς) α ἀν(ὰ) [ε
/λι(βὸς) ἐχό(μ.) ἀ̣ρχό(μ.) νό(του) κλ(ήρου) (ἑπταρούρου) Χ[ο(μήνιος
/βο(ρρᾶ) ἐχο(μ.) ἀρχο(μ.) ἀπη(λιώτου) Δη[
/λι(βὸς) ἐχο(μ.) ἀρχο(μ.) βο(ρρᾶ) Ψεṿ[
/νό(του) ἐχό(μ.) ἀρχό(μ.) ἀπη(λιώτου) ⟨κλ(ήρου)⟩ (ἑπτ[αρούρου)
/τοῦ αὐτοῦ]
/βα(σιλικῆς) β∠ ἀν(ὰ) [ε
λι(βὸς) ἐχό(μ.) ἀρχό(μ.) νό(του) κλ(ήρου) [

(fragment b)

Col. III

. . . .

]. .[ο]υς
ἀ]ρχ̣[ό(μ.)] ἀ[πη(λιώτου) ± 10] ιβ [ἀν(ὰ) δ∠γ´ιβ´
λ̣ι(βὸς) ẹχό(μ.) ἀρχό(μ.) β[ο(ρρᾶ)] Πνεφερῶς Πẹτειμούθọυ ε∠ ἀν(ὰ) δ[
ἀπη(λιώτου) ἐχό(μ.) ἀρχό(μ.) νό(του) Ὧρος καὶ Φαγάτης Μικίωνος
ιϛ (ὧν) [
βο(ρρᾶ) ἐχό(μ.) Πνεφερῶς Ὥρου καὶ Ὧρος καὶ οἱ μέ(τοχοι) θ ἀν(ὰ) δ∠̣γ´ι̣β̣´
βο(ρρᾶ) ἐχό(μ.) ἀρχό(μ.) ἀπη(λιώτου) Ὧρος Ὀρσείους ϛ∠ ἀν(ὰ) δ∠γ´ιβ´
λι(βὸς) ἐχό(μ.) Ἁρφαῆσις Πετεσούχου δ∠ ἀν(ὰ) δ∠γ´ιβ´

λι(βὸc) ἐχό(μ.) Cọκ̣μ̣ῆνιc Πετεcούχου καὶ οἱ μέ(τοχοι) ̣ [ἀν(ὰ)] δ∠γ́ιβ́
[λι(βὸc) ἐχο(μ.)] . [ἀν(ὰ)] δ∠γ́ιβ́
λι(βὸc) ẹχ̣ọ́(μ.) ἀ̣ρ̣χ̣ọ́(μ.) ν̣ọ́(του) [Ὀ]ν̣ν̣ῶφ[ρ]ιc Πετεαρψενήcιοc
γ⟦∠d⟧ ἀν(ὰ) δ∠γ́ιβ́
[βο(ρρᾶ) ἐχό(μ.) ἀρχό(μ.) ἀπη(λιώτου) Πετοcῖριc] Π̣ετενεφιείουc καὶ
οἱ μ̣ẹ́(τοχοι) ϛ∠ ἀν(ὰ) δ∠γ́[ιβ́]
λι(βὸc) ἐχό(μ.) ἀρχό(μ.) βο(ρρᾶ) Λύκοc Ζωπυρίωνοc δ ἀν(ὰ) [δ]∠γ́ιβ́
νό(του) ἐχό(μ.) ἀρχό(μ.) λι(βὸc) Πετεῆcιc Θώνιοc ε ἀν(ὰ) δ∠γ́ιβ́
ἀ̣πη(λιώτου) ἐχό(μενον) ἐγβαῖ(νον) βο(ρρᾶ) ἐξαγωγοῦ ∠
ἀπη(λιώτου) ἐχό(μ.) ἀρχό(μ.) βο(ρρᾶ) Ὀννῶφριc Ὥρου καὶ Μεγχῆc εd ἀν(ὰ)
δ∠γ́ιβ́
νό(του) ἐχό(μ.) Π̣ετ̣ẹῆcιc Τεῶτοc εd ἀν(ὰ) δ
νọ́(του) ἐχό(μ.) Τεῶc Πετεχῶντοc εd ἀν(ὰ) δ
ν̣[ό(του)] ἐχ[ό(μ.)] Ὀννῶφριc Ὥρου καὶ Μεγχῆc εd ἀν(ὰ) δ∠γ́ιβ́
νό(του) ἐχό(μ.) κλ(ήρου) ἐφόδου μεταβεβη(κότοc) εἰc τὴν κα(τοικίαν)
Ἀcκληπιάδου τοῦ Ἀcκληπιάδου ιβ
[νό(του)] ἐχ[ό(μενον)] κ[λ(ήρου)] ἐφόδου μεταβεβη(κότοc) εἰc τὴν κα(τοικίαν)
Πέτρων Θέωνοc
τὸ λο(ιπὸν) τοῦ κλ(ήρου)
[νό(του)] ẹχ̣ọ́(μ.) Πετεῆcιc Τεῶτοc ε (ὧν) γ ἀν(ὰ) δ, β ἀν(ὰ) γ
ν̣[ό(του)] ἐχ[ό(μ.)] Μαρρῆc Πετεχῶντοc η ἀν(ὰ) δ
νό(του) ἐχό(μ.) Ἀθεμμεὺc Πετεcούχου ιε ἀν(ὰ) δ∠γ́ιβ́
νό(του) ἐχο(μένη) πεφαραγγωμένηc α

(fragment c)

Col. IV

] ∠
]ε
]ῶντοc ϛ ἀν(ὰ) δ∠γ́ιβ́
κλ(ήρου) (ἑπταρούρου) Χο(μήνιοc) Ἁρυώτη]c Ἁρυώτου ϛ∠
[τοῦ α]ὐτοῦ βα(cιλικῆc) α ἀν(ὰ) ε
[νό(του) ἐχό(μ.) κλ(ήρου) (ἑπταρούρου) Χο(μήνιοc) Ἁ]ρμιῦcιc Cοκονώπιοc ϛ∠
[νό(του) ἐχό(μ.) Μα]ρρ[ῆ]c̣ Μαρρείουc βα(cιλικῆc) β∠dή ἀν(ὰ) δ∠γ́ιβ́
[νό(του) ἐχό(μ.)] κλ(ήρου) (ἑπταρούρου) Χο(μήνιοc) Ὧροc Ἁρφαήcιοc ϛ∠
τοῦ αὐτοῦ βα(cιλικῆc) α ἀν(ὰ) ε, (γίνονται) ζ∠
[νό(του) ἐχό(μ.)] ἀ̣ρχό(μ.) ἀπη(λιώτου) κλ(ήρου) (ὀγδοηκονταρούρου)

Λέοντοϲ τοῦ Λεοντίϲκου ˋτὸ λο(ιπὸν) τῶν μʹ ιε
[λι(βὸϲ) ἐχό(μ.) ἀρ]χό(μ.) βο(ρρᾶ) κλ(ήρου) (ὀγδοηκονταρούρου) [Δ]ώρου
τοῦ Πετάλου ιε
[νό(του) ἐχό(μενον)] ἐγβαῖ(νον) ἀπη(λιώτου) παρὰ τὴν προγεγεω(μετρημένην)
ϲχοι(νίον) τὸ λο(ιπὸν) τῆϲ διώρυ(γοϲ) ˋκαὶ χώ(ματοϲ)ʹ γ
νό(του) [ἐχό(μενον)] κλ(ήρου) ἐφό(δου) Πτολεμαίου τοῦ Μενίϲκου τὸ λο(ιπὸν) δ
[± 19] . δ̣[ιώρ]υ(γοϲ) β
ν[ό(του)] ἐχό(μ.) ⟦ἀρχό(μ.) λι(βὸϲ)⟧ Ἀθε̣μμεὺϲ Πετεϲούχο[υ] ⟦κ⟧ε∠ ἀν(ὰ) γ
νό(του) ἐχό(μ.) ˋἀρχό(μ.) λι(βὸϲ)ʹ Πύρριχοϲ Ἀπύγχιοϲ ⟦ ± 16 ⟧
⟦ζ ἀν(ὰ)⟧ ϛ ἀν(ὰ) γ
ἀπη(λιώτου) ἐχό(μ.) ἀρχό(μ.) ˋβο(ρρᾶ)ʹ κλ(ήρου) (ὀγδοηκονταρούρου) Δώρου
τοῦ Πετάλου ι
νό(του) ἐχό(μ.) ἀρχό(μ.) ⟨λι(βὸϲ)⟩ ἱερᾶϲ γῆϲ Ϲοκνεβτύνιϲ θεοῦ μεγά(λου)
διὰ τῶν ἱερέων ιε
ἀπη(λιώτου) ἐχό(μ.) κλ(ήρου) (ὀγδοηκονταρούρου) Διοδότου τοῦ Ἀπολλωνίου
τὸ λο(ιπὸν) κβ
ἀπη(λιώτου) ἐχό(μ.) ἐγβαί(νουϲαι) βο(ρρᾶ) παρὰ τὴν προγεγεω(μετρημένην)
χώ(ματοϲ) ἐκτὸϲ μιϲ(θώϲεωϲ) καὶ διώρυ(γοϲ) ϛ

Col. V

ἀπη(λιώτου) ἐχο(μ.) ἀρχο(μ.) β[ο(ρρᾶ)] ἀπὸ τ̣ῶν περὶ̣ [τὸ]ν Ἰβιῶ(να)
τῶν (εἰκοϲιπενταρούρων) πε(δίων)
Ὀννῶφριϲ Πετε̣χῶ̣ντοϲ βα(ϲιλικῆϲ) [
ἀπη(λιώτου) ἐχό(μ.) ἀρχό(μ.) βο(ρρᾶ) κλ(ήρου) (ὀγδοηκονταρούρου) Δώρο̣[υ]
τοῦ Πετάλου [
νό(του) ἐχό(μ.) Ἀθεμμεὺϲ Πε̣[τ]ε̣ϲούχου βα(ϲιλικῆϲ) ε ἀν(ὰ) γ
νό(του) ἐχό(μ.) ἐγβαί(ν.) λι(βὸϲ) Πολίτιοϲ [Ὀν]νώφριοϲ β̣α̣(ϲιλικῆϲ) θ∠ ἀν(ὰ) γ
νό(του) ἐχό(μενον) ἐξαγωγοῦ ∠
νό(του) ἐχό(μ.) κλ(ήρου) (ὀγδοηκονταρούρου) Κ̣αλλικράτουϲ [τ]οῦ Φιλοξένου ν̣α
νό(του) ἐχό(μ.) ὑπολό(γου) ἐ̣μ̣βρόχου τ̣[οῦ] ἀπὸ τοῦ μ (ἔτουϲ) ζ
νό(του) ἐχό(μ.) ἐγβαί(ν.) ἀπη(λιώτου) ἐξαγωγ[ο]ῦ β
νό(του) ἐχο(μ.) ἀρχο(μ.) λι(βὸϲ) . . . . ι
ἀ̣π̣[η(λιώτου)] ἐ̣χό(μ.) ἀρχό(μ.) νό(του) ὑπολό(γου) ἁλμυ(ρίδοϲ) τοῦ̣ [. . . . . . .]
(ἔτουϲ) δ̣

[βο(ρρᾶ)] ἐχό(μ.) ὑ[πο]λό(γου) ἐμβρό(χου) τ̣ο̣ῦ̣ ἕ̣ω̣ς̣ [τοῦ λθ] (ἔτους) ια
β[ο(ρρᾶ)] ἐχό(μ.) ἀρχ[ό(μ.)] λι(βὸς) ὑπολό(γου) ἁλμυ(ρίδος) τ̣ο̣[ῦ ἀ]π̣ὸ̣
τοῦ μ (ἔτους) ιβ
ἀπη(λιώτου) ἐχό(μ.) ἱερᾶ̣[ς] γῆς Σούχου θεοῦ̣ [με]γά(λου) μεγά(λου) διὰ
Σαραπίωνος
τοῦ [Σ]α̣ραπίωνος κ[αὶ] τ̣ῶν με(τόχων) κ
ἀπη(λιώτου) ἐχό(μ.) ⟦ἀρχ̣[ό(μ.)]⟧ ὑπολό(γου) ἁλμυ(ρίδος) τοῦ ἕω[ς] τοῦ
λθ (ἔτους) ιβ
ἀπ[η(λιώτου)] ἐχό(μ.) ἀρχό(μ.) β̣ο̣(ρρᾶ) ὑπολό(γου) ἐμβρό(χου) τοῦ ἕως τοῦ
λθ̣ (ἔτους) ι
νό(του) ἐχό(μ.) ἀρχό̣(μ.) ἀπη(λιώτου) \`ὑπολό(γου)´ χέρσου τῆς ἕως τοῦ
μ (ἔτους) ε
λι(βὸς) ἐχό(μ.) ⟦ἀρ⟧ ὑπολό(γου) τοῦ ἕως τοῦ λθ (ἔτους) κατεξυ(σμένου) ε
λι(βὸς) ἐχό(μ.) ἀρχό(μ.) β[ο(ρρᾶ) ὑ]π̣ολό(γου) ἁλμυ(ρίδος) τοῦ ἀ[πὸ το]ῦ
μ (ἔτους) ε

Col. VI

(*c.* 5 lines lost)
ἀπὸ βορρᾶ καὶ λι(βὸς) (ὧν) ἐν τ[ῶι καλουμένωι Κερκεούρει λι(βὸς) πε(ριχώματι)]
ἀρχό(μ.) βο(ρρᾶ) ἱερᾶς γῆς Σοκ̣[νεβτύνιος θεοῦ διὰ τ]ῶν ἱερέων
κοινῆι ιδ
νό(του) ἐχό(μεν) ἀρχο(μεν) ἀπη(λιώτου) . . . . . . [
λι(βὸς) ἐχό(μ.) ἀρχό(μ.) βο(ρρᾶ) ⟦νό(του) ἐχό(μ.)⟧ Παπνεβ̣τ[ῦνις
βα(σιλικῆς)] β ἀν(ὰ) δ∠γ´ιβ´
νό(του) ἐχό(μ.) Παπνεβτ[ῦνις βα(σιλικῆς .] ἀ̣ν̣(ὰ) δ∠γ´ιβ´
Σοκνεβτύ̣ν̣ι̣[ος θεοῦ διὰ]
νό(του) ἐχό(μ.) Πετερμοῦθις Ἀ̣[μεν]ν̣έ[ως βα(σιλικῆς) .] ἀν(ὰ) γ∠
νό(του) ἐχό(μ.) Πετερμοῦθις Σιεφμοῦτος ζ∠ ἀν(ὰ) δ∠γ´ιβ´
νό(του ἐχό(μ.) Σοκμῆνις Πετεσούχου καὶ οἱ μέ(τοχοι) ζ∠ ἀν(ὰ) δ∠γ´ιβ´
νό(του) ἐχό(μ.) Ἁρβῆχις Ἑργέως ι ἀν(ὰ) δ∠γ´ιβ´
νό(του) ἐχό(μ.) ἱερᾶς γῆς ἐλ(ασσόνων) ἰβίω(ν) τροφῆς δι' Ἑργέως καὶ
τῶν με(τόχων) β
νό(του) ἐχό(μ.) Πετοσῖρις Ὥρου βα(σιλικῆς) γ ἀν(ὰ) δ∠γ´ιβ´
νό(του) ἐχό(μ.) Πετοσῖρις [Ἁ]ρκοίφιος βα(σιλικῆς) γ ἀν(ὰ) δ∠γ´ιβ´

νό(του) ἐχο(μένη) ἀρχο(μένη) ἀπη(λιώτου) ὑπολό(γου) ἁλμυ(ρίδος) ἀπὸ
τοῦ μ (ἔτους) α∠
λι(βὸς) ἐχό(μεναι) ἀ̣ρ̣χό(μ.) β̣ο̣(ρρᾶ) ⟦ἐχό(μ.)⟧ Κέντις Ὥρου ιδ ἀν(ὰ) δ∠γ′ιβ′
νό(του) ἐχό(μ.) Μαρρῆς Πακύρριος δ ἀν(ὰ) δ∠γ′ιβ′
νό(του) ἐχό(μ.) ἀρχό(μ.) λι(βὸς) Ἁρφαῆσις Πετεσούχου η ἀν(ὰ) α
ἀπη(λιώτου) ἐχό(μ.) ἀρχό(μ.) βο(ρρᾶ) ὑπολό(γου) τοῦ ἕως τοῦ λθ (ἔτους)
κατεξυ(σμένου) κ
λι(βὸς) ἐχό(μενον) ἀρχό(μενον) ἀπη(λιώτου) τὸ λο(ιπόν)
λι(βὸς) ἐχο(μένη) ἐγβαί(νουσα) βο(ρρᾶ) παρὰ τὴν προγεγεω(μετρημένην)
σχοι(νίον) διώρυ(γος) α̣
λι(βὸς) ἐχο(μένη) ἀρχο(μένη) βο(ρρᾶ) ἡ κεχω(ρισμένη) πρό[σ]οδος διὰ
γεω(ργοῦ) Πετεσοκονούριος
τοῦ Κεφάλωνος ἀπὸ τοῦ μθ (ἔτους)
νό(του) ἐχό(μ.) ὑπολό(γου) ἁλμυ(ρίδος) τοῦ ἀπὸ μ (ἔτους) ζ

Col. VII

[νό(του)] ἐχό(μ.) ἐγβαί(ν.) βο(ρρᾶ) ὑπολό(γου) τοῦ ἕως τοῦ
λθ (ἔτους) κατεξυ(σμένου) κβ
[νό(του) ἐχο(μένη)] π̣ερίστασις κώ(μης) νό(του)
[(γίνονται)] τ̣ο̣ῦ̣ περιχώ(ματος) (ἄρουραι)
(Blank space of *c.* 2 cm.)
ἀπὸ βορρᾶ καὶ ἀπη(λιώτου) (ὧν) ἐν τῶι καλουμένωι Κερκεούρει ἀπη(λιώτου)
πε(ριχώματι)
νό(του) κ̣α̣ὶ̣ ἀ̣πη(λιώτου) νό(του) μὲν ἀπὸ τῶν περὶ Θεογο(νίδα) πεδίων
ἀρχό(μενον) ἀπη(λιώτου) ἀπὸ τῶν περὶ Ταλὶ πε(δίων) διώρυγος Φίλωνος ∠d
βο(ρρᾶ) ἐχο(μένη) ἀρχο(μένη) ἀπη(λιώτου) ὑπολό(γου) ἁλμυ(ρίδος) τοῦ
ἕως τοῦ λθ (ἔτους) α∠
λι(βὸς) ἐχό(μ.) ἀρχό(μ.) βο(ρρᾶ) ἱερᾶς γῆς Σούχου θε(οῦ) μεγά(λου)
μεγά(λου) διὰ Ἀπολλωνίου Ποσει(δωνίου)
καὶ με(τόχων) δ∠
νό(του) ἐχό(μ.) ἀρχό(μ.) ἀπη(λιώτου) ὑπολό(γου) ἁλμυ(ρίδος) τοῦ
ἐν τῶι ν (ἔτει) δ∠
λι(βὸς) ἐχό(μενον) ὑδραγωγοῦ d
λι(βὸς) ἐχό(μ.) ὑπολό(γου) ἁλμυ(ρίδος) τοῦ ἀπὸ τοῦ μ (ἔτους) δ
λι(βὸς) ἐχό(μ.) ἐγβαί(ν.) βο(ρρᾶ) \`ἀρχό(μ.) βο(ρρᾶ)′ ὑπολό(γου)

ἀβρό(χου) ὑψη(λοῦ) τοῦ ἕως τοῦ λθ (ἔτους) β
νό(του) ἐχό(μενον) ἀρχό(μενον) ἀπη(λιώτου) ὁδοῦ τῆς ἀγούσης εἰς Ταλὶ ∠
λι(βὸς) ἐχό(μενον) ἀρχό(μενον) νό(του) Ἰσιείου συ(μπεπτωκότος ?) d
βό(ρρᾶ) ἐχό(μ.) ὑπολό(γου) ἁλμυ(ρίδος) τοῦ ἀπὸ τοῦ μ (ἔτους) ι
βο(ρρᾶ) ἐχό(μ.) ἀρχό(μ.) λι(βὸς) κλ(ήρου) (ὀγδοηκονταρούρου) Καλλικράτης Πτολεμαίου ιϛ
βο(ρρᾶ) ἐχό(μενον) ὑδραγωγοῦ d
βο(ρρᾶ) ἐχό(μ.) ⟦ἀρχό(μ.) ἀπη(λιώτου)⟧ ὑπολό(γου) ἁλμυ(ρίδος) τοῦ
ἀπὸ τοῦ μ (ἔτους) β
βο(ρρᾶ) ἐχό(μ.) ἀρχό(μ.) ἀπη(λιώτου) ὑπολό(γου) ἁλμυ(ρίδος) τοῦ
ἕως τοῦ λθ (ἔτους) ζ
λι(βὸς) ἐχο(μένη) ὑπολό(γου) τοῦ ἀπὸ τοῦ μ (ἔτους) α
λι(βὸς) ἐχό(μ.) ἀρχό(μ.) νό(του) Πετεῆσις Τεῶτος ε ἀν(ὰ) γ
βο(ρρᾶ) ἐχό(μ.) Φμούεις Παθήβιος δ∠ ἀν(ὰ) δ
βο(ρρᾶ) ἐχό(μ.) ἀρχό(μ.) ἀπη(λιώτου) ὑπολό(γου) ἁλμυ(ρίδος) τοῦ
ἀπὸ τοῦ μ (ἔτους) β
λι(βὸς) ἐχό(μ.) εἰσβαί(ν.) βο(ρρᾶ) παρὰ τὴν ⟨προγεγεω(μετρημένην)⟩
ἀβρό(χου) ὑπολό(γου) ἁλμυ(ρίδος) ἀπὸ τοῦ μ (ἔτους) β

Col. VIII

(*c*. 3 lines lost)
βο(ρρᾶ) ἐχο(μεν) ἀρ̣[χο(μεν) λι(βὸς)
ἀπη(λιώτου) ἐχό(μ.) ἱερᾶς γῆς Σοκνεβτύ̣ν̣[ιος θεοῦ]
διὰ τῶν ἱερέων κο̣ι̣[νῆι
ἀπη(λιώτου) ἐχο(μ.) Κατῦτις Κατύτιος [
ἀπη(λιώτου) ἐχο(μ.) ἀρχο(μ.) νό(του) Φαῆσις Ἁρυώτου [
βο(ρρᾶ) ἐχο(μ.) ἐγβαι(ν.) ἀπη(λιώτου) παρὰ τὴν προγεγεω(μετρημένην)
ὑ[δραγωγοῦ
βο(ρρᾶ) ἐχό(μ.) ἀρχό(μ.) ἀπη(λιώτου) ὑπολό(γου) ἁλμυ(ρίδος) τοῦ
ἐν τῶ[ι . (ἔτει) θ, (ὧν)]
α ἀν(ὰ) δ∠γʹιβʹ, η ἀν(ὰ) β∠
λι(βὸς) ἐχό(μ.) ἀρχό(μ.) νό(του) κλ(ήρου) ἐρη(μο)φύ(λακος)
μεταβεβη(κότος) εἰς τὴν κ̣[α(τοικίαν)]
Νεκτενίβιος τοῦ Ὥρου ι
βο(ρρᾶ) ἐχό(μ.) ἀρχό(μ.) ἀπη(λιώτου) ὑπολό(γου) ἁλμυ(ρίδος) τοῦ

ἀπὸ τοῦ μ (ἔτους) ϛ
λι(βὸς) ἐχό(μενα) τὰ περὶ Ταλὶ πεδία. Ἀμμωνίου τοῦ̣
Ἡρακλείδου ἐφόδου μ̣εταβε̣[β]η(κότος) εἰς τὴν κ̣[α(τοικίαν)
λι(βὸς) ἐχό(μ.) ἀρχό(μ.) νό(του) κλ(ήρου) ἐφόδου μεταβεβη(κότος)
εἰς τὴν κα(τοικίαν)
Δημητρίου τοῦ Ἡρακλείδου ιβ
τοῦ αὐτοῦ βα(σιλικῆς) δ ἀν(ὰ) δ∠γ´ιβ´, ⟨(γίνονται)⟩ ιϛ
βο(ρρᾶ) ἐχό(μ.) ὑπολό(γου) ἁλμυ(ρίδος) τοῦ ἀπὸ τοῦ μ (ἔτους) β
βο(ρρᾶ) ἐχό(μ.) ἐξαγωγοῦ β
βο(ρρᾶ) ἐχό(μ.) ἀρχό(μ.) ἀπη(λιώτου) κλ(ήρου) (ὀγδοηκονταρούρου)
Ἀμμωνίου τοῦ Ἀπολλωνίο̣[υ
λι(βὸς) ἐχό(μ.) ὑπολό(γου) ἐμβρό(χου) τοῦ ἀπὸ μ (ἔτους) θ̣[
λι(βὸς) ἐχό(μ.) \`ἀρχό(μ.) νό(του)´ ὑπολό(γου) ἐμβρό(χου) τοῦ ἐν
τῶι να (ἔτει) ϛ ἀν(ὰ) δ̣∠γ´ιβ´, κβ[
βο(ρρᾶ) ἐχό(μ.) Λύκος Ζωπυρίωνος η ἀν(ὰ) δ∠̣γ´ιβ´, .[
ἕως τῶν περὶ τὸν Ἰβιῶ(να) τῶν (εἰκοσιπενταρούρων) πε(δίων) βο(ρρᾶ) καὶ
λι(βὸς) [
ἀπὸ νό(του) καὶ ἀπη(λιώτου) (ὧν) ἀνὰ μέσον ὄντος τοῦ προγεγεω(μετρημένου)
ὕ[
ἐξαγωγοῦ

66 Πτολεμαίου: π corr. from α 70 ϛ corr. from γ 112 ἀ̣ρχο̣(μένης) βο̣(ρρᾶ) corr. from νό(του) 116 λι(βὸς): read νό(του) 132 λι(βὸς) corr. from νό(του) 140 ἕως: ε corr. from α. λθ corr. from μ 141 λι(βὸς) corr. from βο(ρρᾶ)

1–13 These properties are described from a different orientation in **1120**. 38–47 and the mutilated **1118**. 3 ff. The sketch on p. 149 is offered as one way of combining the descriptions (but cf. the caveat **1116** introd.).

1 ἱερᾶς γῆς ἐλ(αςςόνων): sc. ἱερῶν, cf. **88**. 61; for the restoration, **1118**. 3–4, **1120**. 38. The property meant is an ibis shrine, located in the northern part of the Third Perichoma according to **62**. 24.

3. ἐχό(μεναι): this word occurs approximately a thousand times in **84**, **85**, **826**, **830**, and **1116–21**, always in the abbreviated form εχ̂. The meaning is clear enough (**84**. 16 n., **86** introd.), but the vocalization is rather problematic. In Roman surveys in which the word is written in full, it is the adverb ἐχόμενα (SB I, 4325, ii, 4 and often; P. Ryl. II, 378. 11 and 16; l. 5 of the text should have been restored ἀρ]χομένων rather than ἐ]χομένων); and the same is apparently true of P. Petrie II 36. But in the Kerkeosiris surveys ἐχο(μ.) is clearly parallel to the participles abbreviated παρα( ) (e.g. **1118**. 68), ἀρχο( ) (16 below), and ἐγβαι( ) or εἰςβαι( ) (41). Of these the first does have an adverbial form, παρακειμένως, but not with the requisite meaning 'lying along side of'; and the others do not form adverbs. One must assume therefore that ἐχο(μ.) is in our texts an adjective. The editors of vols. I and III. 2 treat this adjective as in agreement with the category of land, ἐχο(μένης) for βα(σιλικῆς), ἐχό(μενος) for κλ(ῆρος), and the like. But there can be little if any doubt that the referent is actually ἄρουραι, which appears frequently in **1116** and sporadically in **85**, and with

κλῆροc of Ἁρχῦψιc, and βαcιλική	βαcιλική, 4 ἄρουραι	ἱερὰ γῆ ἐλαccόνων 5 ἄρουραι
κλῆροc of Ἀμμώνιοc Ἀπολλωνίου, also called Ἀπολλώνιοc Ἀπολλωνίου 18 ἄρουραι	βαcιλική leased to Πετεcοῦχοc θεόc, 5	
	κλῆροc of Ἀπολλώνιοc Πτολεμαίου, 7	
κλῆροc of Διονύcιοc Πυρρίχου 18⅜ ἄρουραι	βαcιλική, 2	
	¼ ἄρουρα of παράδειcοc ἔρημοc	

few exceptions (fractions, λο(ιπὸν), and properties whose extent is not given) is to be understood throughout. So **526**.

4 cπό(ροc) ἀρά(κωι) ἐν με(λανθείωι): I take this to mean that aracus was grown interspersed among black cumin plants; the phrase seems not to occur elsewhere. The doubtful μ could equally well be read as π but ἐν πε(δίωι) *aut sim.* seems pointless and no other resolution suggests itself.

5 ἀρχό(μεναι) βο(ρρᾶ): see **84**. 16 n. In all surveys of this archive except **1116**, use of ἀρχόμεναι is limited to instances when the survey team took a right angle in proceeding to the next parcel of land; but as **1116** shows, this is not inherent in the sense of the word, which means simply 'forming all or part of the boundary of the next property'. Given 6 parcels arranged as in the sketch p. 150 a surveyor moving from A to C would describe the latter as βορρᾶ ἐχόμεναι in respect to A and ἀρχόμεναι ἀπηλιώτου or λιβόc in respect to E or F respectively. It could also be described as ἀρχόμεναι βορρᾶ to B or ἀρχόμεναι νότου to D, but only in **1116** would that be stated in a line which began βορρᾶ ἐχόμεναι.

κλ(ήρου) : in comparable passages the editors of vols. I and III. 2 write κλ(ῆροc) (e.g., **84**. 20), but the genitive is necessary, since κλ(ήρου) is a category of land parallel to ἱερᾶc γῆc and βαcιλικῆc. Κλ(ηρουχικῆc) would also have seemed possible, but **85**. 72 and **1116**. 75 show that the word abbreviated κλ( ) is not feminine.

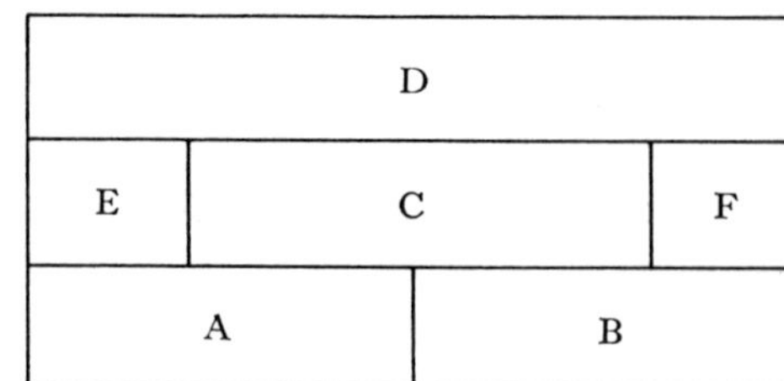

(ἑπταρούρου): grammatically this is gen. of possession, a cleros belonging to a 7-aroura cleruch. The editors of vols. I and III. 2 seem to understand the word as an adjective agreeing with κλῆρος (e.g. **84**. 198); but (ἑπταρούρου) is parallel to φυλακίτου in **84**. 124, ἐφόδου (**84**. 176), ἐφόδου μεταβεβη(κότος) (**84**. 113), and [χε]ρσεφίππου (**84**. 181). In **1116**. 75, ἱππαρ[χ]ικοῦ κλ(ήρου), the word order is significantly different.

Χο(μήνιος): Χο(μηνιακός) would also seem possible (**61**(a). 140), but cf. ἑπτ. τῶν Πτολεμαίου (**1118**. 40), ἑπτ. τῶν Ὥρου (**1120**. 15), and τριακοντάρουρος Φυλέως (**1110**. 49).

βα(σιλικῆς) ∠ ἀν(ὰ) ε: cf. p. 8.

9 διὰ Πετεσούχου: so **1118**. 6. Later the property was farmed by one Harphaesis; cf. **1120**. 40 and **93**. 62, where the extra $\frac{1}{8}$ aroura is προ( ) (cf. **1107** introd.).

10 ς is almost surely a mistake for ζ, the figure given in **1120**. 41, inasmuch as this plot reckoned at 7 arouras, plus the 17 located in **1119**. 38 and 79, will account for the whole of the man's allotment. The description of the land in **62**. 155 f. should be interpreted as γεω(μετρηθεῖσαι) β̄ γ̄ βο(ρρᾶ), i.e., surveyed in the Second Perichoma and the Third North, which is correct.

17 If this refers to the machimos Ψενῆσις Στεφάνου it must register Crown land rented in addition to his cleros, which was located elsewhere (**84**. 45 = 222).

30 ἀπη(λιώτου): after ἀρχό(μεναι) β[ο(ρρᾶ) in the line above one expects νό(του), but this cannot be read and would be inconsistent with the following ἀρχό(μεναι) νό(του). Perhaps a line with the orientation νό(του) ἐχό(μεναι) ἀρχό(μεναι) λι(βός) has dropped out.

46 A blank space was left between κλ(ήρου) and ἐφόδου. The rest of this man's property is located in **1118**. 108, 111 and parallel texts.

48–9 Petron had 15 arouras located in this perichoma (**62**. 146), divided into two plots of 8 and 7 (**1118**. 91 n.). But the orientation of the property is stated differently in other texts, so that I cannot tell which parcel is meant here.

53 πεφαραγγωμένης: 'gullied'; cf. P. Gurob, p. 44.

57 ff. Cf. **1118**. 164 ff.

60 βα(σιλικῆς) β∠δή: in **1118**. 167 the same lot is said to measure 3 arouras.

65 σχοι(νίον): in comparable passages the editors of vol. I wrote σχοι(νίου) (cf. **84**. 110, 139, 179, 190), but the accusative is required; Mayser II. 2, p. 330.

66 This property is located in the Themistou Perichoma according to **62**. 66, but that probably refers only to the 20 arouras in **84**. 177, not the 4 here. Such carelessness is common in **62**; cf. introd.

68 ⟦κ⟧ε∠: the cancellation of κ is probable but not quite certain.

71 This is apparently the land referred to in **1118**. 176, but the area is there given as 8 arouras.

74 Cf. **1118**. 178, where there are only 20 arouras.

78–9 Restore probably β ἀν(ὰ) γ and η; cf. **1122**. 43, 49.

81 In **1118**. 182 the tenant's name is spelled Πόλιτος and the area of the land is 10 arouras.

94 τῆς: the usual article after ὑπολό(γου) χέρσου is τοῦ. Probably the scribe simply forgot to correct τῆς after inserting ὑπολό(γου); but τῆς may have been intentional; cf. **1118**. 202, 205.

97 For the order in which perichomata were surveyed at Kerkeosiris see introd. to this text; cf. **1127**. For the restoration, cf. l. 124.

100 This line is a later insertion into the text.

101 ⟦νό(του) ἐχό(μ.)⟧: there is no mark of erasure, but the marginalia are obviously intended to replace this.

103 A later insertion. We are probably to understand νό(του) ἐχό(μεναι) Σοκνεβτύνιος θεοῦ διὰ Πετερμούθιος τοῦ Ἀμεννέως βα(σιλικῆς) ι ἀν(ὰ) γ∠. Cf. **84.** 161, where different boundaries are given; **1118.** 135–6.

111 A later insertion.

118 ἡ κεχω(ρισμένη) πρό[σ]οδος κτλ.: the reference is to land originally ὑπόλογος which was brought into cultivation as κεχωρισμένη πρόσοδος in 122/121 B.C. and leased at a low rent to Petesokonouris and others. Its total extent was 16½ arouras, but only a fraction of that will have been located here. Cf. **61**(b). 9 ff.; P. Yale 58.

125 A later insertion. The original text, without this line, may be paraphrased as follows: 'The survey proceeds from the north and east of the property just surveyed, and encompasses the so-called East Kerkeouris Perichoma. Starting from the arable area about Tali, and forming the eastern boundary of the property next to be surveyed, is ¾ aroura of the canal named after Philon.' The insertion was intended to add the southernmost and easternmost limits of the survey: on the south, the fields of Theogonis; on the east, presumably those of Tali. But the complement to νό(του) μέν was never written, probably because the mention of Tali in the next line was felt to make further detail superfluous.

135 συ(μπεπτωκότος?): in **84** the same abbreviation is regularly resolved συ(μπεριειλημμένου), 'included', but there it is applied to properties ἐκτὸς μισθώσεως which have been counted in the area booked to a man, and which must therefore be subtracted from that area before rents can be calculated (**84.** 17 and often). But that does not apply in the present case, and we need an explanation also why the priests connected with the shrine are not named; this συ(μπεπτωκότος) would provide. If the Isieion owned by Dionysios son of Pyrrhichos was in a similar state of collapse (**62.** 48), that would explain its absence from the list of shrines in **88.**

143 For an ancient sketch of the property see **1123.** 7.

151 A later insertion.

152 The only other instance where the (previously) assigned rent of derelict land is still registered in these surveys is l. 166 below, concerning ἐμβρό(χου) τοῦ ἐν τῶι να (ἔτει); but one hesitates to restore the same date here because **74** and **75** do not mention the formation of salt land in year 51.

157 Ammonios son of Herakleides is named only here. I suspect a slip for Demetrios son of Herakleides.

166 Refers to land flooded by a break in a major dike near Theogonis and Tali, **74.** 38–40.

169 Restore perhaps ὑ[πολόγου καὶ].

1118. LAND SURVEY

P. Teb. 173 r | 105 × 27 cm. | 117/116 B.C.

Parts of 9 columns from a survey similar to the preceding and following. The perichomata surveyed are: Third North (2–68), Fourth (69–124), Themistou (125–58) and Pao( ) (159–end).

1118 postdates two cleruchic land cessions in year 54 of Euergetes (cf. 60–1 and 142–3 with **64**(a). 60–5), but antedates another cession of year 2 of Soter (cf. 91 with **30.** 1, **64**(a). 73). Therefore only 2 regnal years can be considered for the text: 54 = 1, and early 2. The latter is excluded by a comparison of lines 74–5 and 77–80 with **1103.** 174–5, 276–7, and lines 133–4 and 150–2 with **63.** 9–16. As in the case of **84**, the verso was later used for another survey (**1120**).

1118 should be studied in conjunction with those portions of **84**, **1117**, and **1120** which cover the same area in different years (see p. 141). Restorations not otherwise explained are taken from those texts.

Col. I

γίνονται τοῦ περιχώ(ματος)
(Remainder of column blank)

Col. II

. . . .
[ ] εdή
βο(ρρᾶ) ἐχό(μ.) ἀ̣ρ̣χ̣ό̣(μ.) [ἀπη(λιώτου) ἱερᾶς γῆς ἐλ(ασσόνων)
διὰ] Πνεφερῶ(τος)
τ̣ο̣ῦ̣ Π̣[ετειμούθου καὶ τῶν ἀ]δ̣ελ(φῶν) ε
λι(βὸς) ἐχό(μ.) ἀρχό(μ.) [βο(ρρᾶ) Χῦψις] Π̣ε̣τ̣ε̣σούχου βα(σιλικῆς) δ̣
νό(του) ἐχό(μ.) [Πετεσο]ῦ̣χ̣ο̣ς̣ θε(ὸς) διὰ Πετεσούχου βα(σιλικῆς) ε
[νό(του) ἐ]χ̣ό̣(μ.) κ̣[λ(ήρου) ἐφό(δου) ± 6]. . . . τοῦ Ἀπ. . . . .
[ ].μ.( ) κ
[ ]
βο(ρρᾶ) ἐ[χο(μ.) ἀρχο(μ.) ἀπη(λιώτου)]
λι(βὸς) [ἐ]χο(μ.) [ἀ]ρ̣[χο(μ.)]
παρα(κειμεν) [ ]
[ ]
νό(του) ἐχό(μ.) [κλ(ήρου) ± 8]ο̣υ Ἀπ. . . . . υ[
[τοῦ αὐτοῦ] βα(σιλικῆς) [
νό(του) ἐχο(μεν) [
νό(του) ἐχό(μ.) κ̣λ̣(ήρου) (ἐπταρούρου ?) [Χο(μήνιος)] Ἀπῦγχις
Ποώριος [ς∠]
νό(του) ἐχο(μ.) [± 7 Πε]τεσούχου καὶ οἱ μέ(τοχοι) βα(σιλικῆς) [

Col. III

. . . .
].
]η
]γ
]γ

] ∠̣d
]
]
].
]ϛ∠
]. δ
]β

(*c*. five lines lost)

] ἐ̣χ[ο(μ.)] ἀρχο(μ.) ἀπη(λιώτου) Κατῦτις Κατ̣ύτιος [βα(ϲιλικῆϲ)
λι(βὸϲ) ἐχο(μ.) ἀρχο(μ.) νό(του) τοῦ αὐτοῦ Κατύ[τιοϲ βα(ϲικιλῆϲ)
νό(του) ἐχό(μ.) ἀρχό(μ.) ἀπη(λιώτου) κλ(ήρου) (εἰκοϲιαρούρου)
Χο(μήνιοϲ) Ἀκρίϲ[ιοϲ Ἀκριϲίου ὃν με(τειληφέναι)]
Χομῆνιν τὸν υἱὸν ιθ
λι(βὸϲ) ἐχό(μ.) ἀρχό(μ.) νό(του) κλ(ήρου) (ἑπταρούρου) Χο(μήνιοϲ)
Φατρῆϲ [Ὥρου] ϛ∠
βο(ρρᾶ) ἐχο(μ.) ἀρχο(μ.) ἀπη(λιώτου) Ὀρϲῆϲ Ὀρϲείουϲ .
[λι(βὸϲ) ἐχό(μ.) ἀ]ρ̣χό(μ.) νό(του) κλ(ήρου) (ἑπταρούρου) Χο(μήνιοϲ)
Μεϲταϲῦτ̣[μιϲ Ὥρου] ϛ∠
[τοῦ αὐ]τοῦ βα(ϲιλικῆϲ) β..
].....[
] Ἁρ̣μ̣[αχό]ρ̣οϲ Θ̣ο̣τορτ̣α̣ί̣[ου
ἐχό(μ.)] ἀρχό(μ.) βο(ρρᾶ) κλ(ήρου) (ἑπταρούρου) τῶν Πτολεμαίου
Μ̣αρρῆϲ Παάπιοϲ [ϛ∠]
[νό(του) ἐχό(μ.) ἀρχό(μ.)] λι(βὸϲ) κλ(ήρου) (ἑπταρούρου) Χο̣(μήνιοϲ)
Θοτεὺϲ μι(κρὸϲ) [Φολήμιοϲ ϛ∠]
τοῦ αὐτοῦ βα(ϲιλικῆϲ) α, (γίνονται) ζ∠
[λι(βὸϲ) ἐ]χό(μ.) κλ(ήρου) (ἑπταρούρου) Χ̣ο̣(μήνιοϲ) Φαεῦ[ϲ] Ϲοκέω[ϲ ϛ∠]
τ[οῦ αὐτοῦ βα(ϲιλικῆϲ) α, (γίνονται) ζ∠]

Col. IV

. . . .

].[...].[
[νό(του)] ἐ̣χ̣ό̣(μ.) [ἀρχό(μ.)] ἀ̣πη(λιώτου) κλ(ήρου) (ἑπταρούρου)
[Χο(μήνιοϲ) Παῶπιϲ Πετεϲούχου δ∠]
λι(βὸϲ) ἐχο(μ.) {[ἀ]ρχο(μ.) βο(ρρᾶ)} Θοτορταῖϲ Πετοϲίριοϲ β[α(ϲιλικῆϲ) ε∠]
λι(βὸϲ) ἐχό(μ.) ἀρχό(μ.) βο(ρρᾶ) κλ(ήρου) (ἑπταρούρου) Χο(μήνιοϲ)

῟Ωρος ῞Ωρου ϛ∠
τοῦ αὐ(τοῦ) βα(cιλικῆc) α∠, (γίνονται) η
ν[ό(του)] ἐχ[ό(μ.)] δ̣ιώρυ̣γο̣ς̣ d
νό(του) ἐχό(μ.) ἀρχό(μ.) ἀπη(λιώτου) κλ(ήρου) (ἑπταρούρου) Χο(μήνιος)
῟Ωρος Ὀρcενούφιος ϛ∠
λι(βὸc) ἐχό(μ.) κλ(ήρου) (ἑπταρούρου) Χο(μήνιος) Φο̣λ̣ῆμ̣ιc Νεκτενίβ̣ι̣οc ϛ∠
λι(βὸc) ἐχό(μ.) ἀρχό(μ.) νό(του) κλ(ήρου) (ἑπταρούρου) Χο(μήνιος)
Cοκονῶπιc Πάcιτοc [ϛ]∠
βο(ρρᾶ) ἐ̣[χό(μ.) ἀρ]χό(μ.) ἀπη(λιώτου) κλ(ήρου) (ἑκατονταρούρου)
Πρώταρχοc Διονυcίου ι
[το]ῦ̣ αὐτοῦ [βα(cιλικῆc)] ∠
[λι(βὸc) ἐχό(μ.) κλ(ήρου) (ἑπταρούρου) Χο(μήνιος) Πορεγέβθ]ιc
Ἀπύγ[χι]οc ϛ∠
[τοῦ αὐτοῦ] βα(cιλικῆc) γ, (γίνονται) θ∠
[λι(βὸc) ἐχό(μ.) κλ(ήρου) (ἑκατονταρούρου)] Πολέμωνοc τοῦ Ἀμμωνίου [κ]
[λι(βὸc)] ἐ̣χό(μ.) κλ(ήρου) (ἑκατονταρούρου) Μελάνιπποc Ἀcκληπιάδου
ἀπὸ τοῦ (πρότερον) Πο̣λ̣έμωνοc τοῦ Ἀμμωνίου ι
λι(βὸc) ἐχό(μ.) κλ(ήρου) (ἑκατονταρούρου) Ἀπο̣λ̣λ̣ω̣ν̣ί̣ου τοῦ Διονυcίου κε
λι(βὸc) ἐχό(μ.) κλ(ήρου) (ἑκατονταρούρου) Πρώταρχοc Διονυcίου ι
λι(βὸc) ἐχό(μ.) ἀρ̣χ̣ό̣(μ.) νό̣(του) ἐξαγωγοῦ διώρυγοc γ
βο(ρρᾶ) ἐχό(μ.) ὑ̣π̣ο̣λό(γου) τοῦ ἕωc τοῦ λθ (ἔτουc) ι∠
βο(ρρᾶ) ἐχο(μ.) διῶ̣ρυξ ε∠
βο(ρρᾶ) ἐχό(μ.) ὑπολό(γου) ἐμβρόχου τοῦ ἕωc λθ (ἔτουc) γ
παρα(κειμ.) βο(ρρᾶ) ἐχο(μ.) ὁδὸc β
βο(ρρᾶ) ἐχό(μ.) ἀρχό(μ.) ἀπη(λιώτου) ὑπολό(γου) τοῦ ἕωc λθ (ἔτουc)
κατεξυ(cμένου) β
λι(βὸc) ἐχό(μ.) ἀρχό(μ.) νό(του) τὰ περὶ τὸν Ἰβιῶ(να) τῶν
(εἰκοcι⟨πεντ⟩αρούρων) πεδία
βο(ρρᾶ) ἐχό(μ.) Πετερμοῦθιc Cιεφμοῦτοc βα(cιλικῆc) γ∠
βο(ρρᾶ) ἐχό(μ.) ἀρχό(μ.) ἀπη(λιώτου) ὑ̣πολό(γου) ἁλμυ(ρίδοc) τοῦ
ἀπὸ τοῦ μ (ἔτουc) γ∠
λι(βὸc) ἐχ[ό(μ.)] ἀρχό(μ.) βο(ρρᾶ) ὑ̣[πο]λό(γου) ἐμβρόχου τοῦ ἕω̣ς̣
το̣ῦ̣ λ̣θ̣ (ἔτουc ?) ε̣
ν̣ό(του) ἐχό(μ.) Πετεcοῦ(χοc) θε(ὸc) διὰ Πετοcίριοc τοῦ
Ἀμμενέωc βα(cιλικῆc) ϛ∠

Col. V

. . . .

[ἀπη(λιώτου) ἐχό(μ.) ἀρχό(μ.) βο(ρρᾶ)] Ἁρφαῆ[c]ι[c Πετοcίριοc]
    β[α(cιλικῆc) α∠d]
ν[ό(του)] ἐχ[ό(μ.)] κλ(ήρου) (ἑπταρούρου) Χο(μήνιοc) Πᾶcιc μ[έ(γαc)]
    Καλατύτιοc ς∠
  τοῦ αὐτοῦ βα(cιλικῆc) β, (γίνονται) η∠
νό(του) ἐχό(μ.) κλ(ήρου) (ἑπταρούρου) Χο(μήνιοc) Πᾶcιc μι(κρὸc)
    Καλατύτιοc ς∠
  τοῦ αὐτοῦ βα(cιλικῆc) ạ, (γίνονται) ζ∠
ṿ[ό(του)] ἐχό(μ.) ἀρχό(μ.) ἀπη(λιώτου) Κέντειc Ὥρου βα(cιλικῆc) ιδ
λ[ι(βὸc)] ἐχό(μ.) ἀρχό(μ.) νό(του) κλ(ήρου) (εἰκοcιαρούρου) Χο(μήνιοc)
    Φμέρcιc Ὥρου ε
  τοῦ αὐ(τοῦ) βα(cιλικῆc) α, (γίνονται) ς
βο(ρρᾶ) ἐχό(μ.) ἀρχό(μ.) ἀπη(λιώτου) κλ(ήρου) (ἑπταρούρου) Χο(μήνιοc)
    Ἁρφαῆcιc Ὥρου ς∠
λι(βὸc) ἐχό(μ.) Θῶνιc μι(κρὸc) Κεντείcιοc βα(cιλικῆc) γ∠
λι(βὸc) ἐχό(μ.) ἱερᾶc γῆc Cοκνεβτύνιοc θεοῦ μεγά(λου) μεγά(λου)
  διὰ τῶν ἱερέων κοινῆι οε
[λι(βὸc) ἐ]χό(μ.) κλ(ήρου) (εἰκοcιαρούρου) Χο(μήνιοc) Ἁρμιῦcιc
    Πτολεμαίου ιθ
[λι(βὸc) ἐχό(μ.)] Ὧροc Πετώṿτοc βα(cιλικῆc) ε
[λι(βὸc) ẹχό(μ.) ἀρχό(μ.) νό(του)] κλ(ήρου) ἐφό(δου) μεταβεβη(κότοc)
    εἰc τὴν κα(τοικίαν)
  Πέτρωνοc τοῦ Θέων[οc] ἀ[πὸ] ιε̄
βο(ρρᾶ) ἐχό(μ.) Πᾶcιc Πετεcούχου [βα(cιλικῆc)] δ
βο(ρρᾶ) ἐχό(μ.) {ἀρχό(μ.) ἀπη(λιώτου)} κλ(ήρου) (εἰκοcιαρούρου)
    Χο(μήνιοc) Κεφαλᾶc Πετεcούχου ιθ
  τοῦ αὐτοῦ βα(cιλικῆc) β, (γίνονται) κα
βο(ρρᾶ) ἐχό(μ.) ἀρχό(μ.) λι(βὸc) Πᾶcιc Πετεcούχου βα(cιλικῆc) δ
λι(βὸc) ἐχό(μ.) ἀρχό(μ.) νό(του) ⟨κλ(ήρου)⟩ (ἑπταρούρου) Χο(μήνιοc)
    Ἁρμιῦcιc Πετεcούχου ς∠
βο(ρρᾶ) ἐχό(μ.) ἀρχό(μ.) ἀπη(λιώτου) Πετῶυc Μαρρείουc βα(cιλικῆc) ζ∠
λι(βὸc) ἐχό(μ.) Ἀρcῦτμιc Λύκου βα(cιλικῆc) ε∠
λι(βὸc) ἐχό(μ.) κλ(ήρου) ἐφό(δου) μεταβεβη(κότοc) εἰc τὴν κα(τοικίαν)

Πέτρων Θέωνος τὸ λο(ιπὸν) τῶν ιε̄
λι(βὸς) ἐ̣χ̣ό̣(μ.) ἀ̣ρ̣χό(μ.) βο(ρρᾶ) Πᾶcιc Π̣ε̣τ̣ε̣c̣ούχου βα(cιλικῆc) ζ
ν̣ό(του) ἐχό(μ.) ἀρχό(μ.) ἀπη(λιώτου) κλ(ήρου) (ἑπταρούρου) Χο(μήνιος)
Πετεcοῦχος Τοθῆc ϛ∠

Col. VI

(One or two lines lost)

]ε̣[
ἐχό(μ.) ἀρχό(μ.) ἀπη(λιώτου) κλ(ήρου) ἐφό(δου)] μεταβεβη(κότος)
εἰc τὴν κα(τοικίαν)
['Ακουcιλάου τ]οῦ 'Αcκληπιάδου ϛ̣
[λι(βὸc) ἐχό(μ.) ἀρχό(μ.) βο(ρρᾶ) κλ(ήρου) φυ(λακίτου) μετα]β̣εβη(κότος)
εἰc τὴν κα(τοικίαν)
Μ[ά]ρ̣ω̣νος τοῦ Διονυcίου γ
νό(του) ἐχό(μ.) κλ(ήρου) (ἑκατονταρούρου) 'Αcκληπιάδηc 'Αcκληπιάδου ιβ
νό(του) ἐχό(μ.) \`ἀρχό(μ.) ἀπη(λιώτου)' κλ(ήρου) ἐφό(δου) μεταβεβη(κότος)
εἰc τὴν κα(τοικίαν)
'Ακουcιλάου τοῦ 'Αcκληπιάδου δ
λι(βὸc) ἐχό(μ.) κλ(ήρου) (ἑκατονταρούρου) 'Αcκληπιάδηc 'Αcκληπιάδου
ἀπὸ τοῦ Π[ο]λ̣έμωνος τοῦ 'Αμμωνίου ι
λι(βὸc) ἐχό(μ.) κλ(ήρου) (ἑκατονταρούρου) 'Απολλοδώρου τοῦ Πτολεμαίου κ
λι(βὸc) ἐχό(μ.) ἀρχό(μ.) νό(του) κλ(ήρου) φυ(λακίτου) μεταβεβη(κότος)
εἰc τὴν κα(τοικίαν)
Μάρωνος τοῦ Διονυcίου ζ
βο(ρρᾶ) ἐχό(μ.) ἐξαγωγοῦ [d]
βο(ρρᾶ) ἐχό(μ.) κ̣[λ(ήρου) (ἑκατοντ]αρούρου) 'Ηρώδηc 'Ηλιοδώρου [
β̣[ο(ρρᾶ) ἐχό(μ.) ἀρχό(μ.) λι(βὸc) ὑπο]λ̣ό̣(γου) ἐμβρό(χου) τοῦ ἀπὸ
τοῦ̣ μ̣ (ἔτους) [η]
π[αρα(κείμ.) ἀπη(λιώτου) ἐχό(μ.) ἀρχό(μ.) νό(του) ἐξαγωγοῦ [d]
[βο(ρρᾶ) ἐχό(μ.) κλ(ήρου) φυ(λακίτου)] 'Ακουcιλάου τοῦ 'Απολλω-
ν̣ί̣ο̣υ̣ [ἀπὸ ῑ]
β[ο(ρρᾶ)] ἐ̣χ̣[ό(μ.)] ἀρχ̣[ό(μ.) ἀπη(λιώτου) κλ(ήρου) (ἑκατονταρούρου)
'Απολ]λ̣οδώρου τοῦ Πτο(λεμαίου) [μ]
λι(βὸc) ἐχό(μ.) ἀρχό(μ.) ⟨νό(του)⟩ ὑπολό(γου) ἐμβρόχου τοῦ ἀπὸ τοῦ
[μ (ἔτους) δ]
βο(ρρᾶ) ἐχό(μ.) ἀρχό(μ.) ἀπη(λιώτου) κλ(ήρου) φυ(λακίτου) 'Ακου-

ϲιλάου τοῦ Ἀ̣[πολ(λωνίου) ζ]
παρα(κειμ.) λι(βὸϲ) ἐχο(μ.) ἐγβαι(ν.) ἐπὶ νό(του) διῶρυξ [
λι(βὸϲ) ἐχο(μ.) ὑπολό(γου) χέρϲου τῆϲ ἕωϲ λθ (ἔτουϲ) α
λι(βὸϲ) ἐχό(μ.) ἀρχό(μ.) νό(του) ὑπολό(γου) ἐμβρό(χου) τοῦ ἕωϲ
λθ (ἔτουϲ) ε
βο(ρρᾶ) ἐχό(μ.) ἐξαγωγοῦ διῶρυξ δ
χέρϲου τῆϲ ἕωϲ τοῦ λθ (ἔτουϲ) ε∠, (γίνονται) θ∠
βο(ρρᾶ) ἐχό(μ.) ⟨ἀρχό(μ.) λι(βὸϲ)⟩ ὑπολό(γου) ἐμβρό(χου) τοῦ ἕωϲ
λθ (ἔτουϲ) γ
ἀπη(λιώτου) ἐχό(μ.) κλ(ήρου) (ἑκατονταρούρου) Ἀθηνίων Ἀρχίου ιγ
ἀπη(λιώτου) ἐχό(μ.) {ἀρχό(μ.) νό(του)} κλ(ήρου) (ἑκατονταρούρου)
Ἀϲκληπιάδου τοῦ
⟦βο(ρρᾶ)⟧ Πτολεμαίου κδ
ἀπη(λιώτου) ἐχό(μ.) ἀρχό(μ.) νό(του) ἱερᾶϲ γῆϲ̣ [Ϲο]ύχου θεοῦ
με(γάλου) διὰ Πετε[
τοῦ Πετειμούθ[ου] ⟦δ̣⟧ ε∠̣

Col. VII

(Four or five lines lost)

β̣ο̣(ρρᾶ) ἐ̣χό̣(μ.) [Ϲοκνεβτῦνιϲ θεὸϲ]
διὰ Πετερμ[ούθιοϲ τοῦ Ἀμεννέωϲ βα(ϲιλικῆϲ) ι]
βο(ρρᾶ) ἐχό(μ.) οἱ γεωργ[οὶ κοινῆι
βο(ρρᾶ) ἐχό(μ.) ἀρχό(μ.) ἀπη(λιώτου) ὑπολό(γου) ἐμβρόχ[ου του
ἐν τῶι να (ἔτει)
λι(βὸϲ) ἐχό(μ.) ἀρχό(μ.) νό(του) Φ̣α̣ῆ̣ϲ̣ιϲ Φίβιοϲ [καὶ οἱ μέ(τοχοι)
βο(ρρᾶ) ἐχό(μ.) ὑπολό(γου) ἐμβρό(χου) τοῦ ἀπὸ μ (ἔτουϲ) ε
βο(ρρᾶ) ἐχό(μ.) ἀρχό(μ.) λι(βὸϲ) ὑπολό(γου) ἐμβρ[ό]χου [τοῦ . . . .]
(ἔτ) ιβ
ἀπη(λιώτου) ἐχό(μ.) ἀρχό(μ.) νό(του) κλ(ήρου) (ἑκατονταρούρου)
Ἀκ[ουϲιλάου] τοῦ
Ἀϲκληπιάδου τὸ (πρότερον) Θέωνοϲ τοῦ Θέωνοϲ λ
βο(ρρᾶ) ἐχό(μ.) ἀρχό(μ.) λι(βὸϲ) κλ(ήρου) (ἑκατονταρούρου) Ἡρώδηϲ
Ἡλιοδ[ώρο]υ κ
ἀπη(λιώτου) ἐχό(μ.) Ὧροϲ Πετῶτοϲ [βα(ϲιλικῆϲ)] κβ
[ἀπη(λιώτου) ἐχό(μ.)] ἀ̣ρ̣χό(μ.) νό(του) κλ(ήρου) (ἑκατονταρούρου)

ʽΗρώδης ʽΗλ̣[ιοδώ]ρ̣ου ϵ
[βο(ρρᾶ) ἐχό(μ.) ἀρχό(μ.) ἀπη(λιώτου)] ὑπολό(γου) ἐμβρό(χου) τοῦ
ἀπὸ τοῦ [μ (ἔτους)] θ
[λι(βὸς) ἐχό(μ.) ἀρχό(μ.) νό(του) κλ(ήρου)] (τριακονταρούρου)
χερςεφίππ[ου]
[Πάνταυχος Πανταύχου] ἀπὸ λδίξλβ
(*c.* 6 lines lost)
ν[ό(του)] ἐχ[ό(μ.)] ἱερᾶ̣[ς γῆς Coύχου θεοῦ μεγά(λου) διὰ]
᾿Απολλ[ωνίου τοῦ Ποςειδωνίου καὶ]
Cαραπί̣ω̣[νος τοῦ Cαραπί]ω̣νος ξ
νό(του) ἐχό(μ.) ἀρχό(μ.) ἀπη(λιώτου) διώρυγο̣[ς τὸ] λ̣ο̣(ιπὸν]
τῶν γ̄ (ἀρουρῶν)
λι(βὸς) ἐχό(μ.) ὑπολό(γου) ἐμβρό(χου) τοῦ ἀ[πὸ] τοῦ μ (ἔτους) ιθ
παρα(κείμ.) λι(βὸς) ἐχό(μ.) κλ(ήρου) (ἑκατονταρούρου) Λεπτίν[η]ς̣
Cτρατονίκου κϵ
ʽΗφαιςτίων Cτρατονίκο̣υ [. .].[. .]. .ϵ
παρα(κειμένη) λι(βὸς) ἐχο(μ.) ⟨ἀρχο(μ.) νό(του)⟩ διῶρυξ Πολέ{λε}μωνος
χώμα(τος) ⟨ἀπὸ⟩ ιδ̄
παρα(κειμ.) βο(ρρᾶ) ἐχο(μ.) ἀρχο(μ.) λι(βὸς) διῶρυξ ἐξαγωγὸς τὸ
λο(ιπὸν) τῶν ιδ̄
ἀ̣π̣η̣(λιώτου) ἐχό(μ.) κλ(ήρου) (ἑκατονταρούρου) Λυςίμαχος Πύρρου μ
ἀ̣π̣η̣(λιώτου) ἐχό(μ.) ἀρχό(μ.) βο(ρρᾶ) κλ(ήρου) ἐ̣ρ̣η(μο)φύ̣(λακος)
Λ̣α̣γῶς Διοδώρου ι

Col. VIII
(*c.* 8 lines lost)
ἀ[πη(λιώτου) ἐχο(μ.)] ἀρχο(μ.) [νό(του)
βο(ρρᾶ) [ἐχο(μ.)] ἀρχο(μ.) λι(βὸς) ὑπολό(γου) ἐμβρό(χου) τοῦ
ἀπὸ τοῦ μ̣ [(ἔτους)
ἀπη(λιώτου) ἐχ[ο(μ.)] Cενθεὺς ʽΑρκοίφιος βα(ςιλικῆς) .
ἀπη(λιώτου) ἐχό(μ.) ἀρχό(μ.) βο(ρρᾶ) κλ(ήρου) (ἑπταρούρου) Χο(μήνιος)
ʽΑρυώτης ʽΑρυώτου ϛ∠
τοῦ αὐτοῦ βα(ςιλικῆς) α, (γίνονται) ϛ∠
νό(του) ἐχό(μ.) κλ(ήρου) (ἑπταρούρου) Χο(μήνιος) ʽΑρμιῦςις Cοκονώπιος ϛ∠
νό(του) ἐχό(μ.) Μαρρῆς Μαρρείους βα(ςιλικῆς) γ
νό(του) ἐχό(μ.) κλ(ήρου) (ἑπταρούρου) Χο(μήνιος) ῟Ωρος ʽΑρφαήςιος ϛ∠

τοῦ αὐτοῦ βα(ϲιλικῆϲ) α, (γίνονται) ζ∠
νό(του) ἐχό(μ.) κλ(ήρου) (ὀγδοηκονταρούρου) Λέοντος τοῦ Λεοντί⟨ϲ⟩κου ιε
παρα(κείμ.   ) ν̣ό̣(του) ἐ̣χ̣ό(μ.   ) χῶμα καὶ διώρυγος ε
ν[ό(του) ἐχό(μ.) κλ(ήρου) ἐφό(δου) Πτολεμαίου τοῦ Μενίϲ[κου τὸ
λο(ιπὸν) τῶν κδ̄]
ν̣ό̣(του) ἐ̣χο̣(μ.) Ἀθεμμεὺϲ Πετεϲούχου βα(ϲιλικῆϲ) [
[νό(του) ἐχο(μ.)] ἀρχο(μ.) λι(βὸϲ) Πύρριχοϲ Ἀπύγχιοϲ βα(ϲιλικῆϲ) [
[ἀπη(λιώτου) ἐχό(μ.) ἀρχό(μ.) νό(του) ἱερᾶϲ γῆ]ϲ̣ Σοκνεβτύνιοϲ
θε(οῦ) με[γά(λου) μεγά(λου)]
[διὰ τῶν ἱερέ]ω̣ν κοινει ιε
β[ο(ρρᾶ) ἐ]χ̣[ό(μ.)] ἀρχ[ό(μ.)] λι(βὸϲ) κ[λ(ήρου) (ὀγδοηκονταρούρου)
Δώ]ρου τοῦ Πετάλου η
ἀπη(λιώτου) ἐχό(μ.) κλ(ήρου) (ὀγδοηκονταρούρου) Διοδότου τοῦ
Ἀπολλωνίου κ
παρα(κείμ.) ἀπη(λιώτου) ἐχό(μ.) ἐγβαί(ν.) βο(ρρᾶ) χώ(ματοϲ) γ
διώρυγοϲ β, (γίνονται) ε
ἀπη(λιώτου) ἐχό(μ.) Σενθεὺϲ Ἁρκοίφιοϲ βα(ϲιλικῆϲ) β
ἀπη(λιώτου) ἐχό(μ.) ἀρχό(μ.) βο(ρρᾶ) κλ(ήρου) (ὀγδοηκονταρούρου)
Δώρου τοῦ Πετάλου η
νό(του) ἐχό(μ.) Πόλιτοϲ Ὀννώφριοϲ βα(ϲιλικῆϲ) ι
νό(του) ἐχό(μ.) κλ(ήρου) (ὀγδοηκονταρούρου) Καλλικράτηϲ Φιλοξένου να
νό(του) ἐχό(μ.) ὑπολό(γου) ἐμβρό(χου) τοῦ ἀπὸ τοῦ μ (ἔτουϲ) η

Col. IX

(One or two lines lost)

]. ἱερᾶϲ γῆ̣[ϲ Σούχου θεοῦ μεγά(λου) διὰ]
[Ἀπολλ]ωνίου τοῦ Ποϲιδ̣[ωνίου
ὑπο]λό(γου) ἐμβρόχου [
] χέρϲου τῆϲ ἀπὸ τ[οῦ
]. . . ἕωϲ τοῦ λ̣θ (ἔτουϲ)
]. . κλ(ήρου) (ὀγδοηκονταρούρου) Καλλ̣[ικράτηϲ
]. . .[. . .]. .[
ἐχο(μ.) ἀρ]χ̣[ο(μ.)] νό(του) Ἁρφαῆϲιϲ [
[βο(ρρᾶ) ἐχο(μ.) ἀ]ρχο(μ.) λι(βὸϲ) Μαρρῆϲ Πακύρριο̣[ϲ
[
ἐχο(μ.)] ἀ̣ρ̣χ̣ο̣(μ.) ἀπη(λιώτου) .[

λι̣(βὸς) ἐ̣χο̣(μ.) . . . . . καὶ οἱ μέ(τοχοι) [
λι(βὸς) ἐχο(μ.) ἱερᾶς γῆς ἐλ(ασσόνων) ἰβίω(ν) τρ(οφῆς) δι' Ἑρ[γέως
καὶ τῶν με(τόχων)
παρα(κειμ.) [λι(βὸς) ἐχ]ο(μ.) δ̣ιῶρυξ [
λι(βὸς) ἐχό(μ.) . . . . τοῦ μ (ἔτους) ζ
ἡ κεχ]ωρισμένη πρόσοδος β∠
βο(ρρᾶ) ἐχο(μ.) ἀρχο(μ.) λι(βὸς) Ἀρβῆχις Ἐργέως βα(σιλικῆς) [
ἀπη(λιώτου) ἐχο(μ.) ἀρχο(μ.) νό(του) ὑπολό(γου) χέ(ρσου) τῆς ἀπὸ
τοῦ μ (ἔτους) [
βο(ρρᾶ) ἐχο(μ.) Σοκμῆνις Πετεσούχου καὶ οἱ μέ(τοχοι) βα(σιλικῆς) [
βο(ρρᾶ) ἐχο(μ.) Πετερμοῦθις Σιεφμο̣ῦ̣[τος βα(σιλικῆς)
βο(ρρᾶ) ἐχο(μ.) ἀρχο(μ.) ἀπη(λιώτου) ὑπολό(γου) χέρσου τῆς ἀπὸ τοῦ
μ̣ (ἔτους ?) [
βο(ρρᾶ) ἐχο(μ.) Παπνεβτῦνις Σοκέως β̣α̣(σιλικῆς) [
βο(ρρᾶ) ἐχο(μ.) ὑπολό(γου) ἁλμυ(ρίδος) τοῦ ἀπ[ὸ τοῦ μ (ἔτους)
βο(ρρᾶ) ἐ̣χο(μ.) ἀρχο(μ.) λι(βὸς) Σ[ο]χ̣ώτης [
(Breaks off)

102 Τοθοείους 123 ἀπη(λιώτου) corr. from νό(του) 130 ἀπη(λιώτου) corr. from λ 159 ἀπη(λιώτου) corr. from παρα(κειμένη)

1 γίνονται τοῦ περιχώ(ματος): since comparison of the properties named in ll. 2 ff. with the same holdings in **62** shows that those lines refer to the Third Perichoma North, the basin meant here is no doubt the Third South (cf. **1117** introd.). Ample space was left after περιχώ(ματος) for a summary of the land categories in the basin, such as is found in **85**. 104 ff., but no such summary was ever filled in. So also in **84**. 138, 192; **1116**. 40, 101; **1117**. 123.

3–7 Cf. **1117**. 1 ff. with notes; **1120**. 38 ff.

7 **1117**. 10 and **1120**. 41 have κλ(ήρου) ἐφό(δου) Ἀπολλωνίου τοῦ Πτολεμαίου, which was certainly not written here. It is tempting to read Πτολεμ]α̣ί̣ο̣υ̣ τοῦ Ἀπο̣λ̣λ̣ω̣ν̣ί̣ο̣υ̣, which fits the traces very well and would be an accidental inversion of the names of father and son.

8].μ.( ): not παρα(δείσου) ἐρ]ή̣μο̣(υ).

30 ff. Cf. **1120**. 63 ff.

30 Probably [βο(ρρᾶ)] should be restored at the beginning of the line and [γ] at the end; cf. **1120**. 63.

31 Restore probably [ε]; cf. **1120**. 64. νό(του) is a mistake for βο(ρρᾶ).

32 ὃν με(τειληφέναι): the construction is explained by such passages as **79**. 63, Σεύθου τ[οῦ] Δωσ⟨ι⟩θέου ὃν γρ(άφει) ὁ κω(μο)γρ(αμματεὺς) μετειληφέναι κτλ. (probably from Magdola; for Kerkeosiris cf. **1113**. 20–1).

40 (ἑπταρούρου) τῶν Πτολεμαίου: i.e. a soldier enrolled by the scribe Ptolemaios son of Petenoupis (**1108**. 137), with whom most references associate one Xenon (e.g. **1110**. 215). In **1120**. 69 the same man is called (ἑπτάρουρος) τῶν δι' Ὥρου; cf. **1120**. 15 n.

47 Restored from **1120**. 79. The remaining 2 arouras of this cleros are located in **1119**. 50; cf. **62**. 301–2, where [ζ̅ βο(ρρᾶ)] δ̣∠ should be read.

48 Cf. **1128**. 40 n.

50 α∠: the same man or his successor rents only 1 ar. later, **1120**. 81.

56 Protarchos has no Crown land in **1120**. 82.

62 Ἀπ̣ο̣λ̣λ̣ω̣ν̣ί̣ου: **1120**. 87 has [Ἡλιό]δ̣ωρος Διονυςίου; but Heliodoros had no more than 10 ar. left by the time of this text (**62**. 130), and in any case Ἡλιόδωρος is not a satisfactory reading. **1120** is in error.

64 The canal is described in **1120**. 89 as παρα(κείμεναι) λι(βὸς) ἐχό(μεναι) ἐγβαί(νουςαι) ἀπη(λιώτου). The texts diverge from this point, but begin to parallel each other again at l. 74 = **1120**. 92.

67 This is probably the ὑπόλογος ἔμβροχος referred to in **84**. 68 despite the difference in extent (3 ar. vs. 5¼).

69 The survey now enters the Fourth Perichoma; cf. **84**. 65 ff. Lines 74–86 of **84** were omitted from the editio princeps. They read

74 [νό(του)] ἐχό(μ.) κ̣λ̣(ήρου) [(ἑπταρούρου)] Χ[ο(μήνιος)] Παςῶς μέ(γας) Φανήςιος ϛ∠
75 [τοῦ] αὐ(τοῦ) βα(ςιλικῆς) α ἀν(ὰ) ε
76 νό(του) ἐχό(μ.) κ[λ(ήρου) (ἑπταρούρου)] Χ̣[ο(μήνιος)] Ὀρςῆς Ἁ[ροννήςιος] ϛ̣∠
77 τοῦ α[ὐτοῦ βα(ςιλικῆς) α ἀν(ὰ) ε, (γίν.) ζ∠]
78 νό(του) ἐχό(μ.) κλ(ήρου) (τριακοντ[αρούρου) Χο(μήνιος) Ἁρυώτης Φαεῦτος ε]
79 τοῦ [αὐτοῦ βα(ςιλικῆς) . ἀν(ὰ) ε, (γίν.) .]
80 νό(του) ἐχό(μ.) κλ(ήρου) (ἑπταρούρου) [Χο(μήνιος) Ἁρφαῆςις Ὥρου] ϛ∠
81 νό(του) ἐχό(μ.) \`ἀρχό(μ.) [λι(βὸς)´ Κέ[ν]τι[ς Ὥ]ρ[ο]υ̣ β[α(ςιλικῆς)] β
82 π[αρα(κειμ.) ἀπη(λ.)] ἐχό(μ.) κλ(ήρου) (ἑπταρούρου) Ἁρφαῆ[ςις Ὥρο]υ τὸ λο(ιπόν)
83 τοῦ αὐτοῦ ⟨βα(ςιλικῆς)⟩ β ἀνὰ̣ [ε
84 ἀπη(λ.) ἐχό(μ.) ἀρχό(μ.) βο(ρρᾶ) [Ἁ]ρ̣φαῆςις Πετοςίριος βα(ςιλικῆς) α∠d ἀν(ὰ) δ∠γ́ιβ́
85 νό(του) ἐ[χ]ό(μ.) [κλ(ήρου) (ἑπταρούρου) Χο(μήνιος) Πᾶςις μέ(γας) Κ]α̣λατύτιος ϛ∠
86 [τοῦ αὐτοῦ βα(ςιλικῆς) β ἀν(ὰ)] ε̣, (γίν.) η∠

The property of the elder Pasis son of Phanesis (l. 74) is given from a different orientation in **1120**. 59. The restoration Ἁρφαῆςις Ὥρου in 80 seems required by the parallels (**1118**. 84, **1120**. 102); but as the 6½ ar. here constitute the whole of his cleros I do not see what can be meant by τὸ λο(ιπόν) in 82.

72–3 **84**. 72 mentions only 2 ar. salty land instead of 3½, and omits the 5 ar. ἔμβροχος.

75 βα(ςιλικῆς): the editors of **84** are wrong in considering this land to be ἱερά (note to l. 74). Cf. Crawford, *Kerkeosiris* 100; Shelton, *Crown Tenants*, pp. 121–4.

76 Restored from **84**. 84 quoted above.

77 ff. Cf. **84**. 85 ff., **1120**. 98 ff.

80 Pasis farms no Crown land in **1120**.

81 Κέντεις = Κεντῖςις **1120**. 100.

82 ἀρχό(μ.) νό(του): this change of direction does not take place in **84**. The texts parallel each other again at 86 = **84**. 91.

89 Ὧρος Πετώυτος βα(ςιλικῆς) ε: surely the land rented by Harmiysis and farmed by Harphaesis in **84**. 95.

91 The figure which was never filled in after ιε should be η. Cf. **1120**. 108, where the land has been transferred to Didymarchos son of Apollonios. **84**. 98 is confused.

92–6 The rental of Crown land in **94**. 99–102 and **1120**. 111 is different.

97–8 These are sons of the tenants in **84**. 104–5.

100 The figure left unwritten after ιε is ζ; cf. **1120**. 116.

103 If ε̣ is rightly read, this is no doubt the Crown land rented by the god Petesouchos and farmed by Petesouchos son of Pakyrris in **84**. 111 and **1120**. 121.

113 κ: only 18 in **84**. 122, but the correction in l. 132, τὸ λο(ιπὸν) τῶν ξ μ⟦β⟧ indicates that the reading here is preferable. It was not previously known that Apollodoros was a hekatontarouros; cf. Uebel 177 n. 4. This suggests that the texts which date his cleros to the 34th year of Philometor are correct, since the other known allotments of year 31 went to ogdoekontarouroi.

120 ἀπὸ ῑ]: cf. **84**. 130, ἀπὸ ῑ γ; but in this text the 2nd numeral was probably not filled in; cf. 91, 100, 149, 153, 158, 172.

122 Restored from **84**. 133.

124 This διῶρυξ is probably the canal described in **84**. 137 as παρα(κείμ.) λι(βὸς) ⟨ἐχό(μ.)⟩ ἐγβαί(ν.) νό(του) καὶ βο(ρρᾶ) ἐξαγωγοῦ β, but **84**. 136 mentions a ὑδραγωγός which is omitted here, making

restoration of the numeral hazardous. The ἐξαγωγός in **84.** 137 marks the boundary between the Fourth Perichoma and the Themistou. This text does not note a change of perichoma, but l. 131 shows that such took place, since the property listed is located not only in **84.** 152 but in **62.** 91 f.

125–9 Cf. **84.** 142–7, where the data are often different.

133 f. The names of the priests in **84.** 155 are Peteimouthes and Mestasytmis.

135 ff. Cf. **84.** 161 ff.

137 *οἱ γεωργ[οί: Ἀνεμπεὺς Πετοςίριος βα(ςιλικῆς) ϛ*, **84.** 162.

149. The number left unwritten after *λδιϛλβ* is *κ*; cf. **84.** 175.

151–2 The two men are entered separately in **84.** 184–5, where their combined holdings are only 43 ar.

155–6 It is natural to take these lines as referring to the property which in **84.** 187 is booked to Heliodoros son of Menodoros. This is certainly right in the case of Leptines, who received 25 ar. of Heliodoros's property in 119/118 (**61**(a). 7); but the remaining 15 were transferred not to Hephaistion son of Stratonikos but to Maron son of Dionysios. The word after *Cτρατονίκου* is very probably [*χέ*]*ρ*[*co*]*υ*, the figure probably *κε*, dittography from the line above. Hephaistion owned only 10 ar., taken over from Heliodoros son of Dionysios (**64**(a). 104 f.). Even if the name here is a mistake for *Μάρων Διονυςίου*, the expected *ιε* cannot be read.

157 ⟨*ἀπὸ*⟩ *ιδ*: l. 158, *τὸ λο(ιπὸν) τῶν ιδ*, shows that ⟨*ἀπὸ*⟩ must be inserted here.

158 This canal marks the boundary between the Themistou Perichoma and that whose name is abbreviated *Παω*( ), since the cleros of Lysimachos son of Pyrrhos (159) is located there in **62.** 63 f. Cf. **84.** 193.

164 ff. Cf. **1117.** 57 ff.

167 Cf. **1117.** 60 n.

172 *τὸ λο(ιπὸν) τῶν κδ*]: 4 arouras according to **1117.** 66, but that will not have been filled in here; cf. 120 n.

173–4 The figures in **1117.** 68 and 70 are 5½ and 6 ar.

176 *κοινει*: Mayser I, pp. 128 ff.

177 This seems to be the same property as **1117.** 71, but the area there is said to be 10 ar.

178 *κ*: or perhaps *κ*⟨*β*⟩. Cf. **1117.** 74.

182 *Πόλιτος*: *Πολίτιος* in **1117.** 81. The 9½ arouras there plus ½ ar. of drainage ditch in l. 82 seem to have been combined for the 10 ar. here.

184 Only 7 ar. in **1117.** 84.

190 *Καλλ[ικράτης*: presumably the son of Philoxenos, since K. son of Ptolemaios is wholly accounted for in **1117.** 137.

1119. LAND SURVEY

P. Teb. 215 50×31 cm. 115/114 B.C.

Part of a survey of the Second Perichoma at Kerkeosiris, noteworthy for the regularity with which crop information is given.

In lines 38 and 79 Apollonios son of Ptolemaios is listed as still in possession of land to which his son succeeded by year 4 of Soter II (**1113.** 35); the transfer of Crown land from Cholos son of Sisouchos to Demetrios son of Sentheus mentioned ll. 58–60 occurred in year 2 (**1103.** 128–30). Possible years for **1119** are therefore late 2, 3, and early 4: of these year 2 is excluded by such passages as 18 and 70–1 vs. **1110.** 201 and 57–60, and year 4 by 70–1 vs. **1113.** 12–15.

Col. I

(*c.* 13 lines lost)

]ρcείουc βα(cιλικῆc) δ ἀν(ὰ) δ∠γʹιβʹ
Ἁρμαχ]ọ́ροc Ἁρ[μα]χόρου βα(cιλικῆc)
]β̣
]ι̣οc βα(cιλικῆc) α ἀν(ὰ) β∠ cπό(ροc) (πυρῶι)
] . [. .]c βα(cιλικῆc) β∠ ἀν(ὰ) δ cπό(ροc) (πυρῶι)
] . ιοc βα(cιλικῆc) β∠ ἀν(ὰ) δ cπό(ροc) (πυρῶι)
] β[α(cιλικῆc)] ∠ ἀν(ὰ) δ cπό(ροc) (πυρῶι)
] β̣α̣(cιλικῆc) ι ἀν(ὰ) ∠ cπό(ροc) (πυρῶι)
] δ̣ ἀν(ὰ) δ∠γʹιβʹ cπό(ροc) (πυρῶι) γ
] . . . . . (ὧν) cπό(ροc) (πυρῶι)
]
] (πυρῶι)

Col. II

ἀπη(λιώτου) ἐχό(μ.) Πετεcοῦχοc Χ̣ε̣ύριοc βα(cιλικῆc) γ ἀν(ὰ) δ∠γʹιβʹ
ἀρά(κωι) κα(τανενεμημένωι)
ἀπη(λιώτου) ἐχό(μ.) ἀρχό(μ.) νό(του) κλ(ήρου) (ἑπταρούρου) Χο(μήνιοc)
Ὀννῶφριc Μεcταcύτμιοc
γ ἀν(ὰ) γ∠
ϛ∠ cπό(ροc) ἀρά(κωι) κα(τανενεμημένωι) γεω(ργὸc) Πετερμοῦθιc
Μαρρείουc
βο(ρρᾶ) ἐχό(μ.) ἀρχό(μ.) ἀπη(λιώτου) Πετεcοῦχοc Χεύριοc βα(cιλικῆc)
δ ἀν(ὰ) δ cπό(ροc) (πυρῶι)
λ̣ι̣(βὸc) ἐχο(μ.) ἡ κεχωριcμένη πρ(όcοδοc) διὰ Πετοcίριοc
τοῦ Νεοπτολέμου β (πυρῶι)
λι(βὸc) ἐχό(μ.) ἀρχό(μ.) βο(ρρᾶ) ˋἀν(ὰ) (μέcον) διώρυ(γοc)ˊ κλή(ρου)
(ἑκατονταρούρου) Πρώταρχοc Διονυ(cίου) ι (ὧν) ἀρά(κωι) ε
φαcή(λωι) ε
γεω(ργὸc) Χεῦριc
νό(του) ἐχό(μ.) ἀνὰ (μέcον) ὑδρα(γωγοῦ) Πορτειοῦc μέ(γαc) Τεῶτοc
βα(cιλικῆc) ϛ (ὧν) γ ἀν(ὰ) γ
γ ἀν(ὰ) β∠ (ὧν) cπό(ροc) (πυρῶι) γ τήλε̅ι̅ α φαcή(λωι) β
νό(του) ἐχό(μ.) Κολλούθηc Παπνεβτύ(νιοc) βα(cιλικῆc) β ἀν(ὰ) δ cπό(ροc)

κρι(θῆι)
νό(του) ἐχό(μ.) Πετεσοῦχος Ὀρσενούφιος βα(σιλικῆς) β ἀν(ὰ) δ σπό(ρος)
ἀρά(κωι) κα(τανενεμημένωι)
νό(του) ἐχό(μ.) ἀρχό(μ.) ἀπη(λιώτου) Μεστασῦ(τμις) Πετεσούχου βα(σιλικῆς)
α ἀν(ὰ) α τή(λει)
παρα(κειμ.) λι(βὸς) ἐχο(μ.) ὑδρα(γωγοῦ)
λι(βὸς) ἐχό(μ.) ἀρχό(μ.) βο(ρρᾶ) Ἁρμιῦσις Πετοσίριος βα(σιλικῆς) δ∠ ἀν(ὰ) δ
(ὧν) κ(ριθῆι) β∠
φασή(λωι) α τή(λει) α
νό(του) ἐχό(μ.) Μεστασῦ(τμις) Πετεσού(χου) βα(σιλικῆς) ε ἀν(ὰ) β∠
σπό(ρος) (πυρῶι) δ τή(λει) α
νό(του) ἐχό(μ.) ἀρχό(μ.) ἀπη(λιώτου) Πετεσοῦχος Πετοσίριος βα(σιλικῆς)
δ ἀν(ὰ) δ (ὧν) (πυρῶι) β χό(ρτωι) β
λ[ι(βὸς)] ἐχό(μ.) ἀρχό(μ.) βο(ρρᾶ) Ἁρυώτης Φαήσιος βα(σιλικῆς) ι ἀν(ὰ) δ
(ὧν) σπό(ρος) (πυρῶι) ϛ
φασή(λωι) β ἀρά(κωι) α τήλει α
[νό(του)] ἐχο(μ.) ἀρχο(μ.) ἀπη(λιώτου) ἡ κεχω(ρισμένη) πρ(όσοδος) διὰ
Θεογένους β∠ σπό(ρος) κρι(θῆι)
π[αρα(κειμ.)] λι(βὸς) ἐχο(μ.) ὑπολό(γου)
λι(βὸς) ἐχό(μ.) ἀρχό(μ.) νό(του) κλή(ρου) ἐφό(δου) Ἀπολλωνίου τοῦ
Πτο(λεμαίου) ιδ (ὧν)
σπό(ρος) (πυρῶι)
βọ(ρρᾶ) ἐχο(μ.)
βο(ρρᾶ) ἐχο(μ.) ἀρχο(μ.) λι(βὸς) Πορτειοῦς Τεῶτ[ος
σπό(ρος) (πυρῶι)

Col. III

[ἀπη(λιώτου)] ἐχό(μ.) ἀρχό(μ.) νό(του) κλή(ρου) (ἑπταρούρου) Χο(μήνιος)
Ἁρψάλ̣[ις Στεφάνου] ϛ∠ (ὧν)
σπό(ρος) (πυρῶι) γ∠ χό(ρτωι) γ γεω(ργὸς) Ἐρα̣[θρῆς ?
[βο(ρρᾶ) ἐ]χό(μ.) Μεστα̣σῦτμις Πετεσούχου β[α(σιλικῆς)] δ∠ [ἀν(ὰ)
σπό(ρος) (πυρῶι) δ κ(ριθῆι) ∠
βο(ρρᾶ) ἐχό(μ.) Τοθοῆς Ἀγοννούφιος βα(σιλικῆς) δ∠ ἀν(ὰ) δ∠γ′ιβ′ (ὧν) [ ] γ
ἀρά(κωι) α∠
βο(ρρᾶ) ἐχο(μ.) Φαῆσις Ἁρυώτου βα(σιλικῆς) α ἀν(ὰ) δ∠γ′ιβ′ σπό(ρος) (πυρῶι)

βο(ρρᾶ) ἐχό(μ.) κλή(ρου) (ἑπταρούρου) Χο(μήνιος) Παῶπις Πετεσούχου β
c[πό(ρος)
γεω(ργοὶ) Μεγχῆς καὶ ῾Αρμαχόρος
[βο(ρρᾶ)] ἐχό(μ.) ἀρχό(μ.) ἀπη(λιώτου) ἱερᾶς γῆς Σούχου θεοῦ μεγά(λου)
μεγά(λου) διὰ
Πετενεφιείους ε σπό(ρος) (πυρῶι)
[λι(βὸς)] ἐχο(μ.) ἀνὰ (μέσον) ὑδρα(γωγοῦ) Παaλομοῦνις ῞Ωρου βα(σιλικῆς)
⟦β⟧ \`α´ σπό(ρος) [με]λ̣ανθεί(ωι)
β[ο(ρρᾶ)] ἐχό(μ.) \`ἀρχό(μ.) ἀπη(λιώτου)´ Τοθοῆς ᾿Αγοννούφιος βα(σιλικῆς)
λ ἀν(ὰ) δ∠γ´ιβ´ ἀσπόρου
λ̣ι̣(βὸς) ἐχό(μ.) \`⟦ἀρχό(μ.)⟧´ ῟Ωρος Κεντίσιος βα(σιλικῆς) ε ἀν(ὰ) δ∠γ´ιβ´
(ὧν) (πυρῶι) γ φα(κῶι) β
λι(βὸς) ἐχό(μ.) ⟨ἀρχό(μ.) βο(ρρᾶ)⟩ ἀνὰ (μέσον) ὑπολό(γου) ᾿Ιλῶς ῞Ωρου
βα(σιλικῆς) ε ἀν(ὰ) γ (ὧν) σπό(ρος) (πυρῶι)
νό(του) ἐχο(μ.) ⟦Χολῶς Σισούχου βα(σιλικῆς) α ἀν(ὰ) δ∠γ´ιβ´⟧
νό(του) ἐχό(μ.) Δημήτριος Σενθέως βα(σιλικῆς) δ ἀν(ὰ) δ καὶ τὴν (πρότερον)
Χολῶτος α ἀν(ὰ) δ∠γ´ιβ´ (γίνονται) ε, (ὧν) σπό(ρος) (πυρῶι)
νό(του) ἐχό(μ.) Πετοσῖρις Πετενεφιείους βα(σιλικῆς) ε∠ ἀν(ὰ) δ∠γ´ιβ´
(ὧν) (πυρῶι) γ
ἀρά(κωι) α∠ φα(κῶι) α
νό(του) ἐχό(μ.) ᾿Οννῶφρις ῞Ωρου βα(σιλικῆς) δ ἀν(ὰ) δ∠γ´ιβ´ σπό(ρος) (πυρῶι)
νό(του) ἐχό(μ.) Πορτειοῦς Τεῶτος βα(σιλικῆς) α ἀν(ὰ) δ σπό(ρος) (πυρῶι)
νό(του) ἐχό(μ.) ῟Ωρος Πετεσού̣χου καὶ Φαῆσις βα(σιλικῆς) δ∠ ἀν(ὰ) δ∠γ´ιβ´ (ὧν)
σπό(ρος) (πυρῶι) β∠ κ(ριθῆι) α τήλει α
νό(του) ἐχό(μ.) ῟Ωρος ᾿Ορσείους βα(σιλικῆς) ζ ἀν(ὰ) δ∠γ´ιβ´ (ὧν) σπό(ρος)
(πυρῶι) β ἀρά(κωι) γ τή(λει) β
νό(του) ἐχό(μ.) Πετεσοῦχος ᾿Ιμούθου βα(σιλικῆς) δ∠ ἀν(ὰ) δ∠γ´ιβ´ (ὧν)
σπό(ρος) (πυρῶι) β∠
φα(κῶι) α τήλει ⟦β⟧ α
νό(του) ἐχό(μ.) ἀρχό(μ.) ἀπη(λιώτου) κλή(ρου) (ἑκατονταρούρων) Διοδότου
καὶ ᾿Απολλωνίου οἱ β̄
Μικίωνος ι∠δ´η´ σπό(ρος) (πυρῶι) γεω(ργὸς) ῾Ηρα(   ) Μενίπ⟨π⟩ου

Col. IV

λι(βὸς) ἐχο(μ.) ἀρχο(μ.) ν̣[ό(του)] Πνεφερῶς Ὥρου βα(σιλικῆς) ⟦σπό(ρος) . ⟧
σπό(ρος) (πυρῶι)
κρι(θῆι) α
βο(ρρᾶ) ἐχο(μ.) Ἁρμιῦσις Πετοσίριος σπό(ρος) (πυρῶι) σπό(ρος) (πυρῶι)
βο(ρρᾶ) ἐχο(μ.) Παᾶπις Πετοσίριος σπό(ρος) κρι(θῆι) σπό(ρος) (πυρῶι)
βο(ρρᾶ) ἐχο(μ.) Πετῶς Ἁρχύψιος σπό(ρος) (πυρῶι)
βο(ρρᾶ) ἐχο(μ.) Σισόις Πετοσίριος σπό(ρος) (πυρῶι)
βο(ρρᾶ) ἐχο(μ.) Πνεφερῶς Ὥρ[ο]υ (ὧν) σπό(ρος) (πυρῶι)
(Blank space of *c.* 6 cm.)
λι(βὸς) ἐχό(μ.) ἀρχό(μ.) ⟨νό(του)⟩ κλή(ρου) ἐφό(δου) Ἀπολλωνίου
τοῦ Πτο(λεμαίου) γ χέ(ρσου)
βο(ρρᾶ) ἐχό(μ.) Σισόις Πετοσίριος αλαγης βα(σιλικῆς) α ἀν(ὰ) γ
σπό(ρος) (πυρῶι)
βο(ρρᾶ) ἐχο(μ.) ἡ κεχω(ρισμένη) πρ(όσοδος) διὰ Θεογένους δ∠ (ὧν)
(πυρῶι) β∠ κ(ριθῆι) β
βο(ρρᾶ) ἐχό(μ.) ἀρχό(μ.) ἀπη(λιώτου) κλή(ρου) (ἑκατονταρούρου) Πρώταρχος Διονυ(σίου) ιε (ὧν) σπό(ρος) (πυρῶι) ι ἀρά(κωι) ε
γεω(ργὸς) Χεῦρις
λι(βὸς) ἐχό(μ.) ἀρχό(μ.) νό(του) κλή(ρου) (ἑκατονταρούρου) Ἀπολλωνίου
τοῦ Διονυ(σίου) κε (ὧν) (πυρῶι) ιε ἀρά(κωι) ι
γεω(ργὸς) Ὧρος Κεντίσιος
βο(ρρᾶ) ἐχό(μ.) κλή(ρου) (ἑπταρούρου) Χο(μήνιος) Φθαῦς Πετεήσιος δ∠ (ὧν)
ἀρά(κωι) β∠ φασή(λωι) β
γεω(ργὸς) Θῶνις
βο(ρρᾶ) ἐχό(μ.) κλή(ρου) (ἑκατονταρούρου) Πρώταρχος Διονυ(σίου) ε
σπό(ρος) φασή(λωι) κα(τανενεμημένωι)
γεω(ργὸς) Θῶνις
βο(ρρᾶ) ἐχό(μ.) ἀρχό(μ.) ἀπη(λιώτου) Τοθοῆς Σενθέως βα(σιλικῆς) γ ἀν(ὰ)
δ∠γ´ιβ´ (ὧν) (πυρῶι) β φα(κῶι) α
λι(βὸς) ἐχό(μ.) Θῶνις Κεντίσιος βα(σιλικῆς) β ἀν(ὰ) δ∠γ´ιβ´ σπό(ρος) φα(κῶι)
λι(βὸς) ἐχό(μ.) κλή(ρου) (ἑπταρούρου) Χο(μήνιος) Φθαῦς Πετεήσιος
τὸ λο(ιπὸν) β σπό(ρος) φα(κῶι)
γεω(ργὸς) Θῶνις
λι(βὸς) ἐχό(μ.) κλή(ρου) (εἰκοσιαρούρου) Χο(μήνιος) Πετεῆσις Πάσιτος ιθ

τοῦ αὐ(τοῦ) βα(ϲιλικῆϲ) β, (γίνονται) κα, (ὧν)
ϲπό(ροϲ) (πυρῶι) ιγ φα(κῶι) γ ἀρά(κωι) γ γεω(ργὸϲ) Θῶνιϲ

Col. V

λι(βὸϲ) ἐχό(μ.) \`ἀρχό(μ.) βο(ρρᾶ)´ Ποτάμων Ἀ[μεννέωϲ
ν̣ό̣(του) ἐχό(μ.) κλή(ρου) (ἑπταρούρου) Χο(μήνιοϲ) Χ[εῦριϲ Ϲοχώτου
γεω(ργὸϲ) Ὧροϲ

The following fragments are inventoried as belonging to Col. V.

(fragment b)

] Ὧροϲ [
]. ἐ̣χο(μ.) .[

(fragment c)

] ϲπό(ροϲ) (πυρῶι) γεω(ργὸϲ) Π[
]..[

(fragment d)

ἐ]χο(μ.) ἀνὰ (μέϲον) ὑπολό(γου) κα̣ὶ̣ [
] ἐχό(μ.) Μεϲταϲῦτμιϲ Π[ετεϲούχου
(πυρῶι) ε φα(κῶι) ε
] ἐ̣χο(μ.) ἀνὰ (μέϲον) ὑπολό(γου) καὶ διώρυ(γοϲ) ἡ κεχ[ω(ριϲμένη)
πρ(όϲοδοϲ) διὰ
]. ἐχό(μ.) \`ἀρχό(μ.) νό(του)´ Ἁρμιῦϲιϲ Πετῶτοϲ βα(ϲιλικῆϲ) β ἀν(ὰ) δ∠γ´ιβ´
β[ο(ρρᾶ)] ἐχό(μ.) \`ἀρχό(μ.) λι(βὸϲ)´ κλή(ρου) (ἑκατονταρούρου) Ἡρα-
κλείδου τοῦ Ἐτ[φεμούνιοϲ ι (ὧν)]
(πυρῶι) ζ ἀρά(κωι) γ γεω(ργὸϲ) Πετεϲοῦχοϲ
[ἀ]πη(λιώτου) ἐχό(μ.) κλή(ρου) (ἑκατονταρούρου) Ἀθηνίωνοϲ τοῦ Ἀρ[χίου
[γεω(ργὸϲ)] Πετ̣εῦριϲ
Ϲο]κνεβτύ(νιοϲ) θε[οῦ

. . . .

19 2nd δ corr. from γ 24 1st γ corr. from ἀν(ὰ) 55 ἀπη(λιώτου) corr. from βο(ρρᾶ) 61 ε∠: ε corr. from δ 62 α∠ corr. from β 70 οἱ: read τῶν 82 Lower stroke of aroura sign in (ἑκατονταρούρου) corr. from π

15 κα(τανενεμημένωι): from the passages in this papyrus alone one might think of κα(θόλου), but cf. **61**(a). 191, **67**. 18, 23, and other references to κατανέμειν in Index XII of vol. I.

17 γ ἀν(ὰ) γ∠ perhaps Crown land rented by Onnophris in addition to his cleros, inserted here very clumsily by the scribe. If so, the rent is unusual; see p. 8.

20 Cf. **61**(b). 16; **1117**. 118 n.

22 ἀν(ὰ) (μέcον) διώρυ(γοc): supply οὔcηc.

25 τῆλει: the stroke above the last letters of this word is very common in the Menches archive.

38 The remainder of the cleros is located in l. 79 below and **1117**. 10 (cf. note) = **1120**. 41.

50 The remainder of the cleros is located in **1118**. 47 = **1120**. 79.

55 λ: not α, despite **1103**. 69. But it is surely a copyist's error for that figure, since **1128**. 68 indicates that this man leased only about 6½ arouras this year.

58–60 Cf. **1103**. 128–30.

72–8 The figures for these lines were never filled in.

73 Presumably meant as an insertion to go with l. 72 or 74.

74 cπό(ροc) (πυρῶι): repeated by mistake, unless one of the (πυρῶι)'s is a slip for some other crop.

80 αλαγηc: cf. **1104**. 19 n.

88 φαcή(λωι) κα(τανενεμημένωι): beans are not likely to have been raised for grazing – at least no instance of it has come to my notice – but accidental damage from flocks let into the field is possible. The expansion κα(θόλου) would avoid a reference to grazed beans, but is not likely to be correct (15 n.).

95 The figures given for the crops total only 19 arouras, the size of the cleros. Evidently the sowing for the Crown land has been omitted.

112 Co]κνεβτύ(νιοc) θε[οῦ: perhaps but not necessarily followed by μεγάλου or μεγάλου μεγάλου.

1120. Land Survey

P. Teb. 173v — 105 × 27 cm. — After 113/112 B.C

Parts of 8 columns from a survey of Kerkeosiris, written on the back of **1118**, and covering the Third Perichoma South (1–37), the Third North (38–91), and the Fourth (92–end).

Evidence for the date is contradictory: line 65 names the successor of Chomenis son of Akrisios, and so is later than **98**. 65 (year 5 of Soter II, **1147** introd.), while 110 shows Kephalas son of Petesouchos still in possession of the cleros he had lost by the time of **98**. 67. There are, then, two possibilities; either the scribe of **98** forgot to name Chomenis's successor, in which case **1120** will fall into year 5 after the removal of Chomenis but before that of Kephalas; or the scribe of **1120** has overlooked the removal of Kephalas. Only the latter choice will do, because **1120** cannot be dated to year 5: Hergeus son of Peteimouthes has taken over the ibis shrine which was still run by his brother Pnepheros in year 5 (l. 38 vs. **1114**. 5), the holding of Harmachoros son of Thotortaios in 67–8 exceeds the totality of **1107**. 285, and Chomenis son of Akrisios was still competent to farm Crown land that year (**94**. 12).

Col. I

Perhaps one line lost.

].
] β
]οc ξϛ

] ξ
]
] . γ
] . ι̣ ἀν(ὰ) β∠
] Π̣τολεμαίου ἡ κ̣εχω(ριcμένη) πρ(όcοδοc) β
] ἀν(ὰ) δ∠γ´ιβ´
] . .

. . . .

Col. II

] . γ( ) γ̄ ἀ[ρ]χ[ο(μ.)] β[ο(ρρᾶ)] Ἀκουcίλαοc Μενίππου β̣α̣(cιλικῆc) .
[νό(του) ἐ]χό(μ.) ἀρχό(μ.) λι(βὸc) Μαρρῆc Πετοcίριοc βα(cιλικῆc) β∠
ἐπιc(κεφθεῖcαι)
ἀπη(λιώτου) [ἐ]χό(μ.) κλ(ήρου) (ἑπταρούρου) Χο(μήνιοc) Ἀμο̣ύ̣ν̣ιοc
Τ̣εφ⟦.⟧νάχθιοc ϛ∠
ἀπη(λιώτου) ἐχό(μ.) ἀρχό(μ.) β[ο(ρρᾶ)] κλ(ήρου) (ἑπταρούρου) Χο(μήνιοc)
Πτολεμαῖοc Cενθέωc γ
νό(του) ἐχ[ό(μ.)] ⟨ἀρχό(μ.) ἀπη(λιώτου)⟩ κλ(ήρου) (ἑπταρούρου) τῶν Ὥρου
Ἁρμάιc Πατορcείουc
cπο(ρίμου) ϛ∠ ἐπιc(κεφθεῖcαι) (πυρῶι) δ φα(κῶι) β∠ γεω(ργὸc) Θ[έω]ν
λ̣ι(βὸc) ἐχό(μ.) ἀρχό(μ.) λι(βὸc) Πτ̣ο̣[λεμ]αῖοc Ὀρcείουc β̣α̣(cιλικῆc) [
βο(ρρᾶ) ἐχό(μ.) [ ] Ἁρμάιοc [
β[ο(ρρᾶ) ἐχό(μ.) ±6] . . . . . ιο( ) Καμ̣ . [
Τεῶc μι(κρὸc) Πετεχῶντοc τὸ (πρότερον) Ἀμούνιοc τ[ο]ῦ
Πικάμιοc
ἀπη(λιώτου) ἐχό(μ.) ἀρχό(μ.) βο(ρρᾶ) κλ(ήρου) (ἑπταρούρου) τ̣ῶ̣ν̣ Ὥ̣ρ̣ου
Ἁροννῶ̣φ[ρ]ι[c Ὥρου ϛ∠]
ἐπιc(κεφθεῖcαι) δι[ὰ cχοι(νίου) ±8] (ὧν) (πυρῶι) . [

. . . .

Col. III

νό(του) ἐχό(μ.) ἀρχό(μ.) ἀπη(λιώτου) [κλ(ήρου) (ἑπταρούρου) Χο(μήνιοc)]
Πᾶcιc Cοκονώπιοc ϛ[∠
τοῦ αὐ(τοῦ) β[α(cιλικῆc) ∠] ἀν(ὰ) εγ´, (γίνονται) ζ
λι(βὸc) ἐχό(μ.) ἀρχό(μ.) βο(ρρᾶ) Ἁρμιῦcιc Πετεcούχου βα(cιλικῆc) β
ἀν(ὰ) δ∠γ´ι[β´]

νό(του) ἐχό(μ.) κλ(ήρου) (ἑπταρούρου) Χο(μήνιος) Ἁρψῆθις Κολλούθου ϛ[∠
νό(του) ἐχο(μ). ἀρ[χο(μ.) λι(βὸς)]ς Φατρείου[ς
ἀπη(λιώτου) ἐχο(μ.) Ἡρ[± 11]ητρίου [
[ἀπ]η̣(λιώτου) ἐχ[ο(μ.)] Πετενε̣φι̣ή̣ρ̣υ̣ς̣ ἱερᾶς Σούχου [
ἀπη(λιώτου) ἐχό(μ.) {ὑπολό(γου) ε} ἀρχό(μ.) ν̣ό̣(του) Πετε{τε}σοῦχος
θεοῦ διαμ[
Πετοσίριος βα(σιλικῆς) ζ
βο(ρρᾶ) ἐχο(μ.) ἀρχο(μ.) λι(βὸς) Πετε̣ν̣εφι̣ῆς . . ἱερᾶς Σούχο[υ
ἀπη(λιώτου) ἐχό(μ.) Ἁρμιῦσις Πετεσούχου βα(σιλικῆς) β[
ἀπη(λιώτου) ἐχό(μ.) ἀρχό(μ.) βο(ρρᾶ) [Ὧρος] Παώπ̣ιος κλ(ήρου)
(ἑπταρούρου) Χο(μήνιος) [ϛ∠
[νό(του)] ἐχο(μ.) ἀρχο(μ.) [
].[
. . . .

Col. IV

βο(ρρᾶ) ἐχό(μ.) ἀρχό(μ.) ἀπη(λιώτου) ἱερᾶς γῆς ἐλ(ασσόνων) δι᾽
Ἑργέως τοῦ Πετειμούθου ε
λι(βὸς) ἐχό(μ.) ἀρχό(μ.) βο(ρρᾶ) Χῦψις Πετεσούχου {β̣} βα(σιλικῆς)
δ ἀν(ὰ) δ∠γ´ιβ´
νό(του) ἐχό(μ.) Πετεσοῦχος θεὸς δι᾽ Ἁρφαήσιος βα(σιλικῆς) ε ἀν(ὰ) γ
[νό(του)] ἐχό(μ.) κλ(ήρου) ἐφό(δου) Ἀπολλωνίου τοῦ Πτολεμαίου ζ
ν̣[ό(του)] ἐχό(μ.) ἀρχό(μ.) ἀπη(λιώτου) Διονυσίου τοῦ Πυρρίχου παρα(δείσου)
ἐρή(μου) d
παρα(κείμ.) λι(βὸς) \`ἐχό(μ.)´ κλ(ήρου) (τριακονταρούρου) μεταβεβη(κότος)
Διονυσίου τοῦ Πυρρίχο(υ) ιηdή
τοῦ αὐ(τοῦ) βα(σιλικῆς) β ἀν(ὰ) ε, (γίνονται) κdή
λι(βὸς) ἐχό(μ.) ἀρχό(μ.) νό(του) κλ(ήρου) (ὀγδοηκονταρούρου) Ἀπολλωνίου
τοῦ Ἀπολλωνίου ιη
βο(ρρᾶ) ἐχό(μ.) ἀρχό(μ.) ἀπη(λιώτου) κλ(ήρου) (ἑπταρούρου) Χο(μήνιος)
Ἁρχῦψις Πετοσί(ριος) [ϛ]∠
λι(βὸς) ἐ[χ]ό(μ.) ἀρχό(μ.) βο(ρρᾶ) κλ(ήρου) (ὀγδοηκονταρούρου)
Διοδότου τοῦ Ἀπολλωνίου [
βο(ρρᾶ) ἐ[χο(μ.) ἀ]ρ̣χο(μ.) ἀπη(λιώτου) διώρυ(γος) [
λι(βὸς) ἐχο(μ.) ἀ̣ρ̣χ̣ό̣(μ.) . . ( ) Π̣ε̣τ̣ερμοῦθις Ὥρου βα(σιλικῆς) ϛ[

[. . ( ) ἐχό(μ.) κλ(ήρου) (ἑπταρούρου)] Χ̣ο̣(μήνιος) Ἀ̣π̣[ῦ]γχις
Ποώριος [ϛ∠
]ϲ Ὥρου βα̣(ϲιλικῆϲ) [
ο]υ β[α(ϲιλικῆϲ)] ζ ἀν(ὰ) δ∠γ́ιβ́
] Ἁρμιύϲιος βα(ϲιλικῆϲ) ε ἀν(ὰ) δ∠γ́ιβ́
λι(βὸϲ) ἐχό(μ.) ⟨ἀρχό(μ.) νό(του)⟩ Ἡ̣ρ[ακλῆϲ] Πετάλου βα(ϲιλικῆϲ) ζ∠
ἀν(ὰ) δ̣∠̣γ́ιβ́
βο(ρρᾶ) ἐχό(μ.) ⟨ἀρχό(μ.)⟩ ἀπη(λιώτου) Ὧροϲ Ἀπύγχιοϲ βα(ϲιλικῆϲ)
β[∠]δ̣ ἀν(ὰ) δ∠γ́ιβ́
λ̣ι̣(βὸϲ) [ἐχό(μ.)] Τεῶϲ Ὥρου βα(ϲιλικῆϲ) γ ἀν(ὰ) δ∠γ́ιβ́
[λι(βὸϲ)] ἐ̣χό(μ.) ἀρχό(μ.) βο(ρρᾶ) Ἰ[ν]α̣ρῶ̣ϲ Παῦτοϲ βα(ϲιλικῆϲ) ε ἀν(ὰ) δ∠γ́ιβ́
νό(του) ἐχό(μ.) ⟨ἀρχό(μ.) ἀπη(λιώτου)⟩ κλ(ήρου) (ἑπταρούρου) Χο(μήνιοϲ)
Νεκτενῖβιϲ Ὥρου ϛ∠
λι(βὸϲ) ἐχό(μ.) ἀρχό(μ.) νό(του) κλ(ήρου) (ἑπταρούρου) Παϲῶϲ μέγ(αϲ)
Π[ανήϲιοϲ ϛ∠]
[βο(ρρᾶ)] ἐχο(μ.) ἀρχο(μ.) ἀπη(λιώτου) ο̣[

. . . .

Col. V

λι(βὸϲ) ἐχό(μ.) ἀρχό(μ.) νό(του) κλ(ήρου) (ἑπταρούρου) Χο(μήνιοϲ) Ὧροϲ
μι(κρὸϲ) Κολλούθου ϛ∠, ὃν με(τειληφέναι)
Ἁρϲενθὲν Ϲιεφμοῦτοϲ
βο(ρρᾶ) ἐχό(μ.) ἀρχό(μ.) ἀπη(λιώτου) Κατῦτιϲ Κατύτιοϲ βα(ϲιλικῆϲ) γ
ἀν(ὰ) δ∠γ́ιβ́
λι(βὸϲ) ἐχό(μ.) ἀρχό(μ.) βο(ρρᾶ) τοῦ αὐ(τοῦ) βα(ϲιλικῆϲ) ε ἀν(ὰ) δ∠γ́ιβ́
νό(του) ἐχό(μ.) ἀρχό(μ.) ἀπη(λιώτου) κλ(ήρου) (εἰκοϲιαρούρου)
Χο(μήνιοϲ) Ὅμηροϲ Ἀκρίου ιθ ἐπιϲ(κεφθεῖϲαι)
λι(βὸϲ) ἐχό(μ.) κλ(ήρου) (ἑπταρούρου) Χο(μήνιοϲ) Μεϲταϲῦ(τμιϲ) Ὥρου ϛ∠
παρα(κείμ.) ⟨λι(βὸϲ)⟩ ἐχό(μ.) ⟨ἀρχό(μ.) νό(του)⟩ Ἁρμαχόροϲ Θοτορταίου
β̣[α(ϲιλικῆϲ) γ∠ ἀν(ὰ) δ∠γ́ιβ́
βο(ρρᾶ) ἐχό(μ.) ἀρχό(μ.) ἀπη(λιώτου) τ̣ο̣[ῦ αὐτο]ῦ γ
λι(βὸϲ) ἐχό(μ.) ἀρχό(μ.) βο(ρρᾶ) κλ(ήρου) (ἑπταρούρου) τῶν δι' Ὥρου
Μαρρῆ(ϲ) Πα[άπιοϲ] ϛ∠
ν̣ό̣(του) [ἐ]χ[ό(μ.)] ἀρχό(μ.) ἀπη(λιώτου) κλ(ήρου) (ἑπταρούρου) Χο(μήνιοϲ)
Θοτεὺϲ Πολή(μιοϲ) [ϛ]∠

τοῦ αὐ(τοῦ) βα(ϲιλικῆϲ) α ἀν(ὰ) ϵ, (γίνονται) [ζ∠]

λι(βὸϲ) ἐχό(μ.) κλ(ήρου) (ἑπταρούρου) Χο(μήνιοϲ) Φαεὺϲ Ϲοκέωϲ ϛ̣∠̣, τοῦ αὐ(τοῦ) [βα(ϲιλικῆϲ) α] ἀν(ὰ) ϵ, (γίνονται) ζ∠

ἐπιϲ(κεφθεῖϲαι) διὰ ϲχοι(νίου) λι(βὸϲ) ἐχό(μ.) ἀρχό(μ.) νό(του) κλή(ρου) (ἑπταρούρου) Χο(μήνιοϲ) Παϲῶϲ Ὀρϲείου[ϲ] ϛ∠

τοῦ αὐ(τοῦ) βα(ϲιλικῆϲ) α ἀν(ὰ) ϵ, (γίνονται) ζ∠

βο̣(ρρᾶ) ἐχό(μ.) κλ(ήρου) (ἑπταρούρου) Χο(μήνιοϲ) Πεϲύθηϲ Παχῶτοϲ ϛ∠

τοῦ αὐ(τοῦ) βα(ϲιλικῆϲ) α ἀν(ὰ) ϵ, (γίνονται) ζ∠

βο(ρρᾶ) ἐχό(μ.) ἀρχό(μ.) ἀπη(λιώτου) Ὀ̣ν̣νῶφριϲ Πετερμούθιοϲ κλ(ήρου) (ἑπταρούρου) Χο(μήνιοϲ) ϛ∠

λι(βὸϲ) ἐχό(μ.) ἀρχό(μ.) βο(ρρᾶ) κλ(ήρου) (ἑπταρούρου) Χο(μήνιοϲ) Ὧροϲ Θοτορταίου ϛ∠

ἐπιϲ(κεφθεῖϲαι) διὰ ϲχοι(νίου) τοῦ αὐ(τοῦ) βα(ϲιλικῆϲ) α∠ ἀν(ὰ) ϵ, (γίνονται) η ἐπιϲ(κεφθεῖϲαι)

νό(του) ἐχό(μ.) ἀρχό(μ.) ἀπη(λιώτου) κλ(ήρου) (ἑπταρούρου) Παῶπιϲ Πετεϲούχου δ∠ ἐπιϲ(κεφθεῖϲαι)

λι(βὸϲ) ἐχό(μ.) Θοτ[ο]ρταῖοϲ Πετοϲί̣(ριοϲ) βα(ϲιλικῆϲ) ϵ∠

[λι(βὸϲ) ἐχό(μ.) κλ(ήρου) (ἑπταρούρου) ± 10] ϛ∠

τοῦ αὐ(τοῦ) βα(ϲιλικῆϲ) α̣ [ἀ]ν̣(ὰ) ϵ, (γίνονται) ζ∠

. . . .

Col. VI

βο(ρρᾶ) ἐχό(μ.) ⟨ἀρχό(μ.) ἀπη(λιώτου)⟩ κλ(ήρου) (ἑκατονταρούρου) Πρώταρχοϲ Διονυϲίου ι

λι(βὸϲ) ἐχό(μ.) κλ(ήρου) (ἑπταρούρου) Χ[ο(μήνιοϲ)] Πορεγέβθιϲ Ἀπύγχιοϲ ϛ∠

τοῦ αὐ(τοῦ) βα(ϲιλικῆϲ) γ ἀν(ὰ) ϵ, (γίνονται) θ∠

λι(βὸϲ) ἐχό(μ.) κλ(ήρου) (ἑκατονταρούρου) Μελάνιπποϲ Ἀϲκληπιάδου ι ἐπιϲ(κεφθεῖϲαι)

λι(βὸϲ) ἐχό(μ.) κλ(ήρου) (ἑκατονταρούρου) Πολέμων Ἀμμωνίου κ ἐ̣[πιϲ(κεφθεῖϲαι)]

λι(βὸϲ) ἐχό(μ.) κλ(ήρου) (ἑκατονταρούρου) [Ἡλιό]δ̣ωροϲ Διονυϲίου [

λι(βὸϲ) ἐχό(μ.) κλ(ήρου) (ἑκατονταρούρου) [Πρώταρχοϲ Διονυϲίου ι

παρα(κειμ.) λι(βὸϲ) ἐχο(μ.) ἐγβαι(ν.) ἀπη(λιώτου) [διώρυγοϲ

ἀρχο(μ.) νό(του) καὶ ἀπη(λιώτου) ἁ̣λ̣μ̣[υ(ρίδοϲ)

βο(ρρᾶ) ἐχο(μ.) ἀρχο(μ.) [ἀπη(λιώτου)

λι(βὸς) ἐχό(μ.) ἀρχό(μ.) [βο(ρρᾶ) Πετεσοῦ(χος) θε(ὸς) διὰ
Πετοσίρ]ιος τ̣ο̣(ῦ)
Ἀμεν̣[νέως βα(σιλικῆς) ϛ∠
νό(του) ἐχό(μ.) κλ(ήρου) (ἑπταρούρου) Χ[ο(μήνιος)] Ὀρσῆς Ἁροννῆς ϛ∠
τοῦ αὐ(τοῦ) βα(σιλικῆς) α ἀν(ὰ) ε, (γίνονται) ζ∠
νό(του) ἐχό(μ.) ⟨ἀρχό(μ.) λι(βὸς)⟩ κλ(ήρου) (τριακονταρούρου)
Χο(μήνιος) Ἁρυώτης Φα[εῦ]τος ε ἐπισ(κεφθεῖσαι)
ἀπη(λιώτου) ἐχό(μ.) ⟨ἀρχό(μ.) βο(ρρᾶ)⟩ Θῶνις μι(κρὸς) Κεντίσιος
βα(σιλικῆς) [
νό(του) ἐχό(μ.) κλ(ήρου) (ἑπταρούρου) Χο(μήνιος) Πᾶσις μέ(γας)
Καλατύ[τιος] ϛ∠̣
νό(του) ἐχό(μ.) κλ(ήρου) (ἑπταρούρου) Χο(μήνιος) Πᾶσις μι(κρὸς)
Καλατύτιος [ϛ∠
νό(του) ἐχό(μ.) ⟨ἀρχό(μ.) ἀπη(λιώτου)⟩ Κεντῖσις Ὥρου βα(σιλικῆς)
[ιδ ἀν(ὰ) δ∠γ´ιβ´
λι(βὸς) ἐχό(μ.) ἀρχό(μ.) νό(του) κλ(ήρου) (εἰκοσιαρούρου) Χο(μήνιος)
Φμ[έρσις Ὥρου ε
βο(ρρᾶ) ἐχό(μ.) ἀρχό(μ.) ἀπη(λιώτου) κλ(ήρου) (ἑπταρούρου) Χο(μήνιος)
Ἁρφ[αῆσις Ὥρου ϛ∠
⟨λι(βὸς) ἐχό(μ.)⟩ Θῶνις [μι(κρὸς) Κεντίσιος βα(σιλικῆς)

Col. VII

παρα(κείμ.) λι(βὸς) ἐχό(μ.) ἱερᾶς Σοκνεβτύνεος οε
λι(βὸς) ἐχό(μ.) κλ(ήρου) (εἰκοσιαρούρου) Χο(μήνιος) Λυσίμαχο(ς) Χομήνιος
τὸ (πρότερον) Ἁρμιύσιος
τοῦ Πτολεμαίου ιθ
[λ]ι(βὸς) ἐχό(μ.) ⟦ἀρχό(μ.) νό(του)⟧ Ὧρος Πετώυτος βα(σιλικῆς) ε ἀν(ὰ) δ∠γ´ιβ´
λι(βὸς) ἐχό(μ.) ἀρχό(μ.) νό(του) κλ(ήρου) ἐφό(δου) μ̣ετα(βεβηκότος)
Διδυμάρχου τοῦ Ἀπολλω(νίου) η̣
βο(ρρᾶ) ἐχό(μ.) ἀρχό(μ.) λι(βὸς) Πᾶσις Πετεσούχου βα(σιλικῆς) δ ἀν(ὰ) δ∠γ´ιβ´
ἀπη(λιώτου) ἐχ[ό(μ.) ± 16] κλ(ήρου) (εἰκοσιαρούρου)
Κεφαλᾶς Πετεσ(ούχου) ιθ
[τοῦ αὐ(τοῦ) βα(σιλικῆς)] γ ἀν(ὰ) ε, (γίνονται) κβ
[βο(ρρᾶ) ἐχό(μ.) ἀρχό(μ.) ἀπη(λιώτου) κλ(ήρου) (ἑπταρούρου) Χο(μήνιος)]
Ἁ̣ρ̣μιῦσις Π̣[ετεσ(ούχου)] ϛ̣∠

[λι(βὸς) ἐχο(μ.) ἀρχο(μ.) νό(του)] Πᾶσις Πετεσούχο(υ) βα(σιλικῆς) [
[βο(ρρᾶ) ἐχο(μ.) ἀ]ρ̣χο(μ.) ἀπη(λιώτου) Πετῶς Μαρρείους [β]α̣(σιλικῆς) [
[λι(βὸς) ἐ]χ[ο(μ.)] Ἁρς̣ῦτ̣μι̣[ς] Λύκου [
λι(βὸς) ἐχό(μ.) κλή(ρου) ἐφό(δου) μετα(βεβηκότος) Διδυμάρχ[ο]υ τοῦ
Ἀπολλωνίου ζ
λι(βὸς) ἐχό(μ.) ἀρχό(μ.) βο(ρρᾶ) Πᾶσις Πετεσούχου βα(σιλικῆς) ζ̣
τοῦ αὐ(τοῦ) β̣α(σιλικῆς) α
νό(του) ἐχό(μ.) ἀρχό(μ.) ἀπη(λιώτου) κλή(ρου) (ἑπταρούρου) Χο(μήνιος)
Πετεσοῦχο(ς) Τοθείους [ς∠
λι(βὸς) ἐχό(μ.) ὑδρα(γωγοῦ) • γ∠d / γdί̇ς́λ́β β (γίνονται) ζίς́λ́β́
λι(βὸς) ἐχό(μ.) ἀρχό(μ.) βο(ρρᾶ) Πετεσούχου θε(οῦ) διὰ Πετεσούχο(υ)
τοῦ Πακ̣ύ̣[ρριος ε
νό(του) ἐχό(μ.) ἀρχό(μ.) ἀπη(λιώτου) κλ(ήρου) ἐφό(δου) μετα(βεβηκότος)
Ἀκου(σιλάου) τοῦ Ἀσκλη(πιάδου) [ς
λι(βὸς) ἐχό(μ.) [ἀρ]χό(μ.) βο(ρρᾶ) κλ(ήρου) φυ(λακίτου) μεταβεβη(κότος)
Μ̣άρων Διονυσίου [γ
νό(του) ἐχ̣[ό(μ.) κ]λ̣(ήρου) ἐφό(δου) μετα(βεβηκότος) Ἀσκλη(πιάδης)
[Ἀσκλη(πιάδου) ιβ
[νό(του) ἐχό(μ.) ἀρ]χό(μ.) [ἀπη(λιώτου) κλ(ήρου) ἐφό(δου) μετα(βεβηκότος)
Ἀκου(σιλάου) τοῦ Ἀσκλη(πιάδου) δ

. . . .

Col. VIII

(*c.* 3 lines lost)

λι(βὸς) ἐχο(μ.) . . . [
παρα(κειμ.) λι(βὸς) ἐχο(μ.) α̣ρ̣χ̣ο̣(μ.) νό(του) διώ̣[ρυγος
βο(ρρᾶ) ἐχό(μ.) ἀρχό(μ.) λι(βὸς) κλή(ρου) (ἑκατονταρούρου) Ἀθην̣ί̣ω̣ν̣ [Ἀρχίου
ἀπη(λιώτου) ἐχό(μ.) κλ(ήρου) [ἐφό(δου)] μ̣ετα(βεβηκότος) Ἀσ[κλ]η(πιάδης)
Ἀσκλη(πιάδου) [ἀπὸ τοῦ Πολέμωνος ι
ἀπη(λιώτου) ἐχο(μ.) ἀρχο(μ.) νό(του) ἱερᾶς γῆς Σού[χου
δ̣ι̣ὰ̣ Πετειμούθου Πε̣τ̣[εσούχου
[βο(ρρᾶ) ἐ]χ̣ο(μ.) [ἀρ]χο̣(μ.) λι(βὸς) . . . . υ . . . [
[ἀπη(λιώτου) ἐχό(μ.) κλ(ήρου)] (ἑκατονταρούρου) Β̣α̣κ̣χίου [τοῦ Μουσαίου
[ἀπη(λιώτου) ἐχο(μ.)] Μεστα[σῦτμις

Slight traces of a few more lines.

4–5 The 60 arouras may refer to pastures leased by the γεωργοὶ κοινῆι (**1103**. 115 n.), the 66 to Aphthonetos son of Hebdomion (cf. **62**. 30).

12 ἐπις(κεφθεῖcαι): that is, the area of the land had been checked recently by survey.

14 The remainder of the cleros was located near Areos Kome (**1110**. 202).

15 (ἑπταρούρου) τῶν Ὥρου: in this text the machimoi enrolled by the scribes Ptolemaios and Xenon (**1118**. 40 n.) are described as τῶν Ὥρου or τῶν δι' Ὥρου. This is perhaps the Horos referred to as the original enroller of a number of machimoi who were later transferred to the laarchy of Chomenis, *PPt* 2531.

17 The second λι(βόc) is a mistake for νό(του).

23 ἐπις(κεφθεῖcαι) δι[ὰ cχοι(νίου): for the restoration see l. 73. Cf. Hero Alexandrinus, *Geometrica* 2: Egyptian land surveys are carried out ποτὲ μὲν τῷ καλουμένῳ cχοινίῳ, ποτὲ δὲ καλάμῳ, ποτὲ δὲ καὶ ἑτέροιc μέτροιc; cf. Crawford 35 f.

24 According to **62**. 248 this property was in the north part of the 3rd perichoma; but since other properties both before and after this entry lay in the southern portion, it is most natural to suppose that this lot did so as well and that βο(ρρᾶ) in **62**. 248 is an error for νό(του).

29 Ἡρ[ακλείδηc Δημ]ητρίου would fit. A son of Δημήτριοc Ἡρακλείδου?

30 The usual way of describing sacred land is ἱερᾶc γῆc τοῦ δεῖνοc θεοῦ διὰ τοῦ δεῖνοc; for the present word order, in which ἱερᾶc Cούχου stands parallel to βα(cιλικῆc), cf. e.g. **85**. 56, 115, as well as l. 33 below.

33 The traces after Πετẹνεφịῆc are {.

38–41 Cf. **1117**. 1 ff. with sketch in notes; **1118**. 3 ff.

38 Ἑργέωc: the parallel texts show that this is not the land under Hergeus's name in e.g. **1110**. 28, but refers to the ibis shrine elsewhere controlled by Pnepheros son of Peteimouthes (**1110**. 31), who was no doubt an older brother of the man here. The patronymic of the other Hergeus is not known.

40 Cf. **1117**. 9 n.

42–3 This survey lists for Dionysios a cleros of $18\frac{3}{8}$ arouras *plus* $\frac{1}{4}$ ar. of garden land gone desert. In **62**. 48–50 the latter is said to be part of the former, and other deductions as well reduce the given extent of cleros to $17\frac{3}{8}$.

45 Ἀπολλωνίου τοῦ Ἀπολλωνίου: so written for Ammonios son of Apollonios also in **1108**. 27.

59 Or perhaps (ἑπταρούρου) ⟨Χο(μήνιοc)⟩. Similar negligence in l. 79.

63 ff. Cf. **1118**. 30 ff.

65 Ὅμηροc Ἀκρίου: the name Ἄκριοc is not elsewhere attested. Very probably we should read Ἀκρι⟨cί⟩ου, in which case Homeros will be the brother of Chomenis.

79 Cf. **1118**. 47 n.

86 ẹ[πιc(κεφθεῖcαι): to judge from an earlier transcript, ἐπιc( ) was clearly visible in 1969. Today κϛ would be the most obvious reading, but even by 116/115 Polemon held only 20 arouras.

87 Cf. **1118**. 62 n.

91–103 The left margin of the column was shifted to the right from l. 91 on to avoid the ends of the long lines of Col. v.

92 With this property the survey enters the Fourth Perichoma.

94 Ἁροννῆc: nom. for gen., as **1118**. 102.

105 f. The transfer of Harmiysis' property to Lysimachos may have resulted from the former's failure to pay his half-artab tax (**64**(a). 141).

107 This land was rented by Harmiysis in **84**. 95.

114–15 The figures for Petos and Harsytmis in **1118**. 97 and 98 are $7\frac{1}{2}$ and $5\frac{1}{2}$ arouras.

118 Probably refers to the entry below, not above.

120 The canal is described in **84**. 110 as λι(βὸc) ἐχό(μ.) ἐγβαί(ν.) νό(του) παρὰ τὴν προγεγεω-(μετρημένην) cχοι(νίον) ὑδρα(γωγοῦ) ∠d. In view of the dimension stated there, it is most unlikely that the following sketch (cf. **1122** introd.) refers to the canal; it is presumably intended for Petesouchos's land, cleros and basilike combined, as in **1122**. 25–6.

The symbol which replaces β on the right side of the sketch is a mere dot, hardly an omicron: ὁ(μοίωc), as is frequently transcribed in similar instances (e.g. *WChr* 231 and 234), is not suggested palaeographically and is linguistically dubious: P. Iand. VII 135 indicates that the vocalization was *πρὸc ἴcον*. Exactly similar dots are used for the same purpose in Demotic surveys (e.g., O. Med. Habu 152); and like the symbols for deduction, the dot is probably a Demotic borrowing.

129 [*ἀπὸ τοῦ Πολέμωνοc ι*: cf. **1118.** 112, where the boundaries are stated differently. This is the only property held by Asklepiades not already accounted for in 124 = **1118.** 108 = **84.** 118 and **1117.** 46.

1121. Land Survey

P. Teb. 255 — 14 × 26 cm. — Late second century B.C.

This concluding column from a document similar to the foregoing, despite its slight extent, contains a complete survey of the perichoma Psinara( ), totalling 437½ arouras. The land was of exceptionally poor quality: 8½ arouras were salty (3), 77½ water-logged (4, 7, 9), 321½ sanded over (10, 11); and a further 10 arouras of garden land are no doubt part of the holdings of Souchos, which other texts call *ἔρημοc* (cf. **60.** 39–40). Apart from the last-mentioned property, the perichoma contained no sacred land, separate revenue, or productive Crown land, and only two cleruchic allotments.

καὶ τὰ περὶ .[

ἀπὸ βορρᾶ καὶ ἀπη(λιώτου) (ὧν) ἐ̣ν̣ λα(χανείαι) οὔcηc ι, κα(ταλείπονται) γῆc ἐν τῶι καλο[υμένωι]

Ψινα(ρα) περιχώ(ματι) ἀρχό(μεναι) λι(βὸc) ὑπολό(γου) ἁλμυ(ρίδοc) ⟨ἀπὸ τοῦ⟩ μ (ἔτουc) η∠

ἀπη(λιώτου) ἐ̣χ̣ό(μεναι) ἐμβρόχου ὁμοίωc ια

ἀπη(λ.) ἐχό(μ.) κλ(ήρου) ἐρη(μο)φύ(λακοc) Πτο(λεμαῖοc) [C]αραπίωνοc ι

ἀπη(λ.) ἐχο(μ.) ἀρχο(μ.) νό(του) κλ(ήρου) (ὀγδοηκονταρούρου) Δ̣ώρου τοῦ Πετάλο̣υ̣ [ι]

βο(ρρᾶ) ἐχό(μ.) ἐγβαί(νουcαι) λι(βὸc) ⟨ἀρχό(μ.) ἀπη(λ.)⟩ ὑπολό(γου) ἐμ[βρό]χ̣ο(υ) τοῦ ἀπὸ τοῦ μ (ἔτουc) κδ∠

λι(βὸc) [ἐχό(μ.)] ἀ̣ρχό(μ.) νό(του) τὰ [περὶ τ]ὸ̣ν̣ Ἰβι[ῶ(να)] τῶν (εἰκοcιπενταρούρων) πε(δία)

βο(ρρᾶ) [ἐχό(μ.) ὑπ]ο̣λό(γου) ἐμβρό(χου) ἕωc λθ (ἔτουc) μβ

[βο(ρρᾶ) ἐχό(μ.) ἐφ]ημμιcμένηc ρ̣λ̣ε∠ή

[βο(ρρᾶ) ἐχό(μ.)] νομῶν τῶν πρὸc χ̣α̣(λκὸν) ὁμοίωc ροε∠dη

[(γίν.)] ἐφη(μμιcμένηc) τκα∠

[(γίν.)] τ̣ο̣ῦ̣ περιχώ(ματοc)   (γίν.) τῆc κώ(μηc)

Traces of a further line in a 2nd hand are perhaps not part of this list.

1 Perhaps a later insertion, to judge from **187** verso, where the perichoma is introduced from a slightly different direction with the words ἀπὸ βο(ρρᾶ) καὶ λι(βὸς) (ὧν) ἀν(ὰ) (μέσον) οὔσης. . .ης καὶ τὰ περὶ Ταλὶ πε(δία).

2 λα(χανείαι): cf. **60**. 39; **86**. 43, 50. The only land ἐν λα(χανείαι) explicitly mentioned at Kerkeosiris elsewhere is 1¼ aroura on the outskirts of the village (**60**. 39), but it does not seem at all likely that the size of that area would have fluctuated. Probably these 10 arouras are part of the 20 belonging to Souchos, which are elsewhere described as παράδεισος and ἄμπελος (**60**. 38; **61**(a). 158), terms which are also applied to the 1¼ ar. of village land.

3 Ψινα(ρα): the fullest writing of the name is **60**. 43.

6 ι: restored from **187** verso.

11 νομῶν τῶν πρὸς χα̣(λκόν): these likewise (ὁμοίως) belong to the ἐφημμισμένης and are to be contrasted with those pastures which brought a grain rental. Cf. **60**. 41–3, νομῶν τῶν πρὸς χα[λκὸν] διοικουμένοις ἣν ἐφημμίσθαι διὰ τὸ πα(ρακεῖσθαι) τῶι ὄρι (ἄρουραι) ροεδή περὶ Ψιναρα( ). Cf. p. 2; **1103**. 115 n.

13 The totals were not filled in; cf. **1118**. 1 n.

1122. Land Survey

P. Teb. 187 | 34 × 29 cm. | Late second century B.C.

Three columns from a detailed survey of Kerkeosiris comparable to **86**, **87**, **150**, and **1123**; for the format, see introd. to **87** and P. Lond. 267 (II, p. 129; illustrated plate 45). Properties are represented schematically by a horizontal line marked with the four dimensions of each lot, expressed in schoinia; where opposing sides are equal, the measurement of one is given as a dot which functions as a ditto sign (**1120**. 120 n.). The standard order in which boundaries are listed in Ptolemaic Egypt is South, North, East, West. There is no evidence for or against the view that the top figure in these sketches is the southern boundary and the left-hand side figure the eastern. Since the conventions used in calculating with the often very complicated fractions which occur are not clear to me, I have rarely attempted restoration of figures.

Lines 1–35 parallel **1117**. 57–63 = **1118**. 164–70; lines 36–54 parallel **1117**. 75–80. Holdings which are stated as simple blocks in the summary texts are here sometimes subdivided into a number of small contiguous parcels; presumably this practice was intended to help minimize the errors inherent in the formula used for calculating areas (cf. Crawford, 12–13).

A mutilated column on the verso, containing a survey of the Psinara( ) Perichoma similar to **1121**, is not reproduced here.

Traces of a column to the left; then:

[ἀπη(λιώτου)] ἐ̣χό(μεναι) ἐγβαί(νουσαι) ἀπη(λ.) παρὰ τὴν προγεγεω(μετρημένην) σχοι(νία) β∠ιϛ´

κλ(ήρου) (ἑπταρούρου) Χο(μήνιος) Ἁρυ⟨ώ⟩της Ἁρυώτου ϛ∠

ε∠dιϛ´ —— ∠ηιϛλβ´ / ∠ιϛλβ´ —— •, (γίν.) γ∠dιϛλβ´ (πυρῶι)

ἀπη(λ.) ἐχό(μ.) ἀρχό(μ.) νό(του) ήίϛ $\frac{\bullet}{\angle \text{ήίϛλ΄β}}$ •, (γίν.) ή

βο(ρρᾶ) ἐχό(μ.) ἀρχό(μ.) λι(βὸς) τοῦ αὐτοῦ

ίϛ $\frac{\angle}{\bullet}$ ή, (γίν.) λ΄β΄ξ΄δ

ἀπη(λ.) ἐχό(μ.) ἐγβαί(ν.) βο(ρρᾶ) παρὰ τὰ περὶ τὸν Ἰβιῶ(να) τῶν (εἰκοσι-πεντ[αρούρων)]

πε(δία) σχοι(νίον) αή ⟦ἀρχό(μ.) βο(ρρᾶ)⟧ α $\frac{\alpha\angle\text{ή}}{\bullet}$ ......

(γίν.) αή

ἀπη(λ.) ⟨ἐχό(μ.)⟩ εἰς[βαί(ν.) . . (   )] παρὰ τὴν προγεγεω(μ.) ṣχοι(νίου) ∠ή

Ἁ̣ρ̣υ̣(ώτης) κ̣λ̣(ήρου) dίϛ $\frac{\alpha}{\bullet}$ . . , (γίν.) ή̣ξ̣δ̣

(πυρῶι)

νό(του) ἐχό(μ.) ἐγβαί(ν.) παρὰ τὴν προγεγεω(μ.) σχοι(νίον) α Ἁρυ(ώτης) κλ(ήρου) (ἑπτ.) Χο(μ.) τὸ λο(ιπὸν) τοῦ κλ(ήρου)

α̣∠dήίϛ $\frac{\angle\text{ήίϛλ΄β}}{\angle\text{ίϛλ΄β}}$ adίϛ, (γίν.) αήίϛ

(γίν.) τοῦ κλ(ήρου) ϛdήίϛ (πυρῶι) γεω(ργὸς) [

[νό(του) ἐχό(μ.)] Ἁρμιῦσις Σοκο̣ν̣ώπ̣ιος ϛ∠

[ ]. d $\frac{\text{adήίϛ}}{[\ \ ]\text{ήίϛλ΄β}}$ [ ]ήίϛλ΄β, (γίν.) ζήίϛλ΄β

(γίν.) (traces)

νό(του) ἐχό(μ.) εἰσβαί(ν.) λι(βὸς) παρὰ τὴν πρ[ογεγεω(μ.) σχοι(νι   )]ίϛ . . μο(   )

ϛ̣λ΄β Μαρρῆς Μαρρείους [βα(σιλικῆς)] β̣∠ḍή ἀν(ὰ) [δ]∠γίβ

Col. II

δ∠ $\frac{\bullet}{\angle\text{ήλ΄β}}$ δήλ΄β

(γίν.) β∠dή φα(κῶι)

δ ἐν τοῖς αὐ(τοῖς) πε(δίοις)

νό(του) ἐχό(μ.) κλ(ήρου) (ἑπτ.) Χο(μ.) Ὧρος Ἁρφαήσιος ϛ∠, βα(σιλικῆς) α ἀν(ὰ) ϵ, (γίν.) ζ∠

· adήίς / [ ] δ∠, (γίν.) ζ∠ίς

νό(του) ἐχό(μ.) [. . βαί(ν.) παρὰ] τ̣ὴ̣ν̣ π̣ρ[ο]γ̣εγεω(μ.) cχοι(νία) δ∠
[κλ(ήρου) (ὀγδοηκονταρούρου) Λέοντος τοῦ Λεοντ]ίcκου τὸ λο(ιπὸν)
τοῦ κλ(ήρου)
+ ∠, (γίν.) ḍ φα(κῶι)

] α∠ίς /]. . α, (γίν.) αλ́βξδ
] d / α∠ίς α∠, (γίν.) βίς
] βdή / . . β∠, (γίν.) ε∠dήλ́β
π]αρὰ τὴν προγεγεω(μ.) cχοι(νία) βίςλ́β
] • /]ḍή̣ίςλ́β ∠ίς, (γίν.) β∠d χό(ρτωι)
] ιβή (ὧν) ἀρά(κωι) θ φα(κῶι) γή· (γίν.) τοῦ κλ(ήρου)
ν̣ό̣(του) ἐχ̣ό̣(μ.) . . β̣α̣ί̣(ν.) ἀπη(λ.) παρὰ τὴν προγεγεω(μ.) βdήίςλ́β
χώ(ματος) καὶ διώρυ(γος) ς
∠ ι∠dίςλ́β / • d, (γίν.) . . .
χ̣ώ̣(ματος) β, διώρυ(γος) β
ἀπη(λ.) ἐχό(μ.) εἰcβαί(ν.) παρὰ τὴν προγεγεω(μ.) cχοι(νία) η∠dλ́β
Ὀ̣ν̣ν̣ῶ̣φ̣ρ̣ις Πετεχῶ(ντος) βα(ςιλικῆς) β ἀν(ὰ) γ
α [ ] / [ ] [ ], (γίν.) [
ἀπη(λ.) ἐχό(μ.) ἀρχό(μ.) βο(ρρᾶ) κλ(ήρου) (ὀγδοηκονταρούρου) Δώρου
τ[οῦ Πετάλου]
ἀπὸ (ἀρουρῶν ?) . . . . . ς̣ • / d •, (γίν.) η

(Traces of 2 lines)

ἀρά(κωι) traces
ἀπη(λ.) ἐχό(μ.) εἰcβαί(ν.) [. . ( ) παρ]ὰ [τὰ πε]ρὶ τὸν Ἰβιῶ(να) τῶν
(εἰκοσιπενταρούρων) [πε(δία)]

cχοι(νίον) α∠ή̣ ̣ ̣[Ἀθεμμεὺc Πετεcο]ύχ[ου]

βα(cιλικῆc) ϵ ἀν(ὰ) γ

(Traces of 1 line)

                                                    ∠dή́ί́ϛ́
νό(του) ἐχό(μ.) α ̣ ̣ ——————————— • (γίν.) ∠dίϛλ́β́
                                                      •

                        ∠ή́ί́ϛ́
]λ́β́ ——————————— •, (γίν.) ή́λ́β́
                          ή
                        adή́

Lines 1–15. 'Adjoining on the east, projecting $2\frac{9}{16}$ schonia east of the property previously surveyed, $6\frac{1}{2}$ arouras of an allotment for a 7-aroura cleruch of Chomenis, Haryotes son of Haryotes, measuring $5\frac{13}{16} \times 5\frac{13}{16} \times \frac{23}{32} \times \frac{19}{32}$ schoinia, total $3\frac{27}{32}$ arouras, in wheat. Adjoining on the east, forming a southern boundary of the next lot, another bit of the allotment measuring $\frac{3}{16} \times \frac{3}{16} \times \frac{23}{32} \times \frac{23}{32}$, total $\frac{1}{8}$ aroura. Adjoining on the north, forming a western boundary of the next lot, belonging to the same man, another bit of the allotment measuring $\frac{1}{16} \times \frac{1}{8} \times \frac{1}{2} \times \frac{1}{2}$, total $\frac{3}{64}$. Adjoining on the east, projecting $1\frac{1}{8}$ schoinion north of the fields around Ibion Eikosipentarouron, another bit of the allotment measuring $1 \times (?) \times 1\frac{5}{8} \times 1\frac{5}{8}$, total $1\frac{1}{8}$. Adjoining on the east, receding ... of the property previously surveyed for $\frac{5}{8}$ schoinion, another bit of Haryotes' allotment, measuring $\frac{5}{16} \times (?) \times 1 \times 1$, total $\frac{9}{64}$ (?), in wheat. Adjoining on the south, projecting 1 schoinion beyond the property previously surveyed, the remainder of Haryotes' allotment as a 7-aroura cleruch of Chomenis, measuring $1\frac{15}{16} \times 1\frac{5}{16} \times \frac{23}{32} \times \frac{19}{32}$, total $1\frac{3}{16}$. Total for the allotment, $6\frac{7}{16}$ arouras, in wheat, farmed by NN.'

6 The figure ή has the very unusual form ζ̂, which recurs under the horizontal stroke in l. 53.

20 The last word in this line is puzzling, but ἐρήμο(υ) seems possible.

24 δ̅: presumably not Fourth Perichoma, since **1117** and **1118** locate all these properties in the Pao( ), and this is confirmed for the following cleruchs by **62**. 211, 71, 76. A date seems unlikely if not impossible. Perhaps this information was copied from some fourth roll or column.

28 τὸ λο(ιπὸν) τοῦ κλ(ήρου): 15 arouras according to **1117**. 63 = **1118**. 170, but only $12\frac{1}{8}$ seem to be accounted for here.

35 (γίν.) τοῦ κλ(ήρου): the figure was not filled in; cf. **1118**. 1 n.

37 ϛ: 5 in **1118**. 171, 6 as here in **1117**. 75.

38 The total is probably γ and a fraction, in disagreement with both l. 37 and 39.

39 χ̣ώ(ματοc) β, διώρυ(γοc) β: the figures are clear, though 2 short of the expected total.

1123. Land Survey

P. Teb. 86v — 20 × 29 cm. — Late second century B.C.

A papyrus containing a land survey of Arsinoe, **86**, was later brought to Kerkeosiris, where its verso was used among other things for the column printed below, of interest chiefly for its treatment of $4\frac{1}{2}$ arouras of Crown land held by Phmouis son of Pathebis (**1117**. 143). Cf. **1122** and texts there cited.

γ∠ή̣ί́ϛ̣́ξ̣́δ̣́

                                                                                                      β̣ή̣
βο(ρρᾶ) ἐχό(μεναι) ἀρχό(μεναι) λ̣ι̣(βὸc) [.] ̣ ̣(   ) ∠ήλ́β́ ——— .....
                                                                                                      ∠̣ḍίϛ́

ἀπ̣η(λιώτου) ἐχό(μ.) ἀρχ̣[ό(μ.) νό(του). .].νε.χω(   ) διὰ cχοι(νι   ) dή.

βο(ρρᾶ) ἐχό(μ.) ὑπ(   ) • —— α∠d / • —— ∠dή, (γίν.) ∠d.

(γίν.) ϛdή῾ξ῾δ

βο(ρρᾶ) ἐχό(μ.) ʼἐγβαί(νουcαι) λι(βὸc) παρὰ τὴ̣[ν] π̣ρ̣ογεγεω(μετρημένην) cχοι(νίου) ∠dή῾ιϛ Φμούειc Παθήβιοc δ∠ ἀν(ὰ) δ.

α∠dιϛ —— • / βdήλβ —— •, (γίν.) δdι῾ϛ῾ξ῾δ (ὧν) . . . .

φα(κῶι) τὸ λ̣ο̣(ιπὸν) δι῾ϛ῾ξ῾δ

β[ο(ρρᾶ) ἐ̣χό(μ.) ʼἀρχό(μ.) λι(βὸc)ʼ εἰcβαί(ν.) λι(βὸc) παρ[ὰ] τὴν ʼἀγεω(μέτρητον)ʼ τοῦ cχοι(νίου) ή῾ιϛ

α∠ή —— αή῾ιϛλβ / αdή῾ιϛ —— ∠dή῾ιϛ, (γίν.) α∠ή̣[ι]῾ϛ῾ξ῾δ

(γίν.) ϛλβ. πλ(είω) α∠.

ἀπη(λ.) ἐχό(μ.) ἐγβαί(ν.) νό(του) παρὰ τὴν προγεγεω(μετρημένην) cχοι(νία) βdήλβ

ὑπολό(γου) ἁλμυ(ρίδοc) τοῦ ἀπὸ τοῦ μ̣ (ἔτουc) β. [131/130

dή —— γ∠ή / • —— d, (γίν.) ἁλμυ(ρίδοc) αήλβ.

βο(ρρᾶ) ἐχό(μ.) ἐγβαῖ(ν.) λι(βὸc) παρὰ τὴν προγεγεω(μ.) cχ[ο]ι(νίου) ∠dή῾ιϛ τὸ λο(ιπὸν) τοῦ ὑπολό(γου)

αή῾ιϛ —— αή῾ιϛ / α∠ —— α, (γίν.) α∠ήλβ.

βο(ρρᾶ) ἐχό(μ.) εἰcβαί(ν.) ἀπη(λ.) παρὰ τὰ περὶ Ταλὶ πε(δία) cχ̣ο̣ι(νίου) ∠̣ḍή῾ιϛ.

τ̣ὸ λο(ιπὸν) ή —— • / βή —— •, (γίν.) d῾ξ῾δ

(γίν.) τοῦ ὑπολό(γου) γι῾ϛ.

Lines 6–20. ʻAdjacent on the north, projecting $\frac{15}{16}$ schoinion west of the property previously surveyed, $4\frac{1}{2}$ arouras taxed at 4 artabs per aroura, held by Phmouis son of Pathebis, measuring $1\frac{13}{16} \times 1\frac{13}{16} \times 2\frac{13}{32} \times 2\frac{13}{32}$ schoinia, total $4\frac{21}{64}$ arouras, of which . . . the remainder in lentils. Adjacent on the north, forming a western boundary of the next lot, receding $\frac{3}{16}$ schoinion west of the unsurveyed land, a further parcel measuring $1\frac{5}{8} \times \frac{15}{16} \times 1\frac{7}{32} \times 1\frac{7}{16}$, total $1\frac{45}{64}$, grand total $6\frac{1}{32}$ arouras, $1\frac{1}{2}$ in excess (of the proper $4\frac{1}{2}$).

ʻAdjacent on the east, projecting $2\frac{13}{32}$ schoinia south of the previously surveyed property, 2 arouras of salt land which has been declared derelict since year 40 (of Euergetes II), measuring

$\frac{3}{8} \times \frac{1}{4} \times 3\frac{5}{8} \times 3\frac{5}{8}$, total $1\frac{5}{32}$ arouras salt land. Adjacent on the north, projecting $\frac{15}{16}$ schoinion west of the property previously surveyed, the remainder of the derelict land, measuring $1\frac{3}{16} \times 1 \times 1\frac{3}{16} \times 1\frac{1}{2}$, total $1\frac{21}{32}$. Adjacent on the north, receding $\frac{15}{16}$ schoinion east of the fields about Tali, the remainder, measuring $\frac{1}{8} \times \frac{1}{8} \times 2\frac{1}{8} \times 2\frac{1}{8}$, total $\frac{17}{64}$ aroura. Total derelict, $3\frac{1}{16}$ aroura.'

3 It does not seem possible to construe the traces as *Πετεῆϲιϲ Τεῶτοϲ* (**1117**. 142).

ϲχοι(νι): usually the abbreviation in these texts refers to the measure *ϲχοι(νίον)* but here perhaps *ϲχοι(νιϲμοῦ)*, 'surveying' is meant.

4 *ὑπ( )*: *ὑπ(ολόγου)* or *ὑπ(οδοχείου)* (**86**. 15 etc.). The latter is perhaps preferable, since references to *ὑπόλογοϲ* usually include the period in which the land went out of cultivation; and that word is usually abbreviated *ὑπολό(γου)*, as 14 and 16 below.

6–11 Cf. **1117**. 143.

6 The end of the line must state that $\frac{1}{4}$ aroura was left unsown or put to some crop other than lentils, to judge from l. 7.

9 *ἀγεω(μέτρητον)*: cf. **87**. 38 n.

11 *πλ(είω) α∠*: that is, 6 arouras surveyed is $1\frac{1}{2}$ more than $4\frac{1}{2}$ officially booked to Phmouis (cf. **1107** introd., **1125**, p. 11). $\frac{1}{32}$ aroura in the total earlier in the line is ignored.

12–20 Cf. **1117**. 144.

16 *τὸ λο(ιπὸν)*: inaccurate, since a third parcel is mentioned in ll. 19–20.

20 *γίς*: right was $3\frac{5}{64}$.

1124. Land List

P. Teb. 233v | 21 × 21 cm. | 115 B.C. or later

Portions of two columns from a list of persons leasing small parcels of Crown land at 5 artabs per aroura, written on the back of **1127** and in the same hand as that text. With two exceptions (10, 16), the persons involved are known to have been cleruchs; and as the rate charged is commonly associated with Crown land rented by cleruchs adjacent to their own allotments (p. 8), it is likely that lines 10 and 16 refer to cleruchs as well. Comparable texts are **1103**. 264–86 and **98**. 1–26, both of which list parcels at $5\frac{1}{3}$ artabs.

The mention of Archibios son of Horos in l. 12 shows that **1124** is no earlier than year 3 of Soter II (cf. **1143**. 16; his predecessor and no doubt father Horos son of Orsenouphis was still active in year 2, **1110**. 191). On the other hand, Sokonopis son of Pasis (13) requires a date before year 5 (cf. **1147**. 153 f.), unless the line is to be continued *Cοκονῶπιϲ Πάϲιτοϲ [ὃν μέ(τειληφέναι) Μαρρῆν Ἁράπιοϲ.*

. . . .

[Παῶ]ṭιϲ Πẹτ̣ẹịọụϲ ή ἀν(ὰ) ϵ
[Νϵκ]ṭϵνῖβιϲ Ὥρ[ου] γ̄ βο(ρρᾶ) ∠̣ḍ ἀν(ὰ) ϵ
Παϲῶϲ μι(κρὸϲ) Πạνήϲιοϲ ∠d ἀν(ὰ) ϵ
Πϵτϵϲοῦχοϲ Πϵτϵϲούχου ∠ ἀν(ὰ) ϵ
Χομῆνιϲ Ἀκρ[ιϲίου] γ̣̄ βο(ρρᾶ) β ἀ(νὰ) ϵ
Φατρῆϲ Ὥρου γ̣̄ βο(ρρᾶ) ∠ ἀν(ὰ) ϵ

Μεcταcῦτμιc Ὥρου γ̄ β(ορρᾶ) α ἀν(ὰ) ϵ
Μαρρῆc Παάπιοc ∠ ἀν(ὰ) ϵ

Col. II

. . . .

[Ἁρμιῦcιc Φ]ατρε̣ί̣ο̣υ̣c̣ [
Ἁρ[υ]ώτηc Μαρρείουc [
διαφορεῖται
Ἀρχ̣ί̣β̣ι̣ο̣c Ὥρου γ̄ βο(ρρᾶ) [
Cοκονῶπιc Πάcιτοc [
Φορεγέβθιc Ἀπύγχιοc γ̄ βο(ρρᾶ) [
διαφορεῖ(ται)
Ὧροc {τοῦ} Πετοcίριοc δ [
Παcῶc μέ(γαc) Πανήcιοc . [
Ἁρυώτηc Φαεῦτοc [
Πᾶcιc μέ(γαc) Καλατύ(τιοc) [

1 *Παῶ]πις Πε̣τ̣ε̣ί̣ο̣υ̣c*: usually called the son of Petesouchos, but cf. **63**. 222.

2 Nektenibis son of Horos here is the machimos, not the homonymous catoec, since the latter had been replaced by Ptolemaios son of Apollonios no later than 116/115 B.C. (**63**. 81).

10 Haryotes occurs only here.

11 *διαφορεῖται*: cf. 15. 'He disputes it' or 'it is disputed' (cf. LSJ s.v. IV) seems the most probable meaning; cf. **87**. 3, 5 *μὴ εἶναι γρ(άφει)*. It is no doubt significant that both entries with this notation are bracketed.

16 A Horos son of Petosiris occurs often in this archive as a Crown tenant (Index VI, s.n.). This may be a homonym, or the same man. Cf. **1115**. 162–5 n. The incorrect *τοῦ* after *Ὧροc* originated in the confusion of erasing an earlier entry and replacing it with this one.

1125. Report on Improperly Occupied Land

P. Teb. 149 | 13 × 25 cm. | 116/115 B.C.

The exact nature of this carelessly drafted report is somewhat obscure because of the difficulty of deciphering and construing the heading, but it is clear that the persons listed are to be held responsible for a rental of 5 artabs per aroura on small pieces of land which they have reclaimed (*κατειρ[γάcθαι]*, l. 3). The phrase *εὑρῆcθαι πρόc τιcιν γεωργίοιc* (3) suggests that the land was in excess of that for which the men had been booked, the high rent therefore being set as a penalty. The detailed list of Crown holdings for the same year in **1103** sheds no light on the matter.

Ἔτους β, παρὰ Μεγχείους κω(μο)γρ(αμματέως). ἔστιν τὰ ẹ̓[γνωσ-]
μένα ἐξ ἐπισκέψεως ὑπὸ Μαρρείους
τοῦ τοπογρ(αμματέως) \`εὑρῆσθαι´ πρός τισιν γεωργίοις κατειρ[γάσθαι]
αὐτοὺς ⟦ạ̔̂ṣ δ̣ẹδ̣ṿ( ) \`τ´⟧ ὧṿ ἐστιν . . κα( ) ιδ∠ (ὧν) ἐκφό(ριον) (πυροῦ) οβ[∠]
Ἁρμιῦσις Πετοσί(ριος) πρ.( ) κ. . με ( ) d (ἀρτ.) ad
Ἁρυώτης Φαῆσιος ∠ (ἀρτ.) β∠
⟦Ἁρṣῦτμις Λύκου ∠ (ἀρτ.) β∠⟧
Ἀθ̣εμμεὺς Πετεσούχου ∠ (ἀρτ.) β∠
Ἁρμαχọ́ρος Ἁ̣ρ̣μ̣α̣χọ́ρ̣[ο]υ ḍ (ἀρτ.) [ad]
Θῶνις Ὀρσενούφιος d (ἀρτ.) ạ[d]
Θῶνις Κεντίσιος d (ἀρτ.) ad
Κατῦτις Κ̣ατύτιος ḍ (ἀρτ.) [a]ḍ
⟦Ὀννῶφρις Φατρῆς [
Πετερμοῦθις Ὥρου ḍ (ἀρτ. ?) ạ[d]
Π̣α̣[π]ṿẹβṭῦ(νις) Σοκέως ∠ [(ἀρτ.) β∠]
⟦Ν[εκ]τεν[ῖ]β̣ι̣ς̣ [

. . . .

5, 14 d (ἀρτ.) ad corrected from ∠ (ἀρτ.) β∠ 13 Φατρείους

1–2 τὰ ẹ̓[γνωσ]μένα ἐξ ἐπισκέψεως: for the phrase, cf. **82**. 2.

4 αὐτοὺς: has no referent, but must mean the persons listed below. The sentence does not construe. I take the heading to mean in paraphrase: 'Year 2, from Menches, village scribe. Results of an examination by Marres the topogrammateus, in which it was discovered that they (i.e., some Crown tenants) had reclaimed in addition to certain farms 14½ arouras, of which the rent is 72½ artabs.'

. . κα( ): τ̣ὸ̣ κα(θ' ἓν ?) **149**. But this phrase can hardly introduce the statement of a total, as we have here, and τὸ appears impossible. The same objections apply to τὸ κα(τ' ἄνδρα).

5 πρ.( ): πρό(ς) **149**. Of the supposed omicron only a slight discoloration remains. πρẹ(σβύτερος) would also do, though Harmiysis is not among those listed in **1137**. 9–30.

κ. . με( ): the reading of **149**, κẹ (πυρῶι ?) is definitely excluded. Neither κ̣α̣ṭα̣με(μετρημένης) nor κ̣α̣ὶ̣ ọἱ̣ μέ(τοχοι) was written.

1126. List of Tenants of Unwatered Crown Land

P. Teb. 71 v 26 × 30 cm. 114 B.C.

The recto of this papyrus contains copies of two official letters (**26**) as well as a report on the progress of irrigation and sowing at Kerkeosiris up to 9 November 114 B.C. (**71**). The verso text printed below is in all probability a preliminary sketch used in drawing up the latter document. It presents under the title κατ' ἄνδρα τῆς ἔτι ἀποτίστου a list of

14 persons who hold a total of $75\frac{1}{2}$ arouras renting for $371\frac{1}{4}$ artabs. It seems unlikely that coincidence is responsible for the nearness of these figures to the $71\frac{1}{2}$ arouras and $351\frac{1}{2}$ artabs reported unwatered in **71**. 9: the difference, 4 arouras at $4\frac{11}{12}$ artabs/aroura, was no doubt caused by a slight advance in the flood between the time of the verso and recto texts. One lot of just this size and rent is in fact listed in line 10, though the four newly watered arouras need not all have been farmed by the same man.

With the exception of $4\frac{1}{2}$ arouras at 5 artabs apiece (line 7), the rents stated correspond to a rate of $4\frac{11}{12}$ artabs/aroura.

κ̣α̣τ' ἄ̣[ν]δρα τῆϲ ἔτι ἀπο̣τ̣ίϲτου

[Ὥ]ρ̣[ο]ϲ Πετενεφι[εί]ουϲ ι μθϛ´
Πετεϲοῦ(χοϲ) Ϲοκμῆνιϲ ζ λδγ´ιβ´
] Ὀρϲείουϲ ϛ∠ λβ
[Ἀπολλώνι]οϲ Λάγου δ∠ κβϛ´
[Πετε]ϲοῦχοϲ Ὀρϲενούφιοϲ η (ἀρτάβαι) λθγ´
[Ἀ]π̣ύγχιοϲ Πετεϲούχου δ∠ (ἀρτάβαι) κβ∠
Χῦψιϲ Πετεϲούχου γ ιδ∠d
Πετεϲοῦ(χοϲ) Ϲωτη(ρίδου) γ ιδ∠d
Ἁρυώτηϲ Ἀμεννέ(ωϲ) δ ιθβ´
Ὧροϲ Πετ̣ώ̣υτοϲ ε κδ∠ιβ´
Ὀννῶ(φριϲ) Ὥρου ε κδ∠ιβ´
Κεφαλᾶϲ Πετεϲού(χου) ε κδ∠ιβ´
Τεῶϲ Πετεχῶ(ντοϲ) ε κδ∠ιβ´
Πετεῆ(ϲιϲ) Τεῶτοϲ ε κδ∠ιβ´
(γίνονται) οε∠ (ἀρτάβαι) τοαd

3 Ϲοκμήνιοϲ 7 Ἀπῦγχιϲ

1 ἀπο̣τ̣ίϲτου: only here. It corresponds to αἷϲ (sc. ἀρούραιϲ) ἐπικεῖϲθαι τὸ ὕδωρ in **71**. 8. That phrase was understood by Preisigke as indicating land on which water still stood ('Auf dem Acker steht Überschwemmungswasser', WB I s.v. ἐπίκειμαι; but the text opposes those fields to others said to have been βεβρέχθαι, and the opposite of 'watered' land can only be 'unwatered'. For ἐπικεῖϲθαι meaning not 'lie on' but 'lie near', cf. **50**. 6, very probably **61**(b). 169 = **72**. 81, and perhaps **1116**. 38 and 58. In **71**. 8 the word is used in a pregnant sense, 'fail to reach'.

2 The 10 arouras here are Horos's entire holding of Crown land, which he had rented at least since year 1 of Soter II; cf. **1103**. 90, **93**. 44.

4 As the blank space which this text leaves between name and patronymic is of unpredictable extent (cf. **1133**), the number of letters lost cannot be estimated. Of the tenants with the patronymic Orses, only Horos is known to have had $6\frac{1}{2}$ ar. at $4\frac{11}{12}$ situated in one parcel (**1117**. 32), but it is not certain that the $6\frac{1}{2}$ here did lie together.

5 Cf. **85**. 50.

7 The rent charged, 5 art./ar., is very unusual for a non-cleruchic tenant; the area involved is much larger than those in **1125**. Possibly Apynchis was subletting this land from a cleruch (cf.

1103. 65–6 n.); or it may have formed part of a *κατόχιμος κλῆρος*, on which 5 art. was the standard rent (**60**. 105, 107; **61**(b). 257, 293; **64**(b). 21, 23, 26, 28; **70**. 67–71; **72**. 228), and which were sometimes if not always farmed by Crown tenants (**85**, esp. l. 152). But $22\frac{1}{2}$ may simply be an error for $22\frac{1}{6}$, seeing that the total in l. 16 supposes that all the land listed here rented at $4\frac{11}{12}$ art.

9 Cf. **1107**. 320.

10 Cf. **1103**. 126.

11 The holdings of Horos son of Petos underwent a series of changes, but one lot of 5 ar. at $4\frac{11}{12}$ art. is located in **1118**. 89 = **1120**. 107.

16 The figure for rental was achieved not by adding up the individual rents (= $371\frac{2}{3}$), but by multiplying the total land area by $4\frac{11}{12}$ art./ar. Cf. **1103**. 14, 23 notes.

1127. List of Derelict Land

P. Teb. 233 r — 21 × 21 cm. — Late second century B.C.

A listing by *περίχωμα* of salty, dry, and water-logged land at Kerkeosiris. Col. I lists and totals plots of each category within the various basins, and Col. II summarizes this information. The grand total given, $302\frac{1}{2}$ arouras (l. 23), is difficult to explain, since it seems much too small to represent all the derelict land in Kerkeosiris (cf. vol. I, 574–6). Possibly **1127** records only one of the two major divisions of *ὑπόλογος*, namely that which fell out of cultivation after the revolt of 131 B.C. (p. 4). That land was subject to continuous and successful attempts at reclamation over the period of our documentation, and $302\frac{1}{2}$ fits attractively into the series of figures for derelict land *ἀπὸ τοῦ μ ἔτους* known from other years – $427\frac{19}{32}$ in 119/118 (**60**. 76, but cf. n.), $384\frac{19}{32}$ in 118/119 (**60**. 89), $295\frac{3}{16}$ in 114/113 (**74**. 50), $282\frac{3}{8}$ in 113/112 (**75**. 54). Soter's 1st, 2nd, and 3rd years are unrepresented in this series, and **1127** may fall in one of those. Or the proper interpretation of our text may lie elsewhere altogether.

The order in which perichomata are listed is that followed also in **1117–1121**. On the back is **1124**.

. . . .

]. . .[
] αd, (γίνονται) ι∠d [
] . ∠ α ϵ β α α [
] κθ α∠, (γίνονται) . . .[
] χϵ́(ρϲου) ιϛ∠d, α, (γίνονται) ἐμ(βρόχου) . . [
(γίνονται) ἁλμυ(ρίδοϲ) να∠, χϵ́(ρϲου) ιζ∠d, ἐμ(βρόχου) λϵ̣, (γίνονται) ρδd.
ϵ∠̣. γ̄ νό(του) α γ β∠, (γίνονται) ϵ∠.
η̣∠. γ̄ βο(ρρᾶ) α ∠ γ β, ἐμ(βρόχου) β, (γίνονται) η∠ (ὧν) χϵ́(ρϲου) β, ἁλμυ-
(ρίδοϲ) ϛ∠.
δ γ∠ ϵ γ α∠, (γίνονται) ιγ.

Θεμί(cτου) ἐμ(βρόχου) ιε, (γίνονται) ιε.
Παω(   ) χέ(ρcου) ιθ,
ἐμ(βρόχου) ια, (γίνονται) λ (ὧν) χέ(ρcου) ιθ, ἐμ(βρόχου) ια, (γίνονται) λ.
Κε(ρκεούρεως) λ̣ι̣(βὸc) ἁλμυ(ρίδοc) θ, (γίνονται) θ.
Κε(ρκεούρεως) ἀπη(λιώτου) ιδ∠ ϛ ε γ β β, (γίνονται) λβ∠.
Ψ(ιναρα   ) ε∠, ἐμ(βρόχου) ζ,
ἐμ(βρόχου) ξα∠̣, [(γίνονται) ἁλμυ(ρίδοc) ε∠,] ἐμ(βρόχου) ξη∠,
[(γίνονται)] οδ.

Col. II

. . . .

]. .[
Παω(   ) λ (ὧν) χέ(ρcου) ιθ, [ἐμ(βρόχου) ια.]
Κε(ρκεούρεως) λι(βὸc) ἁ[λ]μ̣υ(ρίδοc) θ.
Κε(ρκεούρεως) ἀπη(λιώτου) ἁλμυ(ρίδοc) λβ∠.
Ψ(ιναρα   ) οδ (ὧν) ἐμ(βρόχου) ξη∠, ἁλμυ(ρίδοc) ε∠.
(γίνονται) τβ∠ (ὧν) . .γ.
ἁλμυ(ρίδοc)
χέ(ρcου)
ἐμ(βρόχου) ρκθ∠, χέ(ρcου) λη∠d, (γίνονται) ρξ̣[ηd],
ἁλμυ(ρίδοc) ρλδd.

7 νό(του) corrected from βο(ρρᾶ)   13 λι(βὸc) corr. from ἀπη(λιώτου)   14 2nd β corr. from θ.

2 It is very unlikely that anything has been lost before αd.

3 The first trace looks like β with a superlinear stroke, indicating that the following lots were located in the Second Perichoma. But it is positioned farther to the right than are the perichoma names in lines 7–15; and if the reckoning for a separate perichoma starts here it would follow that the 10¾ arouras of line 2 are not included in the 104¼ of line 6 and that the total 302½ in line 23 cannot be right; for the parcels in lines 6–17 add up to 293¼, leaving only 9¼ arouras to be accounted for elsewhere.

4 Probably nothing has been lost to the right.

6 (γίνονται) ρδd: correct.

7 ε∠: the individual lots total 6½, but the error may lie in the size given for one of the parcels rather than in the total.

8 α∠ γ β: this is salty land, as the end of the line shows. Similarly land of unspecified nature in lines 14 and 15 is ἁλμυρίδοc according to 21 and 22.

ἐμ(βρόχου) β: described later in the line as χέ(ρcου).

16 ἁλμυ(ρίδοc) ε∠ cf. 22 and 8 note.

19 ἐμ(βρόχου) ια: restored from line 12.

23 τβ∠: cf. 3 note.

24–5 The figures omitted here are given in lines 25–6.

1128. Official Accounts

P. Teb. 170 33 × 30 cm. 115/114 B.C.

The presence of Kephalas son of Petesouchos (91) shows that this text antedates **98.** 7 (year 5 of Soter II), and that of Dionysios son of Dionysios (37) shows that it can be no earlier than year 2 (**1115.** 176–7 note). Year 2 is excluded by many passages (cf. e.g. line 74, which indicates a holding of four arouras, with **1103.** 77–8). A comparison of line 71 with **93.** 6–7 indicates that **1128** is the earlier text, since the stephanos cited is correct for the tenant's original holding but ignores an addition reported in **93**; and since there are other reasons to place **1105**+**93** in year 4 (**1105** introd.), we shall not be mistaken in referring **1128** to year 3.

The text has two parts:

I. Lines 1–25. An account headed *κατ' ἄνδρα τῆϲ ἐϲπαρμένηϲ φακῶι* is complete in a single column, listing 21 persons (one of them twice, 18 and 23) who farm a total of 47¾ arouras of lentils. This can hardly represent the full amount of land so used in Kerkeosiris, since known totals for other years range from 163¼ to 232 arouras (vol. I, p. 562); and 47¾ arouras would not be liable even for the 500 artabs rent which was regularly collected in lentils (**1105**, introd.; year 3 was no exception, **1130.** 16 note, 22). The order in which farmers are listed is not alphabetical; the double entry for Peteesis son of Teos (18, 23) may indicate that the data were taken in order from a topographical survey similar to **1119.** Only one of the holdings can be identified elsewhere with any likelihood; cf. 9 note.

II. Lines 26–end. Separated from the preceding column by a blank space 12·5 cm. broad is the beginning of a *κατ' ἄνδρα ϲτεφάνου* which so far as preserved lists 82 Crown tenants (not counting cancellations) together with the amount of wheat due from each for the crown-tax which in **95.** 9 is called *ϲτέ(φανοϲ) γεω(ργῶν)* to distinguish it from various other *ϲτέφανοι* of Ptolemaic Egypt. The rate for this tax suggested by the editors of **93** introd. as 'generally about ½ artaba on the aroura' is so fully confirmed by numerous new references in **1105–1107** that one may safely dismiss the few apparent exceptions in this archive as scribal errors: so e.g. in **93.** 37 f. the papyrus reads as if 10 artabs due probably on 20 arouras in the Kerkeouris Perichoma were the total assessment on 57½ arouras.

The smallest measure used in collecting stephanos was ¼ artab, corresponding to ½ aroura of land. In calculating the amount of tax due from each tenant, smaller fractions might be rounded either up or down according to no detectable system. Some examples of rounding down are: 1¼ art. charged on 2⅞ arouras treated as 2½ (**1105.** 8 ff. = **1107.** 104 ff.); 3¼ on 6⅞ (**1107.** 44 ff.); 4½ on 9⅜ (**1107.** 49 ff.). An example of rounding up: 3½ art. on 6⅞ arouras treated as 7 (**1105.** 47 ff.).

The absence of stephanos from **93.** 55 ff. suggests that Crown land rented by temples was exempt from the charge, perhaps by an extension of the regulation in **5.** 59 ff. Various other cases in which stephanos was not collected can be found in **1105** introd.

The amounts of Crown land farmed in other years by many of the tenants in **1128** are known from **1103–1107**; in most instances the sum recorded here is that expected on their full holdings in those texts at ½ artab per aroura. This indicates that the figures for stephanos in **1128** are not, for example, arrears or part payments, but the total assessment on each tenant for the year. By doubling these figures we are able to determine to within ½ aroura the amount of Crown land each man farmed: the text thus compensates in some degree for our lack of such detailed information concerning year 3 as **1103**, **1105**, and **1107** supply for years 1–2, 4, and 5.

Tenants are listed in the standard, only partly alphabetical order followed also in **94+1107**, **1105+93**, **1132**, and **1133**. The names Horos son of Petesouchos and Harmiysis son of Petosiris occur twice (78 and 103; 27 and 105). Apparently these are cases of homonymity; cf. **1135**. 13 n.

Every entry in the stephanos list bears an x-shaped checking mark to the lower left.

Slight vestiges of a column to the left; then

Col. I

κατ' ἄνδρα τῆϲ ἐϲπαρμένηϲ	
φακῶι ⟦ϲ. . . .⟧	
Φραμῆνιϲ Πετοϲίριοϲ φα(κῶι)	α∠
Ἀνεμπεὺϲ Πετοϲίριοϲ	γ
Κολλούθηϲ καὶ Παπνεβτῦ(νιϲ)	α∠d
Πετεϲοῦχοϲ Ὀρϲενούφιοϲ	α∠
Ἁρμιῦϲιϲ Μεγχείουϲ	β
Τοθοῆϲ Ἀγοννούφιοϲ	α
Ὧροϲ Κεντίϲιοϲ	β
Νικάνωρ Πτολεμαίου	δ
Πετεϲοῦχοϲ Πετοϲίριοϲ	α∠
Πετεϲοῦχοϲ Μικίωνοϲ	α∠
Πετεϲοῦχοϲ Μαρρείουϲ	β
Χῦψιϲ Πετεϲούχου	δ
Τεῶϲ Ὥρου	α
Ἁρμαχόροϲ Θοτορταίου	β
Κεντῖϲιϲ Ὥρου	β
Πετεῆϲιϲ Τεῶτοϲ	β
Νεφερῶϲ Ὥρου	β
Ἁρφαῆϲιϲ Πετεϲούχου	α∠
Νῖνιϲ Φαήϲιοϲ	α

Ὀννῶφρις καὶ Ἑραθρῆς	β∠
Πετεῆσις Τεῶτος	δ
Τεῶς Πετεχῶντος	δ
(γίνονται) μζ∠d	

A blank space 12·5 cm. wide separates Col. I from Col. II.

Col. II

κατ' ἄνδρα στεφάνου	
Ἁρμιύσιος Πετοσίριος	ϛ∠
Ἁρσῦτμις Λύκου	ϛ∠
Ἁρυώτης Φαήσιος	ε
Ἁρμαχόρος Ἁρμαχόρου	β
Ἁρχῦψις Πετεήσιος	α
Ἀθεμμεὺς Πετεσούχου	ια
Ἁρφαῆσις Ὀννώφριος	α
Ἁρμιῦσις Πετεσούχου	γd
⟦Ἁρβ̣ῆχις Ἑργέως	ζ⟧
Ἀνεμπεὺς Πετοσίριος	θ∠
Διονύσιος Διονυσίου	α̣
⟦Δημήτριος Ἡρακλείδου	α⟧
Ἑβδομίωνος Ἀφθονήτου	α
Θοτοραῖς Πετοσίριος	β∠d
Θώνιος μι(κρὸς) Κεντίσιος	α∠
Κεντῖσις Ὥρου	ιγ∠
Κατῦτις Κατύτιος	ιβ̣
Νικάνωρ Πτολεμαίου	ϛ∠.
Ὀννῶφρις Φατρείους	γd
Ὀννῶφρις Ὥρου καὶ Ἑραθρῆς	δ∠
Πετοσῖρις Ὥρου	δ∠
Πετερμοῦθις Ὥρου	ζ
Παπνεβτῦνις Πετοσίριος	βd
Πετερμοῦθις Μαρρείους	ϛ
Πετοσῖρις Ἁρκοίφιος	ε
Παπνεβτῦνις Σοκέως	ε∠̣d
Πετεσοῦχος Πετοσίριος	ε

(γίνονται) ρλγ∠, (ὧν) ζ, λο(ιπαὶ) ρκϛ∠

(m. 2) κβ∠d

Col. III

(m. 1)	*Πετεϲοκονοῦριϲ Κεφάλωνοϲ*	δ
	Παᾶπιϲ Πετοϲίριοϲ	α∠
	Ποτάμων ᾿Αμεννέωϲ	⟦ε∠⟧ \`δ´
	Παυϲῖριϲ Πετοϲίριοϲ	β
	Πνεφερῶϲ Πετεϲούχου	α
	Πετεϲοῦχοϲ Ϲαραπίωνοϲ	β∠
	Πορεγέβθιϲ ῞Ωρου	β∠
	Πετεϲοῦχοϲ Χεύριοϲ	γ∠
	Τεεφῖβιϲ Χεύριοϲ	β
	Χεῦριϲ Χεύριοϲ	β
	⟦*Ταυρίϲκοϲ ᾿Απολλωνίου*	δ⟧
	Τεῶϲ Θοτορταίου	γ
	Τοθοῆϲ ᾿Αγοννούφιοϲ	γd
	Τοθοῆϲ Φαγάτου	∠
	Φαῆϲιϲ Πετοϲίριοϲ	γ∠
	Φαῆϲιϲ Πετεήϲιοϲ	γd
	Φμούειϲ Παθήβιοϲ	β∠
	Φαῆϲιϲ ῾Αρυώτου	δ∠
	Φαγάτηϲ Μικίωνοϲ	β
	Φατρῆϲ Πάϲιτοϲ	ϛ
	Φαῆϲιϲ ῞Ωρου	∠
	⟦*῟Ωροϲ Τιμ⟨ο⟩θείου*	β⟧
	῟Ωροϲ Πετεϲούχου	ε
	῟Ωροϲ Πετῶτοϲ	ι
	῟Ωροϲ Πετενεφιείουϲ	ε
	(γίνονται) ⟦πα⟧ οζ∠	
(m. 2)	ιζ∠d	

Col. IV. A blank space of 7·5 cm. at the top of the column; then

(m. 1)		ζd
	Μαρρῆϲ Πακύρριοϲ	β
	῟Ωροϲ ᾿Ορϲείουϲ	ϛ∠d

	ʼΑπῦγχις Πετεσούχου	β∠d
	ʽΑρμιῦσις Πετεύριος	γ∠
	ʽΑρφαῆσις Πετεσούχου	βd
	ʽΑρυώτης ʼΑμεννέως	β
	Δημήτριος Cενθέω̣ς	β∠
	Κεφαλᾶς Πετεσούχου	β∠̣
	Μαρρῆς ʼΙμούθου	ϛ∠d
	Μεστασῦτμις Cοκέως	α∠d
	Μαρρῆς Πετεσούχου	β
	Νίκων ʼΑμεννέως	ζ̣
	Πετεσοῦχος Μικίωνος	β∠
	Πετῶς Μαρρείους	ια
	Πετεσοῦχος ʼΟννώφριος	⟦δ⟧ β
	(γίνονται) ξδ∠	
(m. 2)	κα	

Col. V

(m. 1)	Cοχώτης Παώπιος	[
	⟦	[
	ʽΩρος Πετεσούχου	[
	ʼΙλῶς ʽΩρου	[
	ʽΑρμιῦσις Πετοσίριος	[
	Θοτεὺς Διοδώρου	.[
	Μαρρῆς Cενθέως [	
	ʽΟρσῆς ʼΟρσείους	δ∠
	Πετενοῦπις Πετοσίριος	γ∠d
	Πορεγέβθις ʼΑπύγχιος	δ∠
	Πετεσοῦχος Cωτηρίδου	δ∠
	Πετερμοῦθις Cιεφμοῦτος [	
	Πετεσοῦχος ʼΟρσενούφι[ος]	β̣[
	Cοκμῆνις ʼΟ̣ρ̣σ̣ε̣ί̣ο̣[υς]	β∠̣
	Τεῶς ʽΩρου	δ∠
	Φμέρσις Cαραπίω[νος	
	Χολῶς Cισούχου [	
	Χῦψις Πετεσούχ[ου	
	Πνεφερῶς ʽΩρου [	

῾Αρμιῦσις Σαραπίω̣[νος

(γίνονται) νδ

λd

(m. 2) κβ

5 Κολλούθης καὶ Παπνεβτῦ(νις): Kollouthes was the son of Papnebtynis, son of Sokeus.

9 ῟Ωρος Κεντίσιος β: probably refers to the land located in **1119**. 56.

19 Νεφερῶς: elsewhere Πνεφερῶς. Use of the Egyptian definite article in such names is rather erratic; cf. e.g. O. Mattha 56. 1 vs. 2, where the editor's note rather misses the point.

22 ᾿Οννῶφρις καὶ ῾Εραθρῆς: these two sons of Horos appear together also in **91**. 9; **1107**. 49; **1130**. 98; and line 46 below. ῾Εραθρῆς = ῾Αραθρῆς, 'Horos the twin'; cf. **91**. 9 and **1139**. 106.

25 Total correct.

27 The same name reappears in line 105.

29 The land on which this tax was paid is probably that of **1119**. 34.

34 For Crown land farmed by this machimos cf. **94**. 1 note.

39 ῾Εβδομίωνος: presumably the son of the 70-aroura cleruch Aphthonetos son of Hebdomion.

40 β∠d: corresponds to 5½ arouras, presumably those located in **1118**. 48 = **1120**. 80; cf. **1103**. 134 and **1137**. 5.

41 μι(κρός) rather than μι(κροῦ) because Θώνιος is more probably a misspelling of Θῶνις than a deliberate genitive in this list.

52 ε∠̣d: the temptation to read εd to correspond with the 10½ arouras of **1103**. 31 and **1107**. 75 should be resisted.

54 ρλγ∠: correct was 133¾, if one omits line 38 but includes line 35. Then line 35 is deducted from the total.

55 κβ∠d: the significance of this figure is obscure. Cf. lines 82, 100, 124.

78 Cf. 103.

81 οζ∠: correct was 71. 77½ includes the cancelled figure in lline 66 and reads line 58 as 5½.

82 Cf. 55 note.

83 ζd: this figure is placed 7·5 cm. down from the top margin. There is no sign of erasure before the number, and it is included in the total in line 99.

The writing in this and the following column takes on a progressively clumsier appearance, but it is not certain that there was a change of hand.

90 Probably refers to the 5 arouras located in **1119**. 59–60.

92 The three plots in **85**. 40, 46, and 52 would give the total of 13½ arouras which are taxed here.

98 The final figure may refer to 4 arouras located in **85**. 139.

99 Total correct, including the 7¼ of line 83.

100 Cf. 55 note.

103 ῟Ωρος Πετεσούχου: presumably different from the man of the same name in line 78, who is found again in **93**. 32 and **1103**. 81; cf. **1135**. 13 note.

105 Cf. line 27.

106 The doubtful figure may be γ̣ to agree with 6 arouras in **1107**. 293, but the reading cannot be verified from the remaining traces.

113 Perhaps β[∠ to follow **1107**. 331.

121 νδ: possibly meant to be cancelled; if so, the 30¼ of line 122 is probably the final total.

124 Cf. 55 note.

1129. Preliminary Account of Grain

P. Teb. 235, 236 — 42 × 29 cm. — 123 B.C.

Numerous papyrus fragments described as **235** and **236** have here been joined to form a single document, as the editors of vol. I suggested might be done (**236**). The text presents a *προδιαλογιcμὸc cιτικὸc ἐπὶ κεφαλαίου* similar to **89**, **160**, and **1130**; cf. also **1131**. Unlike the parallels, it issues not from the *κωμογραμματεύc* but from the *γραμματεὺc γεωργῶν*. Whether this implies that responsibility for making such reports shifted from the latter official to the former some time between 123 (**1129**) and 114 B.C. (**1130**); or whether similar documents were required from both scribes at the same time, can hardly be decided on present evidence. But it may be significant that **1129** omits the list of charges on cleruchs and shrines given in **89**. 48 ff.: the village scribe who drew up **89** was concerned with imposts on land of every description, the scribe of the Crown tenants probably only with those on Crown land. Two cleruchs are indeed mentioned in the present text (63, 65), but presumably only as lessees of Crown land.

Apart from the heading (1–5), the report is divided into two sections: the 'preliminary account' proper, stating the extent of Crown land sown during the year and the rental to be collected thereon (6–11); and an 'appendix of receipts' up to and including Epeiph 10, which occupies at least the following 77 lines.

These receipts fall into four categories:

1. *ἐκφόριον*, rental of Crown land, amounting to 4,858⅔ art. wheat for the year. In addition to wheat itself, payments were accepted in lentils, barley, beans, aracus, and cash. As in later years, lentils were taken at par value with wheat, and barley at the ratio 5 art. barley = 3 art. wheat. Beans and aracus were both valued at 7 art. = 3 of wheat. The conversion formula for cash is not given (cf. **1104**. 2 note). By Epeiph 10, the equivalent of 4716⅙ art. wheat had been collected (39).

2. *τριχοίνικον*, collected in wheat at the rate of $\frac{1}{12}$ art. per aroura on such land as was subject to the charge (cf. **1105** introd.). In year 53, 118/117 B.C., this area amounted to 1092¼ arouras out of 1139¼ leased (**61**(b). 319), yielding a little over 91 art., as the end of that line should be read. Other annual totals known are 94⅔ in 112 B.C. (**75**. 1; the scribe there has erroneously given the total area leased instead of the area subject to trichoinikon), 81$\frac{5}{12}$ or 91$\frac{5}{12}$ in 113 (**89**. 45 note), and 85 in 114 (**1130**. 19+22). In the present text, 80 artabs had been paid by Epeiph 10.

3. *θηcαυροφυλακικόν*, 24 art. barley. It is striking that in **94**+**1107** and **1105**+**93** payments were actually made in wheat. It seems probable that barley originally delivered toward land rent was later diverted to this account. That would be an easy book-keeping procedure, and a relief to the majority of farmers, who raised no barley themselves and would otherwise have had to acquire some to meet this minor charge.

4. *δάνεια*, government loans of seed, which according to **172** had to be returned with a 50% increase by way of interest, the charge which was standard in private loans as well. These loans are of course to be distinguished from the advances of seed grain given

interest-free to most tenants of Crown land (**61**(b). 313–16 n.); cf. **1136**. Of 350 art. wheat due, 244¾ had been paid by (the end of ?) Mesore (76).

As in **89**, monthly summaries of receipts commence from Pharmouthi 1 and are normally broken down into 10-day periods. An exception occurs in l. 17, where revenues for one or two days are recorded separately. As in **1130**, the remainder due at the end of the period covered by the report is followed by a *κατ' ἄνδρα* of those from whom it is to be collected (41 ff., 61 ff.). Account is taken not only of payments made at Kerkeosiris itself, but of giro-transfers from the granaries at Berenikis Thesmophorou, Ibion Eikosipentarouron, and Tebtunis (34–6).

The document concludes with a special section devoted to seed loans, carried into Mesore.

ἔτους μζ, παρὰ Θέω[νος] γραμμ[α(τέως)]
γεωρ(γῶν) Κερκεοσίρεως. π[ροδι]ạλογ[ις]μ[ὸς]
σιτικὸς ἐπὶ κεφαλαίου [τοῦ αὐ]τοῦ ἔτ[ο]υς,
ὑποκειμένων τῶν [ἐγδι]ῳκημένων
ἕως Ἐπεὶφ ῑ. [29 July 123 B.C.
ἐσπαρμέναι ἦσαν ἐṿ [τ]ῶ[ι] αὐτῶι (ἔτει)
γῆς (ἄρουραι) Ἀ Σγ∠ḍ ὧṿ ẹκ̣φ(όριον) (πυροῦ) Ἀ Δωνηβ́
καὶ τοῦ Ἀμφικλείους κ̣[λήρο]υ κδ (ἄρουραι) ξ
καὶ διάφορος μισ(θώσεως) (πυροῦ) ξ/
(γίνονται) (ἄρουραι) Ἀ Σκ[ζ∠d (ἀρτάβαι)] Ἀ Δωνηβ́
ὧν χα[λκοῦ ὧν σί(τος)] λ̣θγ́ίβ́
εἰς ταύτ̣[ας μεμετρῆσθαι ± 5]ωι
Φαρμοῦθι ᾱ ἕω[ς ῑ (πυροῦ)] ψνβd κ(ριθῆς) Σπ [21–30 April
καὶ ἀπὸ ιᾱ ἕως̣ [κ̄] (πυροῦ) κζd κ(ριθῆς) μζγ́ [1–10 May
ἀπὸ κᾱ ἕ[ως λ̄] (πυροῦ) νε [11–20 May
(γίνονται) τοῦ μηνὸς (πυροῦ) ῳ̣κδ∠ κ(ριθῆς) τκζγ́
Παχὼν ᾱ ἕω[ς β̄] (πυροῦ) ρπαγ́ [21–2 May
ἀπὸ β̄ ἕως ῑ (πυροῦ) ϡν[[22–30 May
καὶ ἀπὸ ιᾱ ἕω[ς κ̄] (πυροῦ) τν[κ(ριθῆς) . .]ḍ [31 May–9 June
καὶ ἀπὸ κᾱ ἕω[ς λ̄] (πυροῦ) Σξạ [κ(ριθῆς) .]βd [10–19 June
(γίνονται) τοῦ μηνὸς (πυροῦ) [Ἀ]ψνγ́ κ(ριθῆς) .[. .]ίβ́
(τρι)χ(οινίκου) (πυροῦ) ν, θ[η(σαυρο)φυ(λακικοῦ) κ(ριθῆς)] κ̣[δ] (?)

Col. II

Παῦνι ᾱ ἕως [ῑ (πυροῦ) ρ]ϛ̣ς∠γ́ φα(κοῦ) ρϛθ∠ 20–9 June
δα(νείων) ργ́∠d

ἀπὸ ιᾱ ἕως κ̄ (πυροῦ) υμε φα(κοῦ) ρκζγ´ [30 June–9 July
ἀπὸ κᾱ ἕως λ̄ (πυροῦ) Ϲνε∠γ´ιβ´ φα(κοῦ) ιζ∠d κ(ριθῆϲ) κ∠γ´ [10–19 July
(γίνονται) τοῦ μηνὸϲ (πυροῦ) ωϙϛ∠d φα(κοῦ) τμδ∠ιβ´ κ(ριθῆϲ) κ∠γ´
Ἐπεὶφ ᾱ ἕωϲ ῑ (πυροῦ) ρϛ∠γ´ιβ´ φα(κοῦ) λϛ∠ κ(ριθῆϲ) θ∠γ´ [20–9 July
(τρι)χ(οινίκου) λ, δα(νείων) πβγ´
(γίνονται) τοῦ μ[εμετρη(μένου) (πυροῦ)] ͵Γφπη∠ φα(κοῦ) τπαιβ´
κ(ριθῆϲ) υ[. . . αἱ (πυροῦ) Ϲο]δγ´, (γίνονται) (πυροῦ) ͵ΔϹμγ∠γ´ιβ´
δα(νείων) ρ[πϛιβ´
καὶ χαλκὸν διαγ[εγραμμένον] ὧν [ϲ]ί(τοϲ) [λθγ´ιβ´]
καὶ ε[ἰϲ τὸ π]ερὶ Β[ερ]ενικ[ίδα (πυροῦ)] ρι [φα(κοῦ)] πγγ´
ε.[±7 τ]οῦ Ἰβιῶνοϲ (πυροῦ) θ
καὶ ἐν [Τεβτύ]νι (πυροῦ) ζϛ´, (γίνονται) Ϲθ∠
καὶ Θέωνοϲ τοῦ Θέωνοϲ (πυροῦ) Ϲκγγ´
δα(νείων) μϛβ´, (γίνονται) υλα∠γ´
ὥϲτ' εἶναι (πυροῦ) ͵Δψιϛϛ´, (τρι)χ(οινίκου) π, δα(νείων) Ϲλβ∠d
λοιπαὶ εἰϲ Μεϲ[ορὴ [19 Aug.–17 Sept.
Πολέμαρχ[ο]ϲ . . .[ ] γγ´
Κῶϲ Μαρρείουϲ d
Ψενοβάϲτιϲ Πετε[ ] αιβ´
Πετεϲοῦχοϲ Τ[ο]θο[είουϲ] .∠
Πετεϲοῦχοϲ [

Col. III

Πετοϲῖριϲ Χαιριγένου αιβ´
Ὧροϲ Μαρρείουϲ d
Ὧροϲ Πετοϲίριοϲ θ∠
Ἁρμιῦϲιϲ Πετενούριοϲ φα(κοῦ) ιδ∠d
Ὧροϲ Θοτορταίου .
Ἁρμιῦϲιϲ Ψενεθώτου φα(κοῦ) [
Ὧροϲ Παώπιοϲ α∠
Τεῶϲ Πετεϲούχου φα(κοῦ) γβ´
Πετερμοῦθιϲ Ϲαμῶτοϲ
ἀρά(κου) ιβ (πυροῦ) .
Ἡρακλῆϲ [Π]ετάλου ἀρά(κου) ιβ
φαϲή(λου) [ε]∠, (γίνονται) ιζ∠ αἱ (πυροῦ) ζ∠
Ἁρυώτηϲ [Ἁ]ρυώτου Βερε(νικίτηϲ) ε

(γίνονται) ἐν (πυρῶι) οε∠̣. [λο]ιπαὶ Σ∠
ὧν ἐστίν
Παπνεβτῦνις Ἀσφέως κζ∠ίβ́
Παῆς Πάσιτος α
Νεκτενῖβις Ὥρου ιδ∠d
Πετεσοῦχος Ψενήσιος ιθ∠γ́ίβ́
Δημήτριος Ἡρακλείδου ιθβ́
Πετερμοῦθις Σαμῶτος λϛ
Τεῶς Πετεσούχου ογϛ́
Ἀπολλώνιος Διοκλείους ιδϛ́
Ἡρακλῆς Πετάλο̣υ̣ κα∠d
(γίνονται) Σκϛ∠d πλ(είω)

Col. IV

δανείων ἀπο̣.(   ) τν, (ὧν) με(τρηθεῖσαι)
Παῦνι ἕως ῑ (πυροῦ) ργ∠d [20–9 June
Ἐπεὶφ ἕως ῑ (πυροῦ) πβγ́ [20–9 July
Με[σ]ορὴι (πυροῦ) ιβ [19 Aug.–17 Sept.
Θέωνος μϛβ́
(γίνονται) [Σμ]δ∠d. λο(ιπαὶ) ρεd
[ὧν] ἐστίν·
Τεῶς Πετεσούχου κ[
[γεωρ]γοὶ κοινῆι λ[
Παπνεβτῦνις Ἀσφέως [
[Πε]τεσοῦχος Νεκτενίβιος [
Φ̣αῆσις Ἀγοννούφιος [
Ὧρος Ὥρου Ἀπολλων[
Ἁρμιῦσις Ψενε̣[
Ἡρακλῆς Πετάλου [
Ἁρυώτης Φαήσι[ος
Πετεσοῦχος .[
(γίνονται) ρεd
(m. 2) Ἁρχῦψις Πετοσ[ίριος
Ἀρχετίων Πε. .[
(γίνονται) ἐν κ̣ω̣μ̣ο̣γρ(αμματείαι ?) .[
Six lines washed out.

Col. I. 'Year 47, from Theon, scribe of the (Crown) tenants at Kerkeosiris. Preliminary grain report in summary for the same year, with amounts collected up to and including Epeiph 10 appended.

'In the same year were sown 1,203$\frac{3}{4}$ arouras of (Crown) land with a rental of 4,858$\frac{2}{3}$ artabs of wheat, plus 24 arouras belonging to the cleros of Amphikles (with a rental of) 60 (?) artabs. And the difference between rentals theoretically assigned and practically attainable is 60 (?) artabs. Total, 1,227$\frac{3}{4}$ arouras, 4,858$\frac{2}{3}$ artabs; of which the equivalent of 39$\frac{5}{12}$ art. of grain is to be collected in coinage.

'Towards paying these there were measured in to NN:

'Pharmouthi 1st–10th, 752$\frac{1}{4}$ art. wheat, 280 art. barley. 11th–20th, 27$\frac{1}{4}$ art. wheat, 47$\frac{1}{3}$ art. barley. 21st–30th, 55 art. wheat. Total for the month, 824$\frac{1}{2}$ [*sic* for 834$\frac{1}{2}$] art. wheat, 327$\frac{1}{3}$ art. barley.

'Pachon 1st–2nd, 181$\frac{1}{3}$ art. wheat. 2nd–10th, [at least] 950 art. wheat. 11th–20th, [at least] 350 art. wheat and...art. barley. 21st–30th, 261 art. wheat, ... art. barley. Total for the month, 1,750$\frac{1}{3}$ art. wheat, ... $\frac{1}{12}$ art. barley. Plus 50 art. wheat for trichoinikon and 24 art. barley for thesaurophylakikon (?).'

Col. II. 'Payni 1st–10th, 196$\frac{5}{6}$ art. wheat, 199$\frac{1}{2}$ art. lentils, 103$\frac{3}{4}$ art. for loans. 11th–20th, 445 art. wheat, 127$\frac{1}{3}$ art. lentils. 21st–30th, 255$\frac{11}{12}$ art. wheat, 17$\frac{3}{4}$ art. lentils, 20$\frac{5}{6}$ art. barley. Total for the month, 896$\frac{3}{4}$ art. wheat, 344$\frac{7}{12}$ art. lentils, 20$\frac{5}{6}$ art. barley.

'Epeiph 1st–10th, 106$\frac{11}{12}$ art. wheat, 36$\frac{1}{2}$ art. lentils, 9$\frac{5}{6}$ art. barley, 30 art. for trichoinikon, 82$\frac{1}{3}$ art. for loans.

'Total of grain measured in, 3,588$\frac{1}{2}$ art. wheat, 381$\frac{1}{12}$ art. lentils, [in excess of] 400 art. barley taken as the equivalent of 274$\frac{1}{3}$ art. wheat. Total, 4,243$\frac{11}{12}$ art. wheat, 186$\frac{1}{2}$ art. for loans.

'Plus coinage paid in to the equivalence of 39$\frac{5}{12}$ art. wheat.

'And there were measured into the granary at Berenikis 110 art. wheat, 83$\frac{1}{3}$ art. lentils. At Ibion, 9 art. wheat. And in Tebtynis, 7$\frac{1}{6}$ art. wheat. Total, 209$\frac{1}{2}$ art.

'And from Theon son of Theon, 223$\frac{1}{3}$ art. wheat, 46$\frac{2}{3}$ art. for loans. Total, 431$\frac{5}{6}$ art.

'So that the grand total is 4,716$\frac{1}{6}$ art. wheat, 80 art. for trichoinikon, and 232$\frac{3}{4}$ art. for loans.

'Remainder for Mesore....'

3 *ἐπὶ κεφαλαίου*: the editors of vol. I consistently treat this expression for 'in summary' as if it were a single word meaning 'summary list' (references in Index XII, s.v. *ἐπικεφάλαιον*); and this has been adopted by LSJ, s.v. II. 2, and WB, s.v. But Crönert's observations in *WKlPh* 20 (1903), 456–7 are decisive. In Roman texts *ἐν κεφαλαίῳ* was preferred.

7 *γῆϲ (ἄρουραι)* *'ΑΣγ∠ḍ*: by *γῆϲ* is meant specifically Crown land. The same number of arouras recurs in year 4 of the following reign (**89**. 6), but is there explicitly said to include pastureland, which may or may not be the case here.

ẹḳφ(όριον): apparently not *ẹḳφọ́(ριον)*.

8 This is the earliest reference to the 24-aroura cleros of Amphikles son of Philinos, which returned to the state when he received an equal allotment outside Kerkeosiris. From year 48 to 52 the land went unsown, but from year 53 was devoted to pastures at 1 art./ar. (**61**(b). 110–14 with note; **72**. 35–43). In the present text official rent appears to have been 2$\frac{1}{2}$ art./ar., though this was not in fact collectable (9 n.).

κδ (ἄρουραι): the word order is extremely unusual. Possibly *(εἰκοϲιτεϲϲαράρουρον)*, '24-aroura plot', should be read. The word is not attested elsewhere, but cf. *ἑπτάρουρον* (P. Fay. 118. 25), *δεκόβολον* (PCZ I 59111. 12), and the like.

ξ̣: context demands a figure for the rent. The sign used appears to be a capital zeta similar to the sign commonly used to represent *τάλαντον*. It does not resemble *ξ* in l. 20, but it cannot be taken as *ζ* = 7 in this hand. Traces of the same figure in the line below are too meagre to assist here.

9 *διάφοροϲ*: the only form used elsewhere is *διάφορον*, to which this passage should perhaps be corrected.

The *διάφορον μιϲθώϲεωϲ* was the difference between the last officially assigned rental on a piece of inferior property and the amount for which it could actually be rented (cf. Rostovtzeff, *Kolonat*, 33–4). Since the figures of rent due in lines 7 and 10 are identical, the *διάφορον* here must equal the total rent assigned in line 8.

12 For the restoration cf. **89**. 11, *εἰς ἃς μεμετρῆςθαι κτλ*. The last word will have been the name of the sitologos.

16 *ωκδ∠*: an error for 834½.

17 *ἕω[ς β*: the restoration can hardly be false, yet it conflicts with *ἀπὸ β* in the next line, since *ἕως* and *ἀπό* are normally both used in an inclusive sense.

18–19 The lacunae in these lines include a total of 8 artabs wheat. Cf. next note.

21 [*'A*]*ψνγ*: all but 8 artabs of this figure is accounted for in the preserved text of lines 17–20.

22 *θ*[*η*(*cαυρο*)*φυ*(*λακικοῦ*) *κ*(*ριθῆς*)] *κ*[*δ*] : this reading fits the traces excellently, and in **89**. 39 too the entire charge for thesaurophylakikon was paid in Pachon. But if the reading is right, it is strange that no mention of this payment is made in any of the summaries that follow in lines 30–9.

24 The dot over *ργ∠*d is a check mark.

27 The totals for lentils and barley are correct. That for wheat should have been 897¾.

30 *τοῦ μ*[*εμετρη*(*μένου*): cf. **89**. 27. *Μεμετρημένου* is opposed to the *διαγεγραμμένον* of l. 33.

30–1 The figure 3588½ art. wheat tacitly corrects the mistake in l. 16, but keeps that in l. 27. The other totals are correct so far as they can be checked.

31 *κ*(*ριθῆς*) *υ*[. . . *αἱ* (*πυροῦ*) *Σο*]*δγ*: the wheat equivalent of the barley payment is required to produce the total 4243$\frac{1}{12}$; but it would be hazardous to work back from that to fill in the amount of barley, because the results of such conversions are often only approximate. Expected is about 455⅔ art. barley.

32 *δα*(*νείων*) *ρ*[*πςίβ*: the total of ll. 24 and 29. There is room after this entry for (*τρι*)*χ*(*οινίκου*) *π*, but it is not certain that the restoration should be made

34 *καὶ ε*[*ἰς τὸ π*]*ερὶ Β*[*ερ*]*ενικ*[*ίδα*: sc. *ἐργαςτήριον*; cf. **89**. 12 n. and 71; P. Ryl. II 72. 82 n. The village meant is surely Berenikis Thesmophorou, located near Kerkeosiris, rather than Berenikis Aigialou in the Themistou Meris.

φα(*κοῦ*)]: lentils rather than some other crop because the total in l. 36 shows that this item was taken at par with wheat.

35 There is too much space to read simply *εἰ*[*ς τὸ τ*]*οῦ* or *ἐν* [*τῶι τ*]*οῦ*. The village is no doubt Ibion Eikosipentarouron.

37 *Θέωνος τοῦ Θέωνος*: cf. 75. There was a catoecic cavalryman of this name, but it is hard to see why he should play so prominent a role in an account of this nature. Perhaps the *γραμματεὺς γεωργῶν* himself is meant, though in that case too his role is obscure.

38 *υλα∠γ*: intended as the total of 209½ (l. 36) and 223⅓ (l. 37), ignoring the figure for loans. Right was 432⅚.

39 *'Δψιςς*: the total of ll. 31, 33, and 38, the latter being read correctly as 432⅚. The following totals for trichoinikon and loans sum up ll. 22 and 29, 31 and 38.

40 *λοιπαὶ εἰς Μες*[*ορή*: the difference between the rental collected and that due is 142½ art., but l. 59 implies that 276 should be restored here instead.

55 *ἀρά*(*κου*) *ιβ*: one expects the aracus to be converted into an equivalent amount of wheat (5$\frac{1}{7}$ art., cf. next note; since the fraction $\frac{1}{7}$ is not used with artabs, that would have been rounded off to 5⅙), but the wheat sign which follows is not preceded by *αἱ*, and the number after (*πυροῦ*) is not *ε*.

57 *ιζ∠*, *αἱ* (*πυροῦ*) *ζ∠*: this is the only Kerkeosiris text which envisions the possibility of paying land dues in produce other than wheat, lentils, barley, or olyra, though various crops were acceptable in different villages (cf. e.g. **828**. 13, **832**). The summation of aracus and beans together indicates that they were of equal value. The conversion formula is: 7 art. beans or aracus = 3 art. wheat.

58 *Βερε*(*νικίτης*): not in WB III Abs. 13, but the formation is regular. Cf. **1107**. 331 n., **90**. 26.

59 The total of the amounts paid here and still due (276 art.) ought to equal the figure to be restored in l. 40, but on other grounds one would expect only 142½ there; cf. note ad loc.

70 Right was 228⅓. The point of *πλ*(*είω*) is that the sum of individual entries is greater than the amount outstanding in l. 59, 226¾ [*sic*] vs. 200½ due.

71 *ἀπο*.( ): the dotted letter is probably a raised *μ* or *λ*. Not *ἀπομ*(*ετρηθέντων*), since l. 76 shows that not all of the loans had yet been repaid. *ἀπολ*(*ογιςμός*) would be possible.

84 Perhaps *Ψενε*[*θώτου*; cf. 51.

89–91 The connection of these lines with the foregoing account is not apparent. The name *'Αρχετίων* is new.

1130. Preliminary Account of Grain

P. Teb. 174r 96 × 30 cm. 114 B.C.

A *προδιαλογιcμὸc cιτικόc* similar to **89**, **160**, and **1129**, but dealing with year 3 of Soter II, 115/114 B.C. On the form and content of such documents, see the introductions to **89** and **1129**.

The latest date mentioned in the text is Pachon 29 (l. 61), and it is most unlikely that the collection report extended so far as Payni (4, 32 nn.). In all probability, then, **1130** represents a stage in the collection of land dues some 40 days earlier than **1129** and 90 days earlier than **89**. The amount of rental still owing is correspondingly larger than in those texts: 997 art. in l. 21, vs. 142½ (?) in **1129** (40 n.), and 0 in **89**; and the *κατ' ἄνδρα* of individuals with uncompleted payments is correspondingly longer.

To the four charges collected in **1129**, **1130**, like other texts from Menches' office, adds 4⅔ art. wheat for *κράcτιc Θηβαίων*. As this figure must be substantially smaller than the village total due for the impost (the amount paid in **1105**+**93** alone comes to $7\frac{1}{12}$ art.), it may be that this portion of *κράcτιc* was set aside for some special purpose.

In two other features also **1130** shows closer resemblance to **89** and other documents drawn up by Menches than to the earlier **1129** drawn up by a *γραμματεὺc γεωργῶν*: in the collection of *μίcθωcιc* no crop is mentioned other than wheat, barley, and lentils; and the amount of seed loans due has been stabilized at 120 artabs wheat and 100 artabs lentils (**61**(b). 313–16 n.), as opposed to 350 art. wheat in **1129**. 71.

Several of the unpaid dues in lentils listed in 41 ff. are met in **1134**; for references, see notes there. On the back is **1136**.

[ἔτους γ, παρὰ Μεγχείους κωμογρ]αμματέως
[Κερκεοcίρεωc. προδιαλογιcμὸc cι]τικὸc ἐπὶ κεφα(λαίου)
[τοῦ αὐτοῦ (ἔτους), ὑποκειμένων τῶν] ἐγδιῳκημένων
[ἕωc

[ἐcπαρμέναι ἦcαν ἐν τῶι αὐτῶι (ἔτει) cὺν νομαῖc]
[γῆc (ἄρουραι) 'Αρϛγ∠d, ὧν ἐκφό(ριον) (πυροῦ)] 'Δ̣χξεγ́ίβ́
[ ] (ἀρτάβαι ?) 'Γυκϛ
[ ]γ́ίβ́
[ ]
[ ]
[ ]
[ ].
[ ].ια∠ κρι(θῆc) τ̣
[ ] (τρι)χ(οινίκου) κ

[κ]ράc(τεωc) δβ́
[ ]ν φα(κοῦ) [

. . . .

Col. II

χαλκοῦ ὧ̣ν̣ cῖ(τοc) λθγ́ίβ́
(γίνονται) εἰc (πυροῦ) ʼΓχξηγ́ίβ́
(τρι)χ(οινίκου) ο, κράc(τεωc) δβ́, θη(cαυρο)φυ(λακικοῦ) κρι(θῆc) κδ
λοιπαὶ εἰc τ̣ὴ̣ν κη̄ [15 June 114 B.C.
μιc(θώcεωc) ⳨ϛζ, (ὧν) (πυροῦ) φιζ
φα(κοῦ) υπ, (τρι)χ(οινίκου) ιε.
δα(νείων) (πυροῦ) ρκ, φα(κοῦ) ρ.
με(τρηθεῖcαι) Παχὼν ᾱ ἕωc κ̄ (πυροῦ) ο [19 May–7 June
κᾱ ἕωc κη̄ (πυροῦ) ιζϛ́ [8–15 June
φακοῦ ιβ
(γίνονται) (πυροῦ) πζ̣ϛ́ φα(κοῦ) ιβ
λο(ιπαὶ) (πυροῦ) λ̣β∠γ́ φα(κοῦ) πη
(τρι)χ(οινίκου) .[
π.[
κρ̣ά[c(τεωc)
λο(ιπ) [

. . . .

Col. III

[ὧν ἐcτ]ίν·
Ἁρμιῦcιc Πετοcίριοc καὶ Παυcίριοc φα(κοῦ) γγ́
Ἁρυώτηc Φαήcιοc φα(κοῦ) α δα(νείων) β¯
Ἀθεμμεὺc Πετεcούχου φα(κοῦ) θγ́
⟦ ⟧
Ἁρμαχόροc Ἁρμαχόρου καὶ Τοθοῆc Τοθοείουc
δ∠γ́ (ὧν) (πυροῦ) β∠γ́ φα(κοῦ) β
Θῶνιc Ὀρcενούφιοc (πυροῦ) γ∠γ́ δα(νείων) (πυροῦ) β φα(κοῦ) β, (γίνονται)
(πυροῦ) ε∠γ́ φα(κοῦ) β
Φαῆcιc Πετοcίριοc φα(κοῦ) ιβγ́ δα(νείων) φα(κοῦ) β
Θῶνιc μι(κρὸc) Κεντίcιοc (πυροῦ) γϛ́

Μαρρῆς Πετοσίρ̣ι̣ο̣ς κϛd (ὧν) (πυροῦ) ι φα(κοῦ) ιϛd δα(νείων) φα(κοῦ) β
Κατῦτις Κατύ̣[τιος] φα(κοῦ) ιαd ⟦δα(νείων) ∠⟧
[μ]γ´ίβ´ δα(νείων) (πυροῦ) β φα(κοῦ) α, (γίνονται)
μγγ´ίβ´ (ὧν)
[ ] ⟦(πυροῦ) . . .⟧ (πυροῦ) ζḍ
[ ] . . [. . . . .] κζ∠

. . . .

Col. IV

Παπνεβτ̣[ῦνι]ς Σ[ο]κέως φα(κοῦ) δ∠d
⟦ ⟧
Πετοσῖρις Ἁρκ̣[ο]ίφιος (πυροῦ) ϛ
Π̣ορτεῦς Τεῶτος (πυροῦ) ι
με(τρηθεῖσαι) Παχὼν κη̄ (πυροῦ) ι [15 June
Πετοσῖρις Ὥρου ια (ὧν) (πυροῦ) η φα(κοῦ) γ, (γίνονται) ια
Πετεσοῦχος Πετοσίριος (πυροῦ) δ∠ίβ´
Πετεσοῦχος Χεύριος φα(κοῦ) γ∠
Ποτάμων Ἀμεννέως ⟦(πυροῦ) κ̣⟧ (πυροῦ) ια∠
Πετεσοῦχος θ̣[ε(οῦ)] διὰ Π̣α̣αλομούνιος φα(κοῦ) δ∠γ´ίβ´ δα(νείων) φα(κοῦ) β
Πετεσοῦχος θε(οῦ) διὰ Πετοσίριος τοῦ Ἀμεννέως ιαγ´ (ὧν)
φα(κοῦ) ϛ δ̣[α(νείων)] φ[α(κοῦ) ε]γ´, (γίνονται) ιαγ´
Πετεσοῦχος Πακ̣ύρριος (πυροῦ) ∠
με(τρηθὲν) Παχὼν κθ̄ (πυροῦ) ∠
Πνεφερῶς Πετεσούχου τὸ (πᾶν) (πυροῦ) ζ∠γ´ίβ´
Τεῶς Θοτορταίου φα(κοῦ) γγ´
(πυροῦ ?) ξd

Col. V

Χεῦρις Χεύριος [ ] ∠
Τοθοῆς Ἀγοννο(ύφιος) ζ∠d (ὧν) (πυροῦ) δ̣∠d φα(κοῦ) γ
Τοθοῆς Φαγάτου (πυροῦ) γ̣
Τοθοῆς Σενθέως φα̣(κοῦ) . .
Φαῆσις Πετοσίριος φα(κοῦ) δ̣d δα(νείων) φα(κοῦ) γ
Φμούεις Παθήβιος η∠γ´ (ὧν) (πυροῦ) ϛγ´ φα(κοῦ) β ∠
Φαγάτης Μικίωνος ι∠d, καὶ τ̣ῆ̣ς ἐν
Ἁρψήθι Κολλούθου (πυροῦ) ιγ, (γίνονται) κγ∠̣d (ὧν) (πυροῦ) ιθ∠d

φα(κοῦ) δ
Φαῆσις Ἁρυώτου φα(κοῦ) . . .
Φαṭρ̣ῆς Πάσιτος [
Φαῆσις Νεκτενίβιος (πυροῦ) [±7] (γίνονται) ιϛβ´
Ὧρος Πετεσούχου (πυροῦ ?) μγ´[ιβ´ φα(κοῦ)] ιη, (γίνονται) νηγ´ιβ´
Ὀννῶφρις Τεῶτος [
Τεῶς Πετεχῶντος [

(πυροῦ) οδ∠

Col. VI

[ ] φα(κοῦ) κγϛ´
Ἀπ̣ῦ̣γχις Πετεσούχου φα(κοῦ) β
Ἁρφ̣αῆσις Πετεσούχου φα(κοῦ) β∠
Ἀμεννεὺς Ἀθεμμέως δ∠γ´ (ὧν) (πυροῦ) βγ´ φα(κοῦ) β∠
Δημήτριος Σενθέως (πυροῦ) ⟦φα(κοῦ)⟧ γ∠ιβ´
Ἰλῶς Ὥρου φα(κοῦ) ε
Μαρρῆς Ἰμούθου ιηϛ´ (ὧν) (πυροῦ) ιαϛ´ φα(κοῦ) ζ, (γίνονται) ιηϛ´
Μεγχῆς Δημητρίου θd (ὧν) (πυροῦ) ζd φα(κοῦ) β
Μεστασῦτμις Σοκέως φα(κοῦ) δ
Κεφαλᾶς Πετεσούχου φα(κοῦ) ε δα(νείων) β, (γίνονται) ζ
Νίκων Ἀμεννέως φα(κοῦ) ε
{Πετεσοῦχος Ὀρσενούφιος φα(κοῦ) δ[ϛ´]}
Πετεσοῦχος Ὀρσενούφιος δϛ´ (ὧν ?) (πυροῦ ?) [αβ´ φα(κοῦ)] β∠, (γίνονται) δϛ´

(πυροῦ) κϛ

Col. VII

[Πετεσο]ύχου Μέλας (πυροῦ) δd
[ ] (πυροῦ) α δα(νείων) φα(κοῦ) β, (γίνονται) (πυροῦ) α
φα(κοῦ) β
Π̣ε̣τ̣ε̣σ̣ο̣ῦχος Μι̣κ̣ίωνος κ̣α̣ὶ̣ Ἡρακλείων φα(κοῦ) ε
Πετεσοῦχος Ἰμο̣ύθου ε∠ιβ´ (ὧν) (πυροῦ) γδ̣ φα(κοῦ) βγ´
Ὀννῶφρις Ὥρου καὶ Ἑραθρῆς (πυροῦ) γ
Πετῶς Μαρρείους φα(κοῦ) ι∠d
Πετεσοῦχος Σοκμήνιος δ∠γ´ (ὧν) (πυροῦ) αγ´ φα(κοῦ) γ∠
Σοχώτης Παώπιος ϛ (ὧν) (πυροῦ) γ∠ φα(κοῦ) β∠

Φ[α]ῆ̣ϲιϲ Φίβιοϲ θd (ὧν) (πυροῦ) γd φα(κοῦ) ϛ
Χαιρήμων Πετοϲίριοϲ φα(κοῦ) ∠d
[*Ὧρο*]ϲ̣ *Πετενεφιείουϲ* φα(κοῦ) ε
[ ] (πυροῦ ?) β∠γ´
[*Μεϲτ*]α̣ϲ̣ῦ*τμιϲ Πετεϲούχου* (πυροῦ) ιθίβ´ δα(νείων) φα(κοῦ) κε
Ἁ[*ρβῆ*]χ̣*ιϲ Ἑργέω̣*[ϲ] (πυροῦ) κϛ
Τ[±4]ϲ̣ *Τ*.[ ] (πυροῦ ?) η
Ἁρ[*υώ*]*τηϲ* [ ] (πυροῦ) θ
[(πυροῦ)]

Col. VIII

Πᾶϲιϲ Ϲοκονώπιοϲ [
Ὀρϲῆϲ Ἁροννήϲιοϲ καὶ Πα̣[
Διονύϲιοϲ διὰ Μελα( )
Παϲῶϲ Ὀρϲείουϲ [
Φαεὺϲ Ϲοκέωϲ [
Πεϲύθηϲ Παχῶτοϲ [
Πετεῆϲιϲ Πάϲιτοϲ [
Ὧροϲ Ἁρφαήϲιοϲ [
Ἁρμαχόροϲ Θοτορταίου [
Θῶνιϲ Κεντίϲιοϲ κζ [(ὧν)
Θοτεὺϲ Διοδώρου [
Μαρρῆϲ Μαρρείουϲ β̣[
Ὀννῶφριϲ Πετεαρψενή[*ϲιοϲ*
τνθ

93 κϛ corrected from κβγ´. 95 α in 2nd (πυροῦ) α corrected from β 106 (πυροῦ) corrected from φα(κοῦ) 107 κϛ corrected

1–7 For the restorations cf. **89**. 16. Reasons for placing this text among the Menches papers in preference to restoring a heading modelled on **1129**. 1 are stated in introd.

1 (ἔτουϲ) γ: because the rental in l. 6 is that of year 3 (**69**. 5). According to **69**. 38 n. the same amount was due also in year 4, but cf. **72**. 223 and **89**. 6. At all events the account for year 4 is not this text but **89**, where the figures are different from those given here; and year 3 is further guaranteed by correspondences with **1134**, q.v.

2 ἐπὶ κεφα(λαίου): see **1129**. 3 n.

4 After ἕωϲ supply probably *Παχὼν* λ̄. The last regular day for collection of rent this month appears to have been the 27th (l. 20, λοιπαὶ εἰϲ τ̣ὴ̣ν κη̄, the last for loans the 28th (25). But one expects the date here to be a multiple of 10, since **89, 1129** and **1131** indicate that a 10-day accounting period was generally used in these reports, and a payment as late as the 29th is mentioned l. 61.

5–6 Cf. **69**. 4–5.

7–8 These lines presumably contain a breakdown of the form in which the equivalent of

4665$\frac{5}{12}$ art. wheat was actually to be collected (cf. **89**. 9–10). If so, the fraction at the end of line 8 very strongly suggests restoring *χαλκοῦ (ὢν) cῖ(τος) λθ]γ́ιβ*.

12–16 A record of payments made prior to Pachon 28 (l. 20). Not statements of amounts to be collected because only 20 art. trichoinikon are mentioned in l. 14, whereas 85 were due (19+22).

16 Not *δανείω]ν φα(κοῦ)* because the account for loans is handled separately, ll. 23–8 below.

20 *τὴν κη̄*: of Pachon, since any earlier month would mean a gap of at least a month between this statement of sums still outstanding and the commencement of payments to meet these (l. 52). That is not credible.

23 The heading of the short loan account which extends up to and includes line 28.

30 *Πα̣[ῦνι* not suggested.

32 About 7 cm. of papyrus have been lost after this line, but it is hard to see what they should have contained, since the account apparently did not extend into Payni. Quite likely they were left blank so that the scribe could begin his long *κατ' ἄνδρα* of persons still owing land rent or seed loans (33–124) with a fresh column.

47 No more than 2 short entries plus a column total can have been lost after this line.

62 *τὸ (πᾶν) ζ∠γ́ιβ*: the point of *τὸ (πᾶν)* is that the 7$\frac{11}{12}$ art. are the whole of this man's dues, no instalment having been made up to this time and no arrears remaining for later.

64 The correct total of the preserved figures for wheat in this column is 48$\frac{1}{2}$ art.

71–2 *τῆc ἐν Ἁρψήθι Κολλούθου*: *ἐν* here means 'booked against, owed by', a usage not recognized by LSJ but fairly common in Ptolemaic papyri: Mayser II. 2, pp. 396 f. cites many examples. Phagates is for some reason to be held responsible for dues owed by Harpsethis; it is not clear whether the latter's status as machimos has any relevance here.

80 The lacuna should contain no reference to wheat; cf. 93 n.

93 *(πυροῦ) κϛ*: correct total of the preserved entries for wheat, including that in l. 92.

94 *Μέλαc*: presumably a nickname of the taxpayer rather than undeclined patronymic of his father.

111–18 These persons are all machimoi, with the exception of l. 113. If the name in 108 is *Τ[εῶ]c Τε̣[ῶτοc* a list of cleruchs may have begun at that point.

1131. Grain Account

P. Teb. 238 20 × 25 cm. 115 B.C.

A summary of the amounts of barley, wheat, and lentils received daily by the granary at Kerkeosiris in payment of rental for Crown land. The preserved text deals with Pharmouthi, Pachon, and Payni for year 2 of Soter II; traces of a further column suggest that the full account may have been carried into Epeiph or later. The document is to be compared with the lengthier but less detailed reports from other years printed as **89**, **1129**, and **1130**.

The present papyrus is only a draft, as is indicated by the numerous scribal corrections it exhibits, but there is no reason to doubt the approximate accuracy of the final figures given for each day's income. The following chart serves to translate the data for Pharmouthi and Pachon, and supplies Julian dates. The passage dealing with Payni is too mutilated for use here.

Date	Wheat	Barley
Pharmouthi 3 (21 April, 115 B.C.)		$380\frac{1}{12}$
18 (6 May)	462	
26 (14 May)	$94\frac{1}{12}$	
27 (15 May)	$271\frac{1}{12}$	
29 (17 May)	$229\frac{1}{6}$	
30 (18 May)	$195\frac{7}{12}$	$133\frac{1}{12}$
Total for Pharmouthi	$1,251\frac{11}{12}$	$511\frac{1}{12}$ [*sic* for $513\frac{1}{6}$][1]
Pachon 1 (19 May)	$30\frac{7}{12}$	
2 (20 May)	$71\frac{11}{12}$	
3 (21 May)	$6\frac{3}{4}$	
8 (26 May)	$410\frac{1}{2}$	
10 (28 May)	$65\frac{5}{6}$	
Subtotal to Pachon 10 inclusive	$585\frac{7}{12}$	
11 (29 May)	$66\frac{1}{4}$	
13 (31 May)	$336\frac{5}{6}$	
16 (3 June)	$201\frac{1}{12}$	
18 (5 June)	$74\frac{1}{3}$	
Subtotal, Pachon 11–20	$678\frac{1}{2}$	
23 (10 June)	$117\frac{5}{12}$	
25 (12 June)	$82\frac{1}{6}$	
26 (13 June)	$161\frac{11}{12}$	
28 (15 June)	$183\frac{5}{6}$	
29 (16 June)	$146\frac{1}{12}$	
Subtotal, Pachon 21–30	$690\frac{11}{12}$ [*sic* for $691\frac{5}{6}$]	
Total for Pachon	$1,955\frac{1}{6}$ [*sic* for 1,955 or $1,955\frac{11}{12}$][2]	
Total for both months	$3,207\frac{1}{12}$ artabs[3]	

[1] See note to line 5.

[2] 1,955 is the sum of the subtotals as they appear on the papyrus: $1,955\frac{11}{12}$ is the true sum of the daily entries.

[3] $3,207\frac{1}{12}$ correctly adds up the monthly totals as they stand on the papyrus, but owing to the error in the total for Pachon the true figure would have been $3,207\frac{5}{6}$ artabs.

ἔτους β, παρὰ Μεγχείους κωμογρ(αμματέως) Κερκεο̣ϲ̣ί̣ρ̣ε̣ω̣ϲ̣.
προδιαλογιϲμὸϲ πρ. . . . . τ̣οῦ α̣ὐ̣[τοῦ (ἔτους) ?].

Φαρμοῦθι γ̄ μιϲ(θώϲεωϲ) κ(ριθῆϲ) τ⟦οη⟧ \`πιβ´´
ιη̄ (πυροῦ) υξ̇β, κϛ̄ (πυροῦ) ϙδ̇ιβ´, κζ̄ (πυροῦ) Σο̇αιβ´, κθ̄ (πυροῦ) Σκ̇θϛ´,
λ̄ (πυροῦ) ρϙ̇ε∠ιβ´ κ(ριθῆϲ) ρλγ̇ιβ´, . . (   ) μη(νὸϲ) (πυροῦ) ʼΑΣνα̣∠γ´ιβ´
κ(ριθῆϲ) φιαιβ´.

Παχὼ̣ν̣ ᾱ̣ (πυροῦ) λ∠̣̇ιβ´, β̄ (πυροῦ) οα̇∠γ´ιβ´, γ̄ (πυροῦ) ϛ̇∠d, η̄ (πυροῦ)
υι⟦ε∠γ´ιβ´⟧ \`∠´,

ῑ (πυροῦ) ξε̇∠γʹ, (γίνονται) ἕωс ῑ (πυροῦ) φ⟦ϙ̇α⟧ \`πε∠ιʹβʹ', ιᾱ (πυροῦ) ξϛ̇d⟦. .⟧,
ιγ̄ (πυροῦ) τλϛ̇∠γʹ,
ιϛ̄ (πυροῦ) ⟦τ̣γγʹ⟧ \`Σαιʹβʹ', ιη̄ (πυροῦ) οδ̇γʹ, (γίνονται) ἕωс κ̄ (πυροῦ) χο̇η∠,
κγ̄ (πυροῦ) ριζ̇γʹιʹβ, κε̄ (πυροῦ) πβϛʹ, κϛ̄ (πυροῦ) ρξ⟦βγʹιʹβ⟧ \`α∠γʹιʹβ', κη̄ (πυροῦ)
⟦Σλ̇γ∠γʹ⟧ \`ρπγ̇∠γʹ',
κθ̄ (πυροῦ) ρ⟦ν̣θ̇∠ιʹβ⟧ \`μϛ̇ιʹβ', (γίνονται) ἕωс λ̄ (πυροῦ ?) ⟦ψ̣ν̣ε̣γʹιʹβ⟧ \`χϙ∠γʹιʹβ',
(γίνονται) τοῦ μη(νὸс) (πυροῦ) ʼΑ⳨νεϛʹ,
(γίνονται) τῆс (δι)μή(νου) (πυροῦ) ʼΓΣζιʹβ, ἀφʼ ὧν ἐπεсτάλθαι (πυροῦ ?)
⟦ʼΒ̣τλαγʹ⟧ \`Φαρμοῦ(θι) (πυροῦ) χϙ̇α∠, Παχ(ὼν) ʼΑχλθ∠γʹ',
λο(ιπαὶ) ἐν προχρή(αι) (πυροῦ ?) κδd.

Παῦνι β̄ (πυροῦ) ρϙγ∠d κ(ριθῆс) ιζγʹ, ϛ̄ (πυροῦ) ρζd φα(κοῦ) γ∠d, ζ̄ (πυροῦ) [
κρ̣ι(θῆс) ηβʹ αἱ (πυροῦ) δβʹ, θ̄ (πυροῦ ?) [. . .]. . .γʹ φα(κοῦ) .γʹιʹβ [
(γίνονται) τοῦ μη(νὸс) ⳨ .[, ἀφʼ ὧν ἐπεсτάλθαι Πα]ῦ̣(νι) (πυροῦ) κγ̣ʹγʹ . .[
λο(ιπ) ἐν]
προχρή(αι) (πυροῦ) [

5 κ(ριθῆс) corrected from (γίνονται) 9 πβϛʹ: ϛʹ corrected from ∠d 14 ηβʹ: βʹ corr. from ∠γʹ

Slight remnants of a second column do not merit transcription.

2 The mutilated word is not πρακτορείαс.

5 . .( )μη(νόс): the editors of **238** read τῆс λή(ψεωс) here and τῆс β λή(ψεωс) in line 11, taking the latter to refer only to Pachon, the 2nd month listed in this account. But λῆψιс in the sense of 'period during which receipts were made' is not attested, and τῆс β λή(ψεωс) for line 11 is decidedly to be rejected, since that reading would demand an unwarranted assumption of textual error (cf. note ad loc.). Innumerable passages show that monthly summaries should be introduced by the words τοῦ μηνόс; cf. e.g. **89** *passim*, **1129** *passim*, lines 10 and 15 below. There is no palaeographical problem in reading μη(νόс) here, but the preceding traces are not τοῦ. The second (raised) letter is probably eta, the first probably gamma and almost surely not tau.

κ(ριθῆс) φιαιʹβ: this total ignores the correction in line 3. Right would have been 513$\frac{1}{6}$.

8 ἕωс κ̄: not from the 1st to the 20th, but from the 11th to the 20th.

10 ἕωс λ: i.e., from the 21st to the 30th.

χϙ∠γʹιʹβ: an error for 691$\frac{5}{6}$.

ʼΑ⳨νεϛʹ: incorrect. The total is 1,955 if one maintains the error in the last figure, 1,955$\frac{11}{12}$ if one corrects it.

11 τῆс (δι)μή(νου): the editors of **238** thought this total was for Pachon alone and transcribed the passage as τῆс β λή(ψεωс), presumably meaning 'the 2nd period during which receipts were made'. Since the total in fact refers to both Pharmouthi and Pachon, we need instead an expression for a 2-month period. Reading τῆс (δι)μή(νου) obviates the necessity which would otherwise arise of correcting τῆс to τῶν.

ʼΓΣζιʹβ: this figure perpetuates the error in the total for Pachon. Precise would have been 3,207$\frac{5}{6}$.

ἐπεсτάλθαι: for ἐπιсτέλλω used of grain deliveries, cf. WB I, s.v. 4. Here delivery from the granary to the harbour for shipment to Alexandria is meant.

⟦ʼΒ̣τλαγʹ⟧: this is the total grain shipped away in the 2-month period. It was cancelled and replaced with individual statements for each month.

12 *προχρή(αι)*: cf. line 16. The meaning is doubtful: none of the definitions in LSJ or WB s.v. *προχρεία* has obvious application here.

*κδ*d: the actual difference between $3{,}207\frac{5}{6}$ artabs received (line 11, note) and $2{,}331\frac{1}{3}$ shipped off is $876\frac{1}{2}$ artabs. Taking the figure $3{,}207\frac{1}{12}$ as it stands, the difference would have been $875\frac{3}{4}$.

1132. Account of Rents Due

P. Teb. 169 | 35 × 30 cm. | 115/114 B.C.

Two columns containing the names of Crown tenants with amounts of wheat and lentils: the notation *με(τρηθεῖcαι)* in 10 and 31 indicates payment of the sums listed against the individuals in question; **1132** presumably comes therefore from an account of grain due. The sums are too small to represent rents and taxes of the men involved for a full year, and moreover cannot be directly connected with known plots of land. Most probably, therefore, **1132** is an *ἀπαιτήcιμον* of outstanding rents drawn up after the grain harvest was under way, at a stage when most tenants had already paid the greater part of their land dues; cf. **1129**. 41–58, 61–9; **1130**. 34–124; perhaps also **1138** recto and **1139**. 12 ff.

1132 is unique among the *κατ' ἄνδρα* collection lists of Kerkeosiris in that it specifies not only the total of rent still due, but the use to which the land in question had been put. Under the title *μίcθωcιc* are recorded wheat and lentils to be collected on fields devoted to grain, and the sums described as *νο(μῶν)*, *με(λανθίου)*, and *ἀρά(κου)* are amounts of wheat due on land used for pastures, black cumin, and aracus (cf. vol. I, p. 567). The order *μίcθωcιc*, *νομαί*, *μελάνθιον*, and *ἄρακοc* is invariable, though one or more items may be lacking from a given entry and *μίcθωcιc* may be replaced by its component sums of wheat and lentils. This order is basically that of the summary lists **66–70**: our entry *μίcθωcιc* corresponds to *cῖτοc* in those texts, *μελάνθιον* is classed among the *ἄλλα γένη τὰ πρὸc πυρὸν διοικούμενα*, and *ἄρακοc* is one of the *χλωρά*: see vol. I, pp. 565 ff. In **66–70**, however, pastures are treated after the *χλωρά*, whereas in **1132** they follow the *μίcθωcιc* and are frequently summed up together with it before the minor crops are enumerated; and in the totals at the foot of each column there is no entry for *νομαί*, those sums being included in the *μίcθωcιc*.

A summary of the totals due for each man, with some minor variations, is given by **1133**. 11–34. The two texts were written after year 2 of Soter, since the father of *Πεχῦcιc Κόμωνοc* was still active then (cf. **1133**. 77 with **1110**. 226), and the mention of Kephalas son of Petesouchos (**1133**. 43) requires a date before year 5 (**98**. 67–8). As between the 3rd and 4th year, only the first is possible: $25\frac{2}{3}$ art. are collected for black cumin in ll. 19 and 40, but only 1 aroura renting for 4 art. was so planted in year 4 (**69**. 25).

Col. I

1 *Φαῆcιc Ἁρυώτου φα(κοῦ) δ∠ ⟦(πυροῦ)⟧ με(λανθίου) {(πυροῦ)} ∠γ´, ἀρά(κου)∠, (γίνεται) αγ´, (γίνονται) ε∠γ´*

2 *Φατρῆς Πάσιτος μισ(θώσεως) θ∠γ́ιβ́ (ὧν) (πυροῦ) δς́ φα(κοῦ) ε∠d,*
3 *με(λανθίου) α∠, (γίνονται) ιαγ́ιβ́*
4 *Φαῆσις Ὥρου με(λανθίου) ∠γ́*
5 *Ὧρος Ἀμεννέως με(λανθίου) ∠γ́*
6 *Ὧρος Τιμοθείου εγ́ιβ́ (ὧν) (πυροῦ) γ φα(κοῦ) βγ́ιβ́, ἀρά(κου) ∠*
7 *Ὧρος Πετεσούχου λγ (ὧν) (πυροῦ) γ φα(κοῦ) λ*
8 *Ὧρος Ἰναρῶτος φα(κοῦ) [α], μ̣ε(λανθίου) ∠γ, ἀρά(κου) ∠, (γίνονται) βγ́*
9 *Ὧρος Πατῶτος φα(κοῦ) λε, νο(μῶν) αγ́, ἀρά(κου) ∠γ́, (γίνονται) λζς́*
10 *με(τρηθεῖσαι) Ὧρος [Π]ετενεφι(είους) η∠γ́, ν[ο(μῶν)] ββ́, (γίνονται) ια∠̣, (ὧν)*
11 *(πυροῦ) ς∠ [φα(κοῦ) ε], με(λανθίου) βς́, (γίνονται) ηβ́ \`ἀρ̣ά̣(κου) ∠,*
(γίνονται) θς́ , φα(κοῦ) ε, (γίνονται) ιδς́
12 *Ὧ[ρ]ος Μ[ικ]ί̣ωνος κα∠ (ὧν) φα(κοῦ) ι (πυροῦ) ια∠*
13 *Ὧρος Νεοπτολέμου με(λανθίου) α∠, ἀρά(κου) ∠, (γίνονται) β*
14 *Ὀννῶφρις Μαρρείους εβ́, νο(μῶν) β, (γίνονται) ζβ́, με(λανθίου) α∠, (γίνονται)*
15 *{(γίνονται)} θς́ (ὧν) (πυροῦ) δς́ φα(κοῦ) ε*
16 *Πετοσῖρις Ἀμεννέως δ (ὧν) (πυροῦ) α φα(κοῦ) γ,*
17 *με(λανθίου) βς́, (γίνονται) (πυροῦ) γς́ φα(κοῦ) γ*
18 *(γίνονται) ρν (ὧν) μισ(θώσεως) ρλδβ́, (ὧν) (πυροῦ) λδς́ φα(κοῦ) ρ∠,*
(γίνονται) ρλδβ́, ἀρά(κου) β∠̣,
19 *με(λανθίου) ιβς́, (γίνονται) ιδβ́, (γίνονται) ρμθγ́*

Col. II

20 *Μαρρῆς Παaλομούνιος φα(κοῦ) ε, με(λανθίου) α∠, (γίνονται) ς∠*
21 *Πετεσοῦχος Πακύρριος με(λανθίου) ∠γ́*
22 *Μαρρῆς Πακύρρ[ιος] με(λανθίου) ∠γ́*
23 *Μεστασῦ(τμις) Πακύρριος νο(μῶν) αγ́*
24 *Ὀννῶφρις Τεῶτ̣ο̣[ς] φα(κοῦ) ς*
25 *Τεῶς μέγ(ας) Πετεχῶντος φα(κοῦ) δ̣γ́, νο(μῶν) αγ́, (γίνονται) εβ́*
26 *μ̣ε(λανθίου) ∠γ́, (γίνονται) ς∠*
27 *Τεῶς μι(κρὸς) Πετεχῶ̣ντος μθβ́, νο(μῶν) ββ́,*
28 *(γίνονται) νβγ́, {(ὧν)} με(λανθίου) α̣∠̣, (γίνονται) νγ∠γ́ \`⟦δγ́⟧´ (ὧν)*
(πυροῦ) κγ∠γ́ φα(κοῦ) λ
29 *ἀρά(κου) ∠*
30 *Μαρρῆς Πετεχῶ(ντος) λβ∠d, νο(μῶν) αγ́, (γίνονται) λδίβ́ (ὧν)*
31 *με(τρηθεῖσαι) αὐ(τὸς) θίβ́ (ὧν) φα̣(κοῦ) ⟨ζ∠ιβ́⟩ (πυροῦ) ας́, με(λανθίου) βς́,*
(γίνονται) (πυροῦ) λ̣α̣ḍ, φα(κοῦ) ε

32 *Θέων Πτ[ολεμαίου] φα(κοῦ) κε∠*

33 *῾Ωρος ᾿Ορσείους φα(κοῦ) β, νο(μῶν) ββ́, (γίνονται) δ̣β́*

34 *με(λανθίου) β∠γ́, (γίνονται) ζ∠*

35 *καὶ ῾Εβδομίων [μ]ε̣(λανθίου) γ, ἀρά(κου) ∠, (γίνονται) γ∠, (γίνονται) ια (ὧν)*

36 *φα(κοῦ) ϛ∠ (πυροῦ) [δ]∠̣*

37 *Πετοσῖρις Νεοπτολέμου νο(μῶν) αγ́*

38 *῾Ηρακλῆς Πετάλου κζ∠ (ὧν) (πυροῦ) ι̣ζ∠ φα(κοῦ) ι*

39 *(γίνονται) ρ⟦μθ∠̣[γ́ίβ́]⟧ \`να∠ḍ´ [(ὧν)] μις(θώσεως) ρμd, (ὧν) (πυροῦ) μθ∠γ́[ίβ́]*
φα(κοῦ) ϙγ́, (γίνονται) ρμd

40 *ἀρά(κου) α̣, [με(λανθίου) ιγ∠, (γίνονται) ι]δ∠, (γίνονται) ρνα∠d*

A few letters from a 3rd column do not warrant reproduction.

1 *με(λανθίου)* {*(πυροῦ)*}: it is not altogether certain that (*πυροῦ*) should be cancelled, since the text as it stands can be translated 'for land planted in aracus, $\frac{5}{6}$ art. wheat'; and that is the meaning which is otherwise expected.

2 *μις(θώσεως)*: resolved *μις(θοῦ)* in **169**, but cf. **835**. 10 n.

ιαγ́ίβ́: *ια∠ίβ́* in **169** is a misprint.

6 *Τιμοθείου*: *Τι]μοθέου* **1133**. 15.

8 *᾿Ιναρῶτος*: *᾿Ινα]ρώυτος* **1133**. 17.

9 *Πατῶτος*: *Π]ε̣τώυτος* **1133**. 18.

νο(μῶν): this is the only papyrus of the present volume in which *νομαί* appear to be booked to individual tenants rather than the *γεωργοὶ κοινῆι*. It is of course possible that this is a reversion to the practice of 121/120 B.C., when the pastures were booked to Petosiris son of Horos (**66**. 80); but it seems more probable that the pastures were rented in common and the rent collected from those who used them (cf. **1107**. 345–6). With the exception of 2 art. in l. 14, the only known payments made (**1107**. 346) or due were $1\frac{1}{3}$ art. or twice that; possibly it was the charge for grazing one sheep or goat.

11 *ιδϛ́*: *ιεγ́* **1133**. 19.

18–19 The correct figures were: total, $150\frac{1}{3}$. Grain rental, $134\frac{5}{6}$ (wheat $33\frac{1}{6}$, lentils $101\frac{2}{3}$). For aracus, $3\frac{1}{3}$. For black cumin, $12\frac{1}{6}$. Total of the last two, $15\frac{1}{2}$, grand total $150\frac{1}{3}$. It is striking that Menches was satisfied with his final total of $149\frac{1}{3}$ in l. 19 as a sufficiently close approximation to 150 in l. 18.

22 *∠γ́*: *αϛ́* **1133**. 27.

23 Omitted from **1133**.

31 *αὐ(τὸς) κτλ.*: one expects the remaining payments to be connected with one or more other persons in contrast to Marres just as in l. 35 payments for Hebdomion are listed as the responsibility of Horos son of Orses. That no names follow is presumably due to scribal laxness.

32 Omitted from **1133**.

33–6 Hebdomion is not mentioned in **1133**, all 11 artabs being charged directly to Horos (l. 32).

39–40 The correct figures were: total, including the $\frac{1}{2}$ art. for aracus in l. 29, $177\frac{11}{12}$. Grain rental, $163\frac{5}{12}$ (wheat $75\frac{7}{12}$, lentils $87\frac{5}{6}$). For aracus, 1. For black cumin, $13\frac{1}{2}$. Total of the last two $14\frac{1}{2}$, grand total $177\frac{11}{12}$.

1133. Account of Rents Due

P. Teb. 205 — 49 × 30 cm. — 115/114 B.C.

Four columns from a list of *βαcιλικοὶ γεωργοί* with amounts in artabs. A comparison of 11–34 with **1132** shows that the figures given here represent the sum total of rents due from each cultivator as detailed in **1132**. For discussion and date, see introd. to that text.

Extensive restorations in Col. I are assured for lines 11 ff. by **1132**; supplements to 2–10 are based on the lists of Crown tenants in **93+1105**, **1107+94**, and especially **1128**, which is from the same year as **1133**. A slanting check mark is found to the left of all entries where the papyrus is well enough preserved to confirm its presence.

The papyrus was used earlier for another account which was sponged off to make room for the present text. Liberal space has been left between the name and patronymic of each man – seldom less than 1 cm., and frequently as much as 3. This prevents an accurate palaeographic estimate of the letters lost to the left in Col. I.

Col. I

].ου	[
Χε]ύριος	[
Τεῶς Θοτ]ορταίου	[
Τεῶς Πε]τεσούχου	[
Τοθοῆς Ἀγον]νούφιος	ιθίβ́
Τοθοῆς Φαγ]ᾴτου	∠γ́
Τοθοῆς] Σενθέως	β
Φαῆσις Π]ε̣τοσίριος	δ∠γ́
Φαῆσις Πε]τεῆσιος	δ∠γ́
Φμούεις Πα]θήβιος	βϛ́
Φαῆσις Ἁρ]υ̣ώτου	ε∠γ́
Φατρῆς Πά]ς̣ιτος	ιαγ́ιβ́
Φαῆσις] Ὥρου	∠γ́
Ὧρος Ἀ]μεννέως	∠γ́
Ὧρος Τι]μοθέου	ε∠γ́ιβ́
Ὧρος Πε]τ̣εσούχου	λγ
Ὧρος Ἰνα]ρώυτος	βγ́
Ὧρος Π]ε̣τώυτος	λζϛ́
Ὧρος Π]ε̣τενεφιείους	ιεγ́
[(γίνονται)] Σπ⟦ζγ́⟧η∠γ́	

Col. II

Ὧρọς Μικίωνος	κα∠
Ὧρος Νεοπτολέμου	β
Ὀννῶφρις Μαρρείους	θϛ´
Πετοσῖρις Ἀμεννέως	ϛϛ´
Μαρρῆς Παạλ⟨ο⟩μούνιος	ϛ∠
Πετεσοῦχος Πακύρριος	∠γ´
Μαρρῆς Πακύρριος	αϛ´
Ὀννῶφρις Τεῶτος	ϛ
Τεῶς μέγ(ας) Πετεχῶντος	ϛ̣∠
Τεῶς μι(κρὸς) Πετεχῶντος	νγ∠γ´
Μαρρῆς Πετεχῶντος	λϛd
Ὧρος Ὀρσείους	ια
Πετοσῖρις Νεοπτολέμου	αγ´
Ἡρακλῆς Πετάλου	κζ∠
Πετεσοῦχος Ὥρου καὶ Ἁρυώτης	β
Ἀπῦγχις Πετεσούχου	ιβ∠ιβ´
Ἁρμιῦσις Πετεύριος	ιγ´
Ἁρφαῆσις Πετεσούχου	ιβ´

(γίνονται) Σιζ∠

Col. III

Ἁρυώτης Ἀμεννέως	γ∠ιβ´
Ἀμεννεὺς Ἀθεμμέως	ε∠d
Δημήτριος Σενθέως	δ∠γ´ιβ´
Κεφαλᾶς Πετεσούχου	δ
Μαρρῆς Ἰμούθου	ιζ
Μεστασῦτμις Σοκέως	δϛ´
Μαρρῆς Πετεσούχου	γ∠
Νίνις Φαήσιος	β
Νίκων Ἀμεννέως	λδϛ´
Πετεσοῦχος Ἰμούθου	βd
Πετεσοῦχος Πετεσούχου	νϛ´
Πετεσοῦχος Μικίωνος	ιβ̣´
Πετῶυς Μαρρείους	ιδ∠γ´

Πετεσοῦχος Σοκομήνιος	ζ∠ιβ́
Πετεσοῦχος Ὀννώφριος	β
Ἰλῶς Ὥρου	ιγβ́
Ἁρφαῆσις Πετεχῶντος	κθβ́
Ὧρος Ὥρου	ε∠γ́
(γίνονται) Σκd	

Col. IV

Ἁρμαχόρος [Θοτορταίου ?]	ζd
Ἁρμιῦσις [Πετ]οσίριος	β∠γ́
[Θοτε]ὺς Διοδώρου	εγ́ι̣[β́]
Μαρρῆς Σενθέως	γβ́
Ὀρσῆς Ὀρσείους	ια∠
Πετενοῦπις Πετοσίριος	η∠γ́
Φμέρσις Σαραπίωνος	ζd
Πορεγέβθις Ἀπύγχιος	ι∠̣ιβ́
Πετεσοῦχος Σωτηρίδου	ζς́
Πετερμο̣ῦθις Σιεφμοῦτος	ιγ́
Πετεσοῦχος Ὀρσενούφιος	γγ́
Τεῶς Ὥρου	ς
Φραμῆνις Πετοσίριος	η∠
Χο[λ]ῶς Σισούχου	η
Χῦψ[ις] Π̣ε̣τεσούχου	ε∠
Ὧρος Κεντίσιος	ιε
Π̣νεφερῶς Ὥρου	δ∠γ́
Πτολεμαῖος Σενθέως	εγ́
Πεχῦσις Κόμωνος	εγ́
(γίνονται) ρλζς́	

2–10 For the restorations cf. introd.

11–34 Cf. **1132**. Notes there point out slight differences between the two texts.

39 Correct was $225\frac{1}{3}$.

58 Correct was $215\frac{5}{12}$.

59 *Ἁρμαχόρος [Θοτορταίου ?]*: not [*Ἁρμαχόρου*], who would be out of place so late in the list of cultivators (cf. **1128**. 30). But a *Ἁρμαχόρος Μέλας*, probably identical with either *Ἁ. Ἁ.* or *Ἁ. Θ.*, is found in **1141**. 17 and cannot be altogether discounted here, though elsewhere in the list patronymics rather than nicknames are used.

76–7 Both men are machimoi; cf. p. 8.

78 Correct was $136\frac{2}{3}$.

1134. Account of Lentils

P. Teb. 13v (*b*) 40 × 30 cm. 114 B.C.

A list of persons who paid all or part of their dues for Crown land in lentils (cf. p. 8 and **1105** introd.). Since the collection of lentils did not begin at Kerkeosiris till late Pachon or Payni, it is likely that l. 5 records the first payment of the year. When **1130**, a preliminary grain report for the same year, was drawn up, no more than 10 artabs of lentils had yet been delivered; the remaining 480 to be collected were detailed together with other dues in a long *ἀπαιτήσιμον*, ll. 34–124. Where deliveries made here can be checked against that list, they are usually found to constitute payment in full; see notes.

1134 is the earliest of several documents written on one roll of papyrus; see introd. to **13** and **1140**; **1150**.

ἔτους γ̄ παρὰ Μεγχείους κωμογρ(αμματέως) Κερκεοσί(ριος) [115/114 B.C.
κατ᾽ ἄνδρα τοῦ μεμετρη(μένου) φακοῦ εἰς τὴν μίς(θωσιν)
τοῦ αὐτοῦ ἔτους.
Παχὼν κγ̄ [18 May 114 B.C.
Φαήσεις Πετοσίριος ζ∠ίβ́
κε̄ [± 5 C]ενθέως γ∠γ́ [20
κθ̄ Π̣[ε]τεσοῦχος Cωτηρίδου [[21
᾽Απῦγχις ῾Εργέως β[
᾽Ον[ν]ῶφρις Πετεαρψενήσιος ϛϛ́
(γίνονται) ιγ
λ̄ Πετεσοῦχος ᾽Ορσενούφιος [δ] [22
Κεφαλᾶς Πετεσούχου ε
Φαῆς Πετοσίριος δ∠
῟Ωρος Μικίωνος α∠
῾Αρμαχόρος ῾Αρμαχόρου β
Πετεσοῦχος ᾽Ορσενούφιος β∠
*Πετῶς Μαρρείους ι∠*d
῾Αρμιῦσις Πετοσίριος γγ́ίβ́
Πετεσοῦχος Cοκμήνιος δ∠γ́
῾Αρμαχόρος Θοτορταίου γγ́
Διονύσιος Διονυσίου ιβ́

⟦μη⟧ νβ∠

Lines 1–3 'Year 3. From Menches, village scribe of Kerkeosiris. Detailed account of lentils paid in to meet rental on Crown land for the same year.'

5 Cf. 13 n.

10 ιγ: the total of receipts for Pachon 29, ll. 7–9.

11 δ: restored on the assumption that 52½ in l. 22 is the correct total of the day's income.

12 Pays the dues noted in **1130**. 89.

13 If this line refers to the Phaesis of **1130**. 69, it is an overpayment of ¼ art. But lines 5 and 13 here may both refer to **1130**. 41, in which case the two payments together still leave ⅛ art. owing.

15 In **1130**. 48 this sum is listed against Harmachoros and Tothoes son of Tothoes in partnership.

16–17 So **1130**. 92 and 99.

18 γγʹιβʹ: $\frac{1}{12}$ in excess of the amount due from Harmiysis and his brother Paysiris in **1130**. 84.

19 δ∠γʹ: the entire balance of **1130**. 100, although according to that text only 3½ art. should have been paid in lentils.

1135. Grain Report

P. Teb. 159r — 17·5 × 30 cm. — 112 B.C.

A detailed report from Menches concerning grain delivered to the sitologoi of Kerkeosiris in Pharmouthi of year 5. The column preserved deals only with barley received by *εἰϲδέξιμον* measure on Pharmouthi 18 = 5 May (cf. 7 note); where the can be checked, the payments agree with those in **1107** (for a possible but unlikely exception see 13 note). Deductions for *κάθαρϲιϲ*, which regularly accompany payments by receiving measure (**1105** introd.), are not mentioned here; **1107** shows that they none the less were made.

On the back is **1142**.

Ἔτουϲ ε Φαρμοῦθι, παρὰ Μεγχείουϲ κωμ[ογραμ-]
ματέωϲ Κερκεοϲίρεωϲ. εἰϲδοχὴ κατ' ἄνδρα [τοῦ]
μεμετρημένου ϲίτου Πτολεμαίωι καὶ Πα[. . . .]
τοῖϲ ϲιτολογοῦϲι τὸ περὶ αὐ(τὴν) ἐργα(ϲτήριον), ἀπὸ τῶν γενη(μάτων) τ[οῦ
αὐ(τοῦ) (ἔτουϲ)]
οἱ καὶ ἀντιγραφόμενοι δι' Ὥρου κωμάρχου [καὶ]
Μαρρείουϲ γενηματοφύλακεϲ
Φαρμοῦθι ⟨ι⟩η̅, ἐν αὐτῆι, εἰϲδε(ξίμωι).
/ Παπνεβτῦνιϲ Σοκέωϲ καὶ Κολλούθηϲ κρι(θῆϲ) ιζ
/ Ἁ̣ρ̣μαχόροϲ Ἁρμαχόρου κρι(θῆϲ) ιε∠
/ Τ̣ο̣θοῆϲ Σενθέωϲ [κ]ρι(θῆϲ) ιη∠
/ Ὀ̣ν̣νῶφριϲ Ὥρου φε(   ) κρι(θῆϲ) ιε̣
/ Φαῆϲιϲ Ἁρυώτου κρι(θῆϲ) ιϛ
/ Ὧροϲ Πετεϲούχου κρι(θῆϲ) ιγ
/ Πετεῆϲιϲ Τεῶτοϲ κ(ριθῆϲ) νϛ∠
/

/Πετεςο̣ῦχ̣[οc] Ὀ̣ννώφριος κ(ριθῆc) ϛ∠
/Νικά̣νωρ [Π]τολεμαίου κ(ριθῆc) λδ∠̣
Ἀνεμπ̣ε̣ὺ̣ς̣ Πετοςίριος κ(ριθῆc) .[
Τεῶc Θοτορταίου κ(ριθῆc) [κδ]
Μαρρῆc Παaλομούνιος [

5 τοῖc, ἀντιγραφομένοις 6 γενηματοφύλακος

Lines 1–8 'Year 5, Pharmouthi, from Menches, village scribe of Kerkeosiris. Detailed record of receipts of grain of the crop of the same year paid in to Ptolemaios and Pa..., who manage the granary near Kerkeosiris and whose work is countersigned by Horos the komarch and Marres the crop guard. Pharmouthi 18, in Kerkeosiris, by receiving measure. Papnebtynis, son of Sokeus, and Kollouthes, 17 artabs of barley.'

4 τοῖc cιτολογοῦcι τὸ περὶ αὐ(τὴν) ἐργα(cτήριον): cf. **1129**. 34 note.
5 οἱ καὶ ἀντιγραφόμενοι: cf. **89**. 12 note; **722** introd.
Ὥρου κωμάρχου: cf. **1137**. 9 note.
7 Φαρμοῦθι ⟨ι⟩η̄: the insertion of ⟨ι⟩ is surprising, but necessary in view of the agreement of the figures in lines 10, 12, and 14–16 with corresponding passages in **1107**. To keep the papyrus reading we should have to assume that **1107**, which is apparently to be placed between year 4 (**1106**) and year 6 (**1107**. 57 and 65), nevertheless refers not to the 5th but to some other year (a supposition which also upsets the dating of **1105** and **1128**); and that in this unknown year at least 5 persons delivered on Pharmouthi 18 amounts of barley identical with those they delivered on Pharmouthi 8 of year 5 according to this text. That is too improbable to be true, especially since the error here may be explained either as simple haplography or as a misreading of Φαρμοῦθ(ι) ιη̄.
ἐν αὐτῆι: paid in Kerkeosiris, as opposed to being delivered at another granary for eventual giro-transfer.
10 Cf. **1107**. 163.
11 Cf. **1138**. 9.
12 Cf. **1107**. 174.
13 No barley payment for Ὧρος Πετες[ούχο]υ̣ is recorded in **1107**. 271–4, but there were apparently two persons of this name at Kerkeosiris; cf. **1128**. 103 note.
14–16 Cf. **1107**. 203, 256, and 40 respectively.
18 Cf. **1107**. 151.

1136. ACCOUNT OF GRAIN LOANS

P. Teb. 174v 96 × 30 cm. *c.* 114 B.C.

The verso of **1130** contains in addition to two much-effaced columns of doubtful import the following well-preserved *κατ' ἄνδρα δανείων*, written in a smaller hand than the recto text. The first two columns record the names of persons required to repay loans in wheat and lentils, together with the amount of debt. Under each name are recorded payments made up to and including Payni 1, with a statement of the remainder still owing after that date. Payment in full is indicated by two slanting check strokes under the party's name.

The total amount of wheat owed was 118¾ or 120¼ artabs, depending on whether one reads 8 or 9½ artabs in line 2 (cf. note ad loc.). One entry for lentils is lost (line 48), but the remaining items come to 100 artabs. These figures are practically identical with the annual total for government loans of seed at Kerkeosiris, which had apparently been fixed at 120 artabs wheat and 100 artabs lentils sometime after 123 B.C. (**1129**; cf. **1130** introd.; **61**(b). 313–16 note); there can consequently be little if any doubt that the present text is a complete listing of individuals who had received such loans during one year. The date will hardly have been far removed from that of the recto text, year 3 of Soter II = 115/114 B.C., though that year itself is excluded by the schedule of payments: **1130** shows no receipts for loans in year 3 prior to Pachon, whereas the payments recorded in the present document began in mid-Pharmouthi.

Only a minority of the persons named in Cols. I and II had met their obligations in full by Payni 1. The remainder are listed with the amount still due in Col. III. Remarkably, the names given in Col. III do not always agree with those in Cols. I and II, though the order of listing is clearly the same. The variants are pointed out in the text notes.

There is no obvious connection between the amounts of Crown land known to have been rented by the persons in this account and the size of the loan received.

Several dotted figures and restorations in Col. III can be verified by reference to corresponding entries in Cols. I and II. The following chart will facilitate such reference.

	Cols. I–II	Col. III
lines...	4–5	50
	6–7	51
	8–9	52
	10–11	53
	14–15	54
	16	55
	17–18	56
	19	57
	20–1	58
	22–3	59–60
	24–5	61
	26–7	62
	28–9	63
	30–2	64
	33	65–6
	35–6	67
	39–41	68
	48	69

κατ̣' [ἄν]δ̣ρα δανείων
῾Ωρος Μικίωνος (πυροῦ) ⟦η⟧ `θ∠' φα(κοῦ) δ∠

//με(τρηθεῖϲαι) Παχ(ὼν) θ̄ (πυροῦ) γ, λ̄ φα(κοῦ) δ∠.
῾Ạρφạῆϲιϲ Πετοϲίριοϲ (πυροῦ) ια∠d φα(κοῦ) η ʽ⟦δ∠⟧ʼ
με(τρηθεῖϲαι) Παχ(ὼν) κθ̄ (πυροῦ) ι∠, λ̄ (πυροῦ) ∠ιβ́, Παῦ(νι) ᾱ
φα(κοῦ) δ. λο(ιπαὶ) φα(κοῦ) δ (πυροῦ) αϛ́.
Π̣άτρων Πτολεμαίου (πυροῦ) ϛ φα(κοῦ) ε∠
με(τρηθεῖϲαι) Φạρμοῦθι ιη̄ (πυροῦ) εγ́. λο(ιπαὶ) ⟨(πυροῦ) β́⟩ φα(κοῦ) ε∠.
῾Ḥρακλῆϲ Πετάλου (πυροῦ) ιε φα(κοῦ) ε
με(τρηθεῖϲαι) Παχ(ὼν) ιδ̄ (πυροῦ) ιε. λο(ιπαὶ) φα(κοῦ) ε.
/῾Αρβῆχιϲ ῾Εργέωϲ (πυροῦ) ι φα(κοῦ) ι
με(τρηθεῖϲαι) Παχ(ὼν) κθ̄ (πυροῦ) ε φα(κοῦ) ι. λο(ιπαὶ) (πυροῦ) ε.
Φαῆϲιϲ Πετοϲίριοϲ φα(   ) (πυροῦ) δ φα(κοῦ) γ
//με(τρηθεῖϲαι) Παχ(ὼν) ιδ̄ (πυροῦ) δ, λ̄ φα(κοῦ) γ.
῾Ω̣ροϲ Πετεϲούχου (πυροῦ) ι φα(κοῦ) η
με(τρηθεῖϲαι) Παῦ(νι) ᾱ (πυροῦ) ι. λο(ιπαὶ) φα(κοῦ) η.
Πετεϲοῦχοϲ Ϲαραπίωνοϲ (πυροῦ) β φα(κοῦ) α.

Παυϲῖριϲ Πετοϲίριοϲ (πυροῦ) α φα(κοῦ) β
με(τρηθεῖϲα) Παχ(ὼν) κζ̄ (πυροῦ) α. λο(ιπαὶ) φα(κοῦ) β.
Θέων Πτολεμαίου (πυροῦ) γ φα(κοῦ) β

Δίκαιοϲ (πυροῦ) β φα(κοῦ) β
[μ]ε(τρηθεῖϲαι) Φαρμοῦ(θι) κζ̄ (πυροῦ) β. λο(ιπαὶ) φα(κοῦ) β.
/[Φ]αῆϲιϲ Νεκτενίβιοϲ (πυροῦ) γ φα(κοῦ) β
με(τρηθεῖϲαι) Φαρμοῦ(θι) κζ̄ (πυροῦ) γ. λο(ιπαὶ) φα(κοῦ) β.
᾿Απῦγχιϲ Πετεϲούχου (πυροῦ) γ φα(κοῦ) α
με(τρηθεῖϲαι) Παχ(ὼν) κᾱ (πυροῦ) γ. λο(ιπὴ) φα(κοῦ) [α].

Col. II

/Μαρρῆϲ Πααλαμού[νιο]ϲ (πυροῦ) β φα(κοῦ) β
μ̣ε̣(τρηθεῖϲαι) Παχ(ὼν) ιϛ̄ (πυροῦ) β. λο(ιπαὶ) φα(κοῦ) β.
῾Α̣[ρυ]ώ̣τηϲ μέ(γαϲ) Φα̣ήϲιοϲ (πυροῦ) γ φα(κοῦ) β
[μ]ε̣(τρηθεῖϲαι) Φαρμοῦθι ιη̄ (πυροῦ) γ, λο(ιπαὶ) φα(κοῦ) β.
Μαρρῆϲ Πετοϲίριοϲ φύ(λαξ) (πυροῦ) γ φα(κοῦ) β
με(τρηθεῖϲαι) Παχ(ὼν) θ̄ (πυροῦ) γ. λο(ιπαὶ) φα(κοῦ) β.
/᾿Ο̣ν̣ν̣ῶ̣φριϲ Φα̣τρήουϲ (πυροῦ) β φα(κοῦ) δ
/Θῶνιϲ ᾿Ορϲενούφιοϲ (πυροῦ) β φα(κοῦ) β.

//[με(τρηθεῖcαι)] Παῦ(νι) ᾱ (πυροῦ) β φα(κοῦ) β.
Ἡραḳλῆc Πτολεμαίου (πυροῦ) β φα(κοῦ) α
με(τρηθεῖcαι) Φ̣α̣ρμ̣ο̣ῦ̣(θι) ιη̄ (πυροῦ) β. λο(ιπὴ) φα(κοῦ) α.
Ὀννῶφριος Πετεαρψενή(cιοc) (πυροῦ) γ φα(κοῦ) α
//μ̣ε(τρηθεῖcαι) Φαρμοῦ(θι) κζ̄ (πυροῦ) γ, Παχ(ὼν) κθ̄ φα(κοῦ) [α].
[Μεγ]χῆc κω(μο)γρ(αμματεὺc) (πυροῦ) κγ φα(κοῦ) κε
με(τρηθεῖcαι) Παχ(ὼν) κγ̄ (πυροῦ) β, κ̣[.] (πυροῦ) ιε, (γίνονται) ι̣ζ,
κ[.] (πυροῦ ?) β, κζ̄ (πυροῦ) γ∠̣ḍ, λ̄ φα(κοῦ) βd,
(γίνονται) (πυροῦ) κβ∠̣ḍ. λο(ιπαὶ) (πυροῦ) d φα(κοῦ) κβ∠d.
Θ̣ε̣ο̣γένηc φα(κοῦ) γ
//[με(τρηθεῖcαι)] Παχ(ὼν) λ̣̄ φα(κοῦ) γ.
Κ̣εφαλᾶc Πετεcούχου φα(κοῦ) α
//με(τρηθεῖcα) Παχ(ὼν) λ̄ φα(κοῦ) α.
[Φ]αῆcιc Πετοcί(ριοc) κυψα( ) φα(κοῦ) β̣
// Παῦ(νι) ᾱ φα(κοῦ) β.
Τ̣ο̣θοῆc Ἀγοννώφιοc φα(κοῦ) [

Col. III

ὀφείλ(ουcιν) εἰc τὴν β̄ τοῦ [
/Ἁρφαῆcιc Πετοcί(ριοc) (πυροῦ) αϛ́ φα(κοῦ) δ̣
/Φραμῆνιc Πετοcί(ριοc) (πυροῦ) β́ φα(κοῦ) ε∠
/Ἡρακλῆc Πετάλου φα(κοῦ) ε
/Ἁρβῆχιc Ἑργέωc (πυροῦ) ε̣
/Ὧροc Πετεcούχου φα(κοῦ) [η]
/Πετεcοῦ(χοc) Cαρα(πίωνοc) (πυροῦ) β φα(κοῦ) α
/Παυcῖριc Πετοcί(ριοc) φα(κοῦ) β̣
/Θέων Πτολε(μαίου) (πυροῦ) γ φα̣(κοῦ) β̣
/Μαρρῆc Μαρρείουc φα(κοῦ) β
/Φαῆcιc Νεκτε(νίβιοc) φα(κοῦ) β
//με(τρηθεῖcαι)
/Ἀπῦγχιc Πετεc̣ο̣ύ̣(χου) φα(κοῦ) α̣
Παaλαμοῦνιc Ὥρου φα(κοῦ) β̣
/Ἁρῦώτηc μέ(γαc) Φαή(cιοc) φα̣(κοῦ) β
/Μαρρῆc Π̣ε̣τ̣ο̣cί(ριοc) φύ(λαξ) φα̣(κοῦ) β
/Ὀννῶφριc Φατρή(ουc) (πυροῦ) β φα(κοῦ) δ

//με(τρηθεῖcαι)
/Ἡρακλῆc Πτο̣λε̣(μαίου) φα(κοῦ) α̣
/Μεcταcῦ(τμιc) Πετε̣c̣ο̣ύ̣(χου) (πυροῦ ?) δ̣ φα(κοῦ) κ̣β∠δ̣
/Τοθοῆc Ἀγοννο̣ύ̣φι̣ο̣c̣ [
/⟦ φα(κοῦ) . .⟧

16 φα(κοῦ) α: α corrected from β 48 Ἀγοννούφιοc

1 κατ̣' [ἄν]δρα δανείων: in **174** is printed the curiously contradictory title κα[τ' ἄνδ(ρα) ἐπι-κ]εφα(λαίου) δανείων.

2 ⟦η⟧ ʽθ∠': 9½ appears to be a correction of 8, but the double strokes with this entry indicate payment in full at 8 art., and the name is not found among the debtors of Col. III.

5 (πυροῦ) αϛ': a later addition by the same scribe, hence the unusual order of lentils before wheat; cf. l. 50. The figure is incorrect: right was ⅝.

6 Π̣άτρων Πτολεμαίου: corresponds to Φραμῆνιc Πετοcί(ριοc) in 51.

12 φα( ): added to distinguish this man from his homonym Φαῆcιc Πετοcί(ριοc) κυψα( ) in l. 46. φα(λακρόc) seems likely.

20 Δίκαιοc: only here in the archive. It corresponds to Μαρρῆc Μαρρείουc in l. 58, for which it is not a bad translation.

26 Μαρρῆc Παaλαμού[νιο]c: corresponds to Παaλαμοῦνιc Ὥρου in l. 62, no doubt this man's father.

30 φύ(λαξ): not φυ(λακίτηc), since he is not among those listed in **1108–1115**. Probably identical with the γενηματοφύλαξ of **1135**. 6.

39 [Μεγ]χῆc κω(μο)γρ(αμματεύc): corresponds to Μεcταcῦ(τμιc) Πετε̣c̣ο̣ύ̣(χου) in l. 68, possibly Menches' brother.

46 κυψα( ): cf. 12 n. No really convincing expansion suggests itself, though κυψά(λη), a clay jar used for storing grain, might perhaps be used as a humorous nickname.

47 The double strokes alone serve instead of με(τρηθεῖcαι).

49 After τοῦ probably Παῦνι is to be restored, since the latest date recorded in Cols. I and II is Payni 1 (ll. 15, 34, 47).

51, 58, 62, 68 Cf. ll. 6, 20, 26, 39, notes.

1137. Tax Lists

P. Teb. 214 45 × 30·5 cm. Late second century

That the surviving text was once preceded by at least one column is shown by the opening word καί and by the total for lentil-bearing land in l. 7, which is 354 arouras in excess of the amount accounted for in the first 6 lines preserved. The papyrus includes the following:

I (lines 1–7). 27½ arouras distributed to four Crown tenants διὰ τὸ τὴν γῆν παχάνοπα̣ γε̣γονέναι. Rent is charged at 1 artab the aroura. To judge from l. 7, the whole was planted in lentils.

II (8–31). A list headed καὶ οἷc μεμέρικεν ἀπ[ὸ] τῶν πρεcβυ(τέρων.). Possibly the distribution made (by the epimeletes) was of parcels of land to be cultivated, but the fractions show that the figures here are in artabs; these may be rents due, but there are no doubt other possibilities. Two persons are listed twice, Herakles son of Petalos (12, 27), and Harbechis son of Hergeus (16, 24).

A. Tomsin, 'Étude sur les πρεϲβύτεροι des villages de la χώρα égyptienne', *BAB* 38 (1952), 117 n. 1 doubts on grammatical grounds whether πρεϲβυ(τέρων) here can refer to persons, and suggests a reference to πρεϲβύτεροι κλῆροι. But the latter did not exist at Kerkeosiris, and our list contains no person who could not have ranked among the village elders. Horos the komarch is so ranked in **13**. 4–5, and Teos son of Petechon (23), very probably in **1095**. 3.

III (32–43). A list of persons who each paid 1 artab barley for an unspecified purpose. Five of the ten recur in **1138**: l. 33 = **1138**. 65; 35 = 76; 38 = 77; 39 = 78; 41 = 79.

IV (44–67). A list of persons who were required to pay lentils, or, less probably, from whom lentils should be accepted if offered. These names reappear, for the most part with the same figures, in **1138** Col. 1 verso; lines 45–55 correspond to **1138**. 43–52; 56–64 to 55–62; 65 and 66 to 54 and 53.

V (68–77). A list of persons who make payment in a commodity which is not named but is presumably barley, since in line 78 the total paid is converted into 25 artabs of lentils. Such conversion would probably not have been carried out if wheat, equal in value to lentils, had been paid, and these three were the only crops acceptable as Crown dues at Kerkeosiris at this time.

Three figures preserved (75–7) are identical with the full sums owing from the individuals concerned in lines 59, 58, and 65. It is striking that if one refers back to the entries in lines 44–67, and in every case supplies the figures which are there noted as due in lentils as here paid in barley, the total will be 41$\frac{3}{4}$ artabs barley; which equals 25·05 artabs of lentils converted on the ratio 5:3.

VI (79–82). Three persons from whom small payments of an unspecified nature are taken.

VII (83–91). Mathematical notes in the bottom margin of the papyrus, the connection of which with the main text is not always clear.

Col. I

καὶ ο⟨ἷ⟩ϲ μεμέρικεν ὁ ἐπιμελητὴϲ
διὰ τὸ τὴν γῆν παχάνοπα̣ γ̣εγονέναι
———
Ὧροϲ Τιμοθείου (ἄρουραι) δ (ἀρτάβαι) δ
Πετεϲοῦχοϲ Πετεϲού(χου) ια (ἀρτ.) ια
Θοτορταῖοϲ Πετοϲίριοϲ ε∠ (ἀρτ.) ε⟨∠⟩
Ὀρϲῆϲ Ὀρϲείουϲ ζ (ἀρτ.) ζ
(γίνονται) κζ∠, (γίνονται) φακῶι τπβ∠

καὶ οἷϲ μεμέρικεν ἀπ[ὸ] τ̣ῶν πρεϲβυ(τέρων)
Ὥρου κωμάρχου ϛβ
φυλακείτου ε

Ἡλιοδώρου ιε
Ἡρακλείους Π̣ε̣[τ]ά̣λ̣ου ηγ´
Τήρους ϛβ´
Ὧρος Κεντείσιος γγ´
Πολέμωνος ε
Ἀρβῆχις Ἐργέως ε
Ὥρωι Πετεχῶντι ε
Πάτρωνι γγ´
προφήτου ιϛβ´
κωμογρ(αμματέως) κα

Col. II

Ἀρφαῆσις Πετεχῶντος γ
Ὧρος Μικίωνος δβ´
Τεῶς Πετεχῶντος καὶ οἱ ἀ̣δελ̣(φοὶ) ιζ
Ἀρβῆχις Ἐργέως ε
Ὧρος Πετώυτος θ
Ἁρμιύσιος Σενθέως ζ
Ἡρακλῆς Πετάλου ζ
Ὀρσῆς Ὀρσείους β
Πετεσοῦχος Πετεσού(χου) β
Ζώπυρος α∠
(γίνονται) νηβ´

καὶ τῶν μετρη(σάντων) κρι(θήν)
Κατῦτις Κέντιος α
Ὀρσῆς Ὀρσείους α
Πνεφερῶς Ὥρου α
Χαιρήμων Πετοσί(ριος) α
Φαῆσις Πετεήσιος α
Παπνεβτῦνις Σοκέως α
Μαρρῆς Παλλάμου α
Πετεσοῦχος Σαραπίωνος α
Κέντεις Ὥρου α
Πετεσοῦχος Ἁρυώτου α
(γίνονται) ι, (γίνονται) ξηϛ´

Col. III

καὶ ὧν δεῖ παρα̣δ̣ε̣χ̣θῆναι φα(κόν)
Ἁρμιῦσις Π̣ε̣τ̣ο̣σίριος ε∠
Κατῦτις Κ̣α̣τ̣ύ̣τ̣ι̣ο̣ς̣ γ
Πετοσῖρις Ἁ̣ρ[κ]οίφ(ιος) γ
Παπνεβτῦν[ις] Πετοσί(ριος) β
Πετεσοῦχος Πετοσί(ριος) ε∠̣
(m. 2) με(τρηθεῖσαι) ιθ̄ δ, λο(ιπὴ) α∠
(m. 1) Τεῶς Θοτορταίου α
(m. 2) λο(ιπὴ) α
(m. 1) Τοθοῆς Ἀγοννούφιος γ
Φατρῆς Πάσιτος ε∠
Μαρρῆς Πετεσούχου α
Πετῶυς Μαρρή(ους) ι
Ὧρος Πετενεφιῆς γ
Μεγχῆς Δημη(τρίου) α∠d
Ἁρμιῦσις Ἁρμιύσιος β∠
Φαῆσις Φίβιος β∠
Χαιρήμων Πετοσί(ριος) α∠
(m. 2) με(τρηθεῖσα) α, λο(ιπὸν) ∠
(m. 1) Χῦψις Πετεσού(χου) γ∠
Πετεσοῦχος Σαρα(πίωνος) αd
Μαρρῆς Ἰμούθου ς
Ἁρφαῆσις Πετεσού(χου) β∠
(γίνονται) ξβ∠

Col. IV

(ὧν ?) με(τ.) Τοθοῆς Ἀγοννού(φιος) [
Κατῦτις Κατύ(τιος) [
Παπνεβτῦ(νις) Πετοσί(ριος) [
Φαῆσις Φίβ̣ιος [
Π̣[ετῶ]υς Μαρρή(ους) [
Φατρῆς Πάσιτος [
Ἁρμιῦσις Πετοσίριος [
Ἁρμιῦσις Ἁρμι(ύσιος) ἐγδο( ) σι( ) β∠

Μεγχῆc Δημη(τρίου) ἐδγδο(   ) cι(   ) α∠d
Μαρρῆc Ἰμούθου ς´

ἃ ἐcτιν κε̄ φα(κοῦ)
Πετεcοῦχοc Πετοcί(ριοc) α̣
Τεῶc Θοτορταίου α
Πετεcοῦχοc Cα̣ρα̣(πίωνοc) α̣ḍ
(γίνονται) γd

Col. V (near foot of Col. III)

ἀπὸ (πυροῦ) [. . . .] τ
με(τ.) (πυροῦ) νε[
λο(ιπαὶ) Σ[

Col. VI

(ὧν) νηϛ´, λο(ιπαὶ) ρξβϛ´

Col. VII

καὶ ἐλ(   ) cτεφά(νου) ι
(τρι)χ(οινίκου) ια
πρα(κτορικοῦ) ιδ
(γίνονται) λε, (γίνονται) [ρ]ϙζϛ´

Col. VIII

ἀνθ' ὧ(ν) παραγρ(αφῆc) ρπαγ´, λ̣ο̣(ιπαὶ) (ἀρτάβαι) ιε∠γ´

17 Πετεχῶντοc   57 Πετενεφιήουc

2 παχάνοπα̣: this obscure term occurs only here.

9 Horos is attested as komarch from 118/117 (**67**. 73) to 112 (**1135**. 5).

15 The only two persons named Polemon known to us at Kerkeosiris were the catoecs Polemon son of Ammonios, and the brother of Menches who served as epistates.

31 The right total for ll. 21–31 was 58⅛; cf. 43, 86 notes.

33–42 For corresponding lines in **1138** see introd.

39 Παλλάμου: Πααλο̣μο̣ῦ̣ν̣ιοc in **1138**. 78.

43 Both totals are correct, provided that one reads 58⅛ in l. 31 rather than the erroneous text; cf. **1129**. 30–1, 39 notes.

45–66 For corresponding lines in **1138** see introd.

67 ξβ∠: right was 63½.

68–78 Supplements are probably to be taken from ll. 44–67; cf. introd.

75 εγδο(   ) cι(   ): cf. **112**. 117, Διονυ(cίωι) Ἀκουcιλάου μαχί(μωι) ἐγδο(   ) β. A connection with ἐκδοχεύc or ἐκδοχή seems likely; then probably not just cί(του). Is ἐν cι(   ) (**1150**. 6) relevant? A smooth sense could be obtained from ἐγδοcί(μωι) sc. μέτρωι, but palaeography speaks against this, and the measure is not elsewhere attested.

76 εδγδο(   ) cι(   ): probably the same expression as in l. 75, so that the first δ should be cancelled.

83–6 The natural interpretation of these lines is: out of a lost figure 300 art. is taken as due; 55 or more were paid, leaving 200 or more due. From this is subtracted 58⅛, leaving 162⅛. The last part of the calculation then requires supplementing l. 85 as 220⅓; but 220⅓ plus l. 84 cannot yield 300.

86 *νηϛ́*: the correct total of ll. 9–31.

87 *ελ(*): cf. **1103**. 295 n.

91 *παραγρ(αφῆc)*: 'liabilities'; cf. WB s.v.; P. Giss. I p. 28. Line 90 is regarded as due, l. 91 as owed, leaving a balance of 15⅝ art. in the black.

1138. Tax Lists

P. Teb. 197 — 30 × 30·5 cm. — 114/113 B.C. or later

The recto of this papyrus preserves two columns of names followed by amounts in artabs. The names are for the most part those of simple farmers, though at least three cleruchs (1, 6, 34; cf. 39, and 37 n.) and the god Mestasytmis occur as well. In view of this intermingling, it is most probable that the account records dues of some sort owed on Crown land. It has not proved possible to connect these with any known parcels, and as the amounts listed are often very small it seems quite likely that **1138** recto is an *ἀπαιτήcιμον* of rents still owing after the harvest was well under way; cf. **1132** introd.

It is practically certain that the account ended with the second column printed below, since this is followed on the right by a blank space of about 8 cm., four times the width of the intercolumnar area. But the papyrus must have continued with at least one further text, since a trace of ink, apparently from a check mark, is still visible on the far right-hand edge. Whether Col. I represents the start of the list cannot be determined.

The verso, written in a second and more careless hand, is less enigmatic. A comparison of Col. I verso with **1137** Col. III leaves little if any doubt that this text too lists persons required (or permitted) to make grain payments in lentils (cf. **1137**. 44). All the names in **1137**. 45–66 recur here, usually with the same figure owing. Some differences probably indicate that the two lists refer to different years.

Similarly the names and figures of **1137**. 33, 35, 36, 38, 41, and probably 39 (cf. l. 78 n.) reappear in Col. II verso. This strongly suggests that both texts list persons who have made payments in barley (**1137**. 32).

1138 cannot have been drafted earlier than year 4 of Soter II, when the god Mestasytmis took out a lease of Crown land at Kerkeosiris (**72**. 24 ff.).

Col. I

Διονύcιος Διονυcίου ιγ∠
/ *Θ[ο]τορταῖος Πετοcίριος* ⟦δ∠d⟧ \`ι̣´ (?)
/ *Πετῶc Πετε̣ήcιος ε∠*
/ *Μαρρῆc Πετοcίριος ε*
/ *'Αθεμμεὺc Πετεcούχου ∠*
/

Μεστασῦτμις "Ωρου ζ∠
Μεστασῦτμ̣ις θε(ὸς) διὰ Ἀ̣πολ̣λωνίου α∠
Νικάνωρ Π̣τ̣[ολ]ε̣[μ]α̣ί̣ο̣υ̣ ∠γ´
Ὀννῶφρις "Ωρου φε( ) αγ´
Πετερμο̣ῦ̣θ̣ις Μαρρείους εḍ
Πετεσοῦχος Σαραπίωνος .
Παπνεβτῦ(νις) Πετοσίριος [[α∠]] `δ̣´
Φαῆσις Πετοσίριος [[β]] `γ´´
Φαῆσις "Ωρου ∠d
Ὧρος Ἀμεννέως ∠d
Ὧρος Τιμοθ̣είου ∠̣
Ὀννῶφρις Μαρρείους [[.γ´]] `δγ´´
Πετοσῖρις Ἀμ̣εννέως [[δ]] `α´
γ´ιβ´ ξd νδιβ´

Col. II

Ὧρος Πετεσούχου γ
Ὧρος Ἰναρῶτος [[αγ´]] `∠´
Ὧρος Πετῶτος ϛβ´
ϛβ´
Ὀννῶφρις Τεῶτος καὶ Τεῶς δ∠γ´
Ὧρος Πετεχῶντος ιβd
Ὧρος Ὀρσείους ∠
Ἡράκλειος Πετάλου ε
Νίκων Ἀμεννέως .
Ἁρφαῆσις Πετεχῶ(ντος) .
Ἑραθρῆς "Ωρου .
Ν̣ίνεις Φαήσιος ε
Πτόλλις Ὀρσείους ∠γ´
Πετενοῦπις Πετοσίριος ∠d
Πορεγέβθις Ἀπύγχιος ∠
Χῦ̣ψις Πετεσούχου ∠̣
Καμῆς Ἁρφαήσιος κ̣∠
Νουμήνιος [.]γ´
Πᾶσις Πετεσούχου . .

῾Αρμιῦϲιϲ Πετεϲούχου η
῾Αρβῆχιϲ ῾Εργέωϲ ϛϛʹ
φαγʹ οδβʹ (γίνονται) ρ⟦κη∠d⟧ \`λδ∠γʹʹ
πδβʹ

Col. I verso

(m. 2) ῾Αρμιῦϲιϲ Πετοϲί(ριοϲ) ε∠ δ
Κατῦτιϲ Κατύτιοϲ ⟦δ⟧ \`γʹ
χ ⟦Πετοϲῖριϲ ῾Αρκοίφ(ιοϲ) εγ⟧ {γ}
Παπνεβτῦ(νιϲ) Πετοϲί(ριοϲ) β
Πετεϲοῦχοϲ Πετοϲί(ριοϲ) ε∠
Τεῶϲ Θοτορταίου α
Τοθοῆϲ ᾿Αγοννούφιοϲ γγʹ β
Φατ[ρῆϲ Π]άϲιτοϲ ε∠̣
⟦ . . [±7] . . . ϲ .⟧
[Μαρρῆϲ] Πετεϲούχου ⟦β⟧ \`αʹ
῾Αρφαῆϲιϲ Πετεϲούχου β∠ β
Μαρρῆϲ ᾿Ιμούθο̣υ ⟦ζ∠⟧ \`ϛʹ ϛ
Πετῶϲ Μαρρείουϲ ι⟦β̣∠̣⟧ ι
῟Ωροϲ Πετενεφιείουϲ γ γ
Μεγχῆϲ Δημη(τρίου) α̣∠d
῾Αρμι̣ῦ̣ϲ̣ι̣[ϲ] ῾Α̣ρμιύϲιοϲ θ∠
Φαῆϲ[ιϲ Φ]ίβιοϲ θ∠
Χαιρ[ή]μων Πετοϲί(ριοϲ) ⟦β∠⟧ \`α∠ʹ
Χῦψιϲ Πετεϲούχου δ
Πετεϲοῦ(χοϲ) Ϲαραπίωνοϲ θ
(γίνονται) πη∠γʹιʹβʹ

Col. II verso

῾Αρμιῦϲιϲ Πετοϲί(ριοϲ) α
Κατῦτιϲ Κ̣έ̣ν̣τ̣ι̣ο̣ϲ̣ α̣
Πετοϲῖριϲ ῾Αρ̣κ̣ο̣ί̣φ̣ι̣ο̣ϲ̣ β
Παπνεβτῦ(νιϲ) Πά̣ϲ̣ι̣τ̣[οϲ] α
Πετεϲοῦχοϲ Π . [±5] ∠
Μαρρῆϲ Πετεϲού[χου] α
Πετῶϲ Μαρρ̣ε̣ί̣ο̣υ̣ϲ̣ β

Μαρρῆς Ἰμο̣ύ̣θ[ου] α
Ὧρος μέ(γας) Κε[ντί]ς̣ιος β
Ἁρμιῦσις [±5]. . ς̣ ∠
Φαῆσις Φα[ήσιος] ∠
Χαιρήμων Π̣ε̣τ̣ο̣σ̣ί̣(ριος) α
Πνεφερῶς Ὥ̣[ρου] α
Παπνεβτῦ(νις) Σ̣ο̣κ̣έ̣ω̣ς α
Μαρρῆς Πααλο̣μ̣ο̣ύ̣ν̣ι̣ος α
Κέντις Ὥρο̣υ̣ α
(γίνονται) ιζ∠

56 1st γ corrected

2 ⟦δ∠d⟧ \`ι' (?): no ink has been lost, but the interpretation of the traces is doubtful. The mark which I have taken to be an iota may be nothing more than an ink smear. Assuming that ι is correct, it remains uncertain whether the scribe intended the final reading to be 10, $10\frac{1}{2}$, or $10\frac{3}{4}$.

9 φε( ): this mysterious abbreviation recurs in **1135**. 11.

11 The figure after *Σαραπίωνος* may have been β corrected to ∠d or vice versa.

12 δ̣: slightly preferable to ∠.

17 The figure before the cancelled γ́ is obscure because of one or more attempts to rewrite it.

19 The figures $60\frac{1}{4}$ and $54\frac{1}{12}$ may represent column totals before and after corrections (cf. 41 n.). The referent of $\frac{5}{12}$ is quite obscure.

28 The mutilated figure was probably ∠.

36 Found elsewhere only as one of the ξένοι invited to a dining club, **118**. 5.

37 Probably the cleruch Noumenios son of Menneias who appears in **1144**. 40, 64 and **1145**. 3.

41 The cancelled $128\frac{3}{4}$ was the total of $74\frac{2}{3}$ here plus $54\frac{1}{12}$ from l. 19. The remaining figures in ll. 41–2 are obscure to me.

43–63 The very similar list in **1137**. 44–67 is titled ὧν δεῖ παραδεχθῆναι φα(κόν); cf. introd.

43 ε∠ δ: 4 is meant to correct $5\frac{1}{2}$, which is the reading of **1137**. 45.

44 \`γ': the correction agrees with **1137**. 46.

45 εγ: not εγ́. γ was meant to correct ε but was then written farther away for greater clarity. Later the whole entry was placed between curved lines; the failure to include the second γ in the same brackets is presumably due to scribal carelessness.

51 This cancelled entry has no counterpart in **1137**. An ink trace in the column used for corrected figures would suit δ̣, but there is no numeral at the expected position earlier in the line.

52 [*Μαρρῆς*]: cf. **1137**. 55.

63 πη∠γίβ: true total of the corrected readings is $80\frac{1}{4}$.

64–80 Presumably a list of persons making barley payments; cf. introd.

78 In **1137**. 39 presumably the same patronymic is spelled *Παλλάμου*.

1139. Official Accounts

P. Teb. 199 | 132 × 30 cm. | 113 B.C.

This long papyrus contains the mutilated end of an account mentioning stephanos tax, plus eight columns of a list of Crown tenants with amounts in wheat, lentils, and apparently a crop which is abbreviated κω( ). This second list has the appearance of an ἀπαιτήϲιμον: names are listed, followed apparently by amounts due; space was left between names to record payments as made, and several such actually appear, sometimes with the annotation that a further instalment was still due. But the list is dated Payni 10, and these payments were made two days earlier, on the 8th. This is the heart of the harvest season, and collection lists of dues still owing are known to have been drawn up at about this date (**1130**. 34 ff.; **1132** introd.); possibly **1139** was drafted earlier in the month and postdated to the 10th, with the intention of making daily adjustments till that date should arrive. This at least is more plausible than supposing that the payments on Payni 8 refer to a different year, or that the date in the heading is incorrect; and the final list could then serve as the basis for such reports as **1130**, which were generally made up at 10-day intervals (**1130**. 4 n.). But the advantage of such a scheme is not clear to me, and as only two tenuous connections with **93**+**1105** from the same year are apparent (46–7 nn.) the true nature of the account remains doubtful.

The scribe of **1139** is more than commonly given to vulgar spelling errors. Payments on Payni 8 are apparently later additions, but in the same hand.

]μαρχη ϲτεφά(νου)
] Π̣ε̣τεϲ⟨ού⟩χου (πυροῦ) ιβ
Πορεγέβθ]ειϲ Ἀπῦνχιϲ β
]ώτηϲ καὶ Κ̣λ̣ῖτιϲ β
]ϲ Λάτηϲ γ
] ϲω( ) ϲτεφά(νου) ν

]. (πυροῦ) υν
ϲτ]ε̣φά(νου) τκε
] μ
] λε
(γίνονται) υ

Col. II

ἔτουϲ δ Π[α]ῦνι ῑ κατ' ἄνδρα [[4 June 113 B.C.
Ἁρμιῦϲι[ϲ] Πετ{εϲ}οϲῖριϲ [
Ἁρυ̣ώτη[ϲ] Ἁρυώτου [
Ἁρϲῦτμιϲ Λύκου (πυροῦ) ια
Ἀθεμμεὺϲ Πετεϲούχου κγ (ὧν) κω( ) ιβ φ[α(κοῦ)] ια
Ἁρφαῆϲιϲ Ὀννώφρειϲ (πυροῦ) α
Ἁρβῆχιϲ Ἐργέωϲ (πυροῦ) ιδ
Ἁρμαχόροϲ Ἁρμαχόρου φα(κοῦ) β∠

Θῶνις Ὀρσενοῦφις (πυροῦ) ϛγ´
Θῶνις Ὀρσενοῦφις καὶ οἱ μέτο(χοι) φα(κοῦ) λα
Πετερμούθεις Ὥρου ιϛ∠d (ὧν) (πυροῦ) ι φα(κοῦ) ϛ∠d
Κατῦτις Κατύτιος λ (ὧν) (πυροῦ) ιη φα(κοῦ) ιβ
Τοθοῆς Τοθοήους αλο(   ) (πυροῦ) δ

Col. III

Παπ̣νεβτῦνις Σοκέως (πυροῦ) δ∠
δα(νείου) ∠
Ἁ̣ρ̣χ̣ῦψις Πετεῆσις καὶ Τοθοῆς [
Μ̣α̣ρ̣ρῆς Πετοσῖρις κ (ὧν) (πυροῦ) ι φα(κοῦ) ι
[±4] Πετεσούχου Ὡρίωνος (πυροῦ) ι̣δίβ´
⟦ ⟧
Μαρρῆς Πετεσούχου Ἀρυ(ώτου) φα(κοῦ) κϛγ´
Ὀ̣[ν]νῶφρις Φατρήους (πυροῦ) κεγ´ Παῦνι
η̄ (πυροῦ) . . (πυροῦ) ιϛ
[Ὀννῶ]φ̣[ρ]ις Ὥρου κοφὸς (πυροῦ) α
[Πετερ]μούθεις Μαρρήους (πυροῦ) ιγβ´
Πετεσ⟨οῦ⟩χος Νεκτενίβιος (πυροῦ) μ
Τεῶς Θοτορταίου (πυροῦ) ιε
Πετοσῖρις Ἁρκοῖφις (πυροῦ) ∠d
Σοκμῆνις Ὥρου (πυροῦ) ιβ´
// Φμέρσις Σαραπίωνος (πυροῦ) ια (ὧν) ϛd
Παῦνι η̄ (πυροῦ) ε∠d

Col. IV

(c. 2 lines lost)

. . .[
// Παπνε[βτῦνις
Πετοσῖρις Φαή[σιος
Πετεσοῦχος Πετοσῖρις [
Τοθοῆς Ἀοννοῦφις (πυροῦ) ζ∠ίβ´
Φαῆσις Πετεῆσις (πυροῦ) η∠
Τοθοῆς Φαγάτου (πυροῦ) γ´
Φμόις Παθήβεις θϛ´ (ὧν) (πυροῦ) ϛβ´ φα(κοῦ) β∠
Παῦνι η̄ (πυροῦ) ⟦. . .⟧ ε∠γ´ λο(ιπὸν) ∠γ´

Φαγάτηϲ Μικίωνοϲ (πυροῦ) ε∠
Φαῆϲιϲ ʽΑρυώτου (πυροῦ) θϛ´ (ὧν) γρ(αμματικοῦ) α, λο(ιπαὶ) ηϛ´
Μάρων Πετοϲῖριϲ μά̣χ̣ιμο(ϲ) (πυροῦ) κϛγ´ιβ´
ʽΩροϲ ʼΟρϲενοῦφιϲ (πυροῦ) δd

Col. V

(*c.* 3 lines lost)

Π̣ε̣τεϲοῦχ̣[οϲ
Παᾶπιϲ Πετ[οϲῖ]ρ̣ιϲ [
Φαῆϲιϲ ʽΩρου (πυροῦ) ϛ
Κεφαλᾶϲ Πετεϲούχου δ (ὧν) (πυροῦ) α∠ φα(κοῦ) β∠
ʼΑπῦνχιϲ Πετεϲ⟨ού⟩χου φα(κοῦ) β
Πετεϲοῦχοϲ Φαῆϲιϲ ζϛ´
Παῦνι η̄ (πυροῦ) γγ´
ʽΑρμιῦϲιϲ Πετεῦριϲ (πυροῦ) βγ´
ʽΑρφαῆϲιϲ Πετεϲ⟨ού⟩χου δ (ὧν) (πυροῦ) β φα(κοῦ) β
Δημήτρειϲ Ϲενθέωϲ φα(κοῦ) ζ∠
ʼΑμεννεὺϲ ʼΑθεμμήωϲ (πυροῦ) γ
Πετεϲοῦχοϲ ʼΟρϲενοῦφιϲ οἰκοδό(μοϲ) (πυροῦ) α

Col. VI

φ]α(κοῦ) λα∠
].∠
]
[Μεγ]χῆϲ̣ Δ̣ημητρείου (πυροῦ) [
Παυϲῖριϲ καὶ ʽΩροϲ (πυροῦ) ι̣.
Πετεϲοῦχοϲ Μικίωνοϲ (πυροῦ) ϛ
Πετεϲ⟨οῦ⟩χοϲ ⟦Μικίωνοϲ⟧ \`Ἰμούθου´ (πυροῦ) βγ´
Πετῶυϲ Μαρρήουϲ καὶ οἱ ἀδελ(φοὶ) ιεβ´ (ὧν) (πυροῦ) ε φα(κοῦ) ιβ´
Πετεϲ⟨οῦ⟩χοϲ Ϲοκμῆνιϲ (πυροῦ) γβ´
Πετε[ϲοῦ]χοϲ ʼΟρϲενοῦφιϲ καὶ Πετεχ(ῶν) Τεῶ(τοϲ) (πυροῦ) .
Φαῆϲιϲ Φιβίωνοϲ (πυροῦ) εγ´
Πετενοῦφιϲ Πετοϲῖριϲ (πυροῦ) γϛ´
ʽΩροϲ Πετοϲίριοϲ (πυροῦ) δγ´ιβ´
Ϲ̣ο̣υχώτηϲ Παάπιοϲ ⟦(πυροῦ) γ⟧
ʽΩροϲ Πετεϲ⟨ού⟩χου καὶ Πᾶϲιϲ (πυροῦ) ϛγ´
Παῦνι η̄ β∠γ´ λο(ιπαὶ) δγ´

Col. VII

Πετεσοῦχος Μαρρήους θεαγὸ(ς) θ
Μαρρῆς Πααλομοῦνις (πυροῦ) η∠
῾Ạρφαῆσις . . λιξ (πυροῦ) ∠d
[Π]ετοσῖρις ᾿Αμεννέως (πυροῦ) βd
[Π]ετεσοῦχος Πακῦρρις (πυροῦ) α
Πετεῆσις Τεῶτος φα(κοῦ) ιϛ∠d
Τεῶς Πετεχῶντος λβϛ́
᾿Οννῶφρις Τεῶτος κζ∠
῾Αρφαῆσις Πετεχῶντος (πυροῦ) ϛγ́
῾Αρμιῦσις ῾Αρμιῦσις διδέσκα(λος) (πυροῦ) αϛ́
῾Αρφαῆσις Πετοσίριọ[ς . .] . ς ιαϛ́
῾Αρμιῦσις Πετεσούχου ϛγ́ (ὧν) γρ(αμματικοῦ) β λο(ιπαὶ) δγ́
῾Αρμαχόρος Θοτορταίου κβ∠ιβ́ (ὧν) μετρε(ιθεῖσαι)
Παῦνι η̅ (πυροῦ) ι∠ λο(ιπαὶ) ιβ⟨ιβ́⟩
῾Αρμιῦσις Πετοσίριος Πάτρω(νος) θ∠ιβ́

Col. VIII

῾Ḥρ̣ακλῆς Πετάλου φα(κοῦ) λ
Φαῆσις Φαῆσις καὶ Νικάνωρ (πυροῦ) ιβ
᾿Ạπολλῶνις Διοκλείους ϛ∠γ́
῾Ωρος Νεοπτολέμου α∠
Θῶνις μ[έγας Κ]εντίσιος (πυροῦ) λδd
Θῶνις μικρὸς (πυροῦ) α∠ιβ́
γρ(αμματικοῦ) α∠
Θοτεὺς Διοδώρου (πυροῦ) δγ́
῾Αραθρῆς ῞Ωρου (πυροῦ) διβ́
Πᾶσις Πετεσούχου (πυροῦ) κε∠
Πορεγέβθεις ᾿Απῦνχις (πυροῦ) δ∠
Πετες⟨οῦ⟩χος Σωτηιρίδου (πυροῦ) ϛβ́
Νίκων ᾿Αμεννέως κα∠
Μαρρῆς Σενθέως (πυροῦ) ι (ὧν) γρ(αμματικοῦ) β∠ λο(ιπαὶ) ζ∠
Παῦνι η̅ ζ∠ κω(   ) β∠
[Πετε]σοῦχος Σαραπίωνος ιθγ́ (ὧν) γρ(αμματικοῦ) γ λο(ιπαὶ) ιϛγ́

Col. IX

Πνεφερῶc ῝Ω[ρου
Τεῶc ῝Ωρου [
Πραμῆνιc Πετ[οcῖριc
Χελῶυc ⟨C⟩ιcούχο[υ
]ẹ[
[ ]
Κέντιc ῝Ωρου [
῟Ωροc ᾿Ορcείουc θε. . .( ) [
Πνεφερῶc Πẹτẹc̣[ούχου
῾Αρμιῦcιc Cενθέωc [
Θέων Πτολεμαίου [
γẹωργοὶ κοινῇ ν⟨ο⟩μῶ(ν) [
καὶ ἐπὶ τοῦ κα(τοικικοῦ) τά(γματοc) διὰ [Κρίτωνοc
Μελάνιπποc [

34 κωφόc   46 ᾿Αγοννούφιοc   92 διδάcκαλοc   95 μετρηθεῖcαι

1]μαρχη: η is raised, so the word may be abbreviated. But letters are often raised in this and other accounts of the period even when no abbreviation is intended (e.g., the final α of ἄνδρα in l. 12 below); cf. **84**. 32 n.

3 For the spelling cf. l. 108.

4 *Κḷῖτιc*: or *Κα̣ῖτιc*. The name is new in either case. For *Κλῖτιc* cf. *Κλῖτοc*.

5 *Λάτηc*: apparently nom. for gen. Not found elsewhere.

6 cω( ): a tax so abbreviated is mentioned in **95**. 10, where it follows the cτέφανοc γεωργῶν. The editors there suggest cω(ματικοῦ).

11 υ: total of ll. 8–10.

13 Cf. 97 n.

16 κω( ): cf. l. 112. Since κω( ) here is contrasted with lentils, it is presumably produce of some kind and not an impost. LSJ lists several items which might be plausible, the most likely being κώδεια, garlic bulb or poppy head, and κώμακον, an aromatic; but these are not attested in papyri. Or κω( ) would be an easy misspelling of κο(ρίου), coriander. By analogy with fenugreek, black cumin, and beans, however, one would expect dues on land sown with any of these crops to be paid in wheat; and none is known to have been grown in Kerkeosiris.

24 αλο( ): trade name, nickname, or father's patronymic. ἀλο(πώληc) seems likely.

33 The traces after the first (πυροῦ) sign are .

46 ᾿Αοννοῦφιc = ᾿Αγοννούφιοc: for the loss of γ after an α sound, see Mayser I, p. 164. The amount due is that actually paid on Payni 10 according to **1105**. 51.

47 η∠: the sum of **93**. 10 and 12 margin. Coincidence?

52 γρ(αμματικοῦ): cf. **1105** introd.

54 Horos son of Orsenouphis was apparently replaced as a machimos in year 3 of Soter (**1124** introd.), but this text shows that he was nevertheless still living. Cf. **1140**. 90 n.

65 ᾿Αθεμμήωc: for η instead of ε before vowels cf. Mayser I, pp. 76–7.

82 λο(ιπαὶ) δγ́: right was $3\frac{1}{2}$.

85 Not ἀφῆλιξ. The letter before λ is probably α.

92 διδέcκα(λοc) for διδάcκαλοc: Mayser I 55 ff., esp. 58.

97 Ἁρμιῦcιc Πετοcίριοc Πάτρω(νοc): the grandfather's name was probably added to distinguish this Harmiysis son of Petosiris from a homonym in l. 13; cf. **1128** introd.

121 θε...( ): apparently not θεαγό(c) or Θεαγέ(νουc).

126 κα(τοικικοῦ) τά(γματοc) διὰ [Κρίτωνοc: the expansions and restoration are suggested principally by the following name, since the only Melanippos known in this archive is M. son of Asklepiades, one of the catoecic cavalrymen enrolled by Kriton.

1140. Grain Accounts

P. Teb. 13r 40 × 13 cm. 115/114 B.C.

The letter published as **13** is one of a series of documents on a single papyrus. The series apparently began with **1134**; the verso was then used for other accounts, beginning from the lost end of **1134** and proceeding back in the opposite direction from the recto. The final columns of this verso text, Cols. I and II below, were thus written on the back of the initial column of **1134**, against the fibres of the papyrus. Needing more space for these accounts, the scribe added another sheet of papyrus, recto side uppermost, so that Cols. III–V below, unlike Cols. I and II, are written along the fibres. Finally, the verso of the new sheet was used for **13** and **1150**.

Since both **1134** and **13** are dated in year 3 of Soter II, we shall be safe in dating the intervening **1140** to that year as well.

The document contains three different accounts:

1. A list of persons depositing wheat and lentils into their private accounts at the granary (Col. I).

2. A short list of figures of unknown significance (Col. II).

3. A list of persons who pay small sums of wheat for Crown and cleruchic land (Cols. III–V). The list has three parts: the first has no heading (31–84), the second records payments ἐν θη(cαυρῶι) (85–92), and the third records payments εἰc τὸ Coυχιεῖον (43–111). No difference in the nature of the payments to these various destinations is discernible.

1. Seven-aroura machimoi almost invariably pay ½ artab. Two smaller payments lack a check mark and are no doubt only instalments (l. 52, ¼ art.; l. 81, ⅙ art.). A payment of 1 art. in 106 is presumably on behalf of two men.

2. An ephodos with a 24-aroura cleros pays 2 art. (86).

3. An ephodos who had been promoted to the katoikia, but who held only 12 arouras, pays 1 art. (87).

4. Crown tenants usually pay ⅓ art. Exceptions: one person pays ¼ art. (51), ten pay ½ (31–3, 38, 43, 90, 91, 98, 102, 107), and one pays 1 (35). Check strokes apparently indicate that all these payments are correct; the manner of assessment is not apparent.

Payments are often made by one person on behalf of another. Especially common are instances of Crown tenants who pay for cleruchic as well as Crown land. Whether such persons were lessees of the cleruchs does not appear from the text.

The ½-artab tax on machimoi is probably that referred to in **1143** and **1150.** 10 from the same year; for the tax on cleruchs cf. **1144.** 34–40 and **1145**. The tax on Crown tenants does not appear elsewhere, unless **1150.** 9 is an instance.

Remnants of a column to the left; then:

Col. I

↓ εἰc θέ(μα) Παχ(ὼν) θ̄ [3 May 114 B.C.
Ὧροc Μικίωνοc η
Μαρρῆc Πετοcί(ριοc) γ
(γίνονται) ιἀ
κ̣ᾱ̣ [15 May
Ἀπῦγχιc Πετεcούχου γ̇
[ ] Πετεcοῦ(χοc) Πετεcούχου β
Φ̣ραμῆνιc Πετοcίριοc (πυροῦ) β́
(γίνονται) ββ́
Παῦνι ᾱ Θῶνιc Ὀρcενού(φιοc) (πυροῦ) β φα(κοῦ) δ [26 May
Ὧ̣ροc Πετεcούχου (πυροῦ) ι
(γίνονται) (πυροῦ) ιβ́ φα(κοῦ) δ
ς̄ Ὀννῶφριc Φατρή(ουc) (πυροῦ) δ̣ [31 May
Φο̣λῆμ̣ιc Νεκτενίβ̣ι̣ο̣ς̣ (πυροῦ) β
(γίνονται) (πυροῦ) ϛ
(γίνονται) (πυροῦ) λδβ́ φα(κοῦ) δ, (γίνονται) ληβ́
η̣̄ [2 June
Ἡρακλῆc Πετάλου φα(κοῦ) ε
θ̄ Μεcταcῦ(τμιc) Μεcταcύ(τμιοc) φα(κοῦ) ιϛ [3 June
ῑ̣ Φαῆc Πετοcίριοc φα(κοῦ) β [4 June
Μεcταcῦ(τμιc) Μεcταcύ(τμιοc) φα(κοῦ) ιγd
(γίνονται) φα(κοῦ) ιε̣d
(γίνονται) (πυροῦ) π⟦ε∠γ́⟧\`ζγ́´ φα(κοῦ) ξ̣ϛ, (γίνονται) ρνγγ́, (γίν.) Σκβ

Col. II

↓ (πυροῦ)
ιγ́

η
ια
κα̣
γ
ιζ

Remainder blank.

Col. III

→ / ῟Ωρος Πετεχῶντος βα(ϲιλικῆϲ) ∠
/ Τεῶϲ μι(κρὸϲ) Πετεχῶντος βα(ϲιλικῆϲ) ∠
/ Νίκων Ἀμεννέως βα(ϲιλικῆϲ) ∠
/ Ἀμεννεὺϲ Μαρρείουϲ βα(ϲιλικῆϲ) γ′ (ἐπταρουρικοῦ) ∠
/ Θέων Πετεχῶντοϲ βα(ϲιλικῆϲ) α
/ Ἁρυώτηϲ Ἀμεννέωϲ βα(ϲιλικῆϲ) γ′ (ἐπταρουρικοῦ) ∠
/ Κ̣εφ̣α̣λᾶϲ Πετεϲούχου βα(ϲιλικῆϲ) γ′
/ Κόττυοϲ βα(ϲιλικῆϲ) ∠
/ ῟Ωροϲ Κολλούθου (ἐπταρουρικοῦ) ∠
/ Πετεϲοῦχοϲ Ϲωτη(ρίδου) βα(ϲιλικῆϲ) γ′
/ Ἀμεννεὺϲ Ἀθεμμέ(ωϲ) βα(ϲιλικῆϲ) γ′
/ Παπνεβ̣τῦ(νιϲ) Πετοϲί(ριοϲ) βα(ϲιλικῆϲ) γ′
/ Πετεϲοῦχοϲ Τοθοήουϲ βα(ϲιλικῆϲ) ∠
/ Ἁρϲῦτμιϲ Πετοϲίριοϲ (ἐπταρουρικοῦ) ∠
/ Ἁρμαχόροϲ Ἁρμαχόρου βα(ϲιλικῆϲ) γ′
/ Μαρρῆϲ Πακύρριοϲ βα(ϲιλικῆϲ) γ′
/ ῟Ωροϲ ῟Ωρου (ἐπταρουρικοῦ) ∠
/ Πετεϲοῦχοϲ Πααλομού(νιοϲ) βα(ϲιλικῆϲ) γ′
/ Μαρρῆϲ Πετοϲίριοϲ βα(ϲιλικῆϲ) ∠
/ Πετοϲῖριϲ Ἁρκοίφ(ιοϲ) βα(ϲιλικῆϲ) γ′
/ Πετεϲοῦ(χοϲ) Ἰμούθου βα(ϲιλικῆϲ) d καὶ
ὑ̣π̣(ὲρ) ῟Ωρου Φαγώ(μιοϲ) (ἐπταρουρικοῦ) d Ϲοκο(νώπιοϲ) Πάϲι(τοϲ)
(ἐπταρουρικοῦ) ∠, (γίνεται) α /
/ Ἁρφαῆϲιϲ Πετεϲούχου βα(ϲιλικῆϲ) γ′
/ Ἁρυώτηϲ μι(κρὸϲ) Φαήϲιοϲ βα(ϲιλικῆϲ) γ′
/ Διόδωροϲ Κοκκύλου βα(ϲιλικῆϲ) γ′

Φμέρϲιϲ Cαρα(πίωνοϲ) βα(ϲιλικῆϲ) γ́
Φατρῆϲ Πάϲιτοϲ βα(ϲιλικῆϲ) γ́ ⟦βα(ϲιλικῆϲ)⟧ καὶ
[ὑπ(ὲρ)] Ὥρου Θοτορταίου (ἐπταρουρικοῦ) ∠ καὶ
Νεκτε⟨νί⟩ˋβιοϲˊ τοῦ Ὥρου (ἐπταρουρικοῦ) ∠, (γίνεται) αγ́
Θῶνιϲ μι(κρὸϲ) Κεντίϲιοϲ βα(ϲιλικῆϲ) γ́
Πνεφερῶϲ Ὥρου βα(ϲιλικῆϲ) γ́
(γίνονται) ιδϛ́

Col. IV

→ Πετερμοῦθιϲ Cιεφμοῦ(τοϲ) βα(ϲιλικῆϲ) γ́
Ὀννῶφριϲ Πετεαρψενή(ϲιοϲ) βα(ϲιλικῆϲ) γ́
Ὕλλοϲ Πάιτοϲ (ἐπταρουρικοῦ) ∠
Ἁρμιῦϲιϲ Πετοϲίριοϲ βα(ϲιλικῆϲ) γ́
Ἁρχῦψιϲ Πετεή(ϲιοϲ) βα(ϲιλικῆϲ) γ́
Τοθοῆϲ Φαγάτου βα(ϲιλικῆϲ) γ́
Πετοϲῖριϲ Ἁρμιύϲιοϲ βα(ϲιλικῆϲ) γ́
Ὧροϲ Πετεϲούχου βα(ϲιλικῆϲ) γ́
Φμούειϲ Παθήβιοϲ βα(ϲιλικῆϲ) γ́
Ἡρακλῆϲ Πτολεμαί(ου) βα(ϲιλικῆϲ) γ́
Ὧροϲ Παώπιοϲ (ἐπταρουρικοῦ) ∠
Κατῦ(τιϲ) Cιϲούχου βα(ϲιλικῆϲ) γ́
Παϲῶϲ Ὀρϲείουϲ (ἐπταρουρικοῦ) ∠
Ἑραθρῆϲ Ὥρου βα(ϲιλικῆϲ) γ́
Πετερμοῦθιϲ Ὥρου βα(ϲιλικῆϲ) γ́
Θεαγένηϲ Νεο(πτολέμου) βα(ϲιλικῆϲ) γ́
Ποτάμων βα(ϲιλικῆϲ) γ́
Φαεὺϲ Cοκέωϲ (ἐπταρουρικοῦ) ∠
καὶ ὑπ(ὲρ) Ψενή(ϲιοϲ Cτεφά(νου) (ἐπταρουρικοῦ) ϛ́, (γίνεται) β́
Ὧροϲ Ἀμεννέωϲ βα(ϲιλικῆϲ) γ́
Πετεϲοῦχοϲ Πακύ(ρριοϲ) βα(ϲιλικῆϲ) γ́
(γίνονται) ϛ∠γ́, (γίνονται) κγ́

κγ̄ ἐν θη(ϲαυρῶι)
Ἀπολλώνιοϲ Πτο(λεμαίου) ἐφο(δικοῦ) β
Δημήτριοϲ Ἡρα(κλείδου) α
Πᾶϲιϲ Cοκονώπιοϲ (ἐπταρουρικοῦ) ∠

/ Ἀπῦγχιc Ποώριοc (ἐπταρουρικοῦ) ∠
/ Λύκοc Ζωπυρίωνοc βα(cιλικῆc) ∠
/ Πετῶc Μαρρείουc βα(cιλικῆc) ∠ (ἐπταρουρικοῦ) ∠, (γίνεται) α
(γίνονται) ε∠, (γίνονται) κ⟨ε⟩∠γ́
εἰc τὸ Coυχιεῖον
Πετοcῖριc Ὥρου (πυροῦ) γ́
/ Πευκέcτηc βα(cιλικῆc) (πυροῦ) γ́
/ Μαρρῆ(c) Κ̣[α]λατύτιοc (ἐπταρουρικοῦ) (πυροῦ) ∠
/ (γίνεται) αϛ́

Col. V

→ Ὀρcενοῦφιc ∠
/ Χεῦριc Χε(ύριοc) βα(cιλικῆc) γ́
/ Πετεcοῦ(χοc) Χε(ύριοc) βα(cιλικῆc) γ́
Δίκαλ̣οc βα(cιλικῆc) γ́
Ἀθεμμεὺc βα(cιλικῆc) ∠
Κατῦ(τιc) Cιcούχου βα(cιλικῆc) γ́
Τοθοῆc Ἀγοννού(φιοc) βα(cιλικῆc) γ́
Ὧροc Νεοπτο(λέμου) βα(cιλικῆc) γ́
Θέων ὑπ(ὲρ) (ἐπταρουρικῶν) α
Πύρριχοc ὑπ(ὲρ) αὐ(τοῦ) ∠ (ἐπταρουρικοῦ) ∠, (γίνεται) α
Χολῶc Cιcούχου βα(cιλικῆc) γ́
Παπνε(βτῦνιc) Cοκέ(ωc) βα(cιλικῆc) γ́
Φαῆcιc Πετεή(cιοc) βα(cιλικῆc) γ́
(γίνονται) ζϛ́ μεταβο(   ) ζίβ́

13 δ̣ corrected from β̣ 16 β́ in λδβ́ corrected from d 50 Ἀρκ- corrected from Ἀρφ
59 Νεκτενίβιοc: Νεκτε corrected

1 εἰc θέ(μα) 'for deposit in private accounts'. εἰcδε(ξίμωι) 'by receiving measure', is less likely, though δ and θ are easily confused in this hand.

16 Totals correct, with lentils reckoned at par with wheat.

23 The totals must refer to more than this column. The addition $87\frac{1}{3}+66 = 153\frac{1}{3}$ is correct.

34 (ἐπταρουρικοῦ): sc. κλήρου, if the expansion is correct. (ἐπταρουρικῆc) sc. γῆc and simply (ἐπταρούρου) also seem possible.

62 Total correct.

81 A checking stroke was at first written in front of this name, but was later washed out.

84 ϛ∠γ́: correct was $7\frac{1}{2}$.

κγ́: this must be the sum of Cols. III and IV. Right was 21.

90 Λύκοc Ζωπυρίωνοc: between 118/117 (**84**. 105) and 117/116 (**1118**. 98) Crown land previously held by Lykos was booked to his son Harsytmis; nevertheless Lykos is still alive and capable of paying taxes.

92 Totals correct.

93 *εἰς τὸ Σουχιεῖον*: the granary connected with the shrine of Petesouchos apparently accepted deposits for various purposes, not simply those designed to benefit the shrine. Cf. pp. 9 and 13.

101 *Δίκαλος*: not *Δίκαιος* (cf. **1136**. 20); λ, though damaged, is highly probable. Cf. Byzantine *Δικαλῆς*.

111 *ζϛ*: 6 art. in Col. v plus $1\frac{1}{6}$ from l. 96.

μεταβο( ) : *μεταβο(λήτου)* following **862**. 2–3 n.? Or *μεταβο(λῆς)* as **123**. 12 ff.? On the latter cf. Preisigke, *Girowesen* 117.

1141. Tax List

P. Teb. 219 — 16 × 31 cm. — 113 B.C.

A list of small payments in wheat from *βασιλικοὶ γεωργοί* concerning whom some administrative or judicial decision had been taken (*διακεκρι(μένων)*, line 1). There is no clue as to the nature of this decision or the reason for keeping a separate list of those affected by it.

(ἔτους) δ, Παῦνι κζ. διακεκρι(μένων) ὁμο(ίως)· [13 July 113 B.C.
Φα]μ̣ενὼθ κε̄ [13 April
] διὰ Πετεσοκονόρις (πυροῦ) γ́
] Φ̣α̣ρμ̣ο̣ῦθι δ̄ Θοτορταῖς Πετο(σίριος) ∠ [21 April
Θ]έων Πετεχῶντος α
Πετ]εσοῦχος Χεῦρις α∠
Χο]λῶς Σισούχου ∠
/[Θ]ῶνις μι(κρὸς) Κεντῖτος α
/κζ Ἁρυώτης μι(κρὸς) Φαήσιος α [15 May
/ [(γίνονται) τοῦ] μηνὸς (πυροῦ) ε∠γ́
/[Παχὼν . Ποτά]μων Ἀμεννέως (πυροῦ) α
]δ̄ Π̣ε̣τερμουθις Ὥρου αϛ́
/ιθ Ἀθε̣μμεὺς Πετεσούχου α [5 June
/κ̣ Πάτρων α [6 June
/κδ̄ Πετῶυς Μαρρῆς ∠ [11 June
/ (γίνονται) τοῦ μηνὸς (πυροῦ) δϛ́
Παῦνι ᾱ Ἁρμαχόρος Μέλας (πυροῦ) α [17 June
/η̄ Θεαγένης α [25 June
/ιγ̄ Φαῆσις Πετεήσιος α∠ [30 June
/ Ἁρυώτης μέ(γας) Φαήσιος α
/

(γίνονται) τοῦ μηνὸϲ (πυροῦ) δ∠
(γίνεται) τὸ (πᾶν) (πυροῦ) ιδ∠
καὶ Βελλῆτι ∠, (γίνονται) ιε

1 It is not clear whether anything should be restored before (ἔτουϲ).
3 *Πετεϲοκονόριϲ*: usually *Πετεϲοκονούριοϲ*.
8 *Κεντῖτοϲ*: usually *Κεντίϲιοϲ*.
10 ε∠γ´: includes $\frac{1}{3}$ art. from line 3, although that payment seems to have been made in Phamenoth rather than Pharmouthi.
16 δϛ´: correct was $4\frac{2}{3}$.
17 *Μέλαϲ*: possibly a patronymic, nom. for gen. as l. 15; if so, the man is not known elsewhere. Or *Μέλαϲ* might be the nickname of either *Ἁρμαχόροϲ Ἁρμαχόρου* or *Ἁ. Θοτορταίου*.
22 ιδ∠: totals lines 10, 16, and 21, preserving the error in 16.
23 *Βελλῆτι*: the name recurs in this archive only in **39**. 26

1142. Account

P. Teb. 159v | 17·5 × 30 cm. | 112/111 B.C.

The significance of this list of names with amounts in artabs is altogether unclear; cf. line 1 note.

Written on the back of **1135**, in a different hand from that text. No connection between the two documents is apparent.

κα[..]ντιλογι(   ) [
    ἐν τῶι ϛ (ἔτει) [
Κατῦτιϲ Κατύ(τιοϲ) [
Μαρρῆϲ Πετοϲί(ριοϲ) [
Μαρρῆϲ Πετοϲί(ριοϲ) ε
Πόρτιϲ Τεῶ(τοϲ) ϛ
Πᾶϲιϲ Πετεϲού(χου) ι
Ταυρίϲκοϲ αβ´
Διδυ(   ) Ϲερίφου ε
Ὀννῶ(φριϲ) Μαρρε[ίουϲ] ε
Πετεῆ(ϲιϲ) Τεῶ(τοϲ) ιβ∠γ´
Μαρρῆ(ϲ) Πετε[
Ἡρακλείδηϲ [
,Θῶνιϲ μι(κρὸϲ) [Κεντίϲιοϲ

1 κα[..]ντιλογι(   ): transcribed κα[ὶ ἀ]ντιλογί(α) in **159** descr. The elongated final iota does no doubt indicate an abbreviation, but ἀ]ντιλογί(α) yields no particularly attractive meaning. The

words may equally well be divided *κα[ὶ ἀ]ντὶ λογι(*), if that should be the right supplement for the short lacuna.

4 *Μαρρῆς Πετοσί(ριος)*: it seems surprising to find the same man listed in the line below. Possibly therefore the entry here should be continued [*καὶ μέ(τοχοι)* or the like.

9 *Διδυ(*) *Σερίφου*: only here. The name *Σέριφος* is not found in the *Namenbuch* or *Onomasticon*, though cf. *Σερίφιος*.

1143. TAX LIST

P. Teb. 161 18 × 30 cm. 115/114 B.C

A list of persons required to pay a charge of ½ artab apiece, followed by the names of four Crown tenants. The text presumably antedates a letter on the verso which was written shortly after 3 Mesore of Soter's 3rd year (**16**). On the other hand, the occurrence of Teos the younger, son of Petechon (13) requires a date after 116/115, when his predecessor Amounis son of Pikamis was still active (**1110**. 184).

The charge in question fell on 51 individuals. Since the 35 names which survive are all *ἑπτάρουροι μάχιμοι*, it is natural to suppose that the other 16 were as well. In fact there were 54 machimoi in Kerkeosiris at this period; and as the text follows the usual practice of listing soldiers according to the year in which their cleroi were assigned, two of the absentees can be identified with little chance that their names had occurred earlier in the papyrus. From the list of those who had received land at Kerkeosiris in year 46 of Euergetes II, Ptolemaios son of Sentheus is missing: possibly he was exempted from the impost at Kerkeosiris because the greater part of his cleros was located elsewhere, at Areos Kome. Among the machimoi of year 50 is found neither Komon son of Pechysis nor his son and successor Pechysis: possibly Komon had died and his son had not yet been confirmed in possession of the land. A third man will have been absent from the list of machimoi for year 41.

The nature of the charge is unclear. In their introduction to **16**, the editors of vol. I suggest *γεωμετρία*, which was indeed levied at ½ art. per man; but the same rate is also found for *θέμα*, and neither impost is attested in connection with machimoi as such, but rather with Crown tenants. In all probability we are dealing with the enigmatic charge of **1140**, where a tax of ½ artab on machimoi alternates with one of usually ⅓ art. on Crown tenants. Cf. **1150**. 10.

The connection of the four *βασιλικοὶ γεωργοί* whose names end the document with the preceding text is altogether unclear.

Slight remnants of a column to the left; then:

Col. I

/ *Ἁρμιῦσις Σοκονώπιος*
Τεῶς Τεῶτος

Πᾶσις μι(κρὸς) Καλατύτις
Νεκτενίβιος Ὥρου
Φολῆμις Νεκτενίβιος
Ἀπῦγχις Ποώριος
Κολλούθης Ὥρου
Ὕλλος Πάιτος
Πᾶσις μέ(γας) Καλατύτιος
Ἁρφαῆσις Ὥρου
Κολλούθης Πετοσίριος
Ὀννῶφρις Πετερμούθιος
Τεῶς μι(κρὸς) Πετεχῶντος
Ἁρυώτης Ἁρυώτου
[Χ]εῦρις Σοχώτου
Ἀρχίβιος Ὥρου
Πᾶσις Σοκονώπιος
[Ὀ]ννῶφρις Μεστασύ(τμιος)
Ὧρος Πα[ώ]πιος
Π̣εσύθης [Π]αχῶτος
Σ̣οκο̣ν̣[ῶπι]ς̣ Πάσιτος
Πασῶς μι(κρὸς) [Φ]ανήσιος
Πασῶς Ὀρσείους
Πετεσοῦχος Πετεσούχου
Ὀρσῆς Ἁροννήσιος
Φθαῦς Πετεήσιος
Ἁρμιῦσις Πετεσούχου
Πασῶς μέ(γας) Φανήσιος
Μαρρῆς Παάπιος

Col. II

Ἁροννῶφρις Ὥρου
Ἁρμάις Πανορσείους
Κολλούθης Ὥρου
Παῶπις Πετεσούχου
Ἁρψάλις Στεφάνου
Ψενῆσις Στεφάνου

(*γίνονται*) *να ἀν*(*ὰ*) ∠, (*ἀρτάβαι*) *κε*∠
(*γίνονται*) *ξϛ*

Ἁρυώτης Φαήσιος
Πορεγέβθις Ὥρου
Πνεφερῶς Πετεσούχου
Τεῶς Θοτορταίου

15–20 Because of damage to the papyrus one cannot tell whether these names bore a checking stroke.

31 It is not clear whether there is some significance to the use of a dot here as opposed to the stroke used elsewhere in the text.

36–7 '51 persons at ½ each, total 25½ art. Grand total, 66.' The reference of the last figure is quite obscure.

1144. Grain Accounts

P. Teb. 171 41 × 30 cm. After 116/115

A series of grain accounts written in one hand on both sides of the papyrus.

1. Lines 1–33. A list of Crown tenants with amounts in artabs varying from $\frac{1}{2}$ to $25\frac{5}{8}$. The list is divided into two sections, the first ending at l. 17 and the second at 33. The significance of the division, and of the list as a whole, is obscure, largely no doubt because of undeciphered words in ll. 16 and 33.

2. Lines 34–41. Seven cleruchs who pay 1 or 2 artabs apiece. Cf. **1140**. 86–7, **1145**.

3. Lines 42–94. Crown tenants who pay $\frac{1}{2}$, 1 or 2 artabs apiece for an unspecified purpose. The size of payment is strikingly reminiscent of **97**, where comparable amounts are paid for *ἐπιϲ(τατικοῦ)* and/or *γρ(αμματικοῦ)*.

4. Lines 95–149. Small payments of wheat and barley by Crown tenants in Pharmouthi and Pachon.

5. Lines 150–74. Repayments of state loans of wheat and lentils during Pharmouthi and Pachon.

The text was written after the cession of land to Didymarchos son of Apollonios and Sosikles son of Menneias which occurred in year 2 of Soter II (cf. 34 and 37 with **1115**. 176 ff.). If line 13 indicates that the machimos Maron son of Petosiris was still active (cf. note), then only years 3 and 4 are possible, since Maron is attested in year 4 (**1139**. 53) but is not found in the lists for years 2 or 5 (**1110** and **1147**).

Col. I

πγ∠ιβ́
] *Φανήϲιοϲ β*
] *Ὥρου γβ́*
] *Τεῶτοϲ κε̣∠γ́*
Πετ]*εχῶντοϲ κα∠*
Ἀμεν]*νέωϲ ε*
]*τριοϲ γ∠*
]*τ̣ριοϲ δϛ́*
]*ϲ̣ίωνοϲ β∠γ́ιβ́*
]*δώρου α*
καὶ Πετ]*εϲοῦχοϲ γ*
Πετ]*εϲούχου β∠*
[*Μάρων Πετο*]*ϲ̣ί(ριοϲ) κά(τοικοϲ) γ*
[*Ἀμεννεὺϲ Ἀθεμ*]*μέωϲ δ*
Ἡρα]*κ̣λείδου ι*

] λο(ιπαὶ) . . λο(?) ρμθϛ´ πλ(είω) γ´ιβ´
]∠d
]τος βϛ´
] . ήσιος β∠γ´
]ώτου ε

Col. II

Τοθοῆς Ἀγοννούφιος ζ∠ιβ´
Φαῆσις Φίβιος ϛϛ´
Θῶνις Ὀρσενούφιος ε∠ιβ´
Πετενοῦπις Πετοσίριος ∠ιβ´
Θῶνις καὶ Φαῆσις ∠
Πετεσοῦχος Σοκμήνιος δ
Πετοσῖρις Ἀμεννέως ιαγ´
Ὧρος Πετῶτος ββ´
Θῶνις μέ(γας) Κεντίσιος ϛ
Πετεσοῦχος Παλομούνιος γ∠
Τεῶς Ὥρου δγ´
Πετεσοῦχος Ἰμούθου β∠
(γίνονται) ξδ∠d . . . λο(?) νθd, ἐλ( ) ε∠
Διδύμαρχος Ἀπολλωνίου β
⁄Μ̣ε̣λάνιππος α
Ἀπολλώνιος Πτολεμαίου ἔφο(δος) β
Σωσ̣ι̣κ̣λῆς Μεννείου β
Δημήτριος Ἡρακλείδου β
Π̣[τολε]μαίου τοῦ Πτολεμαίου β
Νο[υμ]ήνιος Μεννείου α
(γίνονται) ια

Col. III

Ὧρος Πετεχῶντος α
Λύκος Ζωπυρίωνος α
Ἀμεννεὺς Μαρρείους ∠
Κόττυος α
Πετεσοῦχος Ἁρυώτου β
Ἁρυώτης Ἀμεννέως ∠

Θέων Δημητρίου α
Μαρρῆς Πετοσίριος ∠
Τεῶς ἀδελφὸς α
Πετεσοῦχος Παalομούνιος ∠
Νίκων Ἀμεννέως α
Πετοσῖρις Ἀμεννέως ∠
Πετοσῖρις Ἁρκοίφιος καὶ οἱ μέ(τοχοι) α
Πετεσοῦχος Πακύρριος ∠
Πετῶς καὶ οἱ ἀδελ(φοὶ) α
Μαρρῆς Πακύρριος ∠
Χολῶς Cιcούχου ∠
Διόδωρος Κ̣οκκο̣ύλου α
Πνεφερῶς Ὥρου α
Πύρρος Cαραπίωνος ∠
⟦Δημήτριος Ἡρακλείδου α̣⟧
⟦ α̣⟧
⟦Ν̣ουμήνιος Μ̣ε̣ν̣ν̣ε̣ί̣ο̣υ̣ α̣⟧
⟦Ἀπολλώ̣ν̣ιο̣ς̣ . . . α̣⟧
Ὧρος Κολλούθου ∠
Θέων Πτολεμαίου ∠
Ἡλιόδωρος α
Πτόλλις Ὀρσείους ∠
Ἕρμων α
Ὧρος Ὥρου (ἑπτάρουρος) α
Ἁρσῦτμις ∠
Μεσταcῦ(τμις) Cοκέως ∠
Παπνεβτῦ(νις) Cοκέως ∠
Πευκέστης ∠
Ἀπολλώνιος Διοκλείους ∠
γεω(ργὸς) Μέλας Πετεσούχου α
Ὀρσενοῦφις θε⟨ο⟩ῦ ∠
Πετεσοκονοῦρις ∠
(γίνονται) κε∠

Col. IV recto

Δῶρος ∠
Θεαγένης α
Πύρριχος α
Πάτρων ∠
Φαῆσις Φίβιος α
Πετεσοῦχ̣[ο]ς̣ Σοκμή(νιος) ∠
Ἀθεμμεὺς α
Πετεσοῦχος Μικίωνος ∠̣
Κατῦτις α
Ἁρμαχόρος Ἁρμαχό̣(ρου) α
Φμούεις Παθήβιος ∠
η∠
Πετεσοῦχος Σωτηρίδου ∠
(γίνονται) θ, (γίνονται) λδ∠

The remaining 15 cm. of the column are blank.

Col. I verso

Ἁρμιῦσις Πετοσίριος Φα(ρμοῦθι) ιη̅ (πυροῦ) . .
Ἁρυώτης Φαή̣σιος Φα(ρμοῦθι) ιη̅ (πυροῦ) .
Ἁρμαχόρος Ἁρμαχό[ρ]ου Φα(ρμοῦθι) ιη̅ (πυροῦ) β
Ἁρμιῦσις Πετεσούχου ιη̅ (πυροῦ) ϛ́
Ἁρφαῆσις Ὀννώφριος Φα(ρμοῦθι) κζ̅ κ(ριθῆς) ∠γ́ιβ́
[Θ]ῶνις Ὀρσενούφ[ιο]ς Φα(ρμοῦθι) ιη̅ (πυροῦ) ϛ́
[Θ]ῶνις καὶ Φαῆ̣ς̣ι̣ς̣ [Φα(ρμοῦθι)] κ̣ζ̅ κ(ριθῆς) α
Θ̣ῶνις μι(κρὸς) Κεντίσιος Παχ(ὼν) ι̣δ (πυροῦ) γ́
[Κα]τῦ(τις) Κατύτιος Φα(ρμοῦθι) λ̣̅ (πυροῦ) α∠ κ(ριθῆς) α∠
[Κα]τ̣ῦ(τις) Σισούχου Παχ(ὼν) α̅ κ(ριθῆς) ∠γ́
[±5] Ὥρου Φα(ρμοῦθι) λ̅ (πυροῦ ?) [.] κ(ριθῆς) γ́ιβ́
[Πετ]ερμοῦθις Ὥρου Φα(ρμοῦθι) ιη̅ (πυροῦ) γ́ιβ́
[Παπ]νεβτῦ(νις) Σοκέως Φα(ρμοῦθι) ιγ̅ (πυροῦ) γ́ιβ́
[Π]ε̣τ̣ε̣ρμοῦθις Μαρρή(ους) Παχ(ὼν) κγ̅ (πυροῦ) β́
[Π]ε̣τ̣[ο]σῖρις Ἁρκοίφιος ιη̅ (πυροῦ) ∠γ́ιβ́
[Π]ετο̣σῖρις Ὥρου Φα(ρμοῦθι) ι̣η̅ (πυροῦ) ϛ́ λ̅ κ(ριθῆς) ∠γ́ιβ́
[Π]ετεσοῦχος Χεύ[ρ]ιος λ̣̅ (πυροῦ) ∠

[Π]ạᾶπις Πετοσίρ[ι]ος Φα(ρμοῦθι) κζ̄ κ(ριθῆς) β́
[Μ]αρρῆς Πακύρρịος ιη̄ (πυροῦ) ∠
[± 5]ις Χεύριος λ̄ (πυροῦ) ∠
[± 6] Πετεήσιος Παχ(ὼν) ιδ̄ (πυροῦ) ∠d
[Φαῆσι]ς Νεκτεṿίβιος κζ̄ (πυροῦ) ∠ιβ́
[± 6] Πετεσούχου [Π]αχ(ὼν) κε̄ (πυροῦ) ς́ κ(ριθῆς) αγ́
[± 6] Χεύριος Φ̣ạ(ρμοῦθι) ιη̄ (πυροῦ) γ́ιβ́
Χ̣ẹῦρịς Τεῶ(τος) κζ̄ κ(ριθῆς) ạ∠γ́
Παχ(ὼν) ᾱ (πυροῦ) .
['Οννῶ]φρịς Ὥρọụ Φα(ρμοῦθι) λ̄ (πυροῦ) β́
[Ὧρος] 'Ορσείους ιη̄ (πυροῦ) β́
[(γίνονται) (πυροῦ)] ịβ∠d κ(ριθῆς) θγ́ιβ́
[Θοτορ]ταῖος Πετοσί(ριος) (πυροῦ) γ́ιβ́

Col. II verso

'Απῦγχịς Πετεσούχọụ λ̄ κ(ριθῆς) αγ́
Ἁρμιῦσις Πετεύριος ιη̄ (πυροῦ) ∠ιβ́
⟦Θοτορταῖος Πετọσ̣ίṛιος λ̄ (πυροῦ) γ́ιβ́⟧
Πετεσọῦχος 'Ιμούθου ιη̄ (πυροῦ) γ́ιβ́
⟦Πετῶς Μαρρείους ιη̄ (πυροῦ) β́ λ̄ αγ́, (γίνονται) β⟧
Σοχώτης Παώπιος ιη̄ (πυροῦ) ∠
Φαῆσις Φίβιος ιη̄ (πυροῦ) ∠ιβ́
Χαιρήμων Πετοσίριος κζ̄ (πυροῦ) ∠
Μαρρῆς Πετεχῶ(ντος) (πυροῦ) αγ́
(γίνονται) (πυροῦ) ςγ́ ⟦β∠ιβ́⟧
(γίνονται ?) (πυροῦ ?) γγ́ κ̣(ριθῆς) αγ́
Ἁρμιῦσις Πετοσίριος Φ̣ạ(ρμοῦθι) ιη̄ (πυροῦ) γ́ιβ́
Μαρρῆς Μαρρείους κζ̄ (πυροῦ) ιβ́
'Οννῶφρις Πετεαρψενή(σιος) κζ̄ (πυροῦ) β́
'Ορσῆς 'Ορσείους κζ̄ (πυροῦ) ∠γ́
Κέντις Ὥρου ιη̄ (πυροῦ) β́ κζ̄ ∠γ́ιβ́, (γίνονται) α∠ιβ́
Πετεσοῦχος Σωτη(ρίδου) Παχ(ὼν) ιδ̄ (πυροῦ) β́
Πνεφερῶς Ὥρου ιη̄ (πυροῦ) β́ Παχ(ὼν) ᾱ κ(ριθῆς) γ́ιβ́
Τεῶς Ὥρου κζ̄ (πυροῦ) ∠γ́ιβ́
Φραμῆνις Πετοσίριος ιη̄ (πυροῦ) γ́

Φμέρcιc Cαρα(πίωνοc) Παχ(ὼν) ιδ (πυροῦ) d
Χολῶc Cιcούχου κζ̄ (πυροῦ) ∠
Χῦψιc Πετεcούχου κζ̄ (πυροῦ) β́
Ὧροc Κεντί(cιοc) κζ̄ (πυροῦ) ∠ιβ́
(γίνονται) (πυροῦ) ηϛ́ κ(ριθῆc) γ́ιβ́

Blank space the width of one column (17 cm.).

Col. III verso

δα(νείων) (πυροῦ) (ἑξα)χ(οινίκωι) Φαρμοῦθι ιη̄
Φραμῆνιc Πετοcί(ριοc) (πυροῦ) εγ́
Ἁρμιῦcιc Πετοcί(ριοc) (πυροῦ) β
Ἁρυώτηc Φαήcιοc (πυροῦ) γ
(γίνονται) (πυροῦ) ιγ̣̄
κζ̄ Μαρρῆc Μαρρείουc [
Ὀννῶ(φριc) Πετεαρψενή(cιοc) [
Φαῆcιc Νεκτενίβιοc [
(γίνονται) η̣̄
Παχ(ὼν) ιδ
Ἡράκλειοc Πετάλο̣υ̣ [
Παλομούνιοc Ὥρου [
Φαῆcιc Πετοcί(ριοc) [
(γίνονται) κᾱ̣
κγ̄ Μεcταcῦ(τμιc) Πετεcού̣[*χου*
κε̄ Ἁρφαῆcιc Πετε̣c̣[*ούχου*
Μεcταcῦ(τμιc) Πετεc[*ούχου*
(γίνονται) ιβ́∠, (γίνονται) κ[
κζ̄ Πετοcῖριc Πετοcί(ριοc) [
Μεcταcῦ(τμιc) Πετεcού(χου) [
*(γίνονται) δ́*d
κθ̄ Ἁρβῆχιc Ἑργέ(ωc) (πυροῦ) ε̣ φ[*α(κοῦ) ι*]
[*Ὀ*]*ννῶ(φριc) Πετεαρψενή(cιοc) φα(κοῦ) β*
(γίνονται) (πυροῦ) ε φα(κοῦ) ι̣β̣
λ̄ Ἁρφαῆcιc Πετοcίρ⟨ι⟩οc ∠ιβ́

48 *τ* in *Δημητρίου* corrected   59 *α* corrected from ∠   66 ∠ corrected from *α*   78 l. *θεόc*
91 ∠ corrected from *α*   134 *β* corrected from ∠

1 Reference unclear.

2 *Φανήσιος*: the only offspring of a Phanesis known in the archive are two machimoi, the elder and younger Pasos.

9]ϛίωνος: the doubtful ϲ might be π.

13 *Μάρων Πετο*]ϛί(ριος) κά(τοικος): for the various ways of naming this individual see vol. 1, pp. 546–7. He is called κά(τοικος) here to distinguish him from a machimos of the same name, **1139**. 53.

16 The traces after λο(ιπαί) are [illegible]. This might mean ἐγ λό(γου), but the final letters can be interpreted as ολ( ) as easily as λο( ). The puzzling word in 33 is different.

17]∠d: perhaps ρμη]∠d, the difference between the total 149⅛ in l. 16 and the $\frac{5}{12}$ which is there called πλ(είω). However this may be, the line is not to be connected with what follows; cf. next note.

33 ξδ∠d: totals lines 18–32.

. . . λο(?): the papyrus has [illegible]. For ἐλ( ) see **1103**. 295 n.

34–41 This list is separated from the foregoing by a blank space sufficient for one line, and the marginal stroke also is apparently meant to mark a fresh beginning.

36 ἔφο(δος): added to distinguish this man from a catoec of the same name.

41 ια: right was 12.

65 The traces after Ἀπολλώνιος may be Πτο(λεμαίου).

78 θε⟨ο⟩ῦ: the false genitive was no doubt inspired by the nearby patronymics.

80 κε∠: correct.

92 η∠: totals ll. 81–91.

94 Both totals correct.

105 Presumably not Kentis or Teos, since these persons are found in ll. 140 and 143 below. Ilos or Pasis would do.

114 The possible supplements are [*Χεῦρ*]ις and [*Τεεφῖβ*]ις. If the apparent alphabetization of the column was carried out strictly, only the latter can be right.

116 [*Φαῆσι*]ϲ: other names with the patronymic Nektenibis are too long for the lacuna.

117 Probably not Chypsis son of Petesouchos, since he is found in l. 147.

118 Cf. 114 n. Alphabetization here would call for [*Χεῦρις*].

122 [*Ὧρος*]: because the alternative, *Ὀρσῆς*, occurs in l. 139.

123 The total for wheat cannot be verified because of the loss of several entries. That for barley is correct.

134–5 The totals are very confused. 6⅓ is correct for wheat, including the amounts that were cancelled; 2$\frac{7}{12}$ looks like a mistake for 2$\frac{5}{12}$, the sum of lines 127 and 129. Then the revised total in l. 135 would be the difference between 6⅓ and 2$\frac{7}{12}$, but this should be 3¾ rather than 3⅓. The figure for barley is correct, repeated from l. 125.

149 Totals lines 136–48.

1145. Tax Account

P. Teb. 145v 113/99 B.C.

The following short text, written on the back of **1115** Col. 1, is included because of its resemblance to **1144**. 34–41. It is followed by an account concerning workmen, written in a second hand and dated to year 15 (of Ptolemy Alexander, 100/99 B.C.). The latter has no apparent connection with the Kerkeosiris tax documents and is not reproduced here.

1145 records payments of 1, 1½ and 2 artabs from cleruchs of varying status, as well as ½ art. from an Orsenouphis shrine. The purpose of the payments, and the relation between the quantities paid and the rank of the cleruchs, remain unclear. But as several of the persons involved make identical payments in **1144**. 34–41, there can be little doubt that some variety of recurring impost is involved.

ἄλλων
Ἀπολλωνίου ἐφόδ[ο]υ β
Νουμήνιος Μεννείου α
Ὀρσενουφιείου ∠
Ἀφθονήτου α∠
Διοδότου τοῦ Ἀπολλω(νίου) β
Διδύμαρχος Ἀπολλωνίου β
θ

2 A dot above the φ of ἐφόδου may be either a check mark or a raised ο representing an initial plan to abbreviate the word as ἐφό(δου). For the size of the payment cf. **1144**. 36.

3 Cf. **1144**. 40.

4 Cf. **98**. 32, **1146**. 35, **1149**. 55.

5 Aphthonetos is presumably the 70-aroura cleruch, son of Hebdomion. If so, it is striking that his payment is smaller than that required from persons with far inferior holdings; but it is not certain that this charge was levied against cleruchic land as such.

7 Cf. **1144**. 34.

1146. Grain Account

P. Teb. 116r 38 × 30 cm. 115/113 B.C.

Two columns from a daybook recording payments of various kinds, but chiefly ἡμιαρτάβιον on cleruchs and shrines. Cleroi held by ἑπτάρουροι μάχιμοι are reckoned at 7 arouras, giving a tax of 3½ artabs; and two εἰκοσιάρουροι pay 10¼ art. as if for cleroi of 20½ arouras, although one of the men (l. 14) in fact held only 15 or 16½ arouras in Kerkeosiris; see p. 11. Two payments by shrines (35 and 36) would meet the full assessment of ἡμιαρτάβιον based on the true area of their land; in 29 f. ⅚ artab of wheat received from an Ibis shrine cannot be more than an instalment on the full dues, if it is intended for ἡμιαρτάβιον at all.

The presence of Thoteus son of Orses and Teos the younger, son of Petechon (14, 18) shows that the text was written after 116/115, when the predecessors of these men were still active (**1110**. 150 and 184). A terminus ante quem is supplied by Sokonopis son of Pasis (23), who was replaced by 113/112 (**1147**. 153).

Concerning the ἡμιαρτάβιον in general, see p. 11 and note 2 below.

Vestiges of a column to the left; then:

Col. I

῾Ωροϲ Π[ετεϲ]ο̣ύχου η
(ἡμιαρταβίου) (ἑπταρούρων) Χο(μήνιοϲ) ᾿Ονν̣ῶ̣φρ̣ιϲ Μεϲταϲύ(τμιοϲ) (πυροῦ) γ∠
(ἡμιαρταβίου) ῾Αρμιῦ[ϲιϲ] Πετεϲούχου (πυροῦ) γ∠
Πεϲύθηϲ Π̣α̣χῶτοϲ (πυροῦ) γ∠
῾Αρψάλιϲ [Cτε]φάνου (πυροῦ) γ∠
Θοτεὺϲ Φολήμιοϲ (πυροῦ) γ∠
Ψενῆϲιϲ Cτεφάνου (πυροῦ) γ∠
Φατρῆϲ ῟Ωρου (πυροῦ) γ∠
᾿Αμοῦ[ν]ι[ϲ Τε]φ[ν]ά̣χθ̣ι̣[ο]ϲ (πυροῦ) γ∠
Πτολεμαῖοϲ Cενθέωϲ (πυροῦ) α∠
῾Αροννῶφριϲ ῟Ωρου (πυροῦ) γ∠
Παῶπιϲ Πετεϲούχου (πυροῦ) γ∠
᾿Απῦγχιϲ Ποώριοϲ (πυροῦ) γ∠
(ἡμιαρταβίου) Θοτεὺϲ ᾿Ορϲείου[ϲ ο]ὗ τ̣ὸ̣ λ̣ο̣(ιπὸν) τοῦ
κλή(ρου) περὶ Τεβτῦ(νιν) (πυροῦ) ιd
(ἡμιαρταβίου) (ἑπταρούρων) Κολλούθηϲ ῟Ωρου τὸ ἐν θέ(ματι) αὐ(τοῦ) (πυροῦ) γ ∠
θέμα(τοϲ) ῾Ηρακλείουϲ Cαρα(   ) (πυροῦ) ε
Τεῶϲ μι(κρὸϲ) Πετεχῶντοϲ (πυροῦ) γ∠
Φολῆμιϲ Νεκτενίβιοϲ (πυροῦ) γ∠

Col. II

῾Ωροϲ Θοτορταίου ἀπὸ θέ(ματοϲ) ῾Ηλι(οδώρου ?) (πυροῦ) γ∠
Νεκτενῖβιϲ ῟Ωρου ἀπὸ θέ(ματοϲ) ῾Ηλι(οδώρου ?) (πυροῦ) γ∠
Πᾶϲιϲ Cοκονώπιοϲ (πυροῦ) γ∠
Cοκονῶπιϲ Πάϲιτοϲ (πυροῦ) γ∠
Μεϲταϲῦτμιϲ ῟Ωρου (πυροῦ) γ∠
῾Αρμιῦϲιϲ Cοκονώπιοϲ (πυροῦ ?) γ∠
῾Αρμιῦϲιϲ Φατρείουϲ ἀπὸ θέ(ματοϲ) ῟Ωρου (πυροῦ) ιd
ὁ αὐ(τὸϲ) (πυροῦ) θ (ὧν) μιϲ(θώϲεωϲ) ε
θ[έ]μα(τοϲ) Μελανίππου (πυροῦ) δ
᾿Ιβιῶ(ν) δ[ι'] ῾Εργέωϲ καὶ τῶν με(τόχων) α∠γ́ (ὧν)
μι(ϲθώϲεωϲ) α   λο(ιπὸν) ∠γ́
Φθαῦϲ Πετεήϲιοϲ (πυροῦ) γ∠
῾Αρυώτηϲ ῾Αρυώτου (πυροῦ) γ∠

(γίνονται) τῆϲ ἡμέ(ραϲ) (πυροῦ) {(ὧν)} (ὧν) (ἡμιαρταβίου)
λο(ιπαὶ) μ̣ιϲ(θώϲεωϲ) ιη
ἐλ(αϲϲόνων) ἱερῶν Ὀρϲενοῦφιϲ θε(όϲ) ∠
Ἰβιῶ(ν) διὰ Πνεφερῶτοϲ β∠
Δημήτριοϲ Ϲ̣ε̣νθέωϲ (πυροῦ) εἰϲδε(ξίμωι) κε
Ἁρμιῦ̣ϲ̣ιϲ Ϲενθε̣ώ̣ϲ̣ καὶ οἱ μέ(τοχοι) (πυροῦ) εἰϲδε(ξίμωι) ιη
] (ἡμιαρταβίου) γ, λο(ιπαὶ) μ̣[ιϲ(θώϲεωϲ)

Remnants of a further column to the right.

2 (ἡμιαρταβίου): for the expansion of the symbol ∟ ō see **768**. 4 n. Other references to the charge are **36**. 9; **61**(b). 323; **64**(a). 80, 121, 141; **89**. 48, 76; **98**. 27, 47; **124**. 44; **135**; **768**. 4, 6; **1049**. 30; **1148**. 7; **1149** *passim*; cf. **1150**. 8; P. Reinach 9 *bis* 9; O. Thebes 11, 13, 16; O. Tait 192, 193, 197, 220, A7; COP 53. 14, 53 *ter* 13; WO 702, 704, 1341, 1527. Cf. Packman, *Taxes* 30 ff. and pp. 11ff. above. See also **1147**. 77 n.

10 α∠: a payment of $\frac{1}{2}$ art./ar. on the 3 arouras this man held at Kerkeosiris. The remainder of his cleros was in Areos Kome.

14–15 ιd: Thoteus succeeded to the cleros of Teos son of Teos, of which only 15 arouras were located in Kerkeosiris, though the addition of a διάφορον ϲχοινιϲμοῦ brought them to $16\frac{1}{2}$ (p. 11). By analogy with the case of Ptolemaios son of Sentheus (preceding note), one would expect ἡμιαρτάβιον to be paid only on land within the jurisdiction of Kerkeosiris: that should yield $8\frac{1}{4}$ artabs rather than $10\frac{1}{4}$. But in **98**. 70 too Thoteus is booked for $20\frac{1}{2}$ taxable arouras.

ο]ὗ τ̣ὸ̣ λ̣ο̣(ιπὸν) τοῦ κλή(ρου) περὶ Τεβτῦ(νιν): cf. **98**. 70. The editors' note there is incorrect in supposing that this phrase 'is out of place and should refer to Phmersis in l. 72'. Both men held part of their cleroi near Tebtunis; the scribe of **98** simply forgot to repeat the information for Phmersis.

16 τὸ ἐν θέ(ματι) αὐ(τοῦ): i.e., grain to pay the tax was transferred from Kollouthes' private deposit at the granary, rather than being delivered directly in kind.

17 θέμα(τοϲ) Ἡρακλείουϲ: a further payment of Kollouthes, to be credited to the account of Herakles (unknown elsewhere).

20–1 ἀπὸ θέ(ματοϲ) Ἡλι(οδώρου?): no other expansion than Ἡλι(οδώρου) will yield a name found elsewhere in these papers; cf. perhaps **91**. 24. The reason why a tax for these men should be paid from Heliodoros' account does not appear, any more than the reason why one Horos should pay for Harmiysis son of Phatres in l. 26.

26 Harmiysis is a 20-aroura hippeus. The first entry is for ἡμιαρτάβιον paid for him by Horos; then 5 art. paid by Harmiysis himself are credited to dues on Crown land rented apart from his cleros, and 4 more artabs are deposited to the account of Melanippos.

30 μι(ϲθώϲεωϲ): i.e. as payment for Crown land rented by the ibis shrine to supplement its income. The remaining $\frac{5}{8}$ art. may be ἡμιαρτάβιον, but if so it was only an instalment, since this shrine had 4 arouras, on which 2 art. were due (**98**. 36).

33 The figures which should have followed (πυροῦ) and (ἡμιαρταβίου) were never filled in.

39 (ἡμιαρταβίου) γ: refers to the payments in lines 35–6. The figure after μ̣[ιϲ(θώϲεωϲ) will have been μγ, if the doubtful number in l. 38 is rightly read.

1147. Tax List

P. Teb. 98. 77–118+245 +247 (UC 2513) — **245**: 32 × 31 cm. **98**+**245**: 114 × 31 cm. — 113/112 B.C.

The papyrus described as **245** in fact contains the concluding three columns of **98**, to which it can be physically joined; and a small fragment catalogued as part of **247**, with a few letters from ll. 141–8 below, also belongs to this text. We reprint here lines 77–118 of **98** with some improved readings, and continue the line numeration into **245**.

On the nature of the document as a whole, see **98** introd. The five columns printed here are concerned with the impost of ¾ artab/aroura levied on *ἑπτάρουροι μάχιμοι* (77–188) and with three catoecic cavalrymen whose *ἀρταβιεία* Menches had agreed to pay if they themselves defaulted (189–97). This undertaking of Menches is referred to also in **75**. 4 ff., where we learn that official uneasiness over the ability of these catoecs to pay their artabieia had arisen when it was learned that their cleroi had become completely unproductive: *τῶν ὑπογεγρ(αμμένων) κλήρων ὄντων ἐν ὑπολό(γωι) διὰ τῆς τοῦ ε (ἔτους) κατὰ φύλλον γεωμετρίας, ἀναδέχομαι πόρον δώcειν τῆς (ἀρταβιείας) τοῦ αὐτοῦ (ἔτους) ἢ μετρήcειν ἐκ τοῦ ἰδίου.* Since the three catoecs and one ephodos whose names follow this heading in **75** are those cited in the present papyrus (**98**. 44 and **1147**. 189 ff.), there can be little if any doubt that both texts refer to the same event of the same year 5, 113/112 B.C.

The text exhibits three hands: the first listed taxpayers together with the sum due from each, leaving space beneath each name to enter payments when made; the second wrote in payments for Pachon and Payni, and the third recorded the single payment in Epeiph (161). Double lines as checking strokes were added by an uncertain hand to indicate completed payments.

The tax due from machimoi was with few exceptions paid in two instalments, one of 3½ artabs on the last of Pachon or early in Payni, and one of 1¾ art. late in Payni. This impost, here called *τὸ (ἥμιcυ) (τέταρτον)*, is discussed on pp. 11 ff.; cf. **1146**. 2 n. and below, n. to l. 77. All data for the catoecs of ll. 189 ff. have been lost.

98. 77 (ἑπταρούρων) ὧν τὸ (ἥμιcυ) (τέταρτον)
Πορεγέβθιc Ἀπύγχιοc εd (ὧν) με(τρηθεῖcαι)
Παχ(ὼν) λ̄ (πυροῦ) γ∠, Παῦ(νι) ιζ α∠d, (γίνονται) εd
Ὧροc Ὥρου εd
με(τρηθεῖcαι) Παῦ(νι) η̄ (πυροῦ) γ∠, ιθ α∠d, (γίνονται) εd
Ὧροc Θοτορταίου εd
με(τ.) Παῦ(νι) β̄ (πυροῦ) γ∠, ιθ α∠d, (γίνονται) εd
Ἁρχῦψιc Πετοcίριοc εd
με(τ.) Παῦ(νι) η̄ (πυροῦ) γ∠

// Πετεσοῦχος Τεῶτος ϵd (ὧν) μϵ(τ.)
Παχ(ὼν) λ̄ (πυροῦ) γ∠, Παῦ(νι) ιθ̄ α∠d, (γίνονται) ϵd
// Κανῶς Πετοσίριος ϵd
μϵ(τ.) Παῦ(νι) ιγ̄ (πυροῦ) γ∠, ιθ̄ α∠d, (γίνονται) ϵd
Ἁρσῦτμις Πετοσίριος ϵd
μϵ(τ.) Παῦ(νι) ζ̄ (πυροῦ) γd, η̄ d, (γίνονται) γ∠

98, Col. VI

// Ἁρς[ενθ]εὺς Σιεφμοῦτος ϵd
μϵ(τ.) Παῦ(νι) ιθ̄ (πυροῦ) ϵd
Ἁρψῆθις Κολλούθου ϵd
Παῦ(νι) ιθ̄ α∠d
// Πετεσοῦχος Τοθοείους ϵd
μϵ(τ.) Παῦ(νι) ζ̄ (πυροῦ) γ∠, ιθ̄ α∠d, (γίνονται) ϵd
// Ὧρος Φαγώμιος ϵd (ὧν) μϵ(τ.)
μϵ(τ.) Παχ(ὼν) λ̄ (πυροῦ) γ∠, Παῦ(νι) ιζ̄ α∠d, (γίνονται) ϵd
// Φατρῆς Ὥρου ϵd
μϵ(τ.) Παῦ(νι) β̄ (πυροῦ) γ∠, ιθ̄ α∠d, (γίνονται) ϵd
// Μεστασῦτμις Ὥρου ϵd
μϵ(τ.) Παῦ(νι) β̄ (πυροῦ) γ∠, ιθ̄ α∠d, (γίνονται) ϵd
Φαεὺς Σοκέως ϵd
μϵ(τ.) Παῦ(νι) ζ̄ (πυροῦ) γ∠
// Θοτεὺς Φολήμιος ϵd
μϵ(τ.) Παῦ(νι) β̄ (πυροῦ) γ∠, ιθ̄ α∠d, (γίνονται) ϵd
// Μαρρῆς Πακούρριος ϵd
μϵ(τ.) Παῦ(νι) β̄ (πυροῦ) γ∠, ιγ̄ α∠d, (γίνονται) ϵd
// Ἁρμιῦσις Σοκονώπιος ϵd
μϵ(τ.) Παῦ(νι) β̄ (πυροῦ) γ∠, ιζ̄ α∠d, (γίνονται) ϵd
Τεῶς Τεῶτος ϵd
// Πᾶσις μι(κρὸς) Καλατύτιος ϵd
μϵ(τ.) Παῦ(νι) ιθ̄ (πυροῦ) ϵd
// Πᾶσις μέ(γας) Καλατύτιος ϵd
μϵ(τ.) Παῦ(νι) ιθ̄ (πυροῦ) ϵd
// Νεκτενῖβις Ὥρου ϵd
μϵ(τ.) Παῦ(νι) β̄ (πυροῦ) γ∠, ιθ̄ α∠d, (γίνονται) ϵd

245, Col. I = **98**, Col. VII

Φολῆμις Νεκτενίβιος εd
// *με(τ.) Παῦ(νι) β̄ (πυροῦ) γ∠, ιθ̄ α∠*d, (*γίνονται*) εd
᾿Απῦγχις Ποώριος εd
// *με(τ.) Παῦ(νι) β̄ (πυροῦ) γ∠, ιθ̄ α∠*d, (*γίνονται*) εd
Κολλούθης ῞Ωρου εd
// *με(τ.) Παῦ(νι) β̄ (πυροῦ) γ∠, ιθ̄ α∠*d, (*γίνονται*) εd
῞Υλλος Πάι[το]ς εd
// *με(τ.) Παῦ(νι)* [̣] (*πυροῦ* ?) *γ∠*, [. *α∠*d], (*γίνονται*) εd
῾Αρφαῆσις ῞Ωρου εd
με(τ.) Παῦ(νι) η̄ (πυροῦ) γ∠, ιθ̄ (πυροῦ) αϛ´
Κολλούθης Πετοςίριος εd
[*με(τ.)*] *Παῦ(νι) ιθ̄ α∠*d
᾿Ονν̣ῶφρις Πετερμούθιος εd
// *με(τ.) Παῦ(νι) η̄ (πυροῦ) γ∠, ιθ̄ α∠*d, (*γίνονται*) εd
Τεῶς μι(κρὸς) Πετεχῶντος εd
με(τ.) Παῦ(νι) β̄ (πυροῦ) γ∠
᾿Αμοῦνις Τεφνάχθιος εd
// *με(τ.) Παῦ(νι) β̄ (πυροῦ) γ∠, Παῦ(νι) η̄ α∠*d, (*γίνονται*) εd
῾Ạ[ρυ]ώτης ῾Αρυώτου εd
// [*με(τ.)*] *Παῦ(νι) β̄ (πυροῦ) γ∠, ιθ̄ α∠*d, (*γίνονται*) εd
[*Χεῦρ*]*ις Σοχώτου* εd
// [*με(τ.) Παῦ(νι)*] *ζ̄ (πυροῦ) γ∠, ιθ̣̄ α∠*d, (*γίνονται*) εd
᾿Ạρ̣χ[ίβ]ιος ῞Ω[ρου] εd
// *με(τ.) Παῦ(νι) η̄ (πυροῦ) γ∠, ιθ̄ α∠*d, (*γίνονται*) εd
Πᾶσις Σοκονώπιος εd
// *με(τ.) Παῦ(νι) β̄ (πυροῦ) γ∠, ιθ̄ α∠*d, (*γίνονται*) εd
᾿Οννῶφρις Μεστασύτμιος εd
// *με(τ.) Παῦ(νι) β̄ (πυροῦ) γ∠, ιθ̄ α∠*d, (*γίνονται*) ε̣d
Πτολεμαῖ[ος] Σ̣ενθέως βd
// *με(τ.) Παῦ(νι) θ̄ (πυροῦ) α∠, ιθ̄ ∠γ´*, (*γίνονται*) *βγ´*

245, Col. II = **98**, Col. VIII

῟Ωρος Παώπ[ιος] εd
// *με(τ.) Παῦ(νι) ιθ̄ (πυροῦ)* εd

Πεςύθης Παχῶτος ϵd
μϵ(τ.) Παῦ(νι) β̄ (πυροῦ) γ∠, ιθ̄ α∠d, (γίνονται) ϵd
Μαρρῆς ʽΑράπιος τὸν (πρότερον) Coκον⟨ώ⟩πιος
τοῦ Πάςιτος ϵd
μϵ(τ.) Παῦ(νι) β̄ (πυροῦ) γ∠, κ̄ α∠d, (γίνονται) ϵd
Παςῶς μι(κρὸς) Φανήςιος ϵd
μϵ(τ.) Παῦ(νι) η̄ (πυροῦ) γ∠, ιθ̄ α∠d, (γίνονται) ϵd
Παςῶς ʼΟρςείους ϵd
μϵ(τ.) Παῦ(νι) η̄ [(πυροῦ) γ]∠, ιθ̄ α∠d, (γίνονται) ϵd
Πετεςοῦχος Πετεςούχου ϵd
μϵ(τ.) Παῦ(νι) η̄ [(πυροῦ) γ∠], (m. 3) ʼΕπεὶφ ϛ̄ α∠d, (γίνονται) ϵd
ʼΟρςῆς ʽΑροννήςιος [ϵd]
μϵ(τ.) Παῦ(νι) ζ̣̄ (πυροῦ) γ∠, ιθ̄ α∠d, (γίνονται) [ϵd]
Φθαῦς Πετεήςιος ϵd
μϵ(τ.) Παῦ(νι) β̄ (πυροῦ) γ∠, ιθ̄ α∠d, (γίνονται) ϵd
ʽΑρμιῦςις Πετεςούχου ϵd
μϵ(τ.) Παῦ(νι) β̄ (πυροῦ) γ∠, ιθ̄ α∠d, (γίνονται) ϵd
Παςῶς μέ(γας) Φανήςιος ϵd
μϵ(τ.) Παῦ(νι) ζ̄ (πυροῦ) γ∠, ι̣θ̣̄ α∠d, (γίνονται) ϵd
καὶ τ[ῶν] δι᾽ ῞Ωρου
Μαρρῆς̣ Παάπιος ϵd
μϵ(τ.) [Παῦ(νι) ̄. (πυροῦ) γ∠, ̄.] α∠d, (γίνονται) ϵd
ʽΑροννῶ̣φρις ῞Ωρου ϵd
μϵ(τ.) Π̣α̣ῦ̣(νι) [̄.] (πυροῦ) γ∠̣, κ̣̄ α∠d, (γίνονται) ϵd
ʽΑρμάις Πανορςείους ϵd
μϵ(τ.) Πα[ῦ(νι)] η̄ (πυροῦ) γ∠, κ̄ α∠d, (γίνονται) ϵd

245, Col. III = **98**, Col. IX

Πεχῦςις Κόμωνος ϵd
μϵ(τ.) Παῦ(νι) η̄ (πυροῦ) γ∠
Κολλούθης ῞Ωρου τὸν (πρότερον) [ϵ]ḍ
Λαβόιτος
μϵ(τ.) Παῦ(νι) ιγ̄ (πυροῦ) ϵd
Παῶπις Πετεςούχ[ου ϵd]
μϵ(τ.) Παῦ(νι) η̄ (πυροῦ) γ∠, κ̄ α∠d, (γίνονται) ϵd

// Ἁρψάλις Στ̣[ε]φάνου εd
μέ(τ.) Πα̣ῦ(νι) β̄ (πυροῦ ?) γ∠, ιθ̄ α∠d, (γίνονται) εd
// Ψενῆσις Στεφάνου [εd]
μέ(τ.) Παῦ(νι) β̄ [(πυροῦ) γ∠], ̄ α∠d, (γίνονται) εd
(γίνονται) Σπ∠, (γίνονται) μαχί(μων) υ

(*c*. 2 cm. blank)

καὶ ὧν ἀναδέδεγμαι τῶν
κατοίκων ἱ̣π̣π̣έ̣ων
Πολέμωνος τοῦ Ἀμ[μωνίου
[
Ἀσκλη[πιάδου τοῦ Πτολεμαίου
[
Μάρων[ος τοῦ Διονυσίου
μέ(τ.) [
(γίνονται) [

Remainder blank.

77 τὸ (ἥμισυ) (τέταρτον): a tax of $\frac{3}{4}$ art./ar. collected from ἑπτάρουροι μάχιμοι, whose cleroi are reckoned at 7 arouras rather than the $6\frac{1}{2}$ entered in land lists. See pp. 11 ff. for a brief history of the charge, which despite its rate was usually called ἡμιαρτάβιον. On that parallel, one might expect the form (ἡμιτεταρταρτάβιον) here (cf. P. Ryl. II, p. 316 n. 1 and **346**. 5 n.); but no artab sign was written here and the name (ἥμισυ) (τέταρτον) apparently recurs in WO 1529. Cf. Packman, *Taxes* 30 ff.

92 Ἁρσ[ενθ]εὺς: not read in *editio princeps*.

147 βd: correct for the 3 arouras this man held at Kerkeosiris. The rest of his cleros was at Areos Kome.

148 βγ́: no explanation for the overpayment of $\frac{1}{12}$ art. suggests itself to me.

188 Σπ∠: this is the correct total of the dues required, not of those actually paid.

(γίνονται) μαχί(μων) υ: obscure. The total of dues from ἑπτάρουροι plus those of the τριακοντάρουρος and εἰκοσιάρουροι (**98**. 76) would be $406\frac{3}{4}$.

189 καὶ ὧν ἀναδέδεγμαι: see the passage from **75** quoted in introd., from which it appears that the charge Menches guaranteed was ἀρταβιεία; cf. **98**. 27 n.

1148. Grain Account

P. Teb. 218 | 17 × 28 cm. | 113/112 B.C. or later

A list of grain payments for various purposes. The ἡμιαρτάβιον on machimoi is calculated at $\frac{3}{4}$ art./ar., a rate which apparently went into effect in year 5 of Soter II, 113/112 B.C.; cf. p. 11.

Top lost.

Παπνεβτῦ(νις) Σοκέως (πυροῦ) ιη∠
ϛπο(   ) αβ̸ κα(θάρσεως) ∠γ́, (γίνονται) β⟨∠⟩
λο(ιπαὶ) ιϛ∠

/Πᾶσις Σοκονώπιος ἀπὸ θέ(ματος) Θέω(νος) (πυροῦ) δ
/Πεσύθης Παχῶτος (πυροῦ) εγ́
(γίνονται) λγϛ́

(ἡμιαρταβίου) (ἑπταρούρων) Χο(μήνιος) /Πετεσοῦχος Πετεσούχου εd
/Τεῶς Τεῶτος εd
/Κολλούθης Ὥρου εd
/Ἁρχῦψις Πετοσίριος εd
/⟦Πασῶς Ὀρσείους ἀπὸ θέ(ματος) Μεγχε(ίους) Πε(τεσούχου ?) ε ⟧
/Παῶπις Πετεσούχου εd
/Ὧρος Ἰναρῶτος ἃς Τε(ῶς ?) (πυροῦ) η
Πετεσοκονοῦρις Κεφάλωνος φα(κοῦ) ι (ὧν)
..( ) δ
Μεστασῦ(τμις) Πετεσού(χου) .... ⟦ϛ⟧ `δβ́'
[   ] αγ́

1 ιη∠: the traces after ι are completely illegible and may not be ink. The text reading is the total of 2 from l. 2 (though that is a mistake for 2½), and 16½ from l. 3.

2 ϛπο( ): the same group of letters usually means σπό(ρος) or σπό(ριμος), but neither of these makes sense here. But the sigma is oddly formed and ἀσπό(ρου) may be meant; cf. **172**.

4 (πυροῦ) δ: Pasis was a machimos. The size of payment suggests dues on ¾ aroura of Crown land rented at 5⅓ art./ar.; cf. p. 8. The amount of Crown land rented by this individual varied: in **98**. 13 he is booked with 1 aroura, in **1120**. 25 with ½.

5 εγ́: probably the rental of 1 aroura of Crown land; cf. last note and **98**. 20.

11 Μεγχε(ίους) Πε(τεσούχου?): the komogrammateus, if the expansion is right.

15–17 The figures add up to the 10 artabs of l. 14.

15 Before δ read probably αὐ(τός).

1149. Account of Payments in Kind

P. Teb. 232 — **232**: 10 × 27 cm. **91** + **232**: 25 × 30 cm. — After 113/112 B.C.

The papyrus described as **232** constitutes the lower portion of the unpublished second column of **91**. We print here the whole of that column from the combined texts, continuing the line numeration of **91**. From l. 29, the document lists persons and shrines paying the *ἡμιαρτάβιον* tax; in the case of shrines, additional payments are made for *εἰcφορά*: cf. pp. 11 ff., 14.

Line 53 shows Petesouchos (son of Pakyrris) farming the *ἱερὰ γῆ* of the god Petesouchos. This text will therefore be later than **98**. 30 (113/112 B.C.), where Petesouchos' brother Marres is still in charge of that land. Col. I of **91** deals with the revenues of two days, the 19th and 20th of an unspecified month, and concludes with a summary of receipts on the 20th. One might therefore expect this second column to refer to the 21st or a later day, but no indication is preserved.

= **91**, 27

Πετεcοῦ[χοc
Δημή[τριοc
(ἡμιαρταβίου) Κολλο[ύθηc *(πυροῦ)* ϵd]
(ἡμιαρταβίου) Ὧροc [*(πυροῦ)* ϵd]
(ἡμιαρταβίου) Ὧροc [*(πυροῦ)* ϵd]
(ἡμιαρταβίου) Πετεcοῦχ[οc *(πυροῦ)* ϵd]
(ἡμιαρταβίου) Πᾶcιc μέ(γαc) [Καλατύτιοc (πυροῦ) ϵd]
(ἡμιαρταβίου) Πᾶcι[c Cοκονώπιοc (πυροῦ) ϵd]
[(ἡμιαρταβίου)
(ἡμιαρταβίου) Φατρῆ̣ϲ̣ [Ὥρ]ου (πυροῦ ?) ϵd
(ἡμιαρταβίου) Θοτεὺc [Φολή]μιοc (πυροῦ) ϵd
(ἡμιαρταβίου) Ψενῆ(cιc) Cτε[φά(νου)] (πυροῦ) ϵ̣ḍ
(ἡμιαρταβίου) Ἀρψάλιc Cτ̣[εφ]ά(νου) (πυροῦ) ϵd
(ἡμιαρταβίου) Ἀμοῦνιc [Τεφ]ν̣άχθιοc (πυροῦ) ϵd
(ἡμιαρταβίου) Πετεcοῦ(χοc) Τοθοή(ουc) (πυροῦ) ϵd
(ἡμιαρταβίου) Ἁρcῦτμιc Πετοcίριοc (πυροῦ) ϵd
(ἡμιαρταβίου) Ἁροννῶ(φριc) [Ὥρο]υ (πυροῦ) ϵd
(ἡμιαρταβίου) Πτο̣λ̣ε̣μ̣α̣[ῖοc Cεν]θέ(ωc) (πυροῦ) β∠
(ἡμιαρταβίου) Ὧροc Ὥρου (πυροῦ) ϵ̣d
(ἡμιαρταβίου) Πορεγέβθιc Ἀπύγχιοc (πυροῦ) ϵd
(ἡμιαρταβίου) Ὧροc {.} Φαγώμιοc (πυροῦ) ϵd
(ἡμιαρταβίου) Ἀκουcίλαοc Ἀπολλω(νίου) φυ(λακίτηc) (πυροῦ) ϵ
(ἡμιαρταβίου) Τεῶc μι(κρὸc) Πετεχῶ(ντοc) (πυροῦ) ϵd
(ἡμιαρταβίου) Ὧροc Θοτορ[ταίο]υ (πυροῦ) ϵd
(ἡμιαρταβίου) Φολῆμιc Νεκτενίβιοc (πυροῦ) ϵd
(ἡμιαρταβίου) Πᾶcιc μι(κρὸc) Καλατύτιοc ϵd
(ἡμιαρταβίου) Πετεcοῦ(χοc) θε(ὸc) διὰ Πετεcού(χου) (πυροῦ) ββ́

καὶ εἰcφορᾶc β∠d, (γίνονται) εγίβ
(ἡμιαρταβίου) Ὀρcενοῦφιc θε(όc) ∠
καὶ εἰcφορᾶc ∠, (γίνεται) α
[(ἡμιαρταβίου)] ἰβίω(ν) τροφῆc διὰ Χε(ύριοc) καὶ τῶν ἀδελ(φῶν) β∠
εἰ̣ς̣φο̣(ρᾶc) . , (γίνονται) .
[(ἡμιαρταβίου)] Ἡ̣ρ̣α̣κ̣λείδηc Ἐφθεμού(νιοc) [φυ(λακίτηc) (πυροῦ) ε]

44 β∠: Ptolemaios son of Sentheus had only 3 arouras in Kerkeosiris, the remainder of his cleros being located in Areos Kome; hence the smaller payment. But it is not clear how the figure 2½ artabs was reached: the proper tax of 3 arouras at ¾ art./ar. is 2¼ art., the amount paid in **1147**. 147

47 The trace after Ὧροc is not μέ(γαc) or μι(κρόc), nor is either term ever applied to this individual.

48 φυ(λακίτηc) (πυροῦ) ε: the rate of ἡμιαρτάβιον levied against the 10-aroura cleroi of φυλακῖται remained ½ art./ar. throughout the period for which we have documentation.

54 εἰcφορᾶc: a tax of this name is mentioned in connection with ἱερὰ γῆ also in **36**. 9 and **853**. 10, 13, and 46. The rate is unknown.

1150. Tax Accounts

P. Teb. 13v (*a*) 40 × 30 cm. 115/114 B.C.

Despite a number of obscurities, the two short accounts printed below are of interest for their reference to payments on behalf of seven-aroura and twenty-aroura cleruchs as well as for the novel impost of l. 5. The text was written on the same papyrus as **13**, **1134**, and **1140**, between the letter **13** and the lentil account **1134**. For a discussion of the format and date of the papyrus, see **1140** introd.

[εἰc]δοχή·
[Μ]αρρῆc φύ(λαξ) ὑπ(ὲρ)
Κολλούθου τοῦ Πετοcί(ριοc) (ἑπταρούρου)
[Π]εcύθηc Παχῶ(τοc) χα(λκοῦ) υν
Φαῆcιc Φίβιοc χι( ) μ̣α( ) β (πυροῦ)

(*c.* 10 cm. blank)

κ̣γ̄ ἐν cι( )
Ἕρμων Ὀρcείουc
ὑπ(ὲρ) (ἑπταρούρου) γ∠
Κατῦ(τιc) Κατύ(τιοc) ὑπ(ὲρ) αὐ(τοῦ) ∠
ὑπ(ὲρ) (ἑπταρούρου) καὶ (εἰκοcιαρούρου) α, (γίνεται) α∠

'Income. Marres, guard, on behalf of Kollouthes son of Petosiris, 7-aroura cleruch. Pesythes son of Pachos, 450 copper drachmas. Phaesis son of Phibis, 2 artabs wheat for...

'23rd (?). In. . . .Hermon son of Orses, 3½ artabs on behalf of a 7-aroura cleruch. Katytis son of Katytis, ½ artab on behalf of himself, 1 artab on behalf of a 7-aroura and a 20-aroura cleruch. Total, 1½ artab.'

2 [*Μ*]*αρρῆς φύ*(*λαξ*): see **1136**. 30 n.

5 *χι*( ) *μα*( ): perhaps *χι*(*ριστικοῦ*) *μα*(*χίμων*). The impost *χειριστικόν* is common enough (cf. **847**. 17–18 n.), and was paid by cleruchs as well as Crown tenants (**1037**. 12); but the phrase *χειριστικὸν μαχίμων* has not occurred before. Instead of *μ̣α*( ), *π̣α*( ) could be read.

β (*πυροῦ*): the word order is odd but the reading is clear. The wheat symbol may have been added as a second thought, to make it clear that the sum was no longer in money as in the line above.

6 Perhaps *ἐν σι*(*ρῶι*): cf. **862**. 3–4, *ἐν τῶι μικρῶι σιρῶι*; cf. P. Lond. 216. 11 (II, p. 186).

8 *ὑπ*(*ὲρ*) (*ἑπταρούρου*) *γ∠*: the size of the payment suggests *ἡμιαρτάβιον* (**1146**).

10 (*ἑπταρούρου*) *καὶ* (*εἰκοσιαρούρου*): expanded in the singular because the payment is so small. Possibly the charge which occurs in **1140** and **1143** is meant.

INDICES

I. KINGS

II. DATES

(*a*) REGNAL YEARS

(b) Months and Days

III. Geography

IV. OFFICIAL AND MILITARY TERMS

V. RELIGION

(a) Gods

(b) Shrines and Temples

(c) Miscellaneous

VI. PERSONAL NAMES

b = brother of
f = father of
gf = grandfather of
ggf = great-grandfather of
gggf = great-great-grandfather of
s = son of
gs = grandson of
ggs = great-grandson of
gggs = great-great-grandson of
⟨ ⟩ enclose alternative spellings

VII. MEASURES AND CURRENCY

(*a*) Measures

(*b*) Currency

VIII. TAXES AND OTHER CHARGES

IX. WORDS

doubtful